Gambling with History

Also by Laurence I. Barrett

THE MAYOR OF NEW YORK

Gambling with History

RONALD REAGAN IN
THE WHITE HOUSE

Laurence I. Barrett

DOUBLEDAY & COMPANY, INC.
GARDEN CITY, NEW YORK
1983

Library of Congress Cataloging in Publication Data

Barrett, Laurence I.
  Gambling with history.

  Includes index.
  1. United States—Politics and government—1981– .
  2. Reagan, Ronald. I. Title.
  E876.B37 1983   973.927′092′4
  ISBN 0-385-17938-1
  Library of Congress Catalog Card Number 82–46057

For Adam, David and Paul—good friends as well as sons—
and for Paulette, the best friend of all, always

Contents

Author's Notes

When I first mentioned to President Reagan in September 1981 that work on this book was well underway, his initial reaction was to roll his eyes toward the cloudless sky. "Another book?" More demands on his time. It took him only a moment or two to get past that tedious aspect of the venture. He asked a few questions about publication plans. "Let's see," he said, "by then we'll have the budget balanced. Inflation will be under control. Interest rates will be down. The Russians will be behaving themselves. The thing in Poland will be solved." Then he paused, enjoying the buildup to a typical Reagan punch line. "That's just Chapter One." He slapped his thigh, flashed that marvelous, lopsided, life-is-wonderful grin, and winked in a conspiratorial way as a couple of other reporters ambled over to the patio of the White House tennis court.

Events dictated different ingredients for the first chapter and several others, though he went two out of five in his mock predictions. Assorted difficulties were already beginning to crowd the Reagan White House on that relaxed Sunday afternoon. Some would worsen over the next fifteen months, as my research and writing continued. Midway through Reagan's term—perhaps his first term, perhaps his only one— it was still not clear whether his presidency would join the succession of political failures that had begun with Lyndon Johnson, or whether he would reverse that trend. The political court of 1984 may exalt him as an Eisenhower or condemn him as a Hoover.

While I'm as fascinated by that verdict as the next fellow in my trade, predicting it was neither the original purpose nor the outcome of this work. Rather the goal was to describe and assess this unusual President's first two years in the White House. Because of how he works and what he set out to do, this assignment inevitably led also to an attempt at what might be called ideological biography of the principal character, and close scrutiny of a few of the people at his elbow.

In writing about so controversial a President, a journalist is bound to evoke disagreement from many readers. In depicting "inside" scenes and treating some of the players' motivations, one is likely to raise questions about methodology (not to mention credibility). Because of these factors, and because many in the audience regard White House reporters as unrelenting partisans, pro or con, it is appropriate to describe briefly my own views, the genesis of this book and how I went about it.

Most of my twenty-five years in newspaper and magazine journalism have been spent examining politicians and their works. Like most others with that résumé, I have followed the route from city hall to state house to Washington, dividing my time as reporter, writer or editor between the politics of elections and the politics of governance. Both ends of that unbreakable American chain fascinate me still. More out of temperament than conscious choice, I have avoided personal commitment to party or specific doctrine since the day, nearly thirty years ago, when a pro-McCarthy majority drove a few of us "progressives" out of the New York University Young Republican Club.

I've never believed, however, that a journalist can really be "objective." To carry that off requires a suspension of judgment beyond the ability of most of us. We can, with effort, be informed aliens monitoring the process, the practitioners and the product through the lens of our own understanding. To be detached from the factions and personalities we write about is necessary. To claim we ignore our own backgrounds and prejudices is pretense. While covering the Goldwater campaign I respected the man and feared his ideas. Reporting on Jimmy Carter's White House, I found myself to the right of it on most issues. With candidate, later President, Reagan, the opposite juxtaposition has usually been the case. Nonetheless, a few of Reagan's basic policies seem to me necessary, albeit unpalatable. Some of his peripheral ideas strike me as either inequitable or inane or both.

Reporters are forever discovering that the public leaders they cover are complicated individuals with internal contradictions. In other words, those in power are like the rest of us, except that their ambiguities can affect the commonweal. Reagan, though a simpler man than most of his predecessors—in both the positive and negative senses of that adjective—has his share of inner paradox. Those whose jobs take them close to a President are frequently asked whether they like the man. The question makes me uncomfortable; when you like someone you too easily discount his flaws. I usually fudge the response. That is particularly difficult to get away with in the case of Reagan because of his nice-guy manner. It is common these days for commentators to trash Reagan's policies, intellect and lifestyle, then to conclude, for the sake of balance, with the observation that he is a decent, charming person. If the first is accurate, the second is irrelevant, even dangerous.

I got to know him well during his 1980 campaign, nearly all of which I covered for *Time*. Intrigued by his views, I repeatedly interviewed him and others about the origin of his ideas. Immediately after the election, I wanted to do a book on that relatively narrow subject. Circumstances dictated otherwise. Later, in close consultation with Sam Vaughan and Lisa Drew of Doubleday—both of whom participated fully in the conception, but are herewith absolved of responsibility for the offspring's quality—I began this larger venture.

Obviously it would not have been possible without a degree of cooperation from the Reagans and some of the President's senior assistants. Several staff members, as a group, agreed that they would assist me in the reconstruction of certain policy decisions. They in turn encouraged a few others to be helpful. Many conversations took place a week or more after the event described, so that the research was segregated from my continuing work as *Time*'s White House correspondent. In addition, I was allowed to attend a number of the meetings normally closed to the press.

We had a clear understanding from the outset, however, that this was in no way an "authorized" book, and that the judgments of policies and individual performances could well be adverse. Reagan's principal subordinates were aware of my approach to issues through my magazine work and many conversations during the campaign and the first few months of the Administration. My commitment was to do a serious, balanced account of their two years in power, with the scales remaining in my hands alone. To their credit, the Reagans themselves and several of their associates continued to cooperate even after the tensions and letdown of the second year set in.

Nonetheless, the arrangement from the beginning was insufficient for the needs of this book. Documentary material—particularly that bearing on national security affairs—was not made available to me on a regular basis. While some of the private meetings were fascinating, I could never be certain how my presence was affecting what was said. Thus it was necessary to reach far beyond the top eight or ten members of the President's staff. Eventually I interviewed some sixty individuals in the White House, several of the executive departments, in Congress and elsewhere. A number of them made themselves available at short intervals over eighteen months. Some sources must remain anonymous, others are quoted at length.

In the relatively few instances in which I was present at a scene described in the book, the account indicates that. Much more frequently, I have relied on the notes and recollections of certain participants. In nearly all of these cases I was able to get corroboration from a second source. On a few occasions when only two or three persons participated in a noteworthy encounter and their accounts to me contained contradictions—such as the final two conversations between Alexander Haig and the President—I have simply reported the differences. I have avoided the technique of "synthesizing" situations. Where I thought it reasonable to include my own insights or suppositions, the reader will find them identified as such. In providing the evolution of some of Reagan's views, and in the profile sections, I relied heavily on my reporting during the presidential campaign. Portions of this appeared in *Time,* as indicated in chapter notes or the text. Much of this material was not published during 1980; a reporter rarely has the space or time to print all he would like on a daily or weekly basis. That is half the reason why we write books.

The cooperation of several of my *Time* colleagues was vital to this work throughout. Henry A. Grunwald, Time Inc.'s editor-in-chief; Richard Duncan, chief of correspondents; and Ray Cave, the magazine's managing editor, allowed me to wear two reportorial hats for a year. Then they permitted me six months of liberty in a busy season so that I could finish the task.

Fellow members of the magazine's Washington Bureau were extremely generous with moral and insight support. Of particular assistance when spirit flagged or insight dimmed were Robert Ajemian, Strobe Talbott, Douglas Brew, John Stacks, David Beckwith and Cassie Furgurson. Lissa August provided research assistance, along with the patience and good humor that are as essential to this kind of enterprise as legible notes. Marcia Baggott served tirelessly as typist and indulgently as spelling consultant. To these associates and to several personal friends who helped fight off the anxiety attacks that often accompany the writing of books, I owe more than I can easily repay.

Gambling with History

1

Two Elections, Four Arguments

"I hope," George Shultz tells Ronald Reagan upon parting for the evening, "I really hope it turns out better than Dan Rather says it will." The President accepts this modest wish from his modest Secretary of State with a noncommittal smile. As Nancy Reagan sees the Shultzes to the tiny elevator that conveys visitors to and from the family quarters of the White House, her husband sinks down on one of the two immense sofas that dominate the sitting room. These pieces, with their bold red floral pattern, are old-shoe for him; for years they filled the living room of the Reagans' Pacific Palisades house.

He focuses once again on the television set. Election night, 1982, had been planned as a casual evening with some friends. The ten couples invited for buffet dinner included close associates of many years' standing and some newer people as well. As her ensign of informality, a set of bright red lounging pajamas serves as Nancy's costume. Reagan is in standard dress for such friendly occasions: his old blue-green tartan blazer, wide red tie held in place by a pearl that must have come from a hyperactive oyster, black slacks. All that is missing is his customary ebullience.

Reagan normally delights in supplying the entertainment. Tonight there is no stream of anecdotes from his show business years, only an occasional quip on current affairs. At ten o'clock on the night of the midterm election it is still too early to know the real body count from the hundreds of battles across the country. But the network projections look dismal. CBS is particularly bearish, talking about a loss of three dozen Republican seats in the House of Representatives. That figure would be the borderline of disaster.

For two months Reagan had taken a gritty approach. He had gone out of his way to make his administration's record as much of a national issue as the variegated midterm election permits. The results would be read as a verdict on his performance as well as a forecast of his ability to govern during the next two years. Even for Reagan, so accustomed to taking bold risks, this was a gamble of some magnitude.

At the moment his pile of chips is diminishing. John Hiler, a House freshman typical of the hard-core conservatives brought in by Reagan's 1980 victory, is declared an early victim in Indiana. Earlier Republican surveys had indicated that Hiler would win easily. Richard Wirthlin, Reagan's pollster for many years, is visibly disturbed. James Baker, the White House Chief of Staff and the man with overall supervision of the campaign effort, is also somber. "These are funny numbers," he remarks. He delays his appearance in the Press Room, hoping for more cheerful news.

Wirthlin's firm, Decision Making Information, had taken its own statewide survey in California and concluded that the Republicans would win the governorship and Senate seat. Now the networks are reporting their own Election Day exit polls, with samplings much larger than DMI's, and saying that the Democrats are ahead in both these important contests. Unaccustomed to being wrong, Wirthlin tries to figure out what's going on. He exchanges whispers with Stuart Spencer, the California political consultant who managed Reagan's own gubernatorial campaigns. Spencer and Wirthlin make some phone checks. Of those evening hours, Wirthlin will say later: "The news was so terribly bad compared with what we thought we knew. It isn't surprising that we were worried."[1]

Watching Reagan watch the tube intently, I realize that I have rarely seen him so subdued. On the eve of losing the Iowa caucuses to George Bush in 1980, for instance, he was determined to be buoyant, to amuse those around him. We flew up on a nine-passenger Saberliner from Palm Beach to Mason City that last weekend before Iowa Republicans made their choice. Reagan, a few aides, bodyguards and reporters. The executive jet was so crowded that one of my colleagues spent the flight seated on the toilet. Reagan was to make a television speech in Des Moines that night, his last big number before the caucuses. His early lead in Iowa had vanished, erased by Bush's energy and Reagan's aloof strategy.

He clearly did not like the text on his lap. For two hours he worked it over, lips pursed, forehead furrowed, half-moon glasses perched on his nose. While the rest of us jabbered, drank, passed around the tray of fruit and cold cuts, Reagan silently sounded out words and phrases as he translated chunks of text into his own shorthand on four-by-six index cards. Finally, when he felt he could do no more with the prose, he took command of the banter. In situations like that the entertainer in him invariably triumphed. The subject of hunting came up. This led to an elaborate tale, a shaggy bear story, in which the quarry turns the tables on the hunter. Reagan played both parts. As the bear, he rose from his seat in the cramped aircraft and glowered down on the trapped rifleman. Then he flipped, draped himself backward over the airliner seat to play the supine hunter looking up at the fierce animal. He interrupted the dialogue to tell us, "You see, this is really a sight gag." When we finally landed, after applauding more Reagan shticks, he still had to face delivering a so-so speech and what would turn out to be his worst setback of the primary season. But his spirits were high. "Well," he said, satirizing the issue then prevalent—his age—"get the makeup ready! Call the girl to dye my hair!"

Now, on the evening of November 2, 1982, I am reminded of his ability to seal himself into a capsule of concentration. Nancy Reagan cannot bear to see her husband even look worried. She curls up on the sofa next to him, kicks off her red slippers, tucks her feet under a pillow embroidered with a large RR monogram, lures his arm around her shoulders. When Roger Mudd says that if he were Reagan he too would have campaigned on a "stay-the-course" line, she chirps, "Did you hear that!" John Chancellor, reporting on opinion surveys, observes that despite Republican reverses, Reagan personally "is in pretty good shape with the voters." That prompts Nancy to slap her husband's thigh smartly a couple of times as if to say, cheer up, honey, it's getting better. He replies with an indulgent hug but his attention remains fastened on the networks as we channel-flip through the evening.

Unpleasant news had started more than an hour earlier, as Reagan monitored two TV sets in his small, crowded study. The initial exit polls from Texas were as bad as those from California. Millicent Fenwick, with whom Reagan had made a campaign appearance in New Jersey, lost her Senate race ("Oh dear," Reagan sighs, half to himself, "I'm sorry"). Senator Lowell Weicker has survived in Connecticut but that is a mixed blessing; Weicker frequently thwarts conservative moves on the Hill and Prescott Bush, George's brother, had made a feckless attempt earlier in the year to get the GOP nomination. Hearing of Weicker's victory over a liberal Democrat, Toby Moffett, Reagan makes one of his few jokes of this long night. "Now control yourself, George," he says to his Vice-President. "Don't cheer." Then, musing aloud about Weicker's opponent in the general election, Reagan takes some solace from the outcome: "I understand that Moffett can be as bad as Jerry Brown." As Reagan measures things, that is very tough talk.

Reagan's political aides, like his wife, try to find silver linings. Jim Baker announces, "We don't believe the exit polls from California." Later, when the votes are actually in, that skepticism will prove well founded; Brown will lose the Senate contest and the Republicans will recapture the governor's chair Reagan once occupied. Barbara Bush also accentuates the positive. "George has just talked with Bill Archer in Texas, and he says Bill [Clements, the Republican governor seeking reelection] has fifty-five percent." The networks have already forecast defeat for this loyal Reaganite, a projection that will turn out to be accurate. There is much more concern about Bob Michel, the House Minority Leader, who had contributed heavily to the Administration's legislative victories during 1981–82. In recognition of that, Reagan appeared with Michel in this staunch centurion's Illinois district, where both blue collar workers and farmers were suffering the hardest of times. Michel's defeat would be both a material and symbolic blow. The raw vote so far looks ominous.

A computer terminal set up for the evening in Reagan's study isn't keeping up with events. Wirthlin makes some calculations of his own. "Michel is winning," Wirthlin says with conviction, "and we've picked up a House seat in Nevada. Your trip gave us a six-point bounce there." Reagan accepts in silence the tribute to his personal pulling power. Wirthlin's prediction will turn out to be sound. Michel will survive the night, though barely. The new House seat created by reapportionment in Nevada will go Republican and an obscure GOP challenger of modest credentials, Chic Hecht, will beat Nevada's venerable Democratic incumbent senator, Howard Cannon.

That is but conjecture when Reagan first hears it. The kaleidoscope of television images is giving him hard facts, hard to swallow. A liberal Democrat, Barney Frank, has beaten a moderate Republican, Margaret Heckler, in Massachusetts. Reagan is surprised. "Did we know she was going to lose?" Both Baker and Wirthlin say yes. Reagan mutters about feminist groups, particularly the National Organization for Women, which this year emphasized issues rather than gender in providing support. "When the woman candidate is a Republican they abandon her," he complains. "Gee, I'm sorry to lose Heckler. She was a good little girl." Half the people in the room are women. Some of them, like Susan Baker, Barbara Bush and Ursula Meese, are sophisticated in politics. Of course no one present makes a point of Reagan's calling an experienced, middle-aged member of Congress a "good little girl," or the connection between that casual remark and his inability to comprehend the mentality of militant feminists.

Because the Washington TV stations cover Maryland and Virginia races closely, we get several renditions of Senator Paul Sarbanes' easy reelection in Maryland. Sarbanes had become a particularly sharp critic of the Administration and earlier there was some frail hope of defeating him. Now, answering a reporter's softball question, Sarbanes utters a few clichés about the "people's victory." Reagan answers the screen: "What are you talking about? The people lost." Getting into the spirit of it, Reagan then says to no one in particular, "D-E-M no longer stands for 'Democrat.' It stands for 'demagogue.'" When a woman TV reporter gives a rundown of defeated Republican governors, Reagan admonishes her video image to "keep the glee off your face, sister!" Then the mood improves as Malcolm Wallop holds his seat in Wyoming; the GOP's control of the Senate is safe.

By ten-thirty, those of the guests who haven't been involved in the campaign, like Shultz and National Security Adviser William Clark, are gone. It is time for the outsider, the writer, to leave also. Reagan will settle down with his political associates for a while. He will stay up much later than usual, watching television from bed until well after midnight, when he calls Deputy Chief of Staff Michael Deaver at home to remark on the confirmation of good news from California. Still, he goes to sleep not knowing exactly how the Republicans have done in Congress.

The top line sunup Wednesday came as something of a relief. In Indiana, John Hiler in fact won; the networks had erred in saying the opposite. The Republicans have lost twenty-six House members—a blow that is serious, but perhaps not fatal to the coalition of Republicans and conservative Democrats that had allowed Reagan to amass a favorable legislative scorecard in 1981–82. The GOP maintained an advantage of eight in the Senate, an outcome marginally better than all the forecasts. But the loss of seven governorships, including Texas and some of the large Midwestern states, was worrisome. The first run of analysis called it a Scotch verdict. The voters were said to have neither condemned Reagan's record irrevocably nor blessed it. While they certainly did not enhance his presidency, neither did they cripple it. But they did reduce his running room, and closer scrutiny of the returns revealed a more threatening message to the White House, as we shall see a bit later.

In brilliant autumn sunshine the morning after, Reagan and Bush talked to reporters in the Rose Garden. "There is a smile on our faces," the President said, "and intentionally so. . . . We have every reason to feel good." Later in the day, in the Oval Office, he was cheerful and vigorous during our hour-long conversation. It was already obvious that he would be under great pressure from some of his allies as well as all his adversaries to make new accommodations on the most important parts of his economic program. Deficit gap was yawning wider than ever, his aides had warned him during the preceding forty-eight hours, and the incoming Congress would be less amenable to his ideas than the old one had been. After analyzing voluminous polling data, Communications Director David Gergen told him that public support for very high defense spending had crumbled. The electorate's tolerance for further reductions in domestic programs was disappearing.

When the subject of his stubbornness came up in our talk, he replied genially, "I don't think I *am* rigid." He had compromised with Congress on some aspects of his programs before, he pointed out. But neither in public nor in private, neither with a writer nor with his inner circle, would Reagan concede that the results of the midterm election or the clear drift of public opinion would alter his direction. The fundamentals would remain the same. "Rigid as far as basic principles, yes," he told me. To a small group of intimates he said, "By God, we came here to change things, not to follow opinion polls."

That defiant mood was vintage Reagan, emblematic of both his strength and weakness. He refused to acknowledge, perhaps even to himself, the difficulties that he and the country still faced. He would not or could not see the critical changes between the two elections, 1980 and 1982. In that denial he found the will to continue going his way, the way he felt was essential. It would take another two months of accumulated bad news, along with intense pressure from advisers and congressional allies, before Reagan confronted some basic decisions in January 1983. He would bend grudgingly, unwilling to surrender his own sense of long-range mission or even to appear to wobble. Steadiness of purpose, he believed, was what the electorate had ordered when it sent him to the White House.

As they repudiated Jimmy Carter in 1980 and elected the most overtly ideological President in the nation's history, the voters had made possible a drastic shift in national politics, a realignment as basic as the one begun in 1932 and ratified in 1934. No serious analyst convincingly argued that 1980 in itself represented a national consensus to move right, or even to install the GOP for a reign of some duration. The presidential election had been a beachhead; 1982 and 1984 would determine whether Reaganism could penetrate the interior of American politics. "When he took office," the conservative political scientist James Q. Wilson wrote, "the only mandate Mr. Reagan had was to be different from his predecessor."[2]

Reagan insisted on a more expansive interpretation. He proved to be different, without doubt, and a much stronger leader. If he could also be successful in satisfying the country's more important short-term needs, he could make palatable at least some of the items on his long-range radical agenda. Elephants would be back in political style, perhaps for a dozen years or more. They would not be the tame pachyderms of the Eisenhower or Nixon years. Rather Reagan wanted the rebirth of an older, fiercer genus resembling the mastodon. This powerful beast would trample big government at home and gore Soviet aggressiveness abroad.

First, however, it had to pull the country back to material prosperity. Here Reagan would defy history. The essentially centrist American electorate has traditionally cared little for radicalism left or right. It cares greatly about chickens in the pot, Fords in the garage, boats on the lake, General Electric appliances doing the work. Reagan chose to attempt two heroic missions simultaneously, trying to meet the economic demands of the moment and his own imperatives for the future. When they sometimes clashed, he usually tried to go with his vision. "If he were playing for the short term," Wirthlin told me, "the kinds of positions he's taken over the last eighteen or twenty months would have been different and probably would have brought us through the fall election in better shape. He is gambling very much on his ability to induce structural social change in the long run. His poker chips on the table are what happens in the short run. And it *is* a gamble."

Reagan had less than two years before his first major electoral test. During that time he reasserted presidential leadership in a way that defied modish laments about the office's inherent weaknesses.* But to be a popular success, Reagan would also have to give the country a keen sense that he was solving its immediate economic difficulties. By the fall of 1982 his vigorous thrusts toward that end had succeeded principally in rearranging the misery. Positive trends were underway, but the results were agonizingly slow. On the eve of the 1980 election, in his final TV speech of the campaign, Reagan could sneer at Carter's mushy record and promise "a new age of reform in this country and an era of national renewal." Two years later, the night before Americans elected the Ninety-eighth Congress, Reagan spoke on television again. He did not flinch from making himself the central issue. But now his tone was defensive, as it had been for several weeks while he cam-

---

* The crux of which is that our constitutional and party systems virtually preclude an effective presidency in the modern era. The latest book-length argument of this theme is *None of the Above: Why Presidents Fail and What Can Be Done About It* by Robert Shogan (New American Library, 1982). Even in John Kennedy's day there was serious analysis along this line, such as James MacGregor Burns's *The Deadlock of Democracy* (Prentice-Hall, 1963).

paigned around the country. "Some have argued," he said that final night, "that our economy is heading over a cliff. Well, they are wrong. Slowly, but surely, we are lifting our economy out of the mess created over the past several decades. We are on the road back."

The lunch bucket remained the principal object of the nation's *angst* during those two years. In 1980 the difficulties were mild recession, pernicious inflation and suffocating interest rates. Two years later, prices were under control, loans easier to get. But the voters who made their selections in 1980 while haunted by inflation went back to the polls spooked by unemployment and all its toxic side effects.

Between elections, their morale oscillated in dizzying fashion. One of the best measures of the public's general confidence in its leadership is the "Right Direction/Wrong Track" survey conducted by Wirthlin's company, DMI.* Shortly before Carter left office, pessimism reigned. Sixty-one percent of the respondents felt we were on the wrong track (versus 26 percent picking "right direction"). Nine months of Reagan's tenure turned that around smartly. But by April of 1982 public sentiment was back in the basement: negativism prevailed, 67 percent to 28 percent. Hints of economic recovery improved matters, though by Election Day the numbers were still bearish, 59 to 33. Surveys by other firms, differently worded, confirmed the general trend. That hard times accounted for this autumnal mood was beyond doubt. Yet detailed examination of voters' attitudes also showed that Reagan was meeting or even exceeding the public's expectations of him in other categories. Reagan was still seen as a leader who might yet deliver what was demanded of him.

In the age of instant mashed potatoes, stir-fried history and microwave politics, Reagan demanded that the country be patient. He confounded those who insisted that early obituaries of his presidency were in order. He rebuffed others who preached that his presidency could survive only by taking fundamentally new directions in 1983–84. He was right to the extent that the halfway point in the case of his administration was too soon to render cosmic judgment. Nonetheless, some significant conclusions could be drawn. Four principal arguments will be made in the course of this narrative:

• Reagan, the first modern President to emerge from a protest movement rather than conventional party process or idiosyncratic personality politics, remained far more faithful to his "ism" than the constraints of incumbency normally permit. The most obvious result was

* The question asked at short intervals of voters: "Generally speaking, would you say things in this country are going in the right direction, or have they pretty seriously gotten off on the wrong track?"

that his brand of radical conservatism would get at least a partial test in power. There were subtle side effects as well. More than any other contemporary leader, Reagan embodied American mythology. With Reagan in the White House, Americans were forced to consider, consciously or otherwise, whether they could, or even wanted to, act out their civic folklore concerning individualism. A second ripple was the threat that Reagan's adherence to ideology would have the effect of sharpening group divisions.

• On the operational level, Reagan, by overplaying his hand particularly in the first eighteen months, inflicted unnecessary pain on the country. He thereby damaged his own standing. By committing some egregious blunders he forfeited, at least temporarily, the opportunity to broaden that political beachhead created in 1980. The large irony is that more adroit and timely responses to economic realities could have reduced the trauma without sacrifice of basic principle.

• Reagan was, nonetheless, an effective President in his first two years. The criteria for this judgment are pragmatic. He saw the need for significant changes in both domestic and national security affairs. He moved vigorously to achieve them. Against difficult odds, he succeeded in some important respects. The wisdom of any number of his decisions is easily challenged. The sum of all of them, in the end, may still be frustration. But even if his administration bleeds itself to death in 1983–84, even if Reagan becomes yet another in the series of one-term dropouts, he will be able to leave behind some important achievements.

• Thus the portrayals of him as a passive figure, as a totem for forces he only dimly understood, miss a critical distinction. It is true that Reagan came to the White House with important flaws in terms of personal capacity. Sometimes his temperament seemed to resemble Coolidge's and his intellect, Harding's. Hence he was a mediocre administrator, ever vulnerable to errors born of indifference or incomprehension. But he could provide unusually clear strategic direction. He could, when the occasion demanded, when his real imperatives were at stake, demonstrate will and vigor that evoked memories of the two Roosevelts. He did not hesitate to use the powers of the office, or of his personality, to pursue the goals he cherished. In the largest sense then, Ronald Reagan was an activist President.

Typically an elected executive—mayor, governor or President—sets his fiscal policy more by the barometer of his current political needs than by the compass of his political beliefs. With Reagan it was the opposite. Two sympathetic academic commentators pointed out at midterm, "It seems fair to say that no incoming administration had ever before staked so much on a specific, comprehensive economic program. In contrast the administration of Franklin Roosevelt . . . was a hodgepodge of political expediency and unresolved economic theorizing." These analysts went on to point out—accurately, I think—that "the ultimate reason for Reagan Presidency's confidence in its multi-year economic strategy lay in the fact that it was founded on a political, not economic, theory."*

Some of the most trenchant commentary on Reagan's difficulties, in fact, came from conservatives who approved, at least in broad terms, Reagan's goals, if not his specific approaches. The economist Herbert Stein, an orthodox Republican and occasional adviser to Reagan, agreed with the President that the new administration had to excise long-term rot. Yet, reviewing Reagan's performance in late 1982 Stein wrote: "Our problems would, I think, be less severe today if Mr. Reagan had acknowledged from the beginning . . . that disinflation would entail a temporary rise of unemployment and if his budget policies in 1981 had not been predicated on a rate of economic growth that would certainly be inflationary. More modesty would have made the policy more credible and helped to slow the inflation with less unemployment."[3]

Only the farthest right Reaganite fringe disagreed with that appraisal. The rest of his subordinates and supporters in the White House and the Congress quietly lamented the loss, at least temporarily, of a large opportunity. Had Reagan been more flexible, more people would have been working in the fall of 1982—and fewer would have voted Democratic.

That does not mean that the Republicans would have captured the House of Representatives or performed other heroics. It *does* mean that they either could have taken a small step forward toward the basic political realignment made possible by 1980, or at least held their ground. Instead they lost yardage, and more of it than was indicated by the number of seats that changed partisan label.

What had given 1980 such significance was Reagan's ability to assemble a coalition far broader than his natural base of conventional Republicans and restless conservatives who lacked a strong party tie. He had captured enough support from blue collar voters, the middle-aged and elderly, and moderate independents to tack together an abso-

---

* The study by Rudolph G. Penner, an economist with the conservative American Enterprise Institute, and Hugh Heclo of Harvard's government department attempted, with considerable success, to synthesize Reaganism and Reaganomics as put into practice by the Administration. The paper was delivered at a symposium at Princeton's Woodrow Wilson School, November 19, 1982.

lute majority of the popular vote in a three-way contest. If he could build on this foundation, he could then make some tenets of what his more fervent admirers called the "Reagan revolution" durable.

Instead, these groups in 1982 began "coming home" to the Democratic Party in significant numbers. Though Republicans, as usual, spent far more campaign money than Democrats, the GOP won several of its most important House and Senate races by slivers. A swing of less than 50,000 votes in five states would have cost the Republicans control of the Senate. They made no progress at all in overcoming the "gender gap," a relatively new element in the equation: in significant proportions, women have begun to vote differently from men. In 1980 and 1982, women were measurably less partial to Republicans than men were. Democrats also benefited from the first increase in voter participation in five midterm elections. Analysts attributed that surprising change to an anti-Reagan reaction among low-income voters and blacks.

These losses were severe enough to create doubt as to whether Reagan, or any Republican, could reassemble in 1984 the vote pool that gave the GOP the White House and the Senate in 1980. The consolation from the GOP's viewpoint was that there remained time to recoup. Reagan, unlike Carter in 1978, was still regarded by the electorate as a strong leader. Thus he could rebuild, though it would be a difficult exercise in political architecture. Three days after the midterm vote, one of the most knowledgeable tacticians in the White House remarked privately, "I am staying up nights trying to get a plan for making this coalition come together again. We're driving away the women, the Social Security thing scares the old folks, we've lost the blacks altogether and the union types are beginning to talk New Deal again."

In this era of rapid changes of public mood and fragile political alliances, no one's coalition is safe from fragmentation very long. For Reagan this was a particular danger from the beginning. His normally agreeable mien and his advisers' efforts to file down some of the most jagged teeth of his philosophy could go only so far. One price a public man pays for holding strong convictions is the arousal of strong feelings. In the spring of 1979, as his strategists planned the campaign to come, Wirthlin conducted a detailed survey of attitudes. The questionnaire contained 146 items and nearly an hour was required for each interview. After studying the results, Wirthlin wrote a report for his boss and his colleagues. "Ronald Reagan," it said, "polarizes those interviewed in this study on more than a dozen personality and interpersonal style variables—more than any other candidate measured."

That quality remained just below the surface of his persona. It was

not necessarily a liability. Franklin Roosevelt evoked powerful sentiments, negative as well as positive, and won four presidential elections.
But FDR, whose style Reagan admired and tried in some ways to
emulate, had the capacity to rally large groups around him even before
World War II imposed a new unity on the country. Those he antago-
nized, sometimes with premeditation, were his own kind, the social and
economic elite. Here Reagan was different. His doctrine, when presented baldly, could frighten and alienate those at the low end of fortune's ladder and others in the political center. Carter in 1980 tried, in
his maladroit fashion, to exploit that. First he said that the election
could be a choice between war and peace, accusing Reagan of being a
warmonger. Then, in a second orgy of excess, he said his own victory
would unify the nation and warned, "If I lose the election . . . Americans might be separated, black from white, Jew from Christian, North
from South, rural from urban."

Carter's hyperbole backfired. Reagan had modulated his own verbiage between 1976 and 1980 and he adjusted it further between the
primary and general campaigns. He refused to live up to Carter's caricature of him. Yet Reagan had to hold his right wing while capturing
other pieces of the spectrum to win. He did that on Election Day,
handsomely. To hold those pieces once in office would be more
difficult. In late January 1981, some of Reagan's senior aides had
finished an internal planning document on near-term strategy which included this admonition:

> Ronald Reagan's support among liberals [in the presidential election] was
> hyped because of their distaste for Carter. We cannot count on them in
> the future. Our ideological appeal must rest fundamentally on our con-
> servatives, but we must broaden our base to include moderates to enhance
> our coalitional strength across the board.[4]

How to do that in practice remained a central dilemma for Reagan's
White House. Making rapid, palpable progress in overcoming the recession would have overshadowed several difficult but politically less
important issues, such as civil rights, the ERA, abortion, classroom
prayer and environmental protection. But when that did not happen,
the Administration began making enemies in organized cadres. Early in
the second year Senator Bob Packwood of Oregon, a moderate who
headed the Senate Republican Campaign Committee, enraged the
White House by remarking in an interview that got wide distribution,
"The Republican Party has just about written off those women who
work for wages in the marketplace. We are losing them in droves. You
cannot write them off and the blacks off and the Hispanics off and the

Jews off and assume that you're going to build a party on white Anglo-Saxon males over forty. There aren't enough of us left."[5]

When the economics of 1982 put him on the defensive, Reagan occasionally made the mistake of letting the raw side of his nature show in a manner almost as mean-spirited as Carter's two years earlier. With White House acquiescence, Senate Republicans removed Packwood from his leadership post as punishment for his brash candor. In one speech to veterans' organizations in October Reagan bunched national defense, crime, morality, abortion and fiscal questions into the same few paragraphs, strongly implying that anyone who disagreed with him on tax policy, for instance, was also against safe streets and godly classrooms. Then he exhaled this puff of old-style Populist smoke:

> For the truth is that Americans must choose between two drastically different points of view. One puts its faith in the pipe dreamers and margin scribblers in Washington; the other believes in the collective wisdom of the people and their commitment to the American dream. One says tax and tax, spend and spend, and the other says have faith in the common sense of the people. The other side believes the solutions to our nation's problems lie in the psychiatrist's notes or in the social worker's file or in the bureaucrat's budget. We believe in the workingman's toil, the businessman's enterprise and the clergyman's counsel.

What clergymen and psychiatrists had to do with fiscal policy was left unstated. So was the identity of the "margin scribblers." Reagan's symbolic foils were as relevant to the real cares of the period as George Wallace's "pointy-headed perfessors" had been fifteen years earlier. When Reagan went on such anti-intellectual detours, he gave credence to criticism like Packwood's. On election eve, in his final appeal for support on network television, Reagan attacked the "big spenders" in Congress for having caused inflation and unemployment, adding, inaccurately and gratuitously: "They even drove prayer out of our nation's classrooms."

This was a blatant attempt to hold at least part of "our conservatives," the segment that cared most about classroom prayer and other so-called "social issues." Reagan was risking losses elsewhere. In fact he was paying a heavy price for the convictions closest to his heart. The goal he clung to most fervently was the "politics of subtraction"—reducing the impact of the federal government on American society. When he took the oath of office on a bright winter day, he broke precedent by speaking from the west side of the Capitol. Thus he looked out toward the Mall, the monuments and the vast rows of huge federal buildings which to his mind had become gauntlets tormenting the spirit of American individualism. It seemed to me on Inauguration Day that the words he spoke with most conviction were these: "It is my intention to curb the size and influence of the federal establishment and to demand recognition of the distinction between the powers granted to the federal government and those reserved to the states or to the people. All of us need to be reminded that the federal government did not create the states; the states created the federal government."

Later his most vigorous fights would be to cut tax rates, and to retain those large reductions though the immediate effect was temporarily disastrous. The rationale of the moment was that a lighter tax burden would combat stagflation. In Reagan's mind the more durable goal was to reduce government's ability to spend, regardless of the economy's condition. He reasoned that in the long run only revenue attrition would compel Congress to discipline itself. In virtually every sector save the military he ordered a general retreat. The wonder is that he actually got some significant movement in that direction. He did not merely check the glacial advance of government intervention; for better or for worse, he began to reverse the trend of the previous half century. Inevitably this offended an array of interest groups dependent on Washington's financial or legal support. In national security affairs, meanwhile, he commanded another important turnabout: he substituted a new armaments program for a new effort to achieve détente with Moscow. The result was a partial return to Cold War anxiety. Some experts regarded this as a high-risk policy, others as a necessity to reduce Soviet mischief. In fact, it was both.

These changes must be measured against the conditions he inherited. The federal government had, by common consent, become impossibly bloated. The economy was in grievous condition; on that, everyone also agreed. There was little argument that the nation's military machine was rusting out. In world affairs, the United States had become tentative, seemingly baffled. Reagan succeeded four failed Presidents. The inhibitions on any administration that sought to move vigorously seemed almost insuperable. That Reagan could walk into such unpromising conditions, dragging the weight of his own considerable flaws, and still move ahead was in itself an achievement. First his enemies dismissed him as an impotent relic of the past—too old, too eccentric, too extreme actually to *do* anything. Ronald Reagan was soon all too potent for their taste.

To me the classic concession along this line came from Nicholas von Hoffman, a stylish writer who never met, or even read about, a President whom he did not attempt to consume with piranha prose. In his long meal on Reagan, we find two revealing passages: "Our most dangerous President came clothed in the civic and political virtues we demand from our public men and seldom get. No one thought it would be the movie actor who would double-cross the nation by taking his own campaign promises seriously and consecrating himself to carrying them out." No one thought Reagan sincere? Well, perhaps no one in the insulated upper stratum of the Bos-Wash village. Von Hoffman again: "Whatever else he may be, Ronald Reagan isn't a political amateur, an accidental figure. By persisting in thinking of him as a vacuous dabbler, we make it easy for him by underestimating him. We are encouraged to underestimate him the more because we think he's weak on his civics, that he gets his facts wrong. Actually, he gets *our* facts wrong; he gets *his* facts right." Just who the "we" are is unspecified. Presumably the pronoun includes, but is not limited to, those who agree with Von Hoffman's conclusion that it is "humiliating to think of this unlettered, self-assured bumpkin being our President."[6]

This critique is cited not because it is unique. Rather it is typical, except for its ferocity, of the shock experienced within the Eastern press and political establishments when the inmates of those closed fraternities began to comprehend that this risible fellow from California, this ersatz cowboy who once sold Borax on television, had not merely glided into the presidency on the waves of his saccharine baritone delivery, but actually had the grit and the smarts to function once there. Jim Wright, the Democratic House Majority Leader, kept a diary during the period in which Reagan was running amuck on Capitol Hill in mid-1981. An excerpt from the entry for June 11:

> His philosophical approach is superficial, overly simplistic, one-dimensional. What he preaches is pure economic pap, glossed over with uplifting homilies and inspirational chatter. Yet so far the guy is making it work. Appalled by what seems to me a lack of depth, I stand in awe nevertheless of his political skill. I am not sure that I have seen its equal.[7]

Wright, who had served in Congress under six previous Presidents, was talking in this passage about Reagan's economic program. Of the changes Reagan has put in place, that is without question the most important. He had been in office only six months when he obtained passage of legislation that actually set in motion a reduction of government social services. However one views the wisdom or equity of that change, it must be classed as historic. One month later the Administration's tax bill turned another corner: for the first time since Calvin Coolidge's day, income redistribution inspired by Washington was going up the social scale instead of down.

The spending priorities of the preceding two decades were also reversed. Reagan did not merely give the Pentagon a larger share of federal resources—that would have occurred under Carter or even Ted

Kennedy in the 1980s. Rather Reagan set in motion long-term changes whereby defense spending would grow as a proportion of the budget (and of GNP) indefinitely while many types of civilian expenditures would shrink in absolute terms after inflation was taken into account.* It will be very difficult for a successor administration to alter this pattern substantially even if it wishes to do so. The federal civilian work force began to diminish for the first time in thirty years. Not only were positions left unfilled; 10,000 employees who fancied that they had lifetime tenure discovered otherwise. The ripple effects were larger for state and municipal workers. The combination of reduced federal subsidies and the recession forced governors and mayors to lay off hundreds of thousands. For the first time since World War II, federal assistance to local government, in real terms, began to diminish.

Nor was this all that Reaganism had wrought. For a full generation, under Democratic Presidents and Republicans, Washington had steadily increased its role as protector of those who were ill used. The feds had been attacking with a variety of legal weapons the inequities imposed on racial minorities, women, the poor and others. That offensive slowed visibly under the new administration.

The environmentalist movement, which had its roots in the Republican progressivism of Theodore Roosevelt, suddenly discovered that the Republican conservatism of Ronald Reagan meant a sharp change of course. On the strength of a backlash against federal control of vast amounts of land, mostly in the West, which came to be called the "Sagebrush Rebellion," Interior Secretary James Watt started to reduce those holdings. In the name of economic expansion it was made easier to develop for commercial use areas previously in preserve status. An example: under previous federal practice, environmentalists seeking to block exploitation of wetlands areas had recourse to five appeal procedures which could stretch over many months or even years. Under the new administration, that was cut to two appeals within ninety days.

Reagan's supporters on the far right frequently complained that he was not moving fast enough to dismantle governmental regulation. Major statutory changes were slow in coming. But in culling existing rules and in enforcement techniques, the changes were stark. In polic-

* Reagan was uncomfortable with that fact. Because of continued growth in Social Security outlays, he could argue that social spending as a whole continued to rise. This was simply untrue in "real" or constant-dollar terms. An internal White House study completed November 12, 1982, measured federal spending in six broad civilian categories. Four of them showed significant net decreases in constant dollars between fiscal years 1981 and 1983. The increases showed by the other two were only a tiny fraction of the growth rate under previous administrations.

ing atmospheric pollution, industrial safety, food and drug standards, the new managers constantly opted for permissiveness rather than stringency. As the Administration sifted 119 different categories of regulations, encompassing thousands of individual rules, it claimed that over a decade its amendments would spare the economy $70 billion in unnecessary expenses. That savings presumably would result in higher productivity and lower prices. Consumer advocates of the Ralph Nader ilk called such claims ridiculous. The relaxation of policing would in the end carry a huge price tag in terms of health hazards and other liabilities. That debate could not be settled immediately; whatever damage being done by reduced enforcement would be gradual and incremental. What could be stated with certainty was that Reagan had reversed yet another steady trend that had run for decades.

In only one sector did Reagan prefer more government intervention than less: the complex, emotion-laden bundle of concerns misnamed the "social issues." Reagan himself carried no burden of personal piety. He sipped an occasional highball, enjoyed a vulgar joke with intimates. But he was also the uncomfortable ally of the politically militant religious right typified by the Reverend Jerry Falwell's Moral Majority. During the 1980 campaign Reagan welcomed that faction's blessing, appeared at some of its functions and committed himself to its agenda. At one press conference during the election year, he even expressed sympathy for the idea that creationism, the pseudoscience derived from a literal interpretation of Genesis, deserves equal treatment with the theory of evolution in public school classrooms.

As President, luckily, Reagan did not have to involve himself in modern versions of the Scopes monkey trial. But he did have to take stands on such touchy subjects as abortion, school prayer and the Equal Rights Amendment. Officials opposed to abortion, and even skeptical about federal assistance to family-planning programs, got second-level appointments in the bureaucracy. Criteria allowing impoverished women to pay for abortions with Medicaid funds were, with the White House's approval, made more restrictive. Reagan also gave at least lip service to proposals that would drastically curtail any woman's right to have an abortion regardless of who paid the bill.

"Faith in God," he told one meeting of religious militants in the White House, "is a vital guidepost, a source of inspiration and a pillar of strength in times of trial. . . . If the President of the United States can pray with others in the Oval Office—and I have on a number of occasions—then let us make certain that our children have the same right as they go about preparing for their futures."

That kind of admonition from the White House was also new. Most of Reagan's recent predecessors had the good sense to stay out of such emotional cockpits. The larger religious community was itself sharply divided over these issues, including classroom prayer. Reagan did not invest a great deal of political capital in these disputes. But he occasionally went the bully-pulpit route in order to keep his franchise with the restive Fundamentalists who waged war on what they called "secular humanism."

It was a tricky business which at times proved embarrassing.* Early on, Reagan even gave nominal support to a doomed piece of legislation, the proposed Family Protection Act, which his pal Senator Paul Laxalt sponsored (albeit with limited enthusiasm). This omnibus Constitutional booby trap, among its other features, would have got Washington involved in the content of school textbooks. It would also have enhanced the influence of local parent organizations over public school curricula. Among the ingredients of this proposal—strongly supported by the Moral Majority and allied groups—was legislative kerosene for book burning. Reagan was hardly responsible for this sort of crusade or all its excesses. Still, in choosing to exploit it for political purposes, Reagan bestowed on this new militance a legitimacy that it had previously lacked.

At the local and even the state level the movement translated into an aggressive anti-intellectualism. In Arkansas and Louisiana, legislators caved in to pressure on the creationism issue, which then had to be fought in the courts. Censorship efforts aimed at anything considered lewd or leftish picked up. The targets included network television as well as school libraries. If such specific clouds of know-nothingism floated far beneath Reagan's radar, the rationale for them did not. Reagan was for "localism." He was for "traditional values." He pined, in public remarks, for the days when Hollywood policed itself by never showing even a married couple in the same bed. He was for the citizenry's right to protect its children from the dangers of required reading lists. In one tiny corner of the new times accompanying Reagan's presidency, atavistic puritanism was making a comeback with his tacit support.

Prominent in the foreground, meanwhile, Reagan took a very active role in reminding America that it was a military superpower and had better act like one again. Reaction to the Vietnam war, budget prob-

---

* For instance, on August 22, 1980, Reagan was the only major candidate to attend a conference on political action staged by Fundamentalist leaders in Dallas. Dr. Bailey Smith, one of the more prominent Southern Baptist ministers, declared that "God Almighty does not hear the prayer of the Jew." Inevitably Reagan had to comment on that when reporters later cornered him. It was a bigger problem for Falwell. Eventually Falwell chose political expedience over his own Baptist-Separatist tenets. He reconsidered his position and announced that God hears everyone's prayers.

lems and other factors had combined during the 1970s to weaken the country's defenses both materially and morally. The risks resulting from this deterioration and from Carter's wobbly foreign policy became clear before the 1980 campaign. Reagan had plenty of company when he argued for restoration.

The debate, unfortunately, later was distorted by preoccupation with strategic nuclear forces and size of the Pentagon budget. These specific issues were open to argument. Reagan, relying on dubious advice, dug too deep a trench for himself on these questions, as we shall see later on. But, more broadly, the Administration was able to make necessary repairs to other parts of the military machine. Just as important, he began to erase the timidity that had set in during the Carter years. The use of American Marines as part of the peacekeeping force in Beirut was one prominent example. A minor revival of covert action operations by the Central Intelligence Agency was a secret kept only medium well. As the post-Vietnam syndrome of gratuitous shame faded, Reagan also capitalized on the changing mood to revive pride in the military. ROTC membership was no longer a stigma, even at Ivy League universities. Congress would still haggle over the outlandish size of his military budget requests, but Capitol Hill was less inclined to tie the eagle's talons with new inhibitions on the use of force.

Any comparison, then, between the autumn in which Reagan was elected and the winter in which he started the third year of his presidency shows changes that made a material difference in the lives of Americans, and in the way government conducts itself. Reagan's administration was still a work in progress. There were enough dangers to give a plausible foundation to the fashionable predictions that his presidency would fail. During the months after the 1982 election some of the battles of the first two years would have to be fought again. The danger of a deadlock between Capitol Hill and the White House was quite real. New leadership in the Kremlin, new strains with the Western alliance and other changes overseas produced another set of challenges.

Reagan, the man who wanted above all else to limit the influence on society of the government he headed, stood at the intersection of all these concerns. Though he was often distressingly estranged from the mechanics of his own government, though he often seemed enthralled by his muzzy vision of what America was and must be again, he remained the very willing instigator of great change. Consciously or not, he acted out the judgment of Harvard's Professor Wilson: "Today, an administration cannot be conservative by doing little, it can only be conservative by doing a great deal."[8]

Yet Reagan also sluffed off what he called the "minutia" of his office. He insisted on a good night's sleep and as much vacation as his schedulers could carve out of the calendar. Rarely did he allow decisions, once made, to weigh on him. Rarer still were the occasions when he allowed defeats to suffocate his optimism. After two years in what is usually described as the world's most difficult job, after one bullet in his lung, the oldest President in American history looked more fit than he did while running for the office. He insisted on conducting the presidency according to his own metabolism. Reagan the man was as much an anomaly in the White House as Reagan the ism was in American history.

2

Rawhide

"Please hold on," the White House switchboard operator says, "he has been trying to get you."

Her tone of voice leaves no doubt who "he" is. Because Ronald Reagan does not suffer from telephonitis where journalists are concerned, I spend the twenty or thirty seconds it takes for him to get on the line in total bafflement. The rare calls this President makes to reporters are to protest something published or broadcast. As of this Sunday in July 1982 I have been out of print for a month, on leave from *Time* in order to write this book. The only thing to do is reach for a pen and wait.

"Hi," he says. "Where did they find you? I hope I haven't interrupted anything." I assure him that he is distracting me from nothing important—as if that mattered. A phone call from the President of the United States, regardless of the subject or hour, pumps up the ego of any political writer. You've made an impression, you say to yourself, he cares what you think.

In this case, Reagan cared what I thought about his personal involvement in White House business and his views of the powers of his office. We'd had a conversation the day before at Camp David during which I tried—with little success—to make him talk introspectively about his metabolism as an administrator, his personal engagement, or lack of it, in the day-to-day conduct of the presidency. It was a relaxed discussion that Saturday afternoon. We sat on wrought-iron lawn furniture on the patio of the main house, Aspen Lodge, looking out on a Technicolor sweep of flower beds that blend into a sloping lawn and, farther down, the woods through which Reagan loves to canter. He was just back from a ride, still clad in a red knit shirt, beige britches and his favorite pair of ancient, cracked English-style boots complete with spurs. In place of the thin gold Corum he normally wore at the White House, an old stainless steel Rolex would tell him the time today.

His cheeks flushed from his ride, his blue eyes clear and his carriage erect as usual, he conveyed more than enough ruddy vigor to justify the Secret Service code name assigned to him: *Rawhide*. (Nancy Reagan's is *Rainbow* and any limousine in which he rides is *Stagecoach*.) At ease and smiling or telling anecdotes in an animated way, he looked easily a dozen years younger than his age. Only when still, or frowning in concentration, did Reagan's phiz advertise its owner's seventy-one years. Questions that challenge the way he operates or raise theoretical matters unfamiliar to him tend to cause that reaction. So the years showed when I suggested that he was far less involved than his predecessors in the ordinary affairs of government and mentioned the commentary of James David Barber, the Duke University political science professor who has written extensively about the character of previous Presidents.

Barber is well known among political cognoscenti, whether or not they agree with his use of psychohistorical techniques or his classification scheme. He puts his subjects into one of four categories: active-positive, active-negative, passive-positive and passive-negative.* The first adjective measures political ambition and the willingness to assert power; the second concerns personal temperament, self-confidence or insecurity, optimism versus pessimism. During the 1980 campaign Barber had pronounced Reagan passive-positive and stuck to that judgment later.[1] Reagan was unfamiliar with Barber's general thesis as well as its specific application to him. After hearing an explanation, Reagan was uneasy with the subject. What did he think his classification should be? "I don't know," he replied. "The 'passive' thing kind of bothers me a little bit, because I do not think that there is anything 'passive' in what we have attempted here—to turn around the whole fiscal approach of government." True enough, though that didn't deal with Reagan's personal involvement.

Reagan went on to talk about his management style, volunteering the familiar analogy to a corporate board of directors in which the company's senior officials—cabinet members here—argue matters out before the chairman. "Those debates get pretty spirited," Reagan said. "And out of that comes what I need to know to make the decision.

---

* In his best-known work, *The Presidential Character: Predicting Performance in the White House* (Prentice-Hall, 1972), Barber was particularly prescient about Richard Nixon's vulnerability to his own personality flaws. He classed Nixon as active-negative, along with Lyndon Johnson.

And that is the only difference between [this administration's cabinet] and a board of directors' meeting. We do not take a vote. I make the decision."[2]

Something about that exchange had gnawed on Reagan, which was uncharacteristic. He was not prone to dwelling on yesterday's policy decisions, let alone yesterday's talk with a writer. But he ruminated overnight. "Listen," he said, "after you left yesterday I was thinking about it, especially the word 'passive' and so forth. I got to wondering about some things. . . . What I should have said to you yesterday was that while I feel as I do about the proper relationship of federal and state government, I feel that those things that are the federal government's responsibility, we damn well do them."

To support that, he mentioned two cases in which the White House had authorized federal authorities to assist state and local law enforcement agencies: the murders of young blacks in Atlanta and the effort to contain the crime spree in southern Florida, an outbreak centered on narcotics traffic. Both were successful, Reagan remarked. The Atlanta killings had stopped with the arrest of a suspect; the crackdown in Florida was producing numerous indictments and the confiscation of tons of illicit drugs. These examples of federal intervention, Reagan felt, showed that his administration could be active rather than passive under the appropriate circumstances. He rested his case. And, as sometimes happened when he dealt with subtleties, he missed the point. His personal involvement and awareness were at issue, not his interest in fighting crime or, much more importantly, his desire to change the face of government. He may have thought of himself as the board chairman, but the fact was that Reagan often hesitated to make decisions, including important ones, when his senior advisers could not agree on a firm proposal.

Neither the conversation at Camp David nor the telephone chat got close to the heart of the matter. Crudely put, the question that lingered through the 1980 campaign and was still unsettling two years later was whether Reagan in the end would be undone by his own shortcomings of temperament. These attributes are distinct from character, which in Reagan's case was as sound as one could hope to find in high public office. He had in him less vindictiveness, guile, ego or cowardice than most men who make it in politics do. Nor did he suffer from that lust for power, for perfect control of all things large and small, that had so distorted the careers of Lyndon Johnson and Richard Nixon. Rather it was the opposite with Reagan. He was afflicted by a surfeit of qualities we normally regard as assets in our leaders: serenity, confidence in himself, his convictions and those around him, the gift of advocacy, faith in the verities he learned when young and in the rhetoric he had used while transforming himself from fading actor to star politician.

Reagan offered a fascinating challenge. It was easy to allow the simplicity of the ideology to mask the complexity of the person.* In fact he could not be squeezed into any schema as neat as Professor Barber's. That Reagan was "passive" on occasion and "positive" often there could be no doubt. He was also steel-stubborn, venturesome and negative at crucial moments. These characteristics, together with a turn of mind that resisted ambiguity the way an immune system rejects alien substances, threatened his presidency as surely as high unemployment did. He harbored misconceptions about situations that went far beyond simple misinformation. This same flaw appeared, with troubling results, in his handling of a few of his subordinates. Yet, though it seems contradictory, some of these same qualities helped him in his public advocacy, in his role as "communicator in chief," to use the current cliché. They contributed to his persona of steadiness of purpose, to the picture of him as a "nice guy" who managed to combine grit and humaneness. These elements will show up repeatedly as specific situations are recounted in the course of this book. Here I will attempt to describe the President's personal strengths and weaknesses apart from the details of program and policy.

In both of Reagan's presidential campaigns, as well as afterward, reporters repeatedly twitted him for making factual errors. Some of these fluffs involving names or statistics were simple slips of the tongue committed under pressure. During the 1980 New Hampshire primary, for instance, he confused Afghanistan and Pakistan a few times. Defending himself against criticism that his budget reductions were hurting the poor, he told editors of the New York *Post* there would still be "five times as many food stamps as there were in 1978."[3] He meant to say twice as many. During a White House press conference on December 17, 1981, he acknowledged that he could not remember the details of a controversial affirmative action lawsuit. When the questioner summarized the litigation, Reagan responded that he saw nothing wrong with the program at issue; in fact, his Justice Department had already announced itself on the other side of the dispute. Once, in a private conversation with several aides, Reagan wondered aloud why the Federal Reserve Board did not simply reduce the prime rate, one of the most closely watched and important measures of commercial interest. Apparently he had forgot, or did not know, that the private banks rather than the Fed set the prime rate.

That little blooper remained secret, but such lapses occurred in pub-

* Chapter 3 deals with Reaganism.

lic often enough to become a running semi-serious joke. Sometimes Reagan was defensive on the subject, feeling that we were nit-picking. His errors gave rise to some dark speculation that because of age, indolence or both, Reagan simply lacked the capacity and energy to absorb what he needed to know. This was not the case. Reagan in fact still possessed a trick memory which, when he chose to use it, allowed him to retain the contents of long briefing papers.

Now and then he astonished his aides by regurgitating complicated material he'd received only a day earlier. On other occasions he made them nervous with his disinclination to prepare seriously for a press conference or interview. Particularly in the early weeks of incumbency, before the criticism about errors irritated him, he preferred to use the prep sessions with his aides for laughs. Or else he would answer during these private briefings with brutal candor, just to get things off his chest. Some of the participants made notes showing both these tactics. One of the sparring questions concerned his hopes for dealing with Peking—what did he intend to accomplish concerning China? He shot back that he planned to turn that backward country into "a land of Laundromats." How would he respond to criticism from Jimmy Carter? "By calling him a little schmuck." What about attacks from the New Right? "Those bastards won't ever be satisfied."

In one of these drills Reagan talked about the Iranian Government in such caustic terms that his assistants feared he would do the same in public. At the time, Iran still held three private American citizens as prisoners. Reagan could not seem to frame a politic response. Finally he said, "Boy oh boy. Don't worry. I won't behave this way at the press conference. I'll faint or I'll start a coughing fit." At the end of the practice match February 6, Ed Meese urged him, "Be dull, Mr. President." Reagan responded, "Being dull is very hard for me." Reagan the showman felt that he was addressing the larger television audience, which was entitled to a performance, rather than the literal-minded journalists in the room with him.

When a subject interested him and he felt that he needed to know more about it, he had no modesty about asking, even when the request allowed a reporter present to note Reagan's shortage of information.*

* On occasion between February 1981 and May 1982 I was able to attend the daily breakfast meetings conducted by Reagan's three senior assistants, Edwin Meese, Michael Deaver and James Baker, the larger staff meeting that followed, and sessions in the Oval Office attended by Reagan and his "troika." I was also allowed into one meeting of the full cabinet and one of the Cabinet Council on Legal Affairs. Reagan at one of the larger gatherings announced my presence to his colleagues with the quip, "Okay, let's go ahead with that phony script we wrote." It was difficult to tell just how much the presence of an outsider altered the proceedings, but Reagan himself seemed unaffected.

One morning in May 1982, when the fiscal '83 budget dispute was in a fogbank of chaos, his senior advisers said they wanted to bring in several experts to brief him on details of the competing plans. "Right," Reagan replied. "That situation always confuses me." During a Cabinet Council meeting a few days later, members discussed changes in the federal criminal code, including one affecting the insanity plea that John Hinckley was using to evade punishment for the March 30 assassination attempt. Reagan followed the lawyerly talk closely, then broke in to say, "This may be a terrible *confession* of ignorance on my part" —he paused for the appreciative laugh at his intentional double entendre—"but if you plead guilty because of insanity, doesn't that mean you are at least committed [to a mental hospital]?" That misimpression was promptly corrected.

Other subjects, including some important ones, simply bored him, and he showed it. At two consecutive morning meetings with the troika, Reagan quickly assumed a look of sealed indifference when Meese brought up the Law of the Sea treaty. "We really need to follow up on this," Meese said, "before the European trip." The issue was controversial because Reagan had decided, early in 1981, that the United States would not sign the treaty negotiated by the Ford and Carter administrations. Advocates of the pact were raising a howl, but the White House was comfortable with its policy and Reagan saw no reason to worry about the critics.

There was an entirely different species of Reaganesque error that caused real difficulty. This virulent variety came not from a verbal glitch or from watching a movie in the White House theater instead of reading briefing papers. Rather it came from fundamental misunderstandings on certain subjects. And these skewed perceptions virtually always complemented his general ideology.

During the 1980 election campaign this showed up in his frequent assertions that Alaska had larger oil reserves than Saudi Arabia. "We're not an energy-poor nation," he said several times during the primaries, "we're energy-rich." Liberate the oil industry from government regulation, he said, "and we won't need OPEC oil." This at a time when the United States was still importing 40 percent of its oil and when no serious expert was predicting total energy independence for many years to come.* He was so intent on asserting the "magic of

---

* In September 1982, the Congressional Office of Technology Assessment reported that the country might get along without energy imports starting in the year 2010—provided favorable trends continued and the synfuel industry was encouraged to develop. The latter could occur only with substantial government involvement. The Congressional OTA is a bipartisan group, which at the time the report came out was headed by Senator Ted Stevens, a conservative Republican from Alaska.

the marketplace" that in his mind, and early speeches, government meddling was the only obstacle to solving the energy problem forever. It took months for his advisers to persuade him to modify this line of talk and he never did acknowledge that federal conservation measures imposed in the late seventies had helped ameliorate the problem. Nor did his administration adopt an activist energy policy except in promoting nuclear projects.

Reagan believed to his marrow that local institutions can and should take responsibility for many of the social services that have been assumed by government. Thus when he once visited Santa Marta Hospital in a Chicano neighborhood of East Los Angeles he talked to some of the nuns about the financing arrangements. Then, in a jubilant tone, he congratulated Santa Marta for operating independently of government payments. If true, that would have been front-page news; it is unheard of for hospitals in impoverished areas that treat most patients on a charity basis to get along without government funds. Several of us cornered the chief physician, who happened to be an active Republican and an admirer of Reagan. He readily acknowledged that 95 percent of the patients' expenses were underwritten by Medicaid or Medicare. Reagan at that time had been governor of California for eight years, when hospital finance was a major controversy. He was the presidential nominee of a national party and the cost of hospital care was a national issue. Yet his idealized notions about voluntarism predominated in his mind.

A candidate can make some excuses for this sort of thing—the strain of travel, sporadic briefings, exposure two or three times a day to rat-tat-tat interrogation by reporters. An incumbent has none of these alibis. He travels rarely. He can summon up expertise easily. His staff tightly controls access by the press. Yet incumbency made little difference to Reagan. To an audience of black teenagers in Chicago, Reagan said, "A few years ago, before the Great Society, poverty was being reduced in this country. . . . And then came the Great Society programs and, strangely enough, with all that government spending, the poverty stopped being eliminated; in fact, it started going up and so did the unemployment rate, particularly in black communities." Census Bureau figures published routinely show that the percentage of Americans, black and white, below the poverty level continued to fall for several years after Great Society programs began. That trend turned only at the end of the 1970s, when a variety of factors had changed and when Johnson's approach had lost its momentum.[4]

In the same vein, Reagan during his press conference of November 11, 1982, explained why he opposed temporary "make-work job programs" then being promoted by Democrats as a response to the unemployment rate of 10.4 percent. During the seven years ending in fiscal '81, he said, Washington spent $66 billion "on the kind of jobs programs that some of them are talking about now on the Hill. And that $66 billion got us nothing but an increase in unemployment. It did not resolve the problem."

As so many of his other statements did, his remarks about the Great Society and stopgap public works contained grains of truth. The 1960s war on poverty never fulfilled the claims originally made for it (though Vietnam distorted the economic situation, making clear analysis difficult). Temporary jobs appropriations are generally inefficient and worsen the federal deficit. However, to argue that the first made *more* families poor while the second *caused* increasing unemployment leaves out so many other factors as to constitute gross deception.

While some economists might give Reagan a few points in debates like these because his determination to attack inflation is a necessary ingredient to any long-term recovery, yet other instances betrayed a comprehension deficiency of hefty proportions. In the fall of 1981, Reagan scribbled a marginal note on a message from a congressman that eventually led to a furor over the Administration's commitment to civil rights. Reagan's casual act caused his administration to reverse the federal government's long-held policy of taking away tax exemptions as a means of penalizing private schools that practiced racial discrimination.* A year later the controversy was being argued before the Supreme Court, with the federal government no longer on the side of the civil rights movement. Reagan several times tried to explain how he had blundered into this mess, all the while insisting that he was determined to combat segregation. His most poignant explanation popped out spontaneously during a Q and A session with a black audience in Chicago: "It was turned around and [critics] said I was trying to provide tax exemptions for schools that still practiced discrimination. I didn't know there were any . . . maybe I should have [known] but I didn't. And it was a total turnaround of what I had intended."

Maybe he should have known that racism is still a reality? Nonetheless, it was a gracious *mea culpa* in its way, delivered in a tone of genuine regret, and most political leaders would not have had the courage to make such a concession. But Reagan's several statements on the subject could not alter two facts: the Justice Department had retreated on yet another front in the civil rights battle and the President had acknowledged a surprising gap in his awareness of conditions in his country. Reagan's visceral dislike for the Internal Revenue Service and all its works—for him a primordial animosity—had outweighed everything

* The so-called Bob Jones case is described in detail in Chapter 24.

else in the balance. He did not pause to ask whether IRS's practice, which had the blessing of three previous administrations, the sanction of the federal judiciary and the tacit approval of Congress, was still necessary. He did not imagine that blacks would object to his move. For him it was a simple case of intrusive IRS agents unjustly persecuting the underdog.

This incident was unusual in the severity of the backlash it caused and in the White House's frantic, though unsuccessful, effort to undo the public relations damage. Yet it was typical of two facets of Reagan's mind-set. He was frequently unwilling to reexamine his opinions even when his original factual basis for them was shaky or when objective conditions changed. Second, he had difficulty seeing the connections between related goals and understanding the tensions between competing needs. Both blind spots showed up more visibly in domestic affairs than foreign policy; in the latter field he adapted to new situations somewhat more easily, perhaps because he was less certain of his own knowledge.

The stay-the-course syndrome, which would become his campaign motto in 1982, was most apparent in his basic economic program. There was a good argument, of course, for constancy of purpose. Reagan and his aides understood that Carter had weakened himself by zigzags. The new group had what turned out to be an exaggerated fear of being "Carterized." But for Reagan this was more than an expedient reaction to his predecessor's failings. Firmness was part of his self-image, part of the Rawhide shtick long before the Secret Service had to choose a designation for him. As things turned out, Reagan in his fiscal program made the mistake of committing himself far too early to too many hard specifics. Then, in the name of constancy, he lashed himself to figures and schedules that could no longer be sustained as underlying conditions of the economy changed rapidly.

For twenty-five years he had preached that only the bungling intrusions and unreasonable levies of the federal government placed bounds on American prosperity. Now that he was reducing both the interference and the tax burden, recovery had to follow. Toward the end of his long march to power, more and more experts as well as many ordinary citizens began to share the general view that government had grown too large for anyone's good—that was no longer a purely conservative creed. Yet during the quarter century of Reagan's advocacy other things were happening in the nation and the world. Reduction of taxes and regulation could no longer, alone, serve as even a theoretical panacea. Rather Washington would have to develop new, more creative incentives to restore productivity. The private sector, business and labor both, would have to cooperate in fresh approaches to creative capitalism.

The so-called structuralists and neoliberals have been making this case for the last few years. When I asked Reagan, the morning after the midterm election, whether he had ever considered their arguments, he said no. "The complexity," he said, "has really been created by government intervention." He pointed out that among countries that have sought to industrialize their economies during the last twenty to thirty years, those that have followed the free-enterprise model have fared better than socialist nations. "Who are the miracles?" he asked rhetorically. "South Korea, Taiwan, Singapore, Hong Kong."[5]

Of course such a comparison, with Asian nations light-years ahead of their African counterparts in cultural and political development, is beside the point. So is the capitalist/socialist contrast as it pertains to the United States, the domestic problems of which have become extraordinarily complex. The fragile international monetary balance, or imbalance, adds yet another layer of frightening challenge. But Reagan is not intimidated. The Rawhide label is so appropriate for him not merely because of his affection for horses, frontier trappings and wide open spaces. It is uncommonly apt because it also connotes faith in American particularity. We found the right values, the correct answers to all the big ones, long ago. They paid off for us in the past. Now we must simply tighten our grip on them. That some of the more important specific questions change with time does not get a lot of attention in this kind of thinking. Reagan concluded this phase of our talk with a very human, and very American, observation:

I often fantasize [about taking] Soviet leaders in a helicopter and just flying around, just kind of let them choose where we go, so it wouldn't look like a planned tour, and be able to point down and say, "Yeah, those houses down there. Yeah, that house with a trailer and a boat on it in the driveway. That's a working man in America. Yes, he lives in that house. He has that boat. He drives that car to work." . . . They could not show me comparable things in their country.

In a literal sense this aspect of American folklore, in which Reagan believes so fully and on which he trades so well, is unexceptionable. No one questions that the American system has produced a better standard of living for most of its citizens than the Soviet system has. Nor does any serious commentator suggest that Yuri Andropov inherited a going economic enterprise that Americans should envy. The pertinent issue, as that worker fails to keep up monthly payments for his boat, is whether a nostalgic view of the powers of unfettered capitalism is helpful in addressing American needs in the 1980s and 1990s.

Our mythology favors the clean, bold stroke. As an outside critic of big government, Reagan always preached the efficacy of that approach. Running the operation is something else, demanding sophistication and a keen appreciation of the color gray. Here Reagan has had severe problems. That became apparent in the conflicts among his senior advisers in the Treasury, the Office of Management and Budget and the Council of Economic Advisers. Because they were all conservative Republicans, more or less, Reagan assumed that they would be compatible. Instead, differences among the monetarists, supply-siders and orthodox fiscalists tended to exacerbate, rather than ameliorate, the built-in tension between the need to check inflation by means of Federal Reserve Board restrictions and the desire to stimulate growth by large, rapid tax cuts. Toward the end of the first year, when the cost of this conflict was becoming clear, I asked Reagan whether the philosophic cleavage among his experts bothered him.

"I think it makes it easier in this sense," he replied. ". . . It's the fact of opening yourself up to the full range of debate with people who feel both ways. That tests your own beliefs. And my own beliefs were not changed." Government, he said, "has no business fine-tuning the economy and so forth, and forgetting that there is no better tuner of the economy than the people out there in the street with their hand in their pocket to buy something, and the laws of supply and demand."[6] That sounded like Keynesianism, 1933 vintage, but I could not bear to muddy the theoretical waters further that day. The point was larger than Reagan's beliefs—it was how to put them into practice in an effective way. This would require very skillful balancing of diverse factors. In this arena Reagan's team needed a coach to serve as arbiter, someone to compel discriminating editing of the playbook as the game progressed. Instead it had an ebullient cheerleader for the original script.

In foreign affairs Reagan was far more willing to make tactical adaptations under tutoring first from Alexander Haig and then George Shultz. While reluctant to admit it, he inched away from the hard-right positions on a number of occasions in order to get arms control negotiations going with the Soviet Union, for instance. In the national security affairs area he clung to the Rawhide persona most closely on the question of military spending, which to him became an item of great symbolism. It was his message to the Soviet Union, and to America's allies, that the United States was a practicing superpower again.

Yet even here there were disconnects in his thinking. I came across a hidden example of that in Reagan's first important personal message to Leonid Brezhnev. Reagan made the State Department bureaucracy nervous when he insisted on composing the letter himself—apprehension, as it turned out, of some validity.

The date was April 24, 1981, when Reagan was still recuperating from the assassination attempt. On the same day the White House announced that Reagan was lifting the partial embargo on grain exports to the Soviet Union imposed by Carter in response to the invasion of Afghanistan. Reagan had opposed the embargo from the beginning, arguing that it was both ineffective in terms of changing Moscow's behavior and grossly unfair to farmers, who needed to maintain a large share of the Russian market. Yet he waited three months before eliminating the embargo. Haig and others insisted that it would be interpreted as a sign of weakness at a time when Washington contended that the Soviet Union was causing more mischief than ever in the world. Reagan nonetheless felt strongly that he had made a political commitment to American agriculture and he had to honor it.

The public announcement that day emphasized that Reagan was fulfilling a domestic campaign pledge, which indeed he was. It also stressed that the change should not be taken as a conciliatory gesture to Moscow; the Kremlin, after all, had not changed its ways one iota. The presidential statement put out to the public concluded with these two sentences: "We will react strongly to acts of aggression wherever they take place. There will never be a weakening of this resolve."

In the family quarters of the White House, meanwhile, the President was polishing, in longhand, his letter to Brezhnev. In ten succinct paragraphs, he defended with simple eloquence America's record as a peacemaker in international affairs ("We used our power and wealth to rebuild the war-ravaged economies of the world, including those nations who had been our enemies . . ."). He also chided Brezhnev obliquely for allowing ideology and nationalism to overshadow the human needs of Soviet citizenry ("Will the average Soviet family be better off, or even aware that the Soviet Union has imposed a government of its own choice on the people of Afghanistan? . . .").

So far, so consistent. Those ten paragraphs, while emphasizing the new administration's desire for peace, confirmed Reagan's stance that it was up to Moscow to take the first concrete steps toward rapprochement. They were of a piece with Reagan's oft-stated determination to send Moscow a firm, steady "signal." But then the eleventh and final paragraph: "It is in this spirit, in the spirit of helping the people of both our nations, that I have lifted the grain embargo. Perhaps this decision will contribute to creating the circumstances which will lead to the meaningful and constructive dialogue which will assist us in fulfilling our joint obligation to find lasting peace."

Those two sentences not only flew in the face of what the Administration said in public it was doing; they also contradicted what the White House, State Department and Pentagon were in fact trying to do vis-à-vis Moscow. But Reagan did not see the connection at the time. The following November 18 he made public most of that letter to Brezhnev in the course of a speech on arms control. The eleventh paragraph, however, was omitted.

Reagan insisted on writing his own scripts whenever possible, though his staff included a full corps of professional writers. They were even more frustrated than previous White House ghosts because Reagan so often injected his own prose, as well as his own ideas, into his more important speeches. In fact he was better at it than the hired help. He was forever shortening sentences, simplifying images, framing ideas in ways that the average citizen could readily understand. By the time he got to the White House he had spent more than fifty years using every communications medium save Morse code and smoke signals. He had been a successful stage actor in high school and college, a pioneer in the young radio business, a journeyman screen performer, a television personality, a speechmaker to audiences of every description, author of a syndicated newspaper column. For the column he depended heavily on a ghostwriter; Reagan knew better how to write for the ear than the eye, which is why so many of his speeches sounded better than they read.

Like any human being, Reagan best enjoyed doing what he did best. That was why he invested much of his energy working with felt-tip pen and legal pad. Some of his associates used that fact to explain why he delegated so many other responsibilities to those subordinates he trusted. He viewed himself as the creator of the message as well as the chief messenger. Everything else was secondary. There was something to that interpretation, and we'll look at others along the way. But about one crucial fact there could be no doubt: Reagan trusted his aides not wisely but too well. He often leaned on them more heavily than their strength warranted. He also stuck with a few of them for the wrong reasons.

For decades, in his private affairs as well as in public life, Reagan had been a tidy organizer, a believer in compartments. "Mommy" wasn't merely his cute nickname for Nancy; discipline was distinctly her department when the children were young. Much more than other actors, he relied on his agent—and once on his brother, Neil—to negotiate his show business deals. Once he had enough money and property to matter, he turned over all management of it to trustees. When his older two children, Maureen and Michael, needed loans, they dealt with Dad's lawyer, William French Smith, rather than with Dad (and they paid interest).

Reagan had little concern about, or knowledge of, the mechanics of political campaigning. Each time he ran, starting in 1966, he turned over control to managers whom he trusted, Stuart Spencer and Thomas Reed in the gubernatorial races, John Sears in the 1976 challenge to Gerald Ford and Sears again at the beginning of the 1980 campaign. This was not a matter of sentiment or loyalty. He never particularly liked Sears, for instance. To others he complained that Sears sometimes made him personally uncomfortable because the strategist had a withdrawn, imperious manner and eventually created conflict within the organization. Because those rivalries could not be resolved, Reagan eventually fired him. But Reagan took Sears on in the first place and kept him as long as he did because other aides personally closer to Reagan, such as Mike Deaver, advised it on the basis of Sears's expertise.

It is generally wise for candidates to turn over much of the tactical responsibility to professionals. Reagan carried this to extremes. He simply could not interest himself in the nitty-gritty, or even the grand strategy, of campaigning. In 1972, while still governor, he served as Nixon's nominal state chairman in California. He was not expected to do much except lend his name and keep an eye on the working pols. One day Nixon called from Washington. There was a problem in one of the more important counties; the GOP leader there was causing difficulties. Ron, the President said, I hope you're on top of that, we need to straighten things out. Reagan put his hand over the mouthpiece and turned to Deaver, who had followed the drift of the conversation. Who's he talking about, Mike? Reagan could not concern himself with such trivia. Nixon, while fighting the Vietnam war, could.

Ten years later, when he lived in the White House, Reagan had changed not at all. He would occasionally submit to lectures about polls and analysis of them when the issue was of immediate concern to him. Otherwise, he put that under the heading of subjects to be delegated. An amusing example of that occurred during the phone conversation we had when he was uneasy over the "passive" label. That same Sunday, July 25, 1982, the Washington *Post* published in its *Outlook* section a long article by Kevin P. Phillips, a Republican theorist whose work has been must reading inside the fraternity for a dozen years or so. His prose can be dense, but his sweeping analysis is invariably provocative. By the time the July 25 *Post* article appeared, his other recent writings had struck a new theme: that support for Reaganism was dissolving and that the dissolution could lead to social upheaval. After Reagan finished telling me what he had called about, he seemed in no hurry to hang up. We chatted about other things.

Knowing that he read the Sunday papers closely, I asked him about Phillips' latest rendition of his latest line. Yes, he'd read it, Reagan said. "Frankly," the nation's First Republican and Conservative added, "I don't understand him at all. I don't know what the hell he is trying to say."

It would have been easy for Reagan to reply that he hadn't read the article yet, or to fudge in some other way. His candor in this instance, born of self-confidence, was as revealing as it was spontaneous. He did not think it was part of his job to parse a prominent writer's reasoning just because the subject was the downfall of the Reagan presidency and the prospective fragmentation of the 1980 Republican coalition. Let Baker, Wirthlin, Meese and Deaver worry about that sort of thing.

Reagan also let others handle the details of implementing his budget cuts. Because he himself remained persuaded that it was mainly "waste, fraud and abuse" being eliminated, he constantly resisted news accounts showing that real people were losing real benefits. David Stockman and others told him that those suffering losses really did not qualify for help in the first place. Thus Reagan was repeatedly unprepared for the increasing horror stories showing the contrary.

The two most damaging situations in which Reagan relied too heavily, too long on his subordinates were the general management of national security affairs, particularly during 1981, and the administration of the Pentagon through 1982. In the first instance he finally acknowledged that the lax system he had favored initially simply was a bust and that his first National Security Affairs Adviser, Richard Allen, should be let go. In the second case, he continued to place an extraordinary degree of trust in Defense Secretary Caspar Weinberger even though Weinberger did little to justify it.

Weinberger had served Reagan well in California as state finance director. There, and later, in the Nixon administration, he got a reputation as a sharp-eyed, efficient administrator who liked nothing better than to eliminate lard from bureaucracy. Though he knew little about military strategy or complex weapons systems, Weinberger was given the Defense post. The rationale: appropriations would be rising steeply and it would be a political plus to have a man in charge who was able to squeeze as much value as possible from those additional tens of billions.

In Reagan's mind, Weinberger was the perfect choice. Many others impressed with Weinberger's earlier reputation agreed. But performance failed by far to match prospectus. Weinberger was never able to get control over his mammoth department or to force the military services to make efficient use of the new resources being poured in. Nor was he able to help Reagan make discriminating judgments about new weapons systems. The Administration had been in nearly two years, for instance, when Weinberger, after false starts, came up with his final proposal for basing the new missile, the MX. The scheme was so poorly thought out that three of the five members of the Joint Chiefs of Staff opposed the deployment method known as "dense pack." The Defense Department and the White House could not sell the idea to Congress, which brusquely rejected it during the special legislative session in December 1982. Meanwhile Weinberger's stubborn refusal during the first two years to yield any appreciable part of the additional appropriations planned—even when the amounts exceeded the percentage increase originally envisaged as a symbolic show of strength—worsened Reagan's deficit problem. When the full record is in, Weinberger may well be regarded as the least effective Defense Secretary since Louis Johnson caused Harry Truman's bile ducts to flood.

Truman parted with his appointee after the damage became evident. Reagan refused to recognize the problem. On June 15, 1981, the President privately met with a number of senators of both parties. The venerable and decidedly hawkish John Stennis of Mississippi, senior minority member of the Armed Services Committee (and its former chairman), spoke up about the budget problem. He questioned the wisdom of going ahead with two strategic bombers, the B-1 and the Stealth, and wondered aloud whether the country could afford so many other new projects.

According to the notes of one of the participants, Reagan replied, "I have great faith in Cap Weinberger. I had him as finance director when the state was on the verge of bankruptcy. The California budget weighed ten pounds. He would come in my office, eyes popping. Then when he was up testifying [to the state legislature] somebody asked him about a specific item. He'd say look at the second paragraph on page 1,038 and you will find the answer. The harsh questioning stopped."

For Reagan, himself so immune to detail, that kind of performance by Weinberger in a different time and a different place was proof positive that if anyone could do the Pentagon job, "Cap the Knife" was that man. This judgment had been made long before, and Reagan saw no reason to reexamine it. Besides, he had a perfect loathing toward making staff changes. Sentiment was not the reason. Despite his amiability and adept touch with people, Reagan was not particularly sentimental about his subordinates. He felt emotionally close to only three or four of them and Weinberger was not "family." Rather it was his sense of tidiness. Weinberger took care of Defense for him the way Lee Clearwater took care of the livestock and stables at Rancho del Cielo back in California.

Reagan so despised turmoil in the ranks that he tended to deny, even to himself, that it existed, or that he might have to impose order. Yet because of his style of operating, because he refused to enforce discipline, that problem has dogged him throughout his political career. I was only dimly aware of that the first time I talked to him privately at the beginning of the 1980 race. We met in his new campaign office, near Los Angeles International Airport, and Reagan did not appear comfortable either in his own small, sterile office or with the subject of the conversation. He sat in a low easy chair on that day, looking his age and then some. The chair was in one corner of the room. He seemed to feel trapped, and visibly drew back from my questions about Sears's rough handling of others who had been with Reagan longer. It was well known that Deaver and Lyn Nofziger had left the organization at Sears's behest, though both maintained nominal ties. I had already seen Deaver and Nofziger, finding each of them understandably bitter over what had happened, as well as fully absorbed in their private pursuits. But Reagan insisted that there was no difficulty, no controversy over Sears's role. In fact, he said of his two old retainers, "The people who are supposed to have left never really left [the campaign organization]." That talk took place on January 2, 1980. Two years and two weeks later, just after he had forced Dick Allen to resign, Reagan said at a press conference, "He is still part of the Administration." By that he meant that Allen had been named a consultant to a part-time advisory group. But Allen never served a single day in that post, and never intended to do so.

In early 1980, Reagan allowed the staff infection to fester for two more months until a showdown between Sears and Meese forced him to make a choice. In late 1981 a number of events finally compelled him to sort out affairs at the National Security Council staff level. And nearly a year after that he was resisting advice from a few of those closest to him who thought that he must reorganize the White House staff in order to improve operations for the second half of the term. After the midterm election, Reagan still was not ready to act. When I reminded him of the protracted difficulties in the foreign affairs sector during 1981, he did not argue. Then we had this exchange:

Question: Why aren't you a stern disciplinarian? Why aren't you more demanding?

Reagan: Well, first of all, I am a believer in delegating. When you pull the string on delegating is when the person . . . is not meeting that responsibility and then you have no choice but to take action. The system, what I had done, worked very well in California. Now and then there are situations that arise and then you have to take some action. But I think there have been others in this office who did not do that and who attempted to dot every "i" themselves and as a result were up to their eyebrows in minutia and detail that kept them away from what really should be done. And I also believe that constant confrontation does not make for a happy command and that in a way it is a sign of weakness . . . [It is better] if you can keep the ship balanced and from rolling too much without blasting someone. Now behind the scenes I have really stomped around a bit about the leak situation, for example, and yet that is a very hard one. I know that every President has faced that problem . . .

That principle is difficult to refute in the abstract. Reagan often exploited it well in practice too. He had a fine team of legislative strategists, for instance, and he gave it the right combination of policy guidance and operational freedom to perform effectively. Reagan had an unusually competent Transportation Secretary in Drew Lewis, a man who could handle the aftermath of the air traffic controllers' strike without constant heckling from the Oval Office. (But Lewis resigned after two years rather than remain in one of the lesser cabinet posts.) There were other specific success stories that could serve as endorsements for Reagan's belief in delegating. But the failures on the other side of the ledger were serious enough to make one doubt whether Reagan really knew what was going on in his own shop or whether he simply trusted to luck and his retainers. Nancy Reagan knew the drill perfectly when she said, "I think that it's the eternal optimist in him, [the attitude] that if you let something go, it will eventually work itself out. Well, it isn't always so."[7] In the White House, it is almost never so.

The *eternal optimist*. Nancy, as usual, had put her delicate finger on her husband's emotional jugular. Just as his experiences as an actor, union president, taxpayer, PR man for a major corporation—rather than any intellectual process—had shaped his specific political philosophy, his own good fortune in navigating the squalls of life brought him to harbor at the White House with an unsinkable belief in happy landings and happy endings. Yes, there were sea monsters and pirates out there, but you could distinguish the evil from the good in life just as easily as you could in the movies Reagan made circa 1940. With some faith, courage and a bit of luck, virtue would triumph. There was no reason why every tomorrow could not be better than each yesterday. Reagan knew that because he had lived it. His brother had lived it. Most of the people Reagan associated with during California's marvelous boom decades had lived it. His was a thoroughly American vision, derived from his own, and his country's, robust youth. This accounted for Reagan's resistance to bad news, for his preoccupation with heroes and heroism, for his tendency to impose the sunny mythology dispensed by the Hollywood of his era upon the realities of the 1980s.

To him it made sense. Many Americans had sailed through adversity. Many have gone farther than their parents and see no reason that their children should not go farther still. The American dream is the happily-ever-after fade-out. Reagan's father Jack was a benign alcoholic who drank and gambled away much of what he earned. But the mother, Nelle, was a cheerful, spirited, religious soul who somehow always turned out to be right when she said that God would provide. When Reagan was growing up the family moved often, changing Illinois towns five times in fourteen years, never once owning a house. But Ronald, the younger son, led the family to California and was barely thirty when he set Jack and Nelle up in their own place at last.

Did he know he was special? Did he believe in his destiny? Well, sort of. Reagan has written and talked extensively about his growing up and loves to repeat certain lengthy episodes almost verbatim. But the treasure chest of anecdotes is bottomless; now and then the listener finds an unfamiliar gem. Reagan was lucky to be able to attend little Eureka College, which he entered a year before the Wall Street crash and the onset of the Great Depression. Neither of his parents had made it to the ninth grade. The family could not afford tuition for him. But Ronald—"Dutch" to just about everyone—had saved money during several summers of work. His steady girlfriend happened to be the daughter of a clergyman of the denomination—Christian Church (Disciples of Christ)—to which Dutch belonged and with which Eureka was affiliated. Though his academic record was mediocre, he got a partial scholarship and a campus job. But perhaps the most interesting aspect of his triumphant college career* came out unexpectedly during a mellow conversation a month after his election.[8] Like Reagan, many of his Eureka classmates would be the first in their families to move up from the working class. High school teaching and athletic coaching were popular career choices. That track required education courses in order to obtain teacher certification. Reagan wasn't sure just where he was headed, but he thought it would be someplace bigger and better than the small western Illinois towns in which he had grown up. It would be something more exciting than a high school classroom or gymnasium.

"I felt strongly enough about this," he reminisced, "that I was afraid that maybe as it came time to leave the ivy-covered walls and go out into the broad world, I might weaken and say, Well, this is easier— yeah, I'll go out and look for a teaching job too. So I deliberately did

* He was a varsity football player and swimmer, a star of the college drama group, a leader in campus politics, an editor of the yearbook and finally coach of the swim team. But he remained an indifferent performer in the classroom, getting by on his ability to cram on the eve of examinations.

not take the education courses . . . By the time I was a senior, there was no way I could become a teacher."

One of Reagan's strengths then, as later, was a willingness to face his own frailties and to match them nonetheless with ambition. When he did graduate he already knew that acting was his real goal, but radio seemed the most plausible way of getting there. He acknowledged that he flinched after his first attempt to find a broadcasting job in Chicago ended in total frustration. He hitchhiked home to Dixon and was tempted to surrender to the mundane. As he recalled it: "My mother told me that the new Montgomery Ward store in town was looking for someone to handle their sporting goods department. I rushed down, unshaven, and I know I must have looked pretty mussed up from hitchhiking home. I talked to a young man there who didn't seem very impressed. He was really looking for someone who was known in the community. The upshot of it was that a former high school basketball star in town much younger than I got the job, which I think paid fourteen dollars a week."

Had he been luckier that day, Reagan might have stayed in Dixon long enough to marry the hometown girl he had been seeing steadily for six years. He certainly would have done well at Montgomery Ward. He might never have gone to Davenport, Iowa, where he got his first break in radio. Later, as a sports broadcaster he would accompany the Chicago Cubs to spring training camp in California, where he managed to get a screen test at Warner Brothers. On the wind of such quirks the optimism of Ronald Reagan sailed on for succeeding decades.

There were storms along the way, of course. Reagan's virtue-will-out mind-set permitted survival without bitterness. When his motion picture career expired, he held his nose and learned television. When his first year as governor turned out poorly, he regrouped and tried different tactics. When his 1976 bid for the presidency failed and most "experts" were sure his last hurrah had been heard, he quietly waited for one more shot.* When he took a surprising beating in the Iowa caucuses and his organization was conflict-riven in January 1980, he recouped with intense personal campaigning in New Hampshire.

That aura of serenity that sometimes made Reagan seem torpid as President had a decided up side. It allowed him to marshal strength and energy for the big tests. His insistence on shunting responsibilities off to his aides caused administrative breakdowns, but that trait also

---

* I was among them. At the beginning of the 1980 campaign I had strong doubts that Reagan could make it. I chose to cover him because I thought he was the most interesting candidate in the field and because I had become intrigued with right-wing politics.

forced subordinates like David Stockman and James Watt to absorb animosity created by Reagan's policies. That allowed the President to retain more popularity, and hence more clout, than he otherwise would have. Intentionally or not, Reagan in this situation—as in some others —resembled Dwight Eisenhower.

More instinctively than intellectually, Reagan understood that illusion is an element of leadership. His sincerity, his belief in himself and in the ancient verities that filled his texts, helped to compensate for the harsher aspects of his programs. What other presidential candidate, on election eve, could cite John Wayne as the essence of the American hero—and even quote the late Duke's wisdom—in what purported to be a serious half-hour television speech? What other incumbent President could quote an apple-pie movie character played by Gary Cooper in an ostensibly serious speech concerning social service? Reagan could invoke that inspirational, and thoroughly irrelevant, soliloquy from *Mr. Deeds Goes to Town* because he had established himself as a first cousin, if not brother, of that model citizen.

Reagan loved to remind Americans that you didn't have to scratch an ordinary citizen very deep to find a hero. In his Inaugural Address he gestured toward Arlington National Cemetery in the distance, recited a roster of historic battles and recalled an obscure World War I battlefield courier, Martin Treptow, who died carrying a message between battalions. In the diary of the young man, who had been a barber before the war, there was a more important message, a pledge "to fight cheerfully and do my utmost, as if the issue of the whole struggle depended on me alone."

How Reagan savored that line, which he delivered with marvelous feeling. How he enjoyed having in the VIP gallery, as he gave his first State of the Union speech, a junior government worker, Lenny Skutnick, who had plunged into the frigid Potomac to save survivors of an airliner accident earlier that month. During the campaign many reporters and some of Reagan's advisers thought that he committed a blunder when he insisted on calling the Vietnam war a "noble cause." But his instincts were better than ours on this score. The country was finally beginning to shake its phobia about Vietnam and needed encouragement.

In Hollywood Reagan had yearned for adventure scripts, what he called "sword and saddle" roles. He was occasionally frustrated when a bigger draw such as Errol Flynn got the part he coveted. Offscreen Reagan's affection for men of action was no less. He had a deep and abiding respect for soldiers, policemen and anyone else who risked his neck for the right cause. Reagan occasionally would feign emotion during a public appearance for effect, but there was no mistaking the real tears that he shed—beyond the reach of cameras—when he placed a wreath at the Tomb of the Unknown Soldier on Memorial Day, 1982. He had difficulty reading his speech afterward. Looking at the honor guards who lined the footpaths among the graves, Reagan whispered to a couple of assistants, "My God, why would anyone want to send these kids off to die?"

After he was fully recovered from the assassination attempt, I found myself seated at his table when the Reagans had a movie-and-dinner social evening. Someone brought up the Secret Service, cueing Reagan for an anecdote. In 1976 he took up an invitation to visit a Secret Service target range and fired a few rounds for fun. He used the pistol marksman's crouch, but the agents who were practicing did not. They stood erect. He asked a couple of them why, got no answer and finally turned to a supervisor. "If we're firing," the man explained, "we're standing between you and the assassin." That is, the agents were drilled to serve as human shields. Reagan was utterly into his story now, and he could have been the admiral played by Fredric March in *The Bridges at Toko Ri* as he finished, "I've loved them ever since. When I saw the film of March thirtieth, Tim McCarthy* was standing up. You wonder where you find men like that."

To some skeptics, this aspect of the Rawhide persona showed Reagan as a law-and-order fanatic or as a war-lover. Of course he did have the typical conservative's disdain for disturbers of the peace, criminal or otherwise. But his affection for heroism was much broader than that. In his mind it was a distinctly American attribute which did not need a uniform or badge as certification. Courage to do the right thing in adverse circumstances was the only ticket of admission needed.

Reagan tried to expand that particular bit of American mythology into everyday life and into his appeals for confidence in his economic program. The fact that he had the ability of a professional actor helped. His skill on television was too obvious to require much commentary here. He consciously underplayed his performances, avoided bluster and bravado. On camera as well as in person, he never attempted to overpower the audience, whether it was large or small. Rather his manner and his sherry-mellow voice invited the listener to come to him. Watching him do a radio spot, you could appreciate his delivery even more. A few aides or technicians or others might hover around him, but Reagan screened them out of his consciousness. He concentrated his words and his gaze on the microphone before him as

* Like Reagan, McCarthy recovered fully. The dinner took place September 30, 1981.

if wooing the woman of his dreams. That quality, the desire for intimacy with his audience, came through.

Neither the message nor the delivery would ever impress the more cerebral of his adversaries. The liberal elite whom Reagan so often used as a foil raged all the more when success sanctified Reagan's skills. The critic Mark Crispin Miller, in an essay on Reagan's video persona, spoke for many opponents when he wrote: "Reagan is 'nice' as Iago is 'honest'—that is, he is extraordinarily adept at affecting tones and postures which people trust without thinking . . . Reagan is considered 'nice,' not because he is nice, but in part because his image answers (temporarily) the emotional needs of quite a few Americans, who, tired of feeling cynical about their leaders, will swallow anything . . . Reagan's image goes down easy, calming his audience with sweet inversions of the truth."[9]

It is a fact that Reagan has benefited from his nice-guy image which, like images of most public people, became inflated. Reagan is in fact quite nice in any number of ways. He is remarkably free of arrogance. He is willing to kid himself. He is abundantly kind to all those in his service, great or humble. When Joe Canzeri joined the campaign to manage travel logistics, Reagan—always slow learning new names—introduced him to another person as "Canzoni." Realizing his error later, Reagan apologized repeatedly, inviting Canzeri to retaliate by calling him "Reegan."* The President could become genuinely distressed when hearing of an instance of injustice to a person in modest circumstances. In that respect he had something of a caseworker attitude, being sensitive to an individual whose name or picture struck him, while capable of being quite insensitive to the problems of large groups. That is a common trait among conservatives, while many liberals have the opposite tendency.

The "nice-guy" element of Reagan's makeup usually covered the small streak of anger in him. That anger showed itself spontaneously now and then, sometimes with jarring effect. But because it was so rarely seen either in public or in private, Reagan could exploit it for theatrical purposes. During a televised debate at the climax of the New Hampshire primary campaign, for instance, he did himself a lot of good when, during a controversy over the format, he successfully defended his right to speak. When the chairman of the event, Jon Breen, tried to cut off Reagan's microphone, Reagan declared hotly, "I paid for this microphone, Mr. Green!" Reagan got the name wrong,

---

* Canzoni became Canzeri's jocular nickname until he left the White House staff. I was kiddingly called Barnett for several months because of a similar Reagan fluff.

but he played the scene beautifully.* In October of 1982, with TV cameras also present, Reagan during a meeting with Republican candidates for Congress suffered some irrational heckling from one far-right nominee. After the dissident repeatedly interrupted Reagan's speech, the President finally snapped, "Shut up!" That order worked. Then, speaking extemporaneously, Reagan proceeded to demolish his tormentor's extremist arguments with clear logic and good syntax. Situations like these allowed Reagan to demonstrate that he was as mentally alert as the occasion demanded.

Once in a while, however, the sour side of the Reagan anger showed itself. When under attack for being unsympathetic to hardships caused by the recession, Reagan occasionally lashed back in a foolish way. In an interview with one group of journalists, he let his scorn for television news coverage show by saying, "It's an entertainment medium and they're looking for what's eye-catching and spectacular . . . Is it 'news' that some fellow out in South Succotash has just been laid off that he should be interviewed nationwide? Or someone's complaint that the budget cuts are going to hurt their present program?"[10] That protest came with ill grace from someone who had got so much mileage from television news. It also diluted the aura of concern for the afflicted that the White House had been trying to perpetuate.

Normally Reagan covered his animosities. To a few aides he might occasionally exhibit pique, tossing his glasses on the desk as a sign of impatience. When some genuine shock penetrated his placidity, a grimace and a few muttered imprecations were enough to vent his ire. Anwar Sadat's assassination, for instance, struck him hard. He paused before a color photograph of the Sadats and the Reagans, taken just a few weeks earlier when the Egyptian President had visited Washington, and said of the killers, "Bastards, those damn bastards."

Otherwise his intimates saw pretty much the same sunny Reagan the public did. This optimism could be turgid at times. It could be frustrating to advisers who recognized it as an obstacle to getting timely responses to new problems. At the same time Reagan was able to use his natural disposition to good advantage. A leader must be able to evoke confidence, even courage, when objective circumstances indicate that apprehension would be the purely logical response. Reagan came to power in a period when the effectiveness of the government was in doubt, when faith in the economic system was dangerously low. A

---

* Breen was editor of the Nashua *Telegraph*, which staged the debate. The dispute was over whether all the Republican candidates could participate, or only Reagan and Bush, as originally planned. Reagan's managers scored a public relations coup by opting to open the debate to the others while Bush peevishly insisted that Breen was in charge.

large part of his response had to be a restoration of popular optimism. The electorate responded to that quality in him when choosing him for the White House. Once there, he had to gamble that he could exploit it long enough to allow his high-risk policies to take effect. Preaching the return of good times was one thing he did very well. By an accident of history, it was a necessary talent in the early 1980s. Reagan was never passive in exercising that talent.

3

Of Jefferson and Hollywood

Shorthand is the most important dialect of politics. Labels such as New Deal, right-wing fringe, welfare state, Great Society, Moral Majority, denote complex movements or periods of historic change. Library shelves fill up with explication of them. Each of these coinages can also stand alone, conveying in a couple of words a symbol that is instantly recognized, if not fully understood. In a culture that fixates on personalities much more easily than on ideas, it is significant that our shorthand so rarely attaches to the names of Presidents.

"Carterism" never emerged as a collection of tenets or as a device of discourse. The Johnsonian domestic agenda had great heft and so did the Nixonian view of geopolitics. LBJ and RMN would have to settle for such adjectival fragments. Neither they, nor Truman, nor Eisenhower, would be awarded the portentous suffix *ism*, which in the alchemy of our dialect converts a politician's rhetoric into a putative dialectic.

"Reaganism," on the other hand, entered the argot before Ronald Reagan entered the White House. It was no mere headline writer's gimmick (too many characters for that) or anchorman's code (no ideas, please, in TV-ese) or opponents' handy target (not frightening by itself). Rather it became a valid point of reference for a simple reason: Reagan had been clear enough, sincere enough, consistent enough long enough for the term to take on meaning. Whether it appealed to you or appalled you, Reaganism meant something to you. Once Reagan captured power, dogmatists and theorists would debate Reaganism's durability. John Lofton, then editor of *Conservative Digest*, dined out indefinitely on the danger that his New Right faction faced a terrible fate: "the worst of both worlds, Reagan without Reaganism." Kevin P. Phillips, preaching from a different conservative pulpit, looked back on the first year of the Administration to pronounce a malediction: "It didn't take a genius to predict on Inauguration Day that Reaganism would unravel."[1] On the other end of the political spectrum, Arthur E. Rowse, a consumer advocate, rushed out a book-length attack on the new administration which he subtitled *The Promises and Perils of Reaganism.*[2] A subdivision of the *ism*, the *omics,* gained currency in scores of publications even before the liberal economist Robert Lekachman brought out *Greed Is Not Enough: Reaganomics.*[3] That term also seemed able to stand without definition.

This ease of identification was not just the product of one articulate advocate's preachments over a number of years. Rather Reagan sprang from a movement, an informal congress of conservative factions, which had last united behind Barry Goldwater. Reagan was not its sole champion as 1980 began. The movement did not unanimously select him; he captured it because he came closest to being a consensus figure among the disparate sects and because he was the best campaigner during the early primaries. Thanks to his 1976 campaign against Ford, he was also the best-known of the right-wing prospects.

Thus Reaganism existed as a promontory on the political landscape before there was a Reagan administration. Some ideological geology must be practiced in examining the layers of that rise. Most importantly, the strata must be looked at from the viewpoint of their personal creator, Reagan, rather than from the perspective of the movement's miners who would try to extract ores of their own choosing.

It is also vital to understand the larger landscape of 1980. Over the previous dozen years or so the great highway of American politics had devolved into a trackless savanna. Assassinations, racial turmoil, Vietnam, Watergate, the energy crisis, inflation, a series of shocks had softened Americans' confidence in their system and their leaders. Their sense of direction, pointing them only toward better times since World War II, had become muddled. At home the citizenry found itself stuck in the ooze of stagflation. Looking abroad, Americans saw only frustration, burdens, danger. Their elected guides seemed to have led them into one swamp after another. On real estate of that kind, any high ground seemed inviting. Reaganism offered firm footing, refuge from the mush. The ism's composition could wait to be examined. Here, it seemed, was a place to go with a confident scout to lead the way.

In making the trip, many of the travelers understandably failed to notice one of the secrets of Reaganism. It was not a *program* in the conventional political sense either during its two decades of gestation or during most of the 1980 campaign. It was not an agenda of firm, in-

tegrated policies. Reagan had many specific proposals, to be sure, some
vivid and even drastic: large tax reductions, rapid expansion of the
military machine, reassertion of American will in the world, reducing
federal regulation of business activity, and the flaunting of "traditional
values" once again. These and other ideas had the virtue of being easily understood one by one. But they did not constitute an intellectually
coherent program. Reagan made no effort, for instance, to reconcile
the sharply conflicting theories of his economic advisers during either
the campaign or the initial months of incumbency. When it was necessary to attach credible numbers to his radical fiscal proposals just after
Labor Day 1980, the main justification of his tax plank—that heavy
rate reductions would quickly stimulate compensatory revenue—disappeared into a black hole without explanation. By that stage, however,
friends and foes alike felt that they understood the thrust of Reaganism
regardless of specific details.

Reaganism above all was, and remains, a set of attitudes. Based on
its progenitor's quite personal view of America's past, as seen through
the prism of his own experiences before he even considered going into
politics, it offered both an interpretation of history and one man's vision of the future. Reaganism would be labeled conservative, arch-con-
servative, or far-right because of the limitations of our shorthand and
because such labels mean different things at different times when applied to different issues. In the Midwest of Reagan's youth, conservatives and progressives both were isolationist while eastern liberals
began to follow Franklin Roosevelt toward foreign intervention. After
several permutations, Vietnam reversed that positioning. Reagan hung
Calvin Coolidge's portrait in the Cabinet Room and revered his record,
but in foreign affairs Reagan tried to emulate, without attribution, the
more muscular instincts of Theodore Roosevelt and, yes, Lyndon Johnson.

When the subject of his philosophy comes up and time permits a discourse, Reagan enjoys taking the long view, usually starting in the
1770s. One Saturday at Camp David in July 1982, when barrages from
his own right wing were beginning to annoy him, he talked of transmu-
tations. Today's liberals, he said, would have been Tories during the
American Revolution because they would have supported "the central
power of the king." By contrast, "the people whom we call conservatives today would have been the liberals [then], the ones fighting the
Revolution." It is a neat debater's point, ignoring the fact that the patriots' ranks included those who favored central authority, such as
Alexander Hamilton, as well as those who feared it, such as Tom
Paine, plus a spectrum in between.

Reagan loves to quote the elite liberal of that day, Thomas Jefferson, particularly the line that runs: "If we let the federal government tell us when to sow and when to reap, we shall soon want for bread." Jefferson knew the score about the relationships between levels of government, and the modern Democrats who claim his legacy are usurpers. They ignore their godfather's preachments on states' rights and the importance of governments "closest to the people." The inconvenient fact that the founder of Reagan's own party, Lincoln, fought a war to demolish the ultimate extension of states' rights is ignored.

It is more difficult to define modern conservatism than Reaganism. Even sorting out the players is a problem. The Old Right predates the Goldwater movement but today is intertwined with its legacy. Old Right foliage remains close to classic conservatism, emphasizing mainstream issues such as fiscal stability and military preparedness. Adhering closely to the Republican Party, its bibles are *National Review* and *Human Events,* which happen to be among Reagan's favorite periodicals.

The New Right, dating back only to 1970, gives greater emphasis to "family issues" such as abortion and school prayer. It contains populist elements that revere George Wallace as much as they detest the Rockefeller clan. The New Right's ties to the GOP are frail and its leaders have occasionally itched to start a new party of their own. *Conservative Digest* is the New Right's principal publication, Jerry Falwell its best-known religious leader.

The neoconservatives constitute a school of thought rather than a political movement. Most of their spokesmen are academic former Democrats who became disillusioned with the party when it turned left in the late sixties. Their support of some of Reagan's positions in 1980 provided an intellectual patina previously lacking in Reaganism. Articles from *Commentary* and *The Public Interest* began showing up in his black attaché case. The conservative stewpot contains other ingredients as well, the most important being remnants of the old congressional wing of the GOP Gerald Ford exemplified in his day; Howard Baker and George Bush are that faction's heirs in the 1980s.

Reaganism is more eclectic than any of these subdivisions. It proceeds from an ideology simultaneously broader and simpler. One large virtue of it is that the spectator feels that he always knows what Reaganism favors or opposes at least on principle. What it is against, virtually on reflex, is as clear as what it is for. "Government," Reagan likes to say, "exists to protect us from each other. We can't afford the government it would take to protect us from ourselves." Example, Mr. President? He answers, typically, with an anecdote. As governor, he rebelled when federal authorities tried to force California to adopt a regulation requiring motorcyclists to wear crash helmets. The "or else" was loss of federal highway funds. Reagan said no. He could accept standards for lights and brakes on the grounds that pedestrian safety was at stake. But if the biker is "damn fool enough to want to ride without a helmet, then that's his business."

During one conversation in early 1980 Reagan challenged the value of weighing every position on a liberal-conservative scale. I responded with a playful question: Could he think of a single public issue of consequence debated by Barry Goldwater and Ted Kennedy on which he would come down on Kennedy's side? Reagan paused, smiled, finally responded, "I think it would be very, very difficult."

If not impossible. Some of his positions might collide with each other as he picked items from one or another of the conservative subdivisions. Execution might sometimes seem unlikely. But Reagan could rise above that, in perceptual terms, because of his ability to convey strong, enduring conviction. Here is where Reagan stood apart from contemporary rivals and from most Presidents going back five decades. To find close competitors among politicians holding fixed principles, one must call the roll of losers: Henry Wallace, Robert Taft, Barry Goldwater, George McGovern. By 1980, disillusioned with the safe center, the country was ready for someone who proposed to lead it *somewhere*. That in proceeding in the new direction it might be going in reverse appealed to some and seemed irrelevant to others.

Phillips, a Republican theorist skeptical about the *ism's* viability, analyzed the vote and concluded: "Unlike prior groupings, the new coalition empowered in 1980 seems to be one whose constituencies are cojoined more by various nostalgias and backward-looking vistas than by shared philosophies for the *future*. If so, and given that the United States has never before tried revolutionary conservatism, I doubt whether this coalition can launch a full-fledged, generation-long, deeprooted party realignment of the sort the country has seen five times before in its political history . . ."[4] But the ordinary voter doesn't make his selection on the basis of future party alignments, or even on the basis of all his candidate's views. All the polling data of 1980 showed that the electorate that put Reagan in power dissented from some of his well-established positions—on abortion, for instance, as well as gun control, the Equal Rights Amendment and even his insistence on cutting taxes at the risk of enlarging deficits.

That dissent mattered less than other factors in the equation. He offered optimism during hard times, and Reaganism provided a rationale for his bullishness. Reagan offered steady leadership, and Reaganism promised predictability. Though the country generally bars ideologues from high office, by now the possession of something at least resembling a vision was more important than the content. That

American voters violated their normal practice by electing a radical was thus somewhat incidental.

Radical, simple, optimistic. If you had to describe the fundamentals of Reaganism in three adjectives, these would do nicely. They are not necessarily pejorative. They could serve as caption for the American patriots' outlook in 1776. Reagan's view of that war, in fact, was one of the ingredients of his credo as it began to have a national audience in 1964, when he campaigned for Goldwater. Later he would refine it, sand off some of the more abrasive or anomalous splinters. For instance, in one version of his 1964 testament entitled *A Time for Choosing* he called the great rebellion "the only true revolution that has taken place in man's history."

If that assertion were true, heirs to other revolutions in every quarter of the globe would have less claim to legitimacy than the Americans— hardly a politic view for someone aspiring to world leadership. Reagan later dropped the line, but not the thought. It showed up again, unbidden, during one of our airborne conversations. Though it was October 2, late in the campaign year, I was still sifting the soil in which Reagan's ideas had grown.* I brought up the Depression, and his long response took us back to the eighteenth century: "We didn't have just an armed revolution, where one set of rulers overthrew the other. We had one of the truly great, probably the only truly philosophical revolution that had ever taken place. [It produced] an entirely new and unique concept of government by the people, that government had no powers except those granted it voluntarily by the people. When I talk about freedom, I think in the larger sense what I'm talking about is, 'Let us recall our heritage and let us realize that unique theory is still the newest idea in man's relations with man.' "

A subordinate element in Reagan's historical sense is divine intervention. Secular-minded rebels everywhere destroyed the royalists' heavenly link; republicans picked up the connection. With less fire and brimstone, but with similar conviction, Reagan, like Jerry Falwell, sees the Deity's hand in America's destiny. He returns to that theme periodically, as he did in his Inaugural Address: "We are a nation under God, and I believe God intended for us to be free. It would be fitting and good if each Inaugural Day should be a day of prayer." This is no mere rhetorical device, no hired speechwriter's bow to the pious. It must always be remembered that Reagan, more than any other politi-

---

* From January through October 1980 I had a dozen interviews with Reagan, the majority of them dealing with the evolution of his ideas. The quotations in this chapter, unless otherwise attributed, are from those talks. With one or two exceptions, later conversations with him dealt with contemporary subjects.

cian at the national level, writes his own script. Even more important is that he believes what he writes.

So the American Revolution by this reading was not simply a striving for independence from a particular monarch and government. It was a blow against the tyranny of government in general and central government in particular. King George III and his ministers were eventually replaced as tyrants by Czar Franklin and his Brain Trust. In between, things were pretty good. Reagan's analysis skirts the period between George Washington and Herbert Hoover, leaving aside any explanation of the nation's difficulties before federal bureaucrats undermined the free enterprise system and individual responsibility. Nor has he ever been much concerned with the failings of state governments. Rather the implicit and constant analogy is between London of the 1770s and what Washington became in the 1930s.

In 1964: "I think we have come to a time for choosing. Two contrary philosophies divide us in this land of ours. Either we believe in our traditional system of individual liberty, or we abandon the American Revolution and confess that an intellectual elite in a far distant capital can plan our lives for us better than we can plan them ourselves."

In his Inaugural Address nearly seventeen years later: "In this present [economic] crisis, government is not the solution to our problem. Government is the problem. From time to time we have been tempted to believe that society has become too complex to be managed by self-rule, that government by an elite group is superior . . ."

Gratuitous complexity is another adversary to be overcome if we are to return to that "traditional system of individual liberty." Reagan set himself up for caricature when he took the oath as Governor of California in 1967. "For many years now," he said, "you and I have been shushed like children and told there are no simple answers to the complex problems that are beyond our comprehension. Well, the truth is there are simple answers. There are just not easy ones." Even after he had held the presidency for eleven months he was willing to defend that assertion, up to a point. "There are many questions," he said during a relaxed conversation while vacationing in California, "that are complicated because of many facets. But there still are hard decisions that are simple. You know that to get from here to there, this is what you should do. And you also know that in doing it, you're going to run into all kinds of flak and it's going to be difficult but it's the only answer."[5]

Simplicity comes up repeatedly in another way. One of his favorite ploys at campaign stops was to gesture to the high school band or some other group of youngsters near the platform. Then he wished aloud that these kids could enjoy the kind of freedom their elders had when they were young. When pressed to elaborate, he would rely, as usual, on anecdote. He worked hard as a teenager; he needed a nest egg for college. "At the end of the week all the boss [a building contractor] had to do was reach in his pocket and take out the cash to pay me—no auditors, no bookkeeping, no withholding of any funds or anything. Much of [the government regulation] we have today is what has made teenage unemployment, particularly lack of summer jobs, so great." No one can beat Reagan at distilling the foibles of government. "I have a pond at my ranch. I built that pond. Now, if I stock that pond with fish, I have to get a license to throw a line into my own pond and catch my own fish."

He insists that he isn't on a nostalgia trip. He acknowledges that the good old days had their problems (though he remembers surmounting them on his own, rather than suffering from them). In any event, he concedes the folly of "seeking the past." And yet, and yet. The embers of yesteryear still illuminate Reagan's forward vision, memories of small-town neighbors caring for each other, of plucky entrepreneurs making it, of the handful of blacks he knew surviving oppressive bigotry with the help of a few good people like the Reagans. Hardship was a retail affair. If there was an underclass somewhere, folks on the prairies had no awareness of it, no name for it. Most everyone you know was an unashamed patriot. Once, when an itinerant orator gave young Reagan a mild case of pacifism, his father, Jack, quickly scourged the alien microbes with a stern lecture on patriotism.

These antecedents of Reaganism, hardly original, formed early, even before he left Illinois. They included assertive pride in country and a becoming confidence that opportunity beckons, even in bleak times, for those energetic enough to seize it. Of course it helped when seizing opportunities to be tall, handsome, healthy, quick-witted, personable, proficient in athletics, Protestant and white. Reagan freely concedes that he came by his later political convictions through his personal experiences, most of them from the mid-forties to the early sixties, before he ran for public office. Eight years as Governor of California (1967–75) taught him tactics and finesse, not philosophy. The theory, and much of the specific verbiage for that matter, were already on the record before he got to Sacramento. It can be found in his 1965 autobiography, *Where's the Rest of Me?*, and in his speeches.

When interviewers, including this one, would later nag him to name specific intellectual gurus, he usually demurred. In one discussion during the transition period, for instance, he shied away from giving an enthusiastic blessing to the writings of Norman Podhoretz on the post-Vietnam syndrome. This despite the fact that he was familiar with

Podhoretz's views on the subject and shared them. Perhaps Reagan, with his canny sense of prospective traps, guessed that the neoconservative editor of *Commentary* would eventually become a critic of Administration foreign policy. George Gilder, the theorist who interweaves social and economic doctrine with startling effect, became for a time the new administration's most quoted current author. Gilder and Reagan both have a romantic view of the American entrepreneur, an estimate that goes far beyond Adam Smith's affection for capitalism's benefits. Gilder preaches:

> Capitalism begins with giving. Not from greed, avarice, or even self-love can one expect the rewards of commerce, but from a spirit closely akin to altruism, a regard for the needs of others, a benevolent, outgoing and courageous temper of mind . . . Not taking and consuming, but giving, risking and creating are the characteristic roles of the capitalist, the key producer of the wealth of nations . . .[6]

Reagan permits himself a pinch of hyperbole now and then, a dab of schmaltz here and there, but he would never go for that kind of self-indulgence. Besides, when David Stockman and others were promoting Gilder's new book enthusiastically in early 1981, Reagan might have sensed that by 1982 the supply-side blossom would be wilting. Thus the President, in public at least, contained his enthusiasm for the suddenly modish Gilder.

Early in his term, however, he made an exception while talking with a pair of writers collaborating on a book describing Reaganomics. The three economic thinkers he cited were Ludwig von Mises, Friedrich von Hayek and Frédéric Bastiat.[7] All of them, predictably, were free-market advocates. Bastiat, a Frenchman dead for sixty years when Reagan was born, "dominated my reading," he observed. Reagan would also point out, when appropriate, that he majored in economics at Eureka College. (The school then had an enrollment of 250 and an economics faculty of one.) Reagan, by his own account, was an indifferent scholar who managed to maintain athletic eligibility. Eureka was hardly the cradle for his later political convictions.

In fact, when he thought about politics at all as a young man, he considered himself a Democrat and an admirer of Roosevelt. Jack Reagan was a liberal Irish Catholic Democrat in the conservative, Protestant Republican towns where the family lived. Jack and his older son Neil ("Moon") found jobs for a time in the burgeoning welfare apparatus of the early New Deal. Neil soon soured on Roosevelt's ways and turned Republican while Ronnie ("Dutch") kept the family faith. It was a subject of friendly argument between the brothers for years to come.

The threat of bureaucracy began to be clear to Reagan, he says, during World War II when he traded in his commission as a Reserve Cavalry officer for an Army Air Corps assignment making training films. Poor eyesight, a chronic problem since childhood, disqualified him from regular duty. In our campaign-year conversations, the same anecdote cropped up at least three times. Captain Reagan was surprised, then appalled, at the administrative sloth of the civilian work force at his military post. The installation had assigned to it 250 civilian workers who shouldn't have been there in the first place. Further, that complement then required a larger administrative section than the one serving 1,300 officers and enlisted men. "I came out of the Army with some questions about bureaucracy," Reagan remarked. Fascinated that this minor incident should have stayed in his mind for nearly forty years, I thumbed through *Where's the Rest of Me?* On page 124 I found the same account, with the same numbers, the same tone of indignation.

Reagan also came out of military service with some grave questions about the equity of the progressive income tax, which then carried a maximum marginal rate of 91 percent. Reagan's contract with Warner's paid him $3,500 a week, a princely salary in the mid-forties. He had a large tax bill on income he had accrued while in uniform. Later, on the General Electric lecture circuit, he would castigate "the myth that our graduated income tax has any resemblance to proportionate taxation. The entire structure was created by Karl Marx. It simply is a penalty on the individual who can improve his own lot; it takes his earnings from him and redistributes them to people who are incapable of earning as much as he can." That particular arrow would disappear from his rhetorical quiver but the thought behind it remained fixed in the bowman's mind.

Far more important to the shaping of his political mentality was what happened to the motion picture business between the mid-forties and the late fifties. Reagan was not just an actor and to him the industry was far more than the cow giving him milk. Reagan loved the movies as an *institution,* as a way of life. Often he was more interested in his larger role in Hollywood—his six terms as president of the Screen Actors Guild—than in some of the ho-hum parts he played before the cameras. He defended the industry's interests against adversity as vigorously as he sought to protect performers' interests in negotiations with the studios. Though vinegar laces his memories, he enjoys reminiscing. One afternoon in early June, between Cedar Rapids and Milwaukee, neither of us wanted to talk about the farmers' problems or other current concerns. We took another trip back to Hollywood, birthplace of talkies and of Reaganism.

He was still a Democrat in 1948, one of those sensible followers of the Donkey who tried to lure Dwight Eisenhower into their party as its presidential candidate. When the general declined, Reagan fell in line behind Truman. Thirteen years before he would officially convert to the Republican Party, Reagan voted Democrat for the last time in a national election. "I discovered that Hollywood was one of the early industries that kind of felt the heavy hand of government. I think it was possibly because Hollywood had such poor public relations. No one was going to go to the rescue of big, fat Hollywood."

One problem was caused by Western European capitals rather than Washington. Starved for hard currency, several countries prohibited American motion picture companies from repatriating earnings to the United States. This limited Hollywood's foreign market. It also forced some producers to shoot films abroad, using overseas revenue in the countries of origin. One result was to reduce jobs in Los Angeles. With other union leaders, Reagan had a personal audience with Truman. They found the President unsympathetic. "I remember him saying, 'Oh, yes, but think of their problems.' He was a little displeased with me when I said that an unemployed crew member in Hollywood is just as hungry as an unemployed crew member in London." The moral of the tale was quite clear to Reagan: his appeal to the President did not deter intrusive governments from making life more difficult for private enterprise. And Truman had sided with the foreign perpetrators rather than with the victims at home.

An even heavier blow fell when Washington forced the major studios to relinquish their holdings in chains of theaters. "That literally destroyed the stability of the motion picture business," Reagan pointed out. In particular, it damaged the large companies and the contract-player system through which Reagan had entered the field and in which he had prospered. His grudge against Washington grew apace. I was fascinated, more than two years after this conversation, to hear Reagan bring up the divestment issue again as we talked in the Oval Office. He used some of the same phrases (". . . destroyed the stability . . .") as we talked about contemporary global macroeconomics and the risks contained in his program. In this interview, on November 3, 1982, he defended his ideas by reaching back to Hollywood and Sacramento to support his belief in the "freedom of the marketplace." He did that often, perhaps as an expedient way of avoiding an unpleasant fact: vintage Reaganism did not address some of the more complicated current economic concerns, such as difficulties in international liquidity and obsolescence in the concepts (as opposed to the equipment) of traditional American smokestack industries.

Hollywood was also the cradle for Reagan's animosity toward Moscow. It had little to do, back then, with the Iron Curtain or the defeat of Chiang Kai-shek. Those and similar offenses would vex him later, in retrospect. At the time Reagan was not much interested in events occurring east of Pasadena or west of Santa Monica. The Screen Actors Guild found itself an injured bystander in jurisdictional disputes among other Hollywood unions, some of which contained Communist elements. The labor wars were disruptive, at times violent. The atmosphere was contaminated further by the beginnings of the investigations of leftist influence in the creative end of the business. According to his own account and the recollections of others, Reagan at the outset was a conventional liberal. He even found himself participating, unwittingly, in a new organization that turned out to be dark pink. At the end, he was carrying a pistol because he thought his life was threatened and he was a committed anti-Communist.

This was all ancient history at the time of the 1980 campaign, of course. There was much else to talk about concerning Moscow. But I was struck by the intensity of his feelings toward the Soviet Union. On another flight between campaign stops I asked him whether that sentiment was rooted in the Hollywood conflicts. Yes, he said, and then he startled me with a different kind of memory lane excursion. Regardless of his tone while speaking from a lectern, Reagan in private almost never shows anger or other vivid emotion to an outsider. Even when challenged with unpleasant questions, he controls himself to a remarkable degree. This time it was different. As he recounted what to him had been a grim period, all traces of amiability vanished. He unleashed no one-liners, no jolly anecdotes. Instead there was a cold fury which had by now survived for thirty years. He spoke slowly:

> I was never favorable toward Communism, but I would admit that coming out of service in World War II, when the Soviet Union had been an ally, I did not see them as an imminent threat. And I must say that I returned to the motion picture industry unaware of what had been going on during the latter war years by way of certain labor unions having been infiltrated by the American Communist Party. And I was unaware and unbelieving until they made their big effort by way of a jurisdictional strike to gain control of the picture business. And I discovered firsthand what was going on. I became during that period the president of the Guild. I sat for seven months, virtually daily, in meetings attempting to resolve the strike that was threatening the whole motion picture business. And I discovered it firsthand—the cynicism, the brutality, the complete lack of morality in their positions, and the cold-bloodedness of their attempt, at any cost, to gain control of that industry.

Reagan was acting as a mediator because the Guild had no direct interest in the strike; the actors would walk out later. His role in that and other phases of the Hollywood struggles, he still believes, injured his acting career. He was never part of the witch-hunting apparatus during the McCarthyite terror, but neither did he waste much sympathy on most of those who were blacklisted. Instead, he thinks that the real victims were the good eggs, like himself. He continued his monologue with bitterness: "Today, the rewriting of history that is going on about that era is the biggest fairy tale since 'Snow White.' The idea that a little band of freethinkers was being persecuted by the motion picture industry—well, they had pretty good control already. They could destroy careers, and they did." Finally, he had no doubt that the effort was directed by Moscow.

His concluding mention of Moscow seemed to be a throwaway line in that conversation, which took place in mid-May. It was not clear then just how personally he viewed jousts with Communists going back to the late 1940s. But in Florida at the end of October, when his victory over Carter was probable if not yet certain, we had another sort of exchange. Two of my *Time* colleagues from New York joined the entourage in St. Petersburg. It was a formal occasion; three tape recorders were in use. The fruits of this session were to be used in our special election issue if Reagan won. Thus he was asked to speak as the President-elect. Some questions dealt with the Kremlin. Asked whether he thought the Soviets preferred Carter's reelection, he replied, "I have to believe probably they wouldn't want me. . . . I get a little treatment in their own press every once in a while, and it's pretty unfriendly. You see, they remember back, I guess, [to] those union days when we had a domestic Communist problem. I was very definitely on the wrong side for them."*

It was a remarkable piece of rumination. To Reagan, there is an element of human vendetta in the geopolitical contest. Because his own visceral animosity began in the 1940s, Moscow's feeling toward him must be mutual. He had originally made the Soviet blacklist not by preaching a hawkish military policy in the 1960s and 1970s, not by denouncing détente and SALT; rather, the Soviets first had his number, as he had theirs, when Josef Stalin was trying to subvert the United States by means of the silver screen. This phase of Reaganism, like much of the rest of it, is a vividly personal emotion. His denunciation of Soviet immorality when he held his first White House press conference had almost as much to do with Stalin's assault on Hollywood as it did with Brezhnev's invasion of Afghanistan.

Reagan's approach to both foreign affairs and economics congealed

---

* This observation went unpublished at the time because the article dealt with his future plans rather than Reagan's past.

during the Eisenhower era. Ike's tenure roughly coincided with the eight years Reagan spent working for General Electric as host of its television series and, more importantly, as the company's messenger to its plant workers around the country. His career in motion pictures had pretty much expired and the GE deal was a godsend. Reagan did much of his own research, collecting snippets and anecdotes that backed up his hardening views. He also began to associate with conservative businessmen outside the entertainment field. Always an admirer of success, he came to respect them profoundly. In 1980, on the brink of winning the presidency, there would still be deference in his voice when he mentioned "Mr. Cordiner," who had run GE during Reagan's stint there. It was never "Ralph" or "Cordiner," but always "Mr." during conversations in which Eisenhower came out "Ike" and Ford, "Jerry."

During that period, and later, when the Goldwater campaign enticed him further into politics, Reagan boldly challenged some of the institutions which most other politicians regarded as positive—or at least permanent—accomplishments of the New Deal. Here Reagan's radicalism began to show. He was skeptical about the compulsory Social Security system, derisive of the Tennessee Valley Authority, hostile to welfare programs. These views would haunt him when he became a national candidate in 1976 and 1980 and he had to adjust his public rhetoric to some extent. But there was no doubt that he continued to view the New Deal's legacy not only as a failure, but as the malign force that distorted public policy for nearly half a century. When we discussed the Republican Party's long decline, he had, as usual, a firm idea:

One reason came out of the Great Depression. There was a loss of confidence in the system itself . . . Democrats came in on the great surge of 1932 and they embarked on the great social reforms and so forth. If you look back in hindsight, you find that these social reforms really didn't work. They didn't cure unemployment, they didn't solve the social problems. But what came from that was a group of people in government, entrenched in government in the permanent structure, who wanted social reforms just for the sake of the social reforms. They didn't see them as temporary medicine as most people saw them, to cure the ills of the Depression. They saw them as a permanent way of life. Now, maybe, the thing that has happened today [rising doubts about conventional liberal approaches] would have happened sooner if we had not had World War II. Everyone's mind was turned to that . . . And incidentally, the only cure for unemployment that came out of all social reforms was World War II, which was a rather expensive way to cure unemployment. Now peacetime came and there was no question about the Democratic Party having solidified its hold on the people.

By Reagan's reading, Republicans then failed to meet the challenge. The GOP's problem was "pragmatism on the part of some, the Republicans who said, 'Look what they're doing and they're staying in power. The only way for us, if we want to have any impact at all, is to somehow copy them.' This was where the split began to grow in the party." Unity was restored by the scourging of the pragmatists, the tinkerers, the Republicans who thought that they could find a place in the sun by managing the New Deal legacy better than Democrats did.

This fundamental issue arose repeatedly once Reagan was in the White House. If Reagan's analysis was correct and the great body of reforms dating from the mid-thirties was illegitimate, then reigniting prosperity was only one immediate goal. The long-term aim must be to reduce the size and influence of the federal government across the board. Private enterprise, once unfettered, would supply the meat and potatoes. Shrinking the government would be the more worthy end when collisions with expedience arose, as they inevitably did. Reagan's faith in capitalism remained pure. So did his confidence that Americans, "the most generous people on earth," would find ways to help their poor relations even without Big Brother's stick prodding the donors.

This would be insufficient for some of Reagan's more fervent supporters. Just as liberals are frequently disappointed once their candidates become incumbents, the collection of activists and special interest groups carrying the shorthand designation New Right would be irked regularly by supposed deviations. They found the appointment of Sandra Day O'Connor to the Supreme Court objectionable because she was ostensibly soft on abortion. Alexander Haig was soft on Moscow. William French Smith was soft on affirmative action. The Old Right shared some of these complaints, along with others: that the Reaganauts were not eliminating government regulations fast enough and that they flirted with selling out Taiwan. Neoconservatives complained about what they perceived to be a return to Henry Kissinger's foreign policy.

Reagan tried to keep the peace with these factions. Occasionally he or his senior advisers met quietly with delegations of frustrated conservatives in the White House to allow the venting of steam. In March of 1981 Reagan attended a meeting of the Conservative Political Action Conference, a group dominated by the Old Right, and gave the troops some inspiration. "Because ours is a consistent philosophy of government," he said, "we can be very clear. We do not have a separate social agenda, a separate economic agenda, a separate foreign agenda. We have one agenda. Just as surely as we seek to put our financial house in order and rebuild our nation's defenses, so too we seek to protect the unborn, to end the manipulation of schoolchildren by utopian planners and permit the acknowledgment of a Supreme Being in our classrooms."

It was good stuff; the crowd at the Mayflower Hotel on Connecticut Avenue loved it. They wanted to believe that Reagan shared their enthusiasm equally for all the entries on their shopping list. Of course he did not and could not. He long ago repented having signed what was then a liberal abortion bill in California, but he could never be as fervid about the Right-to-Life movement as he was in attacking high taxes. He recanted his early support of the Equal Rights Amendment as well, allowing a protracted flirtation with the anti-feminists. But the ostensible dangers of Big Feminism could never engage his interest the way the menace of Big Government did. Reagan would sympathize with these activists, give them some aid and comfort when feasible, appoint some of their leaders to middle-echelon jobs. But he would exploit them as any leader must use factional supporters to serve his own priorities. And he could see the humor of the situation. Once he said, "Sometimes our right hand doesn't know what our far-right hand is doing." Pendleton James, then White House personnel director, mused over that remark and added a kicker: "I know what our far-right hand is doing. It's beating the shit out of me."[8] James at that time was under attack because too many "moderates" were getting patronage appointments.

By mid-1982 Reagan no longer joked about the subject. *Conservative Digest* put out a special issue in July devoted to what it called in the cover slash "the growing conservative disappointment with the President." At the same time, assorted right-wingers, including individuals personally close to Reagan for many years, held "emergency" meetings to organize opposition to a revenue measure he sponsored which contravened supply-side doctrine.

Reagan usually contained his annoyance, but the New Right activists were getting under his skin, particularly the faction led by Richard Viguerie, publisher of *Conservative Digest* and underwriter of half a dozen special-interest groups. Speaking specifically of that complex, Reagan said in one conversation, "Some of them are narrow ideologues. The simple truth is that a number of those [organizations and activists], particularly around Washington, who continue to do this, didn't want me to be the candidate in the first place. So for them to now pose as great Reagan supporters who have been betrayed by me— well, I happen to know that they were looking for other candidates." As Reagan viewed it, the New Right came into his 1980 tent only after other conservatives, such as John Connally and Philip Crane, dropped out of the race for the Republican nomination. Much earlier, the same factions had approached him in 1976 about leading a third-party movement. "And I wouldn't do it," he said with a touch of defiance. "I didn't think it was the thing to do and I guess maybe there is a certain unforgiveness."

By now Reagan would admit, albeit with reluctance, that there were indeed different priorities for the assorted conservative agendas. His central interest was government's impingement on the private sector and the federal-state relationship. "Now," he said, "when you bring up some of those other social issues, they are very vital and very important, but they're a periphery to a philosophy."

Question: "They are not the essence of what you've been crusading about?"

Reagan: "No."

Question: "They are adornments, they are filigree, so to speak?"

Reagan: "Yes."9

Ah, now we had got somewhere. Reagan of course would concentrate on the core and do the best he could within the limitations of incumbency. When his desire for much larger defense spending collided with his need to balance the budget, Reagan held out longer and more stubbornly than any other politician in his place would have. Then he gave a little ground—only because the alternative was paralysis and the surrender of his whole program.

Reagan turned out to be slightly less hawkish in foreign affairs than foes on the left feared and friends on the right hoped. When he found that some items on his wish-list conflicted with others—his opposition to peacetime draft registration, say, versus his desire to show the United States as resolute—he had to make choices. The results, occasionally, were contradictory. He would sell grain to the Soviets in order to keep what he considered a campaign promise, and later he would risk upheaval within the Western alliance by attempting to scotch other kinds of East-West commercial transactions. Those recurring dilemmas, together with his willingness to hire subordinates from the center as well as the right of the party, aroused dark suspicions that he was, after all, merely another pragmatist in power, that he was responding to what Walter Lippmann once called the suction of the center.

Hardly. The idea that Reagan is a California Disraeli, willing to co-opt the opposition by stealing its thunder, cannot stand scrutiny. Nixon, the ultimate pragmatist, understood the Disraeli strategy well. He appointed Daniel Patrick Moynihan to his White House staff and used that Democratic academician to attempt to nationalize the welfare system. Reagan's Democrat was Jeane Kirkpatrick, defender of right-wing dictatorships. Nixon got his second year off to a dramatic start by proposing a great federal crusade against air and water pollution (the program was enacted, though history has given Nixon scant credit for it). Reagan appointed James Watt and Anne Gorsuch, who quickly became the environmentalists' bogeypersons. When it was time for Reagan to come up with a show-stopper for his second act in 1982, he launched his Federalism initiative. Its purpose: to divest Washington of dozens of programs in the welfare, health and education fields. That decision was particularly revealing. It was irrelevant to the country's most pressing problems of that season—serious recession accompanied by a growing federal deficit—but highly relevant to Reagan's main domestic goal.

Though the issue had burned him politically in the past, Reagan took one more whack at the Social Security system in 1981. That effort to reduce costs, uncharacteristically inept, failed utterly. But the fact that he was willing to act out another of his long-held instincts despite the political price was significant. Hoping to establish some rapport with organized labor, Reagan as candidate and incumbent liked to remind blue collar audiences that he was the only former union chief to get a major party's nomination for President. One of the few unions that supported his candidacy was the Professional Air Traffic Controllers Organization. When PATCO struck against his administration in 1981, Reagan not only fired all the strikers, he totally demolished the union. PATCO eventually lost its certification and went bankrupt. But in 1970 when postal workers staged an illegal strike, they were taken back and given a new contract with a pay increase. Their unions have since flourished.

The fact that a man who had once led a strike of film actors took a bold stand against an aggressive civil service union turned out to be good politics. But that risky decision, like others he took, came directly from Reagan's gut. He did not agonize over it, pray over it or even think a great deal about it. Some of his most enthusiastic supporters would occasionally be surprised, or disappointed, at what Reaganism wrought. They mistook his commitment to a set of personal convictions for their own adherence to more complex programs. Sometimes it seemed as if they were let down when they discovered that he wasn't a fanatic. That he was not. As the author of Reaganism, he reserved to himself the right to interpret it as he went along, like a writer-director filming his own script. But the desired ending never changed, nor the main ingredients of the plot. As reels of the record accumulated, Reagan could claim that he was still a Reaganite.

4

The Team

Translating Reaganism from a set of interesting attitudes into firm policies for governance would require prodigious alchemy. Every new President, the morning after election, confronts intimidating reality. He has eleven weeks before he places his hand on the Bible before the Chief Justice of the United States. During that period he must choose his cabinet, oversee the process that will eventually recruit the other four hundred or so policy makers who count—not to mention four thousand retainers in the lower patronage ranks—and make some hard decisions about how his power will be used.

In Reagan's case, the challenges were more numerous. The economy was taking another dip. Iran still held Americans hostage. The Soviet Union seemed on the verge of moving against Poland. Beyond all that, his election was not merely a switch in partisan control of the White House; it was supposed to be a symbol of profound change of direction for the country. The right wing, which had nurtured his political career, had no tradition of public service. There was nothing approaching a Reaganite shadow government, no corps of followers schooled in his ideas and sophisticated in running the tangled mass of agencies and programs called the federal government. Still another twist: Reagan vowed to diffuse power in Washington, to bring back "cabinet government" on the style of the Eisenhower era. That goal, together with Reagan's well-established habit of delegating authority to his immediate staff, made his choice of ministers and courtiers and spear carriers even more crucial to his presidency's success than is normally the case.

Edwin Meese knew all of this even before his "client," as he liked to think of Reagan, announced his candidacy. Meese, the lawyer who had been Reagan's Chief of Staff for six years in Sacramento and eventually rose to the top echelon of the 1980 campaign organization, liked to plan ahead. In November 1979, just as Reagan was entering the competition officially, Meese invited to lunch at the California Club in Los Angeles Pendleton James, a professional hunter of executive talent. Meese asked his old pal to prepare a "what-if" plan for personnel selection. "I promptly forgot it," James recalled later. "The election seemed far away and I figured Ed just wanted to make me feel part of the operation."[1]

Five months later, when the nomination was assured but the larger prize was still iffy, Meese came back at James, demanding his plan. So the headhunter spent a weekend in a Palm Springs hotel room producing a rough outline. The scheme evolved into a complex, phased operation to be carried out between mid-spring and late November. For the serious cabinet prospects, elaborate dossiers would be prepared, as many as eight for each of the more important cabinet posts. During the summer James was quietly brought into the campaign organization, given a separate budget of $80,000* and told to make himself invisible. William Casey, the campaign manager, grumbled that the caper would detract energy from the election effort and, if publicized, make Reagan appear complacent. James rented space in what had been the Bush for President headquarters. Most campaign officials were unaware of his work—even his existence—until the election.

If Ed Meese liked thinking ahead, he liked even more to deal in structure, in organization charts. During the campaign one of his functions was to supervise policy formulation. In that capacity he created a bewildering array of advisory councils, roster upon roster, though few had any influence. To consider high-level personnel selections, he had a group that evolved into the Transition Advisory Committee, numbering twenty, and chaired by William French Smith. A wealthy lawyer and Republican activist, Smith had served as Reagan's personal attorney for many years. A dozen other members of the committee also came from the ranks of Reagan's longtime personal backers—the highly conservative businessmen who had induced Reagan to enter politics in 1965. In this crowd Smith, at age sixty-two, was a kid. Several of the others, including Justin Dart (Dart & Kraft, Inc.), Holmes Tuttle (Ford dealerships and industrial interests), Theodore Cummings† (supermarkets) and Earle Jorgensen (steel and aluminum), were in their seventies and eighties. Dart and Joseph Coors (beer) were well

---

* Meese had to get a special ruling from the Federal Election Commission to allow this unorthodox use of campaign funds.

† Cummings died in March 1982, while serving as Reagan's ambassador to Austria.

known for their commitment to right-wing causes, though Dart also
had a personal relationship with Reagan going back many years.

For most members of this kitchen cabinet, the Reagan tie was as
emotional as it was political. William Wilson (land development and
other interests) was probably the closest to Reagan within this geriatric
set. When the Reagans, during their California years, wanted total iso-
lation, they would journey to the Wilsons' ranch in northern Mexico
and disconnect from the world. The intensity of feeling toward Reagan
had frequently been mentioned in descriptions of the kitchen group. I
was skeptical; these were tough guys, hard-nosed entrepreneurs. And
Reagan, after all, doesn't distribute his affection like jelly beans. A
small incident showed me my error.

At one of the several elegant dinners Reagan attended in Washington
during the transition period, Wilson and I were seated at the same
table. He has a seamed, leathery face. At age sixty-six, he could have
easily passed for a stern sheriff in a "Death Valley Days" episode. Toward the end of his informal speech, Reagan told one of his familiar
patriotic anecdotes. A gunner on a World War II bomber is wounded,
trapped in the belly turret as the stricken plane dives toward doom.
The rest of the crew bails out but the captain crawls to the bleeding
youngster, realizes the hopelessness of the situation and makes a conscious decision to stay with the lad so that he would not die alone. I'd
heard Reagan tell the story before (and would again). It could not
have been new to Wilson either. But tears rolled down his weathered
cheeks and he made no effort to wipe them away.

Thus Wilson and others of the old bunch would serve Reagan
selflessly, even relentlessly, as we shall see. Their transition committee
was filled out by a handful of people more active in public affairs,
though it contained only one incumbent politician—Senator Paul Laxalt of Nevada—along with Meese, Casey, former Treasury Secretary
William Simon, and W. Glenn Campbell, director of the Hoover Institution at Stanford University. The immediate task was to reduce the
lists to just a few candidates for each cabinet slot. Then Reagan would
make his final selections. But as would so often happen in the or-
ganization-chart world, the actual decisions had little to do with the
theoretical structure. Of the committee members, Meese, Laxalt and
Casey were the ones who really mattered. Further, four others—
George Bush, Mike Deaver, James Baker and Pen James—would have
important voices on the back channel to Reagan.

Despite all of Meese's early planning and organizing, the element of
chance came into play often enough to make the selection of cabinet
members the quirky, personal process it usually is. The two most im-

portant meetings took place on November 22 and 24 in Los Angeles. At the first, Reagan spent most of his time listening. In between, he conferred with the smaller group and made a number of decisions. For some of the posts, it seemed as if he had known his man all along. There was little doubt that Smith would go to Justice, which he wanted. That was also the case for Richard Schweiker (Health and Human Services) and Raymond J. Donovan (Labor). "I want Dick Schweiker," Reagan said crisply. "Next."

Inevitably, there were surprises. William Simon had been ticketed for the Treasury. He was popular both among orthodox fiscal conservatives and the avant-garde supply-side clique. However, Simon had a condition before he would return to his former post: he wanted assurances that he would be the preeminent formulator of economic policy. This clashed with the team-play concept dear to the Reaganauts, who were unwilling to make an exception for Simon. This word was informally conveyed to him. At the November 24 meeting, Reagan surprised his advisers by saying, "I've got a bombshell for you. I've just had a message from Bill Simon and he wants his name withdrawn." That development slowed the overall process because Treasury is the third most important cabinet job and because another favorite candidate, Walter Wriston of Citibank, backed off as well. Donald Regan of Merrill Lynch had little support among the economic radicals. He finally rose in the competition largely because he was reassuring to Wall Street and because the committee wanted a well-known name.

The most sought-after prize, as usual, was the State Department. It is difficult to understand why public men hunger for that designation when the record indicates so clearly the recent success rate. But the prestige quotient is high, at least for a time, and a niche in the history books almost assured. Optimists must believe that they will be able to build the influence of a John Foster Dulles or Dean Acheson, escaping the impotence of a Dean Rusk, William Rogers or Cyrus Vance. To be Reagan's Secretary of State seemed promising because the President-elect was hardly an expert in the field and he had loudly announced his intention to reduce the role of the White House National Security Adviser.

William Simon, in fact, had been interested in State as well as Treasury. William Casey suffered the same Foggy Bottom itch, even murmuring privately that if he could not have State, he would just as soon go home to Long Island. That turned out to be a bluff. Caspar Weinberger, despite slim credentials in foreign affairs, had a hankering, though he was willing to take the Defense Department too. George Shultz had been the main prospect for two months before the election;

he was at or close to the top of everyone's list. Yet he did not seem enthusiastic, or so Reagan's advisers told the President-elect. One participant recalled later, "He was sitting up there in San Francisco waiting to be begged. Well, we weren't begging anyone to join the Reagan administration." More relevant, perhaps, was that Meese and others who had worked with Caspar Weinberger in Sacramento wanted him in the top echelon of the cabinet more than they wanted Shultz. To take the two highest-ranking cabinet officers from the same company, Bechtel, seemed awkward.* From the periphery, Richard Nixon contributed one of his occasional pieces of advice: Reagan might find Shultz too soft, too conventional, to make the kind of policy changes Reaganism dictated. Nixon, perhaps thinking of his future access to the Administration, urged through intermediaries that Alexander M. Haig be appointed.

Former aide to Henry Kissinger, former White House Chief of Staff to Nixon, former military commander of NATO, he had obvious credentials. Haig and Reagan had a slight acquaintanceship dating back ten years or so, to the time Governor Reagan did occasional diplomatic chores for the Nixon administration. They saw each other a few times after that and eventually Haig served on one of the 1980 advisory groups, though never in close proximity to the candidate.

Reagan liked Haig's confident style, his tough rhetoric, his record for loyal performance under distressed conditions as Watergate sank Nixon. The general had a feel for how the national security complex worked as well as an "institutional memory" of recent great events. Further, Haig was an expert on NATO and was highly respected by the allies. The perception of Reagan in Western Europe was unfavorable; he was viewed as an irresponsible Cold War rhetorician unlikely to be interested in reviving détente. Haig's appointment would be an antidote to that reputation. While Shultz was still the main contender for State, however, Haig got a different feeler. As Haig recalled it later, Simon informed him that he was under consideration for Defense Secretary. Was he interested? "And I said, 'Well, I'd be surprised because I think it would be the wrong thing for an ex-military man to go into that position.' And he said, 'You mean you wouldn't take it?' I said I think I would not."[2]

In view of what was to befall Haig later, his recollections of the transition period are piquant as well as relevant. In mid-November he got

---

* After he came to the State Department, Shultz insisted that in 1980 he had no inclination to leave Bechtel. "I was very pleased with what I was doing . . . I had no interest in doing anything else and nobody asked me to do anything else," he told me. He passed this word informally to Casey and Simon, who told Reagan.

calls from Dart, Simon and Richard Allen telling him he was Reagan's "prime candidate" for Secretary of State. He didn't discourage the idea, but by his account he didn't grab the line with both hands either: "I wasn't running for it, I wasn't lobbying for it, and, frankly, I didn't expect it. The next thing I knew it became public speculation and a row started here in Washington about Watergate. . . . I expected to hear from the President [but] I didn't until [mid-December]. By then I had been the focal point of attacks on my integrity, a series had been run in the Washington *Post*—the most outrageous charges . . . unbelievable. At that point I said to my wife, I don't know whether the President is going to ask me to join or not, but I'm going to have to say yes if he does, because my good name has been challenged. If I were not to do it, it would reflect that I had something to hide, which I did not and do not. So when the President called me, I said let me think about it a day or two and I called him back and said yes."[3]

Even before Haig's nomination was announced, then, he had the sense of being surrounded, threatened. And even his account of his selection is controversial. Others who were involved recall him as having been actively interested in the job since he realized that a cabinet slot might be available. The brouhaha about his appointment was more complicated than the Watergate baggage, the lingering question about Haig's role in Nixon's defensive maneuvers and in Ford's decision to pardon his predecessor. Right-wingers were exercised about Haig's previous link to Henry Kissinger. And some of Reagan's and George Bush's people wondered whether Haig still entertained ambition for the presidency, as he had in 1979 when he left the Army.

With the heat rising, Reagan's advisers seriously considered recommending that Haig simply be dropped. Reagan himself vacillated briefly and formal announcement of the nomination was delayed. The prospect of a nasty confirmation fight early in the new year, when the Administration would be pressing its priorities and attempting to seize control of the agenda, was repugnant. Before making any decisions, four of Reagan's men—Meese, Baker, Laxalt and James—asked Haig to come down from Connecticut for an unofficial conversation. It took place on the evening of Wednesday, December 10, in the cramped sitting room of James's suite at the Jefferson Hotel. Two of the interrogators were in black tie because of a formal dinner later in the evening. They asked Haig about his health since his coronary bypass operation, about his performance during the Watergate melodrama, including the eighteen-minute gap in Rose Mary Woods's tape. Meese inquired about his presidential ambitions. According to one participant, Haig responded with a question of his own: Can any of you name a Secretary of State since Jefferson who went on to become President?* That's the last job you would want to use as a stepping-stone, Haig pointed out in language that would prove to be all too prophetic; "You come out bruised and scarred."

One participant recalls Haig in that inquisition as "very direct, very cool, very candid," although the atmosphere was highly charged. "We were all hoping that he would pass the test," this Reaganaut said later, "and so was the boss. Reagan wanted a favorable report." Haig himself described the focus this way: "Their concern was Watergate. That was the main thing they asked about. 'Are you clean?' That might have got a little tense."[4]

The "favorable report" he sought in hand, Reagan promptly decided to stick with Haig despite the continuing static on Capitol Hill and in the press. Howard Baker, soon to be the Senate Majority Leader when the new Congress convened, was still worried about serious confirmation problems. One of Baker's aides, on the sly, gave James a "dossier" on Haig that presumably would make Reagan reconsider. The packet contained only newspaper clippings, however, and James decided to forget it. Laxalt, Reagan's closest friend and ally in the Senate, also argued in favor of going ahead with the nomination. To cave in because of threatened opposition would be a sign of weakness that the legislators would seek to exploit in the combat yet to come over many other issues.

On December 16, then, Reagan announced the ninth and tenth of his cabinet selections. Ironically, Haig's designation was paired with that of Raymond Donovan. The rest of the members fell into place during the next few weeks. The finished cabinet—heads of thirteen executive departments plus the Director of the CIA, the head of the Office of Management and Budget, the United Nations ambassador and the U.S. Trade Representative—was different from what the political community had expected and from what Reagan had promised.

Of the seventeen, only three could be described as oriented toward ideology: David Stockman, who had lobbied actively for the Budget Director's job and who for a brief time would be the darling of the supply-side clique; James Watt at Interior, a champion of the "Sagebrush Rebellion," who got the post only because the original choice had run into an insurmountable conflict of interest; and Jeane Kirkpatrick, who would be sent to the United Nations because Reagan liked her neoconservative ideas, but whose influence on policy would be negligible.

* There were five after Jefferson: Madison, Monroe, Adams, Van Buren and Buchanan. According to recollections of that conversation some months afterward, however, no one took up Haig's challenge. His general point was accurate: for more than a century the post had not been a route to the White House.

Most of the others were stolid conservatives rather than radicals, administrators rather than innovators, team players rather than potential stars.

Reagan originally had talked of diversity, of reaching beyond the conventional for innovative talent. Instead he wound up with a crew that was overwhelmingly middle-aged, white, male, Christian and Republican, not much different from the original Nixon cabinet. Kirkpatrick was the only woman and the only Democrat; by the time she was appointed she was a Democrat in name only. Samuel Pierce was the only black and had been chosen for Housing and Urban Development late, when James and the kitchen cabinet had been unable to recruit one of the other black or Hispanic prospects they had considered. Pierce was a stranger to the Reaganauts and would remain so. Four owed their jobs to their direct links to Reagan: Weinberger at Defense, Smith at Justice, Casey at the CIA and Schweiker at HHS. The only appointee to come from the Senate, Schweiker was an oddly sentimental choice by Reagan.

In 1976, when he was considered a progressive Republican, Schweiker had agreed to become Reagan's running mate if Reagan won the presidential nomination. That was a desperate ploy designed to shake loose Ford delegates in the Northeast. The scheme fizzled and his fellow Pennsylvania Republicans more or less ostracized Schweiker for a time. He, in turn, converted to down-the-line Reaganism. Now he would serve in the cabinet with Transportation Secretary Drew Lewis, who in 1976 had held the Pennsylvania delegation for Ford, and who ambled into Reagan's 1980 camp because his very sensitive antennae discerned the winner early.

If the final selection lacked flair, it did demonstrate adroitness on Reagan's part. He did not attempt to stretch his cabinet across all the mainstream political factions, but he avoided the trap of narrow ideological confinement. The sects and trends of his own party were well represented. Malcolm Baldrige at Commerce, Lewis at Transportation and Regan at Treasury, for instance, had strong associations with the moderate Eastern elite—the remnant of the Rockefeller wing. William Brock, the U.S. Trade Representative, had been the party's National Chairman and a middle-of-the-road senator before that. Casey, though a New Yorker, had never been in the Rockefeller orbit. His political lineage went back to Leonard Hall's more orthodox branch of the New York GOP. Though the far right was underrepresented among the cabinet appointees, there were two large compensations for that: Reagan himself at the top and the subcabinet posts below. Reagan intended to police the major decisions. He trusted himself to apply the test of Reaganism when the stakes were large enough. Down at the operating

levels, where multitudes of operational calls and administrative inter-
pretations must be made, the Reagan White House soon began to
require stern tests of loyalty. Professor G. Calvin Mackenzie of Colby
College, studying the pattern of subcabinet appointments in the early
months, concluded:

> Anyone attempting to use the Reagan cabinet as a guide to the ultimate
> shape of his administration could easily have been misled. For it was only
> in the staffing of the operating levels of the subcabinet and the agencies
> that the political and administrative thrust of this administration was fully
> revealed. . . . The hostility of many of these appointees to the programs
> they would administer was a common characteristic of Reagan's choices
> for second-level positions in the departments and agencies . . . There was
> achieved in this second round of appointments an uncommon degree of
> ideological consistency and intensity.[5]

Even before the cabinet nominations could be sent to the Senate
officially in late January, another of Ed Meese's structural concepts
came undone. Meese had hoped to replicate the system Reagan and he
had used successfully in California—a small "super cabinet" at the
point of the pyramid presiding over policy to be carried out by the individual departments at the base. That top stone would consist of three
or four of the most senior cabinet officers—probably State, Defense,
Treasury and Justice—and a like number of White House advisers.
This elite of approximately eight members would be the board of directors over which Reagan would preside as chairman.

It is impossible to say how it would have worked because the plan
was never tried. James Baker, among others, viewed it as a design for
administrative gridlock. He tried to imagine the Secretaries of State and
Defense, say, spending long hours reviewing decisions in the domain of
the Interior, Education and Labor departments. The picture could not
come into focus. Though the scheme received some publicity and
Meese viewed it as workable, Baker early in the transition period managed to sink it. Instead, there would be a series of "cabinet councils,"
or subcommittees of the cabinet, in which heads of departments with
related concerns would refine options for Reagan. In its own sphere,
each body would function more or less the way the existing National
Security Council has in the field of military and foreign affairs. Eventually the White House would establish seven cabinet councils* with staff

---

* Economic Affairs, chaired by the Treasury Secretary; Natural Resources and
Environment, chaired by the Interior Secretary; Commerce and Trade, chaired by
the Commerce Secretary; Human Resources, chaired by the Secretary of Health
and Human Services; Food and Agriculture, chaired by the Secretary of Agriculture; Legal Policy, chaired by the Attorney General; and Management and Administration, chaired by Meese.

work provided by the White House Office for Policy Development. It was through these subcommittees that a species of "cabinet government" would come alive, handling a variety of secondary issues. The big ones would remain in the National Security Council or in less formal White House organisms not contemplated by Meese's original organization chart.

Meese was the ubiquitous Reaganaut during this period, as he had been during the campaign after New Hampshire and would be through the early months of incumbency. In the dowdy office building on M Street, where the new administration was gestating before Inauguration Day, underlings called Meese "Mr. Transition." Policy advisers pushing particular lines, Republicans seeking to return to government, reporters looking for insight constantly sought out the friendly, unassuming former prosecutor and law professor. He seemed to know at least something about everything because he insisted on a role in all phases of the operation. Looking ahead, he saw himself as the bridge between the White House and the cabinet, the horn through which ideas would reach Reagan's ear, the overall supervisor of both the national security and domestic affairs units in the White House. In his spare time, he would serve occasionally as a prominent public spokesman as well.

Here we must pause to consider the dense subject of the White House staff. Journalists covering the presidency regularly sometimes seem obsessed with this topic, tracking the fever graphs of influence and access. Who gets into the Oval Office most often? Who goes to the family quarters in the mansion? Who deserves the credit for a success or the blame for a blunder? Who is poisoning which rival's well? On the human level this preoccupation is easy to understand. It is the staff, not the President or the cabinet, with whom we White House newsies deal, or attempt to deal, day by day. It is they who try to shape our perceptions, to sell the company line, occasionally to airbrush out of the picture their own individual warts. In the insulated, incestuous small-town mind-set surrounding the presidency, there are only two occupations: politics, in the grandest as well as the meanest sense of the term, and journalism, ditto.

The political *Peyton Place* aspects of it aside, the staff must also be viewed on a more elevated plane. No modern President, whether personally brilliant or dull, immersed in detail or detached, adept at public relations or ham-handed, can escape the weight of his staff's performance. The job's responsibilities as well as the bureaucracy's complexity over the last forty years have grown too much for one man to cope sensibly with even the top four or five priorities of the moment, let alone the crushing volume of minor matters that require a presidential nod. Foreign visitors drop in as if the White House were a tourist attraction like the Washington Monument. Before the war Franklin Roosevelt pretty much managed his own press relations by gathering the newspaper reporters who mattered around his desk twice a week and leading them to his preferred line. Now a formal presidential press conference requires at least four or five hours of homework and rehearsal by the principal, and that does not count the dozens of other interviews a President is expected to grant each year. When the unexpected occurs—Israel's invasion of Lebanon, say—the President is expected to make rapid decisions; their effectiveness can be only as high as the quality and clarity of the choices presented to him.

Inevitably, each successive court takes part of its character from the monarch who assembled it. John Kennedy's men, as a group, combined the intellectual edge, the political smarts and personal arrogance of their leader. The Nixon crew shared its boss's boldness of purpose, his cunning and what turned out to be the fatal void where his basic values should have been. The Carterites rivaled their President in good intentions, pious naïveté and an inability to differentiate between the politics of election and that of governance. But that is not all. A White House staff, as it evolves over the months, takes on attributes of its own. If it matures properly and maintains cohesion, it can compensate for a particular President's shortcomings. Or it can, with its own failures, compound his flaws.

Ronald Reagan's staff managed to go both ways, often simultaneously, during the first two years. Parts of it performed brilliantly at times, complementing with tactical dexterity a President whose main strengths lay in conveying a sense of steady purpose, in building confidence that his startling domestic agenda deserved a full opportunity. Other parts just as dramatically failed.

The difficulties took months to surface, except in the national security field where they were apparent from the start. For more than a year, including the transition period, fundamental fault lines lay under the surface. Like its creator, the Reagan staff brought civility, good humor, confidence and more than a few touches of class to the White House. The Administration's successes, lasting into the fall of 1981, discouraged excessive carping. Those of us who adore tales of dissension initially found the pickings slender except for Al Haig's successive agonies.* It was only later, in retrospect, that the severity of the fissures could be appreciated and the damage discerned. By then the early origins of the flaw were obscure.

* The fact that Haig's ongoing difficulty with the White House was the only visible, reasonably dramatic feud during the early months made his situation all the worse for him. Having no other conflict of similar interest with which to toy, the press fastened on this one.

At his moment of victory, the last thing Ronald Reagan wanted to do was to fool with the jigsaw puzzle of staff. He wanted to get to the ranch for some rest. He had to settle the cabinet. Soon he would confront a series of policy decisions. To have to select the top dozen to fifteen advisers and to design their relationship to him and to each other was a chore not to his liking. He would pick the top three and let them worry about the rest. He wanted Ed Meese close at hand, but he also knew by Election Day that Meese's reputation as an administrator was overblown, that Meese had no experience in Washington, that he was not a particularly good judge of political talent. Thus Reagan, a few days before the votes were cast, listened to what seemed to be wise advice from a couple of dispassionate associates. He checked that counsel against the judgment of his most passionate associate, Nancy Davis Reagan, and found that she agreed. Another lawyer, though a relative stranger, would somehow share staff leadership with Meese. The alien was James A. Baker III, fifty, like Meese a lawyer by background, but otherwise dissimilar in many respects. Baker was a wealthy, urbane Texan, deft in political public relations and—most important—possessed of a talent for operations and organization. As Ford's delegate hunter in 1976, he had helped foil the Reagan challenge. As Bush's manager in 1980, he had briefly made the GOP contest interesting. As a Reagan adviser from the convention onward, he had quickly adapted to the Californians' way of doing things. He would be Chief of Staff, Meese would be "Counselor," an amorphous title that Meese more than anyone else would have to define.

Reagan also wanted Michael Deaver, the aide who knew the Reagans best as human beings. Only forty-two when the votes were counted, Deaver had spent most of his adult life in Reagan's service, one way or another. During the post-Sacramento interregnum, while Meese tried the corporate executive life and then switched to the teaching and practice of law, Deaver was co-owner of a political public relations firm. His chief client: Ronald Reagan. Reagan's initial campaign headquarters in late 1979 was the Wilshire Boulevard offices of Deaver & Hannaford.

But now Deaver was ambivalent. He liked life in California, choosing to live with his wife and two children in placid Sacramento rather than Los Angeles, and for the first time in his career he had begun to make real money. His lust for political power was slight. Beyond that, he feared getting in the middle of a Meese-Baker contest for turf. Thus Deaver equivocated, and seriously considered saying no to Reagan for the first time. Through November, when other campaign aides and a few of the reporters who had covered the race were deciding whether to move to Washington with the new administration, several of us who shared that dilemma had a standing joke: if Deaver really says no, Reagan won't go either and we'll all be off the hook.

We were denied that easy way out, of course. While insisting that he would stay only eighteen to twenty-four months, Deaver agreed to carry the subordinate title of Deputy Chief of Staff. He would run scheduling and the President's travels, would take a hand in long-range planning, help with public relations and personnel. Most important, he would ride shotgun against the unexpected adversities that cannot be penciled into a calendar. Deaver would be the chief troubleshooter inside, with low visibility outside. And he would share, with only Baker and Meese during the first year, unlimited access to the President. Soon they became known as the troika, the triumvirate, the big three or, in Haig's phrase, the "three-headed monster."

While the relationship among them would sometimes be vague and uneven, their schedule was codified just two days after the inauguration. Margaret Tutwiler, Baker's executive assistant, prepared a memorandum recording that the three had agreed to meet for the first time each workday at 7:30 A.M. ("Not public," Tutwiler noted). A half hour later the troika would sit down with the senior White House staff. Then at 9:15 the trio would see the President ("Not public," Tutwiler noted again). Between 5:30 and 6 P.M. there would be another session with Reagan and then a final conversation without him. Initially, the troika thought that it could keep at least part of its schedule secret; hence the "not public" marginal jottings. The trio wanted neither the cabinet nor the press to regard the little group as a tight inner circle wielding great influence. Word of their routine soon leaked, of course, creating exactly the anticipated reaction.

Still hidden then was the much more elaborate agreement Meese and Baker had negotiated between themselves during the fortnight after the election. The one-page memorandum they initialed on November 17 was divided into two columns, one headed MEESE, the other BAKER. A third lawyer, unfamiliar with the workings of the White House, might have assumed on the basis of that single typed sheet with handwritten corrections that it gave Meese more power than Baker. It acknowledged that Meese had "cabinet rank" while Baker did not. The idea of a super cabinet was still alive then; Meese would preside over it in the absence of the President and Vice-President. Meese would have responsibility for "coordination and supervision of the work of the Domestic Policy staff and the National Security Council [staff]." Dominion over some of the other presidential provinces, such as the Council of Economic Advisers, would be shared.

The memo was deceptive, however. Even as he scrawled his *OK—JAB III* in the lower left corner of the page, above Meese's initials, Baker knew that the super cabinet idea wasn't feasible. That item thus would be neutralized. Baker insisted on incorporating his West Wing address in the agreement, the "office customarily utilized by Chief of Staff." That seemed petty, but the office is the largest on the floor, other than the President's, and the only one suitable for big meetings. Baker would be host of these, always sitting at the head of his conference table. Another item might also seem picayune to an outsider: "Coordination and control of all in and out paper flow to the President . . ." Deciding what the President sees, and when, can be crucial in the decision-making process. Baker, ostensibly the administrator, was already establishing his claim in policy formulation. Further, he would soon name a talented, sharp policy expert, Richard G. Darman, to handle that paper stream day to day. Darman, who came from the remnant of the party's progressive wing, had no ties at all to the Reaganauts. The third important item in Baker's column: "Hiring and firing authority over all elements of White House staff."

It was subtle, and even the principals were not fully conscious of it, but a rivalry for power was already underway. Without any grand scheme or clear-cut philosophical cleavage, factions would array themselves periodically in an attempt to pull the President in one way or another. Baker was conservative enough in the general sense of the term, but Reaganism was absent from his marrow. Encased instead in Baker's political bones was the pragmatic desire to win. Now that he was on Reagan's team, Baker, as an honorable professional, of course wanted Reagan to prevail. But if prevailing meant zigzagging, if it meant deferring some of the items on the wish-lists of New Right or Old, if it meant tossing only symbolic snacks to the purists instead of the red meat for which they hungered, then so be it.

Agility was one of Baker's strengths. Stockman was ostensibly a Reaganaut ideologue, but he and Baker easily and early worked out an entente because they, with Darman and a few others, quickly recognized the problems of Reagan's economic program. Baker, by and large, recruited Republican professionals to run the staff functions under his jurisdiction. Only two of the nine important slots in that category went to California loyalists (Pen James in Personnel and Lyn Nofziger in Political Liaison). Meese, by contrast, filled almost every significant post on his roster with certifiable Reaganauts, most of them from California.

Eventually the November 17 agreement, like the much more elaborate organization charts, proved to be an inaccurate map of reality as well. Baker's control of staff functions was not nearly as complete as he wanted it to be. He could not really hire and fire at will, for instance. And Meese's direct control over the two policy bodies, domestic and national security, assured a dichotomy that repeatedly would be a cause of contention and delays in decision making.

The contest would have a second theme. Whether in choices of personnel beyond the White House or in policy options, Meese's first instinct was to hold fast to what was familiar to Reagan (and thus to Meese as well). Though laudable enough a goal for the sake of consistency, if no other, that approach offered poor guidance when one Reagan objective, or loyalist, clashed with another. Baker, lacking the sixteen-year-old umbilical cord, often found himself in a paradoxical position. If Reagan was to succeed in getting the government to "break with the past"—one of the early catch phrases—he might have to break with his own past in order to prevail. Reagan would have to shed skins to adapt to his new role and to changing conditions. Baker had no sentimental attachment to obsolete epidermis. Luckily for him, he would often get support from Deaver.

Immediately after the inauguration, a poignant symbolic test occurred. Several members of the kitchen cabinet were in line for secondary jobs while two of the younger members got important posts—Smith at Justice and Charles Z. Wick, eventually, at the International Communication Agency (later restored to its original name, United States Information Agency). But William Wilson, Justin Dart, Joe Coors and a few other old guardsmen wanted something more: an indefinite if vague role close to Reagan. Wilson was the most aggressive in this regard. Outflanking Baker's authority, he obtained a White House credential through Ed Hickey, who headed the White House Military Office under Deaver's control and who knew the Wilson crowd well. From Lyn Nofziger, Wilson obtained use of Suite 180 in the Old Executive Office Building, just across an alley from the West Wing of the White House. There Wilson set up shop unofficially, intending to assure that Pen James be kept straight in personnel selection. Though not on the payroll yet—he was awaiting appointment as the President's special representative to the Vatican, a part-time post—Wilson did want to do the right thing. He obtained the forms that prospective staff members fill out and decided to create a new little organism. In the space provided for the applicant's prospective specialty, Wilson wrote, "Office of the Kitchen Cabinet."

Meanwhile, Wick was awaiting the official call to the ICA directorship. He occupied his spare time by organizing a fund-raising group to finance grass-roots support for Reagan's economic program. This effort involved, among other things, solicitation of businessmen around the country by other members of the kitchen cabinet. Contributions of up to $50,000 each were being requested for the "Coalition for a New Beginning." The effort prompted a variety of legal and public relations questions. Some of those solicited complained of the pressure. "Those guys," said one of the President's political advisers, "hadn't seen anything like that since the fund-raising for Nixon."

Something had to be done, and quickly. Deaver summoned from California political consultant Stuart Spencer, to help persuade Reagan that his old pals were creating problems. That had to be done gently and circuitously, however. So Spencer first alerted Reagan to the danger and then conducted a meeting in the Roosevelt Room of the White House on February 5 ostensibly for the purpose of clarifying what Wick's coalition was supposed to do. Having studied the prospectus, Spencer came in with his own judgment. "The objective of the program remains cloudy," Spencer's memorandum said. "There appears to be a consensus that action should be taken to support the President's program, but the target remains confused." Privately, Spencer informed Reagan: "The thing is a damn disaster. You've got to get them all out of here."

Reagan did have a little chat with Charlie and Mary Jane Wick— Mrs. Wick was active in the effort too—and their coalition was allowed to expire quietly. However, the kitchen cabinet still clung to its beachhead in the Old Executive Office Building. Hints that it was time to go were ignored. Finally, the troika summoned Wilson, Dart, Jorgensen and a few of the others to Baker's office late on February 23. Also present was Fred Fielding, the new White House Counsel, who explained that the kitchen cabinet would have to undergo FBI investigation and submit financial disclosure forms if they continued their "volunteer" efforts. Dart seemed to get the idea at last. One of the participants in the session recalled that Dart turned to his buddies and said, "I think we've been dense. They don't want us around, so let's clear out." It was a lingering departure nonetheless. To speed it along, John Rogers, Baker's deputy for administration, ordered the locks and phones changed in Suite 180.

Reagan tolerated the severance of this tiny strand of his ties with his own past, though he left the task of actual cutting to others. He would continue to enjoy the company of Bill Wilson, Justin Dart and the others on occasion and he was happy to give positions, real or honorific, to those of his old supporting cast who were interested. He would even continue to take phone calls from a few of them now and then, and to hear them out when they pressed advice on him. But in this department, as in some others, he was willing to shed at least swatches of the old skin. He was even willing to court the Washington establishment which he had belabored for so long. Not that he was willing to enlist in it; rather he intended to draft it for his own purposes.

5

Seduction and Blitzkrieg

He resembled nothing so much as a swimmer approaching the cold Atlantic surf in early summer. In the weeks immediately following the election, Ronald Reagan ventured into his new role up to the shinbone, retreated, came back to knee depth, only to return to the shore until he was ready for total immersion. That at least was the pace in public. Older reporters who had watched the tense processions in and out of the Kennedys' Georgetown headquarters in the transition of 1960–61, or the traffic at the Hotel Pierre in New York, where Richard Nixon personally ran his operation in 1968–69, could not fathom Reagan's distance from the action.

It was not merely that Reagan appeared and disappeared, lingered in California for a rest, then visited Washington as if he were a celebrity tourist, then went home again. What was difficult to track was the way Reagan spent his time while visible. Business meetings seemed the exception. He appeared to have detached himself from the cabinet selection process, allowing underlings to announce his appointments. The Iran hostage crisis was approaching another climax but Reagan avoided the subject. When he returned to Los Angeles, he visited his regular barber in Beverly Hills, his old tailor in Hollywood, the family meat locker in Thousand Oaks. Television crews and curious civilians congregated at every stop. "You mean to tell me," Reagan said, "that a farmer doing his work is of this much interest?"[1]

While the Reagans were in Washington their night life eclipsed his workday. The President-elect and the First Lady-imminent started by throwing a party at the F Street Club for fifty of the heftier names in Washington's cultural and civic hierarchy, including the city's superliberal black mayor, Marion Barry, and Joe Hirshhorn, of the museum of the same name. Nancy Reynolds, the Bendix Company executive and former Reagan aide who arranged that shindig and others, recalled with amusement that some of the guests thought they had been invited by mistake; most of them, after all, were Democrats. Reagan explained to Washington *Post* reporter Elisabeth Bumiller, "Well, I decided it was time to serve notice that we're residents." And Mrs. Reagan added, "We wanted to get to know some people in Washington."[2] It was a charming note. Washington is a city of transients. When a Foreign Service officer or an Army colonel is assigned to a tour of duty there for the first time, his wife quickly invites a dozen couples for dinner. Soon the new people receive a dozen invitations in return and their social life is gliding. Of course the Reagans needed only to put out the word that they were available, which Nancy Reynolds did. They went to dinner at the home of George Will, the conservative columnist, and met Katharine Graham, matriarch of the Washington *Post* and *Newsweek,* as well as empress of the limousine liberal set. Then the Reagans attended a party thrown by Mrs. Graham herself, with a politically ecumenical guest list of senators, news executives and such diehard opponents of Reaganism as Vernon Jordan, then head of the National Urban League, and Lane Kirkland, president of the AFL-CIO. George Will and the president of Time Inc., Richard Munro, were also present. Time Inc.'s editor in chief, Henry Grunwald, continued the social season with a dinner party at the Renwick Gallery, one of Washington's fine small museums. Kay Graham, making the cut once again, seemed to be spending more time in Reagan's company than Al Haig was.

Reagan was not simply indulging himself. He was engaged in a shrewd gambit, one of several with the common goal of showing that the country now had a President very different from Jimmy Carter. The Georgia peanut farmer had not only run against business-as-usual; once elected he consciously showed disdain for the symbols as well as the machinery of the permanent government. The Hollywood actor had campaigned even more vigorously than Carter, four years earlier, against the bureaucracy. Now Reagan was saying to the peerage, look, I'm not the enemy. I've come to save you from the ruination we'll all suffer if the system collapses. Don't be frightened. I'm not the political freak you thought. Give me a hand, give my program an open mind, and let's see if we can't work a bloodless revolution here.

In approaching the Eastern elite which had been both his foil and bane for so long, Reagan decided that seduction would produce more satisfactory results than rape. No script girl on her first date with a star ever succumbed so quickly. Reagan was proving, in his own quite personal way, that even though he came from the political fringe, he could

fraternize with the center. That, after all, was the most effective way of
conveying his demands and assuring submission. His slow-motion transit to power got across another point as well. Washington was accustomed to Presidents who wallowed in their jobs, who could not get
enough of the responsibilities and decisions quickly enough. That never
was Reagan's style, never would be. The sooner Washington learned
that he was taking the job on his own terms, the better.

During daylight hours as well, Reagan treated cheerfully with both
the vanquished and his fifth column of sympathizers in Washington.
Edward Kennedy came to call at the government townhouse on Jackson Place where Reagan stayed. This last link to Camelot left talking
about the need for unity. The Reagans visited the Carters; the color
photographs published in magazines show that none of the four appeared at ease. The tourist picture album filled up—Reagan with Warren Burger at the Supreme Court, Reagan with the Republican leadership on the Hill, Reagan with the Democrats on the Senate side,
Reagan with House Speaker Thomas P. O'Neill, the closest thing to a
standard bearer the opposition would be able to muster before the
1982 election.

In his own public statements during the period, Tip O'Neill was cautious, tentative, wary of appearing to be an obstructionist. O'Neill
could have been mistaken for a moderate Republican. He managed one
minor expression of hubris after Reagan visited the Speaker's lair by
giving reporters a rendition of his admonition to the President-elect:
" 'You were governor of a state, but a governor plays in the minor
leagues. Now you're in the big leagues. Things might not move as
quickly as you would like.' He seemed a little surprised when I said
that."[3]

Whatever surprise Reagan may actually have evinced would be nothing to the astonishment that O'Neill and Katharine Graham and Lane
Kirkland and many others would soon experience. While Reagan during the transition continued to act the shy conqueror, decisions of crucial importance were being made. Further, his lieutenants, out of public
sight, were planning a blitzkrieg. Fierce, rapid assault, not courtship,
was the real game plan. Their captain agreed.

A remarkable thing, in retrospect, was that clear strategy emerged
from a disorderly, excessively structured transition organization. Visiting the official headquarters on M Street, one was overwhelmed by the
confusion. More than 1,000 people were involved as paid staff and vol-
unteers. Or was it 1,200? No one could say. Four years earlier, the
Carter group had used only three fourths of the $2 million in federal
funds allocated for transition expenses. Now the Reagan crew decided

that $2 million would not be nearly enough. So they cranked in a surplus left over from the primaries and soon that was insufficient as well. Additional contributions were solicited from private donors to meet costs that would eventually reach $3 million. One division alone, concerned with putting study teams in each of the executive agencies, required six pages of organization charts merely to diagram its own structure. These teams accumulated voluminous reports, volume upon black volume, much of which was to be ignored. Haig, as soon as he had the opportunity, disbanded the group assigned to the State Department and ostentatiously rejected its work.* At the Pentagon, Weinberger ousted William Van Cleave, the hawkish professor who had been the ranking campaign adviser on defense spending and technology. Weinberger subsequently refused to give Van Cleave a postinauguration appointment. When David Stockman became fully involved in budget planning in December, he discovered that little of value had been done. "It was not what you would call 'budget real time,'" he said later. "Rather it was done along the lines of policy abstractions. It was not done in such a way as to ask the question of what could be done to yield savings in eighty-two, eighty-three and eighty-four."[4]

That cumbersome transition structure, presided over by Ed Meese and William Casey, was also an abstraction. Luckily for Reagan, several of his advisers and some designated cabinet officers knew how to cut through the maze. Meese, when he could disentangle himself from the temporary bureaucracy he had created on M Street, also recognized the need for decisive, clear strokes and helped Reagan to move in that direction.

Perhaps the most important single decision had nothing to do with economic policy or foreign affairs per se. Rather it concerned psychology and opportunity. Reading the election returns and the polls soon after, guessing about the mood of the Democrats in Congress, Reagan's strategists came to a quite logical conclusion. Like any newly elected President, Reagan enjoyed more support then than he was likely to have after the first six or eight months. Further, the country in that winter of 1980–81 was particularly receptive to change. Three of the strategists, Richard Wirthlin, the pollster; David Gergen, eventually to become Communications Director; and Richard Beal, an associate of Wirthlin's who would run the White House planning office, drafted the "Final Report of the Initial Actions Project," which opened:

* The head of the State Department transition team, Ambassador Robert Neumann, was given the embassy in Saudi Arabia despite Haig's coolness toward him. Soon after, Haig persuaded Reagan to fire Neumann.

The direction of the country remains unsatisfactory to a majority of Americans. Hoping for change, they elected Ronald Reagan to preside over a restructuring and redirection of public policy for the country. The public sense of urgency requires that the President immediately undertake to steer a new course . . . The momentum of presidential activity—a brisk but not frantic pace in the beginning—emphasizes the sense of urgency and provides the basis for the President's leadership opportunity . . .

That document went on to stress that the first two or three months could be crucial to the entire four years ("How we begin will significantly determine how we govern . . .").* Darman elaborated on one aspect of this approach in a February 21 memorandum to James Baker. The subject: combat with Congress. "Cutting across the legislative strategy and others," Darman wrote, "a plan [is needed] for the preservation of the appearance of the President's continuing strength and effectiveness—the avoidance of association with 'losses,' the association with a planned string of 'successes.'"

By the logic of classic political gamesmanship, both Darman's prescription and the views synthesized by Gergen could not be refuted. They were appropriate to the psychology of the moment, to Reagan's desire for rapid change, to the disheveled condition of the opposition. Concerning the Democrats, Wirthlin later observed, the Reaganauts made an interesting miscalculation. The White House anticipated more effective opposition in the first year than actually materialized. The Democrats were even more cowed by November's defeat, including the loss of their Senate majority, than they appeared. "A lot of Democrats," Wirthlin said, "did look at the election results as a repudiation of the way they had previously handled inflation and related problems. They probably overestimated that aspect of the vote."[5] Not realizing just how wobbly O'Neill and his allies were, the new crowd would trim a few of their proposals in marginal ways.

But boldness and urgency and momentum became the dominant motif. And this had great impact on specific policy. It meant, for one thing, that Stockman would have to move very fast to put together the Administration's drastic overhaul of the fiscal '82 budget already proposed by the lame-duck Carterites. Second, the Reagan White House would focus intensely on the domestic side, more particularly on spending reduction and lower tax rates. Foreign affairs, to the greatest extent possible, would be put on hold. The Administration did not wish

* The document was occasionally mentioned during early 1981, but never published. The "final report" was dated January 29. In fact, it represented a consensus of many of the Reagan advisers' views through the transition period. Both in its affirmative proposals and in its warnings about dangers, the study has held up well.

to diffuse its energy or take any risky initiative that, if it failed, would associate Reagan with losses.

Before too long that path would also lead to great difficulty, to the impression that the Administration lacked any comprehensive foreign policy at all. But the White House clung through most of 1981 to that choice; it would deal abroad only to the extent that circumstances demanded. During the transition, to escape the clamor of what he regarded as "the madhouse on M Street," Fred C. Iklé and several other foreign policy experts moved to a more serene headquarters in the Old Executive Office Building near the White House. Iklé, an academic who had headed the Arms Control and Disarmament Agency under the previous Republican regime, now worked for Allen. Later he would become Under Secretary of Defense for Policy, or head of the "little State Department" in the Pentagon. With several younger associates, Iklé tried to identify the most urgent foreign problems in December and January. The list combined the obvious and the obscure: the American hostages still held in Iran; Poland; the civil war in El Salvador and related problems in Central America; Libya's subversive activities and the Middle East. That last subject actually contained two complex parts: the paralyzed Arab-Israeli "peace process" and instability in the Persian Gulf. A sixth item, more chronic than immediate, was how to deal with the West Europeans' rising anxiety about nuclear arms control—or the prospective abandonment of it by a new American administration bent on a large military buildup.

Haig was eager to move on a number of fronts, but during the transition he was tied down in preparations for his confirmation hearings, which threatened to be difficult. In late January, after the Senate approved his nomination, he discovered that the troika of Meese, Baker and Deaver was in no hurry to launch enterprises in his sector. When he wanted to come out immediately with a comprehensive bellicose statement and policy concerning Central America, Meese and Baker compelled him to wait until late February, after Reagan had made the first two televised speeches on his economic program laying out the basics. Haig was then allowed to proceed. When his rhetoric on the subject reached a high decibel level, fueling popular apprehension that a military adventure was imminent, the troika explicitly instructed him to back off. A middle-level State Department official, John Bushnell, was given the unhappy task of telling reporters that *they* had been overplaying the El Salvador story.

Moscow sent unmistakable signals that it wanted to start doing serious business with the new crowd in Washington. Its experienced ambassador, Anatoly Dobrynin, obviously under instructions from home, had opened communications three weeks before Haig's appointment was announced. Dobrynin met twice with Richard Allen, on November 25 and December 5, for extended conversations over lunch. Memoranda summarizing those talks remained buried; it would have been inconvenient to indicate just how eager the Soviet regime was to begin negotiations.

In the first meeting, Dobrynin took the initiative. He stressed that it was very important for the new President to get off to a good start with the Kremlin. The Carter administration, he complained, began on the wrong foot by trying to discard the specific items concerning arms control to which both sides had agreed earlier. The Americans should also recall that John Kennedy started his relationship with Nikita Khrushchev in an abrasive way. Now there should be a clean slate, the ambassador said in his fluent English. For instance, the SALT II treaty should be "rescued."* Leonid Brezhnev would be willing to consider an early summit meeting. Moscow, its envoy said, hoped that Reagan, unlike Carter, would not see a Russian behind every bush around the world.

In both conversations, Allen discouraged the idea that Reagan would be willing to have a summit meeting anytime soon. He told Dobrynin privately what Reagan had preached in public: SALT II was a dead issue. When the Russian wondered aloud what issues Washington *would* wish to grapple with early, Allen suggested that Soviet involvement in the turmoil of the Middle East and Afghanistan certainly were ripe questions. Communist meddling in the Ayatollah's Iran was troubling to the United States. So was Iraq's invasion of Iran. The new "friendship treaty" between Syria and the U.S.S.R. raised some puzzlement as well.

We can talk about anything Washington wishes, Dobrynin observed. But where do you Americans get the idea that we are threatening your oil supplies? Where are we doing that? The pact with Syria has no secret codicils; it is what it seems to be. Moscow knew nothing of Baghdad's war plans until the day the fighting started. While we're talking about the Middle East, Reagan's rhetoric concerning the PLO seems rather harsh to us. Allen replied that Reagan was committed to Israel's survival. So is Moscow, Dobrynin said. Will the Soviets now be included in the peace process, as Carter had once planned? If so, we could attempt to influence the PLO; we could "advise them."

---

* After failing to interest the Soviets early in 1977 in a drastic new approach to the arms question, involving large-scale reductions in strategic weapons deployment, Carter and Secretary of State Cyrus Vance went back to the formulation that had been shaped under Gerald Ford and Henry Kissinger. The SALT II pact Carter finally signed ran into opposition in the United States, however, and was shelved in 1979 when the Soviet Union invaded Afghanistan.

Toward the end of the second conversation, in which the Soviet envoy's tone was sharper than it had been ten days earlier, Allen brought up Poland. At that point, as during the twelve months to come, Moscow's intentions concerning the Solidarity movement seemed menacing but unclear. We have been restrained, Dobrynin insisted. We do not wish to intervene. Further, we must protest the warnings on this subject by American officials; they are offensive to us. Warnings, Allen replied, are not threats, but it would take a very long time to repair the damage after a Soviet invasion of Poland.

Moscow was also irritated by suggestions in the United States, and particularly by the Reagan circle, that there was a connection between tension on the Polish frontier and Sino-American relations. (There had been hints that Soviet aggressiveness would bring China and the United States closer, perhaps to the point of military cooperation.) "We are not afraid of the Chinese," Dobrynin said. "We can take care of them, though we do not expect them to do anything. We will leave them alone unless they provoke serious trouble." Tongue in cheek, Allen replied that the new Reagan administration would hardly encourage the Chinese to send forces to Poland.

Dobrynin was curious about Reagan's staff and how new relationships would be established. What about Reagan's reputation for delegating authority? What would Edwin Meese's role be? (Meese is the person closest to Reagan, Allen replied.) With the holiday season approaching, Dobrynin delivered a New Year's card that Leonid Brezhnev wanted Reagan to receive.

When Reagan's advisers analyzed these exchanges and put them together with other signals from Moscow, they concluded that the Soviets were eager for at least the appearance of serious negotiations, and perhaps the substance as well. The Kremlin, as it had when earlier Presidents were taking office, thought that it was a good time to wipe the slate clean of the memory of its own mischief—in this case, Afghanistan. The Soviets were indicating willingness to cooperate, but at the same time saying that Washington would have to take some initiative in a new thaw. Without question, Brezhnev wanted to give Reagan incentive to back away from his announced plans to launch a major expansion of nuclear weaponry.

But Washington would not play. In public, there would be harsh rhetoric from Reagan and Haig. In private, the pace of approaching Moscow, and particularly in renewing arms negotiations, would be agonizingly slow. Toward the end of the transition the United States had neither an ambassador nor even a full-fledged chargé in its Moscow embassy. Ambassador Arthur Hartman did not arrive in the Soviet Union until October 1981. At home, the Administration did not get around to nominating the new head of the Arms Control and Disarmament Agency until April; Eugene Rostow would be among the last of the Administration's senior officials designated, and he did not take office until June 1981. It was not merely emphasis on the domestic program that caused this hesitation waltz. The Reaganauts wanted Moscow to understand that it was dealing with new policy as well as new personalities. The Pentagon's refurbishment would have to begin before negotiations did. Meanwhile, Reagan and his people would deal with other issues.

In the main arena, economics, the players moved in a blur of constant action. The mottoes were "break with the past" and "don't be timid." The psychological gambit was to prove that the new crowd actually meant business. Before leaving the Capitol on Inauguration Day, Reagan signed an order to freeze federal hiring. That act was more symbolic than real because exceptions invariably dilute such directives, but the message was clear. In the next forty-eight hours other stringent diktats followed: resignations of holdover officials were accelerated, spending on consultants' services was cut arbitrarily by 5 percent, every agency would have to reduce travel costs by at least 15 percent, procurement of office equipment and furniture was suspended temporarily. Reagan made his first visit to the White House press briefing room to announce a task force on regulatory reform, to be headed by George Bush. Meanwhile, new regulations pending would be held up for review. The White House attempted to eliminate, by executive fiat, the Council on Wage and Price Stability (COWPS) to make two points: rapid elimination of scores of jobs in the Executive Office of the President and a demonstration that the new team would fight inflation with free-market techniques rather than governmental jawboning and ukase. The rush to slice off chunks of bureaucratic sausage was so headlong that the White House had to pull back its order concerning COWPS because it was technically faulty. The flaws were soon corrected, however, and the section of COWPS directly concerned with wages and prices was gone.

These measures and others made for a steady stream of active news copy. But their impact on federal spending was negligible. The "big fixes," as Stockman referred to them, would take time. Meanwhile, Baker and Meese realized that the program rapidly being constructed was so complex, so controversial, so broad in its involvement of diverse departments and competing interests, that a very high degree of coordination would be necessary. Here the White House troika encountered an interesting contradiction. The notion of "cabinet government," along with White House organization charts of which Meese was primary author, tended to diffuse authority. Where the economic program and related measures were concerned, the opposite would be necessary; the White House would have to coordinate closely both policy making and strategy for carrying out decisions. In the first month, organisms that cut across the orthodox lines would begin to form.

On February 17, Meese and Baker sent a memorandum to all cabinet officers and senior members of the White House staff. "To coordinate the efforts of all departments, agencies and offices involved," that document said, "we need to pull together the various plans and activities related to the economic recovery program. . . . The contact person for all material from the White House staff will be Dick Darman. The contact for members of the Cabinet will be Craig Fuller." Occupying adjoining offices in the White House basement, Darman and Fuller at the time were obscure, relatively junior officials. Darman, thirty-seven, had served in cabinet departments during the Nixon-Ford years but was new to the White House. Fuller, who turned thirty that month, was an alumnus of the Deaver & Hannaford firm, and new to Washington. Suddenly they were at the crossroads of the new administration's most important program. In that position they quickly sensed the danger of fragmentation.

In the same February 21 paper in which he stressed the importance of a "planned string of successes," Darman alerted Baker to the need for focused legislative strategy. He pointed out that Treasury, OMB—Office of Management and Budget—and the White House legislative liaison office, headed then by Max Friedersdorf, already seemed to be going off in three different directions. No one was methodically tracking evolving plans—which, Darman said, "will likely be botched if the key players try to carry everything in their heads." Sensing where the action would be and eager to be at its center, Darman volunteered "to call points of conflict, inconsistency, incompleteness, or opportunity to your attention." He concluded by urging "a determination and clarification of specific delegations of authority to negotiate with the Congress on specific matters of procedure or substance. (Aside: Confusion here could prove disastrous.)" Baker was thoroughly receptive to this line of reasoning, out of which was born the Legislative Strategy Group. LSG had no formal charter. Even when the White House organization chart was redrafted in March 1982, to incorporate a number of changes, the LSG appeared nowhere among the thirty-five interconnected boxes. By then, however, it had been in operation for a year and had become a central force affecting both domestic policy and tactics. Though Baker and Meese were nominally cochairmen, the group always met in Baker's large office, and he emerged as its chief. Darman and Fuller provided the staff backup, with Darman as the senior partner.

There would also be a variety of groups formed to handle specific issues, often in informal ways. One early example was the committee put together to find ways to help the depressed automobile industry, more particularly to reduce the number of Japanese cars being imported. This effort between February and April offers an excellent case study of how the new administration coped with sensitive issues over which cabinet officers disagreed. In this case, Reagan's own principles were at war with each other as well. It is worth examining the deft way in which the White House negotiated this obstacle course.

To urban planners, environmentalists and the Ralph Nader school of consumer advocates, the passenger automobile had long since become an evil to be fought. The products of Detroit congested cities, they polluted the air, endangered life and limb. Successive administrations had begun to act out those views, none so vigorously as Carter's, which promoted safety regulations and sought to encourage mass transit projects. Reagan knew the politics of America's enduring infatuation with the automobile. During the campaign he blamed the auto industry's difficulties on Washington's heavy hand. He snickered at efforts to cajole the citizenry into subways underwritten by taxpayers. In one speech to the Detroit Economic Club he called the passenger car "the last great freedom—the freedom to go where we wanted, when we wanted and by the route we chose." That was in May, in Cobo Hall. In September, at a Chrysler K-car plant, he told assembly line workers that Washington must persuade the Japanese, "one way or another," to reduce the influx of their cars into the American market.

This, to be sure, smacked of protectionism, which Reagan abhorred. But the problem in 1980 was acute. The American auto industry that year was accumulating losses that would total $4 billion. Midwest communities dependent on car production were suffering unemployment rates in the 20 percent range. Chrysler was in business at all only because of a special loan program guaranteed by the U.S. Treasury. One quarter of the vehicles being sold in the United States came from abroad, and most of those—1.82 million by the end of 1980—were made in Japan.

Reagan in early February designated Transportation Secretary Drew Lewis, the most adroit politician in the cabinet, to head a task force of nine members to develop a plan. On several points, such as the need to slow down pending safety and anti-pollution regulations, there was quick agreement. But a March 9 memorandum from Lewis to the White House candidly acknowledged that, on the question of import restrictions, "the disagreement within the task force . . . has been documented in detail by the reports of the various members." Lewis himself advocated some form of restraint from the beginning. If that could not be arranged by negotiation, blatantly protectionist legislation might well be enacted; a bill written by Missouri Senator John Danforth had already attracted support. Bill Brock, the U.S. Trade Representative, shared Lewis' pragmatic political approach, as did a few other task force members. But Stockman, Treasury Secretary Donald Regan and Murray Weidenbaum, chairman of the Council of Economic Advisers, defended the free-trade principle. Acting to assist the industry was a bad precedent. It could lead to demands by other special interests. Further, reducing competition might have the effect of encouraging price increases. Regan even predicted that the auto industry would make it into the black during 1981 anyway (a prediction that turned out to be wrong).

As these arguments were rehearsed in a number of meetings, Stockman, Weidenbaum and Regan were at first unaware that the real solution was being worked out secretly. Lewis had been chosen in the first place because Meese knew where he stood. Meese and Baker both also knew that the final result would have to include a reduction in exports from Japan. During February and early March they worked quietly with Lewis and one or two others to cook a deal along those lines. It was a difficult situation, as Lewis later recalled:

> We were caught in a catch-22. Let's put the cards right on the table. The President and the whole Administration espouse free trade, but we had made certain commitments . . . to give some protection, is what it amounted to. How can you be consistent on two directions that are totally inconsistent?[6]

The answer was to make it appear that the United States wasn't imposing a quota, but that the Japanese were "volunteering" to put one on themselves. There was a certain urgency to the situation because the Japanese Prime Minister, Zenko Suzuki, was to arrive for an official visit on May 7. If still unresolved, the auto issue would shadow those meetings. A preparatory visit by the Foreign Minister, Masayoshi Ito, had accomplished little. Ito indicated that Tokyo *required* pressure from Washington in order to be able to rationalize the reductions in exports to its home audience.

On March 19 Reagan was to attend what turned out to be the decisive meeting with his task force in the Cabinet Room. By then Meese and Lewis had a scenario. Stockman and the free-trade faction were just beginning to realize that a deal had already been negotiated. Lewis began the discussion with a summary and said that the best solution would be for the Japanese to come forward with their own plan. Regan, Stockman and Weidenbaum laid down caveats about the need for delicacy. The Budget Director was especially concerned about harming the Administration's larger economic program, an important premise of which was that it would be equitable. "If we give one overt indication that we're willing to depart from the general plan," Stockman said, "then we're going to have irresistible demands from special interests who say they need more [government help]. One of the strengths of the whole program is to get people to set aside their own interests."

Brock responded by reminding Reagan of his promise to the auto workers the preceding September. He went further by suggesting that the Japanese be given a specific number to consider. The President joined the general discussion, as if the conclusion still were not clear. "It would be the wrong thing for me," he observed, "to promise in advance a veto [of the Danforth quota bill]." Instead, Reagan said, we must warn Tokyo in advance that the impetus for protectionism is substantial in Congress. Protectionist legislation would be used as an "or else" to elicit cooperation from Tokyo.

At this point George Bush proposed that Mike Mansfield, the U.S. ambassador to Japan, should convey the word to the Japanese foreign minister. Somehow Reagan missed the cue. After further discussion about the need to preserve the appearance of upholding free trade, Bush repeated the idea: "What's wrong with Mansfield telling them the facts of life?" Now the President responded directly: "I agree. All Mansfield has to do is to tell them there's a firestorm [against the growing volume of Japanese imports]." But, Reagan ruled, no numbers should be conveyed to the Japanese.

That, essentially, was the decision taken before the session began. However, nothing formal was done at that stage. Lewis, worried about leaks, proposed that the meeting end right there, without an official ruling from the President. Reporters, aware that the issue was coming to a climax, had been seeking firm word of a decision. They were to be disappointed. Press Secretary James Brady was summoned to the Cabinet Room, where Reagan informed him simply, "I'm not going to tell you what my decision is going to be." The White House then announced other measures to help Detroit, but remained mute for the time being on the import question. A week later Senator Danforth came in to see the President, urging that pressure on the Japanese be increased. "They will view us as irresolute on many fronts," Danforth argued. Reagan maintained discretion, commenting only that "we're not just sitting here and listening."

There would be further twists and turns over the next month. At the end of April, Brock was in Tokyo—not negotiating, everyone insisted, merely conferring. On May 1, just a week before Suzuki's visit to

Washington, Tokyo announced its very own three-year plan. Initially, exports to the United States would be reduced from 1.82 million a year to 1.68 million. In the second year, if total auto sales in the United States increased, Japan would get a small part of that rise. In the third year, circumstances would be reviewed in light of conditions then. All this was presented as Tokyo's response to the problems of its ally, though no one was fooled.

The White House had acted with dexterity. Both Japan and the free-trade faction of the cabinet were allowed to preserve face. Reagan could claim that he had stuck to his principles and kept a campaign pledge. Meese and Baker had set a significant pattern, which would be repeated in other situations, for cutting through factional problems. But there would be a less cheerful postscript. Despite the façade, the Administration had taken a small step toward protectionism. Later, as economic conditions in all the industrialized countries grew worse, so would the tendency in each nation to protect number one. The American auto industry, meanwhile, continued to have a dreadful year and a sluggish 1982 as well. Detroit's inability to recover would inhibit growth in steel and other businesses. Yes, the new administration had scored a victory, one of several it would enjoy in its first spring and summer. Later, points tallied in the auto game would count for little.

6

Ed Meese:
Counselor and Target

Behind his back they called him Poppin. Though the nickname derived from the cheerful plump creature in the cookie commercial—ready to pop the dough into the oven—it was not used with affection, or by those loyal to Ed Meese. Rather it was a term of derision, spinning off his shape, the unquenchable good humor he displayed in public and his critics' low estimate of his value to the White House.

On rare, very private occasions, Meese would show some of the anxiety corked up within him. He would complain of unfair treatment in the press, or of being made a scapegoat by a colleague. But he permitted few people to see that malaise. In most situations he emitted an affable serenity that is rare among those who ascend the greasy pole of political power. After all, diligence and uncompromising loyalty had raised him high, higher than he ever dreamed he would climb when he was a youngster back in Oakland. He figured then that he might follow his father into the respectable drudgery of local government service. Instead he found a place just a half step down from the throne, first in Ronald Reagan's Sacramento, then in Ronald Reagan's White House.

Meese was grateful. When he said grace at a family dinner, he meant it. When he treated subordinates with unfailing consideration he meant that too. He was so gentle and pleasant a boss that even a temporary secretary in his office who knew Meese only slightly growled at a reporter whose publication had just skewered him. For his own part, Meese offered a mild self-defense before turning cheerfully to the journalist's new inquiries. If smiles could be redeemed in coin, those regularly in the Meese presence would soon be wealthy.

By mid-August of 1981, I had been exposed to this relentless good cheer for twenty months. Still, I was unprepared for just how elevated his mood could be when I visited his suite on the seventeenth floor of the Century Plaza Hotel in Los Angeles. It was the middle of Reagan's long summer holiday and Meese was the ranking aide on duty for a fortnight of it. The tall, stocky figure was frowsy on this Wednesday morning, the nineteenth. His eyes were squinty after a wakeful night, the double-knit trousers rumpled, his collar undone to reveal the top of his undershirt. His short blond hair hadn't encountered a comb since leaving the pillow. But the face, ruddy and wholesome as a successful farmer's, positively radiated satisfaction.

It was the morning after American warplanes shot down two Libyan aircraft over the Gulf of Sidra. Though the Sidewinder missiles found their marks before Meese knew of the engagement, it had been he who received the word from Defense Secretary Caspar Weinberger at 11:05 P.M. Pacific time, he who monitored the situation through the night, he who decided when Reagan should be informed, he who determined when the news should be announced. He was at the center of the action, as he had been many years before when he supervised the quelling of student riots in California. The challenge by Libya, hardly a surprise, had been dealt with firmly. Ed Meese, former lawman, former lieutenant colonel in the Army Reserve, continuing student of military intelligence, constant patriot, could only savor this rebuff to the outlaw Muammar al-Qaddafi. Though not a bloody-minded man, he could only be grateful for having been able to play a role.

The beige hotel phone and the white government phone take turns interrupting our conversation. Al Haig is on the line. They discuss what additional information should and should not be announced. Lyn Nofziger calls next. He has cracked a martial joke, apparently, because Meese replies, "No, we're not going to war. We're just shooting 'em down. We're bringing out the flag that says, 'Don't tread on me.' " A few minutes later Weinberger checks in from the Pentagon. "Good morning," Meese greets his long-time associate. "Didn't get much sleep, did you? I think I got a little more than you. . . . Al thought the way you went on [television] so promptly was very effective. . . . Yes, the whole system worked well. Had anything else happened, we'd have been in a position to handle it. . . ."

As that conversation ends, Nofziger appears in the suite. He also looks unkempt, but not because he was up all night. That is his natural condition. Though not a morning person, the former newspaperman and sometime press adviser to Reagan is almost as chipper as Meese. "This will look pretty good," Nofziger observes. "We didn't turn tail and run."

Viewed as a military operation and as an exercise designed to show

Qaddafi that there was indeed new management in Washington, the little shoot-out over the Gulf of Sidra was successful. But it turned promptly into a public relations downer for Reagan and even more of one for Meese. Technically, Meese had a good case in choosing not to disturb the chief when the news first came in. Action of some kind had been anticipated. It had been over for half an hour when word reached the Century Plaza and therefore there was nothing urgent for Reagan to decide. By waiting five and a half hours to wake Reagan at 4:24 A.M., Meese could then give him a full report and tell him that the large naval exercise was concluding on schedule without further incident.

What Meese forgot was that Americans, and particularly Americans who happen to cover the White House, expect the President to be personally involved with all important events as a matter of principle. These were the first shots fired in anger since Reagan had become Commander in Chief. Not only had he been allowed to sleep when the action was reported, he returned to slumber after hearing Meese's account and remained disconnected until 8 A.M. Long before this incident, Reagan was said to be all too willing to let his aides tend to important affairs. Further, there had also been snide commentary about his four-week sojourn in California. And still further, Meese at this point was the target of stories that he was assuming too much authority, that he was taking on the airs of "deputy President." That these stories were overdrawn was irrelevant. The thesis was out there, awaiting confirmation.

Reagan himself would later joke about the incident at every opportunity. The following November, as he and a few assistants discussed the pending veto of an important continuing resolution—a move that technically would leave some departments without funds and halt some governmental activity—Reagan said, "But Ed, if we do have to go through this thing, I hope you'll wake me up." In fact, the White House became quite sensitive about what was called the "wake-up issue." Announcements were dutifully made each time Reagan was roused from bed to hear some important news, as he was when Leonid Brezhnev died in November 1982.

At the time of the original incident, Meese did not seem to realize that he had damaged his own interests as well as those of the President he tried so earnestly to serve well in all matters. Pentagon reporters would report the real action. White House reporters, slightly bored with the California stay by August nineteenth, would have great sport with Meese's judgment as well as Reagan's blessing of it after the fact. These circumstances prompted one major magazine to report that

Reagan worked only a few hours a day anyway and to savage Meese's general comportment during the California holiday.[1]

Baker and Deaver, far more sensitive to public relations concerns, were unhappy at this outcome. Either of them would have handled matters differently. Other events that occurred during the same period began to strain the unusual troika setup, though this stress was negligible compared with what would happen later. It was during that same fortnight that difficulties arose over the question of defense spending. Weinberger, Stockman and others went to California for meetings to settle the issue, but an impasse developed. Meese, known as the great "synthesizer" and conciliator of internal disputes, failed to press vigorously enough for a solution—or so some of his colleagues would contend. Baker, thinking that a compromise was achieved, went public with numbers that turned out to be wrong.

At the same time, interest rates were soaring. So were estimates of the federal budget deficit over the next few years. Reagan's budget and tax bills, so recently signed into law, would require fixing, and quickly. Yet the revolving cast of advisers in California seemed paralyzed. Meese became one scapegoat. If that judgment was unjust, so was the system that required heroes and goats for every episode. It was Meese, after all, who served as the President's counselor, his senior policy adviser. It was his responsibility to reconcile differences in the cabinet. The fact that Reagan himself was not yet willing to choose among his own conflicting priorities was another matter. Meese took the rap anyway. He thoroughly resented it. Thirteen months later he still insisted that he had been right: "For me the most important thing was the principle that all sides get a fair hearing. It had to be the President's decision and he had to know everything necessary to make that decision in an informed, evenhanded way."[2]

There would be other counts against him, some valid and some not, but nearly all of them leaking out. Meese, as we've seen, had insisted on a share in the direct management of operations. In the first year, both the National Security Council staff and its equivalent for domestic affairs, the Office of Policy Development, reported to him. Further, the National Security Council staff chief, Richard Allen, and the head of the Office of Policy Development, Martin Anderson, were Meese allies. Several of Anderson's ranking subordinates owed their positions to old California connections with Meese. The Personnel Office, responsible for finding talent to fill top jobs throughout the Administration, ostensibly reported to Baker in his capacity as Chief of Staff. But Pendleton James, the Personnel Office director until mid-1982, had known Meese for twenty-five years. Further, Meese as well as Deaver each had a full vote in recommending important appointments for Reagan's final approval.

The NSC and OPD operations during 1981 functioned poorly. The Personnel Office seemed to move in slow motion. At their daily breakfast sessions, Deaver complained frequently to Meese about Allen's performance, about the National Security Adviser's inability to work with the State Department. Later, of course, Deaver would blame Haig for that continuing problem but by then Allen was gone and Haig's departure imminent. Baker became increasingly impatient over OPD's inability to process options for timely decision. What should the Administration's stance be on extension of the Voting Rights Act? What about ending price controls on natural gas? How long before we make a decision on continuing draft registration or ending it? Where are we headed on the Federalism proposal?

Occasionally, and very privately, even Meese became exasperated. In one small meeting he wondered aloud about Anderson's OPD: "What do Marty and those guys *do* over there?" He would try to find out. He would push and prod and hold meetings. But he had surrounded himself with a weak staff during that first year. One high slot on the Meese roster went to Robert Garrick, a Los Angeles public relations man and retired reserve admiral, whose duties were unclear to everyone. The last thing the Reagan White House needed was another PR man. Garrick aroused derision by sending an unsolicited memorandum to all the heavyweights appearing on TV talk programs. Address the interviewers as "Mister" or "Miss," Garrick advised; that maintains dignity and distance. The one star on Meese's staff, Craig Fuller, the cabinet secretary, had come into the orbit through Deaver rather than Meese.

Eventually Meese's colleagues gave him candid advice about his problems and he made some changes, or accepted changes forced by circumstances. He gave up on Allen. Anderson quit in frustration. Garrick and another ranking aide, Edwin Thomas, left the White House. By the time all that was settled, however, Meese's reputation as a mediocre administrator was part of the permanent book on the Reaganauts. In January of 1982, when William P. Clark replaced Allen as the National Security Adviser, Meese was literally cut out of the NSC paper flow. Deaver and Clark managed to exclude Meese from the climax of the Allen affair. Six months later they would do the same thing when they severed Haig's cord. By that late date, the troika as it had existed in the first year was effectively defunct. The exact moment of its demise can be debated. This coroner places the time during the first two weeks of January 1982, when Clark's appointment became official and when Meese took yet another blow—blame for a boner concerning the restoration of tax exemptions for schools accused of racist practices. Baker and Deaver yearned for a realignment of responsibility that would take Meese out of operations altogether. Baker even came to believe that all concerned would be better served if either he or Meese left the White House altogether, so that there could be one Chief of Staff with clear authority.

Because the Reaganauts had made ideology fashionable in Washington, some of the professional spectators interpreted the tug of war within the staff as a struggle between mainstream Republicanism and the new Reaganism. By this reading, Clark's advent favored the latter. Rowland Evans and Robert Novak, whose column sought to track theological shifts of the Administration closely, bought this little myth. Of Clark they wrote: "He is viewed as an instant counterweight to Baker. Insiders expect him to reinforce the fading power of old-time Reagan aide Edwin Meese rather than supplant it."[3] Nothing could have been farther from the truth. Though Clark and Meese had been comrades in Sacramento and shared similar convictions, Clark had long since ceased being a Meese admirer. The main causes of distress were operational technique and personality clashes, not philosophy. As the group labored through the difficult summer and fall of 1982 toward a midterm election that threatened a serious setback, the senior echelon of the White House staff was distracted by what several members expected to be an important reorganization.* Those palpable doubts would become a problem as alliances came into question and one publication after another recorded the increasing *angst*.

Meese himself characteristically refused to acknowledge any change. "It's exactly the same relationship," he said of his dealings with Deaver and Baker in mid-1982. "We are interchangeable."[4] By then some of his colleagues were worried about him. Though Meese generally managed to maintain his affable front to the outside world, those who saw him frequently at close quarters could detect a fatigue of the spirit occasionally bordering on melancholy. That was visible even before his nineteen-year-old son, Scott, died in an auto accident. He continued to spread himself thin, to accept more speaking invitations than he could comfortably cope with, so that he was too often absent from the White House as important matters—Haig's departure, for instance—were coming to a head. Yet at the same time he feared being left out of decisions. One aide sympathetic to Meese observed during this period: "He

---

* A few of the President's advisers thought that he would make some decisions along this line between the midterm election and his return from a New Year's holiday in California. However, Reagan came back from Palm Springs in January 1983 still unwilling to overhaul his immediate staff in any significant way. Once this became clear, the principal players reconciled themselves to living with a system that most of them felt was flawed.

sticks as close to the President as he can. He wants to attend every meeting, even the trivial ones. He seems to want to read the papers on your desk when he drops in. If he notices you talking to somebody from another office, he'll take you aside and say, 'What was that all about? Something I should know?' How do you figure him?"

How to figure Edwin Meese III, and Ronald Reagan's durable affinity for him, had become a favorite game long before the troika died. One well-documented highlight of Meese's career occurred in February 1980 as the New Hampshire primary campaign was ending. A struggle within the organization had been in progress for months, though we only knew parts of the story until the climax. Meese, the policy man, the lawyer far more knowledgeable about criminal justice than about electoral politics or internal vendettas, triumphed over John Sears, a paradigm of adroit political operators. Reagan risked a great deal by firing Sears, along with the experienced professionals loyal to him, well before the nomination was assured. But the choice had become Meese or Sears, and Reagan would not part with Meese.*

In fact, the showdown in New Hampshire was not the first time, and would not be the last, that Meese was the target of other Reaganauts who wanted to remove him from the boss's intimate circle. The conventional folklore about Reagan's successive official families, from his 1966 gubernatorial campaign onward, has them as relatively congenial groups. Most of the members lacked personal ambition or lust for power. They were bound by loyalty to Reagan and, to some extent, by conservative convictions. Compared with some other political entourages—Richard Nixon's collection of feral courtiers, for instance— that pleasant picture is more or less accurate. However, Reagan's men had their own strains over the years and Meese was sometimes the focal point.

By the 1970 election, when Reagan ran for a second term in Sacramento, Meese was serving as the governor's Chief of Staff. He had not participated at all in the first race, four years earlier, or in Reagan's brief flirtation with presidential politics in 1968. Management of the reelection drive was largely in the hands of Tom Reed, an engineer and businessman then serving as Republican National Committeeman from California, and Stuart Spencer, the professional political consultant Reagan's backers first recruited in 1966. Reed and Spencer

---

* The antagonists made some passes at compromise as Nancy Reagan tried to act as mediator. But in the end neither Sears nor Meese wanted to continue living with the other. The struggle was reported in contemporary accounts, including *Time*'s cover story on New Hampshire (the issue of March 10, 1980) and, in more detail, in book-length histories of the campaign, notably *Blue Smoke and Mirrors* by Jack W. Germond and Jules Witcover (Viking, 1981).

had their own differences, but were united on one important item: they wanted Reagan to clean house for his second term, and told him so bluntly. They thought that Meese should be removed from the immediate staff, along with others, arguing that Reagan needed tighter, more efficient administrative technique and fresh ideas. Mike Deaver was already very close to both of the Reagans, but he was subordinate to Chief of Staff Meese. Recalling that period, Deaver said, "There was no doubt in my mind that if Tom won, I would have been out as well."[5] Reed lost, however, and so did Spencer. Their influence in Sacramento declined accordingly. Both later signed up with Gerald Ford, and Spencer became an active adversary of Reagan's in the 1976 nomination fight, only to return to the Reagan fold in 1980.

On the evening of October 29, at the Hyatt Regency Hotel in Dallas, Spencer privately advised Reagan against giving Meese control of the White House staff. Deaver and Spencer then combined to draw Baker into that position, though it was understood that Meese might retain a place of influence. Meese was so shocked when Reagan put this to him the day after the election that a few of the others thought Meese might refuse to serve at all. Instead, he decided to accept Baker's advent and to keep as large a hand as possible in White House operations.

Spencer meanwhile declined the troika's invitation to join the new administration as the full-time head of the political liaison office. But he agreed to serve as an informal adviser and troubleshooter. Reagan and his wife occasionally dined with Spencer because they valued his candid advice. The White House connection did not do Spencer's political consulting firm any harm either. He is a colorful bird in the Reagan aviary—short, banty in his body language in the manner of James Cagney characters, fond of liquor, cigarettes and rough humor, proud of a tattoo on his forearm, *USS Rocky Mountain,* the ship on which he served during World War II ("An old Chinese woman used the needle on me in Honolulu back in forty-five. It hurt like hell"). In at least two of his meetings with Reagan during 1981, on June 26 and again on August 10, Spencer proposed that Meese be given another government assignment. The general tenor of the advice ("You've got good people but you're playing them in the wrong positions . . .") became known to a few others in the inner circle who basically agreed. But Reagan resisted. "He gets that pained look and you don't want to make him suffer," one of Reagan's men said. More than a year later, when Spencer's pessimistic predictions about the troika's usefulness had come true, Reagan was still resisting.

A fair record must show that Meese rejects much of this as simply untrue. Of the conflict with Reed after the 1970 election: "I don't think it ever came to that kind of showdown. No, it never came to a showdown. It came to a disagreement over appointments." The real rivalry, he recalled, was between Reed and Nofziger. "Spencer? I don't know of any animosity. I've never had any towards him. Mike Deaver and Spencer were very much estranged. I may have got some of the fallout from that."[6] Meese pointed out that he welcomed Spencer back to the tent during 1980 and argued that he was happy to see Reed come to the White House in 1982, when Clark drafted Reed for a place on the National Security Council staff. "I have been one of his major supporters in this organization," Meese says of Reed. Meese denies that he was in any way disappointed when he did not get clear command of the White House staff; he neither sought it nor even wanted to be responsible for detail work. He had no idea why anyone would spread such tales.

Those who cover the White House regularly have become inured to Meese's inability to confront this kind of friction. Through most of 1981 he denied that any trouble existed in the NSC staff. He conveys his view of reality with such sincerity, and avoids dumping on others with such scrupulousness, that one sometimes comes away thinking that he, like Reagan, insulates himself from unpleasantness by pretending that it doesn't exist. When I once reminded him that he had misled me on other occasions concerning personality conflicts, he seemed genuinely shocked. The account here of the moves against him and his difficulties with Reed and Spencer was corroborated by enough sources to confirm its accuracy.

Understanding Reagan's loyalty to Meese is more a question of psychological detective work than conventional legwork. One element is clear: Meese, in the human dimension, is Reagan's kind of man. Meese is a fourth-generation Californian. His great-grandfather arrived in the New World from Germany in 1850, crossed the country in a wagon train, later worked as a cabinetmaker. The clan never became wealthy in land or commerce, but by the time Ed and his three younger brothers were growing up in Oakland the family was a fixture in Alameda County's middle-class establishment. The father, Edwin II, was active in the American Legion, the Kiwanis Club, the Lutheran Church. The eldest son got a feel for public affairs early as his father worked as clerk of the magistrate's court and later served a dozen years as the county's elected tax collector and treasurer.

The Meese boys had a strong sense of position and of place. "My father was born in Oakland, my brothers and I were born in Oakland and so were my three children," Ed Meese liked to say. "All Meeses are born in Oakland." The younger three brothers continued to live and work in the Bay area. There was never much money in the family.

As a youth, Ed worked in a drugstore, an iron mill, an oil refinery, a parks department recreation program. College at Yale was possible only because of a scholarship ("The Ivy League wanted more Westerners in the fifties. It was a kind of regional affirmative action"). When he left for New Haven, it was the first time in his life he had ventured east of Reno. Yale's Political Union was a natural goal for a student who had enjoyed the high school debate team, and a newcomer could choose among four factions: Conservative, Bull Moose, Liberal and Labor. He joined the Conservatives without hesitation.

To study law he went to Berkeley and briefly considered becoming a policeman to support himself; while in the Army on an ROTC commission he had enjoyed intelligence work. But law enforcement would wait until he earned his law degree and found a place in the Alameda County District Attorney's office. His attractive blond wife Ursula, whom he had known since adolescence, worked as a deputy probation officer. The young prosecutor handled murder, vice and drug cases, earning a reputation as a tough law-and-order man. In one of the homicide convictions he won, he defeated the flamboyant defense attorney Melvin Belli. Meese's record and popularity in the law enforcement community led to two interesting sidelines: he became an adviser to other jurisdictions on the handling of riots and he went to Sacramento as lobbyist for the state association of district attorneys. Soon after Reagan's victory, he was summoned to meet the governor-elect and then to join the staff with the misleading title of Extradition and Clemency Secretary. That was only part of the job in 1967–68, though the governor did have to rule on controversial capital punishment appeals (one murderer finally went to the gas chamber). The state then was seized with anti-war fever and Meese visited the sites of disorders to work closely with local authorities. Accounts of the period depict him as calm and efficient in the worst turmoil.

Meese grew in the job and Reagan, with his own keen interest in quelling the disturbances, quickly came to respect Meese's judgment on other subjects as well. Years later Reed would recall: "He was very valuable to Reagan. He knew how to stay cool and sensible in difficult situations. He's a hell of a lawyer and a hell of a counselor."[7] Clark at that time was the governor's Chief of Staff, superior to both Meese and Deaver, and eager to leave Sacramento. He would have the principal say in the selection of his replacement. On the personal level, he was much closer to Deaver. Though Meese was the lawman, Clark preferred to use Deaver to mete out staff discipline. Meese's toughness ran thin when he wasn't dealing with lawbreakers or critics of Reagan. But Deaver's ambition for power in the hierarchy was slender, he was

younger than Meese and he lacked the honing of legal training. So
Clark chose a fellow lawyer and Reagan accepted Meese.

Pulled out of his specialty, Meese suffered difficulties as an instant
generalist with broad responsibilities. He was reluctant to delegate authority. He was so eager to make sure that everything was done correctly that he immersed himself in detail without separating priorities
from marginalia. Occasionally Reagan would kid him: "Now, Ed,
don't lose this one on your desk." But that failing seemed minor to the
boss. It was more than offset by other attributes that Reagan found
then, and would continue to find, compelling.

Advisers with ego problems or their own ambitions would occasionally try to prod Reagan away from his own instincts. Or they might
try to force decisions before Reagan was ready to make them. Meese
deftly avoided these gambits. While too conscientious to be a yes-man,
he was also too prudent to get far ahead of his principal. A few others,
such as Baker, would err in that department. Baker not only pressured
Reagan to confront the deficit problem earlier than the President was
ready to act, but he allowed word of what was happening to seep out.
Meese, the veteran Reaganaut, knew the boss's views and metabolism
better. Besides, Meese's private opinions coincided with Reagan's almost completely. It was Meese rather than Baker, Deaver or Darman
who wore a necktie festooned with Adam Smith's profile stitched in
gold thread. It was Meese rather than the others who massaged right-
wing activists when they grew cranky. It was Meese who shared
Reagan's fascination with and respect for the military. When they went
together in May of 1981 to West Point, where Meese's elder son
Michael was getting his diploma and commission, it was difficult to tell
whether the President or his counselor beamed with more pride.

Reagan also admired Meese's willingness to practice as well as
mouth one of the Reaganaut clichés—to "round-table" important questions. Lacking both brilliance and guile, Meese rarely pushed his own
preferences without giving the other side of the argument a full airing.
He had a touch for sorting out complexities so that Reagan could easily grasp the fundamentals of a decision in the making. In Sacramento,
as later, Meese had no intimate friends in the upper echelon, no factional alliances. In fact, while Meese's jolly spirit helped him create
friendly relations with many of his colleagues wherever he worked, and
while he showed intense loyalty to subordinates even when they performed inadequately, he was essentially a loner.

That was still his condition in the White House, particularly after
Martin Anderson resigned. Other alliances, personal or utilitarian,
would form or be renewed. Deaver, Clark and special assistant Helene

von Damm took up the close private friendship they had shared in Sacramento. Baker and Deaver became neighbors and friends as well as allies in many situations. Darman and Fuller, though they dangled off separate lines in the organization chart, collaborated frequently and formed an entente of their own. Meese stood apart from all of that, associating most often with a few subordinates. One newcomer to the Reagan circle who dealt closely with Meese for more than a year said of him: "Does anyone really know Ed? Usually, when you become more familiar with someone, you begin to see the different colors inside. With Ed, you get the feeling that if you stripped off the top layer and did a cross section of the interior, all the slices would be the same color."

Perhaps Reagan identified himself with that side of Meese as well. Each was an amiable loner, compulsively spreading good cheer, friendly to all but friend to very, very few. Like Reagan, Meese enjoyed telling jokes, and like Reagan he occasionally let a good line overcome good sense. When anti-nuclear rallies were building to an intense level, Meese allowed TV cameras to capture him as he asked an audience why the MX missile was like a Hallmark greeting card. Answer: Because if we go to war, we want to send the very best. As usual, White House colleagues who were acutely sensitive to public relations problems winced. And they wondered when the next vacancy on the Supreme Court might occur and whether Meese would consider taking it even though doing so would separate him at last from the man who had raised him up from Oakland.

They figured that Meese would be ambivalent, despite the honor and the advantages. His first instinct would be that Reagan needed him all the more now in the second half of the term. Reaganism also needed Meese, the last keeper of the faith after Anderson, Nofziger and Allen left the White House. Now it was up to Ed Meese to remind his colleagues, as domestic policy decisions were shaped, what Reagan had always stood for on this question or that. Still, the Supreme Court is a good place from which to fan an eternal flame. Meese celebrated his fifty-second birthday when Reagan's third year in office began. At the court, he could influence the course of history for the next twenty years or more. Would Meese be willing to see the troika destroyed in name as well as in functional reality? Perhaps he remembered the night of March 30, 1981, when the action was over and Reagan safely out of surgery. That was the troika's prime, and the time when the full import of the arrangement became clear to all of Washington. After ten o'clock that night the tension was easing. Meese and Baker sat at one end of the conference table in the Chief of Staff's office. Meese stretched out his hand to his companion and said, "I want to tell you it's a pleasure doing business with you." Baker could only respond, "Same here, Ed." Remembering that, could Meese imagine that such solidarity might be rebuilt? With Ed, one of his colleagues observed, you never knew about things like that.

7

"The Thing That Happened to Ronnie"

FBI ballistics tests later would show an interesting aberration. The .22-caliber "Devastator" bullet fired by John Hinckley did not ricochet directly off the side of the limousine. Rather the slug skidded for an inch along the Lincoln's armored right rear panel. The hollow-nosed explosive projectile flattened out, taking the shape of a circular saw blade the size of a dime. As if directed by a malevolent homing device, the bullet deflected off the black metal, found the gap between the car's body and the open rear door, sped under the raised left arm of its target, penetrated his torso below the armpit, struck the top of the seventh rib, glanced off the bone, plunged into spongy lung tissue. By the end of its trajectory, its velocity spent, the bullet no longer sliced neatly like a tiny knife. When piercing the skin it had created a slit that was almost invisible. Now, wobbling through the lower pulmonary lobe, it gouged a hole large enough to accommodate the tip of a surgeon's finger.

Paradox attends every deadly attack on a national leader. Lincoln's murderer never saw service in the Civil War. Robert Kennedy's death helped assure the election of Richard Nixon, who proved to be a very strong friend to Israel. George Wallace was crippled physically, but his ordeal bestowed legitimacy and durability on an otherwise eccentric political career. John W. Hinckley, Jr., arrived at the Washington Hilton Hotel on the afternoon of March 30, 1981, to act out a fantasy created by the industry that had made Ronald Reagan sufficiently famous to enter politics. Without the movie *Taxi Driver,* Hinckley might or might not have found a different outlet for his madness. But without the movie business, Reagan would never have been worth any assassin's powder. Hinckley used ammunition with explosive tips, ostensibly to increase damage to his victims. But had the round that wounded Reagan exploded on contact with the limousine as it should have, it would have splintered to bits before hitting his body.

Other oddities festooned the attempt on Reagan's life. The President of the United States of America was felled by a small, malfunctioning bullet delivered by a small, cheap revolver held by a small, demented loser. The act so totally lacked political or even personal motivation that it seemed an ignominious way in which to nearly lose the nation's leader. Yet this apolitical quest for stature had the eventual effect of certifying the hunter's lunacy in court while allowing the hunted to display, for the first time in his life, a kind of personal heroism that instantly improved his political standing. The shooting would have other ripples as well. It would test a White House staff that was still learning to mesh its gears. It would create new difficulties for a Secretary of State already off to an uncertain start. It would show Nancy Reagan at her wifely best. It would display the personal bravery of Secret Service agents when bullets fly while demonstrating bureaucratic sloth in their agency and the FBI when brains rather than viscera must react. One could savor all of this only after that long, warm, wet day. A few minutes before 2:30 P.M., when Hinckley got off six rounds within three seconds, nothing was clear, not even the fact that the President had been shot.

Three seconds, three casualties strewn on the pavement: Secret Service agent Tim McCarthy had turned to face the gunfire while remaining upright, as his training dictated, and took a bullet in the chest; District patrolman Thomas Delahanty was struck in the neck before he could react; Press Secretary James Brady, who had moved into the wrong position just an instant before, was hit in the forehead above the left eye. The fourth victim neither fell nor staggered. Instead, Ronald Reagan was shoved into the limo by the chief of his Secret Service detail, Jerry Parr, who then threw himself over the President and ordered the driver to take off immediately. Like McCarthy, Parr was following his script impeccably. Months later, Reagan recalled those confused moments:

> I never saw the man with the gun. I didn't even know I had been shot. I knew I was hurt. I felt that very badly and then I was bleeding through the mouth. It first came to my mind, with the paralyzing pain as I landed in the car, that I'd broken a rib [in being knocked over by Parr]. And then when the blood started to come out of my mouth, I thought, The rib is broken and it punctured a lung. And I thought that up until the time I walked into the hospital.[1]

Hundreds of times—it seemed to him thousands—Mike Deaver had gone through the motorcade ritual with candidate Reagan, Governor Reagan, President Reagan. As the lieutenant most often at the captain's elbow, Deaver would go from the limousine to the event in which Reagan was to participate and return to the car afterward. It was the same when Reagan left his large audience of delegates to the AFL-CIO Building Trades Council conference in the Hilton. Though Deaver could have the final say on public relations matters when he chose, he has never served as Reagan's day-to-day press secretary. That fact saved Deaver's skin on March 30. Just three days after the shooting, he was able to recite the sequence in a calm, flat tone: "The President and I walked out together with Jim [Brady] just a step behind me. When we got to the curb, to start to the limousine, one of the reporters yelled out a question to the President. So I automatically traded places with Jim so that he could handle the press." Deaver moved to his left, intending to go around the rear of the Lincoln and get into the car on the street side. That was his familiar routine. He could have done it sightless. This time Deaver never made it past the bumper. Those moments he had dreaded for years were upon him:

> When you're in a very tense [crowd] situation, you think about it and you're very alert, looking at people. There was no reason to think about trouble that day. I hadn't taken but a couple of steps when the first shot came over my right shoulder. It was close enough for me to feel the concussion and smell powder. There was no question in my mind. I mean I went *down* because I *knew*. The shots just kept coming and I crouched behind the trunk of the limousine until I could see that the President was in. I was thinking, My God, it's happening. After all those times when you think about it, it's actually *happening*. Those shots kept coming. I saw people going down, not realizing they were hit. I thought they were just protecting themselves.[2]

Like Reagan, Deaver never saw the gunman or the gun. As the armored limousine pulled away, he made for a Secret Service sedan called the control car. So did David Fischer, a young lawyer and Deaver protégé who by this time had served as Reagan's aide-de-camp for nearly three years. "We got in the car," Deaver went on, "and Dave and I grabbed each other and I said, 'My God, Dave, is he all right?' "

The answer was no. But at that moment, and for some agonizing minutes to come, only three people—Reagan, Parr and Drew Unrue, the Secret Service agent at the limousine's wheel—knew it. Parr's first instinct was to direct the motorcade straight south on Connecticut Avenue, bringing Reagan to the physical safety of the White House in two or three minutes. The bleeding and the pain Reagan continued to expe-

rience quickly changed Parr's mind. He decided to divert the motorcade to George Washington University Hospital, less than a mile west
of the White House. Word that shooting had occurred, and then of
Parr's decision to make for the hospital, was sent by radio to the Secret
Service center in the White House basement. But those bulletins indicated that Reagan had not been shot. The President's aides upstairs
were unaware of the violence. Back at the Hilton, one of Brady's junior
assistants, David Prosperi, rushed into the hotel. He found a pay phone
but discovered that he lacked fifteen cents. Charging the call to his
home number, he dialed the White House Press Office, shouted, "This is
an emergency!" and demanded to talk to Brady's principal deputy,
Larry Speakes. Prosperi told Speakes what little he knew: Shots fired at
the presidential party, Brady wounded.

By 2:30 the hospital's emergency room was alerted that the presidential motorcade was approaching and that gunshot casualties were
being brought in. Broadcast and wire service correspondents who had
been in the press pool staked out at the Hilton exit had relayed their
initial bulletins to their offices. Incomplete and initially confusing, the
news rocketed out to the world. Deaver, in a formal statement dictated
the next day for the archives, picks up the tale:

> The President got out on his own and started to walk in with the help of
> agent Jerry Parr. We got inside the doors and through the waiting room
> and just at the end of the waiting room going into the emergency room
> the President went down—slowly—and he was picked up by three or four
> people and they started ripping his clothes off and carrying him at the
> same time, and he seemed to be in a lot of pain. He was grimacing, and
> there was a lot of confusion, obviously, at that point—aides, doctors,
> nurses, Secret Service agents. The only [White House] staff in there were
> myself and Dave Fischer and Dr. [Daniel] Ruge [the President's personal
> physician]. And when the doctors got him on the table I backed off but
> stayed so that I could see what was happening for a couple of minutes. I
> then got Ruge and said, "Tell me what's happening," and he said, "I don't
> know, I think he may have had a cardiac" . . .

Reagan was put on an examining table in Bay 5A at the rear of the
emergency suite. The hospital had a well-trained trauma unit, which
needed all the skill at its command as Brady and McCarthy were also
brought in. John Pekkanen, in a meticulous account of what then happened,* recreated the scene in Bay 5A: "The President lay flat . . .

---

* Pekkanen's story, published in the August 1981 issue of *The Washingtonian*,
was the best published reconstruction of the medical aspects of March 30. Based
on interviews with doctors and nurses who treated Reagan, the article documented what medical writers at the time suspected: the President was in worse
condition than spokesmen for the White House or the hospital let on.

bright lights in his eyes, his brows furrowed, his expression worried. There wasn't any obvious sign of injury, and hospital staffers had received no word in those first confusing minutes that the President might have been injured. 'I feel so bad,' he said, laboring for air."

Reagan's blood pressure was alarmingly low, a symptom of incipient shock. As nurses cut away their patient's new blue pinstripe suit and doctors began a thorough examination, the physicians quickly realized that Reagan's left pleural cavity was filling with blood. They also discovered the inconspicuous slit which told them that he had been hit, and where. Unable to find an exit wound, they knew that the bullet was still in him. Fluids were pumped into his arm while a tube was inserted through an incision between the ribs in order to draw out the pool of blood. X rays were ordered taken. The tiny piece of metal lodged in the lung was spotted immediately. But was it the whole bullet or just a fragment?

The radiologist needed to know the caliber, and quickly. He asked a Secret Service agent, who had no way of knowing at that moment. The Secret Service tries to prevent assassinations; it doesn't investigate them after the fact. The FBI does, so the Service called the Bureau from the emergency room. Initially the FBI would not respond to the request. After the Secret Service insisted, it got an alarming piece of misinformation—that the revolver had been a .38. If true, then there would be more lead in the President than was visible on the chest film. Additional X rays were ordered to search for other fragments. It was only later, while the surgery on Reagan was in progress and the bullet dug out of Tim McCarthy was identified, that the surgeons got the good news that they were contending with a .22 slug.

During that first half hour in the emergency room, while the medical staff was deciding what to do and a second team was working on Jim Brady, the place was a tableau of chaos. Nancy Reagan did not know what to expect when she arrived from the White House, just a few minutes after her husband. She had been in the mansion, on the third floor, when one of her Secret Service agents gave her a fragmentary report of the incident, along with the assurance that Reagan had not been hit. Later that week, she was relatively composed when she started an account of the worst day of her life. "I just took off," she said with an almost apologetic smile. "They were in touch with the hospital and said it was such bedlam there, so much confusion and such bedlam, that maybe it would be better if I stayed here. And I said, 'No, I want to go.' So we got in the car and I didn't know, until we got to the hospital and Mike Deaver told me, that Ronnie had been hit."[3]

When she saw her husband in the emergency room and realized that every breath was a struggle for him, she was devastated. Reagan responded to the panic in his wife's face with the device that has served him well for so many years in so many situations: the relevant wisecrack. With feigned nonchalance, he smiled and said, "Honey, I forgot to duck." There would be many more jokes that day and night, some of them scribbled when the mouthpiece of a breathing device prevented speech. The remark was reassuring to both his wife and doctors, but Nancy couldn't derive much solace. For thirty years they had enjoyed a closeness usually found only on honeymoons. She had babied him, humored his whims, fretted about his career, more than she had with their children. Now he was stricken and she was a helpless spectator. When we talked about those moments, she hugged herself as if to keep from falling apart and she lapsed into the present tense while she relived the fear:

> There's an unreal kind of feeling, it's hard to describe. There's an unrealness to it. You're frightened, sure, of course you're frightened, and especially because he's having trouble breathing and that's frightening. But it just seemed so unreal. And I guess you . . . I guess you, uh, must go into a sort of a—[here she lapsed into silence for a moment]. All you're thinking about is you've got to hold yourself together and not be a bother to anyone so that they can do whatever has to be done. And they put me in a tiny room, tiny little room, really tiny. There was a desk, no examining table, no windows. It was really tiny and hot. There were so many people running back and forth in the halls, and police and doctors and a lot of noise, a lot of people shouting "Get back, get back out of the way." My main thing was I just wanted to see Ronnie. Then after that, when they said I had to leave because they wanted to find out whether there was blood in his stomach, I went into that little room. They told me there was a chapel in the hospital and I went in there.

Soon afterward, Reagan was wheeled to the operating room for surgery that would take just over three hours. Deaver, Meese and Baker saw him off. "Who's minding the store?" Reagan quipped. He did not realize that, in a very real sense, the store had moved with him to George Washington University Hospital. That decision had been made almost instinctively by Meese and Baker, following the primeval rule that the presidency is where the President is—even if he is helpless and about to be rendered unconscious.

When David Prosperi made his "This is an emergency!" call, he shaved a minute or so from the time it would have taken for Baker and Meese to get the word through normal Secret Service channels. Larry Speakes hurried across a narrow hallway to the Roosevelt Room, where several staff members had been discussing tactics concerning the Japanese automobile import problem. He informed David Gergen and Craig Fuller of what he knew, which wasn't much. They checked the news tickers in the upper Press Office, where the report of Brady's injury was spreading panic among the people who worked closely with him. Gergen then rushed to Baker's office in the southwest corner of the wing while Fuller made for Meese's place in the northwest corner. Neither of the senior officials had heard the news. Meese and Fuller glanced at a small computer screen tucked away on a bookshelf. Programmed by the Secret Service, it showed Reagan en route to the hospital.

Within a few moments these officials and others, including Treasury Secretary Donald Regan, gathered in Baker's place. Deaver and Fischer at the hospital were keeping one phone line open. Regan, whose department runs the Secret Service, was being personally informed of events on another telephone. At two-forty he took a call and told the others that they could relax; the President had not been shot. The words were barely out of his mouth, however, when Deaver delivered more accurate information to Baker. Deaver then turned the phone over to Ruge, who told Baker about the location of the wound and gave a quick appraisal of Reagan's demeanor. The President is in pain, Ruge said, but he is "alert and fighting." Baker jotted down on a scratch pad: P HIT/FIGHTING. Another of those present noted that twenty minutes elapsed before the Secret Service informed Don Regan that the President had indeed been shot and was in stable condition. By that time Meese and Baker had decided that at least one of them should be at the hospital. There was no tactful way to decide who would go and who would stay; they went together. Alexander Haig was on his way to the White House. It was agreed that the Secretary of State, as the senior cabinet officer, would be the liaison between the growing group at the White House and the troika at the hospital. George Bush, in Texas to make some speeches, would not be back before nightfall.

Haig moved his colleagues to the Situation Room, a secure, windowless conference chamber in the basement that is part of the National Security Council staff suite. Richard Allen, the President's National Security Adviser, served as the principal staff man and note taker as the ad hoc group collected and performed what tasks it could. The most urgent of these were to monitor the military situation abroad and to discover as quickly as possible whether the assassination attempt had been part of a conspiracy. Obviously these concerns could be linked.

As Defense Secretary, Caspar Weinberger had both the legal and logical responsibility for purely military concerns. From the Situation Room, he kept in close touch with the Pentagon's Command Center. The initial reading, shortly after 3 P.M., was reassuring: military intelligence around the world could not detect any sign of unusual movements by Soviet forces, conventional or nuclear. On the domestic side, Attorney General William French Smith got similar consolation from the FBI. Bureau agents quickly found Hinckley's hotel room. What they learned there, and by other means, pointed toward at least a preliminary conclusion that Hinckley was hardly a trigger man for a subversive group attempting to bring down the government by bloody means.

There were also more mundane chores. Foreign allies would have to be informed by the State Department of what was happening. Max Friedersdorf, then head of congressional liaison for the White House, kept in touch with the legislative leadership. Fuller, who ordinarily served as cabinet secretary under Meese, had already rounded up the department heads. Those who were not needed in the Situation Room would be on call, ready to appear on short notice if necessary.

If the government would not have to respond to a military emergency or chase a network of assassins, it might still have to face a very different complex problem: whether to relieve a seriously injured President of his powers. The Twenty-fifth Amendment to the Constitution, enacted in reaction to John Kennedy's assassination, provided the means to do that, as well as to select a new Vice-President in case a vacancy should occur. Section Two of the amendment had been invoked twice, permitting the appointment of Gerald Ford to succeed Spiro Agnew and then the selection of Nelson Rockefeller as Vice-President to take Ford's place. But Section Three—under which a President temporarily divests himself of authority because of disability—had never been used. Neither had Section Four, which authorizes the Vice-President and a majority of the department heads to declare a President incapable of performing his duties. Under Section Four, the Vice-President can serve as "acting President" for an indefinite period.

In both political and constitutional terms, Section Four can be momentous. It creates at least the theoretical possibility of a legal coup d'etat. Once shorn of his powers, the President might never retrieve them. If a dispute arose, Congress would have to settle it. This could add up to a prescription for political paralysis and constitutional deadlock. Even if the President were able to reclaim his authority, his position could be weakened beyond repair.

Just after the President went into surgery, Baker and Meese found a supply closet near the operating suite. With them was Lyn Nofziger, who had served Reagan intermittently since 1966 and now ran the White House political liaison office. The three sought privacy in the supply closet and briefly discussed the possibility that Reagan might relinquish his powers temporarily. They quickly dismissed the idea. If a military emergency demanding an instant decision arose while he was under anesthesia, the National Command Authority system provided the means for coping. Otherwise, the medical prognosis seemed positive enough to support the presumption that Reagan's mental capacity would be unimpaired after the operation. He could deal with urgent situations. On other matters, it would be "business as usual," a reassuring phrase that several White House staffers would use repeatedly—but not very accurately—for days to come.

That still left Section Four of the amendment, the provision allowing the Vice-President and cabinet to take the initiative. In late afternoon Bush was still in the air, returning to Washington from Texas. Reagan was on the operating table. A shifting cast of cabinet members and White House aides, about three dozen of them before the day ended, continued to man the Situation Room. Fred Fielding, the White House Counsel, had pulled together all relevant information about presidential succession when he first learned of the shooting. He and the Attorney General gave the others a short, factual explanation of how the Twenty-fifth Amendment works. But there was no discussion of whether Section Four should be invoked.

Fielding also had on hand the documents that would have to be signed and sent to each house of Congress if Section Four came into play. Now, a few minutes after four-thirty, Fielding had those papers out. At one end of the oblong conference table he was going over the documents with two of the other participants, Haig and Daniel Murphy, a retired admiral who served as George Bush's Chief of Staff. Most of the others in the room were unaware of what Haig, Murphy and Fielding were doing. However, Richard Darman, a restless and inquisitive sort with a knack for troubleshooting, quickly realized what was happening.

At that early stage of the Administration, Darman had only a middling place in the White House hierarchy along with the title of Deputy Assistant to the President. A number of others in the level just below the troika, such as Gergen, Brady, Friedersdorf, Allen and Fielding, nominally outranked him until later in the year. However, Darman was closely associated with Baker and one of his duties was central to White House operations: Darman personally controlled all papers going to and coming from the President.

When he spotted the implementing documents related to the Twenty-fifth Amendment, Darman also recognized trouble. If the subject came up for general discussion in the Situation Room and word of that got out, it would create questions about Reagan's capacities. Worse, Darman sniffed the possibility, however remote, that the cabinet might actually seize the initiative. He made a quick decision to head off both dangers. Darman quietly told Fielding, Haig and Murphy that neither the subject nor the documents belonged on the table. He suggested that he take possession of the papers. Darman supported that proposal with the half-truth that the Twenty-fifth Amendment was something for the President himself to consider. The others gave in. At that point Darman felt that he needed some backing. He got Baker by phone, told him what had happened, and suggested that Baker authorize him to retain physical possession of the implementing documents. Baker acquiesced, whereupon Darman went to his own office nearby in the basement and locked them in his safe. The issue did not come up again in the larger group and got no attention in the news coverage. That night Smith and Fielding briefed Bush on the technicalities of the amendment.

Secrecy was impossible to maintain on a more blatant source of tension, Haig's role in the proceedings. Baker and Meese had left the Secretary of State in charge at the White House, more or less, but there was little for him to supervise. Aside from monitoring information outside and keeping track of what was happening at the hospital, the Situation Room was a locus of pro forma activity without being an important part of the action. In leaving for the hospital, Baker had even taken the public relations function with him in the persons of Larry Speakes and Lyn Nofziger. Many reporters and television crews installed themselves in an auditorium at George Washington, though others congregated in the White House press area. Baker's approach was that news announcements should come at the hospital; officials at the White House would merely echo them.

Atmosphere in the Situation Room, given the circumstances, was reasonably calm during the first hour. Allen, as the principal staff man and nominal host in his own bailiwick, was efficient and orderly. Weinberger, when he had something to say, spoke calmly, almost inaudibly at times, using a combination of lawyerly language and Pentagon lingo. William French Smith made one very odd decision in midafternoon when FBI headquarters called him with an unanticipated problem. Bureau agents had been dispatched to the hospital to collect evidence for the criminal investigation. That included Reagan's clothing. They came up with a card containing coded material for use by the President in the event he had to communicate by voice with military commanders in an emergency. Representatives of the White House military office demanded that the card be turned over to them, but the FBI agents refused. They bucked the decision up through their superiors and Justice Department bureaucratic levels until it reached Smith in the Situation Room. The Attorney General ruled that the FBI should retain possession. That minor conflict remained secret for months.[4]

While that little blip was attended to and while telephone and wire traffic remained heavy, Haig seemed to some of his colleagues to be taut, roiling in restless energy. "He got that bulldog look of his," one of them recalled later, "but there was nothing for him to bite." At three forty-one, shortly after Reagan was wheeled into the operating room, Haig remarked, "The helm is right here in this chair." The comment did not seem to have much relevance when uttered because the good ship Situation Room was not steaming anywhere. But it would be remembered because of what happened thirty minutes later.

Baker sent Speakes back to the White House West Wing to cope with reporters who remained in the briefing room there. Speakes went directly to the lectern without visiting the Situation Room one level below. He had no fresh information to offer at four-ten; he would not even confirm that Reagan was then undergoing surgery. Further, Speakes had not been instructed on how to respond to questions about the way the government was functioning. When asked whether the military had been placed in "higher readiness," he replied, "Not that I'm aware of." Then this exchange occurred:

> *Question:* Who's running the government right now? If the President goes into surgery and goes under anesthesia, would Vice-President Bush become acting President at that moment or under what circumstances would he?
>
> *Speakes:* I cannot answer that question at this time.

Speakes's briefing was being televised live. The uncertainty of his answers hardly furthered the purpose of Reagan's senior advisers, which was to create an impression of calm certainty at the top. In the Situation Room, Haig and the others watched Speakes on the screen. Weinberger saw only part of the performance because he was placing another call to the Pentagon's command center. Haig glared at the television set, almost as if he were trying to will Speakes into silence. It was obvious to the others that Haig was angry both because Speakes was appearing without the advance knowledge of the Situation Room and because of what he was saying. In a few moments Haig was on his feet. He said nothing to the others around the table, but he used a gesture of unmistakable meaning; he thrust a forefinger at his own chest, then pointed toward the ceiling.

As Haig made for the door, Allen followed. The National Security Adviser considered trying to talk Haig out of it, but thought better of that. Instead, he tagged along. Fuller went to the open line to inform Baker that Haig seemed intent on giving a briefing of his own. Haig got to the Press Room just as Speakes had vacated the lectern. Allen later described the Secretary of State's demeanor: "I was standing right next to him, prepared to catch him. I thought that he was going to collapse.

His legs were shaking as if they were gelatinous. It was extraordinary, absolutely extraordinary."[5]

Nonetheless, Haig at least had some facts to convey. He noted that Bush would soon be back and he confirmed what most of the reporters already knew from unofficial sources: that Reagan was on the operating table. Then, intending to clear up some of the doubt Speakes had left, Haig declared, "There are absolutely no alert measures that are necessary at this time that we're contemplating." When asked, "Who is making the decisions for the government right now?" he gave a reply that would haunt him for the rest of his time in the Reagan administration:

> Constitutionally, gentlemen, you have the President, the Vice-President and the Secretary of State in that order and should the President decide that he wants to transfer the helm to the Vice-President, he will do so. He has not done that. As of now, I am in control here, in the White House, pending return of the Vice-President, and in close touch with him. If something came up, I would check with him, of course.

When seen on paper after the fact, Haig's words would seem unexceptional despite his misreading of the Constitution. He was seeking, logically enough, to assure the world that everything was under control. At the same time, however, Haig was creating problems for his colleagues and himself. His delivery was tense, quavery, as if he were under great stress. Further, his I-am-in-control assertion was an unfortunate echo of an incident just the previous week, in which he had publicly challenged the White House decision to make Bush the chairman of the "Crisis Management Team."* Now he was saying that the "team" was in operation and that he was running it in Bush's absence. Finally, Haig left open the question of invoking the Twenty-fifth Amendment—a subject the White House staff would have preferred to keep buried.

Haig returned to the Situation Room to face an annoyed Secretary of Defense. Weinberger wanted to know why Haig had made a public appearance without discussing it in advance. Further, Weinberger said, Haig's statement concerning military alert status was no longer accurate in technical terms. While Haig had been flying solo at the Press

---

* In the previous administration, the National Security Adviser supervised groups representing different departments that were pulled together to monitor emergencies. Bush got the assignment in March 1981, as part of the new administration's policy of reducing the influence of the National Security Council staff. The designation in any event is more symbolic than real. Even the term was dropped at the end of the year because the White House, for public relations purposes, disliked the word "crisis." Thus Bush later presided occasionally over the "Special Situations Group."

Room lectern, Weinberger had been on the phone with the Joint Chiefs of Staff. There had been no significant change in force movements abroad—no clearly discernible threat, certainly. However, military intelligence had picked up some ambiguous signs concerning Soviet readiness. These were neither alarming nor unique. However, under the circumstances, Weinberger during that phone conversation authorized a modest tightening of precautions in Europe and the Mediterranean. Alert status is measured on a "DefCon" (for Defense Condition) scale of five to one; one represents dire emergency. Commands in various regions can be at different DefCon steps, depending on the local situation. In this case, Weinberger did not approve a change by a full step. The change involved gradations within the level already in effect. The modification was minor, causing no visible flurry in the field, so that the Administration could plausibly deny any apprehension of real threat.

Now it was Haig's turn to be irritated. Why had Weinberger acted on his own? What was his authority? Haig was still tense, speaking with his customary vigor. Weinberger was calm, sure of his ground. Two items were becoming intertwined because of Haig's performance in the briefing. The succession question involving the Twenty-fifth Amendment as well as legislation was in one category, separate from the National Command Authority, which solely concerns control over military forces. Specific command authority is established by each new administration. Though the outlines usually become known, the details are contained in a secret executive order from the President. Weinberger, as he occasionally would do at National Security Council meetings, kidded Haig about his Press Room remarks. But the joshing had a sharp edge to it. Haig either was unaware that he had made an error in saying that the constitutional line of authority runs from the President to the Vice-President to the Secretary of State or he was unwilling to concede the fluff. For the purposes of succession, the Constitution mentions only the Vice-President. Current legislation takes the line from there to the Speaker of the House of Representatives and then to the President Pro Tempore of the Senate. Only after that does the cabinet, starting with the Secretary of State, come into play. In response to Weinberger's ribbing, according to three of those present, Haig responded with one of his trademarked glares, the kind of hard look intended to remind the recipient of his mortality. Then Haig remarked, "You'd better read your Constitution, buddy." He turned to Fielding, whom he had known in the Nixon White House, and referred to his rendition of the Constitution. "Isn't that right, Fred?" he asked. Fielding had no choice in his reply: "No, Al, it isn't." Haig lapsed into silence.

Weinberger's authority concerning DefCon changes was another matter. In the event of an emergency that silences the President, his powers as Commander in Chief fall on the Vice-President. Next in line, Reagan had ruled when assuming office, would be the Secretary of Defense and then the Chairman of the Joint Chiefs of Staff. The Secretary of State is out of that sequence altogether. After the Weinberger-Haig exchange, Fielding and Darman took the Defense Secretary aside. They told him that he had acted correctly, well within his authority. If the issue arose again, they said, they would step forward and cite the language of the relevant presidential directive. However, the argument was over on that score.

Confusion on another, more human level soon replaced it. At four fifty-six, Regan was informed by the Secret Service unit at the hospital that Jim Brady was dead. The Treasury Secretary told his colleagues. Richard Allen, a close friend of the press secretary, suggested a few moments of silent prayer. The men around the table bowed their heads to mark Brady's death. Then, still attempting to keep Capitol Hill abreast of events, the Situation Room informed the Senate Majority Leader's office of the bad news. From there word immediately leaked to the networks, which soon broadcast the misinformation. That was not the only serious boner that had to be corrected. One television network correspondent, misunderstanding an unofficial (but accurate) briefing conducted by a radio reporter,* told his audience that Reagan was undergoing open heart surgery.

Competitive pressure accounted in part for these and lesser mistakes in broadcast reporting. Another factor was that the White House was slow in making information available. As late as five-ten, when Nofziger briefed at the hospital auditorium, he would not confirm that chest surgery was being performed. At that point the operation was more than half over. Nofziger, who had been a press and political adviser to Reagan on and off since 1966, gave a sturdy, understated performance. In contrast to Speakes and Haig, he conveyed calm confidence. It was at his briefing that Reagan's men began using on the world audience the one-liners with which Reagan had been entertaining the emergency room crowd (to his surgeons: "Please tell me you're Republicans"). In fact, Reagan was going through ups and downs of anxiety, which the experienced nurses attending him recognized. But he

---

* Ross Simpson of the Mutual Broadcasting System managed to break away from the crowd of journalists at the hospital and obtain some exclusive material, which he broadcast. He then came back to the auditorium that served as a temporary press center and shared his information. Simpson mentioned chest surgery, which NBC then misconstrued as heart surgery.

refused to let his intimates share his occasional fear. To his friend Paul Laxalt he said, "Don't worry about me. I'll make it."

Of course he did, and he fared remarkably well for a seventy-year-old with a punctured lung who had lost a great deal of blood. But surgery proved to be very difficult, principally because the bullet was elusive. The toll it took on him would be clear only later, and then only to those who saw him close up. After the operation, and the next morning, reporters were led to believe that Reagan was in miraculously good shape. Dr. Dennis O'Leary, the hospital spokesman, told journalists Tuesday of still new witticisms by the nation's First Patient ("If I got this much attention in Hollywood, I'd never have left") and announced with satisfaction: "He's on almost no medication, and at this point in time he really probably does not require an intensive level of medical care. He's doing extremely well." That bullish estimate, to put it charitably, was premature.

Immediately after the operation, Reagan's mangled lung was functioning poorly and blood tests showed an insufficiency of oxygen in his system. This was not at all clear to outsiders as the troika set out to demonstrate that the chief was still in charge. An important piece of legislation—a bill to check the increase in the dairy price subsidy—required his signature. Darman took the document to Baker's home at six forty-five Tuesday morning and the troika had Reagan sign it a little after seven. The signature looked shaky, but it was official. At the time, Reagan was dosed with morphine to relieve the pain.

Later in the week, the President began running a high temperature that gave the doctors some concern. The cause was never to be found, but as the readings hovered between 102 and 103 degrees, it appeared that some kind of serious infection might have set in. This was not reflected in the periodic medical reports from the Press Office. On April 3, for instance, after the fever had begun, a White House handout said: "Over the past several hours, the President has developed a moderate temperature elevation, an occurrence which is considered commonplace at this stage for patients recovering from injuries and surgery of this nature. The President's chest X-ray continues to show the left lung to be fully expanded with no evidence of new changes . . . He feels refreshed and appears well rested after a good night's sleep."

Later that day Dr. Benjamin Aaron, the senior surgeon on the case, decided to do a bronchoscopy. That procedure allows for the removal of infectious material if any is present. It also lets the physician view the inside of the bronchial tubes. Researching his *Washingtonian* article, Pekkanen had discovered that the White House medical office had requested that heavy sedation be avoided if at all possible. No reason was given. It was one of those teasers that stick in the mind. The explanation came a year later, when I reviewed the sequence of events one more time with some of the participants. On the afternoon of April 3, Meese, Baker, Deaver and Darman secretly considered the wisdom of invoking the Twenty-fifth Amendment at that late stage if it became absolutely necessary for medical reasons to put Reagan under anesthesia or even give him a heavy dose of Valium. Tranquilizers are sometimes used to help a patient tolerate use of a bronchoscope. This was four days after the shooting, after the original surgery and at a time when Reagan was ostensibly well on the road to recovery. Yet now, the same senior advisers who had ruled out any temporary transfer of legal authority to Bush on Monday afternoon or evening were seriously considering just that move.

The reason for their discussion was geopolitical rather than medical. Between Monday and Friday the Soviet Union had begun to make threatening moves concerning Poland. Intelligence analysts were again concerned about the possibility of an outright invasion. The troika weighed the possibility of that emergency's arising at a moment when the President was unconscious or disoriented. It was a worrisome dilemma. However, the President's men decided against using the Twenty-fifth Amendment. To do so would cause confusion, they reasoned, and would offset their effort to assure the country, and the world, that Ronald Reagan was on the mend. Back at the hospital, as things turned out, Reagan tolerated use of the bronchoscope without systemic sedation. George Bush never learned that he had come close to being acting President four days after Reagan's chest had been sutured.

The examination found no infection and the high fever continued into the following week before finally breaking. Nancy Reagan was making it her personal mission to coax her uncomfortable, weakened husband into eating meals brought over from the White House. That did not help much. As she recalled it long afterward, she tried some wifely guile: "One night I went into him and said, 'We're going to go out for dinner tonight.' And he said, 'Oh, really? Where?' So I said, 'Oh, a little disco I found on the way to the hospital.' So he said okay and he got out of bed. We went into the next room. I had set up two chairs in front of the television set and I thought if he watched the news maybe I could get some food into him and he wouldn't know it."[6]

She had such a good time telling the story that one felt churlish asking whether the ploy worked. "Not too well," she conceded. In desperation, she asked the Reagans' long-time California cook, Anne Allman, to prepare some of the soups he particularly liked—hamburger soup, split pea, turkey. Friends flying East brought containers of soup with them. That did not work too well either. In fact, nothing much helped until the fever broke and the dosage of antibiotics was reduced. When he got back to the White House on Saturday April 11, Reagan bravely walked from the limousine through the diplomatic entrance facing the South Lawn and then another twenty yards or so to the elevator that would take him to the family quarters on the second floor. He put on a very effective show of good cheer. The casual spectators could not know what those who saw him privately observed during the next few days. This robust, vital man had been horribly drained. One of his aides wondered at the time whether the nation might be in for an ordeal similar to the one suffered during Woodrow Wilson's last difficult months in the White House, when an ailing, disillusioned President was propped up by his loyal wife and a few close assistants. But once out of the hospital, Reagan quickly found his strength again.

In psychological terms, Nancy Reagan seemed to suffer more than her husband. For months she could not even bring herself to mention the words "shooting" or "assassination attempt." Instead, it was "the thing that happened to Ronnie" or simply "March thirtieth." We were in California, five months and three thousand miles away, but tears came to her eyes when our conversation went from the hamburger soup to the actual event. No, she said, she and her husband did not talk about it. Had the terror of March thirtieth receded at all? "No. I've come to the conclusion—I don't know about him, but I've come to the conclusion that it never does recede. I mean, somebody gave me that issue of *Washingtonian*. It was the day the Sadats were arriving [August 5]. And I got through two pages of it and I started to cry. I had to put it aside. I said I'm going to go down to the Sadats and they're going to think I don't want to see them. I'm beginning to think that it never —" She stopped herself and we turned to other matters.

Reagan, on the other hand, talked about his narrow escape from death in a relatively detached way. When he came to after the operation he wanted to know whether the gunman had been caught and whether there was a motive for the shooting ("What's his beef?" was the way Reagan put it). Reagan's four children, starting with the youngest, Ron, gathered at the hospital. Their father warned them to pay close attention to the instructions of Secret Service agents assigned to them. To other visitors he remarked that he still opposed gun control legislation because he felt that regulation simply does not work. At the end of the year we talked about the psychological impact on his wife, which seemed to be lasting indefinitely. "I agree, with regard to her," he said. "I think mine was just a case of [having] to get well physically. When I take off to make a speech and so forth, without her saying anything, I know what a long day it is going to be for her. I just know it by what I can see in her. I wish it weren't that way, but it is."[7]

Two associates of long standing, Paul Laxalt and Stuart Spencer, believed that Reagan was affected more deeply than he knew, or would admit. Laxalt continued to see Reagan frequently during the convalescence. "For quite a time afterward," Laxalt said, "there was a certain sadness. You could see it in his eyes. It wasn't just the physical pain. I think that he was deeply hurt, emotionally, that this could happen to him, that someone would do this to him. Of course he would never talk about this to us. He is always upbeat, cracking jokes. He likes to recall some of the one-liners he used at the hospital."[8] Spencer and Laxalt both argued that the brush with death made Reagan more stubborn than ever in clinging to his principles. As Spencer put it five months afterward, "He's very keen to do what he wants to do. I think he says to himself, 'I'm seventy years old, I almost got killed back in March, I'm not worried about the next election.' It gives him a lot of freedom."[9]

Though he occasionally makes a show of emotion in public to achieve a desired effect, Reagan is consistently uncomfortable in talking about his real feelings on personal matters to anyone except Nancy. He hesitated when I put Spencer's view to him, trying to formulate, perhaps, a suitably cool, controlled response. Finally Reagan replied, "He may be right. It's a reminder of mortality and the importance of time. So it could be. But I have not ever consciously—laying there in the hospital bed and [saying] now I must—" He broke off the thought, apparently unwilling to follow it to its conclusion. Instead he made for safer ground by adding, "I guess I thought I was pretty determined already."

Mother Teresa visited the White House on June 4. She had a private lunch with the Reagans, attended by only one or two others, and toward the end of the meal the holy woman from India spoke with great feeling. "You have suffered the passion of the cross and have received grace," she said, looking directly at Reagan. "There is a purpose to this. Because of your suffering and pain you will now understand the suffering and pain of the world. This has happened to you at this time because your country and the world need you." Nancy Reagan dissolved in tears. Her husband, for once, was speechless.

The impact of March 30 would show itself in a number of external ways clearly enough. Wirthlin, the pollster, concluded that the event, and more particularly Reagan's brave response to it, had a lasting effect on popular perceptions of the President. Public views of this or that policy would gyrate, as they do in all administrations, but respect and admiration for the man's personal qualities were enhanced. The shooting occurred at a time when his first year's economic program was approaching crucial tests in Congress. Popular sympathy for Reagan made it more difficult than ever for the opposition to thwart him. The way Meese, Baker and Deaver had coped made their odd troika arrangement seem workable under keen stress. More subtle challenges would soon begin to show the system's weaknesses. But for the balance of the year, at least, the trio—like the President it served—enjoyed a longer honeymoon than would otherwise have been possible. Whatever doubts had persisted prior to the shooting about Reagan's age were erased. It would take more than a year for Hinckley to be found not guilty by reason of insanity. But only a few days after the shooting, Reagan was acquitted of the charge that he was too old to be President. That verdict would be an asset of great value later, when the oldest President in American history began thinking about 1984.

8

In Search of Great Expectations

The times met Ronald Reagan more than halfway. As he closed in on victory in 1980, his apocalyptic predictions about the failures of big government were coming true. Whether measured in micro terms of the filling station and supermarket or the macro calculations of corporate analysts, the world's greatest economy was in prolonged, painful stall. A gallon of unleaded regular gasoline cost you $1.25 or more in November and you paid $1.58 for a pound of hamburger. Working-class families did not need the Census Bureau to tell them that things were beyond "stagnant" or "flat" or "mushy," to use three of the euphemisms economists favored. Rather the everyday business of making do was palpably more difficult for ordinary people than the year before.

Later, Census Bureau statisticians would confirm in multitudinous tables what had been perfectly obvious at the gas pump and the shop counter. Median family income in 1980 had declined from the year before by $1,400 when translated into real purchasing power. There had also been a small decline in 1979.[1] Burrowing deeper into the numbers, one discovered that by the late 1970s the proportion of families officially classified as living below the poverty line had begun to grow again. Over the course of two decades this doleful measure fell from a high of nearly 21 percent in 1959 to 10 percent in 1978. Now it was inching up, to 10.2 percent in 1979, 11.5 percent in 1980. Poverty, despite geometric increases in diverse social programs, was making a comeback.

Numbers of dollars were not the problem; they continued to increase year by year. But inflation was stealing them faster than a worker could earn them. Between 1960 and 1970, the worth of the dollar as translated into meat, shoes, rent and the other mundane necessities declined to seventy-six cents. That relatively mild rate of shrinkage more than doubled in the 1970s. What was worth a dollar when John Kennedy was elected in 1960 amounted to only thirty-six cents when Ronald Reagan won in 1980. Reagan always got a laugh from campaign audiences by saying that he fainted when his doctor told him that he was "sound as a dollar."

For the affluent who did not have to worry much about the prices of food or gasoline, there were other concerns. The cost of financing a new house took 27 percent of average family income in 1970, an increase of just two cents on the dollar over the previous ten years. At the end of the next decade, it would require 42 percent of average income to meet the monthly expenses on a newly acquired house. At the same time, more and more people who did not feel wealthy were being taxed as though they were. A family at the median income in 1980 ($22,380) found itself with a marginal federal tax rate of 24 percent. That is, a quarter of each additional dollar earned would go to the U.S. Treasury. Fifteen years earlier, that same family's marginal rate was only 17 percent. For the more fortunate, earning twice the median family income in 1980, or just under $45,000, the marginal rate had gone from 22 percent to 43 percent.

Taxes, of course, were only a problem if you were working. By the time the campaign reached its crescendo, unemployment had advanced to 7.5 percent, which seemed high at the time, but was nothing compared with the 15 percent to 20 percent in the devastated auto and steel cities of the Midwest where Reagan spent a good deal of his time chasing (and catching) blue collar votes. As he posed for TV cameras in the "rust bowl" of idle Ohio steel mills, he could, like Ted Kennedy, demand "jobs, jobs, jobs"—and blame Jimmy Carter for the lack of them. Over the objections of his literal-minded economic advisers, he insisted on changing a speech to a Teamsters group in Columbus. The insert he wrote called the condition a "depression." Reagan was challenged, as usual, on technical accuracy. Instead of yielding, he capitalized on the distinction. Over and over again during the long political autumn, he delighted audiences as much with his marvelous sense of timing as with the lines: "If he [Carter] wants a definition, I'll give him one [pause, to build up anticipation]. Recession is when your neighbor loses his job [second pause, as listeners realize he's escalating]. Depression is when you lose yours [another hesitation, to wait out the laugh]. And recovery [longish pause now]—recovery is when Jimmy Carter loses his!" Always, everywhere, Reagan blamed Washington for everything.

Only smart politics, the hard-nosed observer might say. The man was exploiting fears, rendering the complex overly simple, perhaps making the situation worse by painting it darker than the facts. Smart politics it was, without question. By late 1979, even before he announced his candidacy officially, Reagan and his advisers knew that the economy, and specifically inflation, would be their best issue. His strategists already had the broad outline of how Reagan would use it and how he would propose to attack it. On the other charges, however, Reagan could conscientiously plead innocent. The economy was not merely in a temporary pause. It was in serious trouble, had been for years, and the Democrats who tried to deride Reagan for peddling moldy nostrums had nothing better to offer than their own records of discredited analysis, inaccurate predictions and aborted recovery efforts.

An inescapable fact in 1980—a governing fact—was that this great bastion of capitalism simply was no longer working well. The Census Bureau in 1982 would look back and discover that for all but the wealthy, inflation had wiped out a decade's worth of income gains. Americans who discovered early in the 1970s that their country could lose wars as well as win them would now have to digest the reality that the United States was not as wealthy as they'd thought it was. Among the world's fourteen most affluent non-communist nations, the United States in 1960 and again in 1970 ranked highest, by a comfortable margin, in gross domestic product per capita. By 1980 America had fallen to tenth on that list, well behind Switzerland, Sweden, Germany and even little Luxembourg. One key index of vitality, productivity, measures the ratio between the amount of labor invested and the ultimate yield. In the 1960s output was expanding, on average, 2.6 percent a year. In the 1970s the average annual increase was only 1.4 percent and showed signs of further deterioration.

The price of money, like the cost of cars and hamburger, went up and forgot how to come down. That case of amnesia had tragic implications for almost everyone. Interest was becoming prohibitive for the person who wanted to buy a car, build a house, start a business. Ditto for a corporation in need of a new factory or a city in need of another hospital. This exemplar capitalist nation was running short of capital.

For years the Keynesians had hooted at the central premise of what came to be Reaganism, that the federal government was the main cause of stagflation. Now certain realities could not be evaded. In 1960 federal spending accounted for 18.5 percent of the Gross National Product. That proportion expanded gradually over twenty years to 23 percent although defense spending, in relative terms, went down. The main reason was the boom in benefits, some for the poor and some for everyone. Many of these programs, such as Social Security, were now called "entitlements" because they were immune to the annual appropriations process. Instead they ran on statutory formulas; as a rule, actual spending year by year far exceeded the estimates made when the program went into law. It became commonplace to watch spending for unemployment benefits, disability, pensions of all kinds, food stamps, Medicare and other health-related activities double or triple every few years. Taxes were also increasing, but never quickly enough, so that the federal deficit became chronic. To cover the shortfall, the Treasury was constantly competing with private borrowers for capital, a competition which helped keep interest rates and inflation up. The poor and the working class, the ostensible beneficiaries of so many of the government programs, were also the most vulnerable.

Reagan was not exactly the only politician who recognized that inflation of over 12 percent was ruinous. Nor was he alone in understanding that the federal government had grown obese, wasteful, a drain on the private sector. The defects of twenty years of federal deficits were widely acknowledged by 1980. Carter had made some stabs at economy measures. He made a serious start on reducing federal regulation of the airline and trucking industries. Carter, after all, had run in 1976 against the impacted New Deal mentality of his own party. By 1980 another Democratic subspecies, sometimes called neoliberal, was forming. It spoke a language barely comprehensible to Tip O'Neill. As for Reagan's Republican rivals, they all grasped the fundamentals of the problem as well as, or better than, the Californian. John Anderson even had the courage to demand a reform of the indexing formula by which Social Security benefits were increased automatically. The others savaged him for that during the Illinois primary, with George Bush self-righteously leading the offensive, but all of them knew Anderson was correct. He soon left the GOP.

What set Reagan apart was that he had been shouting alarms years earlier than the others. In general terms at least, they were catching up to him in recognizing the great satan of inflation and in acknowledging that federal taxation and federal regulation had gone too far. The second, and politically more potent, factor that separated Reagan was his prescription. It was soothing, initially devoid of harsh medicine. Running against Gerald Ford for the 1976 Republican nomination, Reagan had not been required to develop a highly detailed economic platform. He was for lower taxes, more economical government, a balanced budget and other items that allowed him to paddle in the mainstream of conventional conservatism. The difference then was that Reagan would paddle more vigorously than Ford, would turn back certain programs to the states, would actually move the fiscal canoe toward the right bank instead of merely talking about doing so. In 1980 Reagan had new, more palatable specific proposals.

A strange thing had happened to the party in 1978. Desperate for a compelling issue, the GOP leadership, conservatives and moderates alike, latched onto the idea being promoted by Congressman Jack Kemp of Buffalo and Senator William V. Roth of Delaware. The Kemp-Roth bill, calling for across-the-board reductions in income tax rates for three successive years, was the nose of a camel called supply-side economics.* This doctrine, in broad outline, is neither as arcane nor as alien as some commentary suggests. It holds that those who supply goods and services—that is, workers, entrepreneurs and investors —must be given greater incentives than have been available to them in recent years to produce goods and services. More spendable take-home pay, more profit on innovation, more reward for risk would stimulate healthy economic growth. Expanding *supply* would create its own demand.

Government's role is to enhance incentive by reducing taxation and regulation. Simple. One huge catch is how this can be done without turning the fire of federal budget deficits into an all-consuming conflagration, thereby frying to a crisp any hope of reducing inflation. The initial supply-side response was that increased economic activity would broaden the tax base quickly enough to provide adequate revenue despite lower tax rates. This would become the central riddle of Reaganomics.

A second catch, less obvious but just as important, is the dubious assumption that simply creating opportunities for greater private-sector investment will automatically lead to creative and productive expansion. This faith in the "magic of the marketplace" ignored several developments of the previous decade or more: increasing irrationality in industrial labor relations, failure to maintain adequate technical training levels in the work force, the tendency among those controlling capital to use spare resources for speculation and acquisition rather than productive investment, the inability to maintain stability in international trade and exchange rates. Neither the main thrust of supply-side doctrine nor Reaganomics even attempted to address these issues in any serious fashion.

* By common consent, the term slipped into usage after it appeared in a paper presented by Professor Herbert Stein on March 25, 1976, to a conference of business leaders. Formerly chairman of Nixon's Council of Economic Advisers and later a part-time consultant to Reagan, Stein mentioned "supply-side fiscalists" to describe those who wanted deep tax cuts as a means of increasing real GNP. *The Wall Street Journal* then picked up the label. Stein himself first used the phrase in a neutral, analytical tone. Later he became a stern critic of what he came to believe was a dangerous "cult."

Two other legs of today's supply-side stool are to de-emphasize monetarism as practiced in recent years and reconnect the currency to a fixed base—preferably gold. According to this version of the theory, fiddling with the money supply, which is the Federal Reserve Board's stock-in-trade, is obsolete because no one believes that it can produce durable stability. Thus interest rates have continued to gyrate, particularly since the Nixon administration cut the dollar's last tie to gold in 1971.

These fundamentals clash with monetarism and orthodox conservative thinking in a number of ways. The most important is that supply-siders, like some old liberals, pooh-pooh the urgency of balancing the federal budget. Hence they also assign a lower priority than the other, more familiar two sects do to spending reductions. The greater supply of goods, stimulating economic growth, would soon produce the added revenue needed to curb the government's deficit. Thus, while the other schools start with austerity—putting their emphasis first on "wringing out inflation" by monetary manipulation, spending cuts or both—the supply-siders start with steep tax cuts.

The Republican leadership going into the 1978 midterm election let in the camel's nose, the Kemp-Roth tax proposal, as a political gambit. The GOP National Committee even chartered an airliner (the "Republican Tax Clipper") to carry leading spokesmen including Reagan around the country to preach the gospel. The plane went to eight cities, but the idea failed to fly. Reagan, getting his positions honed for the 1980 race, had some reservations about Kemp-Roth. He wanted assurance that the bill was not a formula for yet higher deficits and decided that he would embrace it only if it were tied to spending cuts. Meanwhile, John Sears, his campaign manager, was negotiating with Kemp on a more pragmatic level. With the right wing of the party divided, Sears wanted Kemp in the Reagan fold. This effort brought both Kemp and his supply-side colleagues closer to Reagan's ear for a time, particularly while more orthodox Republican experts were either on the fence or supporting one of Reagan's rivals for the nomination.*

But Reagan never espoused the entire supply-side doctrine. He rarely used the term during the campaign and periodically, under the influence of other advisers, he seemed to veer away from the theory. Once the nomination was assured in early spring, virtually the entire corps of Republican economists signed up with Reagan. Kemp was edged away from the center of influence, along with his allies. In their place came more prominent—and more conventional—advisers such as Alan Greenspan, Arthur Burns and Milton Friedman. Nonetheless,

* A detailed account of Sears's courtship of Kemp can be found in *The Reagan Revolution* by Rowland Evans and Robert Novak.

Kemp, assisted by a young, unknown Michigan congressman named David Stockman, exerted some influences within the GOP platform committee at the Detroit convention, as did Senator Roth. The final document endorsed the Kemp-Roth bill, more or less, along with a specific commitment to a 10 percent reduction in personal income tax rates beginning January 1, 1981. But the platform was also an amalgam of competing Republican economic views. It called for a balanced budget, restraint on spending, larger expenditures for defense.

Reagan at this stage was the target of conflicting advice. The more orthodox experts and pleaders, particularly those associated with big-business lobbies in Washington, wanted the priorities to be corporate incentives such as accelerated depreciation of plant and machinery, along with a balanced budget. Academic economists such as Friedman and Burns emphasized austerity and control of the money supply. The supply-siders, with their populist tinge, clung to the notion of comprehensive, drastic tax cuts. On one point there was agreement: as the general campaign got underway, the candidate would have to present a cohesive, credible position, including numbers, because Carter would hammer at Reagan for being irresponsible. The press would be skeptical. So too would be Wall Street analysts, whose reactions were vital to how markets responded to Reaganomics. This conflict over credibility would become a pattern stretching through the campaign, the transition and incumbency.

In early September, as the general election drive began in earnest, the Reaganauts faced up to arithmetic. Reagan met with his advisers at Wexford, the Virginia hunt-country estate rented for his use while in the East, on September 3. Even then Reagan was already weary of the internal debate. Further, he was irritated about recent news coverage that had depicted him as wavering on the tax proposal. As a personal matter, Reagan abhors being seen as inconsistent. He hates even more being accused of consciously going back on his own word. And Reagan, like any smart politician in the business of selling ideas, always chooses the option that can be explained in the clearest terms possible.

At the Wexford meeting then, as he would at other crucial decision points in November and January, Reagan brusquely overruled the more orthodox faction that was suggesting an amber light on what was known as the "ten-ten-ten" scheme—successive annual reductions of 10 percent each in personal income tax rates beginning in 1981. Reagan felt that he was already committed publicly to the main element of the Kemp-Roth bill. The fact that Kemp's personal influence on Reagan had receded was irrelevant. When one or another of the advisers suggested caution, or raised the possibility that, given the raging inflation rate of that period, the ten-ten-ten scheme was too risky, Reagan shrugged off the advice. Recalling that process nearly two years later, one of the advisers who regretted that he had not flashed the amber light more brightly during the transition put it this way: "You look at all the stories being published about backing and filling and they give the impression that Reagan was changing back and forth. That's wrong. The people around him were changing, or some of us were. We were having doubts, and the news coverage reflected that. Reagan hardly moved at all. At one meeting [in January] Reagan got a little impatient with us. He said, 'Listen, you guys are talking to each other and no one is asking me what I think. I'm sticking with it [the ten-ten-ten approach].' "

The Wexford conference led to the speech and fact sheet Reagan delivered in Chicago on September 9. Greenspan and Martin Anderson did the principal work on the backup paper, using as their economic base line a set of assumptions that had just been published by the Senate Budget Committee. They selected that foundation because the committee, then under Democratic control, would be considered a credible source. However, the Budget Committee projections of economic activity were on the optimistic side. This allowed Greenspan and Anderson to arrive at a bottom line for the Reagan program that looked good, but in fact stood on sand. Reagan would cut both personal and business taxes, increase defense spending, reduce waste and achieve a balanced budget by fiscal year 1983. That was the minimum achievement predicted. Reagan also promised additional efforts at cost cutting which, if successful, would produce a budget *surplus* of $23 billion in fiscal year 1983. Neither the economists' tables nor the candidate's speech on September 9 emphasized drastic cuts in actual government services. When Reagan talked about curbing spending that day, as during the rest of the campaign, the emphasis was on melting fat. Said Reagan:

> Waste, extravagance, abuse and outright fraud in federal agencies and programs must be stopped. Billions of taxpayers' dollars are wasted every year throughout hundreds of federal programs, and it will take a major, sustained effort over time to counter this. Federal spending is now projected to increase to over $900 billion a year by fiscal year 1985. But through a comprehensive assault on waste and inefficiency, I am confident that we can squeeze and trim 2 percent out of the budget in fiscal year 1981, and that we will be able to increase this gradually to 7 percent of what would otherwise have been spent in fiscal year 1985. Actually, I believe we can do even better. My goal will be to bring about spending reductions of 10 percent by fiscal 1984 . . . This strategy for growth does not require altering or taking back necessary entitlements al-

ready granted to the American people. The integrity of the Social Security
system will be defended. . . . This strategy *does* require restraining the
congressional desire to "add on" to every old program and to create new
programs funded by deficits . . .

The speech was not merely another piece of stump rhetoric. It is
worth recalling now because it was Reagan's definitive campaign statement on his economic program and because it established the main
outlines, if not all the important particulars, of what the new administration set out to do the following winter. For the rest of his own program, he was not that fussy. He depended on his advisers for the car-
pentry, even though they themselves were divided.

But soon Reagan would have to make a very important adjustment,
one that would increasingly shadow his term in office and play a dominant part in the critical 1982 midterm election. He would have to acknowledge tacitly that attacks on "waste, extravagance, abuse and outright fraud" would merely save small change. Heavy billions could be
eliminated only by going after actual programs. Philosophically, this
was hardly a problem for the new President because, as we've seen,
Reagan was basically hostile to the content of the New Deal–Great
Society legacy as well as to its price tag. The politics of the situation
was something else. That would be increasingly difficult as real people
began to lose real benefits to which they had become accustomed.

The catalyst for what would become one of the great issues of the
Reagan years was David Stockman, whose influence had increased during the late stages of the campaign. Nonetheless, in mid-November,
when the President-elect summoned his senior advisers to Los Angeles
for a review of economic policy, Stockman was absent, at least physically. He had not yet climbed quite high enough. But his ideas were
present in the form of a twenty-three-page memorandum he had
prepared for Kemp, who was to be the only radical present at a session
dominated by Republican centrists and conventional conservatives. Entitled "Avoiding a GOP Economic Dunkirk," and later referred to uni-
versally as the "Dunkirk memo," the document was remarkable for
several reasons. It depicted the current situation as even more bleak
than the Republicans had charged before the votes were counted. It attacked the Federal Reserve Board's policies as carried out by Chairman Paul Volcker as an abject failure. It raised the danger that both
inflation and high interest rates would persist, bringing doom to Reaganomics even before the program got a fair trial and doom to the Republican resurgence in the 1982 elections. One of the ways to avoid this
fate was to press much harder than the Reagan campaign had envisioned
for enduring budget control, to thin out dramatically the commodity
supplied by Washington for what Stockman derided as "the coast-to-

coast soup line" of federal programs. Unless the new administration acted decisively and immediately, the memo described "intense polarization between supply-side tax cutters and the more fiscally orthodox." It also envisioned "demoralization and fractionalization of GOP ranks" generally.

On taking office, Stockman proposed, the new administration should declare a national emergency. This, to stimulate prompt and drastic action by Congress. The refrain of the entire paper reflected a fear shared by Stockman and a few of the other intellectuals around Reagan—an apprehension that unless the new crowd could rapidly change the gloomy mood of the financial markets and the country at large, unless it could make bankers and brokers and underwriters and union leaders and corporate chairmen and all the other players in the great game *believe* that the economy would improve, then there could be no improvement. Then the Reagan conservatives might suffer the same fate as Margaret Thatcher's conservative policies had in Britain. "Thatcherization," Stockman warned, "can only be avoided if the initial economic policy package simultaneously spurs the output side of the economy and also elicits a swift revision of inflationary expectations in the financial markets."

Expectations. That word, along with *credibility,* became a virtual obsession. Modern government cannot turn in a trice. Stockman's thesis, then as well as later, was that while the country waited months for new legislation, and then awaited the real impact of that legislation more months hence, it would have to hold on to some hope. That was needed to make interest rates fall, thereby encouraging a recovery, thereby keeping the revenue flow strong, thereby holding the deficits within reasonable bounds, thereby lessening the competition for credit, thereby closing the circle by pushing interest rates down even further. To keep that process rolling, there had to be confidence.

After two decades of deficit trauma, there was skepticism abroad that anyone could balance the budget, or even start a strong trend in that direction. After several years of spurts and chokes in Federal Reserve Board practice, there was also skepticism that anyone could achieve the steady, moderate growth in money supply which the monetarists said was necessary for a new day. After so many years of predictions and expert analysis gone awry, there was doubt that any of this was really well understood by anyone.

Here we should pause to note the role of the Federal Reserve Board, or Fed, because it is always controversial in times of stress and became even more so starting in 1979. The Fed is the closest thing we have in our decentralized system to a central bank for domestic affairs. Though its seven members, or governors, are presidential appointees, they serve

fixed terms that do not coincide with the President's. Congress has
granted the Fed independence of both the executive and legislative
branches so that its operations ostensibly can be free of momentary political exigencies. Those operations, totally mysterious to the vast majority of citizens affected by them, have great impact on the availability
of credit in the private banking system. For instance, the Fed controls
the amounts of money that private institutions must keep on reserve,
and thus out of circulation. The Fed also buys and sells government
securities. When it chooses to buy from banks, funds are pumped into
the credit circulatory system. When the Fed sells, cash is withdrawn
from general use and interest rates are pushed upward.

The process has grown far more complex than this simple description indicates. By layman's logic, credit should be easy when the Fed
expands the money supply, and that is often the case. However, money
market logic in troubled times is something else. Rapidly expanding
money supply is a signal of future inflationary pressure. Lenders, to
protect themselves from losses in subsequent months and years, will
demand a higher rental price for their money today. Thus the weekly
bulletins on the state of money supply can make casual readers of the
financial pages cross-eyed in confusion. News that money supply—
expressed as M-1, M-2, M-3 or L to denote different aggregates—is
constricting for the moment is often interpreted as bullish for both the
stock and bond markets. The opposite is also true; the markets suffer if
money supply spurts. Yet if constriction is too severe (and no one
seems sure just where severe becomes too severe), the markets can also
turn bearish.

In October 1979, with the approval of the Carter White House,
Volcker set out to throttle inflation regardless of the short-term effects
on interest rates. The growth rate of money supply would be moder-
ated and, presumably, made more predictable. This, along with other
steps, would dampen overall economic activity at least temporarily.
The effect of the Fed's strategy would be ameliorated by strict control
of the federal deficit; the smaller the deficit, the less competition there
would be for credit that was already being made scarce, and hence the
less upward pressure there would be on interest rates. Reagan himself
and his more orthodox advisers accepted the necessity of Volcker's
stabilization policy, though the supply-side faction found it obnoxious.

Not only would it be extremely difficult to coordinate the Fed's approach with the expansionary thrust of the Administration's tax program, it would also be tricky for the Fed to achieve the exact modula-
tions in money supply that it sought. When economists looked back on
the record of 1980–81, they discovered that actual money supply performance ran above the Fed's new targets the first year and below them

in the second year. The short-term swings were violent. Milton Friedman, the dean of monetarist economists and one of Reagan's advisers, wrote of this period: "My complaint about monetary policy is not that it has been 'too tight' or persistently 'too easy,' but that it has alternated erratically between the one and the other. Average monetary growth over the past two years has been fairly good—but it is worth recalling the six-foot man who drowned trying to cross a river that averaged five feet in depth."[2]

It is also worth noting that the Fed, though ostensibly nonpolitical and beyond the reach of the White House, pumped more money into the economy in 1980, an election year, than its own published targets called for. That probably had the effect of postponing the recession, originally anticipated in early 1981, until the second half of the year. Further, when the new administration proclaimed its desire for decreasing money-growth targets, those goals indeed were lowered. Then actual performance ran still lower.

We have taken this short excursion into the arcane world of Fed practices in order to explain an important dichotomy in the Reaganauts' thinking as Inauguration Day approached. They were trying to put together a program of credible specific measures that would achieve that magic goal of positive expectations in the equity and credit markets. In doing that, they combined strands of three lines of thought: supply-side radicalism, with its emphasis on rapid economic growth; monetarism, with its emphasis on slow, steady expansion of money supply in order to pinch off inflation; and standard Republican conservatism, which favored fiscal austerity. Theoretically, these elements could complement each other. But they could also create contradictory tensions. The latter was more often the case in 1980–81.

The tight money policy already put into effect by Volcker was having dramatic effects even before Reagan took office. In December, the prime rate hit a paralyzing high of 21.5 percent, putting loans beyond reach for most potential borrowers. This would impede supply-side policies. Nonetheless, Stockman hoped for a stampede of the bulls, to provide a psychological lift. The Dow Jones industrial average did spurt ahead for a time, hitting 1,004.7 on January 7, its highest point in four years. In poker parlance, investors were betting on the come, gambling that Reaganomics would deal winning hands though at the time the cards were still being shuffled.

Now, after Christmas, Stockman was presiding over the economic deck. Stockman had acquired an encyclopedic knowledge of budget matters during his years as a congressional committee aide to John Anderson and two terms of his own in the House. Restless and ambitious, Stockman at age thirty-four had already roamed the ideological map.

He had come to rest for the time being among the neoconservatives. At the same time he carried on a heavy flirtation with the supply-side crowd.

The first priority was a thorough overhaul of the budget Carter had already officially proposed for fiscal '82, the budget year beginning October 1, 1981. If major changes could be made, then the new administration would have a chance to approach its domestic goals. The clock was running, and Stockman with it. Murray Weidenbaum, who would become chairman of the Council of Economic Advisers, had not even been nominated at the turn of the year. Donald Regan would take over the Treasury, but he was new to Washington and had to line up a large bureaucracy. Stockman was far ahead of the other two in knowing what had to be done. His immediate predecessors in the Office of Management and Budget had been primarily technicians, with only limited influence on large policy decisions. Stockman in the beginning would be everything: formulator of policy, administrator, advocate before congressional committees and the press. He would extract Reaganomics from Reaganism.

The White House was eager to get out at least the main outlines of its program by early February, with the full details to come a month later. Before that February statement could be made, however, the Administration had to take a new look at the economic assumptions on which its revised budget would be based. This ritual requires the experts to predict, or guess, where certain key indicators will be in subsequent years—nominal GNP, inflation, real GNP, employment, interest rates. All of these bear heavily on the budget. A one-point change in unemployment can alter the deficit figure by more than $25 billion because of the effect on tax revenue coming in and extra benefits going out.

Quietly, Reagan's people already had made some concessions to an unpleasant reality: the figures proclaimed with confidence the previous September were not holding up. The Senate Budget Committee projections had been faulty. Stockman quickly realized that a balanced budget in fiscal '83 would be impossible; that pledge was moved back one year. It would also be impossible to cut spending in the budget year already begun, fiscal '81, by the 2 percent Reagan had pledged. Stockman would settle for a few token trims. The real test would be fiscal '82, so most of the energy focused on that. Even while Stockman and the other players in late January were struggling, haggling, occasionally shouting at one another, over the economic assumptions, the Budget Director was maneuvering to push back the effective date of the personal income tax rate reduction from January 1 to July 1. Every time he looked at the figures he realized that the pool of red ink was more menacing than anyone had been willing to concede.

To get an agreement on the key assumptions, representatives of three offices must be involved: Treasury, OMB and the Council of Economic Advisers. In this case, outside experts also served as consultants. The principal conflict arose first between Treasury officials who spoke for different economic schools, supply-siders and what became a temporary union between Stockman and Weidenbaum at the end of January.

In organizing the Treasury, the White House had created a kind of balanced ticket. Donald Regan himself was a businessman rather than an economist or a theorist. He had only a limited voice in choosing his chief subordinates. The new under secretary for monetary policy was Beryl Sprinkel, a strict monetarist of the Friedman school. The under secretary for tax policy was Norman Ture, a supply-sider, and the assistant secretary for economic policy—the department's designated theorist—was Paul Craig Roberts, a vociferous supply-sider who, as an aide to Kemp, had helped draft the original Kemp-Roth bill. Stockman and his own economic adviser, Larry Kudlow, brought in John Rutledge of the Claremont Economics Institute. The Claremont econometrics model would be used in place of the Wharton School model that had been employed by the Carter administration. Greenspan participated as another interested outsider.

Accounts of what then happened are about as numerous as the participants, who numbered a dozen. Roberts, after he quit the government in disgust a year later, wrote an acerbic article in which he accused Greenspan of clinging to outmoded ideas as a security blanket. Greenspan, Roberts argued, refused to stray far from the Phillips curve, the traditionalist concept that makes inflation and unemployment an either-or proposition. In Roberts' view, Greenspan unduly influenced Stockman, convincing the Budget Director that the assumptions would lack credibility if they departed too far from conventional forecasting techniques. Further, Stockman was obsessed with his own institutional interests—"Stockman seemed to decide that his success indicator was the budget deficit, not the tax cut or the inflation rate."[3] Roberts blamed Stockman, and "the Keynesianism that hovered over the exercise," for skewed assumptions that ultimately caused the severe 1981–82 recession.

Roberts' argument is fascinating, but represents a small minority view within the Administration and the general economists' fraternity. The assumptions that finally emerged in February were skewed, to be sure, but for different reasons. Weidenbaum, with no theoretical ax to grind, was probably closest to the truth with his recollections: "It was a forced marriage. The supply-side people insisted on [forecasting] rapid growth in real terms and the monetarists insisted on rapid progress in bringing down inflation. Each of them would go along with a set of numbers as long as their own concern was satisfied. The monetarists weren't that concerned about growth and the supply-siders weren't that concerned about inflation."[4]

That appraisal came a year after the fact and six months before Weidenbaum resigned. A microeconomist best known for his research on government regulation, Weidenbaum arrived late for the initial negotiations on economic assumptions. Long afterward he would confide privately that he was so shocked at what he found that he seriously considered resigning even before unpacking the cartons in his new office. He had the same urge a few months later, when the assumptions were reviewed and retained for political reasons, though by then everyone knew that they were specious. Never a decisive power in the Administration, Weidenbaum endured frustration each time his Council of Economic Advisers participated in the forecasting ritual because the numbers were sculpted to create the desired effect. It happened again the following year as the fiscal '83 budget was prepared, and for the third time Weidenbaum fought the urge to resign as a matter of principle. When he finally did quit in the summer of 1982, however, he spared Reagan the embarrassment of a public brouhaha. As Weidenbaum looked at it, the published assumptions would have been even more irresponsible in his absence than they were with him there, and he took some satisfaction from the conviction that he had held on as long as he could for the sake of the Administration.

When Weidenbaum arrived, in mid-debate, he was particularly disturbed that some of the participants wanted to set the growth projections very high. The point of that was to allow a revenue forecast indicating a balanced budget despite the tax cut. Even in the adjusted version, after compromises, the Reaganauts went with a "real growth" figure—that is, GNP with inflation taken into account—of 1.4 percent.* That turned out to be nearly twice the actual figure at the end of 1981. Just as troublesome were the "out-year" growth projections for 1982–86, which ran ahead of predictions by most other experts. The Administration was also too optimistic in forecasting unemployment, which rose rather than fell. Ironically, inflation went down faster than the final February consensus predicted, and that too was a problem. While a lower inflation rate was a central goal, the speed with which it

---

* As measured by comparing the rate in the year's fourth quarter to the preceding fourth quarter.

fell surprised the experts and had a dampening effect on government revenue.

"I make no bones about it," Weidenbaum conceded. "We came up with an extremely optimistic forecast. But there's a difference between an extremely optimistic forecast and one that's off the wall."[5] Weidenbaum continued to insist, nonetheless, that the practice of making assumptions is serious business and that the new administration's first attempt produced results within the realm of possibility. "Was it technically feasible? I think so," he said. "But everything had to work well."

That was the professional economist talking. Stockman, a politician and a radical reformer fully sharing Reagan's sense of mission, had a certain contempt for economists and their scenarios. While he confirmed the main outlines of Weidenbaum's account, including the split between monetarists and supply-siders, as well as the final resolution of the issue, Stockman had a more pragmatic explanation of what had happened. At least he did in the summer and fall of 1981,* when the nature of the game had changed dramatically. By then Stockman was waging a desperate fight within the Administration to combat prospective deficits that threatened to overwhelm Reagan's program. He also was under increasing attack from assorted adversaries outside. He seemed torn between acknowledging his own errors and placing blame on others, or on circumstances.

"I wasn't quite as sensitive [as he later became] to the degree to which the budget position, the deficit, was driven by economic assumptions," Stockman said in one of our conversations late in the year. "Our assumptions were inordinately optimistic. I think everyone recognizes that. So, in a sense, they allowed us to fool ourselves into thinking that we had solved the budget gap after the tax cut." Yet Stockman made his own statement sound disingenuous, to put it charitably, when we returned to the subject, at his prompting, in another talk. The difference between the Wharton econometric model, with which Reaganomics could never be made to seem feasible, and the Claremont model was irrelevant, Stockman insisted. "The Claremont model is no better or no worse than anything else. We hand-doctored that one just the way the

---

* During this period, I had three long conversations with Stockman—on August 24, October 10 and October 31—with the understanding that the information would be used solely for this book. I was unaware then that Stockman the previous winter had begun what turned out to be a much longer series of embargoed interviews with William Greider, who published a controversial article on Stockman in the December 1981 issue of *The Atlantic Monthly*. That piece touched only briefly on the "assumptions" process of the previous winter. In the relevant passage, Stockman defended the exercise as "based on valid economic analysis."

previous administration doctored the Wharton model. They're absolutely doctored. We sat up there [in the OMB conference room] arguing whether the GNP rate for the third quarter should be 3.5 or 5. To quote Murray Weidenbaum, 'my visceral computer' [has the last word]. He sat there one day"—here Stockman chuckled and slapped his own belly, impersonating his colleague—"he sat there and said, 'It's right here.' . . . We had about eight days to put the forecast together. It takes about twenty days to put the budget together after you have the forecast. Nobody could agree on a forecast in meeting after meeting after meeting. Finally Murray and I sat right here at this table and split the differences and said, 'This is it.' "

If there had been fewer arguments, or if the group had been able to spend three to four weeks on the assumptions, as the normal budget calendar allows, then the product would have been better, Stockman went on. (A few weeks after Stockman said that, the next budget round started and the same kind of problems arose, with similar results.)

Others familiar with the way budget-making goes in Washington agree that it is customary to shade figures to produce a desired result. This time the circumstances were quite different, however, because the Reaganauts were introducing a revolutionary program. As we have seen, they were acutely aware of the need for credibility. Without it, their proposals would not even get a hearing in Congress. Stockman in the early days was genuinely persuaded that it could all work, given some public confidence. Thus it was worth a gamble. The deadline for the assumptions had to be met if the Administration was to maintain its rapid pace. That was a functional requirement. Second, the numbers had to seem feasible to Capitol Hill, to Wall Street, to the press. "The decision had three parts," Stockman observed. "One part was error, one part haste, one part conscious contrivance."

The depths of the difficulty remained private at the time, though the published figures aroused some skepticism. Reagan himself was unaware of the severity of the wrangling that had gone on, and of just how dubious were the figures on which his specific proposals would be based. But Reagan did now accept the need for deep cuts in many programs. Just about everything except the Defense Department, the main component of Social Security and a handful of other benefit programs were fair game. The President gave Stockman considerable freedom to decide what would be sliced and by how much. The department heads, reading the clear signals from the White House, in most cases offered little resistance.

A week before leaving office, Carter, as required by law, had officially proposed his fiscal '82 budget. It called for an expenditure of

$739 billion, with a deficit of only $27.5 billion, or half the shortfall expected for fiscal '81. Even delaying the effective date of the first round of the personal income tax reduction until July 1, thereby postponing the second and third installments by six months each as well, the Reagan tax proposal was calculated at reducing revenue by about $60 billion in fiscal '82. Together with the planned rise in defense spending, the tax cut meant a deficit considerably higher than Carter had proposed. Reagan and his advisers did not consider it a serious problem provided—and this would become a crucial proviso—that they could legitimately show the deficit declining in fiscal '83 and approaching the vanishing point after that.

Could they? There were some doubts among the cognoscenti even at that early point. Richard Darman, culling material from all the participating groups in order to construct the briefing papers the President saw, felt uneasy. A Harvard M.B.A. with varied experience in business and government, Darman was an agnostic among the monetarists and supply-siders. On February 10 he sent a memorandum to Baker, Meese and Deaver in which he predicted that the program then in the final phases of formation contained three problems. It would encounter political difficulties because the spending targets would affront too many special interests. Second, it was likely to be perceived as inequitable toward the poor and the working class. Finally, and most explicitly, Darman argued that the economic assumptions completed the previous week could not stand close scrutiny. The optimistic projections on real growth and deficit numbers were inconsistent with the presumed falloff in inflation, the increase in defense spending and the realistic prospect of savings elsewhere in the budget.

Darman wasn't the only skeptic, though generally such reservations were muffled. Stockman later would recall a "pioneering mode" infecting all of them, a sense that the obstacles, whatever they were, could be overcome. There was still room for adjustment. There was, without question, a huge opportunity to maintain the political initiative.

At this stage, Stockman had identified $41.4 billion in prospective savings from the "current services" base line. Yet that was not going to be enough. Martin Anderson convened a meeting of the experts on February 16, just two days before Reagan would appear before a joint session of Congress and begin giving the extensive details of the program. By Anderson's calculations, a balanced budget would be impossible before 1986 at the earliest. Additional reductions were discussed and Stockman went back to price them out. This was the origin of the so-called "unidentified savings" that soon began to cause the Administration grief. Stockman insisted that it was only an "accounting problem" rather than a substantive gap. In essence, the Administration was promising that it would come up with more savings in fiscal '83 and '84 in order to keep the deficit line on a downward track. Meanwhile, when the Administration put forward its full '82 revision, on March 10, it was proposing a new total of $48.6 billion in economies apart from the defense budget. It would spend $695.3 billion and wind up with a deficit of $45 billion, or nearly twice the shortfall Carter had projected in January.

The proposed savings did not seem outlandish in a budget of nearly $700 billion. However, the reductions actually would have to come from only a small sector of that very large pie. With defense, the major pension programs and certain fixed obligations off limits, Stockman had less than a quarter of the budget in which to maneuver. Skewed economic assumptions allowed him to claim a reduction of more than $7 billion in debt service, but that was pure illusion. Real savings would have to come from general administration, grants to states and localities and a variety of direct services to the public. It was clear from the outset that the Administration's claim that all of society would share the burden of reductions equitably was specious. Initially, at least, while they awaited the return of prosperity, the lower orders would make most of the sacrifices.

Sensitive to the danger that the plan would be dismissed as manna for the rich, Reagan made a difficult decision concerning his tax proposal. The tax rates then in effect ran from 70 to 14 percent. However, Congress had already put a cap of 50 percent on the marginal rate charged on earned income—wages, salaries, fees for service—as opposed to unearned income, such as interest and dividends. Only on the latter did the marginal rates still range up to 70. It had been generally assumed that the Administration would propose two things: to lower the top rate to 50 percent for all income, unearned as well as earned, and then apply the ten-ten-ten formula across the board. The additional cost to the Treasury would not be severe because the wealthy, who were ostensibly subject to the highest rates on unearned income, usually found ways to shelter that revenue from taxation. In fact, knocking off the illusory top rates presumably would be a large incentive to increase savings and investment of a productive nature. Economists both inside and outside the supply-side sect thought the change was sound tax policy.

It was considered poor public relations, however. Reagan was reluctant to give up on the change. Talking with the troika on the morning of February 12, he complained: "This concern [about appearances] is doing us out of something far more stimulating to the economy than some of these other things." Meese responded that the White House had to be consistent with its pledge of equity. The next day, meeting with his economic advisers, Reagan gave in on the 70/50 issue. However, the option of applying ten-ten-ten to the top rate on earned income was still alive. The original Kemp-Roth bill had neglected to do that because it addressed the full 70-to-14 range. But the White House pulled back from this as well, largely for cosmetic reasons. Kemp exploded, threatening in a conversation with one reporter to introduce his own new tax measure to compete with the Administration's. A phone call from Reagan calmed him down.

A more important defense against the charge of inequity was the concept of the "social safety net." The term was originally given currency in 1978 by Kemp, who thinks that he picked it up from Irving Kristol, editor of *The Public Interest*. It is meant to denote basic benefits that conservatives concede are necessary to protect "the truly needy" from dire want. As it prepared to counter attacks from liberals, the White House Press Office asked Stockman for a list of programs that the Administration would not attempt to cut. Against his better judgment, he mentioned six or eight—there later would be disagreement over exactly which ones—and the White House put these out. Stockman soon regretted that gambit, which he privately called a publicity gimmick, because reporters assumed that the services mentioned would be immune from all reduction. Stockman knew that he could not afford that luxury. Soon he would have to begin trimming those programs as well, only to provoke indignant stories about holes in the safety net.

These distractions in the first winter of Reaganomics hid something more important. Despite internal Administration disputes, despite the overestimate of the opposition's strength, and despite some initial skepticism that the program could work, the Administration was in fact making progress. It was advancing on two tracks, one obvious and the other more subtle. Reagan himself was living up to his record as a superb salesman of his ideas. Meanwhile his aides were making a reputation of their own as shrewd lobbyists and strategists. Together, Reagan as public advocate and his men as private operators were surrounding their political goals even as their economic targets remained elusive. They would achieve the first in a glorious spring and summer of victory while chasing the second, season after season.

9

Euphoria

The Democrats were scared. While the new crowd at the White House managed to cover its concern about the validity of Reaganomics, the Democrats allowed their fear, their divisions, their lack of effective leadership to show during that first long season. For Reagan it must have seemed a remarkable transformation in the rules of engagement. The truism throughout his political career until then was that the opposition always made the mistake of underestimating him. Suddenly he was being regarded as an irresistible force. The perception had the impact of reality. That fact would affect the legislative scorecard, the economy and more. It would change, at least for a time, the balance between the executive and legislative branches of government.

The fright that afflicted the Democrats was easy to understand. As a political personality, even as a mouthpiece, Jimmy Carter evaporated after his defeat. History may rehabilitate his record, but to his party in 1981 he was a non-person. Robert Byrd, never a commanding figure when he led the Democratic Senate majority, became a negligible factor as lord of the minority. That left the House of Representatives and its shambling Speaker, Tip O'Neill. Ostensibly he had a fifty-three-seat advantage when the Ninety-seventh Congress convened* but that number was deceptive. Right-wing Democrats, known as the Boll Weevils and loosely aligned as the Conservative Democratic Forum, could muster a rebel band of two to three dozen on certain issues. O'Neill also had to worry about the constancy of a handful of youngish members

* The division in January was 242 to 189, with four vacancies. When they were filled, the count became 243 to 192. The Republicans held the Senate, 53 to 46; Harry Byrd, Jr., the conservative Virginian, classified himself independent.

who were neither Southern conservatives nor traditional urban liberals. Stockman called them progressives and thought that he could do business with a few of them, such as James Jones, the Budget Committee chairman.

O'Neill's public statements were laced with anxiety. He told one audience of fellow Democrats: "Because of our inability to reduce inflation between 1978 and 1980, as well as the most unfortunate and avoidable increase in unemployment in 1980, we suffered a major defeat at the polls. In fact, it was our worst setback since 1952. Too many Americans, including many members of our own party, felt that inflation was reducing their standard of living and the economy offered no prospect for the future . . . Consequently, we lost the White House, the Senate and thirty-three seats in the House of Representatives."[1]

The Speaker and other party leaders talked openly of their biggest fear: that the 1980 results might prove to have been the preamble to what political scientists call a "realigning election"—a swing in party power that could shift the balance for a generation, as 1932 and 1934 did for the Democrats. The Democrats found the omens nerve-racking. The New York Times synthesized the findings of several pollsters and reported that the GOP was attracting more allegiance than it had at any time in the previous twenty-eight years.[2] There were rumors that several House Democrats would officially change parties; only two actually defected during the year, but their decisions added to the leadership's distress.

The Democrats attempted to offer their own alternatives and sometimes the combat grew fierce. But O'Neill relinquished one of the great powers of his office, control of the legislative schedule. He promised to allow final floor votes on both major parts of the Administration's program—spending reductions and the tax bill—by midsummer. Afterward O'Neill's political adviser, Kirk O'Donnell, explained why: "What the Democrats did, in extraordinary fashion, was to recognize the cataclysmic nature of the 1980 election results. The American public wanted this new President to be given a chance to try out his programs. We weren't going to come across as being obstructionists."[3] Thus Reagan, though facing a divided Congress, would have a better chance in his first year to work his will than Carter ever had in dealing with two houses controlled by his own party. The flip side of that opportunity: Reagan would find it difficult to evade ultimate responsibility if his programs failed.

Reagan initially approached Congress with a cattle prod in one hand and an olive branch in the other. He insisted on rapid action and on controlling the legislative agenda to a greater extent than recent Presidents had been able to do. At the same time, in the early months, he muffled his own combative instincts. Bipartisanship became a byword for cosmetic purposes and tactical reasons as well. The White House, no less than the Democratic hierarchy, was looking toward 1982.

The olive branch was prominent when Reagan gave his first television speech from the White House on February 5. The Inaugural Address two weeks earlier had been intended to set a general tone. Now Reagan intended to give a detailed diagnosis of the nation's economy while reaffirming the broad outlines of his prescriptions. Most of all, he wanted to keep the speech simple. His audience was the electorate, not members of Congress, economists or journalists. The legislators were going home a few days later for the Lincoln's Birthday recess; Reagan wanted them to hear from their constituents.

Two competing texts were in hand forty-eight hours before the speech, but Reagan wasn't happy with them. He felt that they were too complicated, too dense. Though normally a sound sleeper, he awoke around 4 A.M. on February 4 and spent twenty minutes or so putting fresh prose on a yellow legal pad. When the new version was reviewed later, one of his aides remarked that the text was devoid of attacks on the Democrats, the liberals, the "big spenders." In fact Reagan implied that most everyone had contributed to the mess ("Some government programs seemed so worthwhile that borrowing to fund them didn't bother us . . ."). He still preached radical change. All the fundamental tenets of Reaganism received their due. Yet, even more than he had on his inaugural day, Reagan now spoke as the leader rather than as the challenger, and as one concerned about how his compassion quotient would be perceived:

> Our aim is to increase our national wealth so all will have more, not just to redistribute what we already have, which is just a sharing of scarcity. We can begin to reward hard work and risk-taking by forcing government to live within its means . . . Let us join in a new determination to rebuild the foundation of our society, to work together, to act responsibly. Let us do so with the most profound respect for that which must be preserved as well as with sensitive understanding and compassion for those who must be protected.

That was the effect Reagan wanted, and most of his advisers agreed. Forbearance toward his political foes did not come easily, however. To the assistant who had noted the benign tone, Reagan responded with a laugh: "Listen, if I were making this speech from the outside, I'd kick their balls off." Instead, Reagan was keeping the Democrats impotent by more subtle means. His best device, as usual, was his skill in conveying his message. To bring home the impact of inflation, he decided on a prop. He fished a dollar bill out of his own pocket and borrowed a quarter, a dime and a penny from David Fischer. The 1960 dollar had deteriorated in value to thirty-six cents, and the television camera zoomed in to depict that transformation in the manicured fingers of the President of the United States.

Boffo. No other critique of that presidential debut in prime time was possible. The Democrats' fears were reinforced. In mid-month Reagan went to Capitol Hill for his first speech to a joint session of Congress. Originally the White House planned it as an informal State of the Union address, in which Reagan would talk in broad terms about both international and domestic affairs. That idea was shelved for two reasons. The new administration did not yet know precisely what it wanted to say about foreign policy. More importantly, with each passing day Reagan's advisers became even more persuaded of the need to focus all attention on the economic program.

When Reagan again stressed cooperation between the White House and Congress ("I'm here tonight to ask you to join me in making it *our* plan. Together we can embark on this road . . .") the applause was so long and loud that Reagan had difficulty continuing. "I should have arranged to quit right there," he quipped, evoking still more applause. Again he promised to protect the poor, listing seven programs that would be left intact.* Again he introduced a device for making the problem vivid to the average citizen. The national debt was then about to pass the one-trillion-dollar level. Translating that into a stack of thousand-dollar bills, Reagan had calculated while polishing the speech, would make a pile of currency sixty miles high. The White House checked with the Bureau of Engraving to be sure and learned that the President had been close; the stack would be sixty-seven miles high. Stretching out his empty hand to the television cameras and the members of Congress, the old actor created an image of bank notes reaching to the sky.

Courtship went on away from the TV cameras as well. In order to prevail in the House, the Reaganites would have to pry at least twenty-six members away from O'Neill—provided that the Republicans voted as a solid bloc. The task seemed difficult, but not impossible. Max Friedersdorf, then chief of legislative liaison, and his deputy on the House side, Kenneth Duberstein, scattered small favors far and wide—tickets to Kennedy Center performances, passes which lawmakers

---

* There was a glitch between the White House and Stockman's office. Reagan cited old-age benefits under Social Security, Medicare, home relief, veterans' pensions, meals for pupils from low-income families, Head Start, and the summer employment program for teenagers. OMB was uncertain about some of those and had offered instead the main component of welfare, unemployment benefits and railroad retirement pensions. As it turned out later, most of these ten did suffer some reductions anyway.

could give to favored constituents for special White House tours, cuff links carrying the presidential seal (worth about $4.50 wholesale; the Republican National Committee picked up the tab for such doodads). And of course there was the presidential presence. In small groups members of Congress were brought in to chat with Reagan, some to have coffee, some for lunch, some for state dinners when a distinguished visitor from abroad was being entertained.

Jack Brooks, the crusty Democratic chairman of the Government Operations Committee who had never got on well with Carter, came out of the Oval Office in such a benign mood that he took Duberstein aside to give a bit of friendly advice. What Reagan should do next, Brooks said, is buy back the yacht *Sequoia,* which Carter had sold as a symbolic economy measure, so that he could entertain on the Potomac.* Ralph Hall, a freshman Democrat from Texas, became one of the best-wooed of the Southerners. A genial lawyer and banker, Hall appreciated Reagan's calm approach. "It's kind of like you were going on a hunting trip or playing golf with someone who's trying to do business with you," Hall said after maximum exposure, including a trip to Camp David. "Dealing with him is like dealing with another businessman."[4] Hall would vote with the Administration on several key issues; Brooks, closer to the House leadership, would not.

Duberstein, patrolling the House constantly, began to pick up some surprising indications of sentiment. The Boll Weevils were willing, even eager in some cases, to go for bigger budget reductions than Reagan was asking. Even more surprising was that a few Northern Democrats were making soft, but unmistakably friendly noises. Eugene Atkinson, a Kennedy supporter in 1980, indicated through an assistant that he would like to keep in touch with Duberstein. Later, while back in his home district in western Pennsylvania, Atkinson was about to appear on a local radio talk show when a White House telephone operator tracked him down. The President wanted to chat about Atkinson's stand on the budget bill. Well then, would Reagan consent to being hooked into the live broadcast and do his talking on the air? Reagan hesitated, but went ahead. Atkinson not only voted with the White House; this erstwhile Kennedy liberal became one of the two Democrats who announced conversion to the GOP.†

In legislative terms, the initial test would come on the First Budget Resolution for fiscal '82, which normally would not have been a high stakes exercise. As a rule that measure, enacted in mid-May, serves as

---

* In fact a group of businessmen friendly to Reagan did buy the boat, intending to lend it to the President on request, but the White House let the opportunity pass.

† Running for reelection as a Republican in 1982, Atkinson was defeated.

a broad but nonbinding outline of Congress' revision of the budget proposed by the President. Later, the Second Budget Resolution gets down to cases. Meanwhile, Congress acts on separate money bills, each one of which actually provides funds for specific purposes. Now it would be quite different. The Republicans, following Stockman's scenario, were pressing for a "reconciliation" measure as well. The term is misleading. In congressional argot it does not connote compromise. Reconciliation legislation is supposed to impose firm ceilings on what each committee can then do with the actual money bills.

Though the difference sounds technical, it was in fact an important power play. If the White House succeeded, it would inhibit the individual committee chairmen from pumping up spending measures according to their own proclivities. The reconciliation tactic, never before imposed on a First Budget Resolution, would alter the way Congress spends money. It would reduce both the chances for excessive expenditures and the leverage that outside interest groups normally exert in the committees with jurisdiction over their concerns.

Jim Jones, the Democratic Budget Committee chairman, had a different approach. He and his allies drafted their own budget resolution, somewhat different from Reagan's, so that the Democrats would not merely be saying "no." Rather, they would be offering what they hoped would be recognized as a responsible alternative. The Jones version envisioned a more modest tax reduction, a smaller increase for the Pentagon and less of a cut in social programs. Nonetheless, the Jones measure followed the Administration's in its general direction. Even before the first important vote of the year, the new administration had won a victory. The Democrats accepted the drift of Reaganomics even though they tried to dig in against the specifics. Thus the White House already controlled the agenda. Now the question was whether Reagan would split differences here and there.

In the White House Legislative Strategy Group, attention had already leapfrogged to the tax bill, which would be considered after the First Budget Resolution. The memorandum handed around alluded to the Boll Weevils at that stage as "an unorganized group of thirty." The Conservative Democratic Forum could not be counted on. The consensus in the LSG was that the White House probably would have to make a substantive compromise on Reagan's tax proposals, perhaps giving up the third installment of "ten-ten-ten." The more ground given on spending cuts, the weaker the Administration's position would be on the tax issue. Meanwhile, a minor rebellion arose on the Republican-controlled Senate Budget Committee. There three junior Republicans of the New Right persuasion were bucking the Administration budget bill because it failed to go far enough in spending cuts. Stockman's gambit of promising additional but unspecified savings for the "out years"—1983 and 1984—had proved unpersuasive.

That development strengthened the instinct already prevalent in the LSG: avoid any compromise on the spending package until the last possible moment. Reagan himself, though not involved in the group's day-to-day maneuvers, agreed in principle. While recovering from the assassination attempt in early April, the President was even more detached from the strategy sessions than before. But Baker and Darman knew his feelings, which were to press as strongly as possible for the Administration's program rather than to buy the Jones bill or to compromise halfway between.

In the first weeks of spring, Jones and the other Democratic leaders were slow to catch on to what was happening. The greenest Democratic member of the House Budget Committee, Phil Gramm of Texas, renewed what had been a close personal association with Stockman in the Ninety-sixth Congress. Gramm, thirty-nine, began his second term in the House when Reagan took office. A husky, articulate conservative who had taught economics at Texas A & M, Gramm had once collaborated with Stockman on a monograph concerning hospital costs. They had also helped produce a Republican alternative to Carter's fiscal '81 budget, a document from which Stockman drew heavily in proposing spending reductions for '82. Like some of the other Southerners from districts that had voted heavily for Reagan,* Gramm thought that the Administration proposal failed to go far enough. Now he was willing to help the Administration thwart Jones.

The instrument would be a "bipartisan" substitute for the Jones measure, incorporating most of the Administration proposals. Gramm would cosponsor it with Delbert Latta of Ohio, the senior Republican on the Budget Committee. That, at least, was the scheme blessed by the White House. Some of the House Republicans had doubts. The new Republican leader, Robert Michel of Illinois, was doing an excellent job of maintaining party cohesion. But formal collaboration with Democrats, even Boll Weevils, was difficult for some of the older elephants.

"A lot of Republicans were suspicious," Gramm said later. "I could understand how they felt. Del Latta had worked for twenty years in the House to have a Republican budget pass. Here I was, an upstart second-term Democrat, getting a lot of play [from the Administration]."[5] Latta was ready to dump the deal, particularly when he discov-

* Many of the House Democrats who supported Reagan in the 1981 session were reflecting sentiment back home. Gramm was typical. Carter carried his sixth district in east-central Texas by two points in 1976. Reagan won it by eleven points in 1980.

ered that Gramm's name was going to go first in the bill title. One morning as negotiations stalled the two had a loud argument in the back of the committee hearing room. Gramm felt that it was up to the White House to get Republican members into line. At 5:30 A.M. on April 9, Stockman phoned Gramm at home. All right, the Budget Director said, the deal is set. You will introduce the new bill in committee today and Latta will take it to the floor when the time comes. Other details were also cleared up. But when Gramm got to the committee chamber, he discovered new reservations on the Republican side. "I was sitting there feeling a little foolish," Gramm recalled. "I was sitting there in the committee room wishing I was back at Texas A & M. I was saying to myself 'bipartisanship doesn't work.' "6

George Bush did work, however. Alerted to the latest difficulty, Bush phoned Latta and explained that the President, still convalescing, was counting strongly on Latta's cooperation. That was stretching it, because Reagan was quite detached from the intricate maneuvering. Stockman, meanwhile, talked to several other Republicans, emphasizing that if the White House trusted Gramm, they could as well. Late in the day, finally, all hands consented. The Gramm-Latta substitute, carrying the Democrat's name first and Reagan's full blessing, was officially launched. Back at the LSG, a principal agenda item at the April 15 meeting read: "What further needs to be done to rebut the talk of compromise?" The decision was to deny, at every opportunity, that the Administration was willing to yield any ground at all.

The Reaganauts had the opposition surrounded, engulfed. Keeping in close touch with the White House Office of Public Liaison, then run by Elizabeth Dole, the U.S. Chamber of Commerce and other business-oriented organizations lobbied vigorously in selected House districts. Now that one of their own was cosponsor of the bill, the Boll Weevils began to unite behind it. A few moderate Republicans from the Northeast had some doubts. Their region, after all, would benefit less than others. Toward the end, James Jeffords of Vermont was the most recalcitrant of these so-called Republican Gypsy Moths. Duberstein spent hours with him, finally suggesting a strategy. Jeffords could satisfy the home folks by voting first for yet another alternative budget, a third option doomed to failure anyway. When that liberal bill was defeated, Jeffords could then switch to the Gramm-Latta measure. Jeffords agreed to think about it.

O'Neill showed every sign of caving in. During the April recess he visited Australia and New Zealand rather than continuing the fight. On April 27, after his return, he held a dispirited press conference in his office. Not since McKinley, he said, have we had an administration so overwhelmingly for the wealthy. But he conceded that the Jones bill was in trouble. "I know when to fight and when not to fight," he observed. Mail to his own office was five to one in favor of Reagan. The next day, his convalescence nearly completed, Reagan made a triumphal return to center stage with another address to Congress—televised live in prime time, of course. Still sore, still weakened, Reagan gave a magnificent performance. He knew the country was with him. How could it not be? Exactly four weeks earlier he had lain in the emergency room of George Washington Hospital, gasping for air, bleeding profusely inside. Now he was back at work, thanking the country for its prayers and letters and flowers, reading a note from a second-grader in Long Island who admonished the President, "Get well quickly, or you might have to make a speech in your pajamas." Then the inevitable transition line: "Thanks to some very fine people, my health is much improved. I'd like to be able to say that with regard to the health of the economy."

He still talked unity and cooperation. "Tonight I renew my call for us to work as a team," he said, "to join in cooperation so that we find answers which will begin to solve all our economic problems . . . These policies [in Gramm-Latta] will make our economy stronger, and the stronger economy will balance the budget, which we're committed to do by 1984." He defined cooperation as passage of his program now that it carried the name of a Democratic cosponsor. The Jones measure gave the Administration roughly 75 percent of what it had asked, both in spending and tax reductions, but Reagan would have none of it. He didn't need to split the difference, even though the Democratic bill promised a smaller short-term deficit.

By the time the first climax came on May 7, what had appeared to be a reasonably close contest turned into a rout. The key vote was 253 to 176. Every Republican, including Jeffords of Vermont, stayed with the President. Not just forty Democrats defected, as expected, but sixty-three. There was talk now of the Administration owning an ideological majority in the House of Representatives. Suddenly the "realists" who had insisted that the Administration would have to compromise on the tax bill were reconsidering. Most important of all, Ronald Reagan had reminded the country that presidential leadership was not dead after all. It had been in a coma, perhaps, and he was finding ways to rouse it.

It took just five days for the Administration to miscalculate the amount of trump in its hand. Reagan and his advisers, without sufficient preparation, decided to strike boldly at what had become a chronic dilemma—the imminent rupture of the Social Security system. The imperative was valid beyond question. Everyone acknowledged that the main fund, supplying "old age and survivors'" benefits, was going broke. The Carter administration had tried to cope by imposing a large increase in payroll deductions. Though painful for both workers and employers, that move was intended to ensure solvency for four or five decades. Now, three years later, shortfall was again a clear and present danger. The fund on which thirty-six million pensioners depended would simply run out of money in a year or two unless changes were made.

Taken together, the history, philosophy, politics and mathematics of Social Security deserve a book of their own. What started during the New Deal as a modest attempt to shield the elderly from destitution evolved into a complex of benefit programs with runaway costs. Congress not only added new features periodically, it repeatedly underestimated the long-range price of them. When automatic benefit increases pegged to the Consumer Price Index were introduced in the early seventies, costs streaked to the stratosphere. During that decade, old age and survivors' benefits increased by roughly 500 percent, to $120 billion, while the Disability and Medicare payouts went up by even higher proportions. Because of the population trend, fewer and fewer active workers were underwriting increasing and proliferating benefits to more and more recipients.

Reagan, going back to the early sixties, was skeptical about more than the actuarial soundness of Social Security. He had reservations about one premise: compulsory participation. These doubts gave him trouble in both the 1976 and 1980 campaigns, so he muted them. In 1980 he promised repeatedly both to protect the long-range integrity of the system and to maintain benefits for those already receiving them. He avoided explicit commitments concerning future beneficiaries, though that could have been inferred.

Now, in the spring of 1981, the Administration had several options. J. J. Pickle, head of the House Subcommittee on Social Security, was beginning work on long-range proposals, and got in touch with Health and Human Services Secretary Schweiker. What was the Administration's stance? The Pickle bill was likely to be relatively modest and to have little impact on the overall budget problem. But the White House could have waited for that measure to emerge. Another alternative was strictly temporary—to transfer cash from the solvent Social Security subdivisions to the insolvent ones while working out a long-term solution. A third choice was to go for broke now with an omnibus reform package of major proportions.

Martin Anderson favored the third course on philosophical grounds. It was sound Reaganism to begin turning Social Security away from the welfare directions it had been taking. Schweiker, then in charge of the parent body of the Social Security Administration, simply wanted to attack the biggest single problem in his immediate domain. Stockman stood somewhat apart. He had worked marginal Social Security reductions into the budget and they remained part of the Gramm-Latta package. But initially he was not keen for a distracting, separate controversy over Social Security reform while the main Administration program was still at issue.

In mid-spring, Stockman's view changed. Interest rates were not falling as he had hoped. Though the Dow Jones industrial average hovered just over 1,000 for a time—it hit a high of 1,024 on April 27 before beginning another descent—bulls obviously were not taking over the stock market. Private analysts continued to express doubts about the Administration's ability to meet its balanced-budget targets in succeeding years. The public confidence on which Stockman had been banking was still invisible. If the Administration showed the brass and the skill required to prevail over the Social Security lobby—well, that would demonstrate a genuine commitment to change and renewal. Besides, he would be able to carve out hefty savings, though Social Security reform could not be packaged that way. Proposed changes would have to be presented as serving only the interests of the Social Security system and its beneficiaries. Stockman joined with Anderson and Schweiker.

The Legislative Strategy Group, which had been preoccupied with winning the Gramm-Latta fight, got the bulky report of Schweiker's task force on Saturday, May 9. A cabinet council meeting, with Reagan in attendance, was scheduled for Monday. The proposals were complex and far-reaching. One of the changes would discourage early retirement by reducing the benefits of those leaving work before age sixty-five. Another would eliminate certain peripheral benefits. A third would lower the proceeds available to "double-dippers"—those who retire early from government jobs, then contribute to the Social Security fund for only a brief period while working in the private sector. A fourth aimed at trimming the checks of those retiring in 1987 and later regardless of age. One of the few sweeteners: eventually, enough would be saved to allow a reduction in payroll deductions.

Trying to analyze the dense proposal in a hurry, White House aides discovered that while the proposed changes would assure solvency, they added up to twice what was necessary. Put another way, Reagan would now be open to the charge that he wanted to "balance the budget on the backs of the elderly," which is exactly what he had promised not to do. Further, the LSG could not envision many Democrats leaping in to support an administration plan along these lines.

The HHS proposal, along with caveats drafted by Darman, went to

Reagan late Sunday. At the Monday meeting, Schweiker assured the President that most of the changes would be "grandfathered." That is, current recipients would not be affected much. Then another possibility was discussed: adding to the pool of current contributors to the system by extending coverage to government workers. At this point, Reagan allowed his old doubts about Social Security to come to the surface. One of the problems with the whole system, he said, is the way it takes resources from the capital pool. Thus any suggestion to get more workers into the Social Security tent disturbed him. Why, he asked, don't we think of a way to let people bail out instead? Why not give employees the option of putting their money into private pension funds? The point was more rhetorical than serious, though it represented Reagan's visceral feeling. The answer is that withdrawal by millions of workers would produce an instant crisis, forcing Washington to pay benefits out of general revenue.

James Baker and others with good political radar thought that Reagan would follow his custom and refrain from making a decision on the spot. In the interim, the proposals might be modified, or tactics for presenting them worked out. But this time Schweiker and Anderson were making what sounded like compelling arguments for speed. Schweiker wanted the Administration to lead the Social Security charge rather than allow Jake Pickle's subcommittee to get out front. Besides, if Congress took the initiative, the final product might involve a raid on the general Treasury. Anderson, normally not a forceful advocate in such meetings, on this occasion made two effective arguments. If you go ahead with this, he told the President, you will be restoring both the long-term and immediate integrity of the system; no other President has managed to come close to doing that. Second, he said, there will be enormous budget implications on the positive side of the ledger. The economic recovery program will get a large boost. Reagan had heard enough. He asked for changes in a couple of the items and approved the rest.

The announcement was set for the next day, May 12, so Baker immediately called an LSG meeting and invited Schweiker to attend. Schweiker insisted that he could assure Democratic support. The Administration would not have to carry the full burden alone. "This is a bipartisan initiative," he said with great emphasis, "*bipartisan.*" The others challenged his judgment. "Damn it!" Schweiker replied, "I spent twenty years in Congress. I should know how things work."

Feeling queasy, Baker ruled that the announcement should come from HHS, in Schweiker's name, in order to put distance between the idea and the President. Darman even suggested that the Social Security Administration put out the news at its headquarters in Baltimore, to as-

158 GAMBLING WITH HISTORY

sure minimal coverage. The next day Schweiker got his moment in the sun of TV lights.

Then reality came crashing down. The Social Security lobby cried rape. In both houses of Congress, on both sides of the aisles, members competed to denounce the Administration's proposal. The Republican leadership on the Hill informed the White House that under no circumstances could a bill incorporating the Administration's ideas be enacted. To assure that the message was clearly understood, the Republican Senate voted, 96 to 0, to reject the plan on principle. For the first time since the election, Democrats had the Administration on the defensive over an important issue, and demagogic rhetoric polluted the air.

Reagan was affronted. He wanted to fight for the program personally. He considered making a request for network time to answer the attacks, to explain the merits of his proposal. The troika talked him out of that. Better to retreat on Social Security, they advised, than to risk the rest of the domestic program in a controversy the White House would doubtless lose. So Reagan gave in, grumbling. In the future he would talk less about amity between the White House and the Hill. The exchanges with O'Neill would become more acidic. Reagan suspected, quite correctly, that he had been sandbagged.

The Democrats were proud of it. The incident allowed O'Neill to charge, over and over, that Reagan was guilty of a "breach of faith" with the elderly. Others took up the cry. Kirk O'Donnell, the Speaker's political aide, looked back on the episode with delight. "That was the only bright spot for us then," he said. "You bet they were ambushed. They were absolutely taken to the cleaners. It was after that when the 'fairness' question became serious."[7]

Of course much more than politics was involved. Stockman would continue to nibble at the edges of Social Security, biting out a billion here or there, but it was soon obvious that no basic reform would be possible until 1983 at the earliest. Meanwhile, expedients would be used to slide past bankruptcy. Stockman's search for credibility and confidence was thwarted, and not for the last time.

Reagan never resigned himself to what had happened, and apparently never accepted the connection between Social Security and the economic recovery program. At the end of the year, without mentioning the issue, I asked him the cliché holiday-season question. With the benefit of hindsight, was there anything he would have done differently? He replied at length:

The one thing, of course, was the handling of the Social Security thing. We did not want to introduce Social Security at the time we did because we didn't want it to appear as a part of . . . cutting government expenses or anything. Social Security is a separate problem. It is on the road to bankruptcy and has been for years. And no one has had the guts to stand up and do something about it . . . I don't know whether we were had or whether someone on the other side, the committee chairman [Pickle] had good intentions and then somehow couldn't make good, but he demanded to know what we were going to do and what we were going to propose . . . And thinking that if they were that anxious to get at the problem too, that whatever we proposed would then be kind of a basis for negotiations, that we'd start from there and have a bipartisan approach to this. There was no such thing . . . They never touched it. They never offered a single suggestion to it. They just started a campaign that I was out to destroy Social Security . . .

It was the kind of defeat that can blow out an administration's tires no matter how much momentum it has going. Nonetheless, the White House managed to regroup. The Reaganauts thought that their next challenge, after the Social Security debacle in mid-May, would be to cut a deal on a revenue measure encompassing most of the Reagan tax program. For more than a month in the White House, on the Hill, at the Treasury, serpentine negotiations had been underway in search of a winning combination.

Before that effort could be carried through, however, a drastic detour had to be taken. Stockman's Office of Management and Budget had been monitoring the work of House committees after the passage of the Gramm-Latta bill. OMB discovered that the Democratic-controlled committees were systematically deviating from the ceilings set by the First Budget Resolution. With an assortment of gimmicks, the Democrats were crafting authorization bills that would save significantly less than intended. Because these measures affect not only the upcoming fiscal year but subsequent budgets as well, the Administration's hope of creating a downward trend in deficits would be in worse jeopardy than ever. The alterations being worked into legislation, Stockman calculated, amounted to nearly $48 billion over the next three fiscal years, or one quarter of the savings projected when Gramm-Latta was approved in May. In fact, the whole deficit strategy was already in serious danger, as Stockman and several of the others well knew. If the Administration allowed further attrition, the larger game would end then and there, even before the tax bill came to a vote.

One alternative was to wage guerrilla warfare, bill by bill, on the House floor and then in House-Senate conference committees. A much bolder option was to engineer another single test, similar to the Gramm-Latta vote in May. This procedure had little precedent. O'Neill, having regained his nerve, was ready to fight. The House Republican leadership was uncertain whether it could defeat the Speaker again. Some of the Boll Weevils and Gypsy Moths would be squeamish about another round of single combat, another exercise in subordinating the power of Congress to the will of the President.

In mid-June the Legislative Strategy Group mulled the problems. Reagan would have to decide, and quickly. The schedule was getting crowded. President José López Portillo of Mexico was coming to visit. Israel had just bombed Iraq. The tax bill still had to be honed. The Reagans were determined to take a brief trip to California late in the month. In July the President would undertake his most important foreign excursion up to that point when he attended the annual Economic Summit in Ottawa, a trip that required substantial preparation.

Late on June 17, Darman drafted a memorandum summarizing the arguments pro and con on the question of what was now being called Gramm-Latta II. That served as a companion to a document from Stockman outlining the math involved. Baker and Darman hoped to get a decision from the President the next morning at a session to be attended by them and other advisers. Darman's paper listed reasons for going ahead, building to this clincher: "If we are successful with Gramm-Latta II, the perception of your leadership and commitment will be strengthened, the traditional House Democratic leadership will be weakened and the prospects of building upon the new bipartisan coalition will be enhanced." As usual, more than the immediate issue was at stake. As usual, the winning-streak mentality was a large factor.

But the Darman memo also conceded the dangers, which Baker insisted that Reagan understand thoroughly: "The votes for Gramm-Latta II are not there now, and it will take a major effort to get them . . . the strategy is risky. If it does not succeed, it will play as a major Administration loss—with an associated loss of momentum that could have adverse effects on other elements of your program."

The memo's final section urged the President to take the risk and to inform the Boll Weevils of his decision by midday. Reagan did not need long to decide. One of the participants jotted down the outcome tersely: "Decision—have lunch w. Boll Weevil ldrship—then *go.*"

Go they did. The vote would take place in just a week. Expendable items on Reagan's schedule were cleared to allow him time to work the phones and to see individual House members. Stockman, meanwhile, bargained with Boll Weevils who this time, realizing that the margin would be thin, demanded quid pro quo. Members from Louisiana and East Texas were particularly interested in modifying the Fuel Use Act in a manner that would benefit suppliers of natural gas. Louisiana members, such as John Breaux and W. J. Tauzin, also sought renewed protection for sugar producers in their districts. Knowing that their votes would be critical, Stockman reluctantly agreed—and Reagan confirmed—that the Administration would reverse its policy on sugar.* That old-fashioned bit of legislative leverage led Breaux to provide a memorable caption for the deals being made: "They're not buying my vote, only renting it."

On Wednesday June 24, when Reagan left Washington on his trip west, Duberstein's nose count still showed the Administration several votes short. The Democratic hierarchy was attempting to make the vote a test of party loyalty, suggesting in a letter to all its House members that retribution might follow defection. That tactic cowed some Democrats but angered others. Reagan responded with a personal appeal for support, drafted on *Air Force One,* to all 253 legislators who had voted with him on Gramm-Latta I.

He stopped in San Antonio that day to address the annual convention of Jaycees, one of the organizations that had lobbied diligently for Reaganomics. It was a feisty, stump-style speech, the kind Reagan loves giving and partisan audiences enjoy hearing. Now he was his natural combative self again, castigating the House Democrats as "advocates of a different philosophy, manning the barricades in those puzzle palaces on the Potomac."

O'Neill, the night before, had attacked Reaganomics as destructive to the nation. Now Reagan responded, to loud applause: "Where on earth has he been all these years? And strangely enough, the answer is, right in Washington, D.C., in a most responsible position in government . . . Those who make such charges want to return to the same old discredited policies that set off America's economic high fever in the first place."

Back on the plane, heading for Los Angeles, the presidential party received from the Legislative Strategy Group encouraging word: the gap was narrowing. The tacticians zeroed in on fence-sitters. Reagan called sixteen Democrats that afternoon and evening, then stroked a few Republicans the next morning. He started, typically, by saying, "I know you're in a difficult spot and getting a lot of pressure, but—" When the response was positive, Reagan frequently said, "Well, God bless you."

By Wednesday night the Democratic leadership was employing a shrewd tactic, holding up the "rule"—the parliamentary scenario—under which the votes would be taken. O'Neill's lieutenants, James Wright and Dick Bolling, wanted to deny the Republicans a chance at a single up-or-down decision. That meant there would have to be a

---

* The Administration had been attempting, with spotty success, to reduce agricultural subsidies. The 1981 deal led eventually to the imposition of sugar import quotas for the first time in seven years as a means of forcing prices up.

procedural vote Thursday before Reagan's partisans would have their shot. Both sides now knew that every seat would count. Further, there would be some switching after the first vote on procedure. Reagan reached Breaux while the congressman was dining at the F Street Club; Breaux would still not commit himself that evening. Ralph Hall was sitting down to dinner at the University Club with three like-minded Democrats when the maitre d' brought a phone to the table. This quartet, representing Texas, Oklahoma and Louisiana, was interested primarily in the Fuel Use Act. They had already received an encouraging indication from White House aides that their concern would be satisfied. They were leaning toward Reagan now and told him so.

Thursday morning, waiting to speak at a luncheon meeting at the Century Plaza Hotel, Reagan sat in the drawing room of the nineteenth-floor suite making one last round of phone calls. Deaver was across the room on an open line to Darman, back at the White House, who was providing a minute-by-minute progress report on the struggle. Senator Bob Dole came on Reagan's line, ostensibly to report on another matter—his Finance Committee's handling of the tax bill. Abruptly Dole changed the subject, saying something about the House. Reagan wasn't sure he understood. As Dole repeated his bulletin, Deaver let out a whoop and waved excitedly to his boss. But Darman and Deaver had been scooped. Deaver heard Reagan say to Dole: "Oh my God! You've got the news on the House vote. I just can't believe it!" The Administration had just won the procedural round, 217 to 210. All the Republicans present had remained in the Reagan corral. The Administration got just twenty-nine Democrats, enough to win, but fewer than half the number that had cooperated the preceding month.

Reagan descended to the hotel's Los Angeles Ballroom below ground, the same chamber in which he had greeted his followers on election night, to have lunch with the local taxpayers' association. While doing total justice to his filet mignon, salad and strawberry shortcake, he received additional news from Washington about the continuing contest on the Hill. Portions of the speech he was about to give had to be discarded because they were written with defeat in mind. Craig Fuller drafted new material just before Reagan stood up to proclaim "a great victory . . . the greatest reduction in government spending that has ever been attempted."

Actually, the victory wasn't quite won when Reagan spoke. In the House of Representatives, members and Administration lobbyists now engaged in an orgy of bargaining and last-minute amendments, several of which involved billions of dollars. Tip O'Neill and Jim Wright staged a series of counterattacks that lasted until the following day.

Much of the bickering involved a complex package called the Broyhill Amendment, coming up late in the sequence of tests, all of which were being settled by margins of half-dozen votes or less. The Republicans and the Gramm faction wanted the Broyhill Amendment because it would save $7 billion more over the next three years than the measure it replaced. Stockman, personally monitoring the action from a room near the House floor, recalled what happened next:

> Everybody was exhausted and some members were hitting the streets, heading for the airport. We had won so far by the skin of our teeth. The Boll Weevils got Bob Michel on the floor and said, "Don't offer the Broyhill Amendment because we just can't go through this again." So Broyhill was pulled. The dickering we had done all afternoon was for naught . . . It was one of those decisions made in about four minutes as a result of sheer chemistry—the time of day, the sequence of events, how tired the players are. Basically it was the right decision because if we had lost it, we also might have lost the whole reconciliation bill on final passage.[8]

The omnibus bill itself was a physical monstrosity because segments of it had been patched together so hastily. Figures requiring deciphering appeared in the margin. Somehow the name and telephone number of a staff member who had helped with the drafting turned up in the legislative language. Few members knew exactly what all the provisions meant. The document lacked page numbers and an index. Not merely numbers were involved, but alterations in benefit formulas that would have important impact for years to come. Ralph Hall, who had supplied one of the crucial votes on Thursday, went the other way on Friday. "Basically I couldn't vote for it because I didn't know what was in it," he explained. "What I don't know, I don't like." But by the time the frattered legislators got to the final vote on Friday, everyone knew the outcome. The bill went through by a comfortable margin of 232 to 193 even if no one, including David Stockman, could know exactly how many billions had been added and subtracted until OMB computers reviewed all the changes.

Reagan now was on a truly astonishing roll. In just five months he had begun, in material terms, to alter the course of government. After June 26, little stood in the way of yet another significant change in the way Washington dealt with the pocketbooks of all Americans. The impact of it all was still a mystery. Inflation was moderating at last in the first days of summer, but otherwise the economy showed symptoms of worsening anemia. Stockman's marvelous expectations were yet to materialize. None of these uncertainties deterred the White House from the next major engagement. Winning was fun; it sharpened the appetite for still more victory.

10

The Missing Pony

Curbing expenditures gave Reagan pleasure, but the prospect of obtaining the largest package of tax reductions in history yielded ecstasy. To attack spending is tortuous business. One must navigate the budget maze and decide who will suffer more, who less, from the austerity measures. The tax side of the equation is cleaner. The decisions there involve who *benefits* more and who less. Once the legislation is enacted, the deed is done. Besides, taming the tax ogre was the core of Reaganism's long-term goal. "Government doesn't tax to get the money it spends," one of his favorite lines ran. "Government will always find more needs for the money it gets." Permanent reform required a degree of Treasury starvation.

When Gramm-Latta II was enacted, tax-bill strategy had been evolving for two months. At the same time, orthodox Republicans in Congress, including Robert Dole, chairman of the Senate Finance Committee, and Pete Domenici, head of the Senate Budget Committee, were growing nervous about the deficit problem. Neither Dole nor Domenici was a supply-sider, nor was Majority Leader Howard Baker. They were relatively conventional conservatives, loyal to the party and the President, delighted to be in the majority for the first time in their Senate careers. But they were also practical politicians. It was Baker, after all, who had likened Reaganomics to a "riverboat gamble." They were sure that they could get a huge tax bill through the Senate, but they began to have doubts about the wisdom of it.

On June 4, Domenici visited James Baker and Darman at the White House to convey his anxiety. The Administration's claim of a descending deficit line was no longer believed by anyone in command of simple arithmetic. Instead of a balance in fiscal '84, it appeared then that the shortfall was growing to $60 billion in that year. As the Senate Republicans saw it, this would be politically and economically ruinous. Domenici urged the White House advisers to find additional credible spending cuts or improve the outlook in some other way. Chief of Staff Baker responded that they were working on it.

The Baker axis at the White House, which on this issue included Stockman, Darman, Fuller and Gergen, did not require the danger signal. Stockman and Darman in particular, aware of the threat early, had watched it grow. Now these two discussed a bit of heresy. Standing on West Executive Avenue, the alley running between the Old Executive Office Building and the White House's West Wing, they realized that each had the same questions about the tax bill. Do we really want to lose so much revenue? Do we really want to win in the House of Representatives?

It was possible, they reasoned, to go ahead full tilt in the Senate and take the easy victory while at the same time throwing the game in the House. There a much more modest bill could be passed. Then a compromise would be worked out in the House-Senate conference committee. The Administration would settle for a less grandiose victory than was possible. Tens of billions in revenue would be saved, the deficit problem ameliorated. The effect on interest rates would probably be favorable, giving the economy a boost, and the Administration could hope to approach the 1982 election in a strong position.

Tempting as the self-sabotage ploy seemed, it was never seriously considered in the Legislative Strategy Group. Nor did the idea get to Reagan. Stockman and Darman themselves cooled on it. Taking a dive in the House could not be done secretly. As soon as the news got out, Reagan's image as a firm leader would be damaged. The conservative coalition in the House, always fragile, would suffer because the Boll Weevils would feel betrayed. Some of them had already signed up to oppose their party leadership yet again. Further, the Administration was on record, as of June 4, as being in full support of the Hance-Conable revenue bill, in which the Gramm-Latta legislative tactic was being repeated.* The LSG knew that Reagan's hatred for reversing himself, not to mention his affection for tax reduction, would make him reject any scheme to undercut his own plan.

That tax scheme, however, had undergone remarkable transformation in a few months. Originally the new administration had favored a

---

* Barber Conable of New York was the senior Republican on the House Ways and Means Committee, which originates tax legislation. Kent Hance of Texas, a junior Democrat on the committee, played a role similar to Phil Gramm's in making the measure ostensibly bipartisan.

"clean bill," which in legislative lingo means a measure devoid of complicated ornaments appended to attract factional support. The initial proposal had only two significant parts: the "ten-ten-ten" reductions for individual taxpayers and a drastic improvement of depreciation allowances for business. The latter was designed as a stimulant for genuine investment. For the three fiscal years 1982–84, the entire package was to cost the Treasury roughly $300 billion in revenue loss on a "static" basis—that is, discounting what new income would be derived from additional economic activity inspired by lower taxes.

At the time, the Administration was asking spending reductions of only $197 billion over the same three years. In fact, no one believed that the White House would get that much (it did not). This opening disparity of $100 billion between savings and lost tax revenue was one of the reasons for the continuing skepticism about the Administration's ability to balance the budget.

The concept of a clean bill did not survive long. The Democratic response was to denounce the Reagan approach as irresponsible on the deficit issue and pro-plutocrat on the fairness question. Between March and early June, nonetheless, both sides toyed with the idea of a compromise. The central player on the Democratic side, besides O'Neill, was Danny Rostenkowski of Illinois, the new Ways and Means Committee chairman. Rostenkowski, no less than Jones on the budget issue, wanted paternity of whatever measure was enacted.

Rostenkowski started by hanging tough, declaring in a speech on April 9 that he would push only a one-year tax bill. But as the weeks passed and he watched Jones's position deteriorate on the spending issue, Rostenkowski realized that he might be outflanked by a coalition of Boll Weevils and Republicans. He began to hint that he might be amenable to a two-year bill. Then, in an attempt to establish a coalition of their own, the Democrats took a bold step. They decided to incorporate in their proposal an important supply-side measure: reduction of the top marginal rate on unearned income from 70 percent to 50 percent. This was the idea Reagan had reluctantly surrendered in February for fear of being charged with catering to the wealthy. The gambit's purpose was to attract some House Republicans to the Democratic Ways and Means bill with the lure of the 70/50 change. In the Senate, meanwhile, various members of the Finance Committee began to advance their own pet tax ideas. That is the traditional approach to tax legislation: to use a basic bill as a pickup truck to haul along the desires of assorted special interests. One virtue of genuine compromise between the White House and Rostenkowski would have been to head off a bidding war.

On May 12 Reagan and his advisers held a crucial meeting. The President had before him a detailed memorandum showing that (1) potential revenue loss from the tax bill was worsening the out-year deficit problem to a dangerous point and (2) Rostenkowski might still accept a compromise on a two-year bill. In fact, a draft statement already existed, unsigned, to which the senior members of the two Senate and House committees might agree. Reagan was told explicitly that the three-year bill was going to produce a revenue loss in 1984 of roughly $151 billion and that the implication for the deficit was accordingly grave.

The President did not slam the door on a possible deal. He accepted a modification of the ten-ten-ten scheme, for instance, to offset new features that were being added. Now the individual reductions would be 5 percent the first year and 10 each in the second and third. He welcomed the addition of the 70/50 change, which he had favored all along anyway, and accepted a relief provision for two-earner families —amelioration of the so-called "marriage penalty." Don Regan was authorized to continue dickering with Rostenkowski. However, Reagan also accepted a balancing tactic, described cryptically in the agenda for the meeting as "squeeze Rostenkowski by warming up to Hance." Translation: threaten Rostenkowski with total loss of control unless he meets the White House's demands.

Rostenkowski vacillated for a time, but in a breakfast meeting with the Treasury Secretary on May 28 he finally said no. He would stick with a one-year bill. Administration tacticians decided that they were nonetheless still in a controlling position. At worst they would get the bill they wanted from the Senate, the Rostenkowski measure from the House and then compromise in conference. At best they would trounce Rostenkowski. Dennis Thomas, one of the Treasury Department lobbyists, recalled the mood: "The whole thing defied normal legislative process, in which you would make your proposal and then are delighted if you got three quarters of what you said you wanted. We were in a no-lose position, so we were able to go for broke."[1]

Neither side wanted to seem intransigent, however, so the Democratic leadership agreed to see Reagan on June 1 for one more effort at striking a bargain. The issue, after all, involved tens of billions in tax revenue and, quite possibly, the welfare of the economy. In preparation for the meeting, the LSG prepared a four-page memorandum for the President. The document demonstrated the high quality of the Reaganauts' political intelligence network on the Hill. It also showed the close intersection of personal interests and public policy as it analyzed Rostenkowski's position:

> Some think that he would like to have compromised last week, but that he simply could not control the left side of his committee. He is in a difficult situation. He now runs the risk of being "rolled" in his first time out as chairman of Ways and Means (and with his eye on the Speakership). On

the other hand, by not compromising with us he preserves his position with O'Neill and with the liberal wing of the Democratic party. And if— as they think likely—our economic policies fail, they could become the ultimate winners.

The memorandum, prescient in more ways than one, went on to predict that there would be no deal. The meeting came to nothing. Within three days the White House struck a bargain with the Boll Weevils. Soon the allies were fighting on two fronts as the second round of the Gramm-Latta issue got underway. The conservative Democrats needed reassurance as they wandered still farther from their party's leadership. They also feared wavering among the Republicans because certain Gypsy Moths were restless. On June 4 Reagan sat down to breakfast with several of the Democratic rebels, whose first question was about Republican unity. Reagan assured his guests that Minority Leader Bob Michel would hold the line, and that the White House was committed as well. Said the President: "Five-ten-ten is as far as I can go and I can't retreat any further. We've told that to the GOP leadership [in the House]. We will fight for it."

Breaux of Louisiana expressed a different concern looking toward 1982. "We don't want to wind up as politicians without a party," he said. "We're worried about getting in a position where both Republicans and Democrats oppose us [in their home districts]." The best Reagan could do on that score was to pledge that he would not personally campaign against any Democrat who stuck with the Administration on the major issues. "No way," Reagan said. "I couldn't look myself in the mirror if I went out and campaigned against you."

But there was also no way in which Reagan could respond to the risk, mentioned half in jest by Ralph Hall. "We're in the position," said the freshman member from Texas, "whereby if the GOP holds the House in 1983, they won't need us. If the Democrats hold the House, they won't want us." Reagan could only repeat his pledge to avoid personal campaigning against his new allies.

After Gramm-Latta II was disposed of on June 26, the Reaganauts staged a month-long blitz for their tax bill, reinforced by outside conservative political groups and business organizations. It turned out to be the busiest, most trying period of Reagan's first year in office. Alexander Haig and Jeane Kirkpatrick had the first of what turned out to be a series of public spats. The Ottawa Economic Summit with six allies interrupted the President's domestic lobbying effort. Then the Israelis interrupted the Summit by bombing Beirut; new war in the Middle East seemed imminent. The air traffic controllers were threatening to strike.

The White House was not simply campaigning for a bill. It was still rewriting the tax legislation in order to meet the Democrats' competi-

tion. The House leadership was changing its measure as well, making it
more like the Administration's in some ways. The White House and
Treasury, with an eye on the deficit problem, tried to stretch out the
depreciation benefits being given to corporations. That created a backlash from the Washington business lobbyists, who marched on Jim
Baker with an ultimatum: go back to the original formula or we might
defect to the Rostenkowski bill. They split the difference. Along the
way, the original Hance-Conable measure was revised so drastically
that the new version had to be called Hance-Conable II. It was now a
cornucopia with something for almost everyone: special assistance for
corporations too poor to benefit from the new depreciation allowance
formula, a bailout for the savings and loan associations, a reduction in
the capital gains levy, a big break for American executives working
abroad, a return to favored treatment for recipients of stock options,
concessions for small oil producers. On and on the list of goodies went.

The Democrats all but abandoned their "responsibility" argument.
Their bill, by the time the test came, would have cost slightly *more* in
revenue over the next two years than the Administration measure. Only
in the third year did the equation reverse. In fact, the important
differences in the rival measures finally came down to two. The Democratic rate tables were more favorable to those earning less than
$50,000 a year. More important, the Democratic bill assured only two
successive annual tax cuts, totaling 15 percent, with a third installment
contingent on a "trigger" device. That is, the third installment would
come only if economic conditions were favorable. Hance-Conable II
retained three installments, now five-ten-ten, though the effective date
of the first was pushed back again, this time to October 1, 1981, to
save small change.

O'Neill seemed to be making headway with his claim that his party's
bill was more generous to middle-income families. Reagan, soon after
returning from Ottawa, visited members of the Republican House Caucus. "The Speaker," Reagan said, "boasts that his tax cut of fifteen percent gives a bigger break to the worker than our bill. And if you're
only planning on living for two years, it does." Immediately pro-Administration lobbyists seeded Washington with buttons bearing the
message I PLAN TO LIVE. On July 27, two days before both houses
would vote, Reagan requested network prime time. It was, by common
consent of ally and adversary, his best television performance up to
that time. Reagan was confident, in command of his material, crisp in
his delivery. He framed the gut issue, as usual, in very simple terms:

> If the tax cut goes to you, the American people, in the third year, that
> money . . . won't be available to the Congress to spend, and that, in my
> view, is what this whole controversy comes down to. Are you entitled to

the fruits of your own labor or does government have some presumptive right to spend and spend and spend?

Reagan appealed to his audience to tell their congressmen their feelings. Phone calls and telegrams came in profusion, many from organized groups but some from ordinary citizens as well. The ratio was overwhelmingly in favor of the Administration. One Texas Democrat amused reporters in the House press gallery with a rueful tribute to Reagan's pulling power: "I sure hope he doesn't go on television to promote the elimination of fucking." Bo Ginn of Georgia, who had been ambivalent about which way to go, spoke for many Democrats when he lamented: "The constituents broke our doors down. It wasn't very subtle."[2] The actual votes on July 29 lacked suspense. The Senate went for the Administration 89 to 11—a devastating defiance of Democratic party unity. Only one Republican Senator left the GOP fold. Reagan's victory in the House was solid enough, 238 to 195. He lost one Republican, the maverick Jeffords, while attracting 48 Democrats.

Soon Reagan was off to California for a four-week holiday. While at Rancho del Cielo he invited reporters to his mountain sanctuary to watch him sign both the tax and reconciliation bills. The day was foggy and damp, but Reagan was sunshine incarnate in the denims and boots he wears so comfortably. It was a historic turnaround, he said, after fifty years of going in the wrong direction. He shrugged off a question about deficits and said he was not sure whether a recession was starting or not, though he forecast a "soggy" economy for months to come.

A few days later in Los Angeles he denied vehemently any reevaluation of the '82 deficit estimate. The newly signed legislation provided for total tax reduction of $280 billion over the following three years, roughly the same amount the Administration had sought, though now arranged in a different mix. The reconciliation bill, however, envisioned only $130 billion in savings over the same period, or $70 billion less than originally requested, and less than half the amount of the prospective revenue loss. When he was making his chirpy statements in mid-August, his senior advisers had already informed him in detail that Reaganomics was hitting the reefs. Some kind of major salvage operation would be necessary. He had also been told that OMB's *Mid-Session Review of the 1982 Budget,* published on July 15, was both obsolete and deceptive even before it went to the printer.*

This dour news had been conveyed in a formal Oval Office meeting on August 3, just after passage of the tax act. It was the same day the Professional Air Traffic Controllers Organization started a nationwide

* Each April and July the Administration is required to publish up-to-date estimates of its basic economic assumptions and to give a progress report on the current and upcoming budgets.

strike, and two days before the arrival in Washington of Anwar Sadat, whom Reagan would be meeting for the first time. The President, one of his assistants noted, was not much in the mood for a lengthy confidential meeting in midday concerning economic problems. He had been immersed in that subject for months, done his duty and then some, won his fights. What he really wanted to do was follow Congress out of town, the sooner the better, pausing only to fire the strikers. That was done with dispatch. So the President was a little distracted that day, in the mood to rebel, for once, against the tyranny of his schedule. Impossible, the troika told him. There were some things he had to hear.

Sure enough, Reagan's attention came into sharp focus as he sat down to lunch in the Cabinet Room with the Vice-President, Don Regan and nine others. Stockman, still the most authoritative voice on economic affairs, did much of the talking. The government, he said, was suffering a "fiscal hangover" from the recent legislative binge. He went on, mixing metaphors. "We've only slowed, not stopped, the budget hemorrhage." As the result of the "rolling momentum" of past spending practices, as well as new commitments for defense expenditures, the Administration now faced "a stark gap." Stockman, with his knack for dramatic delivery and speaking italic, warned that Reagan would have to confront *"strategic* choices, *fundamental* choices," even if the tax cuts produced some degree of enhanced economic activity.

The Budget Director posed a number of questions. Should we retain budget balance in fiscal '84 as a stated goal though it seemed unlikely to be achieved until 1987 at the earliest? Should we modify defense spending plans? Should we look for alternative revenue sources? If not, are we prepared to go after deep spending reductions beyond what was originally thought necessary?

His own July 15 Mid-Session Review, ironically, had lowered the prospective '82 deficit slightly, from $45 billion to $42.5 billion. Now Stockman was acknowledging that was rubbish. The deficit was shaping up as $60 billion or more. Unless strong measures were taken, the deficit line would then climb.* Stockman suggested an ascending schedule of spending cuts in addition to what was already planned.

Frowning, Reagan interjected: "We should just say to all the agencies, 'To the rear, march.'"

Stockman tried a touch of disingenuous humor. "So far, this is the good news. What happens if the economic assumptions we've been using turn out to be wrong?" There are those, he said, who think the Administration's forecasts of economic growth, unemployment, interest rates and the rest have been too optimistic. By then, of course, Stockman was one of "those." His July 15 review had maintained the opti-

* In fact, the fiscal '82 budget deficit turned out to be $110.7 billion.

mistic scenario outlined the previous winter. Murray Weidenbaum's Council of Economic Advisers had the nominal responsibility for monitoring those assumptions. Now Weidenbaum willingly shared that power. "As a group," he told Reagan, "your advisers decided that the midyear review should not be changed. It would have confused the tax picture." Translation: had the Administration admitted what it knew when it knew it, the case for gargantuan tax reduction would have been undermined.

Reagan considered the public relations aspect of what he was hearing. If this information were generally known, he said, "Tip O'Neill would be wearing a halo." The Democrats would be vindicated politically. Don Regan wondered aloud whether the Administration, in preparing its next forecast, should go with another optimistic projection or whether it should be "more realistic."

None of this, of course, was a surprise to Reagan. He had received intimations of difficulty ahead, though not of such severity. Now he said that he still wished to aim for a balanced budget in '84. Missing the goal by "a little" should not be a political problem. People will be forgiving, he said, provided that they feel we've worked hard at it. Implicitly, at least, Reagan acknowledged that additional cost cutting would be necessary. He recalled some of his experiences as governor, when he sought across-the-board reductions in administrative expenses.

Meese, trying to sum up the session, said that the White House had only a short time to make some big decisions. They should be taken promptly, so that the cabinet could be given new marching orders. Reagan, still thinking about overhead, asked whether the employment freeze he had imposed on Inauguration Day was still in effect. No, Stockman informed him. The ceilings are low, but the formal freeze had been removed. "Well," Reagan replied, "we're still basically lathered in fat where employment in the federal government is concerned." He suggested forced reductions.

On one point the President was adamant. There must be no perception "by anyone in the world" that he was abandoning the military buildup. That must take priority. At the same time, he said, we might be able to slow the rate of increase. The meeting broke up without clearcut decisions. However, some of the participants came away feeling, first, that Reagan would be willing to consider at least token reductions in the Pentagon budget. Second, he acknowledged, at least tacitly, that other measures would have to be taken as well. But, just as important, the President clearly did not share the sense of urgency Stockman had conveyed.

They could not know it at the time but the men who ate lunch in the Cabinet Room on August 3 and digested Stockman's heavy message were at a turning point. For some Presidents, such bends in the political road are dramatic, almost instantly visible. In Lyndon Johnson's case, the Tet offensive in Vietnam quickly led to Eugene McCarthy's strong showing in the New Hampshire primary. For Richard Nixon, it was John Dean's Watergate testimony. There was nothing so vivid, or so decisive, during Reagan's first two years.

Still, a political wind shear was occurring, made up of gusts from several sources. Within a few weeks Wirthlin detected it in his polling returns. The public was feeling renewed anxiety about where the country was heading. The tone of press coverage began to change. That was partly because of oddities, as we have seen, such as the failure to awaken Reagan with news of the Libyan dogfight. But there was more to it. There was a sense that Reagan's staff, so adroit until that point, had relaxed its grip on the initiative, and hence on events. That the troika physically dispersed during the August hiatus, with only one member on duty with Reagan, was a mistake. That Reagan took four weeks off at one stretch, during which he generated little positive news, was a bigger mistake. "After the tax vote," one of his aides recalled later in the year, "it was like a gun going off at the end of a football game. It was natural that everyone wanted to relax before getting up for the next game."

Circumstances demanded something else. Members of Congress, back home in their states and districts, were getting vehement complaints about interest rates and the growing number of bankruptcies. When Reagan, on August 17 and 18, sat down at the Century Plaza for conferences with his aides, the prime rate had settled at 20.5 percent, far too high for business activity to increase. The average yield for tax-free municipals rose a third of a point in just one day, a startling jag upward, and stood at 12.66, or 3.5 higher than the previous year. The Dow Jones industrial index now was down 100 points from its high in April, and would continue sinking. Unemployment was rising—no one imagined then how high that measure of misery would reach—and GNP was faltering. Later, economists of all schools would agree that the recession of 1981–82 started just as Reagan was winning the tax fight. Stockman's game of expectations was now over, though he would not yet acknowledge defeat even to himself.

Reagan during his first six months had demonstrated mastery over Congress, and to a lesser extent over public opinion. No President, regardless of how adept and knowledgeable he is, can maneuver the national economy as if it were a high-performance fighter plane. The economy is more like a huge hot-air balloon, as much subject to air currents as to the manipulation of its pilot. But even the balloonist can try a few tricks.

For the next seven months Reagan was uncertain as to what tricks to attempt. As conditions worsened and political pressure on him increased, Reagan found himself at odds with his closest aides and with his supporters in Congress as well. Disagreement afflicted the broader circle of his advisers. Reagan frequently was torn between them, just as he had immense difficulty choosing among his own priorities when they came into conflict. During the first half of the year, Reagan was able to exploit his personal assets superbly—his skill as a public advocate, the quality of appearing to be firm but reasonable at the same time, his ability to convey confidence, his seemingly inexhaustible supply of luck. Even getting shot, ironically, had its fortunate side for him. During the next phase some of his faults came to the fore. His disdain of detail cost him, and so did his reluctance to impose discipline on his subordinates. What earlier appeared to be laudable consistency based on principle later came across, on occasion, as stubbornness resting on misconceptions.

His optimism, as genuine a part of his makeup as his love of the outdoors, was a tonic in the gloomy atmosphere of 1980 as well as during the early combat of 1981. Now it helped him to resist the alarms he was hearing. One of the favorite items in his repertoire of stories deals with two little boys, an incurable malcontent and an invincible optimist. The first, given a roomful of toys, abuses every one of them until none of them works. The second, given only a huge mound of manure, digs happily into this redolent gift because he knows "there has to be a pony in there someplace." Reagan told that little tale often enough during private meetings to make "the pony" a code word in the White House for Reagan's resistance to bad news. Trouble was, the pile of manure kept growing while the pony remained elusive.

11

The Fall Offensive

Military spending had to be the target. There was no question about this within the Baker-Stockman faction because, with Social Security insulated, there was no other large cache of funds at which to aim. Further, it was time to rectify a terrifying omission, the result of the velocity with which the White House had hurtled through the first half year. The Defense Department budget had to be coordinated with the rest of the program.

That appeared essential for both fiscal and political reasons. Further economies were required. Through August, civilian spending had taken the hits while Pentagon expenditure plans had ballooned. This was a difficult equation to defend on Capitol Hill as the Administration began to frame revisions to be submitted in the fall. Stockman and Baker reasoned that if large repairs were to be made, it would have to be done between Labor Day and Christmas. Once Congress slipped into election-year mentality, the chances for additional spending cuts or revenue increases would be reduced. Reagan's bargaining position would be improved if he showed some give on his defense priority.

Originally Stockman had thought that Defense Secretary Caspar Weinberger would be an easy mark, that there was so much lard in Pentagon operations that tens of billions could be saved without impeding the actual force buildup Reagan demanded. His gloomy warnings at the August 3 meeting in the Oval Office had been the opening barrage for an assault on the Pentagon. Now, two weeks later in California, a presidential ruling would be obtained on specific figures. With that decision in hand, the White House could put together a package of fiscal changes for prompt submission to Congress when it reconvened after Labor Day.

It seemed to be a reasonable plan. The Pentagon, after all, had gone beyond the Administration's own plans for spending increases. How had that happened? In the quicksand of defense spending, which we can explore here only on the periphery, it wasn't difficult. During 1980 there was a bipartisan consensus that defense required a significant increase. The country's military machinery and force structure had simply run down. The Reaganauts, during the fall of the election year, had estimated that a 5 percent increase in "real" terms—beyond the impact of inflation—would probably suffice. However, when Carter's fiscal '82 budget came out in January showing just that rise, Reagan's people decided that they would have to up the bidding. The Soviet Union would have to learn that the new management in Washington must be taken more seriously than the old. For planning purposes, the real increase for the coming years was pegged at 7 percent annually.

But 7 percent of what base? This was not completely clear in January and February. Should the percentage rise be measured against actual expenditures in fiscal '81? Against Carter's proposal for 1982? Against the somewhat higher 1982 figure that emerged from Weinberger's quick recalculation of the Carter program? Each of these alternatives involved a significant increase over the 1981 outlay of $157 billion. The difference between each spending path was also large—as much as $20 billion in 1983, another $20 billion in 1984, more than $30 billion in 1985 and so on. Weinberger now was insisting on the most grandiose option. That was the one, after all, which had been written into the March budget submission.

Stockman claimed that it was all a mistake—"more my negligence than anything else," he said—because back in March the long-range defense program was still being refined. "The amount of effort and thought that went into the rest of the program," Stockman said privately in late August, "was totally absent in the case of Defense's top line. I thought these were plugs, fillers until we had a program developed. They thought these were sacred commitments that could only be moved in an upward direction, if they got moved at all . . . There has been a total disjunction in the first six months between defense and security policy on the one hand and budget policy on the other. We're now in the throes of threading these two inseparable questions back together again."[1]

The thread kept snapping, however. On August 18, when Reagan sat with Weinberger, Stockman and others in the Century Plaza's penthouse, Weinberger showed no give at all. By then the "FYDP," or Five-Year Defense Plan, was completed. It was based on the highest of the available spending paths. For the fiscal years 1982–84 alone, the period of most concern then for fiscal planning purposes, cumulative defense outlays would rise $92 billion above 1981. Weinberger was not prepared to discuss the impact of a possible reduction from that figure.

Presiding at the session, Reagan clearly did not wish to make a stark choice between his budget and political advisers on the one hand and Weinberger on the other. The President was uneasy with this clash between his own conflicting imperatives, fiscal versus military. He was also distressed at the prospect of choosing between trusted subordinates. The degree of Reagan's confidence in Weinberger, who had served him in Sacramento and as an unofficial counselor later, was something else that Baker and Stockman had not counted on.

That exaggerated respect for Weinberger made it all the more distressing for Reagan when the Defense Secretary insisted that it was impossible to retreat from the numbers already in the budget without damaging the military program in substantive ways. Though James Baker was under the impression that Reagan would order a three-year adjustment of between $20 billion and $29 billion, the President on August 18 made no decision. Instead, he used those figures as guidelines. Could we live with them? What activities would have to be stretched out? Stockman had specific proposals but Weinberger did not. Reagan wanted a compromise. He wanted his Defense Secretary and his Budget Director to come back to him with numbers they agreed upon. So the question was deferred for a week with the understanding that the Pentagon would reexamine its position. Ed Meese would serve as mediator. What happened, and failed to happen, over the next four weeks was the strangest episode of the 1981 budget wars.

By August 26 the entourage was in Santa Barbara because Reagan was at Rancho del Cielo. A meeting of all the advisers was called for that day in cottage number eight at the Biltmore Hotel. Security agents swept the room for bugging devices and then sealed the french doors, making the atmosphere uncomfortably close. Meese presided in Reagan's absence. He came into the session expecting to hear from his old colleague, Weinberger, the details of how cuts might be accommodated. Instead the Defense Secretary gave a lengthy argument in opposition to any significant changes. "We have a hollow army with units not ready for combat," he said. Three hours and twenty minutes later, the group had made no progress; Meese would have no specific choices to lay before the President. His response was to tell Weinberger that the Pentagon must prepare, promptly, analysis of two options. Meanwhile, work on other components of the new fiscal package was put in abeyance.

Weinberger and his deputy, Frank Carlucci, produced their study on

September 3, though Baker, Stockman and Darman did not get it until the following day. The Pentagon had produced charts illustrated with soldiers of varying sizes, each representing a budget target. The one carrying the legend REAGAN in large block letters was a brute of a warrior. The one standing for the OMB approach was a pygmy by comparison. "It could have been worse," Stockman quipped to a colleague. "Mine could have been a woman without a gun." The Defense Department was still fighting a delaying action.

At this stage the anxiety level in the White House was rising. The Congressional Budget Office had a new study out challenging the White House's figures. Congress would be back in session the following week and the LSG was eager to take the initiative. The advance signals were nervous-making. The legislators were getting abuse from their constituents about interest rates. Some congressional leaders began to threaten a statutory attack on the Federal Reserve Board, a gesture that always makes the financial markets even more uneasy. Labor Day weekend slowed the pace a little, though Darman, Fuller and Gergen stayed at it on the last holiday of summer in order to devise a schedule for the first two weeks of what they were now calling "the fall offensive." That schedule called for yet another network speech by Reagan on September 14 in which the President would explain why new moves were necessary. But the agenda for the September 8 LSG meeting indicated the frame of mind. Item number three: "What is the ostensible peg for the '82 changes—financial markets? Congressional appropriations overruns? How do we explain why Gramm-Latta wasn't enough and why we've come back so soon?"

Good questions, but the tacticians had no answers. Nor did they have a Pentagon spending track. The morning after Labor Day, Reagan sat down with the economic experts for yet another look at the defense puzzle and related matters. The meeting wasn't set up to yield a decision—that was hoped for the next day—but Reagan said something that chilled the Baker group: "If it comes down to balancing the budget or [adequate funds for] defense, the balanced budget will have to give way." Later, as the meeting broke up, Reagan repeated one of his constant admonitions: "Worldwide, what we're doing in defense must be seen as different than Carter. It must be a symbol of a change of climate as regards defense." Reagan may have been avoiding total immersion in foreign affairs, but he was not forgetting for a moment admonitions from both Haig and Weinberger that defense spending would have to be rattled loudly for effect overseas.

Preparing for the September 9 meeting and what they hoped would be a firm defense spending decision, Fuller and Darman drafted an elaborate "decision memorandum" for Reagan, along with backup ma-

terial that filled a blue ring binder. By now there were six different reduction proposals, the largest coming from Malcolm Baldrige, the Secretary of Commerce, who advocated knocking out $56 billion from
Weinberger's allotment over three years. Once the meeting began,
Weinberger insisted on giving the President a full briefing, complete
with charts flipped by Carlucci, on why any significant reduction would
be destructive. Stockman responded with his own lecture, his own
charts. While the adversaries rehearsed these now-familiar arguments,
Reagan's felt-tip pen traced paths on the lengthy option paper in front
of him. The meeting ended without resolution; Reagan admonished
Weinberger and Stockman to "work together."

That afternoon, a familiar scene was acted out. Meese and Baker
conferred privately with Reagan in order to elicit the real decision. Still
using the option paper with six alternatives, they agreed on $20 billion
over the three years—the low end of Stockman's proposed range, but
nearly twice what Weinberger had finally been prepared to surrender.
That should have ended the matter. However, neither Reagan, Meese
nor Baker is a sharp-pencil man. The numbers they thought added up
to $20 billion in reduced outlays had come from the wrong columns.*

When Weinberger was called in to the White House the next day,
Thursday the tenth, to hear Reagan's decision, he was pleasantly
surprised. As Weinberger understood the ruling conveyed to him personally by the President, the budget was to be reduced even less, in
immediate cash terms, than his own last offer. "Cap left that meeting a
happy man," one aide said later. The scenario then called for Weinberger and Stockman to get together one last time to decide how the
changes were to be distributed. During a routine gathering that afternoon, the President told his Budget Director, "You'd better be going.
You've got an important meeting with Cap." Stockman left, thinking
that the fix was in for $20 billion in outlays. He returned to the
White House stunned. The deal would have to be renegotiated, he
said, and the President would have to do it.

Jim Baker was now in a difficult spot. He was known to be partial to
Stockman, so it would have been imprudent for him to tell the President that Weinberger had unzipped the bargain. Meese had left town
for yet another of his weekends away. That left Deaver, who knew

* In federal budget practice, an "outlay" is an actual cash expenditure in a
particular fiscal year. Two other types of figures, under the headings of "budget
authority" and "total obligational authority," have different connotations. They
designate spending commitments that will be made in one year but will be paid
out over a number of years. Until this point the debate had been in terms of
outlays, or hard cash. The President had inadvertently switched to budget authority.

even less about the numbers than his troika colleagues. Stockman and
Darman rapidly drafted a two-page summary of where things stood.
Not enjoying the assignment a bit, Deaver went to Reagan in the mansion Thursday evening and attempted to explain the screw-up. He proposed a final meeting between Reagan, Weinberger and Stockman on
Friday morning. That session lasted nearly ninety minutes, during most
of which Weinberger moved not at all. As Stockman recalled it later,
"I said to the President, 'You'd better pick a number. You'd better
make a decision, because our whole fall effort is being held up by our
inability to resolve this.' So he picked thirteen billion dollars."[2]

End of dispute? Not quite. There was still the question of what figure
the $13 billion in outlays would be subtracted from, and how the sav-
ings would be expressed. To take the money from the defense line in
the July 15 budget review would be evasive because that line was already unrealistically low. Here Stockman won a little victory. He, with
the aid of his White House allies, managed to have the $13 billion
translated into new outlay ceilings. This had the practical effect of
adding up to more than $13 billion because of discrepancies in budget
reporting. Put another way, Stockman was able to save a couple of
billion more, though the inaccurate figures which OMB had in circulation made the reduction appear to be less.* Nor could this be done
simply. As still new wrinkles developed, Deaver had to call Weinberger
again later on Friday to relay firm word from Reagan that the jousting
would have to stop. Even on Saturday, while lounging in his swim
trunks beside the pool at Camp David, Reagan himself was still making calls to Weinberger and Stockman to assure that the deal held
together. It was nearly 6 P.M. that evening when Gergen met reporters
at the White House to put out the announcement. It made Reagan
sound like an arbitrator in a dispute between two independent parties
rather than a President making a decision. Even worse, the manner in
which the bizarre incident had been handled strengthened the general
impression that the Administration was unable to control spending.

The tussle over defense appropriations became a metaphor for what
turned into a longer, more complicated struggle over Reagan's entire
program. Climaxes came periodically—proposals extended then re-
tracted, deals with the Hill made, then unmade, a dicey presidential
veto imposed, then upheld, the next year's budget promulgated, then

* But there was no question that Weinberger had prevailed handsomely for the
time being. Defense outlays finally were pegged to increase at an average annual
rate of 8.7 percent in real terms over three years, rather than 7 percent, with
Carter's 1981 budget as the base. In proportional terms, over the course of the
five-year defense plan Pentagon spending was to rise from 24 percent of all federal outlays in 1981 to 37 percent in 1987.

demolished—while the underlying themes remained constant through the balance of the year and well into 1982.

Inflation succumbed to tight monetary policy, but that success, important though it was, diminished in impact as the recession went from bad to dreadful. The White House struggled to find a new grip on events before resigning itself to waiting in hope of better economic and political times in 1983. Meanwhile, from September of 1981 through the following March, Reagan and his closest advisers engaged in a strange wrestling match. The alignments shifted slightly from time to time. But in general, one team consisted of the troika (even after it ceased to function as a unit) and Stockman, Darman and Fuller on the inside, with some help from Commerce Secretary Baldrige, senior Republican senators and some part-time advisers on the outside. The other team was smaller, but had a very strong captain: Reagan himself. On his side was his magic pony, his optimism, plus the diminishing cadre of supply-siders. The chronic issue, only slightly oversimplified, was whether to compromise on basic elements of Reaganomics in order to prevent the entire program from disintegrating under the weight of insupportable deficits.

Mainstream commentators and economists for the most part regarded the pony as a first cousin to that other happy but invisible animal, Harvey the rabbit. That bias was natural. The so-called pragmatists had logic, math, tradition and politics on their side. In winning a far larger tax reduction than they had originally expected to achieve, the Reaganauts had scored a legislative triumph while the country suffered an economic defeat. The tight-money policy held in place by the Fed made it impossible for the tax cut to be converted into economic stimulus any time soon. The recession would be well underway before the revenue bill would have real effect. Making matters worse, the 1981 tax legislation proved to the financial community that unprecedented deficits were coming. The fact that the Treasury would be forced to borrow so heavily served to keep interest rates high much longer than otherwise would have been the case. This in turn prolonged the recession and ultimately lead to an unemployment of more than 10 percent. This was the train of events that would lead ultimately to the Republicans' reverses in 1982.

In the late summer and fall of 1981, Reagan still had time to make some alterations. That he chose not to do so compounded his own, and the country's, problems. He appeared then to have on his side only his little steed and the dogmatists. In fact, as his aides muttered privately about the need to "educate" him, Reagan was relying on something more than his own emotional view of economics. For one thing, the need for more defense spending was genuine. For another, the three

previous administrations had wobbled erratically in their policies, causing confusion in industrial boardrooms, in Wall Street, in central banks
overseas. Reagan reasoned that constancy alone was an important technique in calming nervous markets. And, naïve as it sounded while unemployment grew, Reagan insisted on remembering that he had promised the electorate long-term, durable changes in basic policies. He was
possessed of a quaint notion: exigencies of the moment should not
compel him to cut and run.

In hindsight, from the vantage point of 1983, it is easy to see that
those exigencies were hardly momentary. It is also easy to argue that
Reagan was insensitive to what was happening in the real world. Evidence supporting these retroactive judgments was all too plentiful midway through Reagan's term. But it must also be remembered that conventional equations had long since been stood on their ears. Reagan,
for instance, was being accused of emulating Herbert Hoover while at
the same time being asked to emulate Hooveresque fiscal policy—to
raise taxes while the economy was in a steep downturn. While hardly a
Keynesian, Reagan refused to embrace that idea. Eventually he would
consent to hold its hand.

Adjudication of the Pentagon budget issue was a large disappointment to the Stockman group, as well as to the senior Republicans
in the Senate. The Budget Director had to be joshed into putting out a
brief statement welcoming the compromise. "Write it with your tongue
in your cheek," one of his associates said. The fall offensive, obviously,
was off to a poor start. The speech announcing new proposals, originally planned for September 14, had to be delayed ten days while the
Budget Bureau adjusted to a military cut smaller than it had anticipated.

Cold feet, meanwhile, became the fashionable ailment. Kent Hance,
so recently the triumphant cosponsor of the tax bill, wrote to Baker
and Regan suggesting novel new legislation. He proposed a measure
giving the President the authority to postpone implementation of the
second and third installments of the five-ten-ten program. Richard J.
Whalen, a writer and occasional economic adviser to Reagan, published a sympathetic article containing blunt advice: "Whatever the political compromises imposed by the congressional process, the President's program is itself an uneasy three-sided compromise among
zealous supply-side fiscalists, devout monetarists and skeptical conservative traditionalists, whose policy prescriptions, respectively, are: a)
cut taxes; b) cut money growth; and c) cut 'waste' in government
spending . . . The President does not need a confrontation with
Congress. He needs to make a deal."[3]

The Legislative Strategy Group met over the weekend of September

19–20 and focused on an option summarized in the agenda as "Move struggle to lower the deficit front and center." Meese now agreed with that imperative. The troika assigned Stockman and Darman the task of outlining a drastic proposal for Reagan to deliver in his televised speech. That approach had Reagan emphasizing the deficit problem and meeting it frontally two ways: delay in the effective dates of the second and third installment of "five-ten-ten," and large new spending reductions. That outline never got to Reagan, however, because Stockman tried the idea out on the President informally Monday morning. Reagan responded emphatically that he did not wish to hear that option discussed.

Stockman mounted yet another bad-news briefing for Reagan. The Budget Director was growing frustrated and tendentious. His new fact sheet showed still larger deficits over the coming years. His options carried alarm-bell titles: "Govern First, Revolution Later" and "Hard-Line Anti-Spending Strategy" and "Muddle Through." The first and third utterly repelled Reagan when the group met on Tuesday, two days before the speech. Darman, reluctantly, suggested that Reagan must begin preparing public opinion for the deficits while laying the blame for them elsewhere. He also raised the possibility of "fundamental" changes in the enacted program. Reagan shot back, "Any delay on [reduction of] taxes would be a total retreat and an admission that we were wrong." Going for additional revenue, he said, should be left as a "cushion" for possible use later.

Howard Baker and Robert Michel, joining the meeting, were greeted with a presidential pronouncement that there would be "no retreat." The two congressional Republicans suggested that they take the responsibility for further cuts in defense spending. Reagan turned them down. By now he was settling on a modest package that nonetheless had faint prospect of enactment. It included a 12 percent across-the-board slash in discretionary civilian spending and a "reform" of entitlement programs except for Social Security. Baker and Michel informed Reagan that the latter item had no chance of enactment.

The speech, when finally delivered on Thursday night, carried a different tone from the earlier ones. It was more candid, though Reagan still talked of balancing the budget in 1984. It was also more demanding: "We are going through a period of difficult and painful readjustment. I know that we are asking for sacrifices from virtually all of you. But there is no alternative."

The specific proposal presented to Congress had no prospect of improving matters in fiscal '82, which began a week later. In the White House the package was referred to derisively as "the mouse." However, there was still a chance of taking steps that would affect fiscal years

1983–84, though by now the Administration was subject to increasing
—and conflicting—pressure from the outside.

Just before Reagan's televised speech, the AFL-CIO and the civil
rights movement combined to sponsor a sixties-style protest in Washington. The demonstration attracted about a quarter-million people
who covered the Mall south of the White House, chanting demands for
jobs and the restoration of government benefits (the actual loss of
which began the following month). The day after Reagan spoke, Wall
Street booed. The Dow Jones industrial average fell eleven points, to
824. That indicator was now 200 points below its high of the previous
spring and still could not find bottom. Was Reagan concerned about
stock prices? "No, I don't own any," he said in a peevish tone. What
did he think about Wall Street's lack of confidence in his program?
"That makes us even." Yet Reagan soon had to acknowledge in public
that a "slight" recession was underway; he hoped it would be short and
shallow.

The White House was becoming painfully aware that not only the
twitchy markets, but the larger business community as well still would
not *believe*. Only one phase of the tax program—improved depreciation allowances to encourage capital investment—had been made retroactive to January 1, 1981. Yet plant expansion was not taking place.
The Reaganauts were perplexed. "This administration," Treasury Secretary Regan observed, "has done its job. It has provided just what
American industry said it needed to transform our economy. . . . Yet
I must stand here today and ask: Where is the business response?
Where are the expansion plans? It's like dropping a coin down a well.
All I'm hearing is an empty clink." The President complained in an-
other speech about "Chicken Littles who proclaim the sky is falling."

That judgment was coming to Reagan in private as well as in public.
Stockman's October 25 updating report to the White House was a
study in gloom. Two snatches from his confidential statement, written
in headline style, convey the flavor: *"Revenue Enhancement*—House
and Senate GOP badly split. House fears Ways and Means [Commit-
tee] mischief or are opposed to any consideration of tax increases
under recessionary conditions . . ." Farther down: "The economic recovery program will be aborted by continued financial disorder unless
deficit realistically headed for *$30 billion* or below range by *FY '84."*
At that point, the prospective '84 deficit was $83 billion and headed
higher. (That estimated shortfall was eventually $188 billion.)

Stockman hoped that these alarms would shake things up enough
to produce new departures. Another showdown with Congress, he
thought, might be a good thing. But he was feeling desperate because
of the feedback he was getting from the President. On October 9, for

instance, Reagan remarked to several of his aides, "Maybe we're pan-icking. Maybe instead of a tax increase we should be emphasizing that we should have had the [larger] tax cut we originally asked for. Then we wouldn't be having this recession." Periodically, supply-siders were still getting through to Reagan.

His strategists talked of this as the Ping-Pong period. The September 24 speech and accompanying proposals had constituted the "ping." They hoped that it would evoke a "pong" from Capitol Hill resonant enough to make a difference in forecasts, and hence have an effect on interest rates, which were still hanging high. Domenici, the Senate Budget Chairman, came up with a comprehensive, and controversial, proposal in mid-October. It included a hefty tax increase—$75 billion over three years—plus cost cutting beyond what the September 25 package had envisioned in both military and civilian spending.

A modified version of this went to Reagan, who reacted with ambiv-alence. "It looks to me like buying a pig in a poke and then being hooked," he remarked in one meeting. Revenue measures for 1982 he rejected outright. "To talk about tax increases is literally suicide," he said at another private session with Senate and House Republican leaders. On November 2, when the Domenici plan was still alive, Reagan held yet another conference with Bush and the full economic team. The President was agonizing over the situation. He pulled out some letters from ordinary citizens which urged that he stick to his guns. We should listen to the people more often, he said, then added, "We have to have faith through 1982. We'll wait and see if at the end of 1982 we're in a hole. Then we'll convene a war council." One of his aides timidly reintroduced the possibility of altering the five-ten-ten schedule. "Oh Lord, no!" Reagan expostulated. The Vice-President, in one of his rare comments on this subject, suggested that the Adminis-tration should consider declaring a one-year emergency.

That meeting broke up with no important decision taken. The next day the group convened again, and by then all of Reagan's advisers were telling him that the deficit problem had become insupportable, that they could not come close to achieving what was still being prom-ised in public statements. With an air of resignation, Reagan replied, "That's very obvious, but a larger deficit is the least of our problems. What we have to do is get inflation down and business activity and em-ployment up. If there's a bigger deficit then, the man in the street will say, 'That's okay, things are better.'"

The President gave tentative approval to the Domenici scheme, but by then there seemed to be no realistic prospect of getting it approved. The House of Representatives had little appetite for another major bat-tle so late in the legislative session. At that stage Congress was having trouble passing appropriations bills based on previous authorizations. A conflict developed over a "continuing resolution"—a measure required to provide funds for government operations in the absence of formal appropriations statutes. Later in the month, on the eve of Thanksgiving, Reagan vetoed the continuing resolution because it exceeded agreed-upon limits. The veto, which was promptly upheld by Congress, saved something over $2 billion, but was largely a symbolic act. It demonstrated that Reagan was even willing to suspend some government operations in order to control spending.*

But on November 7, two weeks before that spasm, the political will for what Stockman hoped would be "the big fix" prior to the election year ebbed. The LSG relented in its effort to achieve a deal based on the Domenici plan. Baker and Darman, at a White House luncheon that day, sensed that Stockman was deflated. By then he was aware that an article by William Greider in *The Atlantic Monthly*, containing damagingly candid statements by Stockman, would be out in a couple of days. Soon there would be a new round in the same game, with escalating stakes. Stockman knew that, but he did not know whether he would be one of the players. All that he could be sure of was that his fall offensive had been repelled in the Oval Office and that the Ping-Pong contest with Congress had been called for lack of determination at both ends of Pennsylvania Avenue.

* The White House attempted to hype the veto as a show of presidential grit. In fact, on the basis of detailed research, Reagan's aides knew that all essential services would continue uninterrupted.

12

Dave Stockman:
The Trojan Pilgrim

A victorious general could not have collected more compliments than David Stockman did when he made his debut as Budget Director before the Senate Appropriations Committee. The date was January 27, 1981, and as yet he had done nothing visible in his new post other than talk intelligently about Reaganomics. In response, William Proxmire, a Democrat and Capitol Hill's reigning fiscal skeptic, said, "I think your appointment is one of the best we've had in a long, long time." Jake Garn seconded the motion ("The best possible choice President Reagan could have made . . ."). John Stennis, who came to the Senate just a year after Stockman's birth, told the witness young enough to be his grandson, "I like the way you talk. I think you're going to do some good."

Thirteen months later, Stockman had done a great deal. He was back on the Hill, defending the Administration's fiscal '83 budget. When he appeared before the House Budget Committee, Representative David Obey concluded a ten-minute harangue by saying: "Your stewardship has done incredible damage to the credibility of public service everywhere . . . I have no questions for you because very frankly, I wouldn't believe any answers you gave."

Stockman also testified before the Senate Government Operations Committee on the Administration's Federalism program. John Glenn, normally a stolid, temperate sort, told the witness, "We trusted you last year—the public trusted you and we were deceived, deliberately deceived . . . One of the results of that breach of faith is, the 1982 budget deficit is nearly $100 billion, interest rates over 16 percent, more business bankruptcies than any year since 1933 . . ."

Stockman took Obey's assault in silence. To Glenn he replied that it was the magazine article by William Greider that had created confusion because the author of it had misunderstood the facts. "So the notion that somehow anybody has been misled, anybody has been deceived, anything has been rigged, is absolutely and utterly without foundation . . . I hope because you have brought it up today and I have had a chance to provide this background that you will realize it is not something you would want to talk about in the future."

As usual, Stockman was attempting to overwhelm an adversary with certitude and velocity. Glenn subsided for the moment and gradually the anti-Stockman tirades lost steam, but he could never go back to his golden boy good old days. Don Regan was now used as the Administration's leading economic spokesman and then the White House, in August, appointed Martin Feldstein of Harvard to replace Weidenbaum as chairman of the Council of Economic Advisers. Feldstein, a heavyweight among conservative economists and a critic of supply-side doctrine, would develop more influence than his predecessor. Stockman was still the inside wizard, adroit at tactics as well as numbers. He still quested, like a monomaniacal Arthurian knight, for his big fiscal fix, the stability that would let Reaganomics have its true test. But he was a much diminished champion.

Purity was no longer one of the weapons in his armory. In the early months he was a handy device for the critics of Reaganomics. When attacking the President personally was dicey, Stockman served easily as a surrogate Scrooge as he sought to economize on the school lunch program, unemployment benefits and the stipends of welfare mothers. Cartoonists portrayed him as cold, bloodless. They caricatured his thin face as a mask of indifference, his shaggy graying hair as a thick helmet. In the line drawings the eyes behind his unfashionably large spectacles usually had a deranged quality. (Only Interior Secretary James Watt's phiz made a more suitable subject for satire.) But in that period Stockman at least could claim nobility of purpose. The poor and the working class, after all, were the worst victims of stagflation. The war to end all wars on poverty could only be won by rediscovering durable economic growth.

If Reagan supplied the soul of the Administration's program, Stockman provided the intellect. He seemed to have all the answers, all the zeal. It was Stockman who had been the only member of Michigan's congressional delegation to oppose the federal bailout of the Chrysler Corporation. Reagan himself shifted on that item as part of his courtship of the auto industry. Though Stockman for a time considered a future bid for one of Michigan's Senate seats, he nonetheless opposed putting pressure on Tokyo about its car exports. As we have seen,

Reagan yielded to political needs on that issue as well. As the Administration settled in, I wrote a magazine profile on the new Budget Director. The article's tag line: "In the budget battles that lie ahead, what could damage Stockman most is his determination to be more of a Reaganite than Ronald Reagan."[1] (Writers recall their own prose best in cases that demonstrate prescience.)

What Stockman did to himself, and to some extent to Reagan, in the confessional conversations which Greider published was to surrender the shield of purity. Now he could be attacked for his character as well as his policies. The thinker who had been most fervent and most cogent in defining the strategy of great expectations, which depended on credibility, had blown it. In the process, he became a very easy man to dislike regardless of one's feelings about the proper size of school lunches.

Not that the *Atlantic Monthly* story was the only rap. Once you got to know him, you realized his talent for mesmerizing those intellectually less keen than he—that is, nearly everyone—and the pleasure he took in using that gift. His ability to deceive and to manipulate was just as impressive. Once he helped stage-manage a briefing for Reagan in which the object was to get the President to swallow higher excise taxes. Stockman persuaded Don Regan to carry the brunt of the argument distasteful to the boss. Then, for the amusement of a colleague, Stockman drew a little cartoon depicting puppets. Though the puppeteer was invisible, there could be no doubt who held the strings.

Since he had jerked me around once or twice too, I made a diligent effort to dislike him. A book-length account of an administration, after all, can use a few villains. But my effort was in vain. As I studied his record and as events accumulated, I had to concede that Stockman had done as well as we had a right to expect, given the circumstances. From his Dunkirk memo onward, he recognized more clearly than his colleagues the urgency of the situation as well as its fragility. He was given an unwritten commission to serve as Reagan's vicar for economic affairs—the kind of mandate Haig was denied in foreign policy—and Stockman created a better plan than anyone else in the Administration would have.

That his reach exceeded his grasp, that events and other players including Reagan thwarted him at crucial moments, that his character suffered from some jagged chips—well, yes. At the outset of his mission, when all was blurred motion and giddy optimism, he told me one night, "If this thing doesn't work, I know I'll get the blame." Then he shrugged. "So I'll go to something else."[2] Instead he stayed with it long after it became fashionable in Washington to treat his reputation like the city dump. His command of macroeconomics was not as comprehensive as his early hubris led him (and the rest of us) to believe, but his knowledge of the budget, and the budget process, was astonishingly deep. In twenty-five years of patrolling politics I had encountered only a few practitioners who knew so much about their field and cared even more. His flaws made him vulnerable and therefore appealing. Both as a personality type and as the structural engineer of Reaganomics, Stockman warrants a closer look.

We should start with his *Atlantic Monthly* misadventure, though it is out of sequence, because that was the rebel's Gettysburg, if not his Appomattox. Soon after his nomination, he began a series of interviews with Greider which lasted until the following fall. Stockman, who later claimed that he thought he would remain anonymous, was disarmingly candid as he provided insights on the events we have examined in the last four chapters. The fact that he might have thought his personal tracks would be covered is irrelevant. What he said clearly demonstrated that the Reaganauts were less confident and surefooted in private than their optimistic statements in public indicated. "None of us really understands what's going on with all these numbers," he said at one point.*

Two other statements that gave the Administration's enemies particular aid and comfort concerned the 70/50 controversy and a definition of supply-side doctrine's essence. On the first, he indulged in a bit of hyperbole: "The hard part of the supply-side tax cut is dropping the top rate [on unearned income] from 70 to 50 percent. The rest of it is a secondary matter . . . But, I mean, Kemp-Roth was always a Trojan horse to bring down the top rate." Then Stockman allowed himself to be trapped into accepting a pejorative term: "It's kind of hard to sell 'trickle down' . . . so the supply-side formula was the only way to get a tax policy that was really 'trickle down.' Supply-side is 'trickle down' theory."

The rest of the article told of his disillusionment and frustration in the face of assorted reverses. The whole business was a public relations disaster for several reasons, the largest of which was the confessional tone, which made it seem that he was admitting dirty secrets. The cold substance was something else, rather less sensational. That the Administration's numbers were dicey was established before the article appeared. The phrase "trickle down" is a no-no because it connotes plutocratic policy: if the barons get enough champagne, they will increase the serfs' beer ration. A more acceptable way of getting across the

---

* In a press conference on November 12, the day after advance copies of the magazine became available, Stockman confirmed the accuracy of these quotations while protesting the implications drawn from them.

same idea is to argue that everyone benefits from prosperity or, as Reagan has said, the best social program is the availability of decent jobs. The "Trojan horse" crack was typical of Stockman's frequent use of exaggerated language. The revenue loss from the tax bill had become a major problem for him, and he allowed his irritation to show.

Stockman deepened the hole for himself immediately after he saw Reagan and offered to resign; that conversation, he told reporters, was "in the nature of a visit to the woodshed after supper." He tried to explain away the Trojan horse line by saying that the 70/50 provision had not been in the Administration's first formal proposal. It was the Democrats who proposed it officially in 1981, he said. That was technically true. However, Stockman in his Dunkirk memo had argued vigorously for the 70/50 measure. Reagan himself acknowledged in a speech on June 25, before the bill was approved, how much he welcomed inclusion of that item. With a straight face, Stockman denied that the original economic assumptions had been tampered with to achieve a desired effect. That statement made his friends wince and his adversaries giggle. And now, at a time when he had already put a good deal of distance between himself and the Kemp faction, he declared, "I believe, absolutely believe, that the supply-side theory is workable."

What to make of all this? I was eager to get at Stockman again in private, but he retreated for a time and then failed to show up for a Saturday morning appointment in February 1982. His assistants were astonished when he called in later to explain that he had simply overslept; they could not recall his ever having done that. We got together instead on February 15, when the government celebrated Washington's Birthday. The '83 budget had come out to unanimously bad reviews. There had been yet another wrangle over the mandatory economic assumptions, a dispute so intractable that the combatants finally went to James Baker for arbitration. Whimsically, the Chief of Staff picked a set of assumptions labeled "Troika 12/17" ("Because it sounds like a covert operation," he explained). Both liberal Democrats and conservative supply-siders had selected Stockman as scapegoat of the year.

He looked tense, weary, and smoked even more mentholated cigarettes than usual. A fresh mug of black coffee replaced an empty. Though it was early on a winter morning, perspiration stained his button-down shirt. "Maybe it's catching up with me," he said; "the pace, I mean. I'm not sure I can take this much longer." He insisted that he was letting the criticisms roll off. "But I know at any given time there are fifty people out there sharpening their knives for me." Of course he understood the damage of the Greider episode, "a great inadvertent accident." They had known each other for years and were in the habit of debating the writer's liberalism versus the politician's conservatism.

"Then he said, 'Let's formalize this thing.' We'd meet over at the Hay-Adams and have a good breakfast and good argument to get me rolling on Saturday mornings. I hated coming straight to the office at seven-thirty on the weekend anyway. We never did have a clear understanding on the ground rules."

Perhaps he had been concerned about his role in the history of that first year? "No, self-promotion is a bad rap. I won't claim that I'm pure as the driven snow, but I wasn't worried about history."

But he did seem to suffer a compulsion to explain, as much to himself as to anyone else, why the Administration had so far failed to translate legislative victories into economic success. An interviewer helped that process. His views were evolving, his perception of his own blind spots sharpening. In summer and fall, he blamed himself for not understanding the defense spending problem earlier. Beyond that, he should have gone for much larger budget cuts—at least 50 percent more—in the first round. "We simply left too many stones unturned." Meanwhile, he had lost patience with his erstwhile collaborators: "The supply-siders always had this magic view of the economy. That is, you could go from what was really a mess to nirvana in about a year and a half without any missteps, squeezes, pressures, along the way. I never believed in magic. The same folks who said the tax cut was economic magic are saying now [autumn, 1981] that the total financial disorder we have at the present time can be cured overnight by reestablishing gold convertibility. It's the same view of the world. It's just wrong."[3]

But he had subscribed, more or less, to those views, had he not? In our first long conversation, over a Sunday night dinner in February 1981, Stockman had mentioned Jude Wanniski's book, *The Way the World Works: How Economies Fail—and Succeed,** as having been important in shaping his own views when he entered Congress. Well, yes, increasing free-market incentives still was a necessary condition, but not sufficient. It was a question of pace, and measuring what could realistically be accomplished when faced with the responsibility of wielding power as opposed to the happy task of framing theories on the outside. By February 1982, Stockman had narrowed the focus:

> The absolute key to what went wrong wasn't that you were trying to cut taxes, raise defense spending and balance the budget in a few years. That was feasible. The key was the fourth element, bringing down inflation by monetary restraint. The impact of that wasn't clear at first. It was never understood by me until last summer. There was this view that inflation would give up without a struggle. So we didn't focus on how tight money

* Wanniski, a writer and economic consultant, and his friend Arthur Laffer, the economist, were two of the most prominent supply-side theorists. The book appeared in 1978.

would keep interest rates high, how that would induce a recession, and how lowered inflation itself would cut revenue. None of that was in the equation a year ago.

Now that it *was* in the equation, there would still be no instant magic. The election-year atmosphere of 1982 would work against drastic changes. Soon the Administration would overhaul its own '83 budget, the way it had changed Carter's '82 plan, but for different reasons. And for the time being at least, Stockman would attempt to expiate his Trojan horse sin by continuing to act the tireless Trojan in fiscal wars without end. By early spring his spirits and energy level were up once more. He and his accomplices on the White House staff changed Reagan's mind, at last, about the need for more revenue.

His thirty-sixth birthday, in November 1982, coincided almost exactly with two anniversaries. Just two years earlier, Kemp had taken the Dunkirk memo to California. One year earlier, when Stockman turned thirty-five, the Greider story competed with National Security Adviser Richard Allen's difficulties for news attention and the two events together raised the question of whether the Administration was coming apart. One wondered whether those two dense years had aged Stockman to the point where his much longer intellectual pilgrimage had ended, ironically, close to where it began.

As a teenager he had thought of himself as a Goldwater Republican. He took that view mainly from his maternal grandfather, who was active in county politics. Not that young Dave envisioned himself as going into public affairs in St. Joseph, Michigan, where his father owned a farm. The oldest of five children, he thought that farming would be his career too. He went to Michigan State University, where he found that botany bored him so he switched to history. In that department a young instructor from Brooklyn, Jewish and leftish, got into Stockman's Methodist head while the anti-war movement got into his blood. "This guy, in one semester, succeeded in shattering everything I believed in," Stockman recalled with a rueful grin. At college he regarded himself as a "soft-core radical." He was sufficiently active in demonstrations against the Vietnam war to warrant his own dossier in the files of the Michigan state police. Michigan during that period was one of the seedbeds of the Students for a Democratic Society, which eventually turned violent. Stockman preferred the pacifist approach, channeling his protest through Methodist Church activities.

Campus turbulence began to lose its charms, so he sought refuge in the calmer precincts of theology, specifically in the writings of Reinhold Niebuhr. After graduation, he enrolled in Harvard's Divinity School. The bookish farm boy found Cambridge in the fall of 1968 a seat of "nihilistic radicalism" that appalled him. "I didn't just detach myself from the left, I became anti-radical." Helping him move in that direction was his next mentor, Daniel Patrick Moynihan, who maintained a home in Cambridge while serving in the Nixon White House. Stockman moved in as a kind of mother's helper. When Moynihan came back on weekends, there were long evenings of brandy and political discourse. The young pilgrim was on the move again. "Eventually I became 'Moynihanized' through that process. I was looking for an alternative point of view that was respectable but anti-left. It was a good way station. It was conservative, but not Old Right." Neither was it New Right, which hadn't quite been invented yet. Stockman was in on the ground floor of neoconservatism, and found the digs comfortable.

With his interests moving back toward politics, Stockman grew restless at Harvard. His friends there put him in touch with Illinois congressman John Anderson, who was looking for a bright young staff assistant. Anderson then was beginning his own transition, from the right to the left of the GOP, but the two managed to get on anyway. On the Hill Stockman became a vacuum cleaner for information about energy policy and economic affairs. He had never taken a course in economics —a fact that he still liked to flaunt in 1981—but didn't let that omission impede him. He ransacked the libraries of conservative think tanks. Despite his youth, he quickly rose on Anderson's staff. Long after they had parted company, Anderson recalled his aide's diligence: "Even the elevator operators referred to him as the fellow who was always there. He was determined to spend more time on the job than anyone else. Dave was very proud of his ability to work harder than other people. I remember him telling me once that when he was a boy he could pick strawberries longer than anyone else on his father's farm. In his view, this was a measure of his superiority—his prodigious capacity to outwork everybody."[4]

Anderson was chairman of the House Republican Conference, which had a small research and writing staff. He appointed Stockman, at age twenty-five, director of that group. The job gave him an overview of the full run of issues, as well as House operations. He quickly mastered both. Acquaintances in that period remember him as confident that he could be a better House member than most of the representatives he knew.

That opportunity arose in 1976. Stockman's home district in southwest Michigan was represented by a senior Republican who had made the mistake of remaining loyal to Richard Nixon for too long during Watergate. On his first try at elective politics, just before his thirtieth birthday, Stockman carried the conservative constituency easily. His voting record during the next four years was conventionally Republican, but he identified himself with neither Anderson nor Gerald Ford. His new home was the Republican Study Committee organized by Sam Devine, then one of the staunchest New Right members of the House and a foe of Anderson in intra-party disputes. Anderson and Stockman were now colleagues, both representing Midwest districts with similar interests, but their association was over. "I had the impression," Anderson said later, "that he had swung over completely to the free-market economy as almost an article of religious faith. He left me completely as soon as he was elected to Congress. He left me completely even though I had gone up to his district to help him raise money and to campaign."[5] Stockman could shed patrons as easily as he could alliances and doctrines.

Though Stockman played no role in the early phases of the Reagan campaign, he gladly accepted an invitation to help the candidate prepare for his fall debate with John Anderson. Stockman impersonated his former boss in sparring sessions with Reagan so well that Jim Baker asked for a reprise when Reagan trained for the much more important encounter with Carter. Reagan later quipped that the only debates he ever lost were his dry runs with the fast-talking Stockman, conducted in an outbuilding at the Wexford estate. Reagan liked the boyish congressman, who was then in the process of winning his third election. The talent scouts wanted Stockman to consider taking the Energy Department, but he demurred. He preferred staying in the House to assuming a post which Reagan was pledged to abolish. OMB was something else. There Stockman could use his mastery of the budget process. That was where the action would be. He lobbied for the assignment, and the supply-siders worked on his behalf.

More than most of the other Reaganites, Stockman labored to eliminate or substantially curtail entire programs. He was an equal-opportunity skinflint, seeking to pare activities that benefited the middle class (subsidized college loans, Social Security, Medicare) as well as programs for the poor (welfare, Medicaid, the CETA job program). Given the political balance on Capitol Hill, Stockman was more successful in the latter than in the former. In a few situations he also attempted to reduce direct or indirect federal assistance to corporations and agricultural interests; usually lobbyists managed to blunt those efforts.

Early in the second year, before Reagan was persuaded to undertake his first important mid-course correction, Stockman at a meeting one day watched his latest scheme to attack deficits being shelved. He wrote himself a little memo headed "Things we won't balance the budget on backs of" and then listed the poor, the elderly, taxpayers, the Pentagon and other protected species. His tag line—playing off Anderson's campaign-season attack on Reaganomics—was, "So we balance the budget on mirrors."

At other critical decision points, it was usually Stockman who advocated the bold stroke. It was he who pushed hard for grappling with Social Security early, for pursuing Gramm-Latta II, for cutting the Pentagon budget, for making the 1981 "fall offensive" a wide-angle attack on deficits. Darman usually supported him while Baker tended toward the cautious side. As the fall offensive crumbled, one of the other participants who kept an episodic journal of that period described Stockman as "discouraged re: RR's reaction [up] to this point—and RR's perception that budget cuts'll do the trick (along with the 'pony')."

When the supply-siders and the New Right rebelled at what they saw as a drift toward "moderation" and Nixon-Ford policies, particularly the decision in mid-1982 to go for increased revenue, they identified Stockman as a leading traitor. He was condemned as one of the chief "pragmatists." These attacks missed a crucial element in Stockman's philosophy. He was committed, at least as much as Reagan himself, to shrinking the federal government's role in society. Stockman took as a special mission the sharp reduction in latter-day social programs begun by Lyndon Johnson in the 1960s. These, he felt, carried the original New Deal agenda far beyond what society could afford in both fiscal and spiritual terms. Washington, he conceded, did have an obligation to protect citizens from stark privation. That was the real "social safety net." But the government had no responsibility to assure anyone's comfort. He argued that the feds had no business providing legal services for the poor, or inexpensive lunches for the children of the working class, or subsidies for inefficient industries.

One of Stockman's friends, who collaborated with him in both the fiscal '82 and '83 budget fights, tried to read his mind. "Maybe," he said, "David doesn't want to help the poor. I don't think that he likes them or that he thinks they can be helped much. Of course he doesn't like the rich either. He thinks that they're usually selfish and shortsighted. Whom does he like? People who are very talented and hardworking. He likes people who are like himself."

I could not resist trying this formulation out on its subject. It was the eve of the July Fourth weekend and for once he was relaxed, contemplating a couple of days away with his steady girlfriend. At first he bridled at the description. "It's glib," he said, "superficial." Then, chuckling, he chose his words carefully: "I don't *explicitly* lack sympathy for the poor. Of course, if I had to choose between three groups, the idle rich, the undeserving poor and those who are talented achievers, I'd take the third. It's one thing to have a preference. It's another to have a prejudice."

Undeserving poor? *Idle* rich? Those adjectives had not been in the description. He had either added them subconsciously because that is how he thinks of the two classes, or he was using a debater's trick to change the argument. Perhaps he was doing both. More relevant to public policy, the man who was still translating Reaganomics into specific decisions clearly thought that the wealthy, whether idle or industrious, deserved a better break from Washington. He had spent the previous eighteen months protesting that the Administration's proposals did no damage to the "truly needy." Now, when pushed into a corner, he acknowledged that under Reagan "there has been some restitution to taxpayers and some retrenchment for those receiving tax benefits."

That is a narrow way to look at it, he added. Reduced inflation helped the poor. Industrial revival would help all those of modest means. Besides, he said, over two decades "the government has been involved in income redistribution in a big way. So, yes, on that narrow basis, in 'cashbox' transactions, the government now is giving relatively less to the statistically poor and taking relatively less from the statistically wealthy." He vehemently denied that the rich get hidden subsidies. "If you look at the whole budget of more than seven hundred billion dollars, you can't find one percent going to the rich." What of interest deductions? The dozens of flagrant tax loopholes so recently made even more inviting by the 1981 tax act? Stockman himself had fought them. He had compared the industry lobbyists to gluttonous hogs, insatiable in their greed. Now he said, "Of course there are tax loopholes, but those are correctives to an insane tax system, to bring down the effective tax rates. I think it's immoral to tax anyone over fifty percent." Stockman, one must note, was the least affluent member of Reagan's cabinet. He came to government with no personal trust fund, no going business or flourishing law firm awaiting his return.

So he spoke from conviction, and from his life experience in the independent middle class that earned its own way, either in a family business like his parents' farm, or on a professional's salary. As a workaholic with a high I.Q., he had never wanted for patrons, or for opportunity. After roaming the ideological landscape, he settled in the meadow of Reaganism, where he was attempting to trim the foliage to his own particular design. Cerebral as he always had been, he had until recently been a follower of guides—his Goldwaterite grandfather, that left-wing history instructor from Brooklyn whose name he couldn't quite remember, anti-war activists, Moynihan, Anderson, the supply-side theorists. Now he seemed to have run out of gurus. One of his problems in the Reagan administration was that suddenly David Stockman, in his mid-thirties, was himself looked upon as a guru. He had discovered the difficulties of learning that trade while on the job.

13
Over There

Pursuing their domestic goals at a gallop, Reagan and his immediate circle of advisers decided to approach foreign affairs one step at a time. The world had to know that the new leadership in Washington meant new American policies. But the new team wanted time to frame them. Even more important, the Reaganauts had learned, perhaps too well, from Carter's error of diffusing his efforts. National attention must be made to focus on the economic recovery campaign. Thus foreign initiatives, particularly if controversial, should be avoided when possible.

Events abroad made that strategy seem superficially plausible for a time. With the American hostages safely off the soil of Iran before Reagan left the Capitol grounds on Inauguration Day, there was no longer any dire emergency demanding instant decisions or consuming precious seconds on the evening news. Elsewhere, the list of chronic problems and threats drawn up by the Allen-Iklé group during the transition still existed, of course. They would have to be monitored, and in a few cases ministered to. With the exception of El Salvador, they might, with continued luck, remain on the safe side of the critical mass point for months to come.

Moscow still menaced the Solidarity movement in Poland, but otherwise indicated a desire to deal in a businesslike way with Reagan. The White House issued warnings about the former and demurrals on the latter. The NATO allies were anxiety-ridden concerning U.S. nuclear policy; Haig labored to develop a position in Washington that would reassure them.

Combat between Iraq and Iran was frightening. That, together with the continuing Soviet occupation of Afghanistan and turmoil in Africa

fomented by Libya, served as a constant reminder of danger throughout the long arc reaching from the southern Mediterranean to the In-
dian Ocean. The Administration lacked levers in Tehran and Baghdad;
the antagonists would simply have to shoot it out on their own. At least
the West was fortunate, because of other reasons, that an oil glut was
building; the Moslem fratricide would not worsen economic conditions that were already difficult. Meanwhile, Washington would search
for ways to buttress Egypt and the Persian Gulf states. Picking up on
concepts developed at the end of the Carter administration, the new
men talked of a "strategic consensus" among pro-Western nations in
the Middle East and West Asia.

They followed through on Carter's courtship of Saudi Arabia, hastily
agreeing to consummate a huge military aviation deal. They restored
relations with Pakistan, resuming the sale of arms to that military dictatorship. They squinted at Libya, seeking ways to curb its mischief
and trying some—with bizarre results, as we'll soon see.

Meanwhile, Washington allowed Arab-Israeli negotiations to remain
idling. Washington offered no new policy to deal with the Palestinian
problem. The leaders of Israel, Egypt, Jordan and Saudi Arabia all were
eager for invitations to meet the new President, but neither he nor his
policy advisers were ready. Anwar Sadat probably would have received
the call but for two impediments. He was balking at the resumption of
talks on the issue of autonomy for the Palestinians, and Reagan could
not invite him without also seeing Menachem Begin immediately before
or after. That would inject Washington into the Israeli election campaign. Better to defer the whole business for the time being.

Nonetheless, the Reaganauts needed to display to allies and antagonists across both oceans and borders that a "break with the past" had
arrived in foreign as well as domestic affairs. This would be done, for
the most part in the early months, with rhetoric, gestures and attempts
to demonstrate a holistic philosophy at work. The new team, for instance, promptly withdrew U.S. approval of the Law of the Sea treaty
that had been drafted under United Nations auspices in a tortuous
negotiating process. The agreement, Reagan's advisers felt, would inhibit development of mineral deposits by private interests. The pact
had been a high priority for the least affluent maritime nations. In similar vein, the U.S. delegate to a World Health Organization meeting was
the only one out of 119 representatives to vote against an international
code to regulate the marketing of infant formula. For years there had
been complaints that in regions of low literacy the powdered food was
being used improperly, causing malnutrition and even deaths. But the
pro-business Reagan administration argued that an international rule-
book would impede free trade.

To Moscow, the most important communication combined rapid expansion of American military spending with verbiage to match. Haig made some tough statements about the need for the Soviet Union to demonstrate its reasonableness with specific deeds. But it was Reagan, almost unintentionally, who set the tone. At his first formal press conference, on January 29, the new President showed his shaky grasp of foreign affairs. In discouraging the idea that he would soon enter the arms control negotiations, he strongly implied that his administration would avoid serious talks with the Soviets on that subject altogether unless Moscow changed its behavior in other important respects. "In other words," he said, "I believe in linkage." Later he would have to shelve that belief. Then he was asked his view on the Soviets' long-term intentions. Did he foresee renewal of the Cold War or some possibility of another round of détente? Reagan had not come to the press conference intending to make a policy pronouncement on that topic. Instead of vamping in response, however, he reached into Reaganism for a stock reply:

> Well, so far détente has been a one-way street that the Soviet Union has used to pursue its own aims. I don't have to think of an answer as to what I think their intentions are. They have repeated it . . . the promotion of world revolution and a one-world socialist or communist state, whichever word you want to use. Now, as long as they do that and as long as they at the same time have openly and publicly declared that the only morality they recognize is what will further their cause, meaning they reserve unto themselves the right to commit any crime, to lie, to cheat, in order to attain that, and that is moral, not immoral [then] we operate on a different set of standards.

Did that mean Reagan would deal with the Soviets on the basis of morality as he defined it? Not quite. Among the many decisions to be made during that first winter and spring, three posed particularly interesting tests of how Reagan would adjust Soviet-American relations to square with Reaganism, or vice versa.

• What would he do about the partial embargo on grain sales to the Russians? Jimmy Carter had limited agricultural exports as part of his token protest against the Soviet invasion of Afghanistan. Reagan, from the Iowa caucus campaign onward in 1980, criticized that decision. He said that the embargo penalized American farmers as much as it did the Soviets and that it was unfair to single out agriculture. Farm prices in the United States were in difficulty; the export trade was essential to grain producers. He wanted to be hard on the Russians and at the same time maintain free-trade principles. During his second week in office he answered a question on this subject by saying, "You only have two choices with an embargo. You either lift it or you broaden it."

• What would he do about advance draft registration, another of the symbolic steps Carter had taken in response to Afghanistan? Again, Reagan had made this a campaign issue. The procedure, he charged, was meaningless because in an emergency it would provide no significant advantage for the Selective Service process. He opposed peacetime conscription on principle—a triumph of the libertarian in him over the hawk—and implied that he would do away with the requirement.

• What would he do about the Theater Nuclear Force problem, which was rapidly coming to a head? The West Europeans had agreed to allow the deployment of Pershing-2 and cruise missiles on their territory to offset the new generation of Soviet intermediate-range weapons already in place. But there was a crucial proviso: the United States at the same time would negotiate seriously with the Soviets on the TNF question. Reagan was ambivalent about how quickly to do this. Further, the new civilian leadership of the Pentagon, his appointees, wanted to defer such negotiations indefinitely. For openers, there was merely a change in terminology, from TNF to INF, for Intermediate Range Nuclear Forces.

These three dilemmas gave Reagan great difficulty. On the grain question, Haig vociferously opposed full resumption of exports. Each time it came up in National Security Council and cabinet meetings, the Secretary of State argued, logically enough, that the new administration could hardly establish an image of firmness, or set an example for NATO, by making grain purchases easier for the Soviets. The point of the Reagan approach was to induce changes in Soviet behavior outside its borders. So far there had been none. Soviet troops still occupied Afghanistan. Russian equipment and rubles still allowed Havana, Hanoi, the PLO, and other outlaws to disturb the peace at will. Warsaw Pact forces under Soviet command still menaced the reform movement in Poland. Further, the Soviets were in a cycle of poor grain harvests. They could buy the supplies elsewhere, of course, but that cost them more cash.

Though Haig had support from the rest of the "national security community"—the Pentagon, the CIA, Richard Allen and his staff—on the question, the Secretary of State had to lead the parade. Weinberger, Casey and Allen knew the President far better than Haig did. Thus they understood that on certain questions Reagan would not be moved. Agriculture Secretary John Block, pleading the farmers' cause in discussion after discussion, also sensed where Reagan was heading. Haig succeeded only in delaying the decision until late April. He was able to do that because of Soviet feints at the Polish frontier. When those subsided, Reagan promptly lifted the embargo. The White House cast the decision as fulfillment of a campaign promise rather than as a concession to Moscow. Nonetheless the move caused confusion and Reagan himself, as we've seen, was trying to have things both ways, advertising toughness and conciliation simultaneously.* The prevailing popular impression was that the Soviet Union would be getting its full supply of American feed grains once again simply because it had refrained from a military invasion of Poland. There was no quid pro quo of any kind.

That done, the draft registration question became even more difficult. Though it was a token step, to scrap it while pressing to enhance NATO's strength would seem a wobble. Some of the NATO countries, after all, continued full conscription. On the other hand, sticking with advance registration would require a messy complication that the Carter administration had not got around to addressing: the prosecution of those who refused to register. Reagan initially reacted to this unpleasant choice by doing nothing, which had the effect of leaving the registration requirement in place without indicating violators. Meanwhile, the departments concerned marked time with lengthy reviews of all the policy's implications. It was not until January of 1982 that the Administration announced first that it would retain registration and second that, after a grace period, offenders would face criminal proceedings. The rationale was that in the event actual conscription became necessary, six weeks would be saved in mobilization, not the few days Reagan had talked about disparagingly during the campaign.

In terms of internal debate during the first months, the INF dispute caused the most rancor. Weinberger, Iklé and Richard Perle, the assistant secretary of defense for international security policy, wanted to press ahead with deployment of new missiles on schedule. But they wished to defer the second track, a commitment to undertake negotiations, for at least a year. Perle, a "defense intellectual" who carried the sharpest beak among the new administration's hawks, reinforced Weinberger's own hard-line sentiments. Haig and his advisers at State felt that they needed a strong reaffirmation of Washington's willingness to undertake formal negotiations. Otherwise the anti-nuclear movement, so strong in Western Europe, might be able to scotch the deployment of new U.S. weapons. After three months of contention, Reagan in late April finally came down on Haig's side. Said one of Haig's senior aides soon afterward, "We won, but the blood was visible on the floor. The allies saw it and the Russians understood what was going on. Moscow used that skillfully to play on the fears of the Europeans."

Reagan insisted during 1981 that he was sending the Soviets a "clear signal" of his policies so that there would be no misunderstandings.

* Chapter 2 describes Reagan's personal letter to Brezhnev at the time.

Some of his own advisers disagreed, however. The inability to settle the
defense spending issue quickly and cleanly was a source of confusion.
The State Department complained that the Pentagon hawks prevailed
too often while at the Defense Department there was malaise over what
its leaders considered a revival of détente spirit, Henry Kissinger style.
From the outside, Kissinger himself would later complain about what
his heirs were doing. It would be well into 1982 before Reagan's brand
of Soviet policy became legible.

Even then there were doubts. Richard Pipes, the Harvard professor
who served as White House adviser on Soviet affairs through 1982,
monitored Moscow's views closely. A Pole of Jewish descent who fully
shared Reagan's anti-Soviet passion, Pipes in the spring of 1982 concluded:

> There are two schools of thought in the Kremlin, where they are still
> puzzled by Reagan. Some view him as being as tough as he sounds. Others
> think that he is a more or less conventional American conservative who
> will bargain. But the Soviet leaders do take the arms buildup here
> seriously. They know that they will no longer have a free ride. It was in-
> teresting that the way the PATCO strike was handled impressed the Rus-
> sians. Seeing photographs of a union leader being taken away in chains—
> that surprised them and gave them respect for Reagan. It showed them a
> man who, when aroused, will go the limit to back up his principles . . .[1]

Though they disagreed on several important issues and had little respect for each other, Haig and Pipes had similar views concerning the
Soviets' ambivalent perceptions of Reagan. "They are profoundly disturbed by President Reagan," Haig told me after he left office. "They
don't understand him. Some of his rhetoric has hit the mark and of
course they don't like our arms buildup." But was that lack of understanding good or bad for our side? "Both," Haig said. He argued—in a
reversal of the usual image of him—that it was the White House that
softened at the wrong moments. "We have this terrible habit. The rhetoric is tough. The deeds are a maze of populist reactions."*

The Reagan team from the beginning struggled to produce symbols
of their grit more appropriate than PATCO. One was the prompt
reversal of Carter's human rights policy, which showed up in renewed
associations with right-wing dictatorships from Argentina to Pakistan.
Carter's investment in morality had produced mixed results in any

* He meant reactions shaped by popular opinion. We talked on September 29,
1982, three months after his resignation was announced and at a time when he
was beginning to criticize the Administration in public. His tone was very
different from that of an earlier conversation while he was still at State. Other
quotes from Haig in this chapter, unless otherwise identified, are from the September interview.

event. His administration, for example, had severed the U.S. umbilical cord to the odious Somoza regime in Nicaragua, a move which helped bring to power the Sandinista movement. Washington's reward for that was a government in Managua that soon introduced its own brand of repression at home and began to carry Fidel Castro's water elsewhere in Central America.

Toward the end of their term, the Carter people themselves began to adjust their policy. They still sought, through U.S. Ambassador Robert E. White, to promote a negotiated settlement among the warring factions of El Salvador, but they resumed the supply of military equipment to the interim government of José Napoleón Duarte nonetheless. Duarte was an interesting figure in Latino politics. A moderate with humane instincts, he had in the past bucked the oligarchs and the military. Now he headed an uneasy center-right coalition that was attempting some political and agricultural reforms while at the same time fighting a civil war against a collection of leftist factions that included surrogates of Castro. The pivotal question was whether to continue the war, attempting to cripple the guerrillas by military means, or to seek an accommodation in which all elements would be offered a chance to participate.

White and the Carter State Department thought the military option a fantasy. However, the rebels launched what they billed as their final offensive to topple Duarte just after Christmas. The regime meanwhile had only limited control over its own security forces and over right-wing terrorists who waged war against reformers of all stripes. The result was a three-ring bloodbath. Just before the inauguration, the rebels' big offensive crumbled. Nonetheless, the U.S. Army attaché in El Salvador received word that the Pentagon, the day before Reagan was to be sworn in, was already planning to send in military personnel to train Salvadoran government forces. Much later White would reveal that he attempted to thwart that plan, which could only have been advanced with the approval of the incoming Reagan people.[2] Reagan's advisers had already decided, in mid-January, to drop attempts for a broad compromise as the means for ending the civil war. They would pursue a military solution. Once in power, they promptly fired White and began a crash effort to upgrade the Salvadoran military.

Long before that flash point occurred, Reagan's interest in events south of the border was already high. Gringo conservatives from the West and Southwest have a tradition of concern about Latino affairs that has been lacking in the Eastern foreign policy establishment. Opposition to the Panama Canal treaties was particularly strong in Reagan country, and as a candidate Reagan exploited that issue.

Chauvinism wasn't the only element in Reagan's approach, however.

Early on, he had a genuine desire to spread the blessings of capitalism below the Rio Grande and to improve political relations as well. When he announced his 1980 candidacy he talked of constructing a "North American Accord" in concert with Canada and Mexico. The concept was vague and he never developed it, but the instinct was sound. The three nations, with major interests and problems in common, had good reason to improve the atmosphere among themselves and to do what they could to enhance stability in the rest of the hemisphere. During the transition, Reagan went to Ciudad Juárez on the Mexican border for an unofficial visit with President José López Portillo. López Portillo and Carter hadn't got on well; Reagan's trip was a conciliatory gesture. Just after the inauguration, the first foreign head of government invited to the White House was Edward Seaga, the new Prime Minister of impoverished little Jamaica. Seaga, a political conservative in Jamaica's spectrum, had recently defeated an anti-American leftist incumbent. He was looking for fresh capital from the north; the White House helped to organize a consortium of investors and then agreed to buy Jamaican bauxite for the U.S. strategic mineral reserve. The message to other Caribbean and Central American countries, Richard Allen told a few reporters, was that "Those of you who turn to the West will be rewarded." Soon the Administration began work on what it called the Caribbean Basin Initiative, a package of additional foreign aid and trade concessions intended to revive the region's depressed economies. It would take a year to get it done and then the proposal would encounter delay on Capitol Hill. But Reagan was trying his own free-enterprise version of a good neighbor policy.

While these gestures were being made, the National Security Council watched Duarte's wobbly regime with growing anxiety. Intelligence from Central America in the winter of 1980–81 was mediocre; the CIA had been through a tumultuous period of retrenchment during the Ford and Carter years and would recover only gradually under Reagan's patronage. Latin-American operations in particular had suffered. Meanwhile, in January and February the NSC did not have a very clear picture of the contending forces' relative strength. But the Reaganauts did have a quite vivid image of the impact of Duarte's overthrow by Communist-led insurgents. If El Salvador went under just as the Reagan administration was settling in, Washington's attempt to display firmness would be undermined. The standing of Castro and the Sandinistas would be enhanced. Other countries in deep difficulty, particularly Honduras and Guatemala, would be in greater jeopardy than ever. Haig in particular was concerned that Castro was ready to make a long-term effort to exploit the turbulence in Central America. He felt that the Cubans had to be contained. During 1980 Reagan had elicited cheers from campaign audiences with this declaration: "There will be no more Taiwans. There will be no more Vietnams. There will be no more betrayals of friends by the United States!" Taiwan and Vietnam were on the other side of the world. El Salvador, the new President now said, was part of "our front yard." Certainly it was in the traditional U.S. sphere of influence, and Reagan was pledged to make that influence felt again.

Within the National Security Council, it was Haig who saw the conflict in Central America in the most grandiose terms both as a challenge and an opportunity. Here was the place, he argued, to put down a "marker" clearly visible in Moscow and Havana, as well as in hilly sanctuaries around Central America where other rebels plotted against incumbent regimes. The Secretary of State determined to make El Salvador an immediate test, and to challenge both Cuba and Nicaragua over their material support of the insurgents. "Mr. President," Haig said in private meetings on a few occasions, "this is one you can win."

Haig got little argument, on principle, from his National Security Council colleagues. Weinberger, Casey and Allen all agreed on the necessity of bolstering Duarte. Further, the CIA discerned an arena in which to conduct covert activities—a practice that had declined steeply during the post-Vietnam years of retreat. Soon the CIA was preparing proposals for secret measures to be taken against the Sandinistas in Nicaragua. However, Haig was the only one of Reagan's senior advisers who wished to *declare* El Salvador a vivid test case in East-West terms.

Meese and Baker, fearing a distracting controversy, forced Haig to delay by nearly three weeks, until February 23, the publication of a "white paper" that purported to document outside military assistance going to the Salvadoran insurgents. But the pronouncement was finally made, along with an increase in U.S. military aid. Further—and most important in domestic political terms—Washington went ahead with the plan to send fifty-five "trainers" to El Salvador to assist the demoralized, poorly prepared government forces.

That act, reawakening memories of the "advisers" who began the U.S. presence in Vietnam, detonated demonstrations all over the country, and in foreign capitals as well. Neither the situation on the ground nor actual U.S. policy resembled the Vietnam situation. Nonetheless, the public relations aspect of the program was troubling for the Administration, particularly because Haig implied strongly on a number of occasions that the United States would "go to the source"—Cuba—and perhaps use military measures against Castro. To a group of British journalists, Haig remarked, "We consider Cuban interventionism in this hemisphere on our own doorstep as no longer tolerable, no longer acceptable . . . I'm not trying to turn your knuckles white."³ To American newsmen during this period, Haig said, "How far are we prepared to go to prevent Cuban interventionism, to call a halt? . . . The best answer to that is, we are determined to do so by whatever means are necessary."

The White House troika, aghast at the political backfire, persuaded Haig to tone down. But the fears he unleashed continued to have echoes in a variety of ways for nearly two years. Eventually the French and Mexican governments, both presuming to act as advocates of Third World interests, came out in favor of recognizing the El Salvadoran rebels as a legitimate political force. Seven Ivy League undergraduate newspapers, for the first time since the height of the Vietnam protests in 1969, adopted a joint editorial position demanding the end of all military aid to Duarte and a rejection of the March 1982 election results in El Salvador.⁴ Liberals in Congress used the issue to attack the Administration's foreign policy and to thwart attempts to repeal the Clark Amendment, a hangover from the post-Vietnam syndrome that restricted military assistance to anti-Marxist forces in Angola.

The uproar would have been all the louder had it been known that Haig privately was proposing further steps against Cuba, leading up to possible interdiction of shipping thought to be carrying military supplies from the island to the Central American mainland. Haig's approach envisaged a phased tightening of screws, economic and political to start with, but including military pressure if Castro refused to back off. Here the Pentagon and Haig parted company. Neither the Joint Chiefs of Staff nor the civilian leadership was eager to consider a serious commitment of naval and air units in that part of the world. Combat ships were in short supply because of cutbacks after Vietnam. Other regions, such as the Persian Gulf, had a higher priority as the Defense Department saw it.

So Haig was overruled during a protracted debate of which the world heard only distorted echoes at the time. It still rankled when we talked eighteen months later. He acknowledged that his public allusions to "going to the source" had translated in the secret deliberations to the use of military interdiction " 'if necessary'—and I don't think that it would have been necessary had we done it properly." His former colleagues on the Joint Chiefs of Staff, he argued, were still victims of the post-Vietnam syndrome, the main symptom of which was irrational fear about the commitment of American force no matter how urgent the need and how favorable the geography. Haig's bitterness toward Weinberger and other adversaries in the Pentagon came through clearly:

We build the highest defense capability in the history of this country. We even go beyond, in programming our defense requirements, what is necessary because no one has done the analysis necessary to know what can be spent intelligently. We skew our whole budgetary problem because policy making is not being done properly and the right questions are not being asked. While we're doing this, we refuse, philosophically and compulsively, ever to apply those resources to back up American diplomacy.

Haig was ever out of step with his peers, venturesome when they were cautious and vice versa. Allen, after he left office, called the dispute over Central American policy a "silly confrontation as to who the tough guy in the Administration was." As to Haig's specific ideas concerning pressure on Cuba, Allen said, "It was a plan that might best and most fairly be described as folly."[5]

Meanwhile, the limited steps which the Administration did take helped to stave off disaster in El Salvador without achieving real stability. As deadlock set in, Haig explored more peaceful means of dealing with the entire region. In November of 1981 he met in Mexico with Carlos Rafael Rodríguez, the third man in Cuba's hierarchy, and later dispatched his roving ambassador, Vernon Walters, to see Castro. Haig's assistant for Latin American affairs, Thomas Enders, visited Managua in an attempt to settle differences with the Sandinistas. At times the López Portillo government attempted to act as mediator.

None of these efforts yielded much tangible progress, though without them tension might have been even higher than it was. The Administration continued to try to prove the culpability of the Cuban and Nicaraguan regimes in fomenting trouble throughout the region. While no one doubted that was true in a general way, the Reaganites had difficulty in establishing the specifics of their case and in forming a consensus of support at home. Poll after poll over the two years demonstrated the American public's disinclination to take military action or to get deeply involved in other ways in Central America's conflicts. When the election in El Salvador was finally held, the yield was mixed. That the guerrillas were unable to sabotage the balloting as they tried to do showed clearly that they lacked the popular support often attributed to them. In that sense, it was a modest victory for U.S. policy. However, leftists and some moderates boycotted the polls. Duarte's progressive Christian Democrats lost to right-wing political elements. The winners promptly attempted to halt the land-reform program and threatened worse. Human rights violations continued and so, in sporadic fashion, did the combat.

The Reagan administration's ambassador to El Salvador, Deane Hinton, began to criticize his host government in terms similar to those

White had used in 1980. What progress could be claimed came with
agonizing slowness. The chronic corollary of military stalemate was
blood-spattered political turmoil. Elsewhere in the region, new regimes
in Honduras and Guatemala—the former installed by election, the latter by coup d'etat—were proving to be marginal improvements over
their predecessors from Washington's viewpoint. But the Reaganauts
still groped for the right combination in Nicaragua, seeming to vacil-
late between paramilitary pressure and conciliation. And in early 1983
another spasm of concern about El Salvador began as the rebels became aggressive again.

Though modest in scale, new economic development programs
aimed at ameliorating poverty in the region were begun by Washington.
Fidel Castro remained a source of irritation, as he had for every American President since Eisenhower and likely would for years to come.
The Reaganauts responded in kind, putting new restrictions on trade
and travel, conducting naval patrols in a manner aimed at keeping the
Cubans jittery, stepping up pro-American propaganda. Having demonstrated its willingness to be more aggressive in Central America than
the Carter administration had been, the Reagan team seemed content
to settle for a standoff while coping with crises elsewhere.

While Haig was making a large public issue about Castro's activities
in Central America, the Administration very quietly was mulling ways
to treat a much more volatile adversary, Muammar al-Qaddafi. He had
seized control of the torpid kingdom of Libya in 1969 and transformed
it in name and in character. Qaddafi christened his desert domain the
Socialist People's Libyan Arab Jamahiriya and took as his mission the
promotion of Arab nationalism heavily tinged with Muslim funda-
mentalism.

Despite the country's small population—just over three million by
1982 estimates—Qaddafi had enough petrodollars and more than
enough zeal to underwrite terrorism in three or four continents. Starting in the mid-seventies, when Qaddafi's relationship with Sadat turned
from fraternal cooperation to violent antagonism, Libya's forces actively attempted to subvert its impoverished, backward neighbors,
Niger, Chad and Sudan. Ultimately the Libyan army occupied Chad
for a time and its made-in-U.S.S.R. air force carried out bombing missions across the Sudanese border. With funds and technical assistance,
Qaddafi supported the Ethiopians against the Somalis, the South
Yemenese against the Saudis. After the American embassy in Tehran
was seized, a Libyan mob sacked the U.S. mission in Tripoli, rendering
the building unusable. While all this was going on, remarkably, upward
of two thousand Americans continued to work and live peacefully in
Libya, most of them in the oil industry. Italians and Egyptians also
supplied technical expertise and skilled labor for a country which, on

its own, seemed able to do little except export oil and turmoil. The United States happened to be one of Libya's biggest customers, buying approximately $7 billion worth of crude in 1980.

Reagan came into office affronted by this paradox. Qaddafi was making life difficult for America's closest ally in the Arab world, and American dollars were helping him do it. Further, Libya was doing everything it could to prevent consummation of the Camp David peace plan. Early in February the President asked Haig whether there was any leverage the United States could exert. The Secretary of State, already thinking about his "strategic consensus" scheme, was also eager to find ways of leashing Qaddafi. That question became one of the first submitted to a special interagency group, or IG, in the new administration.*

With the State Department's Middle East Bureau in charge of the policy review, the result was what White House staff members called a mouse—a collection of minor items unlikely either to crimp Qaddafi's style or attract his attention. The proposals were to reduce technical exports to Libya, restrict the issuance of visas, and close the Libyan "people's bureau," or embassy, in Washington. These steps were taken by May, when the Administration issued a nonbinding warning to Americans about the dangers of travel or residence in Libya. At the same time, the small American diplomatic mission that had remained in Tripoli after the 1979 attack on its headquarters was withdrawn.

Those measures seemed inadequate to Reagan and the inner circle of the NSC. They agreed that more must be done to contain Qaddafi. As one participant put it, "We concluded pretty early that we wouldn't be able to do business with him. He is just a bad actor. It was irrelevant to worry about driving him closer to Moscow." Instead, the Administration set out to "put pressure on Qaddafi's environment." There was some dim prospect that a dissident movement within Libya might emerge and eventually oust Qaddafi. The CIA was asked what, if anything, the United States could do to encourage that development. Covert-action specialists suggested scenarios, but if anything came of them the Administration managed to maintain secrecy about the details.

The Pentagon meanwhile proposed some overt pressure. Prior to 1980, the Sixth Fleet in the Mediterranean Sea had been accustomed to extending its summer maneuvers into the Gulf of Sidra. In 1980, the

---

* IG's in the national security field generally were headed by assistant secretaries of State or Defense. Senior interagency groups, or SIG's, were headed by under secretaries or deputy secretaries. In the Reagan administration the system usually was cumbersome and inefficient, rarely producing imaginative or timely results.

Carter administration avoided the Gulf, appearing to honor, at least tacitly, Qaddafi's claim that those waters belonged to Libya. Officially, the United States insisted that the Gulf was an international body of water. Now the Defense Department proposed to reassert that view by conducting a training exercise at the Gulf's northern edge. The White House accepted the idea with one small amendment: rather than hold the drill in July, while the tax-bill fight was still in progress, the Defense Department was asked to wait a few weeks. James Baker wanted no violent distractions during the finale of Reagan's winning legislative season.

Sixteen warships, half the Sixth Fleet's strength at that time, swung south in August after giving routine notice to other maritime powers, including Libya. Though Weinberger would later deny it for the record, the American forces were fully expecting trouble. Reagan personally reviewed the standing rules of engagement and approved their application for these maneuvers. In Los Angeles, White House technicians installed extra communications equipment and more secure phones than usual at the Century Plaza Hotel, where the presidential party would be staying. Reagan's aides wanted to be able to handle a very heavy volume of teletype and phone traffic.

As it turned out, the action on August 19 was over quickly. As a pair of carrier-based F-14 Tomcats swept across the Gulf of Sidra in the direction of the coast, two Libyan SU-22 Fitters closed with them. The Americans said that one missile was fired at them. The peacetime rules of engagement allowed the American pilots to respond according to their own judgment. The Tomcats, combat craft far superior to the Russian-made Fitters, quickly maneuvered behind the Libyans and used only one heat-seeking missile each to destroy the Libyan warplanes.

At the Century Plaza Hotel, the President and his men considered that a favorable conclusion. When he saw his top assistants for the first time the morning after, Reagan performed a bit of pantomime, impersonating a Western gunslinger drawing six-shooters from both hips. Qaddafi claimed aggression in his own airspace and talked of unspecified retaliation. Reagan, by coincidence, visited the aircraft carrier *Constellation* later in the day and told reporters, "We decided it was time to recognize what are international waters and behave accordingly . . . This is the rule that has to be followed—if our men are fired on, they're going to fire [back]." Just six days later, North Korea pegged a ground-to-air missile in the direction of an American SR-71 doing a high-altitude reconnaissance mission over the Sea of Japan. That plane carries no ordnance and the source of the projectile was dozens of miles away. The unpublicized American response was to alter the course of subsequent SR-71 flights to make them closer to, rather than farther from, North Korea. The contingency plan: in case of another attack, American planes would take revenge on North Korean air-defense facilities. However, the North Koreans decided not to test the United States again.

No such restraint was visible at the time in Libya, which continued to sell the United States oil and to give away trouble. Now the Administration had a new Libyan task force at work, this one headed by Robert "Bud" McFarlane, a former Marine colonel then serving as State Department counselor. Immediately after the Sidra incident, Qaddafi signed an agreement with Ethiopia and South Yemen that called for $900 million in Libyan military assistance to those two tendentious clients. Libya also launched a new escapade, operating through Benin in order to infiltrate anti-government units across Niger's southeastern frontier. During this period, when McFarlane visited Egypt, Sudan and Somalia, he discovered high anxiety in all three governments friendly to the United States. Washington planned a series of military exercises on both sides of the Arabian Peninsula in order to demonstrate support for pro-Western regimes. Shortly before Sadat's assassination in October, his Vice-President, Hosni Mubarak, visited Washington and again emphasized Egypt's alarm. Cairo was particularly concerned about pressure on Sudan. What would happen, Mubarak asked his hosts, if Sadat decided that he had to send military forces south to reinforce Sudan, or otherwise became embroiled with Libya? That might make Egypt's coast or its northwestern frontier vulnerable to a countermove. Would the Sixth Fleet provide a sea and air shield against that threat? The White House replied that the United States would take no part in an invasion, but Egypt should be free to protect its own interests as it chose. Yes, the United States would risk a confrontation with the Soviet Union if necessary to guard Egypt's right flank. It was never clear whether an Egyptian land invasion was a serious prospect or a gambit to scare Qaddafi off his adventurous course. Sadat's murder made the question moot.

The threat of terrorism appeared ominous. The attempt on Pope John's life was still fresh in the mind when Sadat was cut down. In Paris, an American diplomat was fired on and a Libyan was suspected. In Rome, the life of U.S. Ambassador Maxwell Rabb was threatened in a convincing manner. In Athens, investigators discovered that Muslim terrorists had staked out American offices. Therefore when the White House, late on November 17, received the first word of a Libyan plot against the President's life, officials were ready to take the warning seriously. Deaver worked until two o'clock the following morning revising travel arrangements for Reagan, who was scheduled to make an important speech at the National Press Club at midday on the eighteenth and then to visit the Library of Congress that evening. The schedule was maintained, with extra security precautions in place.

The initial intelligence had come from an informant whose previous reporting on terrorism had proved accurate. The material was relatively specific. A group of assassins, divided into two teams, was bound for the United States by separate routes. Their targets were Reagan, Bush and Haig, or any one of them. Soon the intelligence services of three allied countries contributed corroboration and additional details. The more comprehensive version said that the hit teams had other targets on their list if they could not get at the first three. The names of Meese, Baker and Deaver were mentioned specifically.

White House reporters from November 18 onward could not help notice the extra security precautions, which included additional Secret Service agents as well as automatic weapons more visible than usual. When inquiries were made, Deaver and others tried to discourage news reporting on the subject. He succeeded with a few news organizations, but the story soon broke and for several weeks Washington had a tantalizing guessing game. Was the scare real? Who leaked the Libyan connection to it and why? Was it a ruse intended to serve as an excuse for drastic action against Libya?

Inside the White House, the threat worsened what was already a tense period in late November. Other unpleasantness was occurring: the Allen affair, the *Atlantic Monthly* article on Stockman, a showdown with Congress leading to Reagan's first veto, news that unemployment had taken its biggest monthly increase of the year up to then, reaching 8 percent. Now the White House could not discover where in the U.S. national security establishment leaks about the Libyan hit teams were coming from, or for what motive. Once the news was out, officials confirmed some of the headlines, denied others, no-commented still others. Qaddafi was interviewed on American television and suddenly the leader of the free world found himself in a demeaning shouting match with the maniacal colonel who styled himself the defender of Islam and oppressed people. Where is the evidence? Qaddafi demanded. Reagan, he said, "is silly, he is ignorant." To reporters in Washington, Reagan said, "I wouldn't believe a word he says if I were you . . . We have the evidence and he knows it."

Aside from the credibility question, which was nettlesome, the White House now had another problem. What became known as the hit-team scare complicated the original goal, which was to penalize Qaddafi for his global offenses. The McFarlane group had been working toward the obvious conclusion: eventual cessation of oil purchases. First, however, the Administration attempted communication one more time. In early

October, a diplomatic note was sent through the Belgians, who represented U.S. interests in Tripoli. The formal message, stiffly worded, said that Washington was willing to discuss resumption of normal relations provided that Libya got out of the terrorism and subversion business. The note was returned without response—a clear diplomatic snub by the Libyan Government.

Five weeks later, however, while the CIA, FBI, and border guards were searching the horizon for "swarthy assassins," the Belgians relayed a message from Tripoli. This note—apparently prepared before the news broke—made no mention of the hit teams and was conciliatory in tone. The Libyan Government, it said, now hoped to put relations with the United States back on a more normal footing. Later, CIA Director Casey told an interviewer that Qaddafi sent a separate, less formal message concerning the assassins. As Casey put it, "Qaddafi sent somebody to say, 'We're going to call them off.' And then he said he was firing people from his intelligence organization, but we find they're still there. . . ."[6]

Now the Administration had some decisions to make, all of them complicated by the continued presence of Americans in Libya. Relatively few had left because of the warnings in May. The White House feared that any new action by the United States might produce a hostage situation on a scale much larger than the one in Tehran. On December 10, Reagan decided that Americans must now be ordered out and given some time to leave. After that grace period, Washington would then halt the purchase of Libyan oil and further limit the export of American drilling equipment. In practical terms these steps would have only limited impact; importation of Libyan oil already had declined sharply for economic reasons (the Libyans charged more than other OPEC countries), and European customers would probably take up the slack. Still, Reagan felt that the symbolism was important and he felt better knowing that American dollars would no longer finance Qaddafi's capers.

That still left the question of the hit teams. What should the U.S. response be if there was an actual assassination attempt? And if that attempt succeeded? Here Reagan secretly decided on a relatively temperate course. An assassination attempt that failed would draw only additional economic retaliation. On the other hand, if an American official were injured or killed, and the gunman identified as a Libyan agent, there would be a prompt military response. It should be a "heavy blow on an appropriate target," Reagan ruled.

The Pentagon proposed air strikes against one or more of the depots at which the Libyans kept Russian-made planes and tanks in large numbers. Reagan responded that he preferred an attack on something more closely identified with the reason for the assault. During the previous year or so, U.S. intelligence had identified twenty-five camps in use at one time or another for the training of terrorists and paramilitary units. Thirteen of these were functioning when Reagan and his aides discussed options on December 10. Reagan accepted the proposal that the largest and busiest of these facilities be obliterated in the event that a Libyan hit team actually staged a hit.

Five days later, Washington responded to the diplomatic note of mid-November. The Administration repeated its demand that Qaddafi stop his attempts to subvert neighboring countries and cease support of terrorism. Concerning the specific assassination scheme, Qaddafi was told that the United States would be "compelled to respond in the strongest terms" if any of its leaders was actually attacked. The Libyan foreign ministry returned the message to the Belgians without an answer or acknowledgment. However, by a separate channel Tripoli informed Washington that it would do nothing to impede the departure of Americans. That word was kept and most of the Americans were gone by February, when oil purchases were cut off.

The mystery of the assassination teams was not solved by the end of 1982. FBI Director William Webster acknowledged that investigators never established that any of the assassins got into the United States. Another official, who had monitored the situation from receipt of the first intelligence warning, said nine months later, "We believe that the two hit teams stopped in mid-passage. We can't be sure why they stopped. But we have good information that both groups made it to this side of the Atlantic."

Had Qaddafi changed his mind on his own? Had Washington scared him off? Had the entire caper been an elaborate disinformation scheme intended to make Washington feel nervous and look foolish? These questions went unanswered. Nor could anyone be certain why Qaddafi, in the months immediately following the hit-team furor, appeared to back away somewhat from his role as troublemaker. Having gone ahead with the first installment of the aid he had promised to Ethiopia and South Yemen, for instance, he delayed subsequent payments. American officials quietly noted a degree of retrenchment on Libya's part as conditions in the world market reduced its oil income. But no one was so bold as to predict that Qaddafi had been tamed permanently. Early in 1983, in fact, he renewed pressure on the Sudan.

By the time the Libyan melodrama occurred, the Reaganauts could not escape deep immersion in a variety of foreign challenges. They had hoped that by then their main domestic goals would have been achieved. Instead, they discovered that they would have to fight those rounds again while other challenges crowded in. An even bigger disappointment, one that astonished and saddened Reagan, was his gradual discovery that the system he had chosen to formulate and carry out his foreign policy was a failure. He would have to make drastic changes while world events moved ever faster.

14

Of Turf and Purges

The question from William Clark seemed simple enough, but George Shultz was startled to hear it. How will I be able to reach you, Clark wanted to know, while you're in Europe? What will your itinerary be? The president of the Bechtel Corporation told Reagan's National Security Adviser that his plans were flexible; he would keep his office informed of his whereabouts if Clark needed to track him down.

Musing about that phone conversation later, Clark would insist that he had no specific reason for pinning Shultz down, no certain knowledge of what would soon happen and how urgently Shultz would be needed. In fact it was Shultz who had placed the call shortly before leaving for Europe on June 16. He wanted to talk about the Middle East, a subject on which he had strong views. He was disturbed about the escalating warfare in Lebanon and the way the Administration— that is, Haig—was coping. As a sometime adviser to the White House, he occasionally volunteered his thoughts.

The call came at a time of keen anxiety for Clark. The presidential party had just returned from Europe and the frail agreements reached at the 1982 Economic Summit were already disintegrating. Tension between Al Haig and the White House senior staff had reached a new peak, leading Clark to believe that the Secretary of State should be replaced as soon as possible. There wasn't much time to consider exactly how or when that should be done, what with the emergency in Lebanon and the climax of the cameo war over the Falkland Islands. Yet the "Haig problem" was now high on Clark's agenda. If Clark managed to cut Haig loose, a replacement would be needed simultaneously. Shultz's call was a reminder. Clark sensed that he might soon have to reach Shultz quickly, and not merely to exchange observations about the difficulty of dealing with the Begin government.

Ten days later there would be other, more historic phone conversations between Shultz and the White House. These transatlantic talks would draft Shultz to be Secretary of State. They would also signal the end of an extraordinary ordeal going back to January of 1981. During those eighteen months Reagan's foreign policy apparatus had sputtered, belched smoke, injured those tending it, confused those observing it from abroad. Richard Allen, one of the early casualties, spoke with an edge after his experience: "The President paid the price. Policy paid the price. The [NATO] alliance paid the price. And it was all done with a willfulness that, to put it charitably, struck me as unusual."[1]

For Allen, the culprit was Alexander Haig, whose presumed obsession with dominating the process was often a flashier—though less important—issue than the policies being debated. The White House senior staff, after ousting Allen and trying to repair grave flaws in the system, came to agree with him about Haig. For Haig, the villains were the troika, Weinberger, Allen, Kirkpatrick and eventually Clark. Even Clark, whom he had occasionally called "Uncle Bill" while Clark served him loyally as Deputy Secretary of State, became one of the obstacles to Haig's conduct of the mission as he saw it. He started out believing that Reagan wanted him to be the President's "vicar"* for national security affairs. Instead he found himself condemned to the role of Ishmael. By his lights, all he was trying to do was manage foreign policy in a rational, orderly way.

Some truth could be found in both these viewpoints. Haig's own aggressiveness was a large factor in the conflicts, and was decisive in his downfall. But it is also true that he was confronted with a system so badly flawed initially that even the most unctuous cookie-pusher would have recoiled. Reagan blinked at that for so long while severe contradictions went unresolved that Haig deserves at least partial absolution.

Reagan and his troika came into office not only innocent about the content of foreign problems, but also naïve about the means necessary to translate Reagan's instincts into operational policy. Neither Reagan nor any of the three ranking advisers in the White House during 1981 had been a practitioner or even a medium-serious student of foreign affairs. Allen did possess some experience in the field, but the power

---

* Haig gave the term currency, but did not claim authorship. He attributed the analogy to Paul Nitze, a national security specialist since World War II, who used it circa 1960 when describing systems for managing the conduct of foreign affairs. Having become prominent under Democratic Presidents, Nitze served Reagan as chief U.S. negotiator at the INF talks with the Russians in Geneva.

distribution devised by Ed Meese kept Allen out of the inner circle. One early source of the difficulties was a misconception shared by Reagan and Meese that national security affairs could be orchestrated without any single player or power center's having a strong hold on the baton. In part that attitude was a reaction to the conflicts in prior administrations. The balance of influence shifts somewhat from President to President, but the general trend since the Kennedy years had been to make the White House National Security Adviser a powerful traffic cop at the congested intersection of diplomatic, military and international economic affairs. Jimmy Carter, typically, never quite decided how to manage that heavy flow. Thus his White House adviser, Zbigniew Brzezinski, and his Secretary of State for more than three years, Cyrus Vance, engaged in an enervating contest for influence.

Observing that, remembering earlier conflicts and clinging to the quaintly appealing notion that he should restore "cabinet government," Reagan had decided long before taking office that the National Security Adviser's role should be diminished. That official and his staff of three dozen experts should be coordinators of decision-making, not creators or executors of policy. Those functions must reside at the State Department. Further, Reagan initially believed that neither the President nor the Secretary of State should indulge in much personal diplomacy far afield. Meese could remember that as early as 1976 Reagan disparaged special missions at that level. What Reagan thought of as "pick and shovel work" should be left to the ambassadors or, when necessary, to designated envoys.[2] The attitude was tidy, but not very realistic.

Restoring the Secretary of State to the stature enjoyed by John Foster Dulles or Henry Kissinger* was one thing. That model could work as well as any other—provided power resided somewhere. The actual effect of the Reagan-Meese approach, however, was to atomize authority. State recaptured a degree of clout in formulating policy, but not enough to make the process move in either an efficient or a creative manner because the Pentagon was allowed considerable influence. The White House stepped back during the first year, so far back that Reagan himself often appeared to be out of the game. Some personal decisions Reagan did make early in his term, such as the resumption of full grain exports to the Soviet Union, conflicted with his general goals. He did not make a comprehensive statement on Soviet-American relations until mid-1982, when he had to enunciate the U.S. position on strategic weapons negotiations. Otherwise the Administration did

* Kissinger had it both ways. While National Security Adviser, he monopolized power in the West Wing basement, rendering Secretary of State William Rogers impotent. When he succeeded Rogers, Kissinger retained influence; Nixon appointed the unobtrusive Brent Scowcroft to the adviser's post.

poorly in expressing its broad policies, and Reagan himself ducked opportunities to explain where he was trying to lead the United States.

He became defensive about criticism on this subject. In a press conference on June 16, 1981, he complained, "There seems to be a feeling as if an address on foreign policy is somehow evidence that we have a foreign policy and until you make an address, you don't have one. And I challenge that. I'm satisfied that we do have a foreign policy. I have met with eight heads of state already, representatives of nine other nations. The Secretary of State is now in China . . . I have been in personal communication by mail with President Brezhnev . . ."

Reagan was confusing the practice of diplomacy with the formulation of policy. Haig's visit to China merely established that the Administration had failed to balance its need to deal constructively with Peking and its desire to continue arming Taiwan. It would be nearly another year before the Administration finally began to resolve that basic issue. In a narrow, literal sense, Reagan was correct—a government can make clear its positions and goals without comprehensive statements from the President. What he overlooked was that his spokesmen all too often were at odds with one another.

Weinberger, confident of his special relationship with Reagan, felt free to announce decisions and views that demonstrated the Administration's internal tensions. The Defense Secretary, for instance, insisted on starting production of enhanced radiation warheads—the so-called neutron bombs—at a time when Haig was attempting, delicately, to assure the rest of NATO that the United States would synchronize its policy concerning intermediate range nuclear weapons with the allies. Haig was habitually reminding his colleagues of the view from the other side of the Atlantic. "Looking at it from the Germans' perspective," he would say. Or, "As Schmidt told me recently . . ." Weinberger had little patience with this line. The Defense Secretary would counter, "We shouldn't have German domestic politics affecting our decisions." To his adversaries, Haig's reflex smacked of traditional State Department squish. He saw it the opposite way. "I believed," he told me later, "that the toughest line against the Soviet Union was to have a unified set of policies within the Western community, including Japan, where policy sticks could be applied in unison, rather than [undertake] unilateral, meaningless American action."[3]

The Pentagon was visibly ahead of the State Department in promoting the military aircraft deal with Saudi Arabia. When Haig, during the summer of 1981, was trying to woo Menachem Begin into a tractable stance, Weinberger went on television to criticize the Israeli Prime Minister. Well into 1982 the State Department and the Pentagon continued to wrestle over important issues, whether it was the specific posture from which to begin strategic arms limitation talks or the best way to respond to the imposition of martial law in Poland.

Reagan zigzagged between the rivals, sometimes favoring one, sometimes the other. Usually he appeared to prefer splitting the difference rather than imposing a coherent view. Meanwhile Haig engaged in side skirmishes with assorted other officials, such as Jeane Kirkpatrick at the United Nations and Eugene Rostow, head of the Arms Control and Disarmament Agency (ACDA). Sometimes the issue was substance, sometimes ego. Always it made the Reagan administration look foolish.

Haig and Rostow got into a public hair-pull over whether ACDA or State had primary jurisdiction in the arms control field. In one round, Haig forced Rostow to cancel a meeting with the Soviet ambassador, Anatoly Dobrynin, on the day the conversation was scheduled to take place. Soon after, on September 2, 1981, Haig's spokesman gave out a formal statement: "The State Department has and will continue to take the lead in this Administration, coordinating policy required to prepare for and support the conduct of arms control negotiations." Haig personally instructed his Press Office to make that declaration of primacy without informing, let alone consulting, anyone at ACDA. The next morning ACDA responded with its own pronouncement, calling the State Department "factually inaccurate" on the jurisdictional question. That particular feud continued into the following year, adding to the difficulty the Administration had in formulating arms control policy and conducting negotiations. After Clark took over the NSC post, Rostow's standing continued to decline at the White House, where he was neither trusted nor respected. That was cold comfort to Haig, who found the general chaos increasingly difficult to tolerate. He complained to a reporter about it, assuming that the conversation was off the record. Instead the interview was published verbatim, including this exchange:

> *Haig:* If you're asking me would I like to see greater discipline . . . the answer is yes. But I don't focus it on Cap Weinberger. I focus it on the cacophony of voices.
>
> *Reporter:* In the White House?
>
> *Haig:* Throughout the Administration. I think we have to tighten up.
>
> *Reporter:* Who has to tighten up?
>
> *Haig:* Well, I think the President.
>
> *Reporter:* But he has to have some instrument in the White House to do it . . . and his National Security Adviser [Allen] is barely visible.
>
> *Haig:* Oh, no. I think his National Security Adviser is trying to do what he feels the President wants him to do.[4]

What the President wanted, or knew, was by no means clear. Reagan himself embellished the image of confusion by occasionally getting his facts wrong at press conferences, or by practicing an overspeak that required later clarification. The reason Reagan originally sent Philip Habib to the Middle East in the spring of 1981 was to ward off an Israeli attack on Syrian forces in Lebanon. The Syrians had installed new Soviet-built surface-to-air missiles that threatened Israel's air superiority. While the diplomat was working on that problem, the Israelis bombed a nuclear reactor in Iraq. Thus the Middle East was Topic A when Reagan prepared for his June 16 press conference, and he was ostensibly well briefed. Yet when the question of the new missiles came up, Reagan said, "They are offensive weapons. There's no question about the direction in which they are aimed. I am speaking now of the Syrian weapons."

By any normal definition, the anti-aircraft rockets were defensive, not offensive. After the press conference Larry Speakes said that it had been a slip of the tongue, which Reagan himself realized. The context of Reagan's statement, however, made it clear that it was his comprehension that had slipped. All too often on delicate questions of geopolitics, Reagan said startling things in order to make a point. On October 1 he was defending the proposed sale of AWACS to the Saudis. A reporter asked what would happen if Saudi Arabia went the way of Iran and the sophisticated aircraft fell into hostile hands. Reagan responded first by saying that U.S. technical secrets would not be compromised even in that event. He would have been on safe ground had he stopped there. Instead, he added, "I have to say that Saudi Arabia—we will not permit it to be an Iran."

How was that again? Was Reagan proclaiming a new doctrine for the Persian Gulf in which the United States would protect the Saudi royal government from internal threat? Well . . . maybe. In the following exchange, Reagan said accurately enough that the West had a crucial stake in protecting sources of oil. Therefore ". . . there's no way that we could stand by and see that taken over by anyone that would shut off that oil." That sounded like an enlargement on Carter's pledge to build a Rapid Deployment Force capable of defending the Gulf states from external aggression. But it was not clear then, and the Administration could not clarify it later.

Haig had known from the outset that amateur night would be a frequent feature of the new administration. Not only were the President and his immediate entourage neophytes in the field; so were the Secretaries of Defense and Treasury. Some of Haig's associates later reasoned that he thought this fact would work in his favor—that Reagan, recognizing his own and his Californians' inadequacies, would give Haig a very long, very weak leash. In one sense that was true much of the time, but the clang of conflicting egos and other distractions tended

to hide two crucial facts. First, the divisions between Haig's group at
State and the civilian Pentagon leadership under Weinberger were fundamental, not merely institutional or procedural. Second, though Reagan's personal instincts usually lay with the Weinberger faction, the
President often came down on Haig's side, or close to it, until the final
weeks of Haig's tenure. Then, in a left-handed tribute to Haig's views,
Reagan appointed as his new Secretary of State a man who in broad
terms shared Haig's "Atlanticist" views on most issues. Nonetheless
Haig, until relieved of his post, had to struggle constantly against elements within the President's official family which he considered benighted. His pugnacious style became debilitating for him and exasper-
ating for those around him.

The fundamental split was the difference between the Eastern Establishment brand of anti-Communism and the Western conservatives' approach. Nixon, abetted by Kissinger, had practiced the former. The
true-believing Reaganites regarded that as a prescription for sellout. In
the Ford and Carter years the litmus issues were SALT, other aspects
of détente and the Panama Canal treaties. On these Reagan had sided
with the hardest-liners. Arms control remained a source of contention
in the early eighties, along with East-West trade, the China question
and the relative importance of the NATO alliance versus a tougher,
more independent line by the United States.

The parallels were not perfect, but the pattern was clear. Haig was
hardly a geopolitician of brilliance. Rather he had been a good student
when he worked for Nixon and Kissinger and now he would be a faithful executor of their foreign policy legacy. His years as NATO's military commander reinforced these lessons. Thus he was a Europeanist
first, a believer in alliances and power balances even if that meant
breaking some of Reaganism's primordial spears. Moscow would pros-
per in direct ratio to the size of rifts within the Atlantic alliance. By
the same token, he understood the necessity of broadening U.S. relations with China. To do anything that would even indirectly encourage
a Sino-Soviet rapprochement could be a historic disaster for Western
interests. The American obligation to Taiwan was of course a sticking
point. "The greatest protection for Taiwan in the long run," Haig
remarked in one conversation, "is a good relationship between Washington and Peking."*

In most respects, then, Haig's ideas were a throwback to the main-

---

* That interview was on September 29, 1982. I was reminded of how much
Haig's thinking was affected by Nixon-Kissinger policy when, on October 11,
Nixon published an essay in the New York *Times* containing the same formula-
tion in almost the same words.

stream policies followed by both parties prior to the Carter detour into moralistic muddle. Of course Haig adjusted for new circumstances and could pursue a more belligerent line in one region or another, as he did in Central America. Concerning the Middle East, he was more tolerant than most of his colleagues—and predecessors—of Israel's militarism. But on balance Haig was a sober practitioner of traditional power politics. This ran against the grain of right-wing thinking, on which neoconservatives, Old Right and New Right united.

"The Perle-Weinberger line," Haig growled in parody once out of office. "Anything Marxist is evil and must be destroyed. The Soviet Union is ready to collapse and if we just apply a few more sanctions, it will. On the one hand we can insist that we're too weak to negotiate with them, and on the other hand, we're strong enough to conduct brittle confrontational policies the outcome of which we might not be prepared to face."[5]

There was a touch of self-serving hyperbole in Haig's later commentary, but he had the essentials correct. In the Pentagon—more on the civilian side than within the Joint Chiefs of Staff—Reagan's men reintroduced a strand of thought that had not been detectable for many years. Though muted and rarely articulated, it was a new version of the Fortress America model, a view that the United States first must rearm and then follow its own national interests. The allies could follow or not. If that meant leaving the Europeans behind, so be it. If it meant an indefinite delay in reaching an arms control agreement, ditto. If it meant risking the Peking connection—well, the bear and the dragon could waltz again if they wished. All this was a strong reaction to a decade of deteriorating U.S. influence abroad, years of frustration in which ungrateful allies thrived under the American military umbrella but refused to support American initiatives vigorously.

On Capitol Hill, this translated into opposition from New Right senators to State Department and ACDA appointees who were considered soft. On the National Security Council staff, though its influence was slight in 1981, it meant an undercurrent of disapproval of Haig's attitudes from Richard Allen and the resident Sovietologist, Richard Pipes. In the Pentagon, it meant dogged opposition to State Department initiatives at several critical junctures. Among the coterie of outside activists, it meant a chronic wail of criticism. *Human Events,* long one of Reagan's favorite periodicals, said it simply in a headline: HAIG MUST GO. The story below lamented that "Haig, the combative warrior with a somewhat quirky personality, has, somehow, been transformed into a pussycat."[6]

Even Kissinger published a pair of articles in which he underscored "the emptiness of the Western reaction to Poland." By implication, Kissinger was criticizing Haig, his erstwhile protégé, who was infuriated by the Op-Ed page pieces. At the same time, Kissinger viewed with alarm the internal division between what he called "a new isolationism and traditional Atlanticism." He warned that the Administration must "master these issues and design a coherent policy."[7]

That had been the cry of assorted critics for months, long before the suppression of Poland's reform movement imposed a difficult test in December of 1981. But how could the Administration sort out complex policy questions when it could not even cope with personality quirks and routine paper flow? Whether Haig's own imperative in a given case was ego or the knowledge that he was better qualified to take charge than the other players—usually it was a mixture of the two —from the outset he acted peculiarly on questions of turf. Before the inauguration he told Reagan that the NSC staff must neither deal with foreign representatives in any way nor conduct press relations of its own. On Inauguration Day Haig gave Meese the draft of a proposed presidential order delineating authority among the agencies concerned with national security affairs. It gave State primacy on all important matters and barely acknowledged the existence of the National Security Council staff. Meese, with Baker supporting him, put aside the draft, ostensibly for review; it went unsigned for a year.

Another newcomer to the group who remained neutral in the subsequent conflict was able to watch Haig and Allen closely. "If Al had been as smart an operator as he was supposed to be," this official said eighteen months later, "he would have seduced Dick at the beginning. He would have taken Dick aside and said something like, 'Look, you and I are the experts and we have a problem with these amateurs. Let's work together.' Dick would have kissed Al's ring and carried Al's water." Instead, Haig went out of his way to show contempt for a man he considered inferior. At private meetings, when Allen had the temerity to make a substantive comment, he got a Haigalian glare and putdown in response. That attitude was visible in public as well. At the White House official dinner for Helmut Schmidt in May, Haig—with reporters within earshot—quipped of Allen: "He has to apologize." Why? "For being Dick Allen."[8]

In Haig's view Allen also had to apologize for the reasons he was where he was. Not only was he Meese's man—a demerit, as Haig saw things—but Allen was also supposed to be a right-wing counterweight to the Secretary of State. During the transition several New Right senators told the Reaganauts that if Haig was to be at State, they wanted someone they knew and trusted in the adviser's post. Allen fit that description. Laxalt informed Meese that the faction would be "more comfortable" with Allen in the White House assignment. Thus Haig was not about to give Allen or Allen's subordinates a break. One important side effect during 1981 was an inability to develop a consistent, effective method for briefing the President daily on national security matters. Haig feared that Allen was using the routine morning briefing period to steer the President rather than merely keep him current. When Haig started to participate frequently, the Defense Department and CIA had the same apprehension about him. For a time Reagan received only written updates, which he would discuss periodically with his National Security Planning Group (NSPG), a streamlined model of the National Security Council.

State Department mid-echelon officials were under strict instructions to withhold policy papers and cable traffic from their opposite numbers on Allen's staff in routine situations. One of Haig's senior assistants had to approve exceptions. Even material from the field designated for the White House was often delayed at State longer than necessary. When Haig planned his first Middle East trip in April, he was disinclined to allow the NSC specialist for that region, Geoffrey Kemp, to accompany him even though such participation was customary. Allen had to get Haig in a mellow moment and obtain his personal permission. In public, Allen continued to insist that all was well, and working according to design. In private, he told me, "My staff sometimes goes crazy about being excluded from some processes."[9]

Haig appeared to take the offensive, and to give offense, on every front, escalating petty matters into titanic conflicts. Early on, he insisted on fighting a budget reduction proposed by Stockman. The specific issue was minor: a reduction of 300 job slots, some of them vacant, in the Agency for International Development. Stockman offered to split the difference at 150 but Haig demanded that this small item be argued before Reagan. To the President, he defined it as a "choice between, on the one hand, disaster, and on the other a judgmental compensation." Judgmental compensation? That was a specimen of what became known as Haig-speak. Not yet understanding the lingo, Reagan ruled against Haig on that occasion.

This sort of thing went on constantly, at every level, on subjects large and small. In mid-June 1982, when the ordeal was almost over, Haig was still fighting skirmishes, still crying wolf. At that point the foreign policy apparatus was consumed by two complex concerns: a new decision on East-West commercial arrangements that infuriated the European allies, and the war in Lebanon. By coincidence, Bill

Brock was to go to the Middle East for routine chores in Egypt and Israel.

The U.S. embassy in Tel Aviv and the State Department's Middle East Bureau both advised Brock to cancel the stop in Israel, which he did. But there was no reason to call off his trip to Cairo. Yet on June 15, the day before he was to leave, Haig called him not once, but twice. He told Brock to stay home. By going only to Egypt, the Secretary of State said, Brock would risk ruining the Administration's entire Middle East policy. Puzzled, Brock called Clark at the White House and asked what to do. Equally puzzled, Clark took time out of his frantic day to make inquiries. He discovered, among other things, that Haig had not even discussed the matter with his own ranking Middle East specialist, Assistant Secretary Nicholas Veliotes (Haig at that point was at odds with Veliotes and tried to avoid dealing with him). Clark ruled that Brock should use his own judgment, and Brock went to Cairo.

At the White House during the difficult first months the troika as a unit could do little to remedy matters. All three members knew that Reagan's interests were being harmed, in both public relations and policy terms. Formulating policy on arms control, for instance, was slow-motion torture. One set of major decisions remained frozen until Clark and McFarlane moved from the State Department to the White House and issued flat orders in Reagan's name. That was something Allen had lacked the authority to do.

Haig's own aides began to lament the absence of a strong NSC adviser to break deadlocks. After the North Koreans fired a missile at an American SR-71, it took two weeks to get an agreement among the Pentagon, CIA and State Department as to how the United States should react. Said one of the participants in those discussions, "It was ridiculous. The NSC should have been all over us, demanding recommendations for a quick decision. Instead, there was nothing." Much more serious was Weinberger's inability until the fall of 1981 to formulate firm plans for the Administration's strategic weapons program. In that case the dissension was primarily inside the Defense Department. Again, Allen had no franchise for intervention. Once the complex of decisions was announced in October, new controversies arose.

Instead of decisions there were leaks about the lack of them, and about the disputes. These, as much as anything else, distressed Baker and Deaver, both of whom were highly sensitive to political public relations. Haig's subordinates, quite obviously speaking for their boss, complained chronically about the way Haig was being treated. Haig personally believed that Baker, Allen and Darman all spread tales about him, though he seemed to be uncertain who the chief White

House "guerrilla" sniping at him was at any given time.* In search of a truce, Baker invited Haig to play doubles on the White House tennis court.

Even in one of the few relatively quiet periods, when it appeared that the system was functioning somewhat better, Haig could not shake the feeling that an antagonist was after him. At the time of my first formal interview with Haig, Allen was gone. I couldn't help remembering his description of Haig, privately expressed in an admiring tone, "Haig has the capability to wind himself up on each and every issue as if it is the most important question of the year. He has an *élan vital* that allows him to coil up and emit energy. It's a remarkable trait."[10]

Haig's conversation with a writer in March 1982 obviously wasn't the most important question of the day for him, let alone the year, but he spoke with a ferocious intensity and concern for detail that was striking. A few of his details turned out to be wrong, though he seemed genuinely convinced otherwise. For instance, he insisted that he, not the Reaganauts, had originally settled on Clark as Deputy Secretary of State. When I expressed skepticism, he asked that I check with Clark personally. The next day one of Haig's assistants called to remind me of the request. As it happened, I had been in touch with Clark during the transition, when he was considering whether to take the job, and had also discussed the unusual appointment with the troika. The vote was four to one against Haig's version, but I went through the motions of checking one more time, with the same result. Haig simply could not believe that he had been euchred into accepting Clark.

Haig spoke at length about the "vicarship theory," explaining that while it was an approach ostensibly favored by Democrats, Eisenhower had given a "vicarship" to Dulles. Kennedy had taken the "essentially Republican" approach of centralizing power in the White House, as Johnson did to some extent as well. Reagan had told him that he would have primacy, that the Secretary of State would be the "principal foreign policy adviser, spokesman and agent." Haig took Reagan at his word, which was indeed offered sincerely. What Haig, the stranger, could not know was that Reagan would leave it to the troika, and particularly Meese, during the first year, to translate that word into practice. When Haig, on Inauguration Day, handed Meese the proposed

---

* Haig, in a fit of exasperation, told columnist Jack Anderson that someone in the White House was running a "guerrilla campaign" against him. He had called Anderson in an effort to shoot down an article about to be published. Anderson spiked the first column but substituted the "guerrilla" story, which included a personal plea to Anderson from Reagan on Haig's behalf. The incident caused a temporary furor, embarrassed Reagan and added "guerrilla" to the Washington lexicon for the rest of Haig's stay. The column appeared November 3, 1981.

order assigning authority, the new Secretary of State was merely acting out what he thought his role was to be. He was also living his memory of the Nixon transition when, as he put it, "we had that problem in wrenching that power away from Bill Rogers the same week before the Inauguration of Richard Nixon."[11]

Fascinating point. One of Haig's problems throughout his stay with the Reaganauts was his inability to purge the bureaucratic reflexes he had learned during his years with Nixon and Kissinger. Someone in his position back then had to do a lot of wrenching to stay alive. Now he was determined to be a wrencher still, not a wrenchee like poor Bill Rogers. Reagan's people did not know what to make of all this. Their reaction was to leak stories that Haig was grasping at power. Haig was flummoxed in his turn. From Reagan, in public and private, he continued to get assurances that the President indeed wanted the Secretary of State to be what Haig insisted on calling the vicar of foreign policy. Later he would say, "I might have thought hard about taking the job had it been the other school of thought." But in the newspapers, and in other ways, Haig found himself diminished, deprecated.

Though Allen was caught on one occasion leaking derogatory information, Haig was shrewd enough to know that Allen wasn't his real nemesis. "It wasn't worth my trouble," Haig said, "to have problems with him because he was somewhat irrelevant organizationally—not of my doing, but because of the structural arrangement. What ostensibly was 'cabinet government' was in reality White House staff domination through fragmentation." So Haig sniffed higher up for the perpetrator(s). The motive? Well, it was "someone who has something to gain from having to adjudicate or correct or manage this difference. You see? And the same thing [happened] when [Allen] disappeared from the scene. Suddenly I started having 'problems' with Mr. Weinberger."

Haig had part of the picture right anyway. From the first spring onward, Reagan's top advisers, and particularly Deaver, doubted that Haig would work out. He just did not fit the Reaganaut mold. He was too difficult to deal with, too mercurial. On the evening of March 24 Deaver was in the mansion with the Reagans watching the network news. Haig was shown protesting to a congressional committee earlier in the day the idea that Bush might be appointed to chair the Crisis Management Team (the selection was announced later the same day, after some mixed signals and after Reagan had personally assured Haig that he had nothing to worry about). Deaver, incensed that Haig would go public with his *angst*, told the President and First Lady that eventually something would have to be done. Later he recalled having used dramatic language: "It's a cancer that will have to be cut out."[12]

But neither Deaver, Baker nor Meese contemplated a move against

Haig at that time. Nor were they methodically scribbling graffiti on his image. It became one of Deaver's special missions during 1981, in fact, to work closely with Clark to remove causes of tension. He had two excellent reasons for doing so. Reagan still respected his Secretary of State and was in no mood to consider a change. Second, departure of so senior an official early in a new administration is a sign of instability. It was mainly Haig's performances in public, routine White House gossip and murmurings within the State Department itself that caused the publicity so distressing to Haig.

Rather than attempting to exile Haig in 1981, the White House staff was trying to housebreak him. Meanwhile, Deaver decided that dumping Allen might be the solution. It was clear to Deaver, and eventually to Baker, that the NSC arrangement was a failure. The idea of a diminished NSC adviser had been taken too far. Further, by the summer of 1981 both Deaver and Baker felt that Allen was inappropriate for the post regardless of the job's stature. Deaver had been uneasy about Allen during the campaign but chose not to buck Meese on the issue. For Baker, disenchantment became complete when Allen was initially given responsibility for selling the AWACS plan and did so poor a job that he had to be relieved of the assignment. Another count against Allen was that his hostility toward Haig had earned him the enmity of Clark, who was still playing the role of Haig's shield. In this aspect of the conflict, neither policy nor ideology was a factor. Deaver, Baker and Clark were primarily concerned about negative publicity and faulty procedure. They were right in believing that Reagan was being ill-served by the organization chart then existing. What Baker and Deaver in particular failed to understand was the effect all of this was having on the substance of national security policy. Meese, more sensitive to these concerns, tended to lean toward the Weinberger view of the world. He also supported Allen longer than the others did.

On the weekend of July 11–12, the Deavers and the Clarks visited Helene von Damm* and her husband at Beach Haven Crest on the Jersey shore. Allen, by coincidence, was relaxing at his own summer home nearby. His weekend would have been ruined had he known the main topic of conversation between his White House colleague and the Deputy Secretary of State. Deaver asked Clark if he would take Allen's job under new ground rules that would elevate the adviser's authority. Yes, Clark replied, if Reagan really wanted him there. Deaver let it go

---

* Von Damm, Reagan's personal secretary in Sacramento, was a close friend of both Deaver and Clark. She came to the White House as the President's secretary with the understanding that she would be given a more important assignment. Later she became Pendleton James's deputy in the Personnel Office and succeeded him in August 1982. Reagan then named her Ambassador to Austria.

at that, wondering when and how he could engineer the switch. Reagan, with his keen dislike of staff friction and his disdain for administrative detail, had largely ignored the organizational difficulties of the NSC system. The rumors and the leaks irritated him, but he assumed that the troika was doing its best to cope. Columnists carped about the decision-making process, but they were always complaining about something. The Ottawa Economic Summit, forecast to be a debacle for Reagan, had turned out well enough. Poland, as Labor Day 1981 approached, was still Poland. Reagan thought that things weren't going badly.

Hence Deaver knew that Reagan would be reluctant to make any important change. Meese would be downright resistant to the idea. Clark would never consent to work under Meese, who had been his subordinate in Sacramento. In any event, the object of the game was not merely to get rid of Allen, but also to strengthen the NSC Adviser so that he would have direct access to the Oval Office and would speak for the President in dealing with agencies outside the White House. This meant removing Meese from the line of authority between the NSC staff and the Oval Office.

For the time being, Deaver merely dropped a hint or two to Reagan. His real opening came in November, when Allen's prior involvement in a petty incident prompted a Justice Department investigation and a major news story.* Tarred by publicity, Allen decided to take a brief leave during which he could defend himself freely. At that point, Deaver made his move.

In a private conversation, Deaver told Reagan that Allen should not be taken back, regardless of how the investigation turned out. Further, Reagan owed it to himself to consult a number of people outside the White House staff about both Deaver's recommendation and the status of the NSC post. The qualification *outside the White House staff* was crucial, because that meant the exclusion of Meese. It turned out to be a tricky business with undertones of the clandestine. Over the course of three weeks Deaver arranged meetings, most of them one-on-one, between the President and Bush, Haig, Weinberger, Regan, Casey and Laxalt. Most of the conversations were held in the residence rather than the Oval Office and none appeared on Reagan's schedule. Bringing in Casey and Laxalt was dicey from Deaver's viewpoint; both had been supporters of Allen early on.

Because Deaver's personal feelings about Allen were known to

---

* The previous January, Allen intercepted a $1,000 gratuity from Japanese journalists when they had a brief session with Nancy Reagan. The money was put in a safe and forgotten. Its discovery later led to an investigation and to other small dents in Allen's reputation.

Reagan, Deaver made no further representations of his own. He didn't
have to, as it turned out. Reagan got the message clearly enough from
the platoon of advisers drafted for the occasion. As the presidential
party was about to leave for a New Year's break in Palm Springs,
Reagan told Deaver that he had made a decision: Allen should be cut
loose. He had two concerns: a new post for Allen and the identity of
his replacement.

Deaver wanted Allen out altogether, but agreed to find some niche
for cosmetic purposes. Concerning the replacement, Deaver submitted
just one name: Clark. Can we spare him at State? Reagan asked. By
this stage we can, the aide replied. Reagan was satisfied.

Meese, meanwhile, was coming to realize that something had to give.
He decided that he would have to cut his losses where Allen was concerned. As he recalled it later: "I made up my own mind in December
that there had to be a change. There was no other way. The situation
and the relationships had become impossibly tangled. I told that to the
President before he went to California at the end of the month and I
recommended that he appoint Bill Clark."[13] Meese at the time had no
way of knowing that Clark would shoulder him out of national security
affairs, though a shrewder bureaucrat would have guessed. Meese was
assigned to break the bad news to Allen, who responded that he
wanted to hear it from Reagan personally. He got that opportunity on
January 4 in an Oval Office meeting. Balm came in two varieties. Allen
was told that it would be better for all concerned if he left because
even though the "case" against him had come to nothing in legal terms,
politically inspired attacks would continue. Second, he was made a
consultant—"for an indefinite period," the White House said—to the
President's Foreign Intelligence Advisory Board. Seven months later,
he cheerfully told me that he had served not a single day in that capacity.

Allen, in any event, instantly became stale news. The focus of attention became the Haig-Clark relationship and the changes Clark made
in the NSC structure. The State Department, from the Secretary's office
to the mid-level bureaucracy, was delighted at first. The new arrangement gave the NSC staff more authority, to be sure, but Clark was expected to use that influence to promote State Department policies. He
had, after all, acquired the limited expertise he commanded from working with Haig. Though a Reaganaut, he had served Haig well, at times
acting as the Secretary's apologist both with Reagan and with reporters.
If Haig had ever read the story of Henry II and Thomas à Becket, he
apparently had forgotten its enduring moral.

Once a Roman Catholic seminarian who had considered becoming a
priest, Clark understood hierarchy. He was working directly for Rea-

gan once again, and Reagan had three large needs Clark would have to fill. The President needed a policy-making machine that functioned well. He needed to be better versed in, and more involved in, national security affairs. Finally, he needed to be *perceived* as participating.

The first item was not at issue. The NSC staff had nowhere to go but up when Clark joined it. Nearly half the members lacked permanent credentials allowing them to move from the Old Executive Office Building to the White House basement at will. Dozens of pending orders, including the one delineating authority among the agencies, had never been revised or officially inscribed. Hangover directives from the Carter administration technically were still in effect, though no longer observed. Clark tackled all this underbrush immediately. He fired or transferred half a dozen of Allen's subordinates, sorted out the paper-flow problem, launched new policy studies, rattled the study groups that had fallen into paralysis.

In terms of presidential education and involvement, Clark resumed the practice of briefing Reagan daily, sometimes twice a day, and often in the company of an expert in a particular specialty. In this process, and in running National Security Council meetings as well, Clark initially met Haig's expectation in one important respect. The new adviser almost never advanced his own feelings on policy matters. He declined to be an advocate. However, Clark took it as part of his duty to remind the other players that Reagan's ideas were paramount. Inevitably, Clark began to trim wings at both the State Department and the Pentagon. Travel abroad by high-level officials, including Haig and Weinberger, now had to be "coordinated"—that is, controlled—by his office. The briefs carried by special envoys were suddenly subject to close White House scrutiny. While this sort of thing went on, the White House quietly put out word that, though Haig was still top foreign affairs banana in the cabinet, Reagan henceforth would control Reagan administration policies.

Haig seemed outwardly content with this for a time, particularly because his views continued to prevail through mid-spring on most of the important controversial questions. But Clark had been in office only a few weeks when the prospect of future difficulties became apparent. The new man warranted a profile in *Time*. The last few lines of the article in the issue of February 15, 1982, meet the author's prescience test:

> The good reviews Clark has been getting during his debut period carry some caveats between the lines. Like Reagan, he has never been accused of being an intellectual. His move to the White House improved a messy operation but has done nothing to redress another chronic problem: the Administration's lack of a strategic world view. Clark so far has been ret-

icent about pushing his own positions on specific issues, or even revealing them. Those who know him consider him an instinctive hawk. Eventually, as he gains confidence, he is likely to reinforce Reagan's own hard-line feelings. If that happens, Haig, who is more flexible, will be less eager to applaud the new master of the West Wing basement.

Which is more or less what eventually occurred. Haig hardly needed a magazine article to keep his anxiety mill grinding. Early in the new year and the new arrangement, when the relationship appeared to the outside world to be more serene than at any time during 1981, Haig had a tranquil conversation with Clark. As Haig recalled it later, they were commiserating with each other about the frustrations of their jobs. Clark remarked that he wished Reagan would let him go home to California. Haig said he intended to leave the Administration later in the year, in a "calm time." Of course Clark had heard Haig mutter about resigning, but on the previous occasions there had been some immediate provocation. This time Haig's discontent was general rather than specific. Clark responded with a laugh. Al, he said, there is no such thing as a calm time in this business.

Clark relayed Haig's remark to Reagan, but there was no reason to believe that a showdown was imminent. Reagan, for his part, preferred that there be no major changes in the Administration until after the 1982 election. In late April, Clark's private assessment was that the "Haig problem" was in remission. Occasional rashes still erupted. Haig and Deaver, for instance, clashed over a relatively minor State Department appointment and Haig insisted on taking it to Reagan for adjudication. The President ruled in Deaver's favor. But when the question of Haig's tenure came up, it was always followed by a second question: Who would replace him? Weinberger was still interested, but his star was no longer as luminous as it had once been. George Shultz? There was always George, of course.

Shultz had a quiet but undeniable appeal. Though not one of the old California circle, he was known and liked by the group and by Reagan himself. His background as an academic, cabinet officer and executive of a multinational corporation was of sufficient caliber and diversity.* By temperament he was a conciliator. The only important current issue on which he and Haig differed sharply concerned dealing with Israel. Shultz favored the exertion of more muscle in order to restrain the Begin government. But Haig thought well enough of him to draft him, in the spring of 1982, as the Administration's special liaison to heads

---

* Shultz earned a doctorate in economics at MIT. Later he taught at and became dean of the University of Chicago Graduate School of Business. He joined the Nixon administration as Labor Secretary and then became director of OMB and Treasury Secretary. At Bechtel, he was Weinberger's superior.

of foreign governments as the allies prepared for the Versailles summit meeting. Haig recalled that fact months later, implying that he'd had Shultz in mind as one possible replacement when that "calm time" arrived—probably after the election in November.[14]

Both in Haig's mind and Clark's then, there was an expectation that there might well be a new Secretary of State before the new year. Clark did not yet view the change as an urgent necessity the way his senior associates at the White House did, but he was beginning to doubt that the arrangement would ever work really well or that Haig could muster any enthusiasm for one of Clark's principal missions: enlarging Reagan's personal stamp on foreign policy. As in everything else he did, however, Clark wanted an orderly transition. If Haig could not stay in the family, Clark hoped for a no-fault separation. "At no time," he said later, "did I have the feeling he would have to be forced out, which he was."[15]

On that point, at least, Clark and Haig agreed. Though Haig had been leaning toward the exit and might well have walked through it later of his own volition, he lost control of the timing and the circumstances of his departure. In their accounts, in Reagan's recollections and in those of three others who tracked events closely, one finds a few discrepancies concerning detail and motivation. Yet four significant facts emerge:

• Haig's resignation was forced at an incredibly inopportune moment in the conduct of foreign policy.

• Clark, Deaver and Baker, in descending order of importance, brought about the switch and were largely responsible for the selection of Shultz.

• Reagan himself remained reluctant to make the change when it occurred. He acted only after his advisers persuaded him that there was no realistic alternative except to move quickly. Even then, Reagan was still insensitive to some of the issues involved.

• The sudden change, following a period in which Haig's influence had been deteriorating, in the short run weakened the State Department's hand on some of the policy matters that had to be faced in the ensuing few months.

None of that was obvious in early April, which was the slow beginning of Haig's abrupt end as Secretary of State. Until then, it appeared as if the new NSC arrangement might work out. "We got on rather well," Haig said of his initial dealings with Clark in the latter's new role, "until we had our first crisis." That was when the world learned where the Falkland Islands were, and that those barren dots of land in the South Atlantic were worth deadly combat. Before that bizarre bloodletting was over, Reagan went to Europe for what turned out to be the start of a new round in a prolonged squabbling with the allies over NATO's economic dealings with the Soviet Union. And while that argument was turning ugly, Israel invaded Lebanon. It was a spring of intense frustration for American diplomacy. Each situation, in its own way, offered evidence of how limited American influence was, even on its ostensible friends. Each case also stoked the Administration's internal tensions. Taken together, on the human level, they provided a choice of last straws for the final collapse of the Haig–White House relationship.

Haig still fought, in his idiosyncratic manner, for the territorial control he thought he had to have to manage these crises adequately. He had already given the world a peek at one of his tactics when he told a columnist, "I haven't changed my style in twenty years that I'm aware of, and that style is to get mad when things go wrong. [Anger] is a management vehicle. I don't know anyone who in a tense period would suggest that I'm a rattle-ass."[16] Now he would drive that "vehicle" ever more recklessly when in the vicinity of the Reaganauts.

That last metaphorical journey began with a real trip, or set of them, as he hurtled back and forth between Buenos Aires and London, attempting to prevent that most gratuitous mini-war. Reagan himself had failed, in a lengthy phone conversation with the Argentinian junta leader Leopoldo Galtieri, to deter the initial invasion. After that, U.S. strategy was straightforward. Haig would attempt to act as mediator. While that effort was underway the United States in its public pronouncements would remain evenhanded. If conciliation failed, the United States would then side with its historic ally against the military dictatorship that had resorted to force. There was relatively little internal dissent from this line except by Jeane Kirkpatrick. At an NSC meeting on April 7, just before Haig's shuttle began, she argued for long-term neutrality. To move to the British side, she said, would diminish U.S. influence in Latin America and make a mockery of the Rio pact, which prescribes cooperation against attack from outside the hemisphere. Haig, already hostile to Kirkpatrick, found her argument the essence of what was wrong with neoconservative foreign policy. He did not have to cut her down on that occasion, however, because Admiral Bobby Ray Inman, representing the CIA in Casey's absence and himself on the brink of retirement, demolished her position. Kirkpatrick's stand was the most wrongheaded he'd ever heard, Inman said. Not only was the Atlantic alliance far more important in strategic terms than the relationship with Argentina's unstable government, but over the long run, acquiescence to the junta's aggressiveness could only encourage more adventures. Argentina would probably have nuclear weapons within a few years, the government's most respected intelligence expert pointed out. Buenos Aires must be discouraged from taking any military option.

There was no doubt in Reagan's mind on this score from the beginning. He never wavered in his support for the Atlantic position or for Margaret Thatcher, the European leader he happened to like best. As Haig went about his work, however, he found the ground beneath him shifting. While it still appeared that evenhanded mediation had a slight chance to succeed, there was some pressure to take a pro-British stand more quickly. Then, when the shuttle failed to produce a compromise, Haig knew that Washington had but one shot left: to scare Argentina back from the brink. All along Galtieri and his colleagues had believed that Britain would not fight. Haig warned them otherwise from the start. Now he announced that Washington would back London with both moral and material support. This, he hoped, might make the junta face reality.

For that tactic to be effective, the Administration had to present a united front. But the Kirkpatrick approach resurfaced. Not only were there leaks questioning the wisdom of what Haig was doing, there were also, both at the UN and in Washington, conversations with Argentinian representatives by American officials other than Haig and his principal deputy for Latin American affairs, Thomas Enders. Kirkpatrick was warned by the White House to be more cautious. At the same time, Clark conferred with the Argentinian ambassador, Esteban Takacs.

With some vehemence, Haig told me: "There were contacts made with Argentinian officials by the White House which were neither discussed with me nor cleared with me and which had the practical effect of confusing the issue at the very time we had taken a dramatic step [in announcing formal support for Britain]. This helped confirm that the outcome [actual combat] would be inevitable." Haig insisted that similar meddling the following month in negotiations concerning Lebanon also confused some foreign governments.

Clark, with equal conviction, challenged that interpretation: "Al Haig, or in his absence one of his senior assistants, knew of every contact I had with foreign officials in advance and approved that communication in advance. They were also briefed after every conversation with foreign representatives."[17]

Checks with other officials corroborated Clark's statement about his own procedure. However, both the White House and the State Department became aware that Clark's relatively bland talks with Takacs received a different coloration when the ambassador reported them to Buenos Aires. Takacs apparently exaggerated the progress he was making in pleading his government's cause. The junta, a benighted group of officers with little experience in either war or diplomacy, might have been encouraged to think that Washington was not supporting Britain as strongly as Haig's public statement indicated. The fact that Takacs had initiated the conversations with Clark, and that Clark agreed to them as a courtesy only because he had already seen British Ambassador Nicholas Henderson several times, made little impression on the junta.

Haig's anxiety mounted further as Kirkpatrick, working through Enders and Clark, got approval in mid-May for a different approach to the peace effort. After talks at the UN, she proposed that Reagan call Thatcher once more while Brazilian President João Baptista de Oliveira Figueiredo, then in Washington for an official visit, get in touch with Galtieri. Haig reluctantly agreed to this effort once arrangements were in motion, though he felt that it was also a confusing distraction. The gambit got nowhere in any case. But the Secretary's ire was reaching the danger zone. While Figueiredo was still in Washington, an additional breakfast meeting was set up between him and Reagan. Haig was not going to be able to attend. At an NSC session the preceding day, Haig had observed Kirkpatrick passing Deaver a note. Concluding that Kirkpatrick was using Deaver to prime Reagan for the breakfast meeting, Haig told Clark that a "conspiracy" was afoot to outflank him.

While most of this maneuvering remained secret, Kirkpatrick's dissatisfaction with Haig's performance did not merely leak out; it gushed into print and over the airwaves. One steamy account in *Newsweek*[18] accurately reported a phone conversation between Kirkpatrick and Haig in which she had called him and his top deputies "Brits in American clothes" and accused them of destroying U.S. influence south of the border. She was also disturbed that her views were not being properly conveyed to the White House.

Clark arranged for her to see Reagan on May 31, Memorial Day. She complained to the President not only about the policy, but about what she believed to be the State Department's poor handling of opportunities at the UN. To Clark she said again that she was tempted to resign—an itch that she, like Haig, flaunted from time to time. Later the same afternoon Haig was called to the White House. Reagan told him that he wanted Kirkpatrick to remain in office. Further, the President said that he personally wanted to know more about what was happening at the UN and how Kirkpatrick saw things. Prompted in advance by Clark, Reagan made the point that the UN ambassador should report *through* the State Department, not *to* it.

Haig absorbed this caning with stifled rage. He had imagined that the

Newsweek story, which was understood to have come from Kirkpatrick's office, would buttress his case to have Kirkpatrick fired. Instead,
the President had singed his tail. Once again he talked to Clark about
resigning. Departure for Europe was forty-eight hours away. No one is
resigning, Clark said. No one is being fired either. Let's just get on with
the job.

Looking toward Versailles, the State Department had hoped to construct a compromise on one source of friction: the West's economic
relations with the Soviet Union and its Warsaw Pact allies. Even
before the imposition of martial law in Poland the preceding December, Washington had been attempting to curb transactions that either
promoted industrial development in the East or increased the flow of
hard currency to Moscow. Repression in Poland had sharpened Washington's effort, but the Western Europeans resisted what they viewed as
needless economic warfare that would penalize them far more than it
would affect the United States. Most attention focused on the Yamal
pipeline, a $10 billion project being built with Western technology.
When completed, it would take natural gas from Siberia to Western
Europe and hard currency to Moscow. Before the Polish crisis, even before Reagan took office, the Europeans had committed themselves to
cooperate in construction as well as to buy the gas it would deliver.

The possible compromise being sketched out would have had the
United States relent in its opposition to the project, already underway,
in exchange for a European concession. In the future, the Europeans
would scale back their participation in such transactions. Further, they
would refrain from granting Moscow credit at concessionary terms. But
the details of this potential accommodation were still hazy as the presidential party headed for France, with subsequent stops in Italy, Britain
and Germany.

Perhaps Haig knew that the pipeline compromise had little chance to
succeed. Certainly he was still bristling from his latest brush with Kirkpatrick and from the knowledge that his most dramatic opportunity to
serve as an international peacemaker had failed. As soon as he saw the
seating arrangements on *Air Force One,* he went into a funk. He
thought that he should have been seated in the second compartment,
directly behind the President's private quarters. Instead that space was
occupied by Clark, Baker and Deaver, along with Carolyn Deaver and
Joan Clark. The Secretary of State found himself in the third compartment with Regan and Darman, neither of whom he liked. Deaver had
supervised the seating arrangements.

Two months earlier there had been a brouhaha when the White
House military office—also under Deaver's control—had assigned what
Haig considered an inferior plane for the first leg of his Falklands shut-

tle. It was a windowless craft with, Haig's party thought, inadequate communications gear. His departure then had been delayed because he did not wish to use the plane. Recalling that snaffle and observing Haig's bulldog glare now on *Air Force One,* Baker murmured to Deaver, "At least he's got a window this time."

Neither Baker nor Deaver by this stage had any interest in placating Haig. From the Secretary's viewpoint, the seating arrangement slight was simply the first part of a pattern that would persist for the rest of the trip. Later, speaking of himself in the third person, Haig told me, "There was some evidence that meetings had been held in the White House about getting rid of Haig *prior* to the European visit. It was very evident to me that there was a strong effort to put burrs under my saddle during that European visit. That didn't bother me . . . My problems were from the beginning substantive."

Haig could not cite the "evidence" he mentioned. A few seconds later he said that what he perceived as protocol slights "horrified" the European host governments as well as American embassies abroad, thereby undermining his position further. But when I asked for examples that were noticed by his foreign counterparts, he replied, "Oh, that's just crapola, gossip . . ." He was obviously torn on the subject. In the book he planned to write, he would make his argument to the court of history on the basis of substantive policy and its execution. Yet as a proud man, one who had played an important role in great events when the Reaganauts were still provincial nonentities, Alexander Haig had emotional difficulty coping with assaults on his dignity.

He continued to glower at what he considered affronts. When the party went to luncheon at 10 Downing Street, he misunderstood the arrangements and assumed that he was to be part of the receiving line. Thatcher corrected him in a stage whisper and Haig blamed the confusion on Deaver. Going from Heathrow Airport in London to Windsor Castle by helicopter, the Haigs were not seated in Reagan's chopper, but in a following craft. "What am I," he muttered to a few of the others, "a leper?"

By that time the fighting in Lebanon had begun. Others in the party believed that what was bothering Haig even more than the protocol folderol was the fact that George Bush, back in Washington, was chairing the Special Situations Group, as the former Crisis Management Team had been rechristened. This rankled. Meanwhile two other incidents involving Jeane Kirkpatrick arose to pollute the atmosphere still more. While the Versailles conference was in progress, a Security Council resolution was pending concerning the Falklands war. Britain was going to veto it and the question for the Administration was whether to join in the veto or to abstain. Kirkpatrick favored abstention as a ges-

ture of conciliation toward the Latin American bloc. The working
group in Washington and the presidential party abroad agreed first to
vote with Britain. Then, as the resolution's wording changed, Haig sent
word via the State Department to have Kirkpatrick abstain. The new
instruction, however, reached New York a few minutes after the votes
were cast. Kirkpatrick then explained in public what had happened.

This immediately caused new rumblings among the group in Europe.
Why the delay in the instructions? Why hadn't Haig communicated
directly with the U.S. mission to the UN? Talking to reporters, Haig
tried to pass the incident off with an arrogant joke. A general, he said,
does not deal with a company commander when there is a corps headquarters in between. That military analogy did not exactly fit with the
fiction of the UN ambassador as cabinet member. He also acknowledged that he had made the decision on his own, without consulting
Reagan.

While that flurry was still in progress, Haig and Clark tangled yet
again over a UN-related issue. By now the Reagan group was at Windsor Castle, guests of the Queen for two nights. On both evenings,
Elizabeth staged formal dinners. As one of them got started, Clark
knew that word from the UN would probably arrive concerning a Security Council resolution to impose sanctions on Israel because of its invasion of Lebanon. He had been warned that it was a violation of protocol for a guest to leave the table once the Queen was seated, so he
arranged for the provisions of the resolution to be brought in to him if
necessary. Chuck Tyson, one of his assistants, took in the cable before
the main course was served. As expected, the UN measure provided for
official sanctions of the kind the United States traditionally opposed.
Nonetheless, Kirkpatrick required specific instructions. Clark wrote
across the top of the wire "Al, what are your recommendations?" and,
as discreetly as he could, sent it down the long table to Haig. The dinner lasted another hour, but Clark got no response.

During the after-dinner amenities in the drawing room, Clark braced
Haig. The President has to decide this, Clark said. What do you think?
Don't worry about it, Haig replied. It's just nuts and bolts. The President doesn't have to be involved. Yes he does, Clark insisted. We've
been through this before.

Indeed they had. Again, they were dealing with management principle rather than substance. There was no question of how the United
States would vote. But Clark was determined, as he observed privately
to his colleagues, "to get Ronald Reagan back into the loop" of foreign
affairs. Haig would have to yield on procedure. He would not make
this decision; rather he would submit his recommendation. In so doing,
he would also submit to Clark as Reagan's surrogate. Haig yielded for

the moment. Of course we must vote against sanctions, the Secretary said. Fine, I'll inform the President, Clark replied.

The incident did not end there. Haig sought out Clark later that evening while the National Security Adviser was dictating memoranda to his secretary, Jackie Hill. In front of Clark's astonished aide, the Secretary of State and the President's National Security Affairs Adviser argued loudly about precedence and Haig's standing in the Administration. Haig, the master of cultivated anger, provoked Clark, the practitioner of lawyerly understatement, to raise his voice. The next day Clark told Deaver, "I said things to Al I never thought I'd have to say."

Haig, for his part, was threatening to return to Washington before completion of the trip. The senior White House staff caucused on that possibility. Obviously it would be poor public relations if Haig abruptly bailed out before the party went to Bonn for a NATO meeting. If necessary, the group decided, Reagan would have to be informed of what was happening (as usual, he was being shielded from irksome "details") and the President would have to calm Haig down. That turned out to be unnecessary because Haig backed off.

It was at Windsor Castle, according to two others watching the melodrama closely, that Clark finally had a "bellyful with Haig." Later Clark himself would bridle at that term and at the attempt to place at a precise moment his decision that Deaver and Baker had been right. Hairsplitting aside, when the entourage was departing Europe, Clark firmly believed that Haig should leave sooner rather than later, regardless of what was going on in the world. Both external events and the interplay between the Secretary of State and the National Security Adviser then combined to accelerate that movement. Haig was now like the less skilled combatant in a judo match; his own weight and momentum would be used to bring him down.

The week after the group returned from Bonn, Reagan went to New York to address the UN's special session on disarmament. Haig accompanied him in order to see several of his opposite numbers, including Andrei Gromyko. While Haig remained in Manhattan for these conferences, Reagan came back to Washington to preside at an important National Security Council meeting. The subject was East-West trade and specifically what new steps, if any, the United States should take concerning European cooperation with the project. The cosmetic compromise reached at Versailles had broken down within days; the allies were not going to alter future trade and credit arrangements significantly. There was also an element of personal pique on Reagan's part, though that was only a minuscule factor in the decision. Helmut Schmidt, Reagan thought, had been rude during the private NATO meetings in Bonn. Reagan felt that the German chancellor had displayed bored indifference while he, Reagan, was speaking to the alliance's leaders.

Reagan wanted a tough response both to Mitterrand and Schmidt, the two who were most resistant on the East-West trade issue. This time Clark was not merely the broker of alternatives. He performed as the catalyst for the "hard option" favored by the Pentagon and opposed by State, Commerce and Treasury: the United States would penalize the European subsidiaries of American firms as well as European companies that continued to cooperate with the pipeline project.

Haig, in New York, knew that decision was coming. He instructed his man at the NSC meeting, Under Secretary Lawrence Eagleburger, to argue the opposition case fully. Then, after being defeated, Eagleburger was to request a delay before the decision was announced so that the Europeans could be informed privately. Haig wanted to make a typical diplomatic damage limitation effort. But the White House desired the opposite effect: an impressive demonstration of Reagan's will. Within hours of the decision, the White House announced what had happened. Said Haig later, "That left me in an untenable position with Mr. Gromyko, who the next morning went into an hour and a half polemic with respect to my disingenuousness the day before when [I had not told him] this was happening."

The pipeline decision occurred on Friday, June 18. Reagan then went to Camp David for the weekend while the State Department was finishing work on crucial new instructions for Philip Habib. The special envoy was desperately trying to achieve an agreement that would both lift the Israeli siege of Beirut and eventually bring about the withdrawal of all foreign forces from Lebanon. The main ingredients of the lengthy cable had already been agreed to by the Special Situations Group representing all the departments involved. The document refined the American approach to the crisis and its aftermath, including proposed means to assist the reassertion of Lebanese governmental authority. American military forces would likely have to play at least a token role as PLO forces left Beirut.

Clark had no objection to the cable's content. But the Pentagon did have reservations over a few details. For that reason, Clark told the State Department to delay dispatch of the cable. He wanted to wait until Monday when it could be "round-tabled" at the White House. Meanwhile he transmitted a copy to Camp David along with a recommendation that the document be held forty-eight hours. Reagan of course agreed, as Clark knew he would.

Whereupon Haig ordered dispatch of the cable despite Clark's contrary instructions. The following September, when I asked him why,

Haig slapped the coffee table between us and expostulated, "It couldn't be held until Monday! I talked to the President [soon afterward]. As a matter of fact the issue was very urgent. It could not be delayed. Habib was on his way through Syria to Beirut. He had to have the instructions. I was faced with bureaucratic blockage from Mr. Clark." Other officials who tracked the negotiations closely acknowledged later that the content of the cable held up well. It became Habib's operating guide during the next phases of his delicate mediating effort.

During those same few days, the Middle East crisis affected Haig's position in another way as well. Menachem Begin was scheduled to visit the White House on Monday, June 21. By this stage Haig was virtually isolated, even within the State Department, concerning the manner in which the Administration should treat the Israeli Government. He believed that a visible rupture with Israel would encourage the PLO and the Syrians to hold out in Lebanon. That, in turn, would escalate the violence. By this reasoning any pressure applied to Begin would have to be both subtle and private. Besides, Israel was still America's main ally in the region and, as Haig reckoned things, alliances must always be nurtured.

Clark now believed that Haig had carried that approach too far. As the White House prepared for the Begin meeting, Clark decided to marshal counterarguments in an unusual manner. On Thursday, June 17, he sent requests to Bush, Weinberger, Casey, Kirkpatrick and the Joint Chiefs of Staff. The "tasking" directive instructed each recipient, on an urgent and confidential basis, to give the White House an opinion on how Begin should be approached. Weinberger took the confidentiality aspect of the request so seriously that he came to the White House to dictate his response to one of Clark's secretaries. The JCS submitted its recommendations on unmarked stationery rather than on the printed form normally used.

As Clark had anticipated, all these advisers differed from Haig. Bush's view was particularly important because the Vice-President was rarely didactic. Reagan valued his opinions, which were usually couched in professional, objective terms. From these several memoranda, Clark's staff distilled recommended "talking points" that competed with the State Department version. Reagan digested all this over the weekend and then copied onto index cards what he intended to use while talking to Begin. On Monday morning, Haig discovered that Reagan was going to depart from the "gentle" option. Still there was confusion as both State Department and Pentagon experts sought to make last-minute changes in Reagan's presentation to Begin before the Prime Minister arrived at 11 A.M.

On that same harried day Clark tightened the screw one more turn.

He made an issue of the Habib cable, bringing the breach of discipline to Reagan's attention. Haig tried to explain it away by citing the situation's urgency. His conversation with the President became broader and even more serious. When Haig recalled it later, his tone was still emotional. As I replayed the tape recording of the conversation, exclamation points and emphasis demanded recognition:

> Monday, when I first spoke to him . . . it was *not* my intention to leave [office] at that time—under *no* circumstances. In the midst of the Middle East crisis? Impossible! But I did want to say that I had serious problems, that they were getting *worse!* I gave him some specific details—not to display problems of *prerogative.* That wasn't involved at all. What was involved was procedural transgressions, if you will, that had profound policy implications—*profound*—especially with respect to the PLO and its presence in Lebanon . . . I came away from [the Monday conversation] feeling that my lack of access to him, on a regular, cordial, intimate basis had long since developed its own momentum. The likelihood of his either accepting what I said to him or acting on it was very slim . . . I did want to get my position stated clearly so that whatever I did *after* November would not look as if it was influenced by contemporary politics.

The next scene in this final act took place Wednesday night at the State Department. A news story the previous morning had revealed some of the internal friction of the European trip, emphasizing the antipathy between Clark and Haig. Though the piece appeared to be based on murmurings from Haig's enemies, Clark professed to be irritated over this latest disclosure of difficulty. He suggested a talk. Much of that conversation, which lasted an hour and forty-five minutes, consisted of a recital by Haig of the events and players most disturbing to him. The sum of it was that meddling by others was making the Secretary's role impossible to perform. Unless matters were put right, he implied strongly, he would have to resign. Each time in the past when Haig had raised that prospect, Clark had pooh-poohed it. Now the response was quite different. You must come to the White House, he said, and tell all this to the President in your own words. It was a milestone. Clark was removing himself as Haig's buffer.

Clark informed Reagan and Deaver of what was happening. Deaver in turn told Baker. The President was warned by his advisers that he might get an ultimatum later in the day, Thursday. That news agitated him. One of the participants recalled Reagan's reaction: "Oh no! What for? What's it all about?" He was not so upset, however, that he was unwilling to consider a short list of possible successors. Deaver and Clark argued that should a resignation occur, the White House must announce a replacement simultaneously. That would be sound public relations at home and abroad. Four names were mentioned: Shultz, Weinberger, Senate Majority Leader Howard Baker and Senator Henry "Scoop" Jackson, a hawkish Democrat whom the Reaganauts had briefly considered as Defense Secretary after the election. Reagan, predictably, was interested in only one of those four, Shultz.

Reagan was primed to receive a resignation that day. Instead, he got from Haig a written bill of particulars which restated Haig's complaints. Only the two of them were in the Oval Office for that afternoon meeting, and a fascinating little discrepancy shows up in their versions of what happened. Haig began his account of that session by telling me, "Please understand that I didn't bring a resignation with me at any time." When I pressed him on that point, Haig acknowledged that "somebody [on the State staff] had drafted one and stuck it in my folder. I had no intention of submitting it. In the first place I hadn't even read it carefully . . . I did tell him that I had a resignation prepared . . . I didn't flash an envelope with a resignation at all."

Neither Reagan nor Haig talked about the atmospherics of that meeting in public. Others told me that the President had found the entire experience unnerving and distasteful. A month later, when the subject came up during a conversation at Camp David, Reagan could discuss it only haltingly, volunteering little. His uneasiness came through in this part of the exchange:

> *Reagan:* . . . he came in and told me [of his dissatisfaction] and he showed me that he had the letter of resignation.
> *Question:* He showed you a letter of resignation?
> *Reagan:* Yes, it was in an envelope and he showed it, kept it in his hand. But then he did [talk about] some of the things that had concerned him about—
> *Question:* He gave you a list?
> *Reagan:* He gave me some of these things and so I said to him, "Before I consider that letter then," I said, "I think we should meet again because I want to have time to look at what you presented to me." And it didn't have a bearing, I didn't think, on this, and so the next day I told him that I was willing to accept his letter of resignation, which he had presented to me . . . It's never an easy time, one of these things.
> *Question:* You mean it didn't have a bearing on policy?
> *Reagan:* No.[19]

The document Haig did give Reagan on Thursday elaborated on what he had told Clark the night before, including an item about Clark having gone out of channels to deal with a Saudi official. That communication, when relayed back to the Middle East, had created the impression that the U.S. Government was divided concerning the negotiations over Lebanon. This had made Habib's mission all the more difficult, Haig maintained.*

None of that made an impression on Reagan. What preoccupied him was the question of whether Haig really had to leave. After the Thursday meeting with Haig, he discussed the situation twice more with Deaver and Clark. Early the next morning, Friday, June 25, Baker joined in for still another conversation about Haig. Reagan still had not shaken off the idea of waiting several months, until after the election. When his advisers said that would not work, Reagan wondered aloud whether they should all think about it at least over the weekend. Clark, fully backed by the other two senior advisers, opposed that also. He argued that the issue had to be settled once and for all, provided that a replacement could be named simultaneously. Even a short delay would probably mean leaks. A long delay would only mean more tension and conflict. Reagan was also told that Haig's allusion to a resignation the previous day had constituted an offer to resign. A presidential letter accepting the resignation was drafted.

There was a huge catch, of course: the question of a successor. By no coincidence at all, Clark knew exactly where to reach Shultz. Until that Friday morning, both men later insisted, Clark had given Shultz no hint of the offer about to come. As Shultz reconstructed the exchange: "I was in the midst of what was my last piece of business on this trip, a meeting [in a London hotel conference room] and I was giving a little talk. When I got through, somebody gave me a note saying that 'George Clark' in the White House would like me to call him. I looked at that and kept on with what I was doing, and I stuck it in my pocket and thought, 'Well, I don't know any George Clark, so there must be some mistake.' I didn't pay any attention. A little while later the secretary came over and said, '*Judge* Clark is calling you, he is on the telephone out here in the lobby.' "[20]

Clark said the President would have "something very important and very confidential" to put to Shultz a bit later. Well, Shultz replied, if it's that important and confidential, I'd better go to the embassy and use a secure phone. Shultz promised to be there about 3:30 P.M. London time (10:30 A.M. in Washington). Clark called at that time, said Reagan was tied up for the moment and finally told Shultz the news: The President would be in touch soon with a formal offer to become Secretary of State. Shultz would not have the luxury of cogitating on the decision; the White House would have to have a firm and prompt

---

* In fact, Clark had seen the Saudi Ambassador, Faisal Alhegelan, on June 18 and again on June 22. When Alhegelan reported—or misreported—these brief talks back to Riyadh, some temporary confusion did result. But Haig's assistants had been kept abreast by Clark and the difficulty was transitory.

reply. If Shultz said yes, the appointment would be announced simultaneously with Haig's resignation. Shultz managed to reach his wife, who was elsewhere in London, before Reagan's call came in. "They said that they had a critical moment on their hands," Shultz remembered thinking. "It was hard to say no under the circumstances."

When the President reached him a short time later, the issue was quickly settled. Soon after that conversation, Reagan attended a National Security Council luncheon meeting in the Cabinet Room. To his colleagues, Haig appeared relaxed, even mellow by his kinetic standards. But neither he nor Clark bothered with the food. After the meal, Reagan asked Haig into the Oval Office. With little ceremony, Reagan told his senior cabinet officer that the resignation offered the previous day was being accepted. There was still a note of astonishment in Haig's voice three months later as he described the moment: "He handed—*he handed me*—a letter *accepting* a resignation which I had never submitted. That's what happened. That's when I said, 'Mr. President, I did not anticipate this in the middle of a crisis. I think it's dangerous and wrong.'" Reagan said that he should stay on for an interim period until his successor was ready to assume responsibility.

Haig asked for time to return to his own office to draft a proper letter of resignation. He said he hoped that an announcement could be withheld until that was done. Reagan was noncommittal on that point. The President somehow forgot to mention that Shultz would be the successor; Haig neglected to ask. After Haig left the White House, Clark relayed that information by phone in time for Haig to work it into his own statement. But the White House insisted on breaking the news first. That way, attention would be divided between the advent of Shultz and the departure of Haig.

Reagan came to the White House briefing room at 3 P.M. with the demeanor of someone who had just lost a close relative. He was on the verge of choking up as he read a short prepared statement. He praised Haig for having served his country "above and beyond the call of duty" all his adult life, and as someone "who has served me so well and faithfully with his wisdom and counsel I have respected and admired for all the time our Administration has been here . . ." The President gave no explanation then, or in his press conference the following week, of Haig's motives. Of course he gave no hint that Haig had been forced out. For his part, Haig went on television later in the afternoon to read his letter of resignation, which accused Reagan, politely, of wobbling: "I believe that we shared a view of America's role in the world as the leader of free men and inspiration for all. We agreed that consistency, clarity and steadiness of purpose were essential to success. It was in this spirit that I undertook to serve you as Secretary of State. In recent months it has become clear to me that the foreign policy on which we embarked together was shifting from that careful course which we laid out. Under these circumstances . . ."

Reagan refused to accept the idea that policy issues had been involved in the difficulty. He allowed in our talk at Camp David only that there were "shadings in there." He insisted that Haig chose to go, that he wasn't pushed. The fundamental reason: "He did have a differing view as to—let's say, as to turf." Was there any way to avoid the rupture? "No, I think that he had—well, I'm not going to say. [If I had] said, 'Why, we'll turn everything upside down and turn it around,' then he might not have [quit], but I had a feeling that he knew the situation couldn't be ideally what he wanted, and therefore he chose to go."

Reagan appeared to believe that. As in some other sensitive and important situations, the President had not tracked the details closely. He gave scant weight to the fundamental policy differences that had existed all along. He believed his trusted intimates, Clark and Deaver, when they told him that Haig was an impossible man with whom to work. Just as Reagan in 1981 had overlooked the importance of the philosophic differences among his economic advisers, he could not understand why his national security crew was unable to act in collegial fashion. In the end, the easiest solution was to dump the odd man out, the troublemaker.

As for Haig, he—like Clark—certainly had a bellyful by June of 1982. Much as he would deny it, there was no question that his bristling personality caused severe difficulties for his colleagues. He would claim that "if I had ever been accused of anything it was of being too much of a team player over the years." But in his previous Washington jobs he had always been a staff man rather than captain. Now he had a different post in a different game with different mates. He never adjusted to that. He could not claim to have formulated any dramatic new interpretation of what American policy should be. There is no evidence that Haig, had he been given the jurisdiction he sought, would have produced historic results. But he was equipped to be a reliable manager of foreign policy and a steadying influence in an administration that often groped for the right levers abroad. Toward the end he was denied the opportunity to make even that prosaic contribution.

The abruptness of his departure may have delayed conclusion of the first Beirut settlement, which was finally achieved in mid-August. Haig would argue that it did extend the bloodletting; that was conjecture for which no proof was available as this book was being finished. The White House did end Haig's lame-duck stewardship before Shultz was confirmed for reasons that remained murky.

Shultz was at once a more cerebral and methodical operator than Haig. He was also a firm believer in quiet diplomacy both in internal deliberations and external negotiations. As he explored his new post during the crisis atmosphere induced by the Middle East, he also had to begin to repair the damage to NATO caused by the pipeline decision. He needed months to become well versed in the arms control negotiations already underway. As he was finding his way, the Pentagon continued to construct obstacles to new approaches that might produce accommodation with the Soviets.

Concerning the Strategic Arms Reduction Talks (START), in fact the American position was altered somewhat to make it even less acceptable to Moscow. The State Department's opposition to that change was feeble. By early October, when Shultz held his first conversations with Gromyko, the State Department was beginning to probe for some new formulation that might break the impasse in the INF talks. By then Shultz was beginning to take hold of the subject. In dealing with the Soviets and NATO both, he was trying in his quiet manner to follow the path that Haig had pursued. He was careful to argue for his viewpoints rather than crusade for them.

15

Mike Deaver:
Images and Exorcisms

The call director emits a steady ring, announcing that the President is
on the line. Mike Deaver rises quickly from the wing chair where he
was ensconced for conversation with a reporter. The move is too sudden for his crippled knee, which needs surgery, and he winces as he
hobbles to his desk and interrupts the insistent bell.

"Yes?" A short pause as he listens, then a laugh. "That's all right
. . . Don't worry about it, really. I've got a spare . . . No, it's really
okay . . . All right. Thank you."

He's chuckling as he eases back into the chair, and explains without
having to be prompted. "See, he broke his glasses so I gave him mine
this morning. He was worried that I wouldn't be able to read and
wanted to return them." Do you have another pair, Mike? "I'm sure I
do somewhere. Shirley is organizing a search." Shirley Moore, Deaver's
assistant in Sacramento and the White House, will be unsuccessful.

I add another example to the long list of services rendered to the
Reagans by Mike Deaver. He was in overall charge of their travel, foreign and domestic. He chose the principal members of Nancy's East
Wing staff and supervised that group out of the corner of his eye. He
presided over Reagan's schedule not only in the mechanical sense but
also in the politics of it. When the President's standing began to
weaken at the end of the first year, it was Deaver who organized a new
informal planning group to determine how to ration Reagan's time for
maximum yield. When relations with black groups went from bad to
calamitous, it was Deaver who started a salvage operation.

When not arranging for the ouster of the National Security Adviser or helping to expedite the Secretary of State's resignation, no task was too small—particularly if it involved Deaver's strong suit, which was cultivation of the image. Throughout the White House West Wing, color photographs of the Reagans festoon corridor walls. Visitors see Reagan riding, conferring with foreign VIP's, speaking to friendly audiences, relaxing with Nancy. These pictures, as one would expect, are uniformly flattering. The displays change constantly, thanks to the prolific output of Michael Evans, the White House photographer, and his assistants. One day near the Press Office, a different kind of photo appears. It is a closeup of Reagan, taken in a rare moment when his face is not animated. In this shot, Reagan's features are slack with what seems to be fatigue or discomfort. This frame gives him all his seventy years and then some. A day or two later the picture is gone, removed at Deaver's personal order. Look, he tells Evans, I've spent a lot of time for many years showing Reagan as robust. What do we want with an official photo that conveys the opposite image?

Images, images. We are at Checkpoint Charlie in Berlin, where two decades earlier American and Soviet armor went eyeball-to-eyeball in one of the more frightening moments of the Cold War. Now it is a pleasant morning in mid-April 1982. On the East German side of the line, a barrel-chested officer in gray rushes from his guardhouse. He shouts and waves his arms as he strides toward us, rapidly closing the fifty or sixty yards. Younger sentries armed with submachine guns stand motionless, adding tension to the tableau. Deaver doesn't move for a few seconds either. In fact, he seems oblivious to the scene he has caused until the chief of his Secret Service detail, Joe Masonis, grips Deaver's arm and guides him back fifteen paces or so, across a broad white stripe in the asphalt. "Hey," Masonis cracks, "I don't want to lose my principal."

Deaver and a few companions had strayed into a narrow sliver of no-man's-land at the famous border crossing. We have spent the last couple of hours visiting sites along the Berlin Wall. In two months Reagan will conduct his grand tour of four European countries and Deaver is responsible for all aspects of planning that venture except the actual diplomacy. Now, with a team of specialists—for security, press arrangements, communications, helicopter logistics, even the President's menu—Deaver is heading an advance mission. This morning he wants to select the particular spot along the Berlin Wall at which Reagan will be seen during the June visit. He seems to appreciate the claustrophobic intensity of Checkpoint Charlie as opposed to the more expansive Brandenburg Gate area and other possible settings. "It's so ugly," he says. "It's so depressing. The contrast between our system and theirs is so stark here."

Two months later, Reagan's motorcade will go to Checkpoint Charlie. Looking bulky because of his bulletproof vest, the President spends only a few minutes outside his limousine, long enough to be photographed, videotaped, recorded. What do you think of the place? a reporter asks. Gesturing toward the wall, Reagan remarks: "It's as ugly as the idea behind it." One hears the echo of Deaver's own reaction.

Images, images. Deaver's own is fuzzy to the outside world. During the first two years, Meese and Baker appeared frequently on television talk shows. They gave speeches from time to time and conducted on-the-record press briefings. Deaver did none of that. He was an expert in no objective discipline, not economics, not foreign policy, not administration, not legal affairs, not national political organization. He rarely immersed himself in any one issue unless a serious problem threatened the Reagans. There lay his expertise: how the Reagans think, feel, react. In difficult situations, his habit was to operate inside, as he did in the Allen situation.

His physical presence contributed to anonymity. In a White House full of people who came across as athletic or stylish or macho or at least California-healthy, Deaver was none of the preceding. A premature shortage of hair made him seem older than forty-two when the Administration came in. Between episodic diets, he leaned toward pudgy, a tilt encouraged by his affection for rich food and expensive wine.* The drab gray suits and muted ties he preferred, the absence of a ramrod to direct his middling frame, a tendency to shuffle even when the knee wasn't plaguing him, a professed modesty about his understanding of complicated issues—all this contributed to a stereotype that Deaver was really a glorified servant to the Reagans, with some doubt attending the adjective.

Of course he had always been concerned about the master and mistress' care, feeding and comfort. He often sided with Nancy in protecting the boss from overwork. Presiding over the advance preparations in Europe, he mentioned to the Italian protocol chief, Marcello Guidi, that Reagan does not eat tomatoes. ("I know that's a problem for Italians," he said while discussing arrangements for an official luncheon in Rome.) Once the real excursion was over, Deaver took some criticism different from the usual rap against him. He was blamed for overloading Reagan's schedule, thereby wearying the elderly traveler. Reagan, after all, nodded off while he and the Pope appeared together on televi-

* In mid-1982, however, inspired by a weight-loss contest devised by Richard Darman, Deaver went on a serious health kick. He shed pounds and acquired biceps. The transformation seemed permanent enough for him to sign a book deal. Because he lacked time, expertise in the subject of nutrition and writing ability, he planned to use a collaborator well versed in nutritional science.

sion and had similar difficulty keeping his eyes open at that luncheon sans tomatoes. The reversal in criticism appealed to Deaver's keen sense of the ironic.

But to imagine Deaver's role as primarily that of a political Jeeves would be like describing an elephant merely as an animal with large ears. With his knack for playing a mellow piano and wry sense of humor, Deaver would sometimes be court jester. His rapport with reporters helped to sell Reagan's line of goods. His unerring instinct for situations in which Reagan would come across well brought the President into settings unusual for him—a working class black high school in Chicago, a temporary dike holding back floodwaters in Fort Wayne —and which yielded yet more positive images. Because of Deaver's perfect loyalty, he could occasionally intervene in policy disputes without institutional interests appearing to color his views. Thus he added his generalist's voice to the Baker-Stockman side of the deficit argument.

Deaver's discriminating antenna was always high, alert for trouble, and he was close enough to act promptly upon receipt of a danger signal. We are in Philadelphia on October 15, 1981, when lobbying on the AWACS vote in the Senate is going into its final, desperate stage. Reagan, after a speech, chats with reporters for a few minutes and makes one of his typical errors of nuance. He implies that even if the Senate votes down the controversial aircraft deal with the Saudis, he might use emergency executive powers to go ahead with the sale. That impression is dangerous; it might encourage wobbly senators to vote no, figuring that they haven't done any lasting damage. Deaver, though no expert in legislative affairs, recognizes the problem immediately. When reporters leave the room, he tells Reagan: "I think we've got to clean this thing up." A quick call to Jim Baker in Washington confirms his instinct. Reporters, already boarding buses outside the hotel, are summoned back. "I think I left the wrong impression," Reagan says as he applies the necessary sanitation.

That antenna was disguised by Deaver's resistance to learning the mysteries of government. Even better hidden was his ferocity when he thought Reagan's interests were at stake. Knowing Reagan's weakness in coping with personnel matters, Deaver performed as talent scout on occasion, a routine enough chore for a political adviser. When someone in the entourage became a liability to the boss, Deaver would attack like an implacable exorcist chasing a demon. Once he even expunged himself for the good of the Reagan cause.

In 1976 Deaver welcomed John Sears to the entourage because he believed that no one in the old circle had sufficient skill or bona fides in national politics. Coming on the 1980 campaign, Deaver felt even more strongly about Sears's value. This time Deaver crossed some of the true-believing Reaganauts who distrusted Sears and helped persuade the boss that Sears was indispensable. Sears, in the summer of 1979, then consolidated his own power in the organization. At his behest, Deaver arranged the departure of Lyn Nofziger. Sears moved next against Deaver himself. In a showdown in front of the Reagans at the Pacific Palisades house, the Sears faction posed an or-else ultimatum. It was going to be a difficult choice for Reagan and his wife, who had affection for Deaver but respect for Sears. Deaver resolved the dilemma before Reagan spoke by resigning on the spot. He would return later, after Meese outgunned Sears in yet another duel—and after Sears's strategy turned out to be a loser in the Iowa caucus campaign, thereby proving that Sears was dispensable after all. It was a classic case of Reagan, the old eternal amateur, discovering that he had reposed excessive trust in a strong-willed expert. Deaver, younger but ditto, had been an accomplice in that error.

It was Deaver, in league with his erstwhile foe, Stu Spencer, who at the end of the campaign maneuvered Meese away from the Chief of Staff's post and Baker into it. Later Deaver became an admirer and sometime ally of Dave Stockman. Yet when the Greider story broke, Deaver immediately told Reagan that Stockman should resign. Baker, arguing that Stockman was essential to the operation, prevailed on that one.

Deaver could be brutal in dealing with associates of long standing. After Meese began to have difficulties at the time of the Gulf of Sidra dogfight, Deaver gave him a little advice. Ed, he said, your profile is too high, you travel too much, your staff is mediocre and reporters think you lie to them. Meese protested that he never lied to anyone. Dammit, Ed, we've been through a lot together in fifteen years, good and bad, and you even bullshit me! Never, Meese protested, I never bullshit you. Deaver insisted on the last word: Ed, you're bullshitting me right now.

Images, images. The first to concede that Meese knew the policy issues far better than he, Deaver nonetheless would cross him when he felt that Reagan's political persona was in jeopardy. It is May 21, 1982, and the big three are having their ritual seven-thirty breakfast in Baker's office. The only difference this morning is that the mess steward pours a fourth cup of coffee; the reporter is being allowed one of his rare auditing visits. The first important item that arises comes from Deaver. He has received a telegram from Benjamin Hooks, head of the NAACP, who is exercised about a court case that started in New York City. There is a dispute about an affirmative action program for city employees and the litigation is making its way up, on appeal, through the federal court system. Reagan's Justice Department is on record against this kind of program, and is considering entering the case on an *amicus* basis—in opposition to the NAACP position. "Where are we on that?" Deaver wants to know.

Meese, who took a special interest in legal affairs, says that the Justice Department is working on the issue. He hints strongly that the decision will favor intervention. "It's a fundamental question," Meese says. "We campaigned on it. We're against reverse discrimination." Baker and Deaver are both uneasy about this. The White House will appear—again—to be unsympathetic to blacks and Hispanics. There has been no consideration of the political and public relations implications. "You can't have this decision in a vacuum," Baker says. Deaver adds: "We're liable to get a blast. All I'm saying is that we shouldn't shoot ourselves in the foot one more time."

Meese agrees that a closer look is warranted. The three take no firm position on that Friday morning. The following Monday they hassle over it again. Finally a larger meeting is held, a decision made: the federal government will stay out of the case.

In this and other situations, Deaver often found himself in what passed for the moderate or even liberal position—in relative terms— within the Administration. He was responsible for general supervision of a new venture by the White House, the President's Task Force on Private Sector Initiatives. The idea was to stimulate private philanthrophy and do-good programs, particularly at the local level. By promoting this activity (but investing no federal money) the Reaganauts would display the humane side of their approach to the needy. Philosophic conservatives wanted the emphasis to be on totally volunteer efforts by local organizations. Instead, Deaver helped recruit corporate executives and big-league activists like John Gardner, the founder of Common Cause. The task force thus followed the route of "corporate responsibility." It even had the temerity to recommend that private enterprise drastically increase its charitable donations. To some conservatives, this smacked of federal coercion though the task force could apply only moral pressure. Usually Deaver avoided attack from the right because of his long tenure in Reagan's service. On this occasion, he became a target of the purists' indignation.[1]

The notion of Deaver as a moderate mole among the Reaganauts is amusing. Whatever political philosophy he possessed was conventionally conservative. He had no reservations about the general tenets of Reaganism and in his personal dealings he was hardly a bleeding heart. In the Carter White House, egalitarianism required that men and women, juniors and seniors, enjoy access to the small gymnasium situated in the Old Executive Office Building. Inspecting the facilities during his first few days on the job, Deaver wanted to look at the gym. He found his way blocked by a heavyset black woman who informed him, without much deference, that it was ladies' day in the exercise room. Deaver promptly had the locks changed and ordered up a new set of rules. Henceforth, only high-ranking staffers could use the gym. So few women qualified by grade among the Reagan appointees that no time was set aside for them. Thus the gym became a male preserve.*

For all of his loyalty and the unquestioned excellence of his public relations radar, Deaver unconsciously failed Reagan in one important respect. He was too much like the boss when it came to thinking issues through—or failing to do so. Reagan suffered from a shortage of cerebral advisers whom he trusted enough to go with. Deaver had the mental equipment, but not the temperament, to delve into the hard business of governance. In a rare moment of whimsical hubris, he once told my colleague Douglas Brew why his felow triumvirs trusted him: "I'm probably not a threat. I don't aspire to either of their jobs. If I had wanted either one, I could have had it."2 If he had been Chief of Staff or principal policy adviser, Deaver would have flopped disastrously. He had too much difficulty separating himself from his affection for Reagan.

Talking about this one night, Deaver became introspective: "You really have only your instincts, all you've been taught and all you've experienced. I lead from my gut when I give advice. More than the others around the President, I talk from instinct."3 But when it came to Reagan his instincts were so protective that professionalism suffered. His surrender to Sears at the beginning of the 1980 campaign was an act of self-sacrifice motivated by the idea that Reagan needed the campaign strategist more than he needed Deaver. But his departure, instead of solving the staff problem, contributed to an increasingly unhealthy situation that damaged Reagan's morale and marred the early months of his candidacy. When he did his exorcism number on Richard Allen, Deaver's instinct led him to promote only one possible replacement, William Clark, because of Clark's strong personal tie with the President (and with Deaver as well). But Clark, despite his year at the State Department, was still a tyro in foreign affairs and could be of only limited help in supplying what Reagan needed most: imaginative, cohesive policies.

To Meese, the lawyer above all, Reagan was a prized client. To Baker, the competitive political operator, serving Reagan was the challenge match of a lifetime and the object was to amass the best possible score card. For Deaver, who had never held a job he cared about be-

---

* Reagan had his own private exercise room in the executive residence.

fore he met Reagan, or had a mentor who influenced him greatly, the relationship was as much filial as professional.

Almost every White House has one or two staff members who have risen to great influence because of their personal bond with the chief rather than political ambition or commitment. That was Deaver's reason for sticking with an occupation that he found unreasonable in its demands and insufficiently rewarding in terms of money. The top echelon of the White House staff can be a dreary place for someone who gets no kick out of power.

Back in Bakersfield, where he grew up, Deaver aspired to nothing more than professional status, interesting work and a good income. The Deavers, like the Meeses, were old Californians who had somehow missed out on the gold of the Golden West. Deaver's maternal grandfather, a German immigrant, made it to the coast by helping to build the Santa Fe Railroad. Once there, he made a career in the car yards while his wife served as principal of a segregated black high school. Home was built on a lot purchased from the original Colonel Baker of Bakersfield.

The next generation did not scamper up the ladder very far. Deaver's father, a college dropout who had health problems, couldn't make a go of his Shell Oil distributorship and ended his working life in a civil service job at Edwards Air Force Base. As a teenager, Deaver yearned for nothing so much as his own car; all the family had was a small truck used in the father's service station. Facile at the piano, Deaver finally earned enough playing in saloons to buy a ten-year-old Pontiac. By then he was attending San Jose State College—the quickest way to get on his bad side is to flaunt an Ivy League pedigree—and thinking about journalism as a career. "But I didn't get along with the professor, and anyway I couldn't write. So I switched to political science."[4]

He was in college during the 1960 presidential campaign and considered himself a Nixon loyalist. His preference four years later was Goldwater, though the 1964 debacle made him reconsider the wisdom of supporting staunch conservatives. He drifted into a job as field man for the State Republican Committee. Deaver was working for State Assembly candidates in the Santa Barbara area in 1966, when Reagan fought George Christopher for the gubernatorial nomination, and Deaver leaned toward Christopher. To Deaver, the moderate with political experience seemed the logical choice over the conservative from the movie business. He met Reagan once in Santa Barbara but experienced no instant conversion. In any event, Deaver's job with the state party prevented him from active participation on either side, a fact which probably changed his life. Bill Clark, scouting for a young talent to work for the incoming Governor Reagan, recruited a loyal young Republican who had ostensibly been neutral in the primary contest.

The newcomer ended up handling scheduling, which involved him in the Reagan family's personal lives as well as politics. Deaver found himself part of a family in more ways than one. The Reagans took a shine to him, Clark played an avuncular role in his life and he started dating a secretary in the office, Carolyn Judy, who became his wife in 1968. Still, Deaver thought he should get out when Clark left. He fancied a career in advertising or public relations, and the contacts he had made in Sacramento would be helpful. He wanted a large house behind his picket fence, and leisure to play with his children when the time came to have some. But he held back. Why? "I don't know. I guess I got more and more attached to the Reagans. I kind of felt they needed me. They have a certain vulnerability that gets to you."[5]

After Sacramento, Meese tried the corporate life and teaching law in San Diego. Deaver went into public relations partnership with another Sacramento colleague, Peter Hannaford, but hardly strayed far from the Reagans. The firm's most important and remunerative client was Ronald Reagan—political advocate, speechmaker, newspaper columnist, radio commentator. Hannaford ghost-wrote the columns and supervised research for the radio spots, most of which Reagan preferred to draft personally. Deaver did a lot of the bookings and often traveled with his once and future boss. The firm began to flourish as it acquired other business, but it—and Deaver—remained inextricably tied to Reagan's political ambitions. The candidate's official headquarters, when he declared for the 1980 nomination, was the Deaver & Hannaford office on Wilshire Boulevard in Los Angeles.

His brief exile, following the dispute with Sears, gave Deaver time to reflect. The separation, and particularly the Reagans' acquiescence to it, had hurt. At the same time it was an opportunity at last to assert independence for the first time. Deaver was uncomfortable with bigness and bustle anyway. Hannaford wanted to build the firm into a national organization. Deaver opposed the idea. The prospect of several offices, a large personnel roster, a constant quest for clients to meet the overhead, repelled him. He didn't even like Los Angeles. Home was still Sacramento, where Carolyn and their two young children, Amanda and Blair, lived. Deaver commuted to L.A. He was planning to strike out on his own, to set up a small consulting business with a few rich customers, when he put aside his plans one more time to go back to the Reagan campaign.

By the time the Deavers came to Washington—reluctantly, he insisted—he had acquired a strong taste for the good life. He made the mistake of complaining in public that he could not make it on his White House salary of $60,662 a year. In a period when the Reaganauts were accused of being callous toward the poor, that hardly helped the image. The Deavers rented a house in the chic Foxhall Road section of town, just down the street from the Bakers, who were millionaires. Private schools are expensive in Washington. In the old days, the solution would have been easy: pals of the President would have put up the money necessary to get a prized assistant through this version of hard times. Post-Watergate regulations made that impossible.

Almost from the time he arrived in Washington, Deaver was wondering when he could finally go it on his own. He had sold his interest in the firm to Hannaford for a piddling $40,000, then watched as his former partner—now with well-publicized access to the new administration—expanded into a national operation as he had hoped to do all along. Carolyn Deaver, a gracious, cheerful pixie of a woman who shared her husband's affection for the Reagans, nonetheless wanted him out of the White House. Stuck with car pooling, heavy social responsibilities and a tight household budget, she gave up jogging and resumed smoking. During the Libyan hit-team scare, Secret Service agents were constantly underfoot. Once Carolyn forgot to alert her bodyguards that she was leaving the house. The agents' chase car pursued her station wagon in reverse for several blocks. It was a nervous time for the Deavers, the winter of 1981–82, and tensions within the troika made the following months edgy as well. "I should wear a priest's collar," complained Deaver, a high-church Episcopalian who took religion seriously. "Everyone tells me their troubles."[6]

Carolyn worried that her husband was being swallowed up by the job, a feeling he occasionally shared. When he was down, Deaver would fret: "Most of my adult life, and all of our married life, has been in Ronald Reagan's orbit. I was on my own just those few months when I was out of the campaign. I kind of enjoyed that. Isn't it time that I became Mike Deaver?"[7] But the 1982 congressional election had to be fought and Reagan needed him then. White House staff organization was still a problem. Deaver, ever the talent scout and exorcist, worked on that as well, though he doubted whether Reagan would accept any significant changes. The agenda for 1983 would be complex and the subject of new conflict. Maybe he should stay for another six or eight months to help get the place working better. Carolyn took a part-time job as a public relations consultant. The knee operation was postponed indefinitely for lack of time; Deaver got by with an occasional injection. The presidency had not made the Reagans any less vulnerable. Besides, Deaver liked the parties, particularly when important people begged him to play the piano.

16

The Middle East:
Dear Menachem . . .

June 7 was a pleasant Sunday in Ronald Reagan's first Washington spring. Events moved at a rapid pace—hard bargaining over the 1981 tax bill, a new fight approaching on budget cuts, a delicate diplomatic mission by Philip Habib underway to avert new fighting in Lebanon—but the Reagan people could still enjoy a day off. The President and First Lady were at Camp David, where he rode horseback and prepared for Monday's visit by José López Portillo of Mexico. Alexander Haig played tennis. Richard Allen was relaxing on his sun deck at home at two-thirty when the Situation Room duty officer phoned.

An alarming message from Samuel Lewis, the U.S. ambassador in Israel, shattered the calm. He had just been informed by Menachem Begin's government that the Israeli Air Force that morning struck far from home, demolishing a nuclear reactor outside of Baghdad. Moments later Allen was on the phone to Reagan at Camp David. The news still had not been officially announced by either Israel or Iraq and Allen had only a summary of Lewis' flash message. Reagan replied: "By golly, what do you suppose is behind that?"[1]

The bombing, its timing, its impact on Washington's peacemaking efforts in the region, Reagan's astonishment—all these would be part of a long, agonizing pattern for this administration. The attack on Iraq was only the first of what would be a growing list of explosions between Reagan and a foreign leader whom he had initially admired, Menachem Begin. These difficulties taxed Reagan's national security apparatus. For Reagan personally, it was a journey of disillusionment and education. It would take many months for him to absorb the lessons. He would learn the risks of relying too heavily on his own untutored instincts. Reagan would also begin to recognize the occasions when only his own personal, vigorous intervention would suffice.

Every President since Harry Truman had faced difficult, often risky decisions concerning the Middle East. While successive administrations continued to assure Israel's survival with material and political support, American policy during the last decade became more diverse. One obvious reason was petro-politics. The cutoff of oil exports in 1973, following the Yom Kippur war, and the rapid rise of prices after that, shocked the nervous systems of industrialized and poor nations alike. The aftereffects are still felt today. Volatility in the Muslim world, symbolized most dramatically by Iran's sudden conversion from friend to enemy of the West, was another trauma with durable scars. No one could predict where the malign influence of Khomeini's Iran or Qaddafi's Libya would be felt next.

Moscow, with its own historic ambitions along its southern border and its oscillating relationships with individual states in the region, exported mischief and armaments to every interested recipient. By the late seventies, it was painfully clear, the Middle East had become the most dangerous arena that any American President would have to face. There was greater risk of a Soviet-American military collision there than in any of the other cockpits. Even if the superpowers avoided confrontation, there was still high hazard to American economic and political interests. There was also the possibility, within a few years, of nuclear combat among the smaller states. Finally, Washington's strong ties to Israel over three decades made it difficult for American diplomacy to maneuver among the Arabs. The Israeli connection was to remain firm. In extremis it would be paramount. But it could no longer be the exclusive focus of American aims. Relations with the Arabs required repair, desperately. Thus, under Nixon, Ford and Carter, Washington periodically applied pressure on Jerusalem to compromise on at least some issues. But Israeli resistance to these efforts, as a rule, was successful.

The Carter administration, thrashing about for a way out of the maze, went so far as to invite the Soviet Union back into the play. That blunder—which struck both Cairo and Jerusalem as ludicrous— nonetheless encouraged entente between Anwar Sadat and Menachem Begin. Sadat's historic departure from Arab solidarity in opposition to Israel led, in turn, to the Camp David agreements of 1978 and then to an Egyptian-Israeli peace treaty. In global terms, that was Carter's most important accomplishment. He said later that he spent more time on the Middle East than on any other foreign issue during his four years. It was a great irony that Carter, the American President whom Israel's partisans liked least, presided over the breakthrough that secured Israel's southern front. Without Egypt, no significant Arab military challenge to Israel would be feasible.

But Camp David was only the beginning of what the parties insisted on calling the "peace process." Other issues would have to be addressed, including the status of the city of Jerusalem, which Israel claimed as its capital but which most of the world did not recognize as such because the eastern part of the city had been captured in the 1967 war. The disposition of the Gaza district and the West Bank of the Jordan River would also have to be settled. Above all else, the multitudinous pawns of the region, the Palestinians, would have to be treated as something other than a refugee problem. Whatever the historic rights and wrongs of their situation—and however cynically they had been treated by the Arab states for more than three decades—they had survived as a people and as a political dilemma. No durable solution would be possible without a settlement of their claims. For the United States, that would mean an indeterminant sentence in the prison of petro-politics. Al Haig, in one of his more reflective moments, captured the American role perfectly: "The United States bears a very special responsibility for the situation in the Middle East. It has been historically so. And anything that occurs in the Middle East, good or bad, the United States tends to enjoy or to suffer from the consequences."[2]

The Carter administration had struggled with these complexities unevenly. After the tremendous high of the Camp David accords and the Cairo-Jerusalem treaty, Washington as mediator had great difficulties trying for the necessary encore. Meanwhile, the monarchy's fall in Tehran, the hostage situation, Libya's brazen adventures and the Soviet invasion of Afghanistan forced American attention toward the larger, regional dangers. During 1980 Candidate Reagan made things no easier. Reagan had always been a firm supporter of Israel. He held a simple, even romantic view of what had become a complex, geopolitical riddle—Israel as brave, besieged and reliably anti-Communist. Further, Begin was not only a courageous fighter; he was by Israel's standards an economic conservative, the first such to lead his country after a succession of Labor Party Prime Ministers. Reagan liked him from afar. In his own domestic political arena, Reagan with a clear conscience exploited the difficulties Carter was having with Jerusalem.

In his most important campaign speech on the subject, Reagan was blithely uncritical of Begin's policies, including the continued insertion of Jewish settlements in disputed areas. Candidate Reagan twitted Carter for selling F-15's to Saudi Arabia—a program President Reagan would soon enlarge—and he sounded skeptical about the future of the Camp David scenario. The most important sentence in his speech was more telling for what it implied than for what it stated explicitly:

"While we can help the nations of that area move toward peace, we should not try to force a settlement upon them." In the cryptology of campaign politics, that line, delivered to an audience of Jewish-American activists, meant that Reagan, unlike Carter, would refrain from twisting arms in Jerusalem.[3]

Though Reagan's position made sense in terms of domestic politics, it was poor geopolitics. One of his foreign policy advisers confided to a reporter later that Reagan's initial stance encouraged Begin to believe that Israel would be relatively free of American restraint. U.S. administrations since 1967 had sought, with uneven vigor, to persuade Israel to relinquish land captured in that year's war. Now it appeared that the new leadership in Washington would relax that pressure significantly. Moshe Arens, a senior Knesset member who later became Israel's ambassador to the Untied States, observed: "If you looked at the gap between the Israeli government and the United States government [on the question of territory], it became smaller when Reagan entered the White House."[4] The Arabs had a similar perception.

During the transition, meanwhile, the Reaganauts had to face difficult realities. When the lame-duck President and the President-elect met in the White House on November 20, one of the items Carter told Reagan about was a pending aircraft deal with Saudi Arabia. Washington had already reached a general understanding with Riyadh on a list of major items to supplement the controversial sale of F-15's agreed to in 1978. It would be up to the new team to decide whether to bring the second deal to fruition. As Reagan's advisers explored that and other questions, they came to agree with a number of conclusions which the Carter people were making late in 1980.

These views were brought together in a National Security Council decision paper drafted by Brigadier General William Odom and signed as "PD 63" by Carter in January. It emphasized the need to broaden relations with any of the Arab states amenable to cooperation with the United States. This view recognized the dangers to Western interests posed by instability in the Persian Gulf region. The United States would have to seek new balance wheels now that Iran had become a hostile force. Riyadh and its smaller, even weaker neighbors would have to be buttressed. Jordan would have to be wooed anew. Egypt would have to be reassured of American fealty because Cairo faced rising opposition from the Muslim fundamentalist movement.

The Palestinian conundrum had existed for more than thirty years. It could wait a bit longer, the new team reasoned. The United States would mark time, awaiting the outcome of the Israeli election in June 1981. If the Labor Party defeated the Likud coalition and Shimon Peres replaced Begin—as most American experts hoped would happen

—Jerusalem probably would be easier to deal with anyway. The United States would continue to encourage fulfillment of the last important part of the Israeli-Egyptian treaty, the return to Egypt of the last third of the Sinai. That was scheduled to take place in April 1982. Otherwise, Washington would put the "peace process" on hold and see what could be done to achieve Haig's "strategic consensus" concerning external threats to the region. It seemed a plausible approach in the winter of 1980–81. Later events showed it to be inadequate.

The regional threat was real enough and demanded action. However, the idea that Arab-Israeli relations would remain static without full involvement by Washington was an illusion. Further, the White House and the Pentagon seriously underestimated the psychological impact on Israel of American arms deals with the "moderate" Arabs. To Jerusalem, the Saudis and the Jordanians were implacable foes, just like the Syrians and the Iraqis, as long as they insisted that a state of war existed between them and Israel. Further, the Saudis still subsidized the PLO, whose terrorist operations continued to exact a blood price in Israel. It was all very well for the United States to fret about the future security of Saudi oil fields. Begin had to worry about the lives of his constituents today.

Finally, the Reaganauts miscalculated the human dimension. Though Begin took a biblical view of Israel's borders and was prone to legalistic hairsplitting as a negotiator, he was also an old guerrilla fighter who, like Reagan, relied heavily on his personal instincts. America was Israel's last important friend. Israel was America's only democratic associate in the Middle East, owner of the only modern military machine in the region—a made-in-America machine, in fact. Begin, one of his aides told me privately, could not understand why he was not invited to Washington soon after the inauguration. He was happy to see Carter out of office; the two had developed a keen, mutual dislike. Begin was pleased with what he had heard from Reagan during the campaign. But he had never met Reagan, had no personal feel for him.

During the transition and into the spring he saw a parade of other leaders conferring with Reagan. Were the problems of Jamaica, Mexico, or Canada more important than those of Israel? Reagan had met casually with Helmut Schmidt during the transition, on short notice, because Schmidt hinted strongly that he wanted a conversation. Similar feelers from Jerusalem were deflected. Maybe it was true that Washington hoped for a Peres victory in June. Why did the new administration not appoint a high-level special envoy, as Carter had employed? In the early months there was no envoy at all, high or otherwise, operating between Israel and Egypt. To one subordinate, Begin made a telling remark. He could not decide what to make of Reagan in the spring of

1981, he said, but he was glad that Haig was Secretary of State. After all, Begin knew that he would be comfortable with Haig. The assistant, who followed U.S.-Israeli relations closely, could not understand that feeling about the new Secretary of State. Well, Begin explained, we sat next to each other at a dinner and we got to know each other. That meeting, it turned out, had taken place in 1974, when Haig worked in the White House and Begin was an opposition leader. But the new President was still a stranger. Did he really know what was worrying Israel?

What caused the most urgent anxiety in Israel between February and April was air superiority. When Foreign Minister Yitzhak Shamir visited Washington in February he got the first broad indication that Reagan was going to carry through on the Saudi aircraft deal. However, Shamir was not told specifically that the sale would include Boeing E-3A Airborne Warning and Control System (AWACS) planes. American pilots already were using these planes to patrol Saudi airspace to the east. These modified 707's, carrying large radar dishes and sophisticated data processing equipment, were far more advanced than the Grumman E-2C Hawkeyes in Israel's inventory. Rather the Administration told Shamir in general terms that the Saudis would be sold airborne surveillance equipment of their own.

The Syrian occupying force in Lebanon meanwhile was beginning to challenge Israel's control of the skies in that sector by installing new Soviet-made surface-to-air missiles (SAM's) in the Bekaa Valley region. Originally, Syria's military had been effective in quelling the civil war between Christian and Muslim forces in Lebanon. Now the Syrians were becoming a material factor in Israel's ability to assault the PLO at will. Jerusalem threatened to attack the missiles unless the Syrians withdrew them voluntarily. Damascus refused, and a new crisis threatened.

To make matters even more difficult for the new administration, the national security apparatus found itself unable to agree on just about anything concerning the Middle East. Within the State Department, there were differences between the regional specialists and the global strategists. Haig and Weinberger disagreed from the outset as well. Weinberger reflected his own experiences as a businessman who had had extensive dealings with the Saudis. He also spoke for the Joint Chiefs of Staff, which for years had been uneasy about extensive U.S. military ties with Israel. That part of the bureaucracy favored stronger Arab connections. The Air Force, in particular, vigorously promoted the most grandiose option available in the Saudi plane deal—sale of the larger surveillance planes, plus improvements for the F-15's already committed and the export of large aerial tankers.

Haig himself saw things differently. Unlike Weinberger, Haig believed that the Begin government had to be treated with the utmost delicacy. He studied carefully the CIA's psychological profile on Begin and knew that outside heat quickly brought the Prime Minister's temper to a boil. Further, Haig had a reasonable grasp of internal Israeli politics. Evidence of American coolness would only strengthen the more bellicose elements in Jerusalem. If we are to pursue the "strategic consensus" idea with the Arabs, Haig argued, then we must be all the more solicitous in massaging Begin.

Thus the Secretary of State was skeptical about going ahead with the larger version of the Saudi deal, even after the National Security Council, on February 27, gave informal blessing to the idea. Word of that soon leaked out—though the type of aerial surveillance equipment was still unclear—and the anxiety level in Israel began to climb. Haig was planning his first trip to the region in early April. Reagan was shot before he left, and before a firm decision was reached on the details of the aircraft deal. Political specialists both at the State Department and the NSC staff had already warned their superiors that sale of the Boeing AWACS would cause a serious backlash in Jerusalem. Preparing for the April 1 NSC meeting, at which George Bush would preside, Haig planned to shoot the deal down, or at least force important modifications. He was well briefed and felt sure of his ground. By the time the meeting took place, however, extraneous events of the previous few days had deflated Haig. He had just been slapped down by the White House over the Crisis Management Team arrangement. Further, he had looked foolish on the day of the assassination attempt. He did not need another controversy at that moment.

Bush was pressing for a consensus. The President needs firm guidance on this, he insisted. Weinberger, cool and well organized, delivered essentially the Air Force brief. Haig, uncharacteristically chastened, responded in a feeble manner by his standards. Weinberger's position carried the day. A few months later, the White House would pay a heavy price for this decision. Meanwhile, Haig departed for Cairo, Jerusalem, Amman and Riyadh, in that order. He told the Saudis that Reagan would fulfill Carter's understanding with them.

Nonetheless, Haig and Prime Minister Begin seemed to get on well. The visitor's main message was different from what Israel had heard from the Carter administration. Washington, the Secretary of State said, hoped to elevate its dealings with Jerusalem to that of a strategic relationship between allies. While the two governments would go into details later, the main theme was the common interest both had in regional stability.

As allies, Haig went on, each party must be sensitive to the interests of the other. In particular, the United States was attempting to get a few of the Arab countries into a firm, if informal alignment against external threat—that is, Moscow. That policy, if successful, would obviously benefit Israel. It would be essential for Israel to show a good deal of restraint in dealing with its neighbors. Military moves by Israel would divert attention and energy from the larger problem. By the same token, the more interested the Arabs became in cooperating with the United States in regional defense, the greater Washington's influence would be. That could only help Israel in the long run.

Begin appeared to be sympathetic. He agreed to prudence concerning one specific problem—the SAM's recently introduced into Lebanon by the Syrians. Begin would withhold military action against these emplacements for the time being; he would give American diplomacy an opportunity to resolve that issue peacefully.

That acquiescence seemed to vindicate Haig's approach to Begin. In the State Department it was called taking the "high road" tactic. That was in contrast to the "rug merchant" mentality, a derisive term used by some of Haig's aides to describe the threat of punishment (less military aid) or rewards (usually more assistance) in response to each Israeli act. To Haig, Weinberger was the preeminent carpet dealer and the Secretary of State hoped to close down that shop. For the time being, Haig had Reagan's full agreement as to the proper game plan concerning Begin.

That explained the President's surprise, two months later, when Dick Allen called him with the news of the Israeli raid on Iraq's nuclear reactor. As in later Middle East crises, superficial appearances were considerably different from the realities. In this case, Reagan had no business being astonished. Iraq's nuclear program had been a subject of concern in both Washington and Jerusalem for two years. The Carter administration had attempted to persuade France and Italy to scale back their technical assistance to Iraq. That effort had been made not merely to placate Israel, but because Washington had a thoroughly justified fear that eventually Iraq would use the reactor's produce for nuclear weapons in addition to peaceful purposes. U.S. intelligence analysts felt strongly that Iraq had the desire and would soon have the means. The French and Italian governments had rebuffed the American request.

Immediately after the June 7 raid on the reactor, Ambassador Lewis sent a long cable from Tel Aviv reminding Washington of that history. Of course the State Department and CIA had not literally forgotten that the problem existed. But when administrations change, institutional memory at the top suffers lapses. The Reaganauts were far less concerned than their predecessors about nuclear proliferation. Before long, the Reagan administration would make it easier for foreign countries to purchase nuclear technology and materials from the United

States. For that as well as other reasons, the National Security Council had not paid much attention to the Iraqi nuclear program and had failed to follow up vigorously with the French and Italians. Direct American influence on Iraq was virtually nil. The government of Saddam Hussein was an anti-American client of Moscow.

If diplomacy was not going to deter Iraq's nuclear progress, precision bombing by Israeli F-16's—supplied by the United States, of course—was the other alternative. No one else in the region would have been happy to see Iraq brandishing a nuclear sword. Of course the timing was awkward. Any military move by Israel made it more difficult for Sadat to carry on with negotiations. Further, Washington's strategic consensus pitch was based on a tacit understanding that the United States would work for Israeli restraint. And the attack took place just three weeks before the Israeli election, which made it appear a cynical move by Begin to restore ebbing political fortunes.

In fact, Haig was neither astonished nor particularly dismayed once he learned that the bombing had caused just one death (that of a French technician) and no significant radiation danger. One reason Israel struck when it did was that delay in the attack would have risked much greater contamination as the plant's supply of raw material increased. Haig and Bill Clark spent the rest of that Sunday afternoon at the State Department monitoring reports from the region. When he realized that the air strike had been a surgical success, Haig relaxed. Well, he said with a wink, it would have to have been done some time or other anyway. A perfunctory statement was drafted. It called the attack a "very serious development and a source of utmost concern." This was mild, in diplomatic dialect. No action against Israel, no stern admonition, was planned initially. In fact, the statement was held until Monday morning because the State Department saw no need to comment officially until U.S. reaction was requested.

By Monday afternoon the raid had produced enough agitation abroad to elicit a stronger pronouncement ("The United States Government condemns . . .") as well as a light slap on the wrist. There was no question that Israel had at least technically violated the Mutual Defense Assistance Agreement of 1952. That pact limits to "legitimate self-defense" the use of weaponry given by the United States or sold on favorable terms.* When these incidents occur, as they have with sev-

---

* Israel is a major military power because of U.S. grants, loans and technical cooperation. On a per capita basis, Israel in recent years has received more assistance from the United States, economic and military, than any other nation. The combined total in fiscal '82 was $2.2 billion, and scheduled to rise to $2.5 billion in fiscal '83. Though part of that consists ostensibly of military loans to be repaid, the United States routinely "forgives" $500 million of that each year. Currently 19.4 percent of all U.S. foreign assistance goes to Israel.

eral other recipients of American arms, the Administration is supposed
to report to Congress whether a violation has taken place. The Turkish
invasion of Cyprus caused a long suspension of all American military
assistance to Turkey. Israel had never been spanked so severely. Now,
in June, the Administration—strictly for cosmetic purposes—undertook a "study" of whether a breach had occurred. In the interim,
Washington delayed shipment of a handful of warplanes.

This was done, however, with a broad wink. It was common knowledge that Washington intended to resume the transfer of F-16's within
a few weeks. Meanwhile, in July, Haig sent Robert McFarlane to Begin
for another chat. McFarlane's brief repeated what his boss had said in
April: allies have an obligation to take each other's interests into account. In diplomatic language, McFarlane complained about the Baghdad raid. He pointed out that the United States was continuing to fend
off efforts to impose United Nations sanctions against Israel, and to defend Israel as best it could against the increasing antagonism of the
Western European allies. Paris and Rome, after all, were upset that
their handiwork in Iraq had been blown to bits. Begin responded that
he understood the message. Just forty-eight hours later, however, the
Israeli Air Force attacked downtown Beirut in retaliation for PLO terrorist attacks. It was one of the biggest strikes up to that time, causing
hundreds of civilian casualties.

When the Beirut raid took place, Reagan and Haig were in Ottawa
for the 1981 Economic Summit meeting. This too would be part of a
doleful pattern. The following December, when Jerusalem formally an-
nexed the Golan Heights area, Haig was at a NATO meeting in
Europe. Begin's move that time came just a day after martial law was
imposed in Poland, preoccupying Washington. The invasion of Lebanon in June 1982 occurred while Reagan was on his big European
excursion. Reagan's early admiration for Begin began to crumble. The
President's cheeks were stinging from what he had to view as serial
slaps. "Boy," he remarked to advisers on a few occasions, "that guy
makes it hard for you to be his friend."

But in the summer of 1981 Reagan continued to try hard. In their
public statements, Reagan and Haig expressed understanding for Israel's predicament. The July raid on Beirut caused continuation of the
hold on aircraft delivery, but the Administration made clear that was a
temporary condition. Sadat arrived for a state visit that turned into a
public relations triumph for the Egyptians. Reagan, ever susceptible to
heroic figures, was thoroughly charmed by his guest. However, Reagan
was also taken aback when Sadat, during a formal toast at a White
House dinner in his honor on August 5, proposed that the United
States begin direct talks with the PLO. Said Sadat: "You can help this

process of reconciliation, Mr. President, by holding a dialogue with the Palestinians through their representatives. This is certain to strengthen the forces of moderation among them . . . It would be an act of statesmanship and vision." One of the television correspondents in the press pool dropped her clipboard at this historic moment in the State Dining Room. Reagan declined to pick up on Sadat's suggestion. The United States would maintain its policy of ignoring the PLO until it abandoned terrorism altogether and recognized Israel's nationhood.

Habib and his deputy, Morris Draper, meanwhile labored to maintain a tenuous cease-fire in Lebanon after the July raid on Beirut. The Syrians, apparently motivated by some mindless desire to end any prospects for a comprehensive settlement, were seriously considering the dispatch of additional reinforcements to Lebanon. Had Damascus gone ahead, a massive Israeli attack on the ground would almost certainly have followed. At this delicate moment, the American mediators scored a quiet coup. They persuaded Crown Prince Fahd of Saudi Arabia—who later succeeded to the throne—to intervene. For several years Riyadh had been relatively passive when it came to exerting direct political influence on other Arab countries. The assassination of King Faisal in 1975 seemed to have pushed the royal family into a corner of caution from which it used its ample supply of petrodollars to buy harmony with its neighbors.

Now there was a change. Fahd realized that his wealthy but vulnerable nation had a large stake in maintaining stability—and in promoting Reagan's diplomacy. Riyadh worked quietly to rein in Damascus. Its diplomats served as middlemen between Habib and the PLO, a role that was vital because Habib was prohibited from dealing directly with the organization himself. One of the Americans involved remarked privately at the time: "We were overjoyed with the Saudi participation and sense of commitment. Fahd moved so quickly we could hardly believe it." Reporting back to Reagan, Habib called the Saudi role "absolutely invaluable and indispensable for our future efforts."

This development confirmed for Reagan the wisdom of going ahead with the AWACS deal despite the difficulties involved. Further, when Fahd came out with his own broad-gauge peace plan later in the year, Reagan spoke favorably of it even though Fahd's approach was clearly unacceptable to Israel. In Washington, the very fact that Riyadh had become active in positive ways seemed a major accomplishment.

A delicate balancing act was now more necessary than ever. Haig realized that the Begin government, which had survived the June election in tenuous fashion, could launch another violent initiative at any moment. Or it might seize on some event to delay the return to Egypt of the last third of the Sinai—a move that would sink the Camp David accords for all time. Simultaneously, the Saudis and the Egyptians had to be kept on a constructive track. If at all possible, Jordan had to be lured into a conciliatory posture. Hence the continued need to lower the temperature of Begin, who periodically warned Washington that he was about to unleash his forces on Lebanon.

After Sadat left town, the Administration allowed a few days to pass and then resumed the supply of warplanes to Israel. In September it was Begin's turn to be guest of honor at the White House. The visit was set up to be a love fest, with the friction of June and July forgotten. Haig told his National Security Council colleagues that he would take care of the difficult business with Begin privately. That would leave Reagan free to massage and reassure the Prime Minister. Thus little pressure was applied on any subject, immediate or long-range. As far as the outside world could make out, the President was doing everything within his power short of dancing the *hora* to demonstrate solidarity with his guest.

One point of disagreement could not be blinked at, however. The Administration was about to begin the formal process of gaining congressional approval of the AWACS deal. Further, the $8 billion transaction would strengthen Saudi air power in other important ways as well. Begin replied that he still opposed that sale on the grounds that it would imperil Israeli security. He would have to state that view in public if asked, but he implied that he would not attempt a major personal lobbying campaign. Then he went to Capitol Hill and appeared on American television shows to denounce the Administration plan with his customary rhetorical force.

Reagan was outraged and Haig embarrassed. Before Begin left for home, Haig flew to New York for a last conversation with the Prime Minister. The Secretary of State tried to caution Begin that he risked a breach with the Administration. Weinberger was proposing a full reversion to the "rug merchant" approach; he wanted the National Security Council to consider an indefinite suspension of military cooperation with Israel unless Begin backed off his opposition to the AWACS deal. At the same time, Ariel Sharon, the Israeli Defense Minister, dropped more hints about attacking Lebanon. Begin told Haig that he had no choice but to fight the arming of Arab states. Concerning major warfare, on the other hand, he said that he took Washington's concern seriously. Translation: Begin would restrain Sharon for yet a while longer.

From Begin's departure in mid-September until the end of October the White House was embroiled in the ugliest of legislative fights. Though major arms sales abroad are the executive's prerogative, they can be blocked by both houses of Congress. Because the Administration had allowed its intentions to leak out the previous winter, the pro-Israeli lobby had plenty of time to mount a vigorous opposition campaign, fueled by moral support from Jerusalem. On the other side, scores of American corporations which had large and growing business connections with the Saudis felt an important pecuniary stake in the deal's success. They began an energetic push in favor of the proposal.

If the President and his most senior advisers had realized the previous winter how intense a conflict they would have to endure in the fall, they probably would not have committed themselves so early. Reagan's own political sense is usually acute enough to spare himself unnecessary combat. But, as we have seen, neither Reagan nor the troika focused on foreign affairs in the early months. Once Reagan had dug in, his competitive instincts as well as the need to preserve the presidency's freedom of action in foreign policy demanded that he fight to win.

On the other side the stakes also appeared high. Jewish-American organizations marshal effective lobbying efforts when the occasion arises. They had lost a similar contest in 1978, when Carter signed the original F-15 deal with Riyadh. That very defeat gave the Israeli lobby strong arguments in 1981. Carter's Defense Secretary, Harold Brown, had assured the Senate Foreign Relations Committee, in writing, that the F-15's would have only limited capabilities. He told the senators, for instance, that auxiliary fuel tanks would not be sold and pointed out that the tanker aircraft then in Saudi Arabia's inventory could not be used for serial refueling.[5] Now the Reagan administration was proposing the addition of exactly the equipment Brown had ruled out, plus much more. That being the case, the White House's current assurances about limitations being placed on the new sale held little water. Further, it was becoming obvious that sophisticated American arms would be going to other Arab countries, with Jordan probably next on the list.

During the spring and summer, while the Administration fumbled in its own public relations and lobbying, Israel's partisans lined up majorities in both houses of Congress against the sale. Bickering and rivalry between Dick Allen's interagency group, which initially was responsible for the project, and the State Department made matters worse. At the end of the summer, Baker's LSG took command and found that the White House had no chance at all of winning a majority in the House of Representatives. Prospects in the Senate were only slightly less grim.

It would be a retail operation, vote by vote, if the Administration was to prevail. Now fully aroused, Reagan understood the stakes. "The President would have done almost anything to avoid defeat on this one," Baker said later. "He would have made himself available twenty-four hours a day if necessary. He felt that he absolutely had to win."⁶ One of the things Reagan had to do was to browbeat fellow Republicans. When he met on September 11 with Senator Bob Packwood, a progressive Republican who had differences with the Administration on a number of issues, the atmosphere quickly soured. Packwood headed a campaign committee that raises funds for GOP Senate candidates and he pointed out that Jewish donors were highly displeased with the AWACS proposal. The Saudis were neither reliable nor popular, Packwood argued, and promoting their interests was hardly smart politics. The White House leaked its version of the encounter, which embarrassed Packwood. Increasingly, the debate took on a "Reagan versus Begin" theme rather than focusing on the intrinsic merits of the arms proposal.

Reagan himself sharpened that aspect of the fight when he opened his October 1 press conference with a prepared statement. "As President," he said, "it is my duty to define and defend our broad national security objectives . . . And, while we must always take into account the vital interests of our allies, American security interests must remain our internal responsibility. It is not the business of other nations to make American foreign policy." The implication of that statement was stark. Opponents of the sale, the President was saying, served Jerusalem, not Washington.

Six days later, Muslim fanatics murdered Anwar Sadat. That too became part of the AWACS argument. On October 7, Reagan held a closed-door meeting with forty-three Republican senators, many of whom had already signed a resolution against the sale. On this issue, legislators affiliated with the New Right were among the most adamant opponents of the White House.* Reagan contended that "the sale is particularly important in light of the tragedy of yesterday." When Slade Gorton, alluding to Reagan's press conference statement, protested that the Israeli lobby did not control his vote, Reagan shot back: "That may be so, Senator, but the world will perceive that they do." Rudy Boschwitz listed Saudi Arabia's failings as a prospective ally. Well, Reagan replied, you could have said the same things about Egypt a few years ago. Both in that session and in one-on-one meetings with Republicans Reagan stressed party loyalty and the President's need for credibility in the conduct of foreign affairs. "Vote against me," he said privately on several occasions, "and you will cut me off at the knees."

* They viewed Israel as an anti-Communist bastion in its region. Also, some of the most militant Protestant fundamentalists involved in New Right causes had swung to a Zionist policy across the board for both religious and political motives. The most prominent example was Jerry Falwell, founder of the Moral Majority, whom Begin regarded as a personal friend as well as an important supporter.

Baker's Legislative Strategy Group came up with a shrewd ploy. During a meeting Sunday night, October 4, in the home of Senator John Warner, White House representatives joined their host and Senator Sam Nunn in drafting a resolution intended to reassure Congress that AWACS would be used only for defensive purposes, and with a degree of American supervision. The White House also wrote a presidential letter containing a number of conditions the Saudis would have to meet in order for consummation of the sale to take place in the mid-eighties. This document was shown to wavering senators and amended several times to meet some of their individual requests. One by one, opponents began to announce conversion to Reagan's side. Roger Jepsen, a New Right partisan and initially one of the most vocal members of the opposition, announced his switch. "A vote for the sale," he said, "is a vote for my President and his successful conduct of foreign policy."[7] In the forty-eight hours before the decision, all the movement was toward the White House position. The final tally on October 28: 52 to 48 in favor of the deal. Said Packwood, who remained a leader of the minority: "It was the battleship against the destroyers, and we were outgunned."[8]

In domestic political terms, it was another gratifying victory for the dreadnought's captain and his skillful legislative navigators. A defeat, moreover, would have shot a torpedo into Reagan's credibility abroad. But the positive gains were distinctly limited. Fahd was not eager to flaunt his ties with Reagan. Soon he would cancel his scheduled visit to Washington. In Jerusalem, the outcome provoked Begin to new militance.

Partly to offset the negative connotations of the AWACS deal, the State Department soon after Begin's visit brokered the beginnings of a new military arrangement between the United States and Israel. With Sharon in the lead, the Israelis sought some specific evidence of their ostensibly elevated status as strategic allies. Weinberger and the Joint Chiefs of Staff were ambivalent about any formal agreement. Nonetheless, Reagan went along with the State Department view. Weinberger was assigned to work out with Sharon what became known as the MOU, or Memorandum of Understanding, which Weinberger signed on November 30. In general terms, the agreement provided for joint training exercises and logistical cooperation, among other things. It was predicated on the assumption that the United States and Israel would cooperate in defending the region from external attack.

Nonetheless, the MOU was bound to make the Arabs unhappy. For that reason, American officials attempted to treat it in as low-key a manner as possible. The Israelis, however, pumped up the MOU in public, emphasizing its utility in projecting their military clout far from home. That political gambit irritated the White House, but only two weeks after the signing American annoyance turned to outrage. On December 14, just as the world was absorbing the news of the imposition of martial law in Poland, Begin obtained passage of legislation that had the practical effect of annexing the Golan Heights.

This bulge into Syrian territory had been acquired during the 1967 war. It was one of the occupied territories retained because of its strategic importance. Because Syria insisted that a state of war still existed and that it would not negotiate with Israel under any foreseeable circumstances, Israel on a number of previous occasions had signaled its intention to convert military control of the district into more formal status. Each time, Washington had persuaded Jerusalem to put off the move. Now, without warning, Begin struck. His decision infuriated the Reagan administration not merely because it occurred so soon after the MOU signing—thereby giving the impression of U.S. complicity—but also because the change in legal status had no bearing on Israel's real security needs. Rather, it was a demonstration of Israeli hubris. Four days later the State Department announced that it was suspending implementation of the MOU. Reagan also put a hold on other arrangements designed to promote the export of Israeli-manufactured military supplies.

In private, Reagan pronounced himself astonished yet again at what could only be interpreted as defiance from the leader with whom he was on a first-name basis. Yet in public Reagan was relatively restrained. It was Begin who had a tantrum before the world audience. He called in Samuel Lewis and read a statement denouncing the Reagan administration, then had an assistant give out the text of the tongue-lashing. Begin went back over events since the Baghdad raid as he saw them:

> You don't have the right, from a moral perspective, to preach to us regarding civilian loss of life. We have read the history of World War II, and we know what happened to civilians when you took action against the enemy. We have also read the history of the Vietnam War, and your concept of body counts. We always make efforts to prevent casualties among civilians, but sometimes this is unavoidable, as happened in the bombing of the PLO headquarters [in Beirut]. Nevertheless, you punished us . . . Now you are once again priding yourselves on punishing Israel. What kind of talk is this, "punishing Israel"? Are we a vassal state of yours? Are we a banana republic? . . . You will not frighten us with punishments. He who threatens us will find us deaf to his threats . . .[9]

It was an extraordinary piece of vituperation to be aimed at a "friendly" foreign government—the government that, quite literally, had assured Israel's survival for decades. Begin also proclaimed the

MOU not merely suspended, but cancelled. Reagan wisely declined to engage in a shouting match. Ed Meese spoke for him, softly: "It's important to understand that the United States remains the best friend Israel could possibly have. We have been disappointed by the events in the last week. We're obviously disappointed by this reaction [by Begin]. Just as with friends, occasionally you may be disappointed, but that doesn't end the friendship."[10]

Nor did it completely exhaust Reagan's patience. He could not afford a major breach for two solid, pragmatic reasons. It would have caused him domestic political turmoil. Further, it would have encouraged, at least in the short run, still more intransigence on Israel's part. The strip of Sinai territory to be returned to Egypt in April was hostage at this point. A faction in Israel taking an even harder line than Begin's was campaigning to retain the Sinai corridor. Theoretically, the Administration could have crippled Israel's long-term military capability and worsened the besieged country's already difficult economic situation. This could have been done by a drastic reduction in American assistance. However, Israel already had enough stockpiled material to wage a final Armageddon. American intelligence strongly suspected that Israel also had at least a few nuclear weapons ready for use in extremis. If there was to be any hope of significant progress eventually, some degree of serenity had to be restored in the new year.

Haig journeyed to Cairo and Jerusalem in January, looking for new ways of reviving talks between the two countries concerning a specific formula under which Palestinians on the West Bank and in Gaza would be granted a degree of autonomy. Hosni Mubarak, Sadat's successor, had been able to consolidate his position in Egypt. Still, Mubarak could not quickly rise to Sadat's stature. Israeli aggressiveness could undermine him altogether. Haig's mission succeeded to the extent that it kept communications open. Jerusalem did calm down for a time. Begin's government would go ahead with its withdrawal from the Sinai on schedule despite the domestic difficulties it caused.

When that was actually accomplished in April, Washington had no new initiative ready. By the spring of 1982 Washington knew that the strategic-consensus policy had got nowhere. Most of the Arab countries were still obsessed with what they viewed as Israel's belligerence. Attention in the Reagan administration was turning back to the difficult question of what to do next to carry out the full promise of the Camp David accords. Bill Clark was hardly an expert on the subject but he knew enough to realize that Reagan's advisers had failed to come up with any workable scheme on which they all agreed—let alone a plan that might seem viable to the parties in the Middle East.

McFarlane, who had moved from the State Department to the National Security Council staff with Clark, did have experience in the region. With the NSC's Middle East expert, Geoffrey Kemp, McFarlane discovered that even within the State Department there were still severe differences. In private, Clark joked that he would offer a reward for anyone who came up with a valid proposal. One of his associates replied that peace in the Middle East would have to wait until amity was restored between Haig and Assistant Secretary Nicholas Veliotes. At one juncture McFarlane speculated aloud that the only way to persuade Israel to make concessions was to install one or two American combat divisions for an indefinite period. That kind of commitment would reassure Jerusalem concerning security. McFarlane's idea raised so many other problems that it quickly died.

Other proposals were floated with two common themes. First, the United States would have to undertake a new initiative; without pressure from Washington nothing would change. Second, no significant movement would be possible unless Israel reversed what had been the trend under the Begin government for nearly five years: tightening Israeli control over the West Bank and Gaza district. Thus the Reagan administration was reinventing the wheel of American policy toward the Arab-Israeli deadlock. Both of these elements had been present and obvious under three previous American Presidents. The real question had always been how to get from concept to execution.

At the beginning of May, Reagan formally ordered a full review of the U.S.-Israeli relationship. Begin was due in Washington for a second visit in mid-June. This would be an opportunity to sort matters out, to begin anew. The White House decided that it would serve carrots to the visitor: an offer to revive the MOU, which had been dormant since the Golan annexation, and to start other forms of military cooperation as well. During Begin's visit the previous September, there had been virtually no discussion of Camp David's next phase. Now there would be. In a positive tone, Reagan and Haig would probe the visitor for signs of conciliation. They would, finally, begin to address the dilemma that had been solved only partially in Carter's time. What would it take to persuade Israel to give up still more of the land captured in 1967 in exchange for still more peace than was achieved in 1978–79?

Neither the MOU carrot nor that fundamental dialogue was to survive until mid-June. Habib's episodic mediation efforts concerning the homeland of his ancestors had failed after more than a year. Israeli armored divisions and Air Force squadrons blew them away, along with Syrian and PLO forces, when Israel invaded Lebanon.

The ostensible reason for the invasion was to end, once and for all, PLO terrorist activities on Israel's northern border. Israeli forces were to clear hostiles from an area forty kilometers north, roughly to the Litani River. In fact, Israel struck at a time when military activities against it were diminishing. Yasir Arafat had been turning increasingly to political gambits rather than terrorism. Elsewhere, for diverse reasons, the Arab world was also less of a military threat to Israel than ever before.

In these objective circumstances, sympathy for the Israeli invasion was scarce everywhere. It disappeared almost entirely when Israeli armor swept aside all in its way and plunged far beyond the Litani, all the way to Beirut. Syria made the mistake of challenging Israeli muscle; its squadrons, boasting some of the best planes the Soviet Union exported, were promptly destroyed. Israel also took the opportunity, as long as a little war was on, to obliterate the SAM sites in the Bekaa Valley. Suddenly Israeli battalions were encircling Beirut, with PLO troops and their families trapped among the Lebanese population. Sharon threatened to move in for a climactic battle that would have to have cost thousands of lives unless the PLO cadres were evacuated from Lebanon altogether.

Habib arranged a cease-fire, then another and another and another as skirmishing back and forth continued. Otherwise American diplomacy seemed for a time to be impotent. Reagan talked of the need for all foreign military forces—Israeli, Syrian and Palestinian—to leave Lebanon. In public, Reagan was no more critical of Begin's actions than he had been the previous summer. But he was thoroughly frustrated. The rationale for restraint this time: if the Administration cracked down on Israel in any tangible way, the PLO might be encouraged to hold out in Beirut indefinitely. That, in turn would likely produce a final battle that would destroy the Lebanese capital.

At the same time, Washington began to give lip service to the proposition that the invasion, unfortunate though it was, had created new and favorable opportunities. If the PLO and Syrians could be forced out altogether, Lebanon might become an independent country again instead of a cockpit in which the dispute of others was fought. Further, Lebanon might then be willing to sign a peace treaty with Israel. Those were merely future prospects. There was no doubt at all that the mini-war had already accomplished another result: the further diminution of Soviet influence. Moscow's surrogates had suffered clear defeat in the air and on the ground. Its weaponry had been destroyed like so many toys. Syria was now dickering with the United States over terms and the Soviet Union appeared to have minimal impact on the ultimate outcome. According to this school of thought—which Israel's partisans promoted—Israel had again done the West a favor, albeit in a perverse, bloody manner.

Inside the White House, that argument was understood. No one could deny that there had been a change in the balance. On the other hand, there had also been a new demonstration that Reagan's ability to restrain Begin had vanished. The latest proof of Israel's military prowess could only make the Arabs more reluctant than ever to reach an overall agreement that Israel could live with. In fact, that may have been one of the Begin government's goals—to create a more favorable military equation while freezing indefinitely any diplomatic movement concerning the West Bank and Gaza. While that freeze continued, Israel would deepen its control over the territories that Begin intended to hold forever.

Reagan personally was both angry and confused. His advisers were divided, as usual, though Haig, now in his final days as Secretary of State, was to a large extent isolated on this issue. Begin was in New York at a UN session, scheduled to see Reagan on Monday, June 21. The White House leaked word that the President might cancel the meeting altogether as a sign of displeasure. That was a bluff. Haig wanted to see Begin first, while both were still in New York, as a preliminary to the Monday conversations in the White House. Clark and Weinberger resisited Haig on that point. They, as well as others, feared that Haig would fail to convey the depths of the Administration's displeasure. In earlier rounds with Begin and other Israeli officials, the rest of the NSC now believed, Haig had not been nearly as candid as he had given his colleagues to understand.

This was a crucial element in the dealings between the two governments from Reagan's accession onward. A large degree of misunderstanding clogged communications. It would continue yet a while longer, as we'll see shortly. After considerable wrangling, Haig was allowed to go ahead with a New York meeting. Ostensibly he was to express to Begin the Administration's determination that restraint had to be restored, a lasting cease-fire achieved and a withdrawal of forces set in motion. For his part, Haig insisted that he had no objection to stern talk provided only that the pressure be applied in secret. "I happen to believe," he told me later, "that I could sit down with Menachem Begin, with a mandate from the President, or the President could, and take him to the woodshed any day of the week—and quietly come out with something constructive."[11] He seemed to believe that he had done that repeatedly, including during his June meeting in New York.

The Israelis had a different impression, or said they did. After Haig left office, Arens and I talked about the communications gap. "The meetings with Haig," the ambassador said, "were far more than cordial. Haig was conveying that he had a battle on his hands inside the U.S. Government [concerning Middle East policy]. He was always very confident that his views would win the day."[12] If the Israeli leaders believed that, they were as naïve about Reagan as the President often was about them.

Over the weekend, as we have seen, Clark—strongly supported by Bush and others—provided a relatively tough line for Reagan to use. The session at the White House on Monday had three phases: a meeting in the Oval Office attended only by the principals and the two ambassadors, Lewis and Arens; then a "plenary" in the Roosevelt Room including a number of other aides; finally a luncheon in the Cabinet Room.

During the first few minutes, with photographers present for some ritual pictures, Reagan wore his rare, somber expression. As soon as the newsmen left, he pulled out his four-by-six index cards and began to read his message to Begin. You've raised serious problems for America in the Arab world, Reagan said. The hostilities must end as quickly as possible. He also linked the immediate peacemaking efforts to prompt renewal of the Palestinian autonomy negotiations. Begin gave no ground at all. He insisted that Israel had been correct to intervene—he refused to accept the word "invasion" as an appropriate description—and he argued that all foreign military elements would have to withdraw in order for the Israelis to pull out.

For the luncheon, the White House had an outside caterer prepare Kosher chicken (baked, with sesame seeds). Otherwise there were no concessions to the guests. Reagan, varying his practice on such occasions, did most of the talking on the American side. Haig was relatively quiet. When the President said that Jordan must be brought into the long-term negotiations, Begin replied abruptly. Where are the Jordanians? he said. They know they can come to Jerusalem anytime they want. We'll let them in. Toward the end of the meal, Weinberger spoke at some length, repeating Washington's determination to make arms deals with Arab nations it considered cooperative and "moderate." That term always angered Begin. He broke in: How can you call the Saudis moderate? Look at their record in support of the PLO and against Camp David. Now it was Reagan's turn to interrupt. He answered Begin the same way he had responded to Rudy Boschwitz the previous October. What you're saying about Saudi Arabia, he remarked, describes Egypt just a few years ago.

The toast Reagan had planned to make at the luncheon went unspoken. He even considered allowing Begin to go unescorted to his limousine, a stark departure from protocol. But Reagan thought better of that. Nonetheless, his remarks during the exit ceremony were short and totally devoid of rhetorical flourishes: "It has been worthwhile to have Prime Minister Begin at the White House again. All of us share a common understanding." Begin spoke twice as long, called Reagan "my friend" and insisted that the talks had been "very fruitful."

Later, American officials tried to persuade reporters that the President had been forceful with Begin, more so than he had ever been with a foreign dignitary. The latter may well have been true, but Reagan's style and his abhorrence of personal confrontation apparently prevented him from conveying his real feelings fully. Just before Begin got to Washington, the Prime Minister had a conversation with Sol Linowitz, who had served as Carter's special envoy to the Middle East. Linowitz, who kept in touch with the Reaganauts on this issue, warned Begin bluntly to expect difficult conversations with the President. Later, through an intermediary, Begin sent a message: you were wrong, Sol; everything went just fine.

For many months, both in Washington and Jerusalem, students of the U.S.-Israeli relationship believed that Begin operated under a serious misapprehension concerning American feelings. The Prime Minister's original instinct about Haig had turned out to be reasonably accurate. Begin mistook that for bland complacence. Reagan's habit of starting letters "Dear Menachem" reinforced that view. Begin himself believed in blunt candor. When angry, he said so in bald terms, as he had in his "banana republic" diatribe in December. Reagan, even during the June conversations, could not bring himself to express the kind of passion Begin understood.

Looking back on the violent summer of 1982, which was to end with Begin feeling shocked and abused, Linowitz mused: "There may have been some tough words [in June] but what was communicated to Begin came as a relief to him. He may have perceived that Reagan was so committed to Israel, and so disengaged from the intricacies of the problem, that he did not see the President as a strong, assertive figure. That explains the present eruption, I think . . . We didn't level with him in ways he understood. We tried to use indirection and that confused him. We have played him, in his mind, ambiguously. And now— pow!—we're hitting him."[13]

The "pows" started in midsummer as Habib and Draper labored to construct a deal whereby PLO units trapped in Beirut would leave Lebanon. This was tortuous work involving not only three combatant parties but also the Saudis, the Lebanese (who were in the process of selecting a new President) and ultimately the French and Italians. Begin had given broad authority to Sharon, who repeatedly ordered air strikes in and around Beirut each time he felt that his adversaries were violating the cease-fire in any way. The repeated attacks not only caused casualties among civilians; they interrupted the negotiations and demonstrated to the Arab world the impunity with which Israel could operate, using—as always—American weapons.

On August 12, as a particularly heavy bombardment stalled negotiations, Reagan telephoned Begin. This time there was no mistaking Reagan's feelings. "I want it stopped," the President said. "And I want it stopped now." Later in the conversation, alluding to a poignant news photo out of Beirut showing a baby who had apparently lost both upper limbs, Reagan said: "The symbol of this war has become a baby without arms."* The tactic worked. Begin called back in twenty minutes to say that the cease-fire was in effect once more.

Finally, on August 19, a firm understanding was reached, including supervision of the PLO withdrawal by American, French and Italian troops. The White House capitalized on the occasion with a Rose Garden announcement by the President. There was no question that without firm intervention by his administration, the combat would have been longer and bloodier than it was. But that was only one part of a new American activism concerning the Middle East.

As George Shultz replaced Haig in mid-July, the White House decided that the time had come to put a comprehensive, long-term American peace plan on the table. During a month-long review, Shultz consulted experts from inside and outside the government. The ideas assembled were all familiar ones, a consensus of what many students of the subject considered the necessary ingredients of Camp David's sequel. The real questions were the emphasis to be placed on various provisions and how vigorously Washington should promote the package.

Had Haig remained in office, most of the same ideas would have been proposed eventually, but in a different manner. Haig did not believe that Reagan should baldly propose actual settlement terms. Shultz, however, agreed with Clark that Reagan himself should make a detailed announcement. The United States would have to speak out with a megaphone, not in stage whispers, and would have to do so in full view of the world. That clashed with the approach Reagan had taken in his September 1980 campaign speech. He had learned a great deal since then both about the Middle East and about the need for his personal involvement at critical junctures. Shultz actively encouraged this vigorous approach concerning the Middle East at least. He had felt

---

* United Press International the following month corrected itself after Israeli authorities located the child. He was recovering from his injuries with both arms intact. The caption on the original picture had been inaccurate. Usually adroit in their press relations, the Israelis lost the publicity contest during the Lebanese fighting. Their forces were constantly shown attacking underdog opponents. Arafat meanwhile gave calm interviews and posed for pictures with cute children.

frustrated over what he considered excessive tolerance of the Begin government's behavior.

Thus, on September 1, the White House interrupted the filming of a comedy series in NBC's Burbank studio so that Reagan could make one of the most important speeches of his presidency. It was thoroughly in keeping with the Reagan style that he was on vacation in California when his advisers decided that it was time to seize the moment. With American, French and Italian combat units standing sentry, the last of the Palestinian guerrillas had just left Beirut.

The specific proposals were intended to strike a careful balance between assurances of Israel's future security and hope that the 1.3 million Palestinians—along with hundreds of thousands of others who might join them—would get something resembling a homeland. The U.S. plan envisaged not an independent Palestinian state, but an autonomous entity in a federation relationship with Jordan. Israel would have to give up most of the territory captured in 1967, but not all of it. Reagan acknowledged the need for adjustments in the pre-1967 borders. Before that war, Reagan pointed out, "the bulk of Israel's population lived within artillery range of hostile Arab armies. I am not about to ask Israel to live that way again."

Reagan demanded that Israel immediately freeze the establishment of Jewish settlements in Gaza and on the West Bank. The Begin-Sharon policy of implanting new outposts had clearly been designed to entrench Israeli authority and control. Now Reagan was asking Israel to begin reversing that process of absorption. The *quid* for that *quo* would be recognition by the Arab world, at last, of Israel's right to exist peacefully. The twentieth century's thirty-year war would be over if all parties agreed to the compromise. Obviously Israel would be making sacrifices, as it did when it gave up the huge buffer of Sinai, along with its oil fields and air bases. Reagan asked something of everyone:

> I call on Israel to make clear that the security for which she yearns can only be achieved through genuine peace, a peace requiring magnanimity, vision and courage. I call on the Palestinian people to recognize that their own political aspirations are inextricably bound to recognition of Israel's right to a secure future. And I call on the Arab states to accept the reality of Israel—and the reality that peace and justice are to be gained only through hard, fair, direct negotiations . . . The time has come for a new realism on the part of all the peoples of the Middle East.

Reagan himself had finally confronted a reality: his responsibility to move boldly in a region where only the United States could instigate positive change. And he had addressed frontally the heart of the matter, the Begin government's long-range intention to retain the West Bank and Gaza. For Israel to retreat from that territory after the investment of so much blood, after the Arab world had tried for so long to erase Israel from the map altogether, would be a wrenching sacrifice. Yet for Israel to refuse to retreat under any circumstances would mean perpetual stalemate and the endless threat of war. Washington fully expected Jerusalem to say no at first. When Lewis delivered the news in advance of Reagan's speach, Begin lamented: "It is the saddest day I have had since becoming Prime Minister."[14]

Shimon Peres, leader of the opposition Labor Party, reacted differently. He called the plan a basis for real negotiations. That temperate position provoked accusations that Peres had conspired with Reagan to bring about Begin's political downfall. Some of the leaders of American-Jewish organizations which routinely defend Israeli interests also found merit in the Reagan position. Both in Israel and among Israel's friends in the United States, the American initiative provoked some serious soul-searching. It was the same in the Arab world. With Moscow joining the chorus, the die-hard "rejectionists" found nothing good to say. But Mubarak was sympathetic, and so was Hussein of Jordan, whose participation would be crucial in any forward movement. "I believe it to be the most courageous stand taken by an American administration ever since 1956," the King said in a BBC interview. "I believe it to be a very constructive and a very positive move, and I would certainly like to see it continue and evolve."[15]

Important as Reagan's thrust was, it was only a new beginning. Neither Hussein nor Mubarak had the stature to speak for the Palestinians in a new round of negotiations. The Arab League, meeting in Fez, came up with its own proposals, which the Begin regime found even more abhorrent than Reagan's. The Knesset supported Begin's stance. At that stage, at least, the focus was on political maneuvering rather than on new carnage.

The lull lasted only a fortnight. In mid-September the Christian President-elect of Lebanon, Bashir Gemayel, was assassinated. He had been the leader of the Phalangist Party and commander of its militia in his country's civil conflict. Then, in an incredible blunder, Israeli forces used that same militia to search for underground PLO remnants in two Palestinian camps, Sabra and Shatila, in West Beirut. The Phalangist forces used the opportunity to massacre hundreds of Palestinian civilians, many of them women and children.* That blood orgy was as much a product of Lebanon's internal vendetta syndrome as anything

---

* The exact number of casualties was never established because some victims were taken from the camps and executed elsewhere. Disinterested estimates put the figure at between four hundred and five hundred dead.

else. But the new turmoil it caused deflected any serious attempt at regional negotiations for the time being.

Reagan responded by sending the Marines back to Beirut. France and Italy contributed troops as well. This time the Allied forces would remain indefinitely while Habib attempted yet again to get the Syrians and Israelis to disengage from Lebanon. Washington's relations with Jerusalem were at a new low during the winter of 1982–83. Israel's standing in American public opinion also suffered, though support in Congress remained strong. Sharon lost the Defense portfolio in the aftermath of the Sabra-Shatila tragedy and was replaced by Arens, a personality less bellicose than his predecessor and better able to deal with the Reagan administration. Yet the Lebanon standoff continued into March, postponing serious consideration of Reagan's plan. There would be no sudden triumph for the peacemakers. Reagan at last was willing to use muscle, to use both battalions of Marines and squads of diplomats. But all he could achieve in the first months of this new assertiveness was the prevention of new calamities.

17

Bear, Dragon and Cawk

Ambassador Thomas J. Watson, Jr., was so eager to leave his post in Moscow that he did not even wait for the new President to take office. Soviet-American relations had worsened appreciably during the Carter years. Now the election of an American President pledged to challenge Communist expansionism threatened to make the freeze still more solid. "I don't think," Watson said as he resigned, "the West has any conception of how dismal the future looks for East-West relations."[1]

Watson's forecast was hardly news to the President-elect. Ronald Reagan had never suffered from bullish expectations concerning either the Russian bear or the Chinese dragon. He was determined to deal with them on his own terms, at his own pace. He anticipated no new day of amity where the Soviet Union was concerned. In 1976 his belligerence had forced Gerald Ford to drop the word "détente" from the campaign-year vocabulary. In 1980 Reagan modulated his own rhetoric slightly for domestic purposes but his ideas remained fixed. Only a restoration of American military strength and political will could force the Soviets to behave reasonably.

Disappointment that this simple approach produced only minimal results was typical of Reagan's education in foreign affairs. Deft political pressure from both Moscow and Peking eventually forced Reagan to practice more subtle diplomacy. Fretful impatience within the American electorate and the Western alliance also pushed him forward when he would have preferred to stand fast. The tension between his own instincts and the realities that crowded him were even greater in the national security field than in the domestic sphere. At the same time, unrelenting friction among his foreign-policy advisers deprived him of the meticulous road map that initially guided his domestic program.

Yet Reagan during his first two years did not take the country into any disastrous adventure. Nor did he burn bridges that might eventually lead to reduced danger abroad. During the Vietnam era American officials who sought a middle way between doves and hawks were called dawks. Reagan created a new hybrid status for himself. He remained a hawk in both inclination and practice, but in every complex test he proved to be a most cautious hunting bird. He could be called a *cawk*. That was his guise, as we have seen, as he dealt with the dilemma of Central America. And he flew in cawk's feathers as he sought to solve the Chinese puzzle, as he dealt with the trauma of Poland and as he circled the meanest thunderhead of all, nuclear arms control.

Besides presidential prudence, which surprised many of his friends and critics alike, another important element was at play where Moscow was concerned. Reagan, as in several other situations, enjoyed good luck. The Soviets were in a relatively passive mode during 1981–82, more interested in diplomacy and propaganda than in taking new military risks. Their geriatric leadership was on the brink of replacement, their economy was seriously troubled and their invasion of Afghanistan had yielded more woe than profit. Like the new boys in the White House the old boyars in the Kremlin performed more probes than adventures.

Leonid Brezhnev's temporary inclination to croon enticements rather than to bellow threats, however, affected the complex triangle of Washington, Peking and Moscow. For many years Washington considered Sino-Soviet hostility an important brake on Russian military ability. The forty-nine Soviet Army divisions manning Asian borders were better off there—from the Western viewpoint—than they would be menacing Europe. Ditto the small portion of Soviet nuclear missiles targeted on China.

During the second half of the campaign year, however, two developments combined to complicate the triangular relationship. Candidate Reagan insisted on rehashing his indignation about U.S. treatment of Taiwan, particularly since the Carter administration in 1979 had restored full diplomatic relations with China. In a series of imprecise statements, Reagan implied that if elected he would somehow do better by Taiwan. This naturally alarmed Peking because the United States is the only real obstacle to the forced reunion of "the Motherland" and the island bastion of Chiang Kai-shek's heirs. While this was going on, the Soviet Union began attempting to thaw its relations with China by means of technology exchanges and expressed willingness to resume negotiations over border disputes and other sources of tension.*

* A new round of talks did in fact begin in October 1982 for the first time in three years. Where they might lead—if anywhere—remained unclear at the end of the year.

The Taiwanese Government, taking heart from the election of one of its strongest supporters in the United States, started to press for a major upgrading of its air force. Specifically, the Taiwanese wanted the F-5G, a new fighter far superior to the F-5E that has been a mainstay of the island's defenses. Peking meanwhile wanted to settle the entire question of American arms sales to Taiwan, an issue that had been unresolved in the 1979 Sino-American accord. Throughout 1981 the Reagan administration marked time on this dilemma. In Haig's mind the priority was to soothe Chinese sensitivities, to demonstrate that the regime of Deng Xiaoping had chosen wisely in 1979, to construct additional economic and perhaps even strategic links with the world's most populous nation. Reagan was sensitive to that need. At the same time, he resisted taking any serious step that could be construed as a betrayal of Taiwan. He was happy to go along with blandishments for the mainland—making the Chinese eligible to buy American weapons, for instance. But that teaser aroused little interest in Peking when Haig presented it during a visit in June.

At the beginning of the new year the Administration belatedly faced up to the need for a decision. Haig, Weinberger and Casey united on a recommendation to Reagan: the request for new F-5G's would be turned down. Instead, the United States would simply replace Taiwan's F-5E's as needed. This would be offered as something of a concession to Peking in hopes of eliciting a positive response. But when Assistant Secretary of State John Holdridge took this olive branch to Peking in January, the response was hostile. An implied Chinese threat to downgrade Sino-American relations—to go back to the pre-1979 level —remained in force.

It took another seven months of dickering, including a visit to Peking by George Bush in May and protracted talks in which the United States was represented by Ambassador Arthur Hummel, before a partially satisfactory deal was struck. It took the form of a nine-part joint communiqué announced on August 17. In it the United States made two significant concessions: to refrain from any increase in military aid to Taiwan in either quality or quantity and to "reduce gradually its [weapons] sales . . . leading over a period of time to a final resolution." Peking reaffirmed its "striving for peaceful reunification of the Motherland" but, as in previous statements, took no pledge to avoid military action forever.

Thus the communiqué was an ambiguous expedient in which the United States yielded some ground while Peking, in putting its chop on a new piece of paper, gave less. Both Alexander Haig and George Shultz favored the pronouncement, the final terms of which were agreed upon during the awkward period when one was replacing the other and the Lebanon crisis was paramount. "Had I stayed," Haig told me the following month, "it probably would have come out the other way . . . There was a growing tendency in the White House to take contrary positions from mine just to be doing so."[2]

The right wing was fast and loud in its attack. Even Barry Goldwater, who had distanced himself from the New Right on other issues, joined in the condemnation. "It's one more little country we have double-crossed," he said of Taiwan.[3] Columnist William Safire called the communiqué Reagan's "greatest foreign policy blunder."[4] When Dan Rather of CBS called the decision an example of "reversed policy," Reagan phoned the anchorman to complain that he had it all wrong. Then, as well as later, Reagan seemed to believe that he had secured a pledge from the Chinese that it would never attempt to take Taiwan by force. Yet the Chinese had not made that explicit a commitment then or earlier. They had given a nod to U.S. sensitivities by allowing the mention of "peaceful reunification" to appear in the same document as Washington's new formulation about military assistance to Taiwan. Thus if Peking suddenly menaced the island, the United States would have legalistic cause to complain—and to reinforce its old ally's defenses. This hardly constituted a major breakthrough, and America hardly needed a communiqué to justify such assistance if an invasion were really threatened.

For the balance of the year, the Administration could show little gain from the deal. Peking's rhetoric continued to be unfriendly. New examples of cooperation in any sphere were scarce. The Chinese maintained a strange indifference to the repression in Poland and were as hostile as ever to U.S. policy in the Middle East. They appeared to be thinking things over, considering whether it was time to edge back somewhat toward the Soviets or to warm up to Washington again. The Reagan administration, for its part, seemed to be pausing as well. The August communiqué had checked the steep slide in relations without reversing it. On that distinctly limited accomplishment the White House had to rest for the time being.

George Shultz, catching up with the job he had been given abruptly, might have wished for a similar recess concerning other problems, but he got no such boon. One of his more difficult tasks was sorting out the diplomatic debris that had accumulated as a result of the imposition of martial law in Poland. As in the Taiwan-China dilemma, Poland was a puzzle in which geopolitics and symbolism were intertwined, and in which the tensions between Reaganism and pragmatism added a separate layer of complexity.

It was in this situation that Shultz's singular style began to emerge. Haig had attempted to get his way by a combination of force and disdain. He tried to overpower his opponents frontally with the weight of his expertise. If that did not work he would try angry contempt. When some other advocate held the floor in meetings, Haig would often fidget, make notes, glare at his adversary and otherwise display his restless energy. His successor, according to a colleague who was able to watch both men at very close range, showed much more self-control. He made his case without drum rolls. When it was someone else's turn to talk, Shultz frequently studied Reagan, apparently gauging the President's reactions to what was being said. Ostensibly Shultz, like Clark, got his seat at the Reagan round table in order to translate Reagan's ideology into workable policy. Unlike Clark, however, Shultz represented one of the institutional powers, the State Department. He knew, for instance, that Clark had erred in June when he encouraged Reagan to apply penalties to British, Italian, French and German firms that were honoring their commitments concerning the Siberian pipeline. That would have to be remedied slowly and subtly, in such a way that preserved face all around. Shultz also had to cope with what his State Department colleagues had known for a year: that the Administration had dug itself into too deep a trench in the first phase of the arms control negotiations. That position would have to be reconsidered if there was to be any chance of an agreement in 1983. Both situations had already taken serpentine twists over several months before Shultz arrived in Foggy Bottom. Like the new Secretary of State, we must look back before going ahead, and as he did, we shall start with Poland.

The reform movement that grew to serious proportions within Poland in mid-1980 was far more significant than the earlier attempts at liberalization in Hungary and Czechoslovakia. Poland's was truly a mass effort from the ground up. Thirty-five years of Communist rule imposed by military strength was shown to have been a failure. It was still an alien influence that many millions of Poles were eager to expel. The speed with which Lech Walesa's Solidarity organization drew popular commitment was a historic demonstration of the Soviet system's inability to win durable loyalty outside its own borders.

From the beginning the Western response was ambivalent. If events in Poland could somehow evolve in an orderly way, they could eventually produce a great bloodless victory for the West. But would Moscow allow that evolution? And what would happen in the meantime? The West, including the United States, had become accustomed to living with and trading with the European Communist bloc. It might not be esthetically pleasing, ideologically consistent or morally satisfying, but it was convenient and safe. Even when the United States had overwhelming nuclear supremacy twenty years earlier, it was not prepared to risk war in order to free Eastern Europe.

That being the case, life—and business—went on. Over decades, perhaps, Western influence would help corrode the chains within the Soviet empire. Meanwhile, violent upheaval threatened existing relationships. It also increased the difficulties of dealing with Moscow on such vital matters as arms control. The West's schizoid attitudes in dealing with the East recurred constantly. On the one hand, there was the tendency to concede the Russians their sphere of influence as a practical matter. Yet when Moscow periodically enforced its influence with tank divisions or the threat of them, most NATO members suffered guilt pangs which expressed themselves in verbal indignation. Since they were not prepared to go to war, their only check on Soviet behavior was the threat of reduced commerce. But that weapon was only theoretical. When the Soviets decided that their vital interests were at stake, they acted as they chose. Their experience told them that the West might not forgive, but it soon forgot.

Thus Washington and its allies watched Poland with a mixture of hope, admiration and anxiety. The suspense over what might happen, and how the West should respond, brought to the surface a closely related question. Was the West doing itself any good in the long term by expanding economic relations with the Soviet bloc? In the 1970s there seemed to be no doubt that the answer was yes. The Europeans particularly saw the Soviet Union and its dependents as valuable trading partners. While détente was still fashionable in the United States, economic ties were seen as paying both mercantile and political dividends. Carter's PD (Presidential Decision) 18, which he signed in August 1977, said that the United States "will seek to involve the Soviet Union . . . constructively in global action" of diverse kinds, including "peaceful, non-strategic trade."* Only after Afghanistan did Carter try to use trade as a weapon.

The Reaganauts' thrust was different in theory, and sometimes in practice. Reagan himself, as we have seen, was willing to increase the sale of grain to the Soviet Union when it suited his domestic purposes, and even willing to get extra mileage from that decision by dangling it to Brezhnev as a token of good faith. In the early months Reagan also went along with some heavy equipment sales despite opposition from the Pentagon. However, Reagan was also pulled in another direction. He was increasingly fascinated with the school of thought that the

---

* PD's—called NSDD's, or National Security Decision Directives, in the Reagan administration—are nominally classified secret while they remain in force, and often afterward for a time as well. However, except for purely military portions, the gist of them and even parts of the text usually can be obtained. Some thematic passages of PD 18 and Reagan's NSDD 32 were made available to me for comparison purposes.

United States was foolish to do anything that might ameliorate the Soviet Union's deep economic distress. The most articulate proponent of that line was the scholar, Richard Pipes, who summarized his rationale this way:

> Now no responsible persons can have any illusions that it is in the power of the West to alter the Soviet system or to "bring the Soviet economy to its knees." These are spurious objectives. What one can and ought to strive for is compelling the Soviet regime to bear the consequences of its own priorities. We should not make it easier for the *nomenklatura* to have its cake and eat it: to maintain an inefficient [economic] system, the failures of which threaten the power and even the stability of the regime and, at the same time, build up an aggressive military force and expand globally. Any attempt to help the Soviet Union out of its economic predicament both eases the pressure for internal reform and reduces the need for global retrenchment.[5]

Pipes and other anti-Soviet hard-liners in the Administration had made that argument all along. Six months before the imposition of martial law in Poland, the United States attempted, at the Ottawa Economic Summit meeting, to detach its European allies from the natural gas pipeline project though some large American companies were also participating. The effort was tepid and attracted little attention at the time. It was also futile for two reasons. Washington's vague proposal to cooperate in the development of alternative energy sources, such as the then-untapped Norwegian fields, was unpersuasive. More importantly, the Europeans—particularly the French and Germans—wanted to expand rather than restrict their trade with the East. That eagerness translated into the granting of bargain interest rates in credit arrangements for Moscow.

U.S. policy increasingly went in the opposite direction. By the time Reagan signed NSDD 32, his administration counted economic measures among the means it would employ to "neutralize efforts of the U.S.S.R. to increase its influence." It was now Washington's official intention to "foster restraint in Soviet military spending and adventurism" as well as "to weaken the Soviet alliance system." That secret policy decision, though not signed by Reagan until May 20, 1982, reflected the trend of thought well underway the previous year as both Washington and Moscow monitored the upheaval in Poland.

In March and early April, as the Polish party leadership wobbled precariously, the Soviets made feints at direct military intervention. Moscow held back, American analysts concluded later, primarily for two reasons. Uncertain as to how the Polish Army would respond, the Soviets worried about the prospect of an actual military campaign instead of just a quick strike against unarmed civilians. Second, Brezhnev for other reasons was already embarked on a typical Soviet "peace offensive," attempting to drive a new wedge between the United States and its allies. An invasion of Poland would demolish that effort.

There was agreement within NATO that Soviet military intervention would demand a strong, unified Western response. This would take the form of economic and political disconnects. But there was no consensus about what, if anything, should be done in the event of a less explicit Soviet move. And, as concern about an invasion ebbed in mid-April, there was no clear plan in Washington about what the United States should do if tensions within Poland continued to simmer at high temperature for months to come. One of those participating in the planning sessions recalled later: "There was agreement that we should do something positive. We considered the question of dangling a massive [economic] aid package in front of the Warsaw government and using it to help Solidarity negotiate its wish list. One thing we could do was to help with their immediate food problem and help to make their agriculture more productive in the long run."

But there was indecision for the rest of the spring and early summer as both the Polish party congress and Solidarity's congress were put off. On an interim basis, the Administration provided a $60 million credit for feed grain purchases. But this increase in assistance was not made conditional on continued tolerance of Solidarity. From discreet contacts with members of the Solidarity leadership, the United States received mixed signals. "We never got sufficient clarity in the second half of the year," said the official who was monitoring events closely. "People in Solidarity argued at different times both for and against help from us." In November, Walesa himself sent word that the United States should do nothing until midwinter, when he hoped to visit Washington. Credit for new American assistance would then go to him and other moderates in the Solidarity leadership. The Administration marked time. Then, on Friday, December 11, Reagan approved an additional $100 million in credits for agricultural purchases, with the understanding that another $600 million would be considered early in the new year. These steps were intended to assist the Polish Government in achieving a measure of stability without increasing dependence on Moscow.

By this stage, however, American intelligence had hard information that Moscow and the Jaruzelski government were on the brink of a "Polish solution"—that is, repression by the Polish Army and police. Well-placed informants described the plan as a "military coup d'etat" against both the surviving party structure and Solidarity's growing influence. Preparations had been underway since early fall. Martial-law proclamations in Polish were secretly printed in the Soviet Union. A quantity of Polish military uniforms was delivered to the Russians. The purpose: to allow Soviet observers to monitor the action once it began without being recognized. The final decision to go ahead with the "coup d'etat" was made Thanksgiving week. Western intelligence, however, was not totally certain of the information it obtained a few days after that. Nor did the CIA have a firm fix as to timing. General Wojciech Jaruzelski himself might not have known the precise day, American analysts speculated later, because he wanted to move in response to specific, dramatic provocation by the union.

In any event, the most sensitive information available to Washington during the first days of December was put on a "close hold" basis. It was withheld from working-level planners and diplomats. No serious effort was made to create a firm consensus with the Western Europeans on a joint response in the event of "gray area" action by Communist authorities—suppression that involved neither Soviet Army divisions moving across the frontier nor widespread bloodshed. Whether a consensus could have been achieved was doubtful. Helmut Schmidt's government in particular had resisted the proposition that a "Polish solution" would necessarily demand a concrete Western response.

On Saturday, December 12, delegates to a Solidarity conference in Gdansk disregarded the relatively prudent policy Walesa had been preaching. They demanded a national plebiscite on Poland's form of government and its military alliance with the Soviet Union. Walesa, in despair, told his colleagues, "Now you've got what you're looking for."[6] So did Jaruzelski. Within hours, Walesa and other prominent Solidarity figures were in custody. The next day martial law was declared officially.

The Reaganauts were not exactly on alert that weekend. Haig was in Brussels at a NATO meeting. Allen, on "administrative leave" for the previous three weeks, was about to be dismissed. Weinberger and David Jones, then chairman of the Joint Chiefs of Staff, were out of Washington. Meese was on one of his speechmaking trips. The President was spending the weekend at Camp David. That left George Bush, James Baker, Mike Deaver and James "Bud" Nance, a retired admiral serving as Allen's interim substitute, as the senior advisers in residence. Bush was about to see his first really serious duty in his capacity as head of the Crisis Management Team.

It was at this point that the name was changed to Special Situations Group (SSG) because the White House became leery of the word "crisis." To encourage the idea that events in Poland constituted a crisis for the West created the logical expectation that the Administration was ready to respond in a vigorous, dramatic way. That was clearly not the case. Reagan, returning from Camp David Sunday afternoon, was cautious: "The United States has made it plain how seriously we would view interference in Poland. We're monitoring the situation. Beyond that, I cannot have any comment."

Haig and Weinberger promptly returned to Washington for one of their classic standoffs. The Secretary of State argued that the initial U.S. response should be relatively low key until what was actually happening in Poland became clear and until the Europeans could be prodded into line. Weinberger, supported by Bush and Casey, supported a vigorous denunciation of the Soviet Union, accompanied by as much concrete action as possible. The result was something of a compromise in phases. A few economic sanctions were imposed unilaterally on Poland but they added up to little. Concerning the U.S.S.R., direct American economic leverage was slight to begin with. The agricultural credits approved the previous Friday for Poland were canceled. Food shipments classified as "humanitarian" continued, however.

Reagan was torn between his desire for clean, bold strokes and the inhibitions imposed by other forces. On the evening of December 23, he dealt in symbolism and warnings in his pre-Christmas speech to the nation. He asked that candles be placed in windows on Christmas Eve to provide "a small but certain beacon of our solidarity with the Polish people." To Jaruzelski and Brezhnev, he said:

> I want emphatically to state tonight that if the outrages in Poland do not cease, we cannot and will not conduct business as usual with the perpetrators and those who aid and abet them. Make no mistake, their crime will cost them dearly in their future dealings with America and free peoples everywhere. I do not make this statement lightly or without serious reflection.

Meanwhile, Reagan conveyed his indignation personally to Brezhnev in a private communication. Moscow, he said, must withdraw its pressure on the Warsaw government or risk serious damage to Soviet-American relations. Specifically, the United States was demanding, in private as well as in public, that martial law be lifted, the political prisoners freed and negotiations between Solidarity and the government allowed to resume. The confidential reply from Moscow was blunt: America must cease fomenting trouble among the fraternal socialist republics. Poland was dealing with its problems in its own way and had the Kremlin's blessing in doing so.

This prompted announcement of a second series of sanctions directed solely against the U.S.S.R. Most of the items were of a token nature, but one category was significant: Washington would cease the export of technical equipment used for oil and gas production and distribution. Reagan was beginning his forlorn war on the Siberian pipeline.

The presidential party was in Los Angeles on December 29, when Reagan announced those steps. By coincidence, I was to see him that afternoon for a conversation in connection with this book. I found him strangely bullish about Poland. "There is reason for optimism," he said, "because I think there must be an awful lot of people in other Iron Curtain countries that feel the same [as the Poles]. In other words, the failure of Communism to provide that workers' utopia that they have talked about for so long has been made evident in Poland. Our job now is to do everything we can to see that [the reform movement] doesn't die aborning. We may never get another chance like this in our lifetime." When I asked if he really thought U.S. pressure could change Soviet behavior toward Poland, he responded without hesitation: "Yes, I do."

What did doing "everything we can" consist of? Obviously it was not going to be a total abandonment of "business as usual." He insisted that while he still believed in "linkage," the INF negotiations already underway in Geneva would continue undisturbed. A meeting between Haig and Gromyko on other matters the following month would take place as scheduled. Reagan was not yet ruling out the possibility of a conference between himself and Brezhnev in 1982. He sounded remarkably tolerant about the uneven support he was getting from Western Europe: "Some countries, where the trade balance [with the Eastern bloc] may be higher, have been worried because they could see sanctions adding to their economic troubles and they don't see any other way out, any other direction to go."

There was some logic in these points. The United States, not to mention the rest of the world, had a huge stake in arms control. Even though Poland provided Reagan a specific excuse for suspending the Geneva talks, he chose to ignore it. And it was certainly true that the Europeans had a larger material interest in East-West trade than the United States did. Then, as later, it was a gaping and embarrassing incongruity that Washington promoted sanctions while continuing to sell the Soviets grain.

Thus Reagan's tempered actions could be justified in a number of ways. What could not be supported at all was his continued insistence that half measures would have more than symbolic effect. Carter had gone further in the case of Afghanistan, invoking the grain weapon, but still the Russians stuck to their guns, literally as well as figuratively, and Moscow's geopolitical stake in Poland was considerably higher. When Reagan talked of the problem's "delicacy" and the need for time in order to secure the allies' support, one could almost hear the voice of Haig—or any other Secretary of State of recent vintage—in the background. Reagan was trying to learn his diplomatic lessons well. He was gritting his teeth, choking back his own impulses, resentful of the criticism from friends that he was being too soft. At one point in our talk he complained about "columnists that I respect who lately are kicking my brains out as if, well, here we are backing away [from Poland] . . . It's like [the charge that we don't have] a foreign policy. We've got a foreign policy and, damn it, it has been working and working pretty well—better than anything we have had for a number of years. This is frustrating . . ."

By the very end of that day's interview Reagan abandoned the diplomatic line for a moment. With an expression of relief, he spoke from the archive of his own convictions: "The hard thing for all of us, I think, is to realize the original mistake was made a long time ago. If the democratic world, if the free world, many years ago, had said to the Soviets they were going to have to prove their system themselves, Communism would have collapsed a long time ago, because the plain truth of the matter is, without the help of the capitalist world, the Soviet Union couldn't live."

Did he propose to lead an international boycott? Obviously he did not. In the weeks ahead Reagan resisted pressure from the right to push the Polish regime into bankruptcy by forcing a default on American loans. To do so would have damaged many Western lenders, though it would also have worsened Moscow's financial problems. Some American industrial exports to the Soviet Union were allowed to continue. George T. Will, one of Reagan's strongest admirers among columnists, lamented: "The Polish crisis is over. But a crisis of American conservatism is at hand. This administration evidently loves commerce more than it loathes Communism."[7] With less passion but more facts, Richard T. Davis, a recognized expert on Eastern European affairs, accused the Carter and Reagan administrations of repeated failures of perception and will. "So far," he wrote at the end of a long, detailed article, "the West has failed the test because it has lacked strong, imaginative, and persistent American leadership."[8]

It is always wise to be wary of "Who-lost-X" inquisitions after a foreign defeat. A year after the imposition of martial law no one had yet made a persuasive case that the Administration could have prevented repression or that, after the fact, it could have made the bullies desist. But it was clear that American policy both before and after was ambivalent to the point of fecklessness. Further, Reagan was unable to contain his frustration in mid-1982.

Gromyko dropped hints to Haig that the yoke in Poland might be partially lifted if Washington displayed a little patience. Meanwhile, as the Versailles summit approached, Washington thought it might make a deal that would curb its allies' future transactions with the Soviets.

When both of these prospects fell through, Reagan lost patience. On June 18, he, Clark and Weinberger overrode the views of the State, Treasury and Commerce departments on the pipeline question. Not only would U.S. obstruction efforts continue, they would be increased. That would mean invoking "extraterritoriality," a concept of dubious legal validity. Foreign subsidiaries of American firms and foreign-owned companies as well would be penalized if they honored their contracts concerning equipment for the pipeline. "A matter of great principle is at stake," Reagan told his advisers during that meeting. "It affects our credibility with our allies and with the Russians." As an aside to a smaller group of aides, Reagan said: "You know this is a tough one. I know what's right in the foreign policy aspect of it, but I hate like hell to hurt American business."

The June 18 decision produced applause from those who had been hissing Reagan's earlier stand. In both practical and legalistic terms, however, the new position was very difficult to support. Lawrence Eagleburger, who represented Haig at the June 18 meeting, warned at that session that the Europeans would simply defy Washington. Weinberger disagreed. Great Britain, the Defense Secretary said, could hardly cross the United States in view of Reagan's strong support in the Falklands war. That turned out to be dead wrong. Thatcher, like her counterparts in Bonn, Rome and Paris, was not about to add to her unemployment problem by canceling heavy equipment contracts.

By early fall it was obvious that Reagan's "great principle" was teetering. Withholding of the American components would delay the pipeline slightly but the project would go ahead. Meanwhile, Moscow enjoyed the spectacle of additional friction among the Western allies. Shultz had recognized the problem immediately. Along with Regan, Baldrige and Brock, he worked quietly to minimize the commercial penalties that might be imposed on foreign companies. He dealt with European foreign ministers on the terms of a compromise. He also began to wean Clark away from the hard-line position on this issue. To save face all around there would have to be some new understanding with the Europeans. Tacitly, at least, Washington would have to drop its opposition to the pipeline project already underway. Something would have to be given in exchange concerning future deals with Moscow. With Schmidt having fallen from power in Bonn, François Mitterrand became the pivotal figure on this issue in Western Europe. One of his principal advisers on international economic relations, Jacques Attali, was considered in Washington to be particularly hostile to American interests. As the host official most involved with arrangements for the Versailles summit, Attali had repeatedly thwarted American purposes.

By late October, however, Shultz had worked out the main features of an agreement with the West Europeans, Japanese and Canadians. The most important point in it was the postponement of any new energy-supply deals with the Soviet Union pending completion of a study of alternative means of meeting the need for imported natural gas or oil. Thus the West was united in suspending judgment, at least for the time being, on whether it would provide a market for the second pipeline which Moscow planned to build later on.

All that remained was the question of how to package the understanding for public presentation. The Reagan administration, naturally enough, wanted a prompt announcement that made a clear connection between the removal of U.S. sanctions and the new agreement among the seven allies. If the news could be let out before the midterm election, so much the better. It would not only be a positive diplomatic bulletin; it would also be a boost for those communities that had lost export contracts—and jobs—as a result of the restrictions. The French, however, objected strenuously. Paris wanted no public connection between the new understanding and the removal of the sanctions. It simply wanted Reagan to surrender his sword on the latter issue while the agreement remained merely a tacit element until some later time.

Washington swallowed hard and remained silent on both ends of the equation for weeks. On October 27 Clark made a secret trip to Paris to discuss a number of other issues privately with Mitterrand. Clark pointedly refrained from bringing up the pipeline question. Toward the end of the conversation, however, the French President raised the issue. The Americans, he said, had been guilty of a kind of "hegemony" and violation of others' sovereignty. He said all the allies must tone down their rhetoric on the subject; he would work toward that end. Nonetheless, he indicated clearly that Reagan must yield. Clark took the occasion to tell Mitterrand that neither Reagan's personality nor his principles would allow the result Paris sought. Nor would Reagan permit the imminent election to force his hand.

The issue remained in limbo for another fortnight. During the week of November 8 Brezhnev died and the Polish Government, having thoroughly crushed Solidarity, decided to release Walesa after eleven months of incarceration. These events had no direct bearing on the pipeline question but did serve to refocus attention on East-West relations. The following Monday, November 15, the new German Chancellor, Helmut Kohl, was arriving in Washington for his first visit since succeeding his adversary, Schmidt. The White House wanted the sanctions problem out of the way before Kohl's meeting with Reagan.

On Friday, the eleventh, cables were sent to the six allies informing them that Reagan planned to announce the general outline of the agreement, together with the removal of the sanctions, during his weekly radio broadcast the next day. London, Bonn, Rome, Ottawa and Tokyo responded promptly and offered no objection. Paris was silent. Saturday morning, about an hour before the scheduled broadcast, Attali conveyed word that Mitterrand had "a few small problems" with the details of the understanding to which representatives of all seven nations had agreed. Attali reported that he was going to speak to his principal momentarily and would be back in touch.

Reagan's response upon hearing that was to tell his aides he was going ahead regardless of what the French thought. Nonetheless, at approximately 11:30 A.M. Washington time—thirty-five minutes before he was to go on the air—Reagan placed a telephone call to Mitterrand. The French President refused to accept the call. Reagan went through with the announcement, though he couched it in terms that might give least offense to the French. Further, the actual text of the agreement remained secret, as the Europeans requested. It was called later the "non-paper," a term for unofficial diplomatic understandings.

Saturday, November 12, 1982, may be notable as the most uncivil day in Franco-American relations since Franklin Roosevelt and Charles de Gaulle sparred during World War II. Not only did Mitterrand refuse to take Reagan's call—a most unusual act of discourtesy between "friendly" heads of state—but later the same day the French Government announced that it was "not a party to the agreement announced this afternoon in Washington." The huffy denial violated the spirit, if not the letter, of the deal Shultz had meticulously negotiated. At about 5 P.M. Washington time, the French embassy informed the State Department that it wished an immediate conference in order to clarify Mitterrand's position. Because Shultz was in Moscow that day for the Brezhnev funeral, the request went to Deputy Secretary Kenneth Dam. He promptly phoned the White House for instructions. Clark's response: you will refuse to see them. It was an unprecedented diplomatic rebuff for America's oldest ally.

Shultz went to Paris the following month to participate in an exercise of mutual face-saving. Both the Americans and the French by this time were ready to act calmly. They decorated the obvious differences between them with diplomatic wallpaper. On that ambiguous note the West weathered the first anniversary of the repression in Poland. Though martial law ostensibly was removed, the reform movement had been effectively destroyed. Nothing the United States had done alone, or in concert with its allies, had had much impact. Within NATO, Reagan had merely begun to force a new consensus concerning East-West trade's relationship to East-West power politics. He would be the host of the 1983 annual economic summit. In Williamsburg he would have another opportunity to persuade the alliance that it needs a new unified policy.

Poignant and historically significant as Poland's agony was, it could not compare in gravity to the threat that has dominated East-West relations for more than thirty years: the risk of nuclear war between the superpowers. The shape and nature of that specter has changed with the decades. It seemed most menacing in the early sixties, when John Kennedy and Nikita Khrushchev confronted each other over Cuba. But even in more relaxed times, it has been ever with us. As additional countries have acquired nuclear know-how and materials, the possibility of a "small" atomic battle—which might then trigger the war to end all wars and end everything else as well—has become a factor. At the same time, nuclear gamesmanship developed into the underlying motif of strategic and political relationships both within the Western bloc and between NATO and the Warsaw Pact countries. The construction, deployment and control of missiles, planes and submarines became a constant in the planning of world leaders much the way the tax code guides the decisions of many businessmen and professionals.

History has imposed different perspectives on the competing alliances. The West started the nuclear age with a weapons monopoly, which it used as the principal line of defense against the overland aggression it feared from the East. Even after NATO lost exclusivity, American superiority served largely the same purpose. The Soviet system started as the inferiority-ridden Avis, determined to catch up. When it finally did so in the late seventies, the military balance was substantially altered. Long before that, however, the game had become laden with surreal ironies. Each of the superpowers built more and better weapons largely for the purpose of neutralizing the other's nuclear arsenal. While strategists oscillated among the fashionable scenarios— such as MAD, counterforce and flexible response*—one underlying theory became prevalent: if either side's principal weapons seemed to be degraded, stability and hence peace would be threatened. Weapons degradation could mean either a high degree of vulnerability to destruction by the other side or an inability to penetrate the adversary's improved defenses.

As early as the 1960 campaign, John Kennedy, as the challenger of

---

* MAD stands for mutual assured destruction, which says the ability to obliterate each other's societies regardless of who attacks first will prevent either side from making the initial strike. Counterforce emphasizes the ability to destroy the other side's nuclear weapons even after suffering an opening attack. Flexible response emphasizes the possibility of a nuclear exchange that might be limited insofar as the types of weapons used and the amount of territory engulfed; in this scenario Armageddon is theoretically avoidable.

the incumbent's record on which Richard Nixon had to run, attacked the Republicans for having allowed a "missile gap" to develop. Once in office, Kennedy discovered that the chasm was illusory. He devoted his military energies thereafter more to the Green Berets than the Strategic Air Command. In that time of extremely high Cold War tensions, concern in Europe about the American "nuclear umbrella" reached a peak. It was not so much the prospect of holes in the shield that was a concern, but whether the Americans would open the umbrella at all merely to defend French or German real estate. Thus France justified the need for its own *force de frappe*. And thus a side issue developed over "theater nuclear weapons." The United States maintained a large army in Europe as hostage to its commitment. A Soviet attack on this force, presumably, would compel a salvo of strategic nuclear weapons from the plains states to the steppes. That prospect, also presumably, would deter the Russians. But once ballistic missile alley became a two-way thoroughfare, once the Soviets could more or less match the Americans in long-range destructive power, a new worry set in for the Europeans. What if neither superpower chose to risk its heartland by attacking the other's territory? In that event, the western front of two world wars would in the third round become very noisy for a few days and radioactive indefinitely.

While these complicated factors were in flux, the Soviet Union continued its large-scale armaments program. Its military tradition was land warfare. Nuclear weapons were viewed as tomorrow's artillery. Thus the Soviets concentrated on land-based missiles, the larger the better, to compensate for the greater precision and variety of American weapons. The United States, by contrast, became wedded to a "triad" of strategic nukes, deployed in ICBM's, submarines and long-range bombers. This distinction would become important in the late stages of the arms race.

Jimmy Carter, a Naval Academy graduate who served on nuclear submarines, came into office with an informed skepticism about military spending. He firmly believed that the defense budget could be cut and that a new arms control agreement would lessen the need for additional fancy weapons. He discarded the Ford administration's plans for rehabilitating a force structure and rebuilding stockpiles that had been depleted during the Vietnam war. Carter canceled the Air Force's B-1 program—which was to supply a new strategic bomber to replace the elderly B-52's—and slowed down other big-bang, big-buck projects. Only toward the end of his term did Carter realize that he had gone too far. He and his Defense Secretary, Harold Brown, then tried to accelerate the controversial MX program, the favored successor of the Minuteman as the mainstay of the ICBM force. In making that deci-

sion, the Carter administration in effect recognized at least the proba-
bility that a "window of vulnerability," as the cliché had it, was about
to open for the most formidable segment of the triad, America's land-
based, long-range missiles.

What did American planners fear would fly through that window?
Thousands of warheads lifted from Soviet missile ranges by SS-18's,
the giant of the Soviet force. This monster, thirty meters long, is twice
the size of the MX. It can hurl eight or ten warheads to the other side
of the world with what is thought to be considerable accuracy. In war-
gaming, therefore, the SS-18 ostensibly degrades the Minuteman. To
cover Europe, meanwhile, the Soviets in the late seventies began to
deploy their SS-20, a mobile, intermediate range rocket. They carry
three warheads each. From bases in the western Soviet Union they can
reach every corner of Europe as well as much of the Middle East. They
have three times the punch and six times the range of the older American intermediate weapon based in Europe through 1982, the Pershing-
1A.

These were the frightening comparisons being used by planners in
1980–81. There were opposing evaluations, of course. Rarely is a
statement made about the nuclear balance that does not elicit a contrary view pronounced with equal vehemence. Experts with respectable
credentials argued that the alarums from the Pentagon were overstated,
that when all factors were taken into account, the United States was
not at all outgunned. The superiority of American submarine-launched
missiles, for instance, compensated for some of the Russians' edge in
land-based birds.

It is beyond the scope of this book to lay out all elements of the argument in exquisite detail. This brief visit to the nuclear game room
and hardware store was necessary in order to outline some of the principal ideas and devices at issue as the new administration confronted
the dilemma of arms control negotiations.

Reagan's position in the 1976 and 1980 campaigns, and during the
transition as well, was consistent, though some of his terminology
changed. Running against Ford for the GOP nomination, he insisted
that the United States had become "number two" in the military competition. The Ford-Kissinger formulation of "equivalency," he said,
really meant U.S. inferiority. Reagan was apprehensive about the SALT
I agreement already in place because it merely confirmed that secondary
status. Four years later, running against Carter, Reagan condemned the
unratified SALT II pact on the same grounds. During that campaign
Reagan was trying to sound less bellicose than he did earlier. He talked
of the need for an American "margin of safety," rather than superiority, but it amounted to the same thing. He stressed that he was eager

for legitimate reductions in nuclear arms, not merely a limitation, but only if the cuts did not leave the Soviet Union in a favored position.

Reagan was setting himself a difficult task as an exercise in logic. In order to persuade Moscow to undertake what he considered "genuine" arms reductions, the Kremlin would have to be given a compelling reason to change course. The best incentive would be fear of American military resurgence in the nuclear field. In one of his detailed policy speeches early in the general election campaign, he summed it up this way: "When we demonstrate our determination not to allow the Soviets to achieve a strategic advantage over us, I believe they will become interested in legitimate arms control." Later Reagan would dig himself in even more deeply as nuclear politics became intense. In his press conference of March 31, 1982, he argued: "The truth of the matter is that on balance the Soviet Union does have a definite margin of superiority, enough so that there is risk. There is what I have called . . . several times a 'window of vulnerability' . . . If they're out ahead, we're behind, and we're asking them to cut down and join us in getting down to a lower level, there isn't much of an incentive [for them]."

In fact, Reagan could get very little support, except from his own civilian Pentagon appointees, for the proposition that the Soviets had a "definite margin of superiority." Yet he found that argument essential to justify the general buildup of both conventional and nuclear forces and his stance toward negotiations. Reagan had quite specific views about the theory of bargaining, whether the issue was an actor's contract in Hollywood, the 1981 tax bill or nuclear arms.

"You have to put down what it is that you honestly believe you want," he told me on one occasion. "I think it's a great mistake to say now, because these people are opposed, I better scale down what it is I want and what I am asking for before I approach them. I do not believe that. I think you propose to them what it is you think can be done. They, in turn, are going to oppose you. I have never believed in jumping off the cliff with the flag flying . . . If you come out of there with three quarters of what it was you went in trying to get . . . I do not think it is a compromise of principle. There are other days and other times to come back again and try to get the rest."[9]

A few moments later we narrowed this down to the hard business of arms bargaining. The problem in the past, he said, was that the Russians could sit back and watch the American Congress eliminate weapons systems proposed by the American President. The Kremlin, in those situations, was getting something for nothing. While Reagan would not admit explicitly that any military proposal of his was being put forward strictly as a bargaining chip, he came quite close:

Okay, suppose we had a weapons system and suppose there was a legitimate argument for canceling it out . . . And at the same time you've got
a negotiating team that is negotiating, hopefully, arms limitation with the
Soviet Union. You don't give that [weapon] up here on your own. You
go to the negotiating table with that and find out what your negotiating
team can get in return for giving it up. And out of this, you can actually
get some legitimate arms reduction.

That private conversation took place in July. On November 22, the
Administration formally announced that it had at last decided on the
means of basing one hundred new MX's; it would use a controversial
system known as "dense pack." Several other alternatives had been
ruled out for either technical, political or fiscal reasons. By this stage,
opposition to the project was growing. Reagan went on television to
defend the need for a major new weapons system on absolute military
terms. Yet he also used the argument—mainly to nudge fence-sitters in
Congress—that only the *threat* of having to face the MX would get
Moscow to negotiate seriously. "They would know," he said of the Soviets, "that we were bluffing without a good hand because they know
what cards we hold—just as we know what is in their hand." Nonetheless, Congress forced a new delay in MX production.

In fact, Reagan was gambling that the Russians would respond by
cutting a deal rather than raising his bet with more weapons of their
own. This approach accounted for Reagan's reluctance to curb the
growth rate of defense spending first proposed by Weinberger in early
1981. Any vacillation on that, the President firmly believed, would
weaken the U.S. bargaining position in the broadest sense, not merely
in any one specific set of negotiations. This attitude also had produced
Reagan's original preference to defer arms control talks, particularly
the strategic phase, until the major components of his military proposals were well on their way to fruition.

While this scenario seemed plausible, it contained several flaws. A
few of his own people at the Pentagon were dead set against arms control because they believed that it could only result in damage to the
United States. They would attempt to impede the process. Further,
Weinberger's inability to frame the strategic arms proposals in a persuasive way made the strong posture Reagan hoped to maintain look
dubious. Finally, political pressure both at home and abroad repeatedly
intruded on the Administration's timetable. Reagan had to attempt to
keep the Russians on hold, advance his military program smartly and
fend off the anxiety of allies overseas and constituents here. The sum of
these factors was a herky-jerky process that lurched along precariously.

Much of the political pressure was a reaction to the large arms buildup. The Administration appeared intent on buying every nuclear weapon conceivable. It pressed ahead not only with the MX, but also with the Trident II nuclear submarine, both the B-1 bomber and the potential successor to that, the Stealth aircraft, and the enhanced-radiation warhead. The ostensible rationale was to restore a stability that presumably had been shaken by the Soviets' military advances. But a strong argument could be made that these weapons, by putting the Soviet nuclear arsenal at greater risk than before, in fact would promote instability. The D-5 missiles to be deployed on Trident, as well as the Pershing-2's, for instance, drastically cut the warning time the Soviets would have in the event of an American first strike. From Moscow's perspective then, stability would be reduced.

The arms buildup was accompanied by a good deal of loose talk about nuclear war by members of the Administration. Reagan at times allowed himself to be trapped into press conference exchanges indicating that he thought waging a limited nuclear war was possible. Theoretically, of course, it *is* possible. The American arsenal must be shaped accordingly. But Reagan lacked sufficient fluency in the subject to handle the issue deftly in public. He was not alone in that deficiency.

Thomas K. Jones, Deputy Under Secretary of Defense, promoted civil defense efforts so enthusiastically that he made backyard shelters sound bombproof ("Everyone's going to make it if there are enough shovels to go around . . .").[10] Richard Pipes believed that nuclear war could be prevented only by planning as if it might well happen. While he tried to be discreet about his views, they seeped out. American military doctrine was readjusted to accommodate the theoretical possibility of fighting a nuclear war of some duration. Weinberger's insistence on producing enhanced-radiation warheads, the so-called neutron bombs, for the stockpile though deployment of them seemed unfeasible attracted worldwide attention—and anxiety. These moves fed the upsurge of anti-nuclear protests and a proliferation of literature on the subject. Both in Congress and at the local level strong drives got underway in favor of various "freeze" proposals—resolutions aimed at halting the arms race in place and worrying about reductions later. One result of all this by late 1981 was widespread popular fear, which showed up in virtually every poll on the subject.*

* The NBC/Associated Press survey in mid-December was typical. It found 76 percent of the public believing that war was "likely" within a few years. That was an increase from 68 percent the previous September and 57 percent in August. A Yankelovich poll commissioned by *Time* reported in the issue of December 28 that, by a margin of 55 percent to 31 percent, Americans believed that deployment of new American intermediate-range missiles in Europe pledged by the Administration would increase the prospect of nuclear combat.

Leonid Brezhnev, meanwhile, was adroitly conducting the most vigorous Soviet propaganda offense in more than ten years. It started at
the 26th Party Congress in February 1981, when Brezhnev proposed a
summit conference with Reagan and offered to negotiate all outstanding differences. There, and in later statements, the Soviet leader
talked in grandiose terms of a moratorium on deployment of new
weapons, of creating a nuclear-free zone in Scandinavia, of freeing the
Third World of the nuclear genie, of renouncing the first use of nuclear
weapons.

It was a logical extension of the messages Dobrynin had imparted to
Allen during the transition.* It was also a typical Soviet ploy: to plead
for peace while engaging in dreadful mischief. Brezhnev was still making war in Afghanistan. He was blatantly violating the Helsinki accords
in his behavior toward Poland. He was concluding a massive increase
in sophisticated nuclear weapons. Joseph G. Whelan, a foreign affairs
specialist at the Library of Congress, published a monograph on this
period in which he observed of the Russian effort:

> It was carried forth against a background of substantial Soviet military
> buildup, particularly of SS-20's in Europe. To observers in Western
> Europe, the offensive seemed to have two over-arching purposes: to di-
> vide NATO by capitalizing on the upsurging anti-nuclear movement and
> in a longer term to isolate the United States and weaken its influence in
> Western Europe.[11]

But Whelan, like other specialists, went on to speculate about
whether Brezhnev's rhetoric, echoed by Gromyko in his United Nations
appearances, contained more than propaganda. Did it also offer a serious prospect of negotiations that might be fruitful? That had been the
upshot in the early 1970s, when similar advances by Moscow contributed to the initial SALT pact. Certainly a large sector of opinion in
Western Europe was swayed by Brezhnev's moves. There the anti-
nuclear forces were even more energetic—and more of a political force
—than in the United States. Reagan occasionally charged that pro-
Soviet forces were behind the massive street demonstrations. That he
was probably correct was irrelevant. The operative fact was that in the
second half of 1981 the United States was losing a propaganda war.
The loss could seriously undermine NATO as well as Reagan's domestic support.

At immediate issue was the deployment of new American intermediate-range missiles, Pershing-2's, along with ground-launched
cruise missiles ("Glicums" or Tomahawks), to offset the Soviet SS-
20's, most of them already in place. In 1979, when the Carter adminis-

* Described in Chapter 5.

tration agreed to supply the new equipment, official European sentiment favored it. Actual emplacement was to begin late in 1983. Now
attitudes were changing. European opinion, influenced by what was
perceived as bellicosity by the Reaganauts, began to waver. Brezhnev
was arguing in public that his SS-20's were merely his nation's way of
offsetting other NATO weapons already deployed. He would view the
Pershing-2/Tomahawk installations as a raise in the betting which he
would have to match by still another escalation.

Washington's inability to counter this line of attack successfully was
a study in frustration. Walter Laqueur, a strategic analyst and historian
regarded as a sturdy hawk, wrote in a mood of lamentation: "The failure of the Reagan administration in this respect has been almost inex-
plicable. Afghanistan and Poland and the deepening economic crisis in
Eastern Europe should have placed the Soviet Union on the defensive.
Instead, it is the United States that has found itself in political isola-
tion, cast as a delirious warmonger forever looking to deploy new
weapons of mass destruction."[12]

A recovery was in progress, but very slowly. As early as April 1981
the Administration agreed in principle that it would honor the "two-
track" understanding reached in NATO two years earlier—that the
deployment of new tactical nuclear weapons would be accompanied by
a good-faith effort at negotiations with the Soviet Union concerning the
same devices. Haig was forced to battle Weinberger over just how enthusiastically to honor that understanding, but he succeeded. Translating that into an actual negotiating policy, however, required a more
arduous contest. The United States would have to undertake a
counteroffensive demonstrating a credible commitment to good-faith
negotiations. It would have to put forth positions that satisfied Western
military concerns while offering at least the possibility of a successful
deal with Moscow. The catchword at the State Department was "negotiability," which meant that the terms should not be so extreme as to
preclude eventual agreement. At the top echelon of the Pentagon, however, "negotiability" meant flabbiness.

The two officials with primary responsibility for developing the INF
position at the working level were Assistant Secretary of State Richard
Burt and Assistant Secretary of Defense Richard Perle. The "two Rich-
ards," as they were frequently called, were both strong-willed, intense
experts in defense strategy. Both qualified as hawks in broad terms.
The huge difference in their attitudes was that Burt believed some degree of accommodation with the Soviets was possible under certain circumstances while Perle doubted that any deal would benefit the United
States. A third specialist who participated in the tortuous decision-making process later said of Perle: "He sincerely opposes arms control on

principle. He believes it is an opiate that lulls us into complacency and so it is anathema to our interests. But he does understand the propaganda value."

Perle and his immediate superior at the Defense Department, Fred Iklé, had considerable influence on Weinberger, who himself had no experience in nuclear gamesmanship. But he would fight their battles in the White House, and in this case fight it well. Under Perle's guidance, the civilian planners at Defense refined the "zero-option" plan. It had the virtue of simplicity for the purposes of public presentation in both the United States and Western Europe. The crux of the proposal: that the Soviets agree to dismantle all their SS-20's—even those based in the Far East—along with other, less important missiles. In exchange, the United States would cancel deployment of both the Pershing-2's and the "Glicums." The two sides would, in effect, revert to a balance similar to that existing five years previous, before the SS-20's were introduced.

Burt, with strong support from Haig and some cooperation from Rostow, believed that the zero option had severe flaws. It would require so much change in the Russian tactical force structure that Moscow would reject it out of hand, just as it had rebuffed a drastic SALT proposal made by the new Carter administration in 1977. Second, even if the Defense Department approach did become a basis for negotiations, it painted the United States into too narrow a corner. Any move up from zero would make it appear that the United States was granting a large concession in principle. The State Department plan, which came to be known as "zero-plus," would put the United States in a more flexible opening position. It would disregard two classes of obsolescent Soviet missiles which the Perle group wanted to include in the package. More importantly, the State Department proposal, while holding zero as the ideal, would start with the proposition that a relatively small number of the new missiles on both sides would be permissible.

This clash was an excellent case study in the differences between conventional diplomacy at the State Department and the restiveness of Reaganauts who still hoped to act out the "break with the past" motif of the transition. Said one of the participants months later: "We recognized that the zero option was something that could be exploited for political and public relations purposes at the time [November 1981]. Of course, we all recognized also that the best option, from the viewpoint of traditional arms control thinking, was something with a medium ceiling. After all, they had deployed the SS-20 and we hadn't matched it. State was afraid of getting too greedy. The crucial thing, once negotiations started, was perception. We had to avoid the appearance of being inflexible while allowing Moscow to appear as the more reasonable party."

Reagan, however, did not see things that way. Having stalled the entire process during the summer and early fall of 1981, the Pentagon group now worked through Weinberger to get a presidential verdict in its favor. Weinberger in turn used Meese as a conduit for an unofficial selling job on the President. The actual talks were to start in Geneva at the end of November and the White House wanted a major publicity flourish in anticipation of that event. The Administration also wished to offset Brezhnev's latest sallies as he continued to woo the Europeans.

The crucial meeting in the White House was set for November 12, just six days before Reagan was scheduled to deliver a speech to the National Press Club. Haig's group did not know it then, but Reagan had already settled on the general outline, if not all the details, of the Pentagon proposal. He did not seem eager to hear the arguments rehearsed in all their specific minutiae. He told both Weinberger and Haig that he had read each of their papers closely. The State Department's zero-plus approach, he said, was like stud poker; Moscow would see too many of Washington's cards face up too early in the hand. Reagan also told one of his stock anecdotes on the subject of negotiating, a tale involving Paul Muni when he acted in Lower Manhattan's Yiddish Theater. Muni once played an idealistic union leader confronting an intransigent employer in the final moments of one act. The script had Muni making a vehement speech demanding concessions for his followers. The curtain was to fall with the adversary responding: "I will give them *nothing!*" That left the resolution for the play's last act. As Reagan finishes the story: "In this instance, Muni made his impassioned plea and the actor playing the manager got so carried away that he said: 'I will give them *everything!*' The curtain came down with great applause from the audience. But the players during intermission had to write a new opening for the third act."*

Returning to business, Reagan attempted a couple of times during the discussion to indicate his attitude. "What I was thinking," he began in his typically indirect way of saying what he was already determined to do, "was why we couldn't do it this way . . ." Then he sketched his version of the zero option. Allen, coordinating one of his last NSC

* This rendition of the Muni tale turned up during an interview with me July 24, 1982, but was the same anecdote he told during the dreadfully serious meeting the previous November 12. It had nothing to do with the issues at hand; Reagan was not supposing out loud that the Soviet negotiators would be converted by the eloquence of their American opposite numbers. I mention it here as an example of Reagan's habit of telling jokes in all types of situations.

meetings, remembered the moment later: "Anyone who knows Ronald Reagan and how he went about making decisions would have quickly concluded that here was Ronald Reagan who had made a decision, and you had better just go ahead and get ready. It was clear that he had been won over [by Weinberger]."[13]

Haig did not give in so easily, however. First he argued that the allies would prefer his approach. Then he and Weinberger clashed on related points. For instance, Perle had insisted that SS-12's and SS-22's be eliminated along with three other types of Soviet missiles. Reagan ruled in favor of the State Department on that item, accepting the argument that Washington should not be "too greedy." Haig wanted authorization to consult with NATO ministers before Reagan's speech to make sure that European leaders would be ready to provide the requisite applause. When Weinberger opposed that idea on the grounds that it might diminish the impact of Reagan's speech, Haig made a show of anger at this example of shortsightedness. Haig prevailed on this detail as well; Burt and Eagleburger were dispatched to Europe to bring allied governments up to date.

To the experts, the contest had been gritty and complex. Neither side was completely comfortable with the outcome, though Weinberger had the best of it by far. To Reagan, however, the basic issue was relatively easy, or so he recalled it in a conversation a year later, when the zero option had produced zero progress. "They weren't adamant at the State Department," he told me, "because theirs was a fear just of what the perception would be in Europe, that we were asking an impossible thing, simply to avoid negotiating." Yes, he had listened to the perception argument, but felt his decision was vindicated for two reasons: the Europeans "thought it was great" and the Russians hadn't broken off the talks. "I thought, you know, the situation was so simple . . . It seemed to me so logical to say, you know, 'Wait a minute, [the SS-20's] are [aimed at] the heart of Europe.' What better than to say, 'You do away with yours and there won't be any Pershing-2's'?"[14] The answer to Reagan's rhetorical question was that it would have been better to start with a position that offered a more realistic prospect of actual agreement.

Finally there was the question of the speech's tone. Here there was a good deal of disagreement that went beyond the simple Pentagon-vs.-State split. There were clashing views within the State Department itself. Iklé, representing Weinberger, promoted a relatively narrow approach concentrating on the INF problem alone. Haig favored a more expansive version that had originated in his European Affairs Bureau, then headed by Eagleburger. This model made Reagan sound forthcoming about all forms of arms control, not merely the INF phase. It would also serve as the official unveiling of the acronym START, for Strategic Arms *Reduction* Talks, as the replacement for SALT (Strategic Arms *Limitation* Talks).*

Again there was a back-channel contest. Weinberger lobbied in favor of a draft of which Perle was the principal author. Haig used Clark, then still his deputy at State, and Clark worked through Deaver to get favorable consideration of the Eagleburger version. An NSC staff member, Dennis Blair, meanwhile composed a third alternative. Reagan read all three and decided that State's approach was best. It served as the basis for his address on November 18, the most important foreign policy speech he gave during his first ten months in office.

Though the hard-news aspect of the address was the zero-option proposal for INF negotiations—which Reagan made sound persuasive—he toured the rest of the arms control horizon as well. He was firm and confident without being tendentious. He spoke to posterity as well as his contemporaries: "This, like the first footstep on the moon, would be a giant step for mankind. We intend to negotiate in good faith and go to Geneva willing to listen to and consider the proposals of our Soviet counterparts."

No single statement could reverse the trend of the propaganda war overnight, but Reagan had made a good beginning. The lead editorials in the next day's New York *Times* and Washington *Post* represented a startling change in the critiques Reagan's military views usually got in those forums. "At long last," said the *Times,* "President Reagan has made a sound and shrewd foreign policy speech. Its primary purpose, of course, was not the catchy proposal to clear Europe of nuclear weapons but rather to brace the West's faith in nuclear deterrence." To the *Post,* it seemed "an awfully good speech . . . He was well prepared, forceful and he made a lot of sense. Serious people in this country, in Europe and in the Soviet Union ought to study his message." Responsible European leaders and commentators responded in the same vein. Moscow, as expected, replied with a loud *nyet* on the specifics, but remained willing to bargain.

At the end of the month, Paul Nitze, one of the nation's venerables in the national security field, arrived in Switzerland to begin what would be a prolonged encounter with his opposite number, Yuli Kvitsinsky. Both men were well schooled in their arcane subject and both

---

* The word "reduction" was important for symbolic purposes; it showed how Reagan was changing the emphasis. As the acronym first percolated up from Allen's staff, it sounded flat: SART. That would not be very catchy, White House advisers concluded. At one meeting James Baker, as ready as Reagan to play for a laugh, wrote a note to a colleague proposing that they consider "Faster Arms Reduction Talks" if a real grabber was sought as an acronym. The problem was solved by using the first two letters of "strategic."

were also held on extremely short leashes by their respective governments. Later they would attempt to break free of those restraints, with
interesting results. But meanwhile they were bound in ritualistic exchanges as both governments continued to maneuver on the political
and propaganda fronts.

Until the full documentary record is available some time in the future, it is impossible to say now with certainty whether a constructive
agreement could have been obtained on the INF question in 1982 had
the United States come in with a proposal more familiar to the Soviets.
Moscow's opening position envisioned a gradual and partial reduction
in its own intermediate missile force provided that the United States introduced no new weapons at all. However, the two sides were so far
apart on basic matters—such as how to count a variety of weapons systems already in place—that a relatively quick deal was probably impossible in the absence of large American concessions.

It is clear in retrospect that the zero-option proposal was made more
as a political gambit than as a serious step in negotiations. A few of the
State Department officials who participated assumed in November that
the Administration would begin to shift in a few months to something
more flexible. They even speculated that soon after the United States
presented its formal draft treaty in early February, there would be an
adjustment in the direction of zero-plus. They were wrong. Reagan was
not prepared to make changes at that early stage. Rather he was willing
to gamble that he could maintain NATO cohesion on nuclear policy. If
he was correct on that score, the alliance would move resolutely toward the deployment of nearly six hundred Pershing-2's and "Glicums"
starting in late 1983. And if that remained a realistic prospect, Reagan
the negotiator reasoned, the Soviets would eventually back down. Moscow, meanwhile, seemed to be betting that diverse political pressures
would dilute Washington's resolve. The Soviets attempted to encourage
that development at every opportunity.

At the same time, the Reagan administration was pledged to move
toward the START round, covering the largest and most destructive
weapons. In his November speech, Reagan had said that the United
States "proposes to open negotiations on strategic arms as soon as possible next year." The Polish repression occurred less than a month
later, providing a new chill, but that was only one factor in the slow
pace of policy evolution. Eugene Rostow, given to more candor than
his colleagues appreciated, observed early in 1982: "There is as yet no
consensus as to how military power should be used, or what it should
be used for."[15] Nor was there anything close to a consensus on a
specific negotiating position with which to begin START. In fact, the

Administration was engaged in a larger, more complex sequel to the internal debate over the zero option.

Poland as well as the power vacuum in the National Security Council staff at the end of 1981 contributed to paralysis in the interagency group working on START. In this debate it was not simply a two-sided conflict between the Burt and Perle groups. Rather there were five institutional players: the State Department, the civilian leadership of the Pentagon, the JCS, ACDA and the group within ACDA that would handle the actual START negotiations. Conventional shadings and relationships were askew. In most administrations, the civilians heading the Defense Department must prod the generals and admirals into line on arms control because the brass is more hawkish. Among the Reaganauts, the opposite was true. Similarly, ACDA, whose raison d'être is arms limitation, is ordinarily to the "left" of the State Department. Now the reverse was the case. Finally, the chaotic condition of the Reagan administration's entire national security apparatus during 1981 had tolerated serious dissension not only between Haig and Weinberger as well as Haig and Rostow; there was yet another skirmish between Rostow and General Edward Rowny, his subordinate in charge of START negotiations.

William Clark and the new men he brought into the NSC in January were aghast at the gridlock they discovered. Interagency groups debating START had been considering eight major, competing options—plus some variations—with nothing resembling a consensus in sight. "It was down to the white-knuckle stage," said one White House official who attempted to sort things out. "The national security community was lapsing into bureaucratic rigidity."

Reagan, while hardly eager to rush into an agreement with the Soviets, nonetheless became impatient with what amounted to stasis on a highly important decision. Throughout the late winter and early spring he felt pressure from the anti-nuclear movement and from members of Congress who sought to exploit that sentiment. Because of the worsening deficit problem, his military budget was also under attack; it would be easier to defend if he could demonstrate genuine interest in arms control. Yet there were recurrent news stories reminding the world that Administration officials could not settle basic questions among themselves. What, for instance, should be the main "unit of account" in a new treaty proposal? That is, should the principal measurement be delivery vehicles, numbers of warheads, or payload? That would turn out to be a crucial question, but there was no quick answer to that or other issues.

Clark, like Reagan, was a novice on strategic technology and strategy. McFarlane, who had some experience in the field, was assigned the day-to-day job of forcing the bureaucracy to move. He and Clark drafted an order which would be designated NSSD 3-82 (for "national security study directive"). It was dated March 3 and dispatched to all the interested agencies. The order concerned both procedure and substance. It set a deadline of May 1 for each participating organization to have a final recommendation completed, with interim dates along the way for preliminary steps. Just as important, NSSD 3-82 described Reagan's criteria for what the opening START position must accomplish: it would have to provide for an actual reduction of weapons, not merely curb the increase; it would have to be simple enough to be understood by the public; verification of compliance would have to be feasible; the concerns of the allies would have to be satisfied; the United States would have to be left with a credible deterrent; it would have to create a negotiating position that could be sustained over a long bargaining period.

On one point there was little dissent. The new American proposal would have to be a distinct departure from SALT I, which had expired, and SALT II, which the United States had shelved after Carter signed it. The underlying assumption in the SALT I agreement was that a rough parity existed between the United States and the Soviet Union when all strategic nuclear forces were taken into account. The Reagan administration considered the SALT regime "fatally flawed" because under SALT I the Soviets had been able to increase their large, land-based missiles appreciably. SALT II would not have altered that enough to satisfy the Reaganauts.

In approaching START, the Pentagon civilians, with some support from Rowny, began with a radical departure.* They proposed that the basic "unit of account" be "throw weight," that is, the payload that each side could deliver against the other's territory. By this measure, the Soviets had unquestionably taken the lead, thanks largely to king-sized missiles such as the SS-18. In proposing an identical limit on throw weight, Iklé and Rowny aimed at forcing the Soviets to eliminate many more existing weapons than the United States would have to discard. The ACDA position put forward by Rostow emphasized limitations on the number of warheads permitted along with restrictions on the throw weight of each projectile. The State Department approach came closest to being an extension of SALT; it envisaged ceilings on

* A retired army general who spoke some Russian, Rowny had been a member of the SALT negotiating team in previous administrations. However, he concluded that the Carterites were giving away too much. He quit the team, retired from the Army and, along with Nitze, campaigned against ratification of SALT II.

the numbers of warheads and missiles deployed, with subceilings as to types.

As in the INF debate, the State Department was attempting to promote "negotiability" without using the term. The Soviets would be most likely to bargain seriously in a framework with which they were already familiar. The Pentagon civilians, by contrast, promoted drastic change, just as they had when they persuaded Reagan to accept the zero option. In meetings and exchanges of position papers throughout April the contenders parried each other's thrusts as Clark and McFarlane attempted to achieve consensus. By this stage the White House was determined that Reagan should be waging his own vigorous peace offensive. They hoped that he would be able to make a major speech on strategic arms in May, then capitalize on that when he went to Europe in early June.

A narrowing of the disagreement began in mid-April. According to a participant who was working for compromise, Rowny began to move away from firm unity with Iklé. Instead of holding out for the throw weight formula as the core position, Rowny proposed making that subordinate. Everyone knows, he told his colleagues, that the Soviets will not give up their throw weight advantage in the near future. However, he went on, they might be more willing to consider doing that later because by the end of the decade the United States could be deploying its new D-5 missile in Trident II submarines. That weapon would neutralize the throw weight disparity. In the interim, however, the Soviets might be expected to nibble only at a proposal dealing with warheads and delivery vehicles.

Rowny's view was the seed from which the two-phase American proposal would sprout. Reagan was keeping in touch with the deliberations, largely through Clark and McFarlane. Weinberger continued to back the Pentagon view that had been pressed throughout by Iklé and Perle, and their argument made a favorable impression on Reagan. What worried Reagan as he reviewed written briefs from Haig and Weinberger—which in this case went through the regular NSC channel rather than sidedoors—was the question of clarity. Reagan wanted to go public with a proposal that would be relatively easy to understand. Most of the previous debate about nuclear arms had concerned missiles and warheads. Would it not be confusing, Reagan asked, to introduce suddenly a new measurement as the main criterion? Haig fed that doubt by emphasizing the need for simplicity. The final proposal, he insisted, must be able to stand under scrutiny of both the general public and the experts who would look for signs of phoniness. Weinberger insisted that State was simply recycling the discredited SALT concepts.

Through March and April the Joint Chiefs of Staff remained delphic.

Air Force General David Jones, then in his final months as JCS chairman, had a cool relationship with his new civilian bosses. He had been appointed by Carter and had acquiesced, grudgingly, to the terms of SALT II. In the last days of April, as the decision deadline approached, Jones and Lew Allen, the Air Force Chief of Staff, began to come into line with the State Department view. The professional soldiers had their own reasons. By setting out a limit of 850 launchers, 5,000 warheads and a subceiling of 2,500 land-based warheads—the numbers at the core of State's position—the Air Force's mission would be simplified. There would be fewer Soviet sites to target and fewer American launch complexes to be manned. To the JCS, the State Department approach had appeal because it made "war-fighting" scenarios easier. The CIA, meanwhile, was reviewing its own position. Casey originally tilted toward Weinberger on general principle. However, the intelligence service had to appraise verification capabilities. As a technical challenge, counting missiles and warheads was simpler than attempting to estimate the adversary's throw weight potential.

All these elements were still in flux when the experts met in the White House Situation Room on Saturday, May 1. McFarlane presided at that session, which was attended by working-level officials rather than department heads. When the JCS, for the first time, made an explicit statement of its position, Burt realized that State's argument would prevail. He then drafted a new position paper for Haig to use at the formal NSC meeting scheduled for Monday, which Reagan would attend.

In this controversy, unlike most of the others, Haig had fought tactfully. Now, at the end, he did not hold out for total victory. Weinberger—at odds with the generals in his own department—took a hard line, renewing his pitch for throw weight as the basic unit of account and adding to that a demand for on-site inspection. We must "challenge" the Soviets, he insisted, using that word several times. On-site inspection was particularly controversial; it was virtually guaranteed to elicit a total rejection from Moscow. That did not trouble Weinberger, who said that "take-it-or-leave-it" was probably the best approach. Haig countered with the "consensus option." That is, the United States should propose a two-phase process. The opening stage would concern itself solely with warheads and launchers. A later installment would involve throw weight. Each segment, however, would entail actual reductions in both sides' missiles, though the Soviets would have to dismantle much more hardware in order to meet the new, lower standard.

Reagan declined to make a firm decision at that session. However, the participants knew exactly where he was heading. There was no question, the President said, that the destructive power of both sides

had to be reduced. But he was still concerned about public understanding and he doubted whether the throw weight scheme would make
sense as the core of the American proposal. Early the next morning,
alone with Clark and McFarlane, Reagan said that he accepted Haig's
consensus option. McFarlane immediately drafted a decision memorandum, which Reagan signed later that day. Detailed communications
were prepared for dispatch both to the Kremlin and NATO chanceries.
The public announcement would come in a major speech Reagan was
already planning to give the following Sunday, Mother's Day, at
Eureka College, where he had received his bachelor's degree exactly
fifty years earlier.

The Reagan Physical Education Center lacked air conditioning on
that warm spring day. The guest of honor was burdened with clothing
both functional and symbolic: a bulletproof vest beneath his suit
jacket, a maroon academic robe on top. By the time he spoke his brow
was damp. In this address Reagan reviewed the full realm of Soviet-
American relations and found it laden with problems and dangers
("What can we realistically expect from a world power of such deep
fears, hostilities and external ambitions? . . ."). Détente as practiced
in the 1970s, he said, had been a failure.

His main theme, however, was hope for a better day. He avoided
making arms reduction sound easy, but he pledged to pursue it with
diligence: "The monumental task of reducing and reshaping our strategic forces to enhance stability will take many years of concentrated
effort. But I believe that it will be possible to reduce the risks of war
by removing the instabilities that now exist and by dismantling the nuclear menace."

Having deflected Brezhnev's invitations for a summit in 1981,
Reagan now talked about a personal meeting in positive terms.* "I
would hope we could arrange a future meeting where positive results
can be anticipated. And when we sit down, I will tell President Brezhnev that the United States is ready to build a new understanding . . . I
will tell him that his government and his people have nothing to fear
from the United States."

As an exercise in rhetoric and political symbolism, the Mother's Day
speech was a great success. Reagan was no longer simply bewailing the

* In April, mainly as a propaganda ploy, Reagan had told reporters that he
hoped for an informal meeting if Brezhnev chose to attend the UN special session on disarmament scheduled to be held in New York in mid-June. Brezhnev
replied that would be inappropriate; the two sides should prepare for a formal,
substantive meeting rather than a casual encounter that would be a sideshow to
the UN conference. He suggested meeting in Geneva or Helsinki in October, but
the White House had no interest.

evils of Communism. Nor was he oscillating in schizoid fashion between predictions of Soviet demise and declarations of American nuclear inferiority. Rather, he was challenging Brezhnev to make good on his flowery talk of accommodation. Less than two months later Rowny was ensconced in Geneva with his Soviet equivalent, Viktor Karpov. After a hiatus of three years Russians and Americans were beginning to consider means of reducing the number of weapons capable of ending the world. Elsewhere in the same city the INF bargaining was also in progress. In Vienna a separate set of negotiations continued concerning conventional forces in Europe. Back home, Reagan the hawk continued to battle for major modernization of his country's military machine. At the same time, Reagan the cawk was investigating the prospects of making that apparatus smaller, if no less deadly. But how serious was that investigation? Did it have any real prospects of success? Or would the process conclude, as it had begun, as an exercise in political gamesmanship?

At the beginning of 1983 one could only detect fragmentary answers, the sum of which were inconclusive. The technical details of the Administration's START proposal, though ostensibly more flexible than they might have been, still demanded far more concessions than the Soviet Union was prepared to consider. In insisting that the emphasis be on land-based missiles, Washington was asking Moscow to reduce the core of its nuclear force while the United States would retain much of its formidable triad. The START outline which Reagan presented on Mother's Day was incomplete. In the weeks that followed, important embellishments were added. For instance, the United States made clear to the world that it would continue—at least for a time—to observe the most important provisions of SALT I and II. This was a conciliatory gesture on the surface, a token of good faith while the talks went ahead. But it was also a defensive measure. In the absence of those restraints, the Soviets could add its stockpile of ICBM warheads faster than the United States.

The unofficial observance of SALT curbs and verifications procedures—in which the Soviets joined—could end at any time. Meanwhile, the Administration fleshed out its formal new proposal in such a way as to make it even more difficult for Moscow to accept. In secret meetings held just after Haig resigned, Reagan agreed to a request by the Pentagon that the SS-18's be subject to a specific subceiling in the U.S. proposal. Rather than simply talking about numbers of missiles and warheads in the first phase of START, the United States would specify that roughly two thirds of the 308 operational heavy launchers be dismantled. Another addition which was kept quiet concerned missiles built but held in reserve, sometimes at Soviet training facilities.

Again at the request of Weinberger's planners, the President agreed that these non-deployed missiles be counted in the overall numbers—and, most importantly, that sites at which they might be kept be subject to on-the-ground inspection. Aimed at avoiding cheating, that last proposition has always mashed Moscow's paranoia button.

Shultz, new at his job and far from knowledgeable about strategic affairs, was able to put up only token opposition. Gradually immersing himself in the subject, he began to play a more active role toward the end of the year. But he was still a nuclear neophyte compared with his predecessor, and disinclined to engage in hand-to-hand combat with Weinberger. The Soviets meanwhile hoped to design an agreement only slightly different than SALT II.

In the INF phase, at least the dim possibility of a break arose under unusual circumstances. In mid-July, after seven months of stylized deadlock, Nitze and Kvitsinsky took what officials later called the "walk on the mountain," or "walk in the woods." The American chief delegate, without specific authorization from Washington, provoked an informal exchange which happened to take place outdoors. The purpose was to probe Moscow's willingness to cut a clean deal along the lines of the State Department's original zero-plus proposal.

Nitze could not make a firm offer. For the record, he was not changing the American proposal officially on the table. Rather, he was inviting the Soviets to react to what they might regard as one American's notion of a feasible agreement. Nitze included numbers in his proposition. What if the United States indeed kept the Pershing-2 missiles out of Europe and introduced, say, just 75 Tomahawk launchers? Each of these devices carries four single-warhead missiles, so that the 75 systems would provide 300 projectiles. And what if the Soviets then reduced the number of their deployed SS-20's facing west to 75? Each SS-20 launcher contains a missile with three warheads, for a total of 225. The difference between the number of warheads, 300 American versus 225 Soviet, would "compensate" for the much greater speed of the Soviet ballistic models compared with the relatively slow cruise weapons.

Kvitsinsky absorbed this line of talk and relayed it to his superiors at home. Nitze immediately informed the White House and ACDA of his gambit. The initial reaction in the Administration was one of keen apprehension. Washington wished to give no official signal that it was offering a concession. Further, with Schultz barely installed, Clark, as a procedural matter, did not want ACDA galloping off on its own. Rostow, independently, had taken his own metaphorical "walk in the woods" at the MBFR conference in Vienna.

On August 24 Clark sent an official memorandum nominally

addressed to Shultz, but intended to serve as a warning to ACDA as well. The document reaffirmed the Secretary of State's primacy in arms control and warned against any unauthorized probes by negotiators. Word of that trickled out in garbled fashion, indicating that perhaps a new turf contest was underway. In fact, Nitze's lone venture was potentially much more important than that.

His report back to the White House provoked a new review within the Administration concerning the possibility of revising the American position on INF. Analyzing the exchange, officials inferred that the Soviet Union, when it did not immediately reject Nitze's "hypothetical" proposition, was possibly indicating that it was ready to move away from its own hard position. Without organizing a cumbersome new interagency review—which doubtless would have led to protracted debate—Shultz and a very small circle of experts reviewed the bidding. In Geneva, meanwhile, Nitze received hints from the Russians that Moscow was willing to continue an informal exchange along the lines he had begun.

The JCS, now under a new chairman, informed the White House that it had misgivings about the specifics discussed by Nitze and Kvitsinsky. The generals were apprehensive about relying on the old Pershing-1's along with new "Glicums." The Pentagon civilian leadership was totally hostile to the Nitze scheme. Nonetheless, Reagan on September 15, signed an NSDD authorizing the internal evaluation to continue. Further, the Soviets were informed that Washington would be interested in hearing any new formulation that they might want to suggest. All this was kept secret for another two months, though European sources eventually divulged the bare fact that confidential feelers had been exchanged.[16] By the time that minor leak occurred, however, the unofficial Nitze-Kvitsinsky line was dead, at least temporarily.

Asked about the Nitze ploy, Reagan told me later in the fall: "Yes, it did come to nothing . . . But at no point had the negotiations—with or without the 'walk in the woods'—at no point has there been any indication that the parties could not get anyplace and were ready to walk away. There was no move to leave those negotiations."

Only a handful of American officials knew the details of what had happened and the information was tightly held. Had a breakthrough been close? "No," Reagan said in a tone tinged with some regret. "It really wasn't. It *really* wasn't."[17] Moscow appeared to have retreated either for its own reasons or because it believed that Washington was backing away.

Yet soon after that appraisal by Reagan, new movement of sorts occurred. In late November, Kvitsinsky had lunch with Nitze and a visiting American senator, Gary Hart of Colorado. While the Russian offered no new formulation during that session, he used a familiar diplomatic technique, "assent by silence," as Nitze gave his own summary of where things stood. In effect, Kvitsinsky was giving advance notice of what his government would announce in December: an offer to reduce Soviet intermediate-range missiles in Europe to roughly the number of deployed British and French weapons, provided that the United States withheld all the new Pershings and Tomahawks. Washington, London and Paris promptly dismissed that proposal. Both the INF and START sessions went into recess at the end of the year still deadlocked.

Preparing for the opening of the 1983 round in late January, the Reagan administration still suffered internal divisions. Clearly the Soviets were maintaining the political propaganda initiative. Yet some ACDA and State Department experts believed that genuine bargaining was possible in the new year—provided that Reagan became more flexible. Whatever their motives, the Soviet leaders had taken some small steps toward compromise. The White House considered the state of play tantalizing. The temptation to make some concessions was great. When the Reagan party returned from the New Year's break in Palm Springs, however, there was still no understanding as to how to respond to Moscow's latest ploys.

More broadly, Soviet-American relations during the fall and winter remained dreary. In Poland, suppression of the reform movement became heavier than ever as the military government officially dissolved Solidarity. Reagan responded by limiting imports from Poland further. When Shultz and Gromyko held their first extensive conversations in New York, there was no sign of progress on any issue outstanding between the two countries. The possibility of a Reagan-Brezhnev meeting was not even discussed.

Some American analysts believed that Brezhnev, who was seventy-five and seriously ill, had hoped to end his reign by concluding a significant treaty with Washington. That, perhaps, was one of the motives of his energetic peace offensive. On October 27, however, he sent out a very different message. In one of the most bellicose speeches he had made in two years, he denounced Reagan for "threatening to push the world into the flames of nuclear war." He told his generals that the Soviet Union would have to increase military preparedness "with due account of the latest achievements of science and art of war." If Reagan thought that the Soviets were unwilling to continue the arms race, he seemed to be saying, then Reagan was wrong. Finally, he promised to pursue vigorously rapprochement with China: "We are doing everything in our power toward this end."[18]

A fortnight later Brezhnev was dead. His Politburo colleagues astonished the West by agreeing on a successor within twenty-four hours. The new General Secretary of the Communist Party, only the sixth to hold that post since Lenin's time, was Yuri Andropov. Until a few months before, Andropov had been head of the Committee for State Security, the KGB, and had presided over the latest suppression of dissent within the U.S.S.R. He opened his Kremlin reign by seconding the tough talk of Brezhnev's final days. But it would take some time to learn just what sort of an adversary Andropov would be.

Thomas Watson's forebodings when he left Moscow in the fall of 1980 had proved all too accurate during the two years that followed. About the most hopeful thing that could be said was the world had been spared threats of actual war between the two superpowers. Moscow and Washington both seemed able to sense what lines could not be crossed with impunity. The Soviets restrained themselves from active involvement in the Middle East. The United States checked its temper concerning Cuba. As the Kremlin viewed matters, it had taken the less extreme option in dealing with Poland. Washington provided a modicum of material and moral support for the Afghan rebels, but at such a low level, and with such discretion, that the Soviets could overlook it. In this tainted atmosphere, the White House wondered about the willingness—and ability—of Andropov to demonstrate flexibility. The Soviets, for their part, were probably as curious as American politicians about whether Reagan would be a one-term President.

18

Bill Clark: The Cavalryman

A whimsical fantasy recurs now and then. Charlie Wick, the show biz entrepreneur whom Reagan has installed as head of the U.S. Information Agency, plans a film biography of Bill Clark. Hearing about the project, the President decides that the lead role would be a perfect vehicle for his own comeback as an actor. Charlie, he tells his old pal, you couldn't possibly find anyone better for the part because I know Bill so well. We have a lot in common. We both love ranching and solitude; we both dislike politics and Washington. We're even about the same height and I'd be willing to knock off a few pounds. Look, Charlie, it would be economical. You wouldn't have to hire a stand-in for the riding sequences and—may the Screen Actors Guild forgive me —I'll do the movie for nothing.

Wick is embarrassed. For the first time in his life, he tries to think of something tactful to say, but fails. So he reverts to his customary bluntness. We gotta think box office, R.W. Besides, you know how you hate dieting. I'll give you the bottom line straight, Chief. We've already signed Jimmy Stewart for the part. Thus reminded of his earlier disappointments in Hollywood and of how he did not achieve real stardom until he switched to politics, Reagan decides on the spot to run for a second term.

One part of this fanciful reverie is true. Clark, at least in his public persona, is the kind of character Reagan enjoyed playing in the good old days (and the kind of role some rival usually got). The strong silent type, as they used to say of Western movie protagonists, Clark makes a habit of overcoming handicaps. Without a law degree, he became a successful lawyer and a high-ranking judge. Without an iota of professional experience in, or academic knowledge about, foreign affairs, he occupied highly sensitive posts at the State Department and White House. After initial Washington news coverage that emphasized the paucity of his knowledge, he tamed the press corps the way a skilled wrangler breaks a mean bronco. The Eastern dudes could not best him.

Over sixteen years, this anti-politician with little use for neckties or celebrity periodically rode to the rescue when the good folks (that is, the Reagans) sent out a distress signal. His habit, after cleaning up the mess, was to canter resolutely into his own private sunset, there to claim the birthright denied him as a child by mischievous fortune. For the Reagans he has been a one-man cavalry squadron to be summoned when trouble encircled the wagon train. But here the plot has an interesting twist. As often as not, Clark has said no and made his refusal stick. That departure from stereotype would be a subtle challenge for the actor portraying him. We can see that box office wasn't Wick's only consideration.

In the flashbacks to early childhood, we find a youngster whom we cannot at all envision as someday occupying one of the most difficult jobs in the White House. He is a fourth-generation Californian, descended from Irish Catholic immigrants. Is it merely coincidence that the Clark family, at the point when we come in, like the Meeses and the Deavers, acquired neither land, gold, oil nor riches in any other form? No, that fact is part of an interesting pattern. The circle of wealthy men roughly his own age who first drew Reagan into politics by and large represented new money and the rightward margin of California politics. Those a generation younger who became the hired help —Meese, Deaver, Clark, Nofziger and others—were strivers on the way up, conservatives in a Main Street, middle-class way. The lucky few like Reagan came West and quickly dug out comfy niches in one corner of California society. Those in more prosaic lines of endeavor might labor for decades, or even generations, to find themselves losing ground rather than achieving status.

The Irish in California did not cling so closely to their folkways as did their cousins in the East. Still, law enforcement was a typical occupation, Democrats the preferred party. Robert Emmet Clark, grandfather of the lad we are getting to know, was a sheriff of local renown in Ventura County, a colorful man with an eighth-grade education and a reputation for probity. In the thirties the Roosevelt administration appointed him a U.S. marshal. Fifty years later Robert Emmet's grandson, William Patrick, would hang the late lawman's Colt .44 and badge on his White House office wall. Robert Emmet's son, William, was also a small-town policeman but he aspired to other things; he would be a rancher.

He worked as a foreman and then went into partnership on his own place. "I lived all my early life on ranches of some sort or other," the younger Bill would recall of the boy in a wistful tone. "It was a very isolated life, unusual for the times. The nearest neighbor was miles away."[1] After World War II the partnership went bankrupt. That reversal of fortune imposed a sense of loss that stayed with the oldest child and only son for many years. The family moved back to Oxnard, where the father became police chief. It was a feisty time and place, with enough organized crime around to make a corrupt cop rich or an honest one famous. Police Chief Clark chose the latter course, helping Earl Warren's crusading crime commission to send several local notables to jail.

That was of limited consolation to young Bill, who had loved the land and hoped for nothing more than to work a prosperous family ranch. But there was no money and no prospect of any. "Dad persuaded me that the only way I could return to the agricultural life would be through the back door, using one of the professions." That was Clark's way of explaining why he eventually became a lawyer. He had no particular affection for that trade, or for bookish matters in general. Until the family went back to Oxnard, the boy had spent only six or seven months a year in school and was behind his contemporaries in classroom attainment. He tried to overcome that deficiency in a Roman Catholic prep school, where he did well enough to win admittance to Stanford. There he was out of his academic league, however. After a difficult year he dropped out—far out—by enrolling in an upstate New York Augustinian seminary. The regimen allowed five hours of sleep a night and two hours of conversation in the afternoon. Otherwise, the seminarians worked under a vow of silence. The priesthood, he decided, was not his calling.

Back at Stanford for another try, his marks, morale and bank account hit bottom at about the same time. So he switched to Santa Clara, a Jesuit University, where he did well enough to enter Loyola Law School in Los Angeles. He might have earned a degree—thus sparing himself a good deal of derision later, when he became a jurist without parchment—but the draft intervened. Once more a Clark discovered an aptitude for police work; as an enlisted man in Germany, he served as a counterintelligence operative. He also met Joan Brauner, a Czech working for the U.S. Army. He came home with a bright new wife and his old dim prospects.

By day he worked as an insurance adjuster. By night he read law at Loyola. In between, he learned the joys of fatherhood; there were to be five children, with little time wasted between arrivals. He was closing in at last on his degree when the dean gave him a choice: become a full-time student or leave. Thus Clark eventually became a lawyer without the blessing of the Loyola clergy; he got through the bar examination on the second try.

The Clark name meant something in Oxnard, so Clark hung his shingle there. Soon there were clients, eventually enough of them to support partners in the practice, and then construction of a professional building with paying tenants. By the early sixties Bill Clark was a young man of substance in little Oxnard (population then: 41,000 and growing fast) where, as far as he knew, he would spend the rest of his life. Two things happened to change that. After clinging to his family's Democratic loyalties through the 1960 presidential election and the 1962 gubernatorial contest in which Pat Brown defeated Richard Nixon, Clark began to look at politics differently. Or to look at it for the first time; he had not been much interested until then. Nearly twenty years later he could not remember having harbored strong feelings about any foreign issue, including Vietnam. Domestic affairs did not make a much stronger impression until Lyndon Johnson's administration began promoting new social services, including legal assistance for the indigent. That struck Lawyer Clark as wrongheaded. He did not fancy federal intrusion into his profession. By 1964, Clark was a Goldwater supporter.

The second change came soon afterward. His work frequently took him north from Oxnard and Ventura County to San Luis Obispo County. There, at last, he found his ranch, 900 acres at the right price. He would divide his time between the law practice and the outdoors. Thus, when the state party in 1966 tried to recruit the new GOP convert to run for the State Assembly, the answer was a prompt no. He was too busy living the life he had dreamt of for twenty years. Other Goldwater fans were rallying around the primary candidacy of Ronald Reagan, whom Clark had never met. One day Reagan phoned to ask him to reconsider running for the legislature. Applying the butter, Reagan talked of how much the party needed strong local candidates. No, thanks, Clark replied, I'm not interested in a political career. Eventually they worked out a compromise; Clark would serve as county chairman for the Reagan campaign only. While the contest was on, they met a dozen times.

The next request was also "temporary." Clark was asked to come to Sacramento for ten weeks during which he would work with Caspar Weinberger on transition personnel matters. That done, Clark tiptoed toward the exit, but Reagan barred the way. He needed a cabinet secretary he could trust. Clark needed to work his ranch and keep up enough of a law practice to meet the mortgage payments. Again, they compromised, Clark would stay, but only for two years.

The first really urgent call for the cavalry came only a few months later. The new team in Sacramento had some grievous difficulties getting organized. On top of that, the governor's Chief of Staff departed abruptly. A firm hand and steady temperament were needed. Clark got the summons. He accepted with the condition that he would still stay a total of just two years. A degree of order was restored to what had been a troubled, faction-ridden staff. At the same time, an important precedent was set. Clark was the great champion of what the Reagan group came to call "round-tabling" of issues before they went to the chief for decision. He also made an institution of the "mini-memo," a four-paragraph format which was supposed to summarize for Reagan all but the most complex issues and recommendations. Meese would continue both practices after he succeeded Clark in 1969. These were habits that kept Reagan highly dependent on his staff.

Clark liked to think that his responsibilities were governmental rather than political. The latter sphere he assigned to Tom Reed. The Chief of Staff also liked to think of Reed as his dutiful subordinate. Then, as later, Reed was an assertive, ambitious sort with his own agenda. One of the few important disputes which Clark lost in Sacramento was over the question of whether Reagan should make even a semi-serious run at the 1968 presidential nomination. Reed was among those pushing Reagan hard to try it. Even though he had Nancy Reagan on his side, Clark ultimately lost that one when he failed to head off the formal nomination of Reagan at the GOP Convention. Before leaving Sacramento, Reagan tried to make Clark lieutenant governor. No, Clark said, that would mean a commitment to politics. The bench was more to his liking and Reagan pushed him up the ladder to the California Supreme Court. There, presumably, he would live happily ever after as a judge and rancher.

For several years he did, once he overcame the widespread skepticism about the extent of his legal learning. But in 1980 the call for help came once more. When the Meese-Sears conflict was reaching its climax, the Reagans appealed to Clark to take the top spot in the organization. That way, perhaps, both Sears and Meese could remain. Nancy Reagan liked the idea and she knew that Sears would live with it. For nearly seven hours on Lincoln's birthday at Rancho del Cielo they went over it from every angle, but Clark kept coming back to one fact. He would have to leave the Supreme Court altogether at a time when the liberal views of Jerry Brown's appointees were threatening to prevail. Further, he had never been involved in a national campaign. Again, he told the chief no. But after the election Meese visited him in

San Francisco with a blunt message: we need you badly as Deputy Secretary of State; the boss is absolutely determined to have you there and you can't let him down.

Clark agonized over it. Not only did he want to remain in California, he knew that he faced a mauling during the confirmation process. We talked on the phone about it during that period. The ambiguous nature of the assignment made him uneasy, he said. And what about the Senate? How rough do you think it would be considering my, er, credentials? One of Clark's adroit techniques with reporters was to tickle their vanity by asking their ideas. We all fall for it. Oh, I replied, a few Democrats will mark you up a little, but only ten or twelve will vote no. Anyway, you're going to take the job. Don't wager too much on that, he insisted. I'm really not sure.

We bet a dinner, but I could hardly be proud of my judgment. Clark performed so poorly during his confirmation hearing that even Charles Percy, the Republican chairman of the Foreign Relations Committee, joined in the howl. "Never again," Percy said, "can we accept a man who professes to have no knowledge in the area for which he was nominated." The floor vote was 70 to 24, the highest number of nays awarded any of the new administration's major appointees.

Once in office, Clark performed the main assignment given him; he made the difficult Haig arrangement work for a time. He may not have known much about diplomacy in the global sense but he was diplomat enough to serve Haig loyally while retaining his own strong ties with all the important members of the White House staff. Further, he buttressed Haig's standing with the press by cultivating some strategically placed journalists.

Haig used Clark only sparingly on big policy issues, but the dutiful deputy was always around to troubleshoot. Early in the first year the Administration wounded itself by nominating Ernest Lefever for the sensitive post of Assistant Secretary of State for Human Rights. His controversial record and public statements caused the Senate Foreign Relations Committee to vote against confirmation. This created an irritating vacuum along with the impression—accurate but inconvenient—that the Reaganauts cared little about humanitarian programs. Clark not only shepherded through a more acceptable candidate for the job, he also constructed a policy position that was at least cosmetically appealing.

When Anwar Sadat was about to leave Washington after his visit in August 1981, Haig was taking a weekend in the country. Haig informed Sadat by phone that the United States was about to resume the supply of warplanes to Israel, aircraft which had been withheld for two months because of Israeli raids on Baghdad and Beirut. Accompanying

Sadat to Andrews Air Force Base, Clark got an earful from the angry
Egyptian President. It would be terribly embarrassing to me, Sadat
said, to have this announced just as I land in Cairo. Why should I
come home from America with good news for Begin? Clark that day
was Acting Secretary in Haig's absence. He knew that Haig had already informed the Israeli ambassador of the imminent announcement,
which was to come from the presidential party then in California.
Clark got to Meese and the two decided to postpone the bulletin for a
few days out of courtesy to Sadat. The incident caused internal friction
invisible at the time. Haig had to do some quick explaining to the Israelis and Reagan was disturbed because he did not learn what was
happening until he heard news accounts of the delay. No one had
thought to keep the President informed of this "detail." But Clark and
Meese had acted correctly; Sadat's position had to be maintained.

While at the State Department, Clark remained a relatively obscure
figure, rarely poking his periscope above the surface in public. He
seemed almost lost in the cavernous office assigned to the Deputy Secretary. He also appeared out of place among the sophisticated, quick
intellects in the national security community. His conversation was
slow, impeded with frequent umm's and er's. His Irish farmer's plain
features often conveyed a look of puzzled concentration. Like many
men whose early habits were formed outdoors and whose hearts have
never become reconciled to desk life, he handled documents with a certain air of wonderment. He had spent half his fifty years in law and
government, but he gave the impression that he was still exploring the
world of paper with a sense of awe. The cowboy boots he usually wore
with somber business suits accentuated his height. They also slowed his
gait and when his arthritic condition was in a bad period, the overall
impression of hesitance was reinforced.

There was nothing cautious about his performance when he moved
to the West Wing basement, however. He cleaned Dick Allen's house
with ruthless efficiency, replacing most of his predecessor's favorite
aides. Working through Robert McFarlane and Thomas Reed, he
bullied, cajoled and prodded the bureaucratic enclaves at State and Defense into moving on matters that had become congealed. McFarlane
forced a quicker pace on strategic arms control policy. Reed intervened
vigorously in the Pentagon, attempting to force a decision on how the
MX was to be deployed. He was also instrumental in choosing a
successor to Air Force General David C. Jones as chairman of the
Joint Chiefs of Staff. That choice was illuminating because Jones was
the epitome of Washington warriors—managerial, diplomatic, politically
sensitive and cautious. Reed brought to the top of the list Army General John W. Vessey, whom the Carter administration had shunted

aside because he opposed the SALT II treaty and plans to reduce U.S. forces in Korea. Vessey was a "mud soldier," a National Guard volunteer who had won his commission fighting at Anzio rather than studying at West Point. Reagan liked the symbolism, as well as Vessey's reputation as a tough field commander, and quickly appointed him.

During his first couple of months at the National Security Council, Clark used his stature to impose what turned out to be a temporary truce between Haig and Weinberger. At one meeting in January, George Bush murmured approvingly to Clark: "Your clients are behaving amazingly well these days."[2] That was only part of the task, of course, the part Clark would admit to. Another, more subtle and difficult assignment was to draw the President of the United States more deeply into the conduct of national security affairs. Here Clark could not legitimately play the role of teacher because of his own shortcomings. Rather he had to be dean of the academy, the administrator and facilitator and expediter. Clark's year at the State Department taught him a great deal, of course, because he had started at first grade level. He had nowhere to go but up. If all his predecessors going back to Eisenhower's time could be considered experts in the field, owners figuratively and sometimes literally of advanced degrees, Clark on the job had earned a high school equivalence diploma.

He and Reagan would continue to learn by doing. As Clark saw things, Reagan's education could progress only by personal involvement. The President had to be encouraged to put his own chop on a variety of decisions and not only ones in which he had a visceral feeling, such as the lifting of the partial grain embargo. Thus when Haig early in the new year dispatched Assistant Secretary John Holdridge to China in another attempt to reach an understanding about the Taiwan arms issue, Clark became concerned. It appeared that State was moving faster than the White House wanted to go at that stage. After reviewing the question with Reagan, Clark intercepted Holdridge in midjourney to give him new instructions from Reagan. When Haig sent Vernon Walters as a special envoy to Havana for a conversation with Castro, Clark again intervened. Walters had already reached Miami when Clark recalled him to Washington. In the Oval Office, Walters received modified directions from Reagan.

At meetings of the NSC and the smaller National Security Planning Group Clark penetrated Reagan's passivity from time to time as the decision point neared. "Mr. President," he sometimes asked, "is that what *you* want to do?" This technique—and the quickening of events abroad —did increase Reagan's interest and activity in the field from early 1982 onward.

In that respect Clark accomplished his mission. He succeeded as well in restoring order, energy and spirit to a National Security Council staff that had become moribund in the latter part of Allen's tenure. Clark's adroit handling of reporters induced press coverage that certified, and often embroidered upon, these accomplishments. One of Clark's cute tactics early on was to tell the world that he would grant no interviews at all. But he continued to see some journalists one by one on a "background" basis and to be quite helpful at times. Because he rationed himself, he became a precious commodity. Very few of us wanted to risk losing him as a valuable source; most coverage of both Clark and his operation was positive.

In his White House post, Clark waited five months before making his first public speech. The opening paragraphs of that talk to a seminar of experts and journalists emphasized Reagan as full-time Commander in Chief. "He views national security as his most compelling responsibility," Clark said, "and he has come to treat it accordingly."[3] The talk attracted only limited attention. Clark was better in the backroom than as a public spokesman. Out of view he could be both skillful and tough. After Haig left, Clark ran into Barbara Walters at a party as she was preparing to interview Haig for an ABC program. Clark, fighting a defensive action against criticism that Haig was beginning to express, suggested to Walters that she pin down the ex-Secretary of State on just what his policy differences with his former colleagues had been. Clark felt it part of his mandate to prove that Haig had left only because of personal and jurisdictional friction. That line, if it could be made to stick, would undercut the more substantive attacks Haig was expected to make from the outside.

Clark was good at this sort of skirmishing, better at defending policy than at creating it. Watching the Administration in action, however, hardly gave the spectator a great deal of faith in the content of what was being done, or not done. Clark proved that he could make the NSC trains run on time during 1982. He was considerably less persuasive in establishing that either he or Reagan knew the best routes to their destinations. Sometimes one wondered if the locomotive crew had a firm fix on what those destinations should be.

His lack of expertise forced Clark to rely heavily on his own aides, occasionally with poor results. In the MX basing decision, for instance, Reed displayed more vigor than judgment in promoting the dense pack option. Reed's ebullient self-confidence was refreshing in the world of cautious bureaucrats, but it made him vulnerable to miscalculation. He underestimated the resistance to the dense pack scheme, an error that led to congressional refusal to appropriate production funds for the missile in December 1982. Thus Reagan started the new year with the appointment of yet another expert panel to review the question of how to deploy the new weapon.

A National Security Adviser with more technical savvy might well have spared the White House that embarrassment. Similarly, when he encouraged Reagan to lead from his spleen on the Siberian gas pipeline issue, Clark helped produce a decision with unfortunate consequences. More dissension was created within NATO than the Soviet Union could have hoped to foment on its own.

Clark was well aware of the limitations of his old chum from Sacramento days, Caspar Weinberger. There were times when Clark put pressure on the Defense Secretary just as he did on Haig. But there was a qualitative difference in how Clark performed his traffic cop's role where Weinberger was concerned. He stood by as Weinberger's top subordinates continued to obstruct efforts to achieve arms control agreements even after basic decisions had been made. The NSC made little effort to promote efficiency in defense spending; more often Clark served as a counterweight to Baker, Stockman and Darman on that score though he sensed that Weinberger was not squeezing his budget hard enough. Reagan was satisfied with his Defense Secretary and Clark could rock only so many boats.

In a Jimmy Stewart movie, the hero's canny intuition and strength of character would combine with synergetic force, leading to a happy ending. Alas, that kind of solution eluded the players in our drama. Horse sense was a necessary but insufficient strength. Public relations guile that could help in domestic politics was of limited use in geopolitics. On volatile issues such as Central America, Clark aligned himself increasingly with Jeane Kirkpatrick and other hard-liners. They steered policy back to the purely military track in El Salvador in early 1983 despite the flaws of Washington's client regime.

At the end of two years in Washington, Clark was at peace with himself. He talked of having reached a "plateau," by which he meant that he had done what was asked of him by Reagan and demanded of him by circumstance. He had fended off chaos in the NSC operation, solved the Haig problem, induced Reagan to become a more active player and helped Shultz to become a full member of the team. When Reagan, shortly after his September initiative on Middle East negotiations, told Clark, well, it's been a while since anyone accused us of not having a foreign policy, the adviser took that as a high accolade. Clark figured it was time to head for the setting sun one last time. Maybe he was right, though Reagan refused to see his point. On this journey, the wagon master wanted the cavalryman around for as long as possible.

19

Death of the Pony

Like playwrights, Presidents often have to struggle with their second act. The curtain raiser has established the premise, the plot, the personalities. Now the creator must sustain a forward dynamism, moving his story (policies) ahead toward a credible conclusion. He must provide something fresh to keep his audience (constituents) involved while maintaining firm bonds with what he has already put on stage.

Reagan during the 1981 holiday season faced a most difficult script problem for his second year. His administration, having already consumed the intellectual capital of the election campaign, groped for new ideas. The streak of legislative victories, though dramatic, was insufficient to the need. Concrete results so far fell short. Events in Eastern Europe and the Middle East during December posed challenges that Reagan foreign policy was unprepared to meet. One of the stars of his cast, David Stockman, and several of the supporting players were suddenly drawing harsh reviews. Most important, the national economy was not yet responding to Reaganomics, the plot line that had dominated act one.

The search for great expectations had found only trepidation. Investment in capital goods was not merely stalled, but continued to creep in reverse. The Commerce Department's "Index of Leading Indicators," considered a reliable harbinger of overall economic activity, showed what seemed to be a favorable blip in December—a rise of six tenths of a point. Secretary Baldrige made the cautious pronouncement that the statistical improvements "suggests that the recession may soon touch bottom." Alas, when these same figures were refined later, it turned out that the index for December had in fact fallen by three tenths of a point. The decline would continue, month by month, into the following autumn.

There was some good news as well, to be sure. Inflation as measured by the Consumer Price Index was being checked much more quickly than anyone had thought possible at the beginning of the year. Also, interest rates finally reached their peak and would soon begin to recede gradually. Each of these favorable developments contained a large catch, however. The descent of inflation was so rapid that it adversely affected tax revenue; this was one of the factors in the deficit boom. The leveling off of interest rates in late 1981, moreover, was still something of an illusion.

Nominal interest rates are what a borrower must pay at any given time. The *real* rates are the difference between the GNP "implicit price deflator" (the best measure of genuine inflation) and the cost of borrowing money. If financial markets are gaining confidence, real interest rates should go down about as rapidly as the inflation rate falls. In late 1981 the opposite was still happening. Using short-term Treasury Bills as one representative guide, it was not too difficult to calculate that the real rate had risen from 5 percent in the second quarter of the year to 5.5 percent in the third quarter to 8.2 percent in the final quarter. That last horrendous number compared to only 3.8 percent in the final three months of the previous year.[1] This was just one measure of how poorly Stockman's psychological warfare had done and what great impact the Fed's stringent monetarism was having.

In immediate political terms, the most dramatic problem was jobs. Unemployment figures gathered as Christmas approached would show a December rate of 8.9 percent, up half a point in just one month.* Translated into people, that meant 9.4 million without jobs, not counting a million or more so-called "discouraged workers" who had dropped from the labor force, and the statistical averages, because they no longer sought employment.

The political consolation of falling consumer prices—down to an annualized rate of only 4.9 percent in December and plunging still further in the new year—could carry Reagan only so far. The Yankelovich firm, doing one of its periodic polls for *Time,* asked voters if they felt better off than they had the previous year. Fifty-nine percent said no and only 36 percent answered yes.[2] That survey and others, however, also showed that the public by and large was still giving Reagan the

* Unemployment grew even worse in 1982, hovering above 10 percent through early 1983—the highest rate since the Great Depression.

benefit of the doubt. There was still an attitude that his approach deserved more time to work.

What troubled Reagan's political strategists were the trend lines, particularly among working class voters who had made so large a difference in 1980, and whose continued support would be necessary to sustain Republican strength in 1982. Richard Wirthlin sent a confidential memo to the White House dated February 2. It reflected his firm's constant opinion tracking during prior months. Like the public pollsters, Wirthlin detected residual patience concerning the Administration's economic program. Then he added a huge caveat: ". . . ratings from blue collar workers, on the other hand, have dropped precipitously over the past year. In February 1981, 75 percent of the blue collar respondents felt that the program would help; now only 51 percent of them feel this way."

To White House political advisers like James Baker and Ed Rollins, findings like these were ominous. To the Administration's economic experts and generalists alike, the worsening deficit forecasts were just as nervous-making. Since the collapse of the "fall offensive" in November nothing had been done to blot up the red ink. Now the Administration was preparing the fiscal '83 budget, to be submitted in February, soon after Reagan's first State of the Union address. The Reaganauts were eager to begin a new campaign to restore fiscal order, and the issues remained depressingly familiar. High defense spending was still an obstacle. The revenue loss resulting from the historic tax-cut bill had to be offset to some degree. Means had to be found to curb the increases in "entitlement" spending. Cost of living allowances (COLA's) tied to the Consumer Price Index remained a politically sensitive problem.

Those dealing with Reagan found him resisting this accumulation of bad economic news and warnings of worse to come with amazing fortitude. He simply did not believe in the long-range forecasts, or so he insisted in both private and public comments. He did believe, devoutly, that the program already in place would soon begin to work.

The famous Reagan humor remained intact, a quality that affected his subordinates as well. At his December 17 press conference, in which virtually every question was based on adversity either at home or abroad, Reagan got a small laugh when he cracked: "I've come to the conclusion that there is a worldwide plot to make my job more difficult almost any day that I go to the office." At the White House Christmas party three days later, someone with a keen sense of irony cast Richard Darman as Santa. A world-class curmudgeon and among the most energetic of those pressing Reagan to adjust his policies, Santa Darman

pulled from his sack a note, typed on White House memo paper, as
Reagan's present.

> FOR THE PRESIDENT:
> Heretofore Missing Economic Forecast Found . . .
>
> Deficit/Surplus
>
> FY '83   FY '84   FY '85
> −50   +75   +200

SANTA

Reagan and Darman traded ho-ho-ho's in front of the White House
staff. In private, they resumed their real roles. Reagan saw his as
defending both the premise and the particulars of Reaganomics. Darman, along with Baker, Stockman, Fuller and the Republican Senate
leadership, saw theirs as "educating" Reagan enough to alter the particulars in order to salvage the premise. Astride his valiant little pony
of optimism, Reagan was in fact surrounded by the subordinates
closest to him.

With briefings, memoranda and meetings with outsiders, the Baker
group tried to win in a winter siege at least part of what they had lost
in their fall offensive. Typical of their tactics was a meeting staged on
December 18, during which five Republican senators, including Reagan's friend Paul Laxalt, tried to get across the message that seemed
obvious to everyone except Reagan and the supply-siders. Majority
Leader Howard Baker started off by emphasizing the political dangers
of allowing high deficits to persist. Not much more could be saved
from discretionary spending, Baker argued: "cutting isn't going to do
the job by itself even if we cut entitlements." He urged that additional
revenue be raised by attacking tax loopholes—including some of the
new ones provided by the 1981 law—and raising excise levies. He also
proposed some pressure on the Fed to relax interest rates. "Paul
Volcker needs to get his foot off our neck for a little while," Baker
remarked.

Domenici, the Budget Committee chairman, told Reagan what the
President always loathed hearing: that prospective deficits piling up
over three years would be larger than those of the Johnson, Nixon,
Ford and Carter administrations *combined*. Domenici, of course, dis-
counted the discredited estimates still circulated by Stockman's Office
of Management and Budget. Like most others on the Hill, Domenici
based his planning on the more bearish figures of the nonpartisan Congressional Budget Office.

Dole, head of the Finance Committee, seconded his colleagues and added some details concerning prospective revenue sources. Like Domenici, Dole was willing to tell Reagan what he preferred not to hear. A Kansas conservative hardly known as a bleeding heart, Dole nonetheless insisted that the Republicans must show more "compassion" for the needy. I don't propose to cut food stamp spending further, Dole said, if Cap Weinberger doesn't do something about the defense budget.

The pessimist in the room from whom Reagan wanted least to hear was Laxalt. Unlike Howard Baker and the committee heads—Mark Hatfield of the Appropriations Committee was present and complaining as well—Laxalt was a certified Reaganaut of many years' standing. Laxalt had not only been a personal supporter and friend; he was a philosophical clone. Yet here was Laxalt lending his support to the orthodox Republicans, the ones who had scoffed at Reagan in 1968, supported Ford in 1976 and opposed Reagan during the 1980 primaries. We have to have credible numbers, Laxalt insisted, pointing toward balance in 1984 if at all possible. Otherwise we will not be able to get additional civilian spending cuts. Further, Laxalt argued, defense spending must bear some of the burden.

If none of this was really new to Reagan, neither was his response. He answered his visitors, all of them well informed on fiscal affairs, as if they were a group of provincial journalists in town for some sightseeing and brainwashing. "I'm in some disagreement," Reagan began. He repeated his view that "the worst thing Congress has done" was to lay out the long-range forecasting process. That was a numbers game and the real math of the situation was impossible to get at. The President insisted that his program really had not started yet and that the Kennedy tax cuts of the early 1960s produced the increased economic activity expected of them.* Concerning the tax cut and revenue, Reagan maintained that it was still his goal to reduce the proportion of GNP extracted by federal taxes. Weinberger, he assured the Senate leaders, was diligently searching for savings that would not impede the military buildup. And if it came to a choice between national security needs versus a balanced budget, Reagan as Commander in Chief would have to come down on the side of defense spending. Anyway, Reagan said, he still believed that more could be saved from general government overhead, perhaps as much as $40 billion.

Neither side was moved. Domenici came back hard, trying to make

---

* The first cut in personal tax rates, 5 percent, had taken effect October 1, 1981. However, the investment incentives for business had been made retroactive to the previous January 1. In his frequent allusions to the Kennedy tax program, Reagan always ignored the large differences in underlying economic conditions twenty years earlier.

Reagan understand that even the most generous estimate of increasing economic activity flowing from the tax reductions would still not close the gap. The recession had caused too large a discrepancy. The meeting ended inconclusively. I have reviewed the highlights of that mid-December session not because it was unique. Rather, it was representative of what Reagan was hearing—and rebuffing—during this period. Soon after his exchange with the Senate leaders, I had an opportunity to talk to Reagan alone about what had become a running debate between him and his closest advisers, with increased revenue at the core of the argument. With infinite patience, he rehearsed the basics of Reaganomics and reaffirmed his determination to stay the course. He agreed with an observation that it might be mid-1982 before he knew whether he was right. Then we talked about the advocates he was opposing:

> *Reagan:* . . . those people who kind of chickened a little when they saw this [recession and deficit problem], they turned immediately to increased revenue. Well, we've had increased revenues. We've had the greatest tax increases in our history in these recent decades, and they never accomplished anything except increased government spending and deficits.
> *Question:* But those who chickened a little, as you put it . . . are among the architects of your original program.
> *Reagan:* Well, yes, but it was when the situation changed that suddenly they wanted to retreat, and my own feeling—you could call it optimism—is, we haven't even seen the program work yet . . . Some of the critics of the program started jumping on it before it was even in effect, before October 1, and literally were saying that somehow our program had something to do with the economic conditions.
> *Question:* I wasn't even thinking about the critics. I was thinking of your own troops.
> *Reagan:* Well—[3]

Some of the more imaginative of the White House chickens, meanwhile, had been trying to hatch a large egg, one with a double yoke. They were looking for a policy initiative that would give the Administration something positive—and new—on which to focus in 1982. While they were at it, they hoped to shape the scheme in such a way as to yield enough additional revenue to make a noticeable dent in the fiscal '83 deficit and beyond. The idea on which they fastened offered yet a third advantage. It was one of Reaganism's core tenets, the beginning of a transfer to state control of governmental functions which the federal government had gradually captured since the New Deal. The program would be called simply Federalism, or sometimes the New Federalism. A more apt title would have been Statism, but that had a negative, regressive ring to it.

Reagan had made that transfer one of his cardinal goals for many years. During 1981 Martin Anderson's Office of Policy Development and Rich Williamson's Office of Intergovernmental Affairs mulled ways to start the process. But the work went slowly and failed to produce a plan that seemed both viable and sufficiently ambitious. On November 16, Deaver began to have occasional meetings of what he called the Communications Strategy Group. Its self-assigned franchise was much broader than public relations. Its larger purpose was to anticipate problems and propose the means—particularly the use of Reagan's time—for meeting them. As usual, Darman and Fuller provided the staff support. The agenda for the first meeting included, under the heading of "Problems (some)," these three items:

• "disarray"
• State-of-the-Union [address] that, as of now, would be short on "the lift of a driving dream"
• few opportunities for legislative "victories" in next six months—and prospect of serious difficulties re, e.g., debt ceiling . . .

Under the heading "Need (some)" were a variety of propositions, including:

• economic program adjustment that resolves the substantive dilemma in a way that is politically and substantively saleable
• strong State of Union—with domestic and foreign program to advance right through '82 elections, and with coherent/thoughtful/first-class domestic and foreign back-up document
• low cost/high payoff initiatives for State of Union (enterprise zones, health research initiative(s)? space? "states-as-laboratories" program? other such

Gradually, attention shifted to the so-called enterprise zones, which Reagan had also talked about during 1980, and to state assumption of domestic programs.* Stockman undertook the task of translating these into hard proposals. In Stockman's hands, Federalism soon became an

---

* The enterprise-zone scheme was one of the few Administration proposals aimed at providing specific help for impoverished inner-city neighborhoods and deteriorating rural areas as well. The main idea was to designate zones in need of help and to encourage business development in them by means of tax breaks and related incentives. The proposal seemed reasonable enough, but it went forward late and still had not been enacted at the end of 1982. It was separate from the Federalism idea, which in gestation included establishment of a small fund to encourage states to experiment with innovative social programs—the so-called "states-as-laboratories" approach. The latter struck some officials as too similar to Great Society thinking and was quietly dropped before the larger scheme was announced.

imaginative, complex scheme, which Williamson would have to sell to
governors and mayors. One major phase involved the so-called "swap"
of large activities. States and localities would assume full responsibility
for food stamp distribution as well as for the main component of welfare, the troublesome program called Aid to Families with Dependent
Children (AFDC). These had traditionally been shared between federal and state authorities. In exchange, Washington would take over
the entire burden of Medicaid, which provides health services for the
poor. Ostensibly, the swap would have simplified administration, promoted efficiency and cost the states nothing.

The second phase envisaged assignment to the states of roughly forty
other specific programs in the social welfare, health, education and
transportation fields, among others. During a four-year transition period, cash to compensate the states would come from a trust fund fed
by the proceeds of certain federal excise taxes. At the end of the four
years, the fund would expire and so would the levies. States could then
choose to impose the taxes on their own—while continuing the programs or some other functions—or states could bail out altogether.

All this was couched in terms of Federalism, a.k.a. Reaganism, with
the purpose of diminishing Washington's role in American society. Individual states would have more leeway in determining what governmental services would be provided (or abolished, in some cases). But
Stockman and his accomplices worked into this long-range program a
short-range device for ameliorating the immediate deficit problem. A
number of excise tax rates would be increased in fiscal '83. That, together with some smaller revenue measures such as the closing of certain loopholes, would have produced some quick cash—$40 billion or
so in the first year.

Some of these plans began to leak out even before the Stockman
group formally put the idea to Reagan in meetings on December 22
and 23. The news accounts depicted the plan as a means of evading
Reagan's resistance to just about any significant revenue measures in
the budget being constructed. The President could still joke about it at
that stage; at the first of the two meetings, as he heard some of the details, he cracked: "The papers are right. You *are* plotting against me."
In fact, he was coming to resent the inference that he was being manipulated on the tax issue.

With the wound of the Greider article still fresh, Stockman chose not
to make the main presentation to Reagan. Don Regan was persuaded
to do it instead. That was a shrewd gimmick because the Treasury Secretary, while mindful of the deficit problem, was not a full member of
the Baker-Stockman faction and was less enthusiastic about new reve-

nue measures. To have him carry the campaign now might impress Reagan more.

In any event, Reagan appeared receptive during the December 23 conference. "I think it's on the right track," he commented. He also harked back to his own much earlier Federalism ideas, which included assigning a portion of income tax collected within each state to finance the assumption of programs. Regan pointed out that would require still other revenue sources to compensate for the loss. The President accepted that and commented genially: "I recognized that you were slipping in the [excise] tax increase." After some further discussion Meese steered the session to a positive conclusion. "This is a go-ahead, Mr. President?" he asked. Yes, Reagan said, authorizing his advisers to put the plan into final shape. The participants also agreed to maintain secrecy more effectively than they had been doing. Reagan signed no decision memorandum and, for the record at least, his options were still fully open.

A month later, on January 20, firm decisions were required. The State of the Union speech would be delivered in just six days and shortly after that the new budget would be unveiled. Reagan, the Legislative Strategy Group, Regan, Stockman and Marty Anderson assembled in the Cabinet Room for a hard look at the fine print of the Federalism idea. For the first time, Anderson argued against the scheme as it then stood. He said that excise taxes should not be raised and that the scope of the Federalism program should be reduced. That tax increase, Anderson felt, violated the spirit of Reaganomics. Reagan responded by saying that relatively small revenue measures for specific, desirable ends were acceptable provided that the total was only a minor proportion of the tax cuts enacted the previous year.

Darman had a detailed decision paper in hand. He went down a checklist of items, with dollar amounts, which Reagan was accepting, modifying or in a few cases rejecting. Yes, there could be a small increase in the minimum tax paid by corporations. No, he would not buy the eight-cent hike on gasoline per gallon; he could live with four cents. Beer would be exempt from additional tax; purchasers of fur, leather goods and other "luxuries" would have to pay more. And so on. The decisions hardly amounted to a major turnaround on the revenue question, but they represented a symbolic change. It could be conveyed as a signal that Reagan was willing to adjust in order to meet altered conditions.

That was on Wednesday, the twentieth. Thursday morning, rumors of the decision leaked into print, again making it appear that Reagan was being euchred into something against his better judgment. He also participated in a White House breakfast with leaders of the United

States Chamber of Commerce. The business community, which had given virtually unanimous support to Reaganomics in early 1981, was divided by the end of the year. Executives of some of the largest blue-chip corporations and Wall Street analysts were terrified by the deficits. Many of them favored the orthodox Republican approach. Groups representing smaller enterprises, for the most part, still resisted any revenue measures. The U.S. Chamber, with a broad, Main Street-minded constituency, was in the latter camp.

Guests at the breakfast gave Reagan two messages. Any tax increase would be a grave mistake; it would be a reversal of what the Chamber's membership at both the national and local levels had campaigned for so energetically the previous spring and summer. It would delay the recovery. Second, Reagan should look more closely for expendable items in the Pentagon budget. The President got the first message much more clearly than the second. Immediately after the meeting, Reagan told his aides that he wanted to review the entire question again. No one came up with new arguments one way or another the rest of that day, however. Thursday evening Darman drafted a new decision document reopening everything that had been settled the day before.

Precisely what changed Reagan's mind remained unclear. Much of the commentary at the time attributed his reversal to the Chamber breakfast, but Reagan heard nothing new there which he had not heard repeatedly from others. Friday morning, before leaving for a Camp David weekend, Reagan told Baker, Meese, Deaver and Clark that he had been troubled by the tax issue for weeks. "I haven't been able to sleep because of this," Deaver recalled Reagan saying. "I just can't do it." Reagan looked relieved. "He stood up and was bouncing again," Deaver said soon afterward. "He felt better down to his toes. He was comfortable again. You shouldn't try to change him on certain basic things and it was a mistake for us to try."[4] To a few other advisers, Reagan explained with a grin: "I just let you think I agreed with you so you'd leave me alone for a while."

In light of what happened later, his turnabout between Thursday afternoon and Friday morning remained a fascinating little puzzle. I took a final crack at solving it during a conversation with him the following November 3. He started a lengthy explanation by saying that technical problems had arisen in the proposed distribution to the states of proceeds from the tax increases. Yet none of the experts involved at the time had considered such difficulties very serious.

When I pointed out that part of the original purpose, in the short run, was to reduce the federal deficit for 1983, Reagan recoiled. "Well," he replied, "I must say this. I had never thought of the Federalism plan as part of balancing the budget. I thought that the only plus for both the local and state governments and ourselves would be one that you could not in advance give figures on. It would be the . . . reduced administrative overhead . . ."

It was a most revealing commentary. Reagan could not have been unaware of the revenue implications of the program; they had been spelled out in the written material and the verbal briefings he received. But he chose to ignore that aspect of the package, as if exploiting it for the purpose of deficit reduction sullied the purity of Federalism's larger goal—the diminution of Washington's role in society as an absolute good in itself. And, because he was still denying the severity of the revenue shortfall, his internal logic led him to avert his eyes from the practical implications of what his advisers proposed to do.

Presidential psychology aside, the reversal in January left the senior White House staff distressed and, at least temporarily, disarmed. The rough outlines of what happened became general knowledge within a few days. Reagan had broken the siege imposed by his own people. Implicitly, at least, he had also given them a warning: don't crowd me. The advisers took that admonition seriously. Meeting in Baker's office, they decided, as one of them put it later, that "the President would have to hear it from others." The "it," of course, was the old litany of reasons why he was wrong.

For the moment, there were other urgent tasks to perform. The State of the Union speech had to be completed. The fiscal '83 budget had to be closed. Reagan went ahead with the Federalism proposal, done up as a major new concept, and also laid out the enterprise-zone scheme. They attracted attention, as planned, but also caused some confusion. It was obvious that the Federalism initiative would be highly controversial. The specifics would be the subject of indefinite wrangling with governors and mayors, many of whom saw as its main effect an abrogation of federal responsibility for the poor. To a considerable extent, they were right.

Had the scheme gone on the table during a time of general prosperity, it probably would have received serious consideration by Congress early in the new year. The proposal, whatever its flaws, did address the serious problem of bifurcated authority and overlapping programs that had become a drain for all levels of government. Coming as it did in the midst of a deep recession, when state and local authorities were already struggling with their own deficits and attempting to swallow the cuts in federal assistance imposed during 1981, Federalism seemed downright irrelevant as well as threatening. Thus it would be shunted aside for the balance of the year.

There was more interest in what Reagan would propose for fiscal '83. That too was clear in the January 26 address. It would be more of the same, with no concession at all to the recession and deficit problems. Reagan sounded more gritty than ever when he gave this pledge in his speech to Congress:

> I will not ask you to try to balance the budget on the backs of the taxpayers. I will seek no tax increases this year and I have no intention of retreating from our basic program of tax relief. I promised the American people to bring their tax rates down and to keep them down—to provide them incentives to rebuild our economy, to save, to invest in America's future. I will stand by my word. Tonight I am urging the American people: seize these new opportunities to produce, to save and to invest, and together we will make this economy a mighty engine of freedom, hope and prosperity again.

Those lines were among the several passages Reagan personally inserted late in the drafting process. He was writing from the heart. In the weeks to come, in speeches to state legislatures on his Federalism program, Reagan repeated the same message over and over. The President was on an anti-tax tear as fervent as any he had indulged in since his speeches for Goldwater in 1964.

To some of his associates Reagan seemed possessed by the conviction that he had to stop the liberals who desired nothing but to "tax and tax, spend and spend," as he put it. On January 29, the last day changes could be made in the '83 budget to be published ten days later (to take effect October 1, 1982), there was a review of some final details. A handful of revenue measures survived, adding up to a piddling $7 billion, compared to the nearly $40 billion prior to his reversal on the excise issue. These were items, for the most part, which Reagan himself had first proposed in 1981, but which had been rejected by Congress. One provision was aimed at improving collection of taxes due on dividends and bank interest by a method similar to ordinary income tax withholding. Reagan bridled at this one. "I've always thought," he remarked, "that withholding is government putting the cost of collecting on the private sector without compensation." Another revenue measure was to improve overall enforcement by strengthening Internal Revenue Service resources. That bothered him, Reagan said, because it seemed intended to increase the burden on taxpayers. He finally accepted both, but only with the proviso that they be presented as attempts to be fair to good citizens who paid their full share. He wanted no implication that his administration was simply tightening screws to improve the Treasury's yield.

The budget that finally emerged was a political impossibility. It called for spending of $757 billion, an increase of just $32 billion over the latest estimate for fiscal '82. Defense outlays, however, would rise

$33 billion. That, together with unavoidable hikes for debt service and other uncontrollable expenses, would mean significant reductions in a variety of "discretionary" accounts. Further reductions in social welfare activities of all kinds would be necessary. Despite the relatively modest overall increase, an '83 deficit of $91 billion was projected—or $89 billion more than the long-range estimate first put on the table the previous March. Further, and most importantly, virtually no one sophisticated in federal budget making believed the numbers. On Capitol Hill, on Wall Street, among economics writers—in Stockman's OMB as well—these figures were taken with shrugs and winks. Gargantuan as the deficit projection was, it was still too optimistic.* Beyond that, Congress in an election year was not going to cooperate in additional domestic economies while allowing the Pentagon to rush ahead full throttle. And Stockman, desperate still to show a declining deficit path, had built into the budget several gimmicks that simply could not be made to work. Republicans and Democrats alike in Congress concluded immediately that major changes would have to be made.

Attacks by the Democrats came, as expected, in partisan profusion. The Republicans were not far behind. Senate Budget Chairman Domenici, whose cooperation was essential, was blunt when he addressed a business group in New York soon after the budget was announced: "The President's plan will not pass Congress in its present form . . . It fails to do enough to cut spending and accepts almost benignly what are malignant deficits."[5] Through the rest of February direct and indirect reaction was uniformly negative. Stock and bond prices fell. The prime rate, which had been declining nicely, began to inch back up. Six national associations representing bankers, builders and realtors took out full-page advertisements in large newspapers, demanding that Reagan change course to avoid "economic and financial crisis."

Reagan was defiant—at least in public. "Let me be honest with you," he told a Washington convention of the National Association of Manufacturers. "I have been a little disappointed lately with some in the business community who have forgotten that feeding more dollars to government is like feeding a stray pup. It just follows you home and sits on your doorstep asking for more." On a swing through the Midwest, he berated the "paid political complainers" and challenged the House Democrats to "put up or shut up." Unlike his advisers,

* In January 1983, a quarter of the way into the fiscal year, the current deficit seemed certain to exceed $200 billion. The principal reason was the slow pace of economic recovery. Even if the new Congress adopted all the austerity measures being planned for submission later in the winter, the '83 deficit could not be trimmed very much.

Reagan was taking his new fiscal plan seriously. "The budget we have proposed," he said, "is a line drawn in the dirt."

Jim Baker and his group cringed at rhetoric like that. Ken Duberstein, recently promoted to head the Legislative Liaison office, knew from his constant patrols of the Hill that in the Administration's second spring confrontation would fail. It would be impossible to reassemble the same coalition that had worked so effectively the year before. In the absence of a united Republican front, rebel Democrats, even if they wanted to, could not fill out a viable majority. This time the Administration would have to attempt to deal with the Democratic leadership, to probe for compromise at the top. That would be a stark change. It would go against the grain of Reagan's every competitive instinct, not to mention some of his favorite policies.

This view was widely shared in the White House. The question was how to persuade Reagan. None of the senior advisers wanted to repeat the public humiliation they had suffered in late January, when Reagan had abruptly broken the siege. None of them wanted to go head-to-head with the President until he was softened up to some extent, or until he realized on his own that a significant change was imperative. So they undertook a tactic similar to Deaver's approach the previous fall when he set out to persuade Reagan that Dick Allen had to be let go. They let others bring the bad news to the chief.

This was not difficult because Deaver and Darman between them controlled most of the traffic, human and documentary, that reached Reagan. Important business leaders who favored a compromise were brought in for private conversations. Supply-siders like Jack Kemp, who opposed any tinkering with taxes, were excluded. The staff, if they could help it, would not permit a repeat of the Chamber breakfast. On the other hand, a luncheon with Commerce Secretary Malcolm Baldrige could be helpful. In that conversation, on March 11, Baldrige informed Reagan of yet another disappointment that made a large impression on the President. For several months, when pressed to back up his optimism about the economy's prospects for recovery, Reagan frequently mentioned a capital expansion plan announced by the Iron and Steel Institute. Now Baldrige told Reagan that the grandiose project had been shelved indefinitely; there was already so much excess capacity in the industry that no one wanted to invest in new plant facilities, particularly while interest rates were still so high.

Sometimes one of these ploys backfired. A panel of outside economic advisers had been on call for consultation since the beginning of the Administration. Among the prominent members were Alan Greenspan, the banker Walter Wriston, Milton Friedman and, until he became Sec-

retary of State, George Shultz. The committee held a long meeting with
the LSG on February 28, the evening before a review session with
Reagan. In the preparatory conversation, Shultz said it would be "no
calamity" to trim Pentagon spending. Further, he seemed receptive to
new revenue measures. Greenspan was even more open to change. He
talked about the possibility of reducing the recently enacted business
tax changes and postponing or dropping the last installment of the five-
ten-ten income tax reduction, though the latter point was anathema to
Reagan. What the White House must do in political terms, Greenspan
said, was to distinguish between the philosophy of Reaganomics, which
had to be retained, and some of the specific details, which could be
changed as necessary.

That was exactly what the White House staff wanted to hear—and,
more importantly, wanted Reagan to hear from a group which he respected. The next day, however, Shultz had the assignment of summarizing the panel's views for Reagan. Ever cautious in his speech, and
leery of setting the boss's teeth on edge, Shultz gave Reagan a sani-
tized version of the consensus. While he called the deficits "unwel-
come," he did not push for strong measures to reduce them. It was wise
to keep the focus on spending reductions, he said, though he felt that
defense was not a "budget issue." Entitlements had to be the target. In
general, he summed up: "You have it positioned very well, Mr. President."

Greenspan was somewhat bolder. He repeated his line about distin-
guishing between the program's philosophy and its details. Sooner or
later, he said, there would have to be a "package deal" with Congress
—that is with the Democratic leaders. But Reagan had heard what he
wanted to hear from Shultz. He told his visitors how happy he was to
get "reinforcement" for his views and his new budget. Baker and
Stockman concluded that the session was a net loss in their effort to
turn Reagan around.

Reagan participated in yet another meeting with the Senate Republican leadership on March 9. Again he was reminded that his budget
would get exactly nowhere unless there was a bipartisan deal including
a far larger revenue component than he had been willing to endorse
until then. Meanwhile, Jim Baker, Darman, Stockman and Regan were
preparing a new pitch, business-like but dense in content, because the
White House was running out of time as quickly as the economy was
slipping further downhill. They had to strangle Reagan's pony.

They secured a memorandum from Howard Baker which summarized the forbidding outlook in the Republican-controlled Senate.
The Economic Policy Advisory Board was convened again, but this
time it met with Regan, rather than Reagan, and the Treasury Secretary recorded the consultants' views in a confidential report to the Pres-

ident dated March 19. In ten numbered paragraphs, Regan conveyed a much more bearish message than Reagan had heard the previous month, including these observations:

2) . . . most members were convinced that the recovery from the current recession would *not* meet the Administration's economic assumptions in the budget. Most felt that real growth and nominal GNP would prove sluggish during much of 1982. The group as a whole were [sic] more gloomy than I have ever seen them.

3) There was agreement that the greatest barrier to a healthy and sustained recovery was high interest rates. The central task facing the Administration was getting interest rates down as soon as possible.

4) Most felt that large prospective budget deficits (1983 and beyond) are the primary cause for the high levels of current interest rates, and that the financial markets are convinced that deficits and prospective deficits matter, regardless of the academic debate on the subject . . .

Stockman prepared a new, thirty-two-page briefing paper labeled "extremely confidential" and dated March 17. With charts, graphs and deadpan prose, the Budget Director pleaded his case yet one more time. Though the document did not say so explicitly, the implicit message was that the warnings contained in his Dunkirk Memo of 1980 were beginning to come true. "Administration policy and political decisions," Stockman now said, "have progressively insulated *90 percent of the fiscal equation* from consideration. Unless all policies are reviewed —defense, tax, entitlement—severe fiscal, financial and economic disorder is increasingly probable." Stockman also pointed out that, in constant dollars, the current military buildup would cost nearly double the increase incurred during the height of the Vietnam war.*

Darman prepared a forty-two-page report, dated March 18, which he gave to Reagan in a blue ring binder. This document was ostensibly free of advocacy. Darman billed it as a "relatively objective review" of reaction of all kinds—from economists, the press, Congress, the financial markets, special interest groups and opinion polls—to the Administration's policy since January. The upshot was unmistakable: the Administration's current course was leading nowhere. Further, popular support for Reagan's specific policies had turned down sharply immediately after the wall-to-wall criticism of the February budget presentation.

Wirthlin, updating the survey report mentioned at the beginning of this chapter, now had figures showing a dramatic change. His November tracking showed 56 percent of the public opting to continue Reaganomics without change and 20 percent believing that those

---

* In constant 1982 dollars, including related foreign aid expenses and military items outside the Defense Department, Stockman showed a comparison of $50 billion for the fiscal years 1964–68, compared with $90 billion for 1981–85.

policies were hurting the country. In late February only 39 percent supported the "continue as is" option—a startling drop of 17 points— and 37 percent now believed Reaganomics was hurting. Only 9 percent thought that White House policies were helping. Jim Baker put an asterisk on that page of his copy and wrote *"erosion"* across the chart.

Darman concluded his review by citing the "general type of package" that might sell in Congress. It included a Pentagon reduction of between $7 billion and $10 billion for fiscal '83 with commensurate cuts later, an additional $15 billion in revenue measures and a rearrangement of proposed spending reductions already requested. "This is not to suggest," Darman added cautiously, "that such a package—if indeed it were feasible—would or should be accepted by the Administration."

All this material was in Reagan's hands on March 19, when he sat down with Meese, Baker and Deaver in the Oval Office. Reagan was about to make one of the most important domestic policy decisions of his presidency but there was no formal options paper on his desk. There would be no cabinet meeting on the subject, no repetitious discussion of details with the economic experts. In fact, nearly all his other advisers, including Regan and Stockman, would remain ignorant of the specific guidelines Reagan gave Chief of Staff Baker during that conversation. First and most importantly, Baker was deputized to open negotiations with Tip O'Neill. The goal would be a mutually acceptable compromise to break the fiscal impasse and allow adoption of a First Budget Resolution more or less on schedule in mid-May. Initially, at least, this initiative would not be presented either to the Democratic leadership or the world at large as "negotiations." Baker's charter would be described in more modest terms: ostensibly he was authorized merely to listen, to explore. However, at the same meeting, Reagan agreed to the specific limits he could tolerate. Baker noted them in a cryptic shorthand on a yellow routing slip which had paste on one edge.

Reagan would agree to scale back the 1983 Pentagon increase by up to $10 billion. He would accept revenue measures of $15 billion beyond the token items already proposed. He would swallow these two pills provided that the House Democrats went along with the $56 billion in spending reductions, or their equivalent, called for in the budget already announced. If it became necessary to shift more of the burden to cost of living allowance reductions, the Administration had to get the House leadership's support in securing them so that Republicans and Democrats could share the political blame.

Essentially, Reagan was going along with the figures outlined in the conclusion of Darman's review. No one could know the limits Reagan was setting, or even that the guidelines existed, because if the figures leaked out they would become the floor from which the White House would have to bargain upward. Reagan insisted that they be the ceiling. At that stage Reagan authorized Baker to inform only one other official, Darman, because he would be deeply involved in the complicated process about to get underway. During the intricate bargaining that took place through the end of April, none of the other players in the Administration or on Capitol Hill were aware that Reagan had set dollar ceilings, let alone what they were.

For Reagan, who placed so high a value on consistency, the change of course that he authorized on March 19 was jarring. In a speech just the day before he had used one of his favorite formulations: "Increasing taxes only encourages government to continue its irresponsible spending habits. We can lecture it about extravagance till we're blue in the face or we can discipline it by cutting its allowance." Now he was opting to raise the allowance.

He could console himself with the knowledge that the adjustment was relatively minor. As Greenspan had suggested the month before, Reagan was now tolerating alterations of detail in order to defend the basic philosophy of his program. He would insist on retaining the five-ten-ten formula and on further civilian spending cuts. Still, he had resisted even these minor concessions for many months. He had turned his back on opportunities to seek a deal with the House Democrats before. He yielded only when the realities of the situation gave him virtually no alternative.

Reagan and his advisers had no way of knowing, in mid-March, whether a bargain could in fact be struck. They knew only that the attempt must be made for the sake of both politics and economics. If paralysis were to persist, they could not allow the Democrats to blame the White House for the ruinous deadlock. That would make too potent an issue in the fall elections. Rather, the White House would have to set up O'Neill and his committee chairmen as the heavies.

Politics aside, it would be a coup if the financial markets and the business community at large saw that the leadership of both parties could find an accommodation leading to lower deficits. That would be a long step toward restoring confidence. The road to compromise would take the travelers through some hairpin turns in the months that followed. The pilgrims at both ends of Pennsylvania Avenue would have to improvise as they haggled, came together, fell out again while blundering along. The next phase of the journey took them nowhere near the promised land of prosperity, but at least they were able to back away from the disaster that threatened in the spring of 1982.

20

Gang Warfare

The site reeked of history and tradition. A century ago Presidents came
to the small, square chamber off the Senate floor to sign legislation
approved late in the session. Now the President's Room looks like a
miniature museum, with portraits of forgotten cabinet officers on the
walls and a heroic montage of New World explorers on the ceiling. For
decades the antique clock adorning the marble mantel has been
stopped at nine forty-five.

At 2 P.M. on April 28, 1982, the occasion bore no resemblance to
custom. The President had come not to sign a bill or to preside at a
ceremony. He was there to bargain, personally, with the Speaker of the
House of Representatives over fiscal decisions affecting the next three
years. The confrontation was without precedent in living memory. Success or failure would influence the national economy's performance,
and therefore the daily lives of millions. It could also have a bearing
on the elections the following fall.

Neither the weight of the stakes nor the unique nature of the moment
affected the two aging Irishmen, Reagan and O'Neill, during the pre-
liminaries. Grudgingly, O'Neill consented to sit next to Reagan for the
obligatory "photo opportunity," but wanted it noted that he would
move to the other side of the mahogany table to join his Democratic
colleagues for the real business. The Speaker had been in politics too
long not to understand that the White House crowd was manipulating
him for its own purposes. He was not a man who gave away points easily.

Reagan too followed his reflexes. In a tense situation with other
strong-willed men, he resorts to humor as an opener. One can only

imagine what the shades of patrician Presidents hovering in the ornate sanctum thought of Reagan's choice of thigh-slapper. It seems that an Irishwoman of limited education is instructed by her doctor to produce a specimen for a laboratory test. Not wishing to display her ignorance, she goes home and asks her Irish neighbor—nasty person though the neighbor is—what a specimen is. A few minutes later she returns to her house bruised and disheveled. Obviously there has been violence. What happened? her husband wants to know. Well, says the simple spouse, when I asked what a specimen is she told me to pee in a bottle. So I told her to shit in her hat and the fight was on.

Of course it's better to hear it in brogue, which Reagan does so well. His unsubtle point was that he and O'Neill should avoid conflict based on misunderstanding. On that score the conferees from the House, Senate and White House succeeded. When the meeting ended in deadlock three hours later, neither side was surprised or unclear about the reasons. Each had put his own priorities and its own electoral interests above the need for consensus. The fiscal process would remain in frightening confusion yet a while longer. *The Wall Street Journal* said it all in a four-deck headline:

Economic Hazard

The Budget Impasse
Threatens to Prolong
High Rates, Recession

Financial Markets May Face
More Turmoil, and Some
Fear Rise in Bankruptcies

But President Scores Points[1]

Those tense hours in the President's Room were the climax of an extraordinary six-week period during which the White House and the congressional leadership of both parties had come quite close to performing a rare act of statesmanship. Had they succeeded on April 28, economic recovery would have started earlier. On this point both the participants and disinterested outsiders could agree. The specific terms of a deal, give or take a few billion dollars, would have been less important than the fact that agreement had been reached. Since the previous September Washington had emitted a steady doleful signal: dysfunction.

The opportunity to end that malady in a single decisive stroke excited Jim Baker. Ordinarily, long, complex projects did not appeal to him. Baker's concentration span set no records in White House annals.

Numbers did not stimulate his adrenal glands. But this venture was different. It was gamesmanship and negotiation for very high stakes. Further, he had a secret that neither his adversaries nor most of his associates would ever learn about. Baker had that yellow routing slip containing the President's limits. Thus he had more authority than his opponents knew. He could maneuver within the franchise given him on March 19 while keeping the threat of presidential disapproval as a check on the other side's demands.

Baker's initial separate contacts with O'Neill, Jones and Rostenkowski were mildly encouraging. None of the Democrats demanded in absolute terms that Reagan give up, or even modify, the third installment of the income tax cut. They seemed willing to consider making some savings on cost of living allowances. Of course there were serious disagreements still. The House Democrats wanted most of the deficit reduction to come from increased revenue and a curb on Pentagon spending. The Administration wanted to keep those changes at a minimum while making economies on civilian spending. In that sense, nothing had changed. But at the end of March the preliminary conversations attended by just a few people indicated some room for compromise.

After a meeting on March 30 in Jim Baker's house, the group was expanded to a total of seventeen representatives from the Administration, Senate and House. O'Neill withdrew from personal participation, putting himself on a par with Reagan as one of the two principals. His chief agent would be Richard Bolling, a shrewd veteran who headed the House Rules Committee. Jones and Rostenkowski also spoke for the House Democrats while Ernest Hollings and Russell Long represented the Senate Democratic minority. As soon as the number of participants was firmly established, the group became known as the Gang of Seventeen.

On April 1 they started a series of long meetings beyond the reach of press coverage—at the Vice-President's residence, Blair House, the Family Theater in the White House basement. OMB supplied budget work-sheet forms. A column on the left listed thirteen categories starting with "Baseline Deficit." Below that crucial item came subheadings for reducing the red ink—trims in cost of living allowances and defense spending, new revenue and all the rest. Appropriately enough, the thirteenth and bottom line was "Remaining Deficit." To the right were three columns, for fiscal '83, '84 and '85. The slots in each column were blank. Success meant filling in those blanks with numbers everyone could live with.

To make the White House position credible to the other side, Reagan's men had to begin by accepting the congressional "baseline deficit" projections, which were more realistic, and therefore higher, than those in the February budget presentation. Then, in meeting after meeting, the participants played with different combinations to get a better—and declining—"Remaining Deficit" line over three years. After the fourth session of the full group, which took place over breakfast at Blair House on April 6, Baker paused to take stock. He was about to fill Reagan in on where things stood. So far he had stayed within his original marching orders. He even had some leeway left in the defense category. A few of the other items were causing difficulty, particularly changes in entitlement formulas and cost of living allowances. Writing marginal notes on his work sheet before seeing Reagan, Baker considered a shortcut. The President was to leave the next day for a short Easter holiday in the Caribbean. Baker wrote to himself: "[Howard] Baker and O'Neill to Barbados for one day. Spur of moment?" That move, Jim Baker suspected, might slice through the details and achieve a quick agreement at the summit. The idea would not fly, however, because the Speaker was too shrewd to risk that. So the skull session went on to give the President a vaguely promising report. The President responded with encouragement to keep at it.

Immediately after the return from Barbados, two Gang of Seventeen sessions were held on April 13. These conversations, the second of which lasted well into the evening, were the most encouraging of all as the Republicans saw it. Darman was able to put together a draft agreement, which the White House hoped would be signed by the President, the Speaker and the Senate Majority Leader. That turned out to be a false spring. The House Democrats began to feel as if they were being trapped into a general understanding of dubious legitimacy. As things were then going, Reagan would get credit for leading everyone out of the wilderness and the Democrats would have to share the blame for lowering pension cost of living adjustments just before the election. Or Reagan might change his mind at the last minute, as he had in January. The larger group went into recess for a few days while informal communication continued.

Duberstein consulted quietly with Rostenkowski, who appeared to be more eager than Bolling to cut a deal. Soon after the conversation, Duberstein made notes for Baker's information.

"We still don't trust each other," Rostenkowski said of the larger group. "Can you deliver the President on this package?"

"Can you promise," Duberstein countered, "the third year [of the personal income tax cut] will be preserved? Then we'll be in the ball park."

"I can't promise that," the Ways and Means chairman conceded.

"We have to be able to assure the President that the third year is at minimum risk."

"I can't say that."

Other channels were even more circuitous. On the morning of April 16, with the official talks still in recess, Jim Baker received a memo from one of his assistants: "Alan Greenspan called. He said that he had talked to Louis Harris [the pollster with Democratic connections] who had been called by Tip O'Neill. Tip wants talks to succeed. He feels he needs protection for November and is fearful they will fall apart. Harris believes Tip needs a personal signal from the President."

The Democrats were becoming more apprehensive than ever, and they had good reason to be. Though the Reaganauts had attempted initially to maintain secrecy, leaks were trickling from both the Hill and the White House. Some of these accounts depicted O'Neill as willing to yield considerable ground on cost of living allowances while getting little in return. If this impression took hold, the Democrats would be surrendering a plump election issue; since the previous spring they had been accusing Reagan of heartlessness toward the old folks. Now the Democrats began to fear that they were being jerked around like puppets. They were being asked to save Reagan from the consequences of his own mistakes. In that rescue effort they would have to accept a full share of political liability of new austerity measures. The heart of Reaganomics meanwhile would be retained and Reagan's capacity for strong leadership reconfirmed.

As the White House negotiators reconstructed it afterward, the House Democrats in mid-April made a strategic decision to pull back. Bolling insisted otherwise. "If they thought that," he said later, "they must have been remarkably insensitive. From the very beginning I repeatedly said that I wasn't going to have any proposition until I thought they had been forthcoming enough for me to feel there were grounds for hope." As Bolling saw it, that day never came. Rather, the White House still was acting out a deliberate strategy to "starve the social programs." Reagan was never willing to go for as much additional revenue as Bolling thought necessary. Nor were the White House representatives prepared to deal in specifics.

"The papers were always their papers. The figures were always their figures. I kept saying that I had to have a whole package and look at the detail. I was looking for the smaller pieces that would tell me who was going to get screwed on health care, food stamps, and all the rest." Yet, at the beginning, Bolling did think they might succeed. He believed that Baker yearned for understanding as much as he did. "If it hadn't been for Jim Baker, I would probably have blown it up pretty early. I think he felt we really needed a compromise because the country needed it. Baker and I understood that." Yet Bolling feared that Baker did not actually speak for Reagan and that the Democrats were being "manipulated" in subtle ways.[2]

These anxieties began to show when the full group gathered again on Sunday, April 18, in the Roosevelt Room of the White House. Darman had his draft agreement ready for discussion. The White House at this stage hoped to make a formal announcement two days later, or at least to be able to agree on a firm schedule. That would allow sufficient time for orderly passage of the First Budget Resolution in mid-May, followed by a new Reconciliation Act and related legislation. Bolling, however, raised a number of objections both on procedure and on substance. The Democrats were unwilling to move as quickly as the White House wished. Further, the House leadership wanted to reconsider the cost of living allowance issue and now believed that the revenue measures would have to yield far more in the first year than the group had previously considered.

Reagan's men realized that the deal was slipping away from them. On Tuesday morning Baker and Darman visited Bolling in his office. He gave them more bad news: he had to consult the House Democratic Steering Committee before going any further. This, the White House knew, would only give O'Neill additional qualms because the Steering Committee was more liberal than the leadership. Any deal made would have to be imposed from the top by the Speaker and his lieutenants. If O'Neill and Bolling went to the rank and file now, they would only get an earful of reasons to back away from the kind of compromise Reagan would accept.

Later in the day, the Gang of Seventeen went through the motions again in the White House Family Theater. The mood was testy. Jones complained about the leaks that embarrassed O'Neill. Hollings remarked: "Maybe it's like the Falklands. We need to shed some blood before the parties will come to an agreement." The senior Democrat on the Senate Budget Committee, Hollings also said he doubted that Reagan would help sell a compromise even if one were reached. Like O'Neill, he was understandably worried about the politics of the transaction. Thereupon Jim Baker brought Reagan down to the White House basement for a few minutes alone with Hollings. The President promised that he would personally promote the package.

But would there be any package? Bolling's behavior indicated not. The White House decided that a personal appeal to O'Neill was in order. The idea would be to stiffen the Speaker's backbone before consultations with a large number of Democratic House members put everything out of focus. Reagan phoned O'Neill, stressing that "it's going to be you and me" making the final decision. O'Neill would have none of it. He would not be pressured into a fast decision, not then. The tone between the two grew tense. When Reagan hung up he told his advisers: "There's no reasoning with him."

On Wednesday, Bolling reported back on his meeting with the Steering Committee. There was no consensus in that group, he said, on dealing with Social Security reductions. Everyone had a strong—and separate—opinion. Rostenkowski said the meeting had been "explosive." If the President came out strongly for cost of living allowance reductions, some Democrats would go along. Of course that was exactly what Reagan would not do. Having been so badly burned on the Social Security issue the previous year, he would approach it now only passively, with prominent Democratic accomplices. "I'm totally dejected," Rostenkowski remarked. And Bolling began talking about alternative schemes for saving money on Social Security—but not in fiscal '83.

From the White House viewpoint, the goal of the game now became drastically different. The prospect for agreement that preserved the fundamentals of Reaganomics was approaching nil. Who would get the blame for the breakdown? If the Democrats could be given the goat's horns, it would be good Republican politics. Just as important, if the Democrats could be put on the defensive in public relations terms, it might be less difficult when the White House entered the next arduous round of budget-making in May.

Three more meetings of the Gang of Seventeen took place, but they merely confirmed the impression of imminent deadlock. In public, meanwhile, Reagan was talking about his willingness to "go the extra mile" in order to avert stalemate. The White House decided that, if necessary, that publicity trip should take Reagan two miles to the Speaker's turf for a personal meeting with O'Neill. The symbolism was excellent; the conservative prophet in the White House, with his excellent record for extracting what he wished from the Congress, was willing to go to the liberal mountain, or at least the Hill, in search of a compromise for the national welfare.

Within the Legislative Strategy Group, Reagan's men now calculated that the chances of real success were no better than one in twenty. Darman on April 27 submitted to his colleagues a two-page chronology of what had happened, the point of which was to paint the Democrats as obstructionists. This would be used as public relations fodder after the little summit. He also wrote a succinct memorandum on where things stood. It captured the gamesmanship of the moment perfectly:

> In order to be able to defend the proposition that RR has "gone the extra mile"—
>
>   1) RR needs to seek to meet with O'Neill, *and*

2) RR needs to make O'Neill a thoroughly reasonable offer—that O'Neill will nonetheless reject on the grounds that he will not agree to protect the third year of the tax cut.

The character of such an offer—and the case it would allow RR to make—are suggested by the attached (If there is a worry that O'Neill might accept such an offer, we need to assess: (a) whether we could accept it; and, if not, (b) how to make it more surely unacceptable to O'Neill without seeming either unreasonable or anti-Social Security).

The backup material laid out three alternative propositions, none of which fit well with either Reagan's or O'Neill's real goals. With a brief-case full of ambiguity then, Reagan and his advisers went the next day to the President's Room off the Senate floor. A year after Reagan had employed intransigence to win a series of legislative victories, he now was determined to prove himself a champion of compromise for political reasons.

Knowing that many fragments would be given to reporters later, both sides indulged in a good deal of posturing. Bolling attacked Reaganomics for having caused "human suffering." Reagan retorted: "Look, my program hasn't resulted in anyone getting thrown out in the snow or dying." The participants even rehearsed old arguments about the equity of the 1981 tax law.

There was an attempt at bargaining as well. Reagan offered to split some of the remaining differences but this evoked little enthusiasm. The President's Room grew as warm as the rhetoric: a century's worth of redecorating had laid too many layers of paint on the windows to permit fresh air. The participants* took a recess to cool off and reconsider their positions. The Republicans had a brief caucus in the Vice-President's Room nearby. During that session Howard Baker made a strong argument that it was time for a final breakthrough effort in order to demonstrate just how far Reagan would go for the sake of compromise. The President should show willingness to delay the effective date of the third tax-cut installment for three months in exchange for a similar deferral of 1983 cost of living allowance payments. This offer, Baker said, might win other concessions as well. If it did not, at least Reagan could be depicted as highly flexible.

When the larger meeting reconvened, the Senate Majority Leader made that proposal. By then, however, O'Neill had declared firmly that Social Security was "off the table" entirely because Reagan was refusing to share paternity of benefit reductions. The President insisted that

---

* Meese and Jim Baker accompanied Reagan to the meeting. When O'Neill brought in a staff adviser, Ariel Weiss, the White House added Regan and Stockman to its side of the table. Bolling and the House Majority Leader, James Wright, flanked O'Neill. Senators Howard Baker and Paul Laxalt were also present.

the idea came from the Senate, not the White House; he might accept it as part of a package, albeit reluctantly. Now, after Howard Baker tried to revive that controversial item in tandem with the tax-cut deferral, Reagan indicated that he might be able to live with both as part of a comprehensive settlement. O'Neill eyeballed Bolling. "Dick?" The Rules Committee chairman came back fast and hard: "We just can't take that." There was some more desultory conversation until O'Neill said: "I think we're all waiting for you to get up, Mr. President." Jim Baker, who had just witnessed six weeks of intense effort come to nothing, salvaged at least a small compromise. "Let's all get up together," he said.[3]

Scapegoat time had arrived. O'Neill told a group of reporters: "The President offered a raw deal to the Democrats and to the American people. He advocated that we continue his economic program, which has brought hardship to millions and brought historic rates of unemployment and business bankruptcy." On a table in the Speaker's anteroom rested a pile of new bumper stickers. The message: VOTE DEMOCRATIC—SAVE SOCIAL SECURITY.

Reagan gave a television speech the following night, claiming that he had made his "best effort to achieve a fair compromise." The President distilled the issue to his own advantage: "Apparently the philosophic difference between us is that they want more and more spending and more and more taxes. I believe we should have less spending, less taxes and more prosperity." To confuse matters just a bit more, the President in that talk began a vigorous campaign for an old conservative chestnut —a constitutional amendment to require Congress to enact balanced budgets. That idea had kicked around for many years. Its effect, if enacted, would be more symbolic than real because it would have to contain escape clauses. There was a rich irony in Reagan's renewed advocacy of the amendment, considering that his tax and defense policies were helping to create larger deficits than ever. The immediate purpose was all too obvious; the deficit problem was prolonging the recession and the White House wanted the country to know how the President felt about red ink.

Reagan's supply-side allies were glad to see the Gang of Seventeen's efforts turn from negotiation to warfare. They wanted no compromise that included revenue increases of any significance. A new political button showed up in Washington within a couple of days of the breakdown. LET REAGAN BE REAGAN, it read. The New Right buttonmen were missing a crucial new element in the equation, however. Reagan, when he authorized Baker on March 19 to explore negotiation prospects and during the weeks that followed, crossed a critical divide in his presidency, and in his psychology as well. More important than his

willingness to seek compromise with O'Neill was his acceptance of the
need to compromise—up to a point, anyway—with his own program.
The events between March 19 and late August would appear to be a
series of separate engagements. As tactical matters, they were. But
there had been a strategic change that remained an underlying constant. Ronald Reagan would accept higher taxes and fight for them
when that became necessary. He would live with somewhat smaller increases in defense spending. He would barter on some of the other
fiscal items. Into the fall, at least, Chief of Staff Baker and his allies
would no longer have to hand-wrestle with their boss on fiscal issues.
For the first time in a year, the White House was united on this score.
It could concentrate all its efforts on a Congress that was decidedly
fragmented.

Spring was slipping away and the calendar demanded that the government of the United States produce a new budget. But whose would
it be? Where would the votes be found for passage even of the First
Budget Resolution? In neither house, on neither side of the aisle, was
there anything resembling a firm consensus.

The Legislative Strategy Group concluded that the Administration
would have to begin where it had some strength—the Senate Republican leadership. The Senate Budget Committee, for the record, swept
the table clean on May 5 by unanimously rejecting Reagan's February
budget proposal. That appeared to be a resounding defeat for the
White House. In fact, the February document had been an irrelevancy
almost from the time of its publication. When Domenici's committee
voted 18 to 0 to shelve it, the senators were merely closing the coffin
lid on a corpse.

The same day that vote was taken, Jim Baker, Darman and Stockman secured Reagan's approval on a set of numbers that were not exactly new. Rather, they resembled the White House's offerings during
the earlier stages of the Gang of Seventeen negotiations. That evening
Reagan's advisers used those figures to strike a deal with their Senate
allies, Howard Baker and Pete Domenici. In practical terms, the White
House was announcing a drastic revision of its proposed fiscal '83
budget, with the inevitable carry-over effects for subsequent years.

In the House of Representatives, the byword was chaos. Competing
proposals rattled about in search of working majorities but found none.
The White House hoped to have a First Budget Resolution through by
the first week of June, so that Reagan would have some home-front
support in his pocket when he went to Versailles for his second annual
Economic Summit. That was not to be. At the end of May the House
considered—and rejected—eight separate budgets. This impotence
could not last long. Congress was already three weeks behind its own

budget calendar. When the Senate bought a version that essentially followed the White House–Domenici model of May 5, the House reluctantly went along. Late in June a conference committee resolved the remaining differences and the House accepted that decision in the most grudging fashion; the vote was 210 to 208.

The Democrats had been defeated yet again. Their mood was one of bitter frustration. "We have a political document," Hollings declared, "that will not stand the light of implementation." Congressman Ted Weiss, a Manhattan liberal, spoke for many of his colleagues of all factions when he said during the final debate: "It is a budget package wrapped in deceit, based on phony figures and erroneous assumptions."[4] In fact, the final budget, whatever its flaws, was far closer to reality than what the Administration first proposed in February. It was based on more accurate—and hence more bearish—economic projections. It showed that the government was coming closer to grappling with harsh reality.

At the same time, the budget resolution raised a very large, serious question. Would the Administration be able to pass the specific tax legislation necessary to make good on the resolution's revenue provision? If it could not, the entire fiscal equation would be destroyed. The deficit projections would head back toward the clouds. This time out, some of Reagan's most loyal conservative centurions would be on the other side. Jack Kemp organized an opposition campaign and initially managed to recruit both Martin Anderson and Lyn Nofziger, two of the most prominent alumni of the Reagan White House. Further, while some business groups supported a new revenue measure in principle, many of their lobbyists would oppose provisions that adversely affected specific interests.

Tip O'Neill was suddenly in a pivotal position. For eighteen months he had suffered defeat after defeat to the point of humiliation. The White House had outmaneuvered him at every turn. Now Reagan could not carry out his latest deal with the Senate Republicans unless the House Democratic leadership consented to supply enough votes to compensate for the defection of scores of New Right Republicans who considered any significant tax bill to be treason. O'Neill had the opportunity to fire a very large torpedo into the battered hull of Reaganomics.

It was tempting. Yet there were heavy considerations on the other side. For one thing, O'Neill and his committee chairmen had argued all along that the Administration went much too far in its original tax reduction program. To go to the sidelines now, refusing an opportunity to redress that problem to some degree, would come across as blatant partisanship at the country's expense. There was another element as well. The measure entitled Tax Equity and Fiscal Responsibility Act of 1982 just happened to contain a series of reforms which do-gooders had long hoped to enact. The 1981 bill had been a Christmas stocking full of toys for special interests. The new legislation took a few of those back, along with some older gifts to the affluent. The bill's impact on ordinary citizens would be limited to increases in cigarette and telephone excises and a few minor items. Thus the Democratic leaders faced a dilemma. Should they make a thrust at Reagan's jugular or should they act the statesmen and trust that the voters would recognize their responsible stance? They decided to take the high road—provided that Reagan made a genuine, visible effort to shove as many Republicans into line as possible. With the election less than three months away, O'Neill certainly did not wish to have any tax bill considered primarily a Democratic measure.

Of course the White House had to comply. It had to do so simply on the voting math in both houses. Many members wanted nothing to do with a tax bill so close to Election Day, no matter what the merits of the proposition. The White House now was constructing a coalition different from the 1981 combination, but the methods were the same: massaging, arm-twisting, deals. The most blatant payoff, aimed at getting a few Republican votes on Long Island, was a promise to continue production of A-10 warplanes. Purchases were to have been phased out because additional models were no longer needed. The White House went ahead with this $350 million barter arrangement at a point when it thought three or four votes would make the difference.

That was one of the more difficult bargains Ken Duberstein had to make. Roughly a dozen Republicans already leaning toward the White House viewpoint came in with another kind of request: they wanted George Bush to make campaign and fund-raising appearances in their districts before the election. Duberstein was happy to commit the Vice-President's time whenever he thought it made a difference. Later, when outsiders asked the White House lobbyist whether the tax bill had "cost" a lot, he had a pat reply: "Not really, but don't expect to see George around Washington between now and November." The Republican National Committee contributed to the effort by threatening to manipulate its campaign subsidies to wavering House members.

Nofziger's defection to the Kemp rebel faction was irksome, particularly because Reagan's colorful old sidekick was adept at attracting publicity. The White House dealt with that swiftly. Nofziger was summoned to the Oval Office, where Reagan told him that he had been naughty. Then Baker and Deaver paid him a surprise visit a few days later. They proposed that Nofziger take a short leave from his consulting firm and return to the White House for temporary service. His as-

signment: public relations work for the tax bill. During his year as
chief of political liaison for Reagan, Nofziger worked in the Old Executive Office Building and felt exiled from the inner circle. Now he was
given a comfortable office in the White House West Wing and daily admittance to high-level meetings.

As the vote approached, Reagan himself worked over Republican
members in large groups and small. The President even postponed his
August vacation in California in order to see the fight through. During
the climactic week of August 16 the Reaganauts were engaged on three
major fronts. Habib's delicate negotiations to bring about evacuation of
the PLO from Beirut were finally coming to fruition. Even further from
home, a communiqué with Peking concerning future Sino-American
relations and U.S. arms sales to Taiwan was ready to hatch. But the
most humanly dramatic exercise in rapprochement of that eventful
week was the joint appearance in the Rose Garden of Reagan and
O'Neill. They came together to give their blessing to the tax bill about
to be acted upon. The white-haired, florid Speaker stood by, looking
suitably bemused by fate's whims, as Reagan praised bipartisan patriotism. "All of us here today are united by something bigger than political labels," Reagan said. "We are all Americans."

Away from the cameras' reach, a degree of cooperation usually reserved for the most delicate of foreign relations issues was in progress.
Reagan was to make one of his traditional television speeches on the
eve of the vote. Originally, the Democrats intended to forego a rebuttal. Then they changed their minds. O'Neill designated Thomas Foley,
the House Majority Whip, for the task. Rostenkowski gave that news to
Duberstein, along with assurances that Foley would refrain from harsh
criticism of Reagan. In fact, both sides agreed to avoid attacking the
other. For the sake of sustaining trust, the White House and the Democratic leadership exchanged advance copies of the Reagan and Foley
speeches. Each found a few objectionable phrases in the other's text.
Duberstein brokered some last-minute editing a few hours before the
speeches were delivered. All the requested changes were made. For just
a little while the combatants were willing to forget that an election was
nigh, that points could be scored. Instead, they shared a practical task:
they had to enact a sensible bill despite the inconvenient timing. They
had to tell the financial markets, at last, that help was on the way.

On August 19 the deed was done with a strange combination of factions. In the House, conventional conservatives loyal to Reagan and
their legislative leaders combined with Democratic liberals and a few
Boll Weevils to produce a vote of 226 to 207. The Administration had
several members in reserve ready to switch if necessary. The Republican rebellion was considerable; 87 GOP Representatives voted nay.

Newt Gingrich of Georgia framed the issue in apocalyptic terms: "This is a fight over the heart and soul of the Republican Party." In the Senate, eleven Republicans broke ranks but nine Democrats went the other way to make up a vote of 52 to 47. Reagan had won the most unusual victory of his first two years.

Just before Congress acted, another crucial event occurred. The Federal Reserve Board decided in July that inflation was sufficiently tamed to permit a loosening of monetarist restraint. Volcker, reviewing that period later, delivered what for him was an expansive estimate in talking to the Business Council: "There is growing evidence that the inflationary momentum has been broken. Indeed, with appropriate policies, the prospects appear good for continuing moderation of inflation in the months and years ahead."[5]

Thus the Fed could tolerate a somewhat higher rate of money growth. Between mid-July and mid-November it cut the discount rate —the interest the Fed charges member banks—from 12 percent to 9 percent. This and other moves in turn encouraged substantial reductions in the prime rate (from 16.5 percent to 12 percent during the same four months) and in other indices directly affecting the availability of loans to businesses and individuals.

Even before the salutary effects of that trend were actually felt, the markets began to react with astonishing enthusiasm. Passage of the new tax bill, which would produce $98 billion in revenue over the following three fiscal years, told speculators and investors to prepare for better times. Bond prices rose smartly. The stock exchanges took off on an exuberant rally that propelled the Dow Jones industrial average up 37 percent between mid-August and early November, when it reached a new all-time high of 1,065. More broadly based indices of stock averages rose by even greater proportions until a sense of sobriety returned later in the fall.

That initial reaction went far beyond reality. The tax legislation, after all, was a necessary expedient rather than a fundamental solution. The deficits would not go away; they would merely be slightly less dreadful than they otherwise would have been. The economy in the fall of 1982 had still not come "roaring back," as Donald Regan predicted it would the previous winter. Instead, it was inching along, showing some vague signs of revival along with symptoms of continued weaknesses in crucial industrial sectors. That analysts and investors were willing to react with such gusto demonstrated how eager the financial community had been for any sign of commonsense leadership from Washington. This was the skyrocket of optimism Stockman had hoped for in the spring of 1981. Back then, it might have softened the approaching recession. Now it could only help begin to repair the damage.

In fact, the Reagan White House had executed a mild mid-course correction under duress. It was six months to a year late in making that move and the economy suffered because of the delay. In modulating his policy, Reagan did succeed in buying himself some more time. But most of the same issues would have to be confronted in his third year and perhaps his fourth as well. It would become a grinding, enervating challenge that would test America's oldest President to the utmost. In 1981 he showed that he was willing to make, and able to win, improbable gambles in order to test Reaganomics. In 1982 he demonstrated that he could hedge his bets a little under compelling circumstances. The voters dealt him a weaker hand for 1983 and he would have to play the game with greater shrewdness than ever.

For nearly two months after the midterm election it appeared that Reagan was either misreading both the politics and economics of the approaching new year or not bothering to read them at all. He was angry when his aides told him that the tortuously slow pace of the recovery was producing yet higher deficit projections—$200 billion or more a year through fiscal '87. Had he known that, he remarked during one meeting, he would never have gone along with the 1982 tax increase. During those tense weeks he was unwilling to consider seriously any change in tactics. He would resist pressure on the Pentagon budget. He would fend off any new revenue measure, immediate or long-term. During private sessions he talked of the need for better salesmanship. He would have to "go directly to the people" and he would have to do it even more effectively than in the past.

What would he tell the citizenry? First, not to panic. Second, that the deficit threat must be fought primarily with further reductions in domestic spending. In the preliminary planning for the fiscal '84 budget (to take effect October 1, 1983), Stockman dutifully drew up alternate plans for cutting civilian programs. The most extreme of these was soon known among the insiders as the "rape, pillage and burn option."

It was something of a charade. Howard Baker on Capitol Hill and James Baker in the White House knew as soon as the votes were counted in November that the position Reagan proposed to maintain was untenable. Were Reagan to send up a budget with a towering deficit and social programs cruelly reduced, he would invite instant, bipartisan rejection in the new Congress. Reagan could not repeat what he had done the previous winter. A good deal had changed. Not only were there fewer pro-Administration votes in the Democratic

House of Representatives, now the leadership of both parties was unwilling to tolerate an extension of pure Reaganomics. Paul Laxalt gave the clearest indication of the new mood when he said in public that the deficit prospect was "terrifying." This time there could be no tampering with the economic assumptions in order to produce more pleasing figures. On the contrary, Chairman Martin Feldstein at the Council of Economic Advisers insisted on bearish assumptions, projections that envisaged only a mild recovery in 1983 (and therefore provided no public relations cushion for the Administration). As Reagan's standing in opinion polls took a new slide in early winter, his ability to hold out diminished accordingly. Gradually, grudgingly, he got the message.

At the turn of the year mainstream editorial writers and columnists, almost in unison, posted death notices on Reagan's ability to lead. The consensus of that chilly season was that Reagan had abdicated responsibility because of his stubbornness. "Disarray" and "chaos" became the favored catchwords. This impression was reinforced in early January when Reagan summarily dismissed Eugene Rostow from the directorship of ACDA at a delicate moment in the ongoing arms control negotiations. Rostow, as we have seen, had been having problems with the White House and State Department for months. But Rostow's abrupt departure made it appear that Reagan was out of touch with the rudder of the most urgent foreign issue confronting him as well as the biggest domestic problem.

The political low point of Reagan's presidency up to that stage, it seemed, would coincide with the second anniversary of his inauguration. But he had survived such tumbles before in his public life. Now he showed all the signs of defying the obituary writers yet again.

One result of Rostow's departure was to consolidate authority in Shultz's hands. The Secretary of State by this stage was catching up with the arms control issue. In his methodical way, Shultz would begin pressing for a more effective policy. Reagan, for his part, satirized the coverage he was getting when he told reporters on January 14: "There has been such *disarray* approaching *chaos* in the press corps with regard to the subject of arms control that I thought before you *unraveled* into complete *disorder,* maybe we should straighten out the entire subject."

While he mulled new policy ideas on that issue, Reagan was moving to prevent another deadlock on the domestic side. Jim Baker's faction, suddenly strengthened by the tacit cooperation of Shultz and Clark, finally cornered Weinberger. Isolated as he had never been before, the Defense Secretary at a critical moment proposed a small but significant moderation in military spending for fiscal '84. Reagan immediately accepted the idea.

An even bigger breakthrough occurred soon afterward when the President and Speaker O'Neill joined in a compromise on the vexing Social Security problem. The bipartisan commission studying that dilemma for the previous year had appeared hopelessly deadlocked. Reagan then made some crucial concessions. He even agreed to expand the membership base by the mandatory enrollment of newly hired federal workers. This provision violated one of Reagan's cherished old ideas: that the program should be voluntary rather than compulsory. But the Democrats gave ground as well and Reagan met them a bit more than halfway. The commission's complex proposal satisfied no one. Rather, it angered virtually all of the interest groups. Now, however, Congress and the White House had the basis for enacting a feasible reform that both maintained benefit levels and made fiscal sense.

Not only did he agree, reluctantly, to accelerated payroll deductions for Social Security, he even went along with a contingency revenue plan, to take effect in fiscal '86, provided that the deficit "monster," as he called it, hadn't been tamed by then. The compensating element, from his viewpoint, was a proposal to throttle all non-military spending increases starting in fiscal '84.

Taken together, these changes added up to a credible program with which to begin his third year. He edited his 1983 State of the Union message in an upbeat mood, confident that he had a package that he could sell. On the second anniversary of his inauguration, he greeted reporters in chipper fashion: "A lot can happen in two years. I can see signs of change everywhere. Judging from this group, I seem to have given more gray hairs than I got during the last two years. I guess you can chalk that up to the luck of the Irish."

Reagan's tactical retreats assured him of neither new legislative victories nor economic nirvana. He would still have to face a contentious Congress, a public increasingly impatient with high unemployment, a right wing thoroughly disenchanted with his ostensible "pragmatism," a press corps that was enjoying its rediscovery of skepticism. And he would have to face himself in the mirror when his fealty to Reaganism was challenged.

He could give himself a clean bill. In his mind he was simply marking time for an interlude before continuing the long march toward the proper destination. He was tired of the diehards, he told me once, who wanted him to "jump off the cliff with the flag flying . . . go down in glory. I don't believe in that . . . I can get a sizable chunk of what I want—all right, I will settle for a compromise and get that. And then

I will come back again later and try for more." Even as he made concessions to those who demanded conventional fiscal austerity in early 1983, Reagan firmly believed that Reaganomics would soon produce a larger boom than his own economists would dare predict. Even the cautious Feldstein quickly had to acknowledge that his official projections had been too glum. The Index of Leading Economic Indicators for February spurted upward in surprising fashion, showing that the recession finally was ending. The Irish luck Reagan liked to joke about worked overtime where world oil prices were concerned. OPEC, Arab-dominated petroleum cartel, was unable to hold its line against price reductions in the new year. That fact would encourage economic recovery to proceed without an early resumption of inflation. The economics major from Eureka College might yet have the last laugh on the owners of Ivy League doctorates.

21

Jimmy Baker: The Foundling

Carried on the breezes of Matagorda Bay, the shouted greeting from a flashy cruiser maybe seventy-five yards away takes on an eerie, wailing quality. *James Addison Baker Threeeeee . . . How youuuuu? . . . You people doin' a grand job up there in Wash-ing-ton . . .*

Jimmy Baker squints through the glare at the source of this compliment. At the moment he is standing crotch-deep in the shallows next to a friend's fishing boat. He is wearing a scarlet mesh cap, the cheap kind with a plastic adjustment for size, an incongruous white business shirt with *JAB III* embroidered on the pocket, wash pants minus belt and old tennis shoes now filled with silt. He doesn't hurry his reply. He is peering toward the larger, fancier craft, the complement of which includes a well-constructed woman in a microscopic bikini. Finally he recognizes the man who continues to shout pleasantries about the White House's successes. Baker barely raises his voice when he replies: "Maybe so, but I can't catch me one damn fish today."

Baker's breeding does not encourage shouting. He has already had a surfeit of backslapping and praise—not to mention questions and suggestions—from Texas friends during this vacation. His mind is on the fishing. He spares some attention from that for the nap he takes every afternoon, or for the occasional tennis doubles he will arrange for the sake of his wife, Susan, who doesn't like fishing.

The fish-free condition of the patch of water in which our party has chosen to cast is visible from afar, it turns out. A single-engine plane makes what seems a risky landing on a sandbar. Walter Fondren steps out to kid Baker about having selected the one location being shunned by the red fish and trout he pursues. Baker blames George Bolin, whose boat we are using, and the visiting Yankee reporter, whose strange accent and costume obviously scare off marine life.

Even in this kind of joshing, Baker has difficulty dealing in false information. Even this bit of hyperbole, bleached white in the Matagorda sun, is too dark a stain to leave uncorrected. He immediately admits that he had poor luck the previous day as well, when he went out with a different captain and no alien aboard. Well, Fondren says, just cruise up a ways and "go round the corner" to the Gulf side. He noticed from the air that folks out there are pulling in more than they can handle.

Baker reacts as if he has just been told how to get the crucial votes necessary to put across an important piece of legislation for Reagan. We scramble back into the flat-bottomed airboat and Bolin makes for the "corner." Now we are in more active water, which laps up to the chest. After five minutes or so of this, I retreat to the boat to contemplate the ravaged condition of my designer jeans; no one had warned me about this wet, sandy mode of angling. But Baker stays at it for another half hour, catching nothing at all.

It is a long weekend in mid-August 1981, seven busy, victorious months into the Administration, and the Reaganauts have dispersed for R and R. The previous month, in Ottawa, Reagan had got through his first economic summit meeting with what seemed to be satisfactory results. War in Lebanon was likely a fortnight ago, but Phil Habib had once more managed to maintain a semblance of peace. A few days ago, at Rancho del Cielo, Reagan signed the reconciliation and tax bills in a triumphant ceremony. Baker, like the other senior advisers, knew that the new economic program required major repairs. In the coming week he would interrupt his holiday for a quick trip to Los Angeles, where, he thought, the group would straighten things out. He had Stockman's figures in his attaché case; time enough to open that on the plane west. One of the few things James Baker had in common with Ronald Reagan was awareness of the value of leisure, and a properly familiar place in which to enjoy it.

For the Bakers in the summertime, that meant Port O'Connor, a small town on the Gulf southwest of Houston, the family's tribal base for four generations. In Port O'Connor wealthy Houstonians coexist with coastal locals and blue collar vacationers. Many of Baker's former business acquaintances and a few kinfolk own houses or condominium apartments near the water.

There is no lack of company for the Bakers or their youngest child, Mary Bonner Baker, a nursery school belle who has inherited Susan's striking blond beauty. Baker, a widower, has four grown sons from his first marriage. Susan has three children from her previous match. One or another of these offspring drop in, but the visitor has trouble keeping track. In the next apartment, Bonner Means Baker, the octogenarian matriarch, is at home for any of the younger generation who care to amble by. Even in these temporary accommodations, rented for the vacation, there is a strong atmosphere of continuity, even permanence.

From first acquaintanceship, when he was running the Bush nomination campaign in the spring of 1980, I had been fascinated by Baker's singularity among political managers. First there were his look and manner. He is not merely handsome in conventional sense, with regular features and a sturdy muscular build; he is also blessed with a delicacy unusual among masculine Southerners who get their best jollies using a fishing rod and shotgun. His hands, large and hairy, seemed appropriate for those tools but his gestures bespeak finesse. His handwriting is ornate. He spits tobacco juice without looking gross. Your standard-issue Texas politicians—Lyndon Johnson, John Connally and Robert Strauss come to mind—conform to the state's stereotype of bluff bravado. They persuade an audience or an interviewer with force and bluster, as if the listeners must be subdued like calfs being made ready for the branding iron. Baker, with his small, shy smile, always tried instead to rope you into a conspiracy of candor. Adroit understatement, laced with bits of fact and insight, make a powerful knot for those accustomed to political hyperbole. It had been Baker's style of persuasion, as much as anything else, that maintained George Bush as a credible rival to Reagan longer than the other Republican prospects. Now he was using the same technique in the White House on Reagan's behalf, with good effect.

We first met in March, soon after Bush's debacle in New Hampshire, which I had covered from the winner's side. A reporter recharges his batteries during the endless primary season by switching planes, so I flew with Bush for three weeks. Startled by the sudden prospect that Gerald Ford might belatedly enter the race, ending his own chances, and hungry for a win somewhere, poor Bush starved during the Southern round of primaries. Out on the road, the candidate sounded truculent, defensive: "I'm going to be in this to the end, all the way to the end . . . If I didn't have enough fiber and enough guts to do this, there would be something wrong with me." And Bush finally was beginning to draw real distinctions between his positions and Reagan's.

Back in Houston, Baker was relaxed. "After we won in Iowa," he observed, as if talking about someone else's campaign, "there was a perception that George was fuzzy on the issues. We didn't move from the 'George who?' to the 'George what?' We should have done something about that. We should have done a lot more to establish what he stands for, but it isn't too late. There are places we can catch Reagan.

It's lonely out there in front and you have to remember Reagan is ac-
cident-prone."[1] There was just enough self-criticism and just enough
plausibility in there to fend off political obituaries.

Reagan's organization was in turmoil at that point because the Sears
crew had just been chucked out. Bush's shop was tidy, Baker's place
secure. When I remarked that Bush's crowd was the only one in the
still-young campaign that had not gone through overhaul, Baker seized
on the point to argue that stability was a great asset.* Of course they
had been close personal friends for more than a dozen years; Bush was
Mary Bonner's godfather. But there was something else, more important, that set Baker apart from the rival tacticians in other camps. In
1976, after all, he had risen high in the organization of a relative
stranger, Gerald Ford, and Baker then was still a tyro in politics.

The difference was that Baker didn't need the work, in terms of either money or status in life. He had inherited a fortune and earned a
good deal more on his own. His great-grandfather, grandfather and father had bequeathed him stature in Houston's legal establishment.
Baker accepted the legacy and built upon it in a different law firm because, in his father's time, Baker & Botts adopted an anti-nepotism
rule.

So Baker had a strong identity apart from politics. He could play the
hired gun, like Sears, but with less at stake personally. Unlike some of
the others, such as Carter's man Hamilton Jordan, Baker was not burdened with heavy political convictions. Like all of his class in Houston,
Baker started as a Tory Democrat. He spent his early career serving
corporations and individuals even wealthier than he; at one time his
firm assigned him to the affairs of Howard Hughes. He considered himself a conservative, in a general way, but in his twenties and thirties
politics was terra incognita. His father and grandfather before him considered it a morally offensive occupation and warned young lawyers
against contamination. Had he lived longer, Bonner Means Baker
remarked of her husband, Jim, he would have stopped Jimmy from
ever going to Washington.[2]

The son did not share that scruple. With him it was more a case of
disinterest. As a practicing lawyer he sometimes forgot to vote. He
bothered turning Republican in 1970 only to help his pal, Bush, run
for the Senate (Bush lost). Public affairs, particularly foreign issues,
simply did not register on him. "I was completely apolitical," he told
one interviewer. "Those things were outside my life."[3] Even after he
was in the White House, having found in Reagan a winner at last, po-

* More than two years later, Baker still remembered this part of our conversation and occasionally mentioned it to others. Being seen in a strong relationship
of mutual loyalty with his principal had great appeal for Baker.

litical philosophy was peripheral to his concerns. The right-wingers outside would fasten on Baker as the arch-bogeyman, the despoiler of Reaganism, the closet moderate determined to infect Reagan's victory with the microbe of conventional, boardroom conservatism.

Such criticism missed the essential point about Baker. He was a player fascinated with the game, the process of competition, rather than with theories of economics or geopolitics. His factual command of some important subjects was limited and occasionally during conversations with him it became apparent that he had only a superficial knowledge of this or that issue. During the first few months of the Administration he would occasionally try to rebut criticism concerning foreign policy by ticking off a list of "accomplishments" that he had noted on the back of an envelope he carried in his pocket. Trying to get him to prove that any of those items was important could be embarrassing.

Baker was the kind of operator common in government who could be keenly perceptive about the politics of a situation, intelligent about the means of getting the job done, but only mildly interested in the intrinsic wisdom of the particular goal. In early December of 1980, when Stockman was still the saint of the supply-siders, Baker maneuvered him into lead position for formulation of the economic program. It was not that Baker was a true believer. On the contrary, when he thought about it all, he was skeptical about supply-side notions. Rather, Baker wanted to get things going in a hurry. Stockman was the best instrument available to do that. It was a shrewd tactical move at the time. In the long run, Reagan—and the country—would have been better off with less speed, more deliberation.

For all his class, for all his concern about propriety, Baker had a swatch of the cynic in him. When the Bush campaign was still in gestation, in 1979, a few of the advisers realized that Bush's chance to win the nomination was minute. If they were fortunate, Bush would do well enough to establish himself as a credible national figure. Then maybe, just maybe, Bush would be considered for second spot. Baker had that in mind from the beginning. Or Bush would be in a good position for 1984. When the possibility of running for Vice-President on a Reagan ticket was put to him privately in those early days, Bush recoiled. It wasn't a matter of pride; he wasn't above the office. Rather, he considered himself above Reagan.

Bush, like the patrician cousins he left behind in New England when he moved to Texas, regarded Reagan as a calcified yahoo, an ideologue unhealthy for the party and the country. When Bush's son, George, ran for Congress in west Texas in 1978, the conservatives already identified as Reagan cadre savaged him as some kind of subversive. They did the

same thing to the father in New England and the South during the
1980 primaries, using Bush's former membership on the Trilateral
Commission as Exhibit A. Bush was justifiably bitter about it. One
night as he was losing the Illinois race, he told a few of us: "I despise
it. It's terrible the way I've been abused. You'd think the national press
would have been more indignant over this sort of thing. It's—well, it's
anti-intellectual, that's what it is. It's worse than the Birch stuff. And
Reagan acquiesces—like he did when his people used it against my son
George."[4]

Reagan had indeed blinked benignly as his centurions repeatedly
fouled Bush. Eventually Bush tried to make an issue of the slurs, but it
backfired. Later, Baker attempted to keep Bush's rhetoric gentlemanly
enough—and his race short enough—to preserve a shot at the vice-
presidential nomination. By this time Bush was confronting the grim
prospect of retiring to Houston and going back to the oil business.
That idea repelled him more than joining up with Reagan. Still, he did
not quite get the point of Baker's strategy. During the Pennsylvania primary Bush was staging a comeback. Baker, who was off the plane more
than he should have been, was not with the group to approve a statement drafted by Peter Teeley, Bush's press aide. Teeley wrote in a line
calling Reagan's tax program "voodoo economics." Bush liked the
phrase, which got some attention.* For once, Baker lost his cool and
warned his subordinates in the organization to avoid such intem-
perance. He knew Reagan already found Bush distasteful. It would be
foolish to set that feeling in concrete.

Even after Reagan had more than enough delegates committed to assure nomination, Bush still fought. He was threatening to contest the
California primary. That would have forced Reagan's organization to
mount an effort there for appearance's sake; he could not afford a
mediocre showing in his home state. The Reaganauts were distressed
(and low on funds as well). Bush was stepping beyond the bounds of
good sense, not to mention party loyalty. A real contest in California
could not affect the nomination, but it could slow down preparations
for the convention and the fall effort against Carter. Baker would joke
later that "we had to beat on George" to get him out. In fact, Baker
acted in a more dramatic fashion than that. With Bush on the road,
Baker simply informed reporters that his candidate was withdrawing
from the California primary. He blamed the decision on a shortage of

* Once in office, Bush rashly denied that he had ever used the term himself,
insisting that it simply had appeared in a press release. Dozens of reporters who
covered him knew better. NBC dug up a film clip showing Bush denouncing
Reagan's plan as "voodoo economics."

money. That announcement—made without Bush's knowledge—effectively ended the Bush presidential candidacy.

Baker justified that brassy means with the end it attained; Bush remained a prospect for Vice-President. In the White House, Baker would have to be more cautious. You cannot cross an incumbent President, even for his own good, the way you can a candidate who has already lost the game anyway. Besides, in the White House Baker would always have to watch his flanks and his back. During the first two years he was never the sole chancellor next to the throne. And during that time he never totally overcame the stigma of having been a foundling on the Reaganauts' steps rather than a natural child of the household.

When he joined the Reagan campaign immediately after the convention, Baker had to be controlled, even wary, because of his alien status. Some of that continued even in the White House. I wondered whether seeing him in Port O'Connor, on home grounds, would show a very different side. There were superficial contrasts, of course. He didn't chew Red Man tobacco in the White House, for one thing, except on Saturday. Nor did he tolerate delays and inefficiency with much patience. In Port O'Connor he frequently had a chaw in his cheek and did not seem to mind at all when things failed to work.

After the trout and red fish have eluded him in the sunshine, he accepts an invitation from an old pal, David Beveridge, to go after flounder by moonlight. This operation is different. We are to use a boat equipped with an elevated propeller because our quarry is found in only the shallowest of waters. Up front there is a powerful light by which we are to pick out the fish. Instead of rods, we will use bifurcated spears. To the visitor, it sounds messy but at least on this expedition I get to stay in the boat. Baker's big concern is an early return; while on vacation, he insists on a full night's sleep in addition to his afternoon nap. Beveridge assures him on that score, but the party, including a relative of Susan's, Beveridge's son and the local game warden who knows all the special channels, is slow to gather. Baker bears with the delay cheerfully.

Finally we race under the stars through salt marshes to the spot where Doug Veach, the warden, is confident that we will find more flounder than we'll know what to do with. Trouble is, Beveridge cannot get the spotlight to work. For twenty or thirty minutes they go at the circuitry, the generator, the switch. Baker, a bottle of beer in hand, plays the interested spectator. "Look at that damn mess of wires," he says. "I wouldn't know where to begin." The light remains dead, the flounder unmolested and eventually we skim back to shore, empty beer bottles clinking. "Well," Baker says, "into bed by eleven. That's something, anyway."

He joshes easily with the stockbroker, Beveridge, and the real estate man, Bolin. In Port O'Connor there are more "hells" and "damns" and "shoots" in his speech than back in Washington. He is one of the boys —almost, sort of. When he goes for an early-morning rendezvous at the home of another friend, Sonny Wallace (industrial piping), the White House Chief of Staff carries two thirds of a melon, the only contribution he can find for what will be an informal breakfast.

But, in fact, Baker is not one of the boys, not these boys. His friends here are property proud, always talking about their possessions, gadgets, new acquisitions. Baker owns neither a boat, a house nor an apartment in Port O'Connor. Beveridge cannot understand this. He touts a particular place up for sale, a condominium with services provided. "It's so easy," Beveridge says. "You just lock it up and walk away. They got maintenance, they got security. They'll probably ask one-fifty. Start at one-thirty and see what happens."

Baker feigns interest for courtesy's sake, but he is not going to bid anything. Later he recalls his father's resistance to buying extra property. Among land-loving Texans, JAB II was a cautious man with investments. The son quotes him: "If there's one thing I don't need it's a pile of rocks somewhere." In 1969 the younger man somehow persuaded the father to buy a 1,400-acre spread south of San Antonio— they named it Rockpile Ranch, of course—but to this day the Bakers have not built a permanent structure on the place. Baker uses tents when he hunts wild turkey and other game there.

"My father was a stern disciplinarian," Baker says. "He wanted things just so. He wanted his son to do things right." Only son, to be precise, and that added an extra layer of demand. Baker & Botts had dealings far beyond the borders of Texas. To expand his horizons, Jim Baker in his day had been sent to the Hill School in Pennsylvania and then to Princeton before being brought back to the University of Texas at Austin for his legal training. Young Jimmy traversed the same route. He even joined the same fraternity Dad had belonged to at Texas, though, by the time he arrived, he had a B.A., discharge papers from the Marine Corps and a beautiful wife from Ohio, Mary Stuart, who happened to be a Republican. All the other pledges were undergraduate freshmen, seven and eight years younger than Jimmy Baker. But he went through the childish hazing because his father wanted it that way, and then kept to himself.

In Port O'Connor, Baker still seems the mature, disciplined officer among ebullient frat kids. At the general store's checkout counter the male customers sport money clips containing large wads. Baker, buying some beer, comes up with a tattered tan billfold from which he carefully extracts a five. It is an act performed with deliberation; the money has been around the family for so long that it is not handled in a cavalier manner.

The Fondrens are having a casual dinner party; all the guests contribute food as well as booze. It is a large, magnificent house of weathered wood, built on stilts at the water's edge. Walter Fondren (oil), the one with the airplane, is a serious deep-sea sportsman with troves of trophies and equipment. The men and women segregate themselves by gender, reuniting only around the buffet. Voices are loud, except for Baker's. He seems to murmur while others whoop. As the celebrity, he is courted, and he tolerates it with grace. A huge television set in the corner features a pre-season football game between the Oilers and the Saints. Interest in this contest is high because Houston's coach has switched to New Orleans, causing ambivalent loyalties back in Texas. Cries from the spectators in front of the screen grow louder as the demonic Saints splatter the watery Oiler defense all over the field. Baker edges as far away from the din as he can get.

Most of the men are in sports shirts and slacks; Baker is wearing a pink knit LaCoste that clings to his torso. Someone remarks that he is one of the very few men in the room whose belly does not hang over his belt. "I don't drink beer in the morning," he replies. Then he flashes his gracious little smile; just joking, it says, no offense intended. Later Susan appraises the sociology of the Bakers in Port O'Connor. "Jimmy Baker can get on with any group," she says. "He's at ease up in New York at '21' or in Washington or down here. But the crowd here makes and spends a lot of money and we're different. Jimmy Baker and I think it's obscene to spend a lot of money for things that aren't important. So some of the people we know think we're kind of stodgy."

If political adversity ever forced Baker back to Houston, he would not go there to practice corporate law. By the age of forty, having attained the goals Jim Baker had set for him, Jimmy was bored. Still, he did not leap into politics. Mary Stuart was dying of cancer in 1970 and he had four young sons to think about. His wife's death was the first emotional calamity—the only one, really—that he ever had to deal with. He no longer knew what he wanted to do with his life. Helping to merge companies and picking out shrewd business investments for himself had lost whatever kick they once provided.

Bush suggested that he run for the House seat that Bush was vacating in order to try for the Senate. But Mary Stuart's condition was worsening and anyway Baker had not fancied himself running for office. He was never a plunger. Every move he made had either been dictated in advance by his father or carefully considered from every angle by the son. Bush finally lured the new widower into the Senate campaign organization as a distraction from grief. Baker worked the Houston area in order to stay close to his boys and discovered that he liked the drill. Nonetheless, he remained with the law firm, antsy as he was, until 1975, when Bush brokered an appointment for him as Under Secretary of Commerce in the Ford administration.

By then Baker had married one of his late wife's best friends, Susan, who by coincidence came from a Texas oddity: a ranching family that had been Republican for many years. Not only that, she cared about politics. With some of their merged brood away at school and some at home, the Bakers moved to Washington. Almost by accident, Baker joined Ford's 1976 campaign organization, where successive problems kept creating vacancies at the top. When the Reagan challenge became serious, Baker served as chief delegate hunter. One of his best contributions was his talent for the retail wooing of uncommitted delegates, a meticulous operation in which Ford's time was rationed for maximum effect.

It is hardly a historic achievement when an incumbent President fights off a rival in his own party, particularly if the adversary comes within an inch of winning the nomination. Nor were records for political gamesmanship set in the general election, when Ford managed to make a close fight of what started out to be a Democratic laffer. Nonetheless, Baker emerged from 1976 with an excellent reputation among the national press corps. With no professional experience in national elections, he had brought a degree of professionalism to Ford's disheveled campaign operation. Further, his personal deftness in dealing with reporters had helped balance the strange adulation Candidate Carter and his advisers managed to elicit from the press (President Carter flopped in that department). There was one serious knock on Baker as manager: he was leery of risks and so careful in committing campaign funds that the loser ended with a surplus in his war chest. Veterans who had resented the newcomer's rapid rise to the top of the Ford organization wondered aloud whether a bolder campaign finale— more television, more travel, more street money, more *something*—just might have saved Ford.

There would be no rational way to answer that question, but it was a reminder of Baker's occasional tendency to excessive caution. That showed up again immediately when he withdrew from consideration as the GOP's new national chairman. He would have taken the post if he could have avoided a fight for it, but competition seemed inevitable. So he went back to Houston, back to the practice of law one last time, but the political virus infected his every organ. He agreed to run for state attorney general in 1978, provided that he could get the Republican nomination without a contest. That hurdle passed, Baker discovered that he had made a serious miscalculation. He had assumed the

Democrats would nominate a liberal, allowing Baker to pitch for Tory Democratic support. But the liberal prospect lost the Democratic primary, leaving Baker to face an opponent indistinguishable from him on the issues. "We did our crying on primary night," Susan Baker recalled. They still had to run hard because Baker suspected that he might try again in the future; he needed a reputation as a game campaigner. He and Susan divided Texas' twenty-two media markets between them. He took the larger ones, she the smaller.

"We really did it," Susan said three years later. "We worked our buns off. Three speeches a day with Mary Bonner in a porta-crib."[5] When they appeared together, Baker would identify himself as the "candidate who brings his own baby to kiss." The voters smiled indulgently and elected the Democrat. Soon afterward advance planning started for the Bush campaign. The old friends and tennis partners began their long zigzag trek to the White House, where one would be a heartbeat away from the presidency, as the old saw goes, but the other would be much more influential as a member of the small privy council.

Baker earned that spot by his performance during the general election. Though outranked by Meese, Casey, Deaver and others, he showed a cool hand as an administrator. Further, he argued strongly that Reagan should debate Anderson and then Carter while some of the others had reservations. Baker represented the Reagan camp in negotiations over ground rules, and did well. Because of his experience in the Ford-Carter debates of 1976, Baker also took charge of preparing Reagan for these crucial encounters on network television.

Here Baker had to face something of an ethical problem. In gathering research that Stockman would use when impersonating Carter in the sparring sessions, a member of the campaign staff somehow acquired an unusual prize: briefing material that the other side was using to get Carter ready for the confrontation. Apparently a Reagan mole in the Carter camp had filched papers containing the main points the President planned to make when he met Reagan for the debate. Stockman, hustling to Washington from his own campaign chores in Michigan, was delighted to find most of his homework done for him as he outlined his own script for the dry run. Later, after the real thing was over, the Reaganauts realized that the papers provided by their informant had included every important item Carter used on the air except one: his reference to his daughter, Amy, in connection with nuclear arms control. The Carter people then, as later, apparently were unaware of this hole in their security.

Baker was fastidious about propriety. Early in his legal career he was interested in trial work but he quickly gave up litigation when he realized that sharp practices were common in that branch of the profession. Now, as a senior adviser to the Reagan campaign, he looked the other way when a dirty trick was perpetrated on Carter. He was grateful not to know the mechanics of it. Months later he was still sensitive enough to be embarrassed when I mentioned the incident during a private conversation. And he was relieved that the matter had remained a secret.*

Soon Baker would face a more serious, enduring test of his long-held style and strengths. For the first time in his adult career, Baker now lived in a world in which his motives and loyalty were frequently attacked. Not only did he have to manage the rugged miscellany that makes up the Chief of Staff's menu—everything from legislative strategy to personnel selection to a quarrel between the White House barber and the official beautician—but he had also to contend with the recurrent accusation that he was undermining Reaganism. This constant sniping was not only a distraction; it became an inhibition as Baker attempted to maneuver around Meese's role in White House operations. Since Meese was a certified Reaganaut more concerned than most of the other advisers with the tenets of Reaganism, disputes over jurisdiction and tactics had a way of becoming muddled with philosophy—though the latter usually was not at issue within the White House staff.

Aware of the problem from the outset, Baker initially took some precautions that protected his flanks for a short time. He brought in other non-Reaganauts suspected of centrist views—Darman, Gergen and Friedersdorf were the most prominent—but he balanced such selections on the other side. It was Baker who recalled Nofziger to the Reagan tent and put him in the sensitive job of chief of political liaison. The point of that was to give the right wing a sympathetic ear in the White House.† As contact man with the governors and senators, another significant job, Baker selected Rich Williamson, who had strong conservative credentials as a onetime strategist for Congressman Philip Crane. Baker also found openings for a few New Right operatives in the subcabinet.

Those efforts were enough, in early 1981, to earn him favorable mention in *Human Events* as an authentic conservative.⁶ He also received kudos from the columnists Rowland Evans and Robert Novak,

---

* At least a couple of reporters became aware of the briefing-book caper months after the event. The story did not make it into print, however. The article I did for *Time* in February 1981 was crowded out by other news and remained in the overset.

† Nofziger exerted only limited influence and resigned at the end of the first year. He was replaced by Ed Rollins, a protégé of his, who was also in the "street-corner conservative" style. But Rollins also was on the fringe of influence.

who tracked the charts of right-wing demonology carefully and pronounced Baker both a competent pol—the Republican version of Robert Strauss, they said—and a sound Reaganaut in most respects.[7] There was a caveat even then, however, because of Baker's discomfort concerning supply-side tax proposals that went beyond what the Administration was willing to support. Later Evans and Novak rescinded their praise and condemned Baker as apostate.

Doubts about Baker escalated rapidly on the right. As the strategist responsible for pushing Reagan's top priorities through Congress, Baker of course favored delay in what he (and, in fact, Reagan) considered secondary issues such as school prayer and abortion. Soon Baker not only was arguing for a curb in the Pentagon spending increases; he allowed himself to be depicted in public as a strong advocate. The same thing occurred in the "Fall Offensive" period, when the Baker-Stockman faction tried unsuccessfully to persuade Reagan to support measures to increase revenue. Just about everywhere the true believers looked, they found Jimmy Baker practicing heresy. When Richard Viguerie's monthly *Conservative Digest* devoted its entire July 1982 issue to attacking the Administration's infidelity, article after article nailed Baker as the most important infidel defiling Reaganism.

Baker's frequent "Who me?" defenses must have been painful for him to make, because he was a proud man with nothing to apologize for. It sounded demeaning when he responded to my general question about his political views this way:

Basically, I'm a late-blooming Texas Republican and a conservative. I got this "moderate" tag because I worked for Jerry Ford and George Bush. Well, maybe I'm more moderate than some on the social issues, but when I came to work in the Ford administration, [Treasury Secretary] Bill Simon said, "Well, it's about time we got some more real conservatives around here" . . . Shortly after the 1976 convention, I got a call from Governor Reagan [who was annoyed that another Ford operative had criticized Reagan's effort on behalf of the Ford ticket]. Then he said, "By the way, I'm told that you and I share a common political philosophy." And I said, "Well, I believe that's right, Governor."[8]

By definition, a White House staff man is supposed to be a buffer, taking political hits the way Secret Service agents are trained to use their bodies to stop bullets aimed at the President. But Baker slipped beyond that function. He himself became a distracting issue, a cardinal no-no in the White House staff guidebook. Clymer L. Wright, Jr., who had served as the Reagan campaign's finance chairman in Texas, used right-wing mailing lists to circulate a letter addressed "Dear Friend of Ronald Reagan" in May 1982. The first two sentences suffice to convey the flavor: "Our beloved President today stands alone under siege. His economic program is being undermined by White House Chief of Staff James Baker." Wright concluded by demanding Baker's dismissal.

Reagan took pen in hand to defend Baker, and himself: ". . . Clymer, I'm in charge and my people are helping to carry out the policies I set . . . There has not been one single instance of Jim Baker doing anything but what I settle on as our policy . . ." Reagan's response, which found its way into print, was an example of another cardinal no-no. A President should not go around telling the world he is in charge of his administration. If he has to do that, he will only reinforce doubts on that score.

Deaver often tried to help the colleague whose appointment he had pushed vigorously in the first place. Not only did Deaver usually side with Baker on specific issues, but in subtle ways he attempted to create a personal bond between the President and the Chief of Staff. When Nancy Reagan went to London in July 1981 for the wedding of Prince Charles and Lady Diana, Reagan was lonely. It was Deaver who came up with the idea of a small, informal dinner party outside the White House. And it was Deaver who suggested that Susan and Jimmy Baker be the hosts. It rained and the guests had to retreat from the Bakers' patio, but Reagan took off his necktie and had a good time. In the fall Deaver encouraged Reagan to hunt with Baker and his father-in-law, Whispering Jack Garrett, at the Garrett ranch. The color photo hanging in Baker's office shows Reagan, Baker, Deaver and Secret Service agent Tom Quinn in a Jeep. Reagan's inscription: "Dear Jim—look at me smile. That was *before* the hunt. Ron." The President had failed to bag a wild turkey.

Doubtless Deaver's subtle touches helped, and Baker's generally adroit handling of day-to-day affairs helped him even more. But the outside pressures were increasing while friction inside the White House over Meese's role worsened. Clark's advent had solved some of the National Security Council problems. At the same time, authority was diffused still further. The troika in its original form was dead. In its place was a quartet that did not operate as a unit. Now there were four seniors with free access to the President and only limited coordination among themselves. Of the four, Baker was still the outsider. Baker could not totally hide his frustration at the organizational arrangements.

"I'm convinced that I still have the President's confidence," he said in mid-1982. "He knows I'm loyal, despite the job Evans and Novak are trying to do on me. I bend over backwards to clear things. I don't try to get out ahead of him . . . You might say I'm not a traditional Chief of Staff in the sense that I'm not *the* closest person to the President. No, I'm not, and I never will be. But I'll tell you this. I'm a lot closer to him now than when I came in, and I think that says something."[9]

That Baker felt it necessary to make such pronouncements also said something. The pressures were getting to him, crimping his style. Even in the best of times, Baker suffered some inner conflict. The cautious, disciplined planner in him would be at odds with the impatient doer prone to act now and ask questions later. While running Bush's campaign, and at times in the White House as well, Baker's political trigger finger would sometimes seem slow. When Senator Bob Packwood, a moderate Republican, went public with sharp criticism of Reagan, Baker was reluctant to retaliate. Indecisive, some of his own subordinates grumbled, no sense of going for the jugular. He personally never made an explicit pitch to Reagan for a reorganization of the White House staff that would isolate Meese from actual operations. Baker, much as he wanted that result, feared being blamed by outside critics either for inducing Meese's departure from the White House or for diminishing Meese's role. Baker tolerated the ritual troika breakfast each morning long after it ceased to be useful. Finally, irritated over what he considered secretiveness on Meese's part, Baker ended the practice. The last of the series was held November 1, the day before the midterm election.

After he was repeatedly burned by the moderate-mole line on him, Baker had to pull back in his efforts to persuade Reagan to fight for a revenue bill in early 1982. Those associated with him, such as Darman and Stockman, had to follow suit. That slowed down the process. Even after that milestone was passed, Baker occasionally suffered seizures of insecurity. On August 15, 1982, he appeared on "Face the Nation," a Sunday talk show, and discussed the tax situation. The next morning's Washington *Post* carried this headline: BAKER: 1981 TAX CUTS HAVE FAILED IN IMPACT. The implication of both the headline and the story had Baker dumping on Reaganomics.

Baker felt that the newspaper story distorted what he had said. Uncharacteristically, he called two *Post* executives to complain about the coverage. Then he acquired a transcript of the television interview and brought it into the morning Oval Office meeting. He intended to prove to Reagan that he had not fouled the nest of Reaganomics. The President waved off the document. He had seen the show and was satisfied with Baker's statements on the air. The small incident evaporated, but the anxiety that had prompted Baker's defensive actions remained.

During that long weekend in Port O'Connor, Baker's bad luck with hook, line and sinker held to the end. On the last afternoon before he had to fly to Los Angeles—where he would be embarrassed by the group's failure to resolve the defense spending issue after he gave the wrong information to reporters—Baker went out one more time. When he came to the tennis court hours later, he could show us only two or three of the most anemic trout ever taken in Matagorda Bay. He was shaking his head, laughing at himself.

"It's still fun," he insisted. "I love just *doing* it. But it's a hell of a lot more fun when you catch something." Back in Washington, Baker would continue to pull in important legislative fish for Reagan. No one could question his skill at that. He would continue to run the White House boat as well. But by the end of the second year the *doing* of it had become a struggle that not even Jimmy Baker could love. Like Meese, Deaver and Clark, he would keep at it because Reagan wanted it that way. When the President decided to ignore advice to reorganize the crew for the 1983 leg of the voyage, Baker dutifully complied. The third year of an administration, after all, usually provides the most challenging test of a President's term.

22

Dick Darman: The Professional

When he was becoming addicted to government service ten years ago, Richard Darman and his wife Kath figured that they needed a proper place to live in the Washington area. They had a townhouse in the District's southwest quadrant at the time, an interesting, marginal neighborhood convenient to the municipal college where she taught English literature to black ghetto kids. But it was temporary, not exactly what they would need for the long run. Darman already was succumbing to the banks of the Potomac as a place to live and a way to live.

Price was not the obstacle it is for most couples in their twenties seeking to sink new roots. Each came from a wealthy New England family. Rather, the problem was site. They wanted space, privacy and, if possible, proximity to water. "I can't understand anyone," Darman says, "who wouldn't want to live on the ocean, by a river, or at least a stream. You feel a bit less trapped where you can see the water."[1] He explored along the Virginia side of the river and found an old twelve-room house, brick and clapboard, on five and a half woodsy acres that sloped down to the river.

Most of the surrounding area was parkland which could never be built on; no real estate developer would thrust unwanted neighbors upon them. But there was a hitch. The owner, terminally ill, was in an institution and his affairs were administered by a trustee. The situation presented some legal difficulties until Darman and the trustee settled on an innovative scheme. Darman offered to rent the house for the rest of the owner's life, with a commitment to purchase it from the estate later.

The price would be fixed at the time of the original deal. Both parties would benefit. The Darmans would have immediate occupancy and an ultimate price unaffected by real estate inflation. From the viewpoint of the seller's estate, the proceeds would be taxed only once rather than being subject to a capital gains levy first and inheritance tax later. The deal was concluded, nature took its course, the Darmans added more rooms to the place and lived happily ever since in the McLean squirearchy.

Darman tells his unusual real estate story with a trace of guilt because he feels that it has faintly ghoulish aspects. Kath Darman, a far gentler soul, doesn't like to be reminded of the arrangement at all. The real moral of the tale is that it shows one more time Darman's knack for solving problems. His hobby, he once said, is thinking, but that is too narrow a term. The avocation which he pursues perpetually also includes planning, scheming, fretting, constructing scenarios that invariably start with the worst case but point to a way out.

Darman came to the transition staff because he had once been a Commerce Department colleague of Jim Baker's. The new recruit wore not a single chevron from the Reagan campaign, though he did work with Baker in helping to prepare the candidate for debates with Anderson and Carter. Darman did not know the President-elect or the Californians. They, however, knew that Darman was not even a conventional conservative like Baker. Rather, he was a tenuous Republican, a survivor of the almost-extinct GOP liberal wing. That he rose from that weak base to become one of the most influential members of the White House staff was a mark of the skill and tenacity with which he practiced his hobby.

The original announcement of his appointment stipulated his rank as Deputy Assistant to the President—one rung down the staff ladder—and described his duties in two sentences: "Mr. Darman will be responsible for assuring the full and fair staffing of all papers intended for the President. He will also be responsible for overseeing the management support systems of the White House and for advising the Chief of Staff on selected substantive issues." As a *deputy* assistant he was a cut below contemporaries whom he thought were not quite up to being his peers. Though he was party to drafting the description of his functions, his role was interpreted by outsiders as that of paper-shuffler and mechanic. That nettled him, rattled his brittle sensitivities, but he realized that this low estate was temporary.

Within a few months the triumvers were describing him as the fourth most important member of the White House staff (William Clark's arrival later demoted him to fifth). The offensive qualifier "deputy" was amputated from his title. He was the progenitor and acknowledged en-

ergy source of the Legislative Strategy Group. He exercised quality
control over most of the material going to Reagan, and Darman's
fingerprints turned up in a variety of other places.

A photo taken in the U.S. delegation office at the Ottawa Economic
Summit shows Darman working at a desk. Standing around him in a
semicircle are Ed Meese, Don Regan, Craig Fuller—and Ronald
Reagan. The spectators seem to be concentrating on Darman while he
focuses on his task. The President added one of his funny captions to
the picture later: "Dick—writing home already? We've only been here
about three hours!" In fact, Darman was drafting "talking points" for
the President to use in conversation with François Mitterrand. Another
photo shows Reagan and Darman on *Air Force One,* huddled over a
document. Reagan's inscription: "Now what happens if I sign that
thing? Or did I already?"

An obsessive workaholic, Darman always knew the answers to such
questions whether posed seriously or frivolously. His influence on the
Reagan presidency rose accordingly. He had difficulty hiding his appetite for more responsibility, just as he was not always able to disguise
his impatience with what he considered mediocre performance by some
of his colleagues. On one occasion Baker had to caution him about
bad-mouthing an official whom Darman found particularly ineffective.
What his colleagues also found galling was Darman's ability to cover
great swatches of terrain with such dexterity. In the fall of 1981, as the
White House prepared to participate in the Cancun conference on
Third World development, State and Treasury were at odds over the
U.S. position on the delicate question of "global negotiations"—the
UN-sponsored process under which the least affluent nations hoped to
pry concessions from the wealthy countries. Darman wrote the basic
policy guidance that allowed the Administration to appear cooperative
without committing itself to going very far. A year later it was Darman,
with Baker, who conducted secret liaison work between the White
House and the bipartisan commission studying Social Security reform.
He was attempting to get enough agreement before the new round of
public debate started so that the Administration could live with the results.

Darman's periscope constantly scanned the horizon for the next set
of demands. Early in the second year, with the agenda of problems
growing, the senior members of the staff and some outside advisers
gathered at Camp David on February 5 for a review. The mission was
essentially political at the beginning of an election year. Several of the
participants drew up papers in advance on specific subjects, such as the
economic outlook, trends in poll results, domestic policy proposals and
the like. Among Darman's contributions were three pages citing prob-

lems and possible approaches to them written in terse, breezy style. The subjects, of course, could have been taken from the front page of any daily newspaper. But Darman poked relentlessly into the core of a variety of difficulties ostensibly outside his immediate concerns. Most of his succinct comments held up quite well a year later.

On defense spending, for instance, he wrote one long sentence: "There is a fundamental incongruity here: requested defense resources are less than amounts necessary to be consistent with declaratory foreign policy, yet more than amounts the political system will now provide." He was similarly prescient when he talked about "strains in the alliance—as Europeans split over responses to Soviets, as leftists reagitate over nuclear arms, as protectionist tensions increase, as U.S. interest rates hamper European economic recovery, as Congress (and others) talk of U.S. troop pull-backs." Other Darman alarums also proved to be dolefully accurate.

The Camp David conference's mission was to provide political public relations strategy for overcoming some of these perceived problems. Darman, as usual, favored wily maneuvers and bold strokes. Three of his domestic PR proposals:

• Hype Federalism for as long as it will play.
• Develop and implement plans for minor (low cost) and symbolic actions for key constituencies—aged, Spanish-surnamed, white ethnics/blue collar, populist/rednecks, (other?).
• Distract attention from economic focus until the economy is clearly turning up—via a combination of foreign and domestic actions . . .

One of his proposed diversions was a Reagan-Brezhnev meeting even though the prospects for agreement on any substantial issue between the two was nil in 1982. Darman acknowledged that, adding: "It is not possible to conclude either a responsible INF agreement or a responsible START agreement in 1982. It might be possible to agree on a 'framework for negotiations'—and, if not a substantial framework, at least a timetable. This would help on several fronts."

Darman was not the only Reagan adviser pushing for some of these items. But he did seem to be alone in being able to diagnose so many challenges in a systematic way. Not that all of his approaches held up. The idea of an early summit meeting of sorts with Leonid Brezhnev was floated in midspring and then hauled down because in diplomatic terms it promised little. On the other hand, the White House did try a number of the diversions aimed at specific interest groups. The Administration suddenly remembered, if only for political purposes, Reaganism's commitment to the school-prayer amendment, outlawing abortion, tuition tax credits for families with children in private schools and similar items attractive to "key constituencies." Reagan's renewed and vigorous personal backing for such New Right agenda items did not get them through Congress.* Nor could the PR campaign distract from the economy's continued difficulties.

Darman's willingness to employ disingenuous gambits for the Reagan cause was not restricted to internal memoranda. Though press relations was outside his nominal jurisdiction, Darman in senior staff meetings was a constant source of proposals for packaging information in a manner beneficial to the White House. Near the end of the Gang of Seventeen negotiations, for which he had been a principal strategist, Darman wrote the internal "guidance" showing how the Administration could best position itself for the expected breakdown of the talks. Then he orchestrated the effort to persuade reporters that Tip O'Neill was to blame. When a newspaper later identified him as having conducted one of the brainwashing "backgrounders," Darman feigned irritation.[2] His annoyance was diluted, however, because he received credit for a ploy that was generally successful. Throughout the tortuous fiscal maneuvers of 1981–82, Darman was Stockman's staunchest ally in the White House. In that role he was brutally candid, and generally accurate, in anticipating the shortcomings of Reaganomics during internal deliberations. At the same time, he was an imaginative interior decorator in papering over these problems for viewing by outsiders.

This agility enhanced his value to the White House. It also distracted attention from what, by Reaganaut standards, was a political deformity. Darman was not merely a descendant of the Northeast progressive faction of the GOP. That liability could be worked off inside the Reagan White House. The President himself, after all, had once been a moderate Democrat. Jeane Kirkpatrick had once been a follower of Hubert Humphrey. David Gergen came from Democratic roots and was a Bush man in 1980. Darman was also tempted to get into the Bush campaign but, ever the realist, backed off when he measured the prevailing wind. No, it was not merely his record as a former protégé of Elliot Richardson that made Darman an alien. His dirty little secret was that he believed in government, including the federal government.

It could hardly have been otherwise. During the Nixon-Ford years Darman held policy-level jobs in four departments. As Richardson traipsed through the cabinet, Darman followed from Health, Education and Welfare to Defense, to Justice and finally to Commerce, where at

* The main obstacle was a coalition of Republican and Democratic moderates in the Senate. Reagan did lobby for the New Right positions in the summer and fall of 1982, but not nearly as hard as he had for his spending and tax proposals, for the AWACS deal or for other measures which he considered far more important.

age thirty-two he became Assistant Secretary for Policy. Along with his mentor, Darman quit the Justice Department in October 1973 as a result of the Watergate "Saturday Night Massacre." While teaching at Harvard, he rejoined Richardson, serving as vice-chairman of the U.S. delegation to the UN Law of the Sea Conference.

In that capacity he was, technically, a Carter administration appointee—the only important member of the Reagan White House staff to have held that distinction. But he withdrew from the negotiating team when he realized that the emerging agreement contained "principles of government and economics fundamentally antithetical to both American ideology and pragmatic experience." He used those words to condemn the draft treaty in the January 1978 issue of *Foreign Affairs*. No less a conservative than Senator Jesse Helms inserted in the Congressional Record praise for Darman's "superb analysis of the major deficiencies of the Law of the Sea Treaty." Darman's substantive objections to the pact seemed more practical than theological. It would have damaged American economic and technological interests and created an unworkably rigid system of governmental control.

Both in his federal jobs and as a faculty member at Harvard's Kennedy School of Government, Darman's intellectual interest was in how to make government more effective rather than simply less of a force in society. This hardly marked him as a liberal in the conventional sense. He was a free-market enthusiast and, while out of office, a managing partner of a highly successful economic consulting firm in Washington. What fascinated him, however, was problem-solving, finding the answers to policy riddles, rather than ideology.

When Reagan's advisers were preparing the Administration's New Federalism proposal, Darman suggested that a separate fund be established as an adjunct to encourage states to experiment with new social programs. That idea died because one of Federalism's real goals was to reduce government activity in this area at all levels, not to stimulate it. Like Stockman, Darman came to realize that the revenue problem created by the 1981 tax bill was even more complex than the ruinous deficits that resulted. Beyond the red ink's immediate bearing on interest rates and the recession was an even more fundamental question: could the government really function properly by reducing the revenue base as much as Reaganomics dictated? Even to harbor the inquiry was heresy, of course. Merely to ask it was to insert *plastique* in the foundations of Reaganism and Reaganomics. In the dozens of confidential budget documents and Legislative Strategy Group memoranda which I was able to examine, that point was never advanced with vigor. Apparently not even Darman and Stockman, bold as they were in many situations, were willing to display that kind of skepticism.

As a civilian, however, Darman had raised that same question when he and a colleague contributed a chapter to a scholarly book called *Business and Public Policy*.[8] The study attracted little notice when it appeared during the campaign year, which was probably a good thing for Darman's political prospects. His chapter included this admonition:

> The interest in limiting the growth of government must also be tempered by realism. The growth of government may be slowed or even stabilized, but it is virtually certain not to be reversed. Aggregate U.S. governmental expenditures taken as a percentage of gross national product remain below the levels of most developed societies, and the opportunities for shrinking are few . . . As long as an image of the possible reversibility of the recent growth of government survives, the necessary adaptations to the inescapable realities of pervasive governmental influence are likely to be postponed.

Had he been a Democrat in the early 1980s, Darman doubtless would have been a leading strategist among the neoliberals, a faction at the toddler stage in politics but beginning to show signs of precocity. Though their tenets and their hierarchy were still in flux, their orientation, as expressed by such youngish senators as Gary Hart of Colorado and Paul Tsongas of Massachusetts, was clear enough. They spoke like efficiency experts rather than theorists. They were less concerned about the size of government than about its effectiveness in addressing challenges. If they could discover some pizzaz and find some way to appeal to particular interest groups, they might yet amount to something as a political force.

As a Republican in the age of Reagan, however, Darman had no such refuge. New Right polemicists repeatedly demanded to know what a Richardson renegade like Darman was doing in a sensitive White House post; after Baker, no other staff member was needled so often. Much more quietly, Kath Darman sometimes wondered the same thing. With her doctorate in English literature, she was immune to the political form of Potomac fever and her intellectual instincts positioned her far from Reaganism. The answers to the question from these dissimilar sources were simple. From the boss's viewpoint, there was a keen need for professionals who knew their way around. For his part, Darman, the government man fascinated with the challenge of making systems work, got more jollies from public service than from any other activity. He had done well enough at teaching, research and business, but none of them provided the action that a high post in the White House or a cabinet agency did.

If Reagan, the man or the idea, remained in power, there would be a continued need for a few good political Marines like Darman, skilled in both policy formulation and tactical combat. Reagan would have to continue to fine-tune Reaganism, to adjust further to realities. Darman, like Baker and Stockman, understood political carburetors. One reason that the "wingers" (short for right-wingers) had so few agents in sensitive posts was that their movement was such a poor training ground for governance. They could raise money and polemical hell for their causes, but even in a conservative Senate they could not raise majorities willing to ride their hobbyhorse issues.

If Reaganism failed, the party's future would be clouded. A resurgence of the old Eastern Establishment faction, in which Darman would find his most natural home, would be unlikely. But there could be some other centrist restoration, and it would need veterans of proven talent. Darman, only thirty-seven when Reagan was inaugurated, had decades before him. Secretary of State was not too high a target some years in the future. He might be an alien now, somewhat confined by that status, but he was also heir to a promising future.

Of course Darman would have to perspire for his legacy. Having always invested sweat and persistence in pursuit of all his goals, he was willing. Darman and his wife have a running argument about their courtship. She insists that they were both out of college when they met at a dinner given by mutual friends in Boston. He maintains that he first saw her seven or eight years earlier, when they attended "Beacon sociables," events that allowed teenage Brahmins to mingle antiseptically while learning to dance. By his account, he was more or less smitten and intermittently attempted to date her during the rest of their prep school and college years. When they were contemporaries at Harvard, Darman contrived to be in the same general science section as she, but she turned down his advances "because I wasn't associated with the esthete culture."[4] Rather, he was choosing between math, economics and government, finally settling on the latter. And later it was he who arranged invitations for the dinner party where, finally, she took a closer look at her distant admirer. Slim, blond and fay, Kath Darman enjoys the story but regards it as something of a fairy tale.

He was less certain of his choice of career at that early stage, though Darman fancied something special. That imperative was imposed on him. He was the eldest of four children whose father, Morton, owned textile mills and other interests in New England. Morton Darman had dutifully gone into his father's business, taking time out only for service in World War II, when he rose to be adjutant general of the Third Air Force and won the Legion of Merit. He expected his first son not only to excel at all things, but also to take his inherited place in the Darman enterprises. The mother, Eleanor, exerted a different influence. After college she had exchanged her ambition to be a physician for a traditional marriage. She was the liberal of the two. When her children were grown, she turned to medical social service, ministering to terminal cancer patients and seriously ill children. The father, politically conservative, was immersed in business. As president of the American Textile Manufacturers Institute, a Washington lobby, he "advised" the government on trade policies that were central to his industry's interests.

As a teenager Darman worked one summer in a family-owned wool processing mill. His job as a "bin boy" was to unwrap fresh shearings for sorting. The stuff arrived heavy with excrement ("It was like unfolding dozens and dozens of huge, hairy, used diapers"). He found the eight-hour stint insufficient to consume his energies and there was little to do in the small mill town. So he worked a second shift each day in the office. The lad soon outgrew any interest he had in textiles or other provinces of the family business empire but he did not exactly rebel. Rather, he would meet Father's demands in other ways. "My grandfather was a perfectionist and made one of my father," he says by way of explaining his own drive. "It was expected that I would succeed in everything I did. I expected it too. I don't think it's wrong for an individual always to think he must try to be number one in performance. Anyway, that's the way I've lived."

At Rivers Country Day School he collected A's in nearly all his courses and R's because he was captain of four varsity teams. As a Harvard undergraduate, he made the dean's list each year and played varsity lacrosse. But after breezing through Harvard's Graduate School of Business he discovered that life at a large management consulting company was dreary. Under no compulsion to earn his fortune just yet, Darman and his new wife went to Britain where he took literature courses at Oxford for a year. He considered becoming a writer. "We'd have tea in some nice little place," Kath Darman recalls, "and Dick would take a napkin and list the stages of his career. Three or four years at this, three or four at something else, always moving ahead."[5] He remembers it differently: "I was having a little trouble getting on track."

Instead of going off to a lonely typewriter in the woods, he went back to Harvard for research in education policy. His group did consulting work for HEW (now Health and Human Services). When Richardson succeeded Robert Finch as Secretary, the new leadership of the department found the Harvard study interesting enough to hire Darman. Sometime later the new recruit discovered a typically Brahmin tie. Kath's grandfather and Richardson's father had a friendship dating back to school days.*

Richardson, a Bay State patrician in the political tradition of the Lodges and the Saltonstalls, found young Darman an able apprentice. Darman, in turn, got high on not only public service but also the kicks of rapid advancement. Like addicts of all kinds, he found that continued gratification depended on constantly increasing doses. Further, he was not one to settle for the private satisfaction of jobs well done. He liked the public record to be clear on every particular along this line. The Darman *vita* he updated in September 1982 consisted of a one-page summary and four more of details. It noted, for instance, that the prep school quarterly on which he worked won an award from the Columbia University School of Journalism. While proud of the successful consulting business he helped manage when Carter's election turned him out of the Commerce Department, that activity was insufficient even when combined with lecturing at Harvard. "He would get nervous," his wife recalls, "worrying about whether he was really accomplishing anything worthwhile."[6]

Like some of his other acquaintances, I sometimes ribbed him about his preoccupations with the pace of his progress and the public reviews of his performance. Once he responded with a couple of anecdotes. His father noticed an unflattering reference to the son in a syndicated column. The item, reflecting right-wing sentiment, said that Darman was unfit to replace Stockman should a vacancy occur at OMB (which happened to be one of the jobs Darman seemed to think suitable as a next step). The incident unsettled Darman when his father mentioned it; the son was reminded that the older man did not have a keen fix on what his White House post really meant. Then the father became ill. "And I remember being ashamed of one thing that went through my mind," Darman went on. "Of course I love him and I didn't want him to die. But it also occurred to me that he couldn't die yet because I still wasn't successful in a way that really meant something to him."

The other story was from his high school athletic days. He played quarterback (of course). In one game that seemed important at the time, he threw a short pass. The receiver then took off on a difficult run of forty yards or so, scoring the winning touchdown. A Boston newspaper, in its summary of prep school sports in the region, got the story backward. It gave Darman credit for a heroically long throw which

---

* The lacework of Eastern Establishment connections is intricate and endlessly fascinating. One of Kath's close friends at school was Katharine Graham's daughter. This tie led to a friendship between Darman and the Washington *Post*'s owner.

ended the game. Darman remembers feeling guilty about the skewed account and imagined that the real hero felt worse. In Washington, Darman occasionally felt like that unsung split end.

That was partly his own fault. In the early months of the Administration, before he had established himself, Darman kept his head down in order to offer less of a target to his New Right tormentors. When I was doing a feature story about the President's typical workday in February, I ran into Darman outside the Oval Office. I didn't know him, or exactly what his role in the operation was, so I suggested that I see him. He reluctantly agreed. When I got to his office, however, this most articulate of men turned almost mute. The conversation went badly; my notes of the encounter have just a few procedural items and a description: "chunky but looks younger than age . . . very tense for no reason . . . nervous laugh . . . serious guy."

Later, when anonymity got too much for him, he exposed himself to the ritual profile stories. For a Washington *Post* reporter, he prepared a lengthy memo in which he anticipated the questions. The writer used it to poke fun at him. For a New York *Times* feature on him and Fuller, Darman allowed himself to be photographed standing on a chair next to his taller colleague. The published picture made Darman appear clownish. Other accounts of the White House staff in 1981 diminished his role in relation to some of his rivals for influence.

All of this grated on Darman needlessly. Baker relied on him heavily and Deaver, recognizing talent when he saw it, became his patron as well. Before long Reagan trusted him. This allowed Darman to relax a bit and let his intricate sense of humor run free. Despite the grinding pace at which he worked, he organized elaborate betting pools before key congressional votes. In the spring of 1981, Darman and Fuller announced the "spring renewal" project, an exercise and weight-reduction program for the White House staff. They constructed detailed charts for the participants' stated goals and final achievements. Voluntary entry fees were converted into a pool for the most successful diet hounds. Darman set the highest target for himself, starved off twenty-eight pounds and won the kitty.

Capers like that earned some approval from a White House staff that appreciated fun and games, just as his competence earned grudging respect. However, Darman could have won an unpopularity contest because of an ego immune to weight loss. Of one official he said: "If I'm still here at the end of two years, I promise you that guy won't be." Darman was, and the other fellow was back in private life. His telling accounts of mediocre performances, conveyed to intimates in privacy, were usually quite accurate—and usually entered the White House gossip carousel.

He worried about not only the shortage of excellence but also the lack of continuity—in his own work and in government service generally. Once I asked him what more he could reasonably ask of his career. This loosed a stream of Darmanesque analysis laced with introspection: "Aside from doing right by my kids,* I'd like to go to my grave knowing that I'd done the whole joint some good. What's 'good'? Nothing that fancy. We often overcomplicate the question. We're still not that capable of doing certain basic things. People keep killing each other, for instance, and it would be good to get them to stop. It would be good to do something more about poverty and disease. But a reasonable time frame for making basic changes is decades. For some things, it's centuries. Significant change is very slow. It doesn't fit within generations, let alone political administrations . . . An administration has two or three years to get things done as a rule. Then you're into the election. A change in administration usually means starting some things over.

"There's no time really to learn from what's been happening. Society may be trying to do something or get somewhere over many years, but there's all this noise in the system, all this flux. There is such a short attention span, so little institutional memory. Who really studies the literature? Far too few. As a civilization we haven't yet institutionalized an effective capacity to learn—to learn about governance. And that's a precondition for doing anything that can be sustained and constructive, on a large scale, about even the most basic problems."

Darman could hardly come up with a solution for that the way he could draw a scenario for lobbying through a difficult bill. But he seemed to be turning outlines over in his mind and he obviously thought that a corps of talented government men above the civil servant level would have to be a part of any brave new world. Whether his own twitchy insecurity would allow him to continue in Reagan's service without exploding because of some real or imagined slight was another question. Toward the end of 1982, when the President was mulling proposals for staff changes, Darman—like a dozen or more of his colleagues—did not know how he would fare. He knew only that he wanted even more of the action than he had. Others felt the same way about themselves, but disguised it better.

How did he feel about his prospects during this period of uncertainty? He ducked a direct answer, but his elliptical response was

* The Darmans had two sons who at the end of 1982 were six and nearly two. Both carried interesting names from the past—William Temple Emmet and Jonathan Warren Emmet. Kath's ancestors included Robert Emmet, the Irish nationalist hanged by the British, and Joseph Warren, who died leading Colonial soldiers at Bunker Hill.

revealing in its way. "Obviously," he conceded, "I have a kind of Potomac fever. But, you know, part of any halfway sophisticated life by this river must be an appreciation of the inevitability of its ups and downs. I'll try a couple of metaphors on you. There's a crude sculpture between the house and the river. It came with the place. On misty mornings, it looks a bit like a migrant Loch Ness monster looming up, looking for prey to have for breakfast. The symbolism is hard to escape.

"Below the monster, you see Little Falls. The river has been making that view better, slowly but surely, for thousands of years. Just downstream, Washington rose in what was a flat mud basin infested with mosquitoes not so long ago. Pardon the triteness, but the river spans a lot of time in a little space. It creates, it destroys, it's easy to misunderstand. Staring at it every day, you have to develop some feel for its rhythms.

"Almost every spring, the Park Police fish out at least one body—another adventurer who went over the falls with a bit too much confidence and was consumed by the river. Someday that river may reach right up to our house. I expect we would have moved along by then. In the meantime, if I suddenly find that I'm forced to stay home, I think I'd enjoy it—at least for a while. It's a beautiful place. And I may have a fair amount of time in which to do one thing or another downstream."

For someone who had started life with solid advantages and made the most of them, Darman seemed inordinately sensitive to downside risks whether the subject was public policy or his private ambition. But in the Washington of the 1980s, that was probably a quite rational attitude, even for someone whose personal prospects stretched beyond the 1990s.

23

FDR Versus Darwin

Uncaring and unheeding, the elephant intended to symbolize the Republican Party stomps about amid a display of dinner dishes. This pachyderm in a china shop soon splinters a plate marked SOCIAL SECURITY. That scene was one of the more amusing and imaginative of the television commercials made by the Democratic National Committee for the fall 1982 campaign.

The elephant spot was a response to a Republican TV ad on the same subject. The GOP version depicted a postman delivering a pension check to a retired couple during the summer of 1982. The payment contains a cost of living allowance increase of 7.4 percent; the narrator drives home the point that the Republican administration has made good on its promise to preserve benefit levels and raises already scheduled.

Thus did the two political parties join in debate of what was generally called the fairness or compassion question. Social Security was an item mentioned often for two obvious reasons. The old-age and survivors component of the program served 36 million Americans in 1982, a group far larger than any other receiving direct government payments. Second, middle-aged citizens approaching retirement age as well as the elderly already receiving pensions vote in significantly greater proportions than do younger Americans. The sum of this political arithmetic was the systematic and hypocritical distortion of a much larger complex of problems. Further, the emphasis on maintaining Social Security benefits intact was a bipartisan disservice to the commonweal because it made all the more difficult the task that would soon

402   GAMBLING WITH HISTORY

have to be done: the curbing of future Social Security benefit increases, among other changes in a system that needed overhaul.

Congressional cowardice thwarted the Administration's initial attempt to deal with Social Security's weaknesses in 1981.* By making the issue so highly political, the Democrats managed to scare Reagan off it in 1982 as well. His retreat, however, did not save him from losing political points on the overall question of fairness. His advisers had recognized this vulnerability since the transition. A strategy paper given him as he took office included this warning: "The image of being . . . narrowly pro-business, and uncaring, could potentially derail the President's aspirations for a new direction for the country."[1]

Foreknowledge helped little. By the time the first year's economic program was enacted, Reagan was losing the fairness argument to the Democrats. "They've done a pretty good job of it," he told one panel of interviewers in early 1982. "I'm a Scrooge to a lot of people and if they only knew it, I'm the softest touch they've had for a long time."[2] Poll after poll supported the assertion that Reagan lacked sympathy for the least affluent level of society. That he was personally generous by his own lights and that he responded when an isolated case of inequity came to his attention—supporting the self-image of a "soft touch"—was irrelevant.

Part of the perception problem was inevitable. Quite apart from the specific need for economies, Reaganism's imperative to begin reducing the federal government's role in society had to affect adversely, at least in the short run, some groups dependent on government assistance. Reagan's assertions that the cuts would be equitable and that the "truly needy" would be protected did not stand up once his proposals began taking effect. By the end of 1982 the point was no longer debatable. The affluent were receiving tangible benefits from Reaganomics, mostly in the form of lower income taxes but in other ways as well. The poor, relatively speaking, were worse off. That was the direct effect of new government policy. Beyond that, the deep recession caused pain to all classes, though the lower orders, as usual, suffered more. Within the business community the main victims of the credit pinch were small operators rather than large enterprises. Tight money was the principal cause for the increase in industrial-commercial bankruptcies by more than 50 percent in 1981, to a total of seventeen thousand, and the final figure for 1982 was certain to exceed that by at least five thousand. Those going under were nearly all entrepreneurial smallfry. Big companies, even those deep in the red, were able to exploit intricate new tax gimmicks.

* Chapter 9 describes that debacle.

Every disinterested expert examination of the impact of Reagan-omics during 1981–82 came to similar conclusions about the inequi-ties.* One can accept, either for argument's sake or out of conviction, the general proposition that government had grown too large. One could also concede the existence of waste in social programs and the urgent need to save federal money. That inflation was the most impor-tant immediate problem when Reagan was elected should also be stipu-lated. Granting those philosophical and practical reasons for spending reductions, one still could not escape the end result: that part of Reaganomics already in place was unfair. If the trends underway con-tinued, the measurable inequities would grow.

Unfair by what standards? At least two, one of which may be ob-solescent while the other remains durable. The criterion that seems to have gone out of fashion is that the federal government has a continu-ing obligation both to protect the least favored members of society from utter want and to encourage, actively, their move up the ladder. The execution of that obligation inevitably involves some degree of in-come redistribution through the tax system and other means. Further, it implies some tolerance of waste. From the mid-seventies onward American taxpayers demonstrated decreasing willingness to maintain that approach, let alone to broaden it. The second standard is more general. It holds that the federal government, and particularly its exec-utive branch, is the force in society best equipped to promote the gen-eral welfare, as the Constitution says. Whether it does so with more dollars or fewer at any given moment is irrelevant in principle. What counts is that the federal government has a duty to enhance the *oppor-tunities* of all classes and regions to obtain decent shares of society's bounty. At the very minimum, Washington should do nothing directly or indirectly to widen disparities caused by circumstance. Reaganomics as it has been put into effect so far falls short of both standards.

It is not necessary to rehearse the entire list of tax, spending and regulatory measures to understand what is happening; a few repre-sentative examples will do nicely. One of the cleanest cuts was the elimination of the make-work program under the Comprehensive Em-ployment and Training Act (CETA). This legacy from the Nixon years was expensive and inefficient. It failed to live up to its original in-

* The most comprehensive and current scholarly work at this writing is *The Reagan Experiment,* edited by John L. Palmer and Isabel V. Sawhill. It was pub-lished in September 1982 by the Urban Institute Press in Washington. The previ-ous February, the nonpartisan Congressional Budget Office put out a study called "Effects of Tax and Benefit Reductions Enacted in 1981 for Households in Different Income Categories." The findings were similar to those of the Palmer-Sawhill book. Work by several individual economists and other commentators followed the same track.

tention—to move hundreds of thousands of its beneficiaries from the ranks of the hard-core unemployed to the stable working class. But it did employ more than 300,000 of the poor in 1980–81. Some of them did move into real jobs, thanks to the experience. The Administration wiped out all 300,000 slots during a period when unemployment in the private sector was climbing rapidly. Only about one quarter of those abruptly put out of work were able to find full-time jobs by late 1982. Some of the others went on welfare, which costs taxpayers money in another way. Others entered the underground economy. Reagan acknowledged the importance of vocational training. However, the Administration had no alternative scheme in place to take up any of the slack caused by CETA's demise. In September 1982, with unemployment about to hit 10 percent, Reagan belatedly applied pressure for passage of a modest new job-training bill, one offering no temporary employment. Reagan signed it with a publicity flourish the following month, but its effects could not be felt until 1983. Meanwhile, tens of thousands of the working poor were made worse off.

A similar result occurred thanks to changed regulations under the Aid to Families with Dependent Children (AFDC) category, the largest component of welfare. AFDC is one of the sloppiest legacies of the New Deal. Administration and financing are divided among federal, state and (in some cases) municipal authorities. It is relatively easy to cheat under this program. Further, the availability of AFDC has been considered an incentive for a father to depart the household in hard times. The only defense of AFDC, which was costing Washington nearly $8 billion a year when the new administration took over, is that government has been unable to agree on a better way to feed and house the destitute.

The rules were tightened in order to force economies on local administrators. The most visible of these changes had the effect of discouraging single mothers with children from working at all. This came about because the program previously had provided partial benefits to poverty-stricken women who earned marginal incomes. As their own earnings grew, they lost some of their allowance. But the old formulas in most states provided an incentive to work in that the women could retain more of their wages than they lost in subsidy. The idea was to keep open the possibility of eventual independence of the dole. The new rules reversed the formulas. That is, the permitted earnings were reduced to the point where tens of thousands of female-headed families were pressured into giving up their jobs altogether or reducing their earnings. The other alternatives were to lie to caseworkers more persuasively or to get work "off the books," thereby paying no payroll tax.

Because formulas vary from state to state, no overall figures were available showing the typical effect. However, the story became a staple of daily newspapers and local TV stations. One case history in Middlesex County, New Jersey, tells the tale. A twenty-eight-year-old woman with three children—no husband, of course—worked as a billing clerk and was learning computer programming. Her net earned income was $585 a month. Under the old rules, in early 1981, she was permitted an additional $350 a month in AFDC stipend and food stamps. The new regulations in effect at the end of the year said she was earning $65 a month too much to allow continued welfare payments. She reduced the number of hours she worked until a new evaluation of her case dictated a further decrease in wages. At that point it became more advantageous for her to ask to be laid off, save the baby-sitting money she had been paying, and get by on a combination of welfare, unemployment benefits and food stamps.

When the Urban Institute did a national survey of AFDC cases, it found that total income of "working poor" families in every state had decreased as a result of the new rules. The degree of reduction varied, depending on how generous the states had been originally. Percentage losses were highest in states where grants had been greatest. In Connecticut, for instance, average benefits dropped 27 percent. In states that started with lower stipends, the drop was small but the reduction allowed recipients to fall below the officially designated poverty line. In twelve states the new formulas yielded greater net income to those existing solely on govenment assistance (usually a combination of AFDC, food stamps and Medicaid) than to those who insisted on continuing to earn marginal incomes. Overall, the number of families pushed below the poverty line as a result of the new regulations amounted to an estimated 137,000.[3]

The programs mentioned so far in this chapter, except for Social Security, go by the bureaucratic label "means tested." That is, recipients can qualify only if they fall below specified levels of income and assets. This type of activity obviously is aimed at the lowest stratum of society. Proportionally, it was the category of government assistance that suffered most heavily in the initial round of budget reductions. Before any of the reductions took place, means tested programs accounted for 18 percent of federal outlays for direct government payments, cash and in-kind, under the broad rubric of social services, health, nutrition and the like. Yet these activities absorbed nearly 40 percent of the cuts in benefit distribution. The Administration was not solely responsible for this distinction. Congress, as we have seen, balked at attacking entitlements available to people regardless of their income or accumulated assets. These include the main part of Social Security, other pension programs, Medicare and veterans' benefits.

This hardly means that workers and other members of the middle to upper middle classes got off free. They were affected by reductions in the duration of unemployment benefits and even deeper reductions in "Trade Adjustment Assistance," which is designed to buffer the impact on those laid off when an industry loses ground to imports. If the economic recovery in 1983 goes at a sluggish pace, approximately 3.2 million of those without jobs will get benefits for shorter periods than would have applied before the new program took effect. Reductions in guaranteed student loans and related programs affect the upper middle class as well as those of moderate means.

Nonetheless, the distribution of sacrifice so far has been demonstrably uneven. While the typical wage earner lost ground in the late seventies because of inflation, recipients of Social Security old-age benefits— regardless of their need—stayed even because of automatic cost of living allowance increases pegged to an index that was artificially high.* Civil service and military pensioners made significant gains, particularly those at the higher end of the pay scale before they retired. In some cases alumni several years into retirement found they were receiving more net income from the government than they would have earned had they remained on the job. Peter G. Peterson, the investment banker and former Commerce Secretary under Nixon, was among those bemoaning these anomalies: "Through all the budget cutting of the past year, these programs were hardly touched. It was the programs actually targeted on the 'needy' . . . that fell most heavily under the budgetary ax. What we have then is a safety net for politicians who are unwilling to ask from the broad middle class an explicit contribution to budgetary control and economic revival. Or, we might say, the safety net is, in fact, a well-padded hammock for collection of middle-class interest groups."⁴ One of the few Social Security items affected was the minimum benefit system that supplies small pensions to those with insufficient earned credits. That was eliminated for new entrants into the system.

Apart from the changes in budgetary allocations and formulas, the new austerity also brought about much tougher enforcement. In principle, that should be welcomed by all honest souls. Which of us, after all, doesn't know a few operators who delight in outsmarting benefit sys-

---

* The increases were determined by the Consumer Price Index, which is calculated on the basis of relatively young families with children. The elderly have different, and generally lesser, expenses. Retired workers rarely seek larger houses, for instance. Yet the cost of living allowances assumed the same spending pattern. As a result, retirees, on average, did better than active workers when inflation was at its worst. In 1970, 18.5 percent of households under the poverty line were headed by persons sixty-five or over. By 1980, the percentage was 14 percent and still falling.

tems the way some people take on crossword puzzles? One of the most abused programs historically has been the disability insurance component of Social Security. It has been too easy to turn an injury or an illness into a long-term income. During the 1970s, federal outlays in this category increased from just under $3 billion to more than $17 billion. At the end of the Carter administration, Congress ordered a more stringent review procedure. The work had not started, however, when the Reaganauts took over. They accelerated the culling operation with such energy that nearly 110,000 families were separated from disability benefits by mid-1982. This gave rise to countless little horror stories as people with real physical or mental handicaps were cut off even if they had no prospect at all of employment. John Svahn, head of the Social Security Administration, acknowledged to one interviewer that some individuals were being jettisoned for insufficient cause. In so large an operation, he said, some mistakes are inevitable.[5]

When tear-jerker stories along these lines were published or broadcast and received enough attention to be thrown up to the White House, the response went along one of three lines: the example cited was anomalous and easily remedied; the action taken was required by law, in some cases a statute that predated the Reagan administration; the individual had not been entitled to the benefit he was receiving in the first place. Reagan himself had a private theory, which he sometimes mentioned to aides, to the effect that welfare bureaucrats contrived such abuses as a means of thwarting reform. When the Agriculture Department tried to economize on school lunches by classifying catsup as a vegetable for the sake of satisfying nutritional requirements, Reagan's first reaction was to suspect that sabotage had been perpetrated by some liberal holdover. Presumably the offender was trying to defeat Reaganomics with ridicule. The new regulation was traced to bona fide Reaganauts, however, and withdrawn after suitable expressions of outrage came from all quarters.

In fact, by reducing assistance to states and localities in a variety of ways and turning up enforcement pressure, the Administration created a new atmosphere for functionaries at the retail level. They had to live with lower budgets and less personnel during a period when hard times produced more applicants for all types of benefits. This, as much as anything else, accounted for the parade of injustices and idiotic rulings that contributed to the feeling that America was entering a new era of heartlessness. As a former city hall reporter who had once covered welfare stories, I was sufficiently fascinated to make a small collection of oddities.

My favorite was a tale given national currency by the columnist James J. Kilpatrick, a rugged conservative and strong Reagan backer.

He told the story of one Mattie Dudley, a cripple since infancy who now, relying on a wheelchair at age sixty-seven, sold newspapers on the streets of Charlottesville, Virginia. Her circumstances qualified her for Medicaid coverage as well as a federal welfare stipend of $280 a month. Like many people with few comforts in this world, she cared about the way she would leave it. Thus she had acquired, sometime previous, a burial certificate worth $1,000. Such instruments bear interest. By and by this "asset" made Miss Dudley too wealthy to continue receiving both Medicaid coverage (which she had not used anyway) and her monthly government check. Technically, the only way she could redeem herself was to sell her ticket to a respectable funeral and use the money for food or rent. Suitably impoverished again, she could resume her rightful place on the dole. Eventually, the case was resolved when the offender agreed to give up Medicaid protection. Charlottesville authorities allowed her to keep her pension and funeral certificate.[6]

Kilpatrick did not attempt to draw any large moral from this squalid incident. He did not connect it with what the President he admired so much was doing, and it might be unfair to construct such a link. Reaganomics did not set out to have Mattie Dudley buried in a potter's field (at public expense, by the way). Dickensian cases turned up from time to time under previous administrations. Yet no one familiar with the way the system works could doubt that the new approach to social services, and particularly to the "working poor," introduced by this administration encouraged exactly the kind of policing that forced so odious a choice on Mattie Dudley. Further, Reagan's HUD and HHS not to mention his grandiose New Federalism program—attempted to give local authorities much more responsibility for administering virtually all social services. Since the New Deal at least Washington had become the protector of the individual against arbitrary harshness. The feds were often clumsy, their regulations frequently senseless and inefficient, but they were a force nonetheless. Now Washington was withdrawing money and attempting to withdraw from the process itself.

Tax policy was the second important element in the fairness equation. The most prominent part of the 1981 revenue bill was the "five-ten-ten" reduction in individual rates. In theory, this applied to all taxpayers equally; everyone's marginal rates would be pared by the same proportion. Of course the wealthy would save far more dollars than those of low or moderate income for the simple reason that the affluent paid many more dollars to begin with. So far, so equitable.

When other details were filled in, that picture changed. The structure of the Social Security payroll deduction is such that, in proportional terms, the burden is heaviest on those in the low and middle brackets.

Thus, in the first year of the program, families earning less than $40,000 a year realized no net tax decrease at all because what they saved in income tax, typically, went to the higher Social Security levy. In the higher brackets there were immediate savings.

The Congressional Budget Office did computer runs to make other comparisons. CBO measured the total change in government benefits and personal income taxes for families in different income ranges once the measures take full effect in 1983. For the entire population, CBO calculated, there would be an average net gain of 3 percent that year. That takes into account the change in *effective* tax rates* as well as the loss or decrease of all types of government benefits. With plus 3 percent as the national norm, CBO concluded that those with household income of $10,000 or less will suffer a net loss of 1.7 percent. Those in the $10,000 to $20,000 bracket gain 1.3 percent, or less than half the national figure. In the range of $20,000 to $40,000, the gain is 2.9 percent, still a touch below the norm. In the highest income reaches, the net gains increase significantly above the national average.

Aggregate statistics, of course, can be toyed with and tortured endlessly. CBO's are subject to qualification. The thrust of that study, however, is reinforced rather than weakened when the rest of the tax bill is taken into consideration. Lowering of the marginal rates on unearned income, from 70 percent to 50 percent with an accompanying cut in the capital gains levy from 28 percent to 20 percent, clearly benefited only the affluent. Other provisions opened, or in some cases reopened, loopholes providing advantages to those already well off. For instance, the 1981 bill restored preferential rates to recipients of stock options from their employers. As this works out in practice, a high-salary executive ends up paying less tax on this form of bonus. Reductions in the gift and estate levies made inheriting large sums fun again. New provisions governing individual retirement accounts were a boon for the middle class. Some of these measures were intended to encourage savings and investment. There was partial evidence by the end of 1982 that this effect was being achieved to some extent.

Larger business enterprises, meanwhile, were able to realize benefits immediately. The 1981 law provided new incentives that were so generous that even the Treasury Department and the Republican-controlled Senate Finance Committee quickly realized that the changes had gone too far. The two most egregious examples were the leasing of certain tax write-offs and the detailed formulas for "accelerated cost re-

---

* The effective rate applies to all of one's taxable income and is the more relevant figure from the individual's standpoint. The marginal rate applies to the tax on dollars earned in the next higher bracket. A change in the marginal rate, of course, has impact on the effective rate.

covery." The leasing provision allowed a company that was breaking even or losing money to sell its tax advantage to a more profitable enterprise. Under this arrangement, both corporations benefited at the expense of the Treasury. The losing company received a windfall not because of efficient operations or because it has made creative capital investment, but merely because of a new loophole. For an administration devoted to restoring "the magic of the marketplace," that seemed to be a straight giveaway.

Accelerated cost recovery is sound enough in principle. It means simply that businesses are encouraged to invest in plant and equipment —which is good for the entire economy—because they will be able to get tax credits for those expenditures quicker than before. As this worked out in practice, however, the rate of acceleration was so steep that in certain relatively common circumstances companies could soon begin deducting more in taxes than they had paid for the equipment. That is, there would be a "negative" tax on these transactions. Not only would this be an unearned reward to the individual company; it would counteract the very effects the Administration had sought in terms of macroeconomics. A confidential Treasury Department memorandum on the subject disclosed that the negative payoff could go as high as 42 percent. The document concluded: "The major implications of large negative tax rates are (1) pressure on leasing and mergers, (2) uneven investment incentives among asset types and among industries, and (3) encouragement of less productive investment. Repealing the acceleration of ACRS in 1985 and 1986 would reduce, but not eliminate, these problems and raise about $20 billion in FY 1987."

The 1982 tax bill dealt with both the leasing and acceleration quirks to an extent. That measure, however, was enacted only under the duress of the deficit threat and not because of any altruistic desire to close loopholes. Further, for the short run, corporations were able to reap the benefits of these boons for a couple of years and retained other advantages that were less blatant. At the same time, the Administration continued to relax regulatory pressure in a variety of ways. Pro-business spokesmen complained that regulatory "relief" was far too slow in coming. That was true if the standard applied was the outright repeal of rules which business found onerous. However, Reagan's appointees moved quickly in reducing the enforcement of regulations concerning occupational safety, consumer protection, environmental pollution and other areas.

With the exception of the 1982 revenue measure, which was an expedient response to the deficit emergency, all of the actions undertaken in the spending, tax and regulatory realms were clear expressions of Reaganism. Though they did not drastically reshape the distribution of wealth—not during the first two years, anyway—they did alter the trends of decades. In small but measurable ways life was made more difficult for the very poor and somewhat easier for the wealthy.

Almost by accident, that same shift was occurring among states and regions as well as among economic classes. Geography has never been evenhanded in its distribution of natural wealth. Nor are geography's effects static. Federal policies from the 1930s onward tended to mitigate slightly the disparities of place, but changing economic conditions and population trends in the 1970s were having pronounced effects beyond the reach of government. Wealth and political power were moving from the Northeast and the Upper Midwest to the Southwest, the West and some parts of the South.

The sum of Reagan policies already in effect, including the increase in defense spending, result in a slight acceleration of the movement already underway. Reductions in federal subsidies of all kinds pinch most in states that can least afford the loss. Tax cuts, both personal and corporate, help most in places where there is the greatest amount of wealth to be taxed. If Reagan succeeds even partially in enacting his Federalism proposal, the leveling effect of federal spending programs will be reduced much further. In that event, a state's capacity to provide social services, education and all the rest will depend much more on its own resources—and less on its pro rata share of federal assistance—than it does today.

Figures available in late 1982 suggested only the beginning of these changes, but the signs were unmistakable. Examining the per capita share of reductions in domestic spending by region, one found a range of $145 to $151 in the Northeast and Midwest. In the Southwest and the West, the losses were lower: from $119 to $136. The national average was $138. These figures, compiled by the Urban Institute from published government sources, take into account only the first round of major budget cuts. The second phase, to be fully felt in 1983, can only accentuate the differences. On the tax side, the regional picture is more mixed because of sharper differences among states. Nonetheless, the greatest beneficiaries on a per capita basis were Texas, California and Colorado while New York, Arkansas and Ohio lagged behind. Thomas L. Muller, a student of regional economic trends, concluded: "On the whole, President Reagan's policies will widen economic and fiscal disparities between wealthy and growing states, on the one hand, and less affluent and economically vital states on the other . . ."[7]

Though the differences in regional impact appear to be an unintended effect of Reaganomics, the result fits with the overall thrust and is totally in keeping with Reagan's fundamental beliefs about individual responsibility. In his view there is an absolute virtue in encouraging a

person or a community to decide how to cope within available resources. He has suggested that people who cannot make it to their satisfaction where they are can "vote with their feet" by moving elsewhere. America, after all, was originally populated, and periodically
reinvigorated, by immigrants who did just that. Fifty years ago a young
man in Dixon, Illinois, who found hometown opportunities unequal to
his ambitions moved first to Iowa and then to California. Today the
restless and the energetic still pursue their dreams by migrating if necessary. What about those who for some reason cannot follow the rainbow? Well, the Reagan administration has made food stamps more
difficult to get and done away with make-work jobs.

A number of writers have likened these attitudes and policies to social Darwinism.[8] Crudely put, Reaganomics encourages the strong to
capitalize on their strength while offering fewer crumbs to those who
are weak, lazy or both. The sustained economic recovery that these
policies are supposed to induce would then provide more opportunity
for everyone. Reagan, with his ambivalent feelings about Roosevelt
and the New Deal, defended himself to a relatively liberal New York
audience this way:

> You know, back in the New Deal days, many critics of Franklin
> Roosevelt accused him of trying to destroy the free enterprise system.
> Well, FDR's answer was simple. He wasn't out to destroy our political
> and economic freedom. He was out to save it at a time of severe stress
> . . . Today, I'm accused by some of trying to destroy government's com-
> mitment to compassion and to the needy. Does this bother me? Yes. Like
> FDR, may I say that I'm not trying to destroy what is best in our system
> of humane, free government. I'm doing everything I can to save it, to
> slow down the destructive rate of growth in taxes and spending, to prune
> nonessential programs so that enough resources will be left to meet the re-
> quirements of the truly needy . . .*

The intent here is not to pass final judgment on either the wisdom or
the effectiveness of Reaganomics. The economic situation that Reagan
inherited was hardly susceptible to a miracle cure and the long-term
trends of taxation and government spending did demand stringent reex-
amination. When economic historians review this period several years
from now, they may conclude that painful purgatives of some kind
were necessary in order to cleanse the system.

* The audience was a meeting of the National Conference of Christians and
Jews in Manhattan on March 23, 1982. Outside the New York Hilton Hotel
while Reagan spoke, a collection of liberal and radical groups staged a large rally
in protest against Reagan policies. The President mentioned the demonstrators'
"passionate conviction" but wondered aloud why they spoke with such a "tone of
hatred."

However, it is impossible to swallow Reagan's absolute refusal to acknowledge the connection between his policies and the major recession of 1981–82, or his insistence that the measures he fought so hard to put in place were fair to all except malingerers and cheaters. Debating these questions with him is an exercise in frustration. After a time one longs to hear Reagan declare some contemporary equivalent of "Let them eat cake." If only he would show brutal candor. If only he would argue that the system needed leeching, that the poor and the blue collars and the shopkeeper on Main Street always bleed disproportionately during such therapy. Reagan would not do that because he doesn't believe it. He will not accept the strong link between his monetary and fiscal policy, tight money and the recession. He will not buy for a moment the proposition that anyone deserving help has been victimized by his spending cuts or that the burden has been spread inequitably.

In one conversation I raised the latter point, setting off a polite fencing match that contained much parry and no telling thrust. Reagan repeated his familiar and unexceptionable arguments about the need to invigorate industry, which required "realistic" tax laws. In the long run the workers will benefit. A bit too stubbornly, doubtless, I continued to probe his defenses. The last segment of this long exchange broke no new ground but perhaps conveys Reagan's attitude better than some of his prepared speeches and rehearsed press conference statements:

Reagan: Well, Larry, you can look at it a different way. There's a low level of income earned [by some] in the private sector . . . and those people were being taxed to provide the [CETA] jobs that in many instances were better than the jobs they had. It was like the cab driver who couldn't afford to send his kid to college [but who] was paying taxes for people making a lot more money to send theirs to college.

Question: Granted . . . I guess I get back one more time to what I think is a fundamental spinoff of the program as enacted. The upper-middle class and the upper class are better off today, right today. I think you'd have a hard time finding any of the "truly needy" or even those on the next rung up who are better off today as a result of what's happened.

Reagan: I would think, if you're drawing the line between those who are on government grants, most of what we've done has been to eliminate those people who never should have been getting benefits in the first place . . . You know, for example, [that] in just the first preliminary check, we found 8,500 recipients receiving Social Security payments who had been dead for an average of seven years . . . Now there is nothing wrong with us stopping that and taking [back] that money that is literally stolen . . . The program was never intended to support them.

I am talking about [helping] the people who pay taxes on their earnings and earn the lower income bracket levels. There is where there is a greater percentage of two-earner families, husband and wife, and we eliminated the marriage penalty so they are getting that break now . . . And the savings thing, the deductions for those people. You and I are not going to run down the street and start putting $2,000 in something because it would be a tax break [as part of the new IRA program]. But for those people, yes, that is a very big benefit. Now take the corporations . . . I don't think that it is an unfair thing. The Steel Institute says that twenty-one of the major steel producers in this country are going to go forward with a $6 billion modernization and expansion program. Who is going to benefit more from that than the laid-off steel workers . . . ?

That talk took place at the end of December 1981, when Reagan still clung firmly to his blinding optimism. Three months later Malcolm Baldrige would tell him that the steel industry expansion program was being deferred and other hard facts would hit home as well. But Reagan's basic attitudes remained intact and he marched through the 1982 election campaign urging, as the Republican TV commercials put it, that Americans "stay the course" with his policies. The Democrats insisted that his course had become a minefield for much of the citizenry and that the time had already arrived to declare Reaganomics a hopelessly regressive botch. That appeared to be a starkly clear contrast.

The popular verdict, as described in Chapter 1, was not totally clear. Neither were all the long-range implications of Reaganomics as circumstances changed and the Administration continued to tinker with details. One interesting political trend did begin to emerge, however, in the 1982 voting pattern. In the late seventies, at the height of the tax revolt, many working-class and other middle-income Americans rallied to the conservative side of that issue. They thus pitted themselves against the poor, the most obvious consumers of direct government services. The recession and two years of Reagan policies appeared to have checked the growth of that gap. Blue collar families were being reminded of the interests they shared with those one or two steps down the economic ladder. Whether that recollection would survive the return of prosperity was a question that fascinated both political parties as they looked toward 1984.

24

Snakebitten: The Race Issue

Thaddeus A. Garrett, Jr., has a presence as impressive as his name. He is lithe, handsome, with a bearing that bespeaks quick intelligence and cocky conviction. Trained as a Methodist minister, he has the knack of pulpit projection that congregants in black churches expect from their clergymen. Still, as domestic affairs adviser to George Bush, Garrett was not accustomed to preaching in the Oval Office. But that was the position in which he found himself on the morning of January 12, 1982, along with another black, Melvin Bradley, who then occupied a junior post in the Office of Policy Development. Though Bradley had worked for Governor Reagan in Sacramento, he too was far down the White House pecking order and rarely saw the President.

Garrett and Bradley were summoned on short notice by Deaver. There had been a blunder the previous week, when the Treasury and Justice departments announced a sudden change in policy concerning the tax-exempt status of private schools with practices considered discriminatory. Reversing its own position and that held by three previous Presidents, the Reagan administration would end the Internal Revenue Service's role as an agent of school desegregation. The Justice Department would withdraw from a lawsuit on the issue pending before the U.S. Supreme Court. IRS rules allowing the revocation of tax exemption once racial discrimination was demonstrated would be erased.

That bulletin came on Friday, January 8, but it took a day for the significance of the change to sink in. Over the weekend, the civil rights movement began to cry foul. The White House professed to be astonished over accusations of racism. Deaver was as surprised as the rest and discovered that the President could not understand the sharp reaction either. But Deaver's political public relations antennae were quivering under the assault. He realized that the President needed the flavor of black sentiment on the subject. Because there were no blacks in senior posts in the White House, the Justice Department, and the Treasury, Deaver called in Garrett and Bradley. Neither could be considered a militant activist, but at least they kept in touch with the black community.

They described to Reagan their own unhappiness with the new ruling and conveyed what they had heard from other blacks. Garrett described a black church service he had attended on Sunday. He recounted the minister's use of the parable of the serpent. A woman finds an injured snake, nurses it back to health—only to be bitten by the ungrateful reptile. Garrett took on a preacher's intonation as he built to the climax: "Reagan is that snake!" The entire black congregation, Garrett concluded sadly, erupted in a chorus of amens.

"The President was astounded," Deaver recalled later. "Until that moment he didn't fully realize how this was being viewed. He was absolutely silent for a moment or two and then he turned to me and said, 'We can't let this stand. We have to do something.' Then he picked up the phone and called Sam Pierce [Secretary of Housing and Urban Development and the only black cabinet member]. He asked Sam to come down and talk over the best way out of it."[1]

There was to be no quick or easy way out of the mess. The attempt to assist segregation academies and schools affiliated with white fundamentalist churches not only clinched the argument for many liberals that Reagan cared little and knew less about the problems of minorities. The incident also shattered what mutual trust remained within the troika after the first year. The press gleefully (and accurately) reported new strains among the big three. Baker, and more particularly Deaver, blamed Meese for failing to avoid unnecessary damage to Reagan. For his part, Meese felt that his two associates were dumping on him gratuitously even though he maintained that his connection with the policy change had been slight. Anyway, Meese thought, Treasury and Justice had only been carrying out the President's wishes. Criticism from black leaders continued relentlessly, even after the White House attempted to make amends. John Jacob, newly installed president of the National Urban League, accused Reagan of having "provided aid and comfort to the racists in our midst" and of having "begun to dismantle the desegregation process in America."[2] Mainstream editorial writers and commentators returned to the controversy repeatedly for weeks. In its February 1 issue, *Time* captioned its analysis piece "The White House Sensitivity Gap." By coincidence, the CBS/New York *Times* poll was taking a new sampling just as the initial story broke. It found that approval among blacks of Reagan's performance, already low (14 percent) the previous September, was down another six points—to the lowest positive rating blacks had given any President in the survey's six-year history. Further, of the 127 blacks interviewed by the CBS/*Times* poll that month, only one answered yes to the question of whether Reagan cared "a great deal" about poor people.[3]

When the White House struggled to get off the hook, the New Right complained bitterly that Reagan's aides were selling out to the liberals. Baker in particular was always sensitive to this kind of criticism. As Baker gloomily surveyed the political debris, he—along with many interested spectators—realized that the incident showed more dramatically than ever the flaws in the White House staff system. But he felt that he had only limited ability to make repairs. Meese, because of the advent of Bill Clark the same month, was losing his turf in the national security area. For Meese it was a wretched period. To an associate he said of the schools case: "On this one, you know, I've taken the whole load." Ever cheerful and bustling as a rule, he seemed suddenly deflated in private conversations. "Good guys," he observed, "take it in the chops a lot of times."

But it was Reagan's chops that absorbed most of the punishment. One of the ironies of the situation was how casually the President had allowed himself to slip again into vulnerability on the subject of race relations. Humane and totally color-blind in his personal attitudes, Reagan was always deeply offended by any suggestion that his conservative views might be tinged with racism. To him racial or religious bigotry was immoral, like Soviet Communism. He had proclaimed that idea for as long as he could remember. When events reminded him, as they occasionally did, that feelings and rhetoric were necessary but not sufficient to establish his bona fides, he would be puzzled, even hurt.

Certainly he had sensed no danger when he personally lit the fuse of what would explode as the Bob Jones case. Nor did Reagan understand the complexities. In the 1960s, as pressure from Washington to desegregate public schools grew more intense, many private institutions were started as part of the white backlash. The trend accelerated with the so-called Christian school movement as fundamentalist congregations—primarily in the South and the Middle West—sought to put up barriers against the threat that Jerry Falwell called "secular humanism." As nonprofit institutions, these schools were fully eligible for tax-exempt status. Contributions to them would be deductible. If they chose, the schools would be spared the necessity of paying Social Security and unemployment insurance levies for their staffs. Tax status could make the difference between solvency and bankruptcy for the newer schools struggling to establish themselves.

Civil rights lawyers tried to attack this device with federal court actions, starting in Mississippi, and were generally successful. Following the judicial consensus, the Nixon administration in 1970 empowered IRS to deny tax-exempt status to institutions found to be practicing racial discrimination. Denial would be on a slow, case-by-case basis, and the IRS never succeeded in fully encompassing the rapidly growing Christian school movement. On the other hand, older institutions predating desegregation rulings were also vulnerable to the loss of preferential tax treatment. None of the institutions was safe from IRS scrutiny. One of the legal defenses which victims of the new policy sought to put up was to argue that the feds were infringing on religious freedom. Bob Jones University of Greenville, South Carolina, maintains that it has an open enrollment policy. During the 1981–82 school year, one of its officials said, the school had about a dozen "yellow and black" students (out of 6,300). "Not many of them apply," he noted. The IRS ruling in this case had been based on the school's prohibition of interracial dating and marriage among students. The Goldsboro Christian Schools of Goldsboro, North Carolina, run by Bob Jones alumni, occasionally admitted a yellow student, but drew the line at black. Both schools justified their rules with Scripture.

These two institutions launched legal appeals against the IRS rulings affecting them, putting the issue back into the federal courts that had already decided in favor of the government in related cases. The Ford and Carter Justice departments had routinely defended the IRS's role. The Reaganites, however, were caught in a dilemma. The religious wing of the New Right had become incensed over the issue, which it viewed as a classic test of Reagan's willingness to fight Big Government's intrusion in the affairs of private groups. To placate that sentiment, the 1980 Republican platform on which Reagan ran promised: "We will halt the unconstitutional regulatory vendetta launched by Mr. Carter's IRS Commissioner against independent schools."*

During the first half of 1981, both IRS and the career lawyers in the Justice Department's Civil Rights Division assumed that they would continue to follow the practice they had inherited, despite the platform. Specifically, the federal government would contest the Bob Jones–Goldsboro suit when it reached the Supreme Court for argument. The White House received some static on the question from Moral

* Elsewhere the platform pledged that the GOP would stand "shoulder to shoulder with black Americans" in combating the "vestiges" of racism, but the document was mute on the question of school integration except where it condemned forced busing as a means of achieving racial balance.

Majority lobbyists, but sidestepped the question. Then, on October 30, Congressman Trent Lott of Mississippi, who had been co-chairman of the 1980 platform committee and in whose home state several schools had a stake in the issue, wrote to Reagan. The letter went through channels, in this case the legislative liaison office, and a summary of it showed up in the "Presidential Log of Selected House Mail" that crosses Reagan's desk regularly. On the left margin of these sheets the name of the congressman appears. In the center, there is a précis of the message. On the right there is a blank column headed "COMMENTS." Next to Lott's name appeared two sentences: "Writes regarding pending cases concerning the tax exempt status of church schools. Indicates that the Supreme Court has now agreed to review the case of 'Bob Jones University v. United States,' and urges you to intervene in this particular case." In the right margin Reagan wrote: "I think we should."

Normally when jottings of this kind indicate some action to be taken, the next step is to have them "staffed out." That is, the appropriate office in the White House checks on the matter and bucks it back to the troika if there is need for any further discussion. In this case, however, nothing was done officially. Instead, a junior member of the legislative liaison office copied the page and turned it over to Lott. He began pressing the Treasury and Justice departments, urging that they live up to the platform, now reinforced by Reagan's marginal note. In late December, Meese was informed that the issue was ready for decision. He neglected to fill in Deaver and Baker until two days before the announcement. At no time was it discussed at length in the White House. Neither Baker nor Deaver kicked around the possible political ramifications. Gergen, even deeper in the dark, lacked any sense of the public relations aspects of it. None of the black staff members was consulted in any way, and no one suggested that it would have deep resonance among blacks. "You know what the biggest trouble was?" Deaver remarked later. "All the input Reagan got was from lawyers. It was all presented as a legal technicality. No one talked about the real meaning."[4]

Immediately after Reagan's meetings with black officials, the White House rushed into a rescue effort. In statements, background conversations and briefings by tax and legal experts, the Administration attempted to persuade skeptical reporters that it was not really attempting to let the institutions in question off the hook. Rather, it was trying to end what it considered the pernicious practice of allowing the IRS, by regulatory fiat, to operate in an extralegal way. Thus it would propose legislation on a priority basis to empower IRS to resume doing what three previous administrations and several court rulings had told the IRS to do in the first place. Meanwhile, the White House conceded, Bob Jones University and the Goldsboro schools would get their tax exemptions at least temporarily while approximately one hundred other institutions would not.

There were three large holes in this argument, particularly insofar as the White House's original intent. First, Treasury Department officials conceded privately, there had been no plan at all to introduce any legislation when the policy change was decided. That came up only after the White House realized that it had erred badly. Second, the IRS was hardly operating as a free-lance social reformer; it had responded to court rulings which in turn were based on voluminous civil rights legislation of the 1960s. Third, for both procedural and political reasons, there was no prospect of getting rapid action in Congress on the bill hastily drawn by the Administration. To this shaky defense, Deaver added another element: he put out the word that the fault had been with the staff, not the President. It was a public relations man's nightmare. His boss would be depicted as either having sold out the civil rights movement knowingly, or having been so out of touch that he foolishly approved a bad decision by his staffers.

Reagan was in a no-win position when he conducted his next full-dress press conference on January 19. The question came at him first in this form: "What happened? Are you responsible for the original decision, or did your staff put something over on you?" Reagan had been prepared to discuss the substance of the issue rather than the whodunit aspect, but he rallied well:

> No one put anything over on me . . . The buck stops at my desk. I'm the originator of the whole thing, and I'm not going to deny that it wasn't handled as well as it could be. But I think that what we actually saw was confusion and it was rather widespread and encouraged . . . We had not anticipated the reaction because we were dealing with a procedural matter. And it was interpreted by many of you as a policy matter, reflecting a change in policy . . . I am opposed with every fiber of my being to discrimination . . .

Later in the exchange Reagan claimed credit for having "prevented the IRS from determining national social policy all by itself." After a follow-up question he again acknowledged that there had been ineptitude, but he finished with a plea: "Don't judge us by our mistakes. I'm probably going to make more of them. But judge us [by] how well we recover and solve the situation." The immediate situation was not solved at all. In February, the U.S. Circuit Court of Appeals in Washington ruled that the Administration could not restore the two schools' tax exemptions until the issue had been fully adjudicated. Congress

meanwhile shelved the Reagan bill, which did not make it out of subcommittee in either house. The case remained on the Supreme Court
docket for later argument. The only real change: the U.S. Government
had withdrawn as an anti-segregation partisan in the case.

Reagan's plea to be judged by results in race-related issues rather
than by a single "procedural" error was a risky request on his part. His
administration, like his campaign, repeatedly demonstrated indifference
to and unfamiliarity with the concerns of blacks and Hispanics. More
or less the same attitude showed in its handling of the feminist agenda.
Quite apart from the economic program, which blacks felt gave them
short shrift, the Administration seemed to miss few opportunities to ignore the wishes of blacks.

Early in 1981 Reagan had a chance to make an inexpensive show of
sympathy for the liberal side of the civil rights cause. A central provision of the Voting Rights Act, dating back to 1965 and almost univer-
sally judged to have been successful in its main purpose, would be up
for renewal in August 1982. Liberals wanted to make the enforcement
section even tougher. A few conservatives hoped either to let it die—
arguing that it was no longer needed—or to weaken certain clauses
affecting states with an earlier history of discriminatory practices. The
Administration could have taken the lead promptly, and avoided a
good deal of controversy, by coming out for a simple extension of the
statute. That way, the White House could have held the commonsense
center of the debate. James Baker and some of Reagan's other political
advisers thought that the sensible route.

Momentum from the civil rights side was strong. In October 1981
the House of Representatives approved a liberal version of the bill, 389
to 24. Clearly the blacks' campaign for legislation with even sharper
teeth than before was attracting very broad support. Nonetheless, the
Administration waffled. Martin Anderson's Office of Policy Development along with a faction at the top of the Justice Department felt that
Reagan should oppose the House's model, but the Attorney General
was still studying the issue, with a deadline of October 1 for delivering
recommendations. When they finally arrived, an impatient Baker tried
to force the issue by having Reagan announce that if the Senate accepted the House version with only slight modification, he would sign
it. A statement to that effect was drafted and presented to Reagan. Before it could be announced, however, Smith hurried to the Oval Office
and talked Reagan out of it. Finally, on November 6, a presidential
statement was put out. "The right to vote is the crown jewel of American liberties," it said, "and we will not see its luster diminished." But
the document was hazy as to specifics.

Reagan raised doubts about his own familiarity with the details even in late January, after the Bob Jones case had focused attention sharply on the Administration's views of racial issues. Reagan prepped for a CBS special to be broadcast January 27, in which he would have an hour-long conversation with Dan Rather. Predictably, Rather asked whether Reagan would sign or veto the House version of the Voting Rights Act extension. The President skidded around the point for a moment, but then said: "I believe that I can support what is the House version. I don't know what's going to happen in the Senate." Rather apparently thought he had a headline, and wanted to make sure. "But if the current House version gets through you would not veto that?" Replied Reagan: "I don't know of anything that is in it that would make me veto it."

During a break in the taping session, however, a couple of Reagan's aides pointed out to him that he had erred. Rather, at their request, brought the subject up again when the taping resumed. "I guess I did misspeak there," Reagan said. What he really meant was that he would accept a ten-year extension of the existing law. Nonetheless, confusion persisted. The Attorney General finally took the unusual step of explaining where the White House stood in an Op-Ed page article three months later.[5] In it, Smith wondered what all the fuss was about. "That simple and straightforward position—to extend the act as it is—is President Reagan's position." The Senate then became enmeshed in a minor filibuster effort by Southern conservatives. But a large bipartisan majority quickly quashed that effort. In June both houses of Congress agreed to a twenty-five-year extension of the statute and amended it to satisfy the civil rights movement. Because it contained one of the changes conservatives had sought, Reagan was able to accept the whole package as if it had been his from the beginning. The White House, making the best of matters, staged a formal signing ceremony of the kind usually reserved for major Administration victories.

In other areas involving government activism, the Reagan administration resolutely marched away from the practices that had become standard over the previous thirty years. The Labor Department promulgated regulations drastically reducing the number of federal contractors required to file affirmative action plans. William Bradford Reynolds, head of Smith's Civil Rights Division, announced that he disagreed with an important 1979 Supreme Court decision in the same area, *United Steelworkers of America* vs. *Weber*. In that case, the Burger court ruled that an employer has the right to establish a voluntary affirmative action program in order to help minority workers advance. The Administration generally did what it could to thwart busing programs. One complicated case originating in Washington State pitted local school authorities who wished to use busing against a new state law inhibiting the practice. The feds came in on the side of the state.

At the Justice Department, career lawyers, many of them liberals, publicly balked at the new approaches. Some of them circulated petitions to their superiors, others quit in well-articulated disgust. One of the defectors, Robert Plotkin, who had been chief of the Civil Rights Division's special litigation section, told an interviewer: "I'd say they're emasculating the civil rights laws as we know them. It's a variant of their economic beliefs—that people should be free to do what they want, that the cream will rise to the top and the rest will fall."[6]

Many of the disaffected were youngish liberals who would naturally oppose any diminution in the existing enforcement apparatus, no matter what the faults. Activist lawyers who made their home at the Justice Department under progressive attorneys general had as their mission more, not less, federal involvement in society. But Arthur S. Flemming, one of the elderly deans of the movement, did not quite fit that mold. An alumnus of the Eisenhower cabinet, Flemming was appointed head of the bipartisan U.S. Civil Rights Commission by Nixon in 1974. Never in the Commission's twenty-four-year history had a new administration fired a chairman; the agency was considered exempt from such routine political changes. Yet Reagan ousted Flemming and replaced him with Clarence M. Pendleton, a conservative black from San Diego who opposed busing for integration. Even after Pendleton and another Reagan appointee were installed on the six-member panel, it issued a long, detailed report demonstrating that spending for civil rights enforcement in all agencies was being cut by nearly one quarter.[7]

In recruiting Pendleton, the Administration at least selected a black with obvious qualifications. He had run an Urban League chapter and handled himself well in public. The White House did not fare so well in nominating another member of the Civil Rights Commission or in its first choice to run the Equal Employment Opportunity Commission, another sensitive post. Searching desperately for blacks who would support Reagan policies, the White House Personnel Office came up with candidates of such meager and eccentric credentials that both nominations had to be withdrawn. But those retreats occurred only after the two individuals, as well as the White House, were thoroughly hosed down with derisive publicity.

Pendleton James, the professional executive talent scout who ran the Personnel Office for the first eighteen months, was candor incarnate when asked how the White House had come up with two such inappropriate prospects for posts in a delicate area. "We panicked," he said.[8] James had the difficult assignment of trying to find minority appointees for an administration that had no natural constituency among either blacks or Hispanics. At the end of his tenure in mid-1982, he produced figures showing only modest accomplishment. Of 4,400 appointive slots —reaching down to what the bureaucrats call "Schedule C," a large patronage category without policy-making authority—the Administration had appointed only 171 blacks and 100 Hispanics. Even that combined figure of 6 percent was misleading because the vast majority were in the lowest stratum of the patronage ranks.

"It has been very difficult," James went on. "We find no friendly voices in the civil rights movement." Black Republicans are scarce, conservative black Republicans in even shorter supply. From the beginning, the White House advisers with political instincts realized that the dearth of minorities would be a nagging problem. The top cabinet appointees came from settings in which they had associated with few blacks or women in high positions. George Bush, one of the few people around Reagan who seemed to care about the issue out of conviction, was informed a day after the shooting that the departments were doing poorly in scouting minority and female appointees at the policy-making level. A cabinet meeting was set for April 2. Would Bush raise the issue pointedly and urge the secretaries to do better? Typically, Bush preferred not to take the initiative; he wanted to give no indication that he was asserting himself while the President was convalescing.

So James brought the matter up and the Vice-President seconded him, according to a participant's notes. "Very candidly," Bush told his colleagues, "we're doing a bad job on this." Figures were mentioned, agency by agency. Commerce Secretary Malcolm Baldrige, who owed his job to his connection with Bush, complained that "it's very difficult to find qualified minority candidates who have no past Democratic ties." Bush replied that the political purity test could be waived in certain cases. Baker backed him up. According to the organization chart, both the Personnel Office and the political liaison shop reported to him (though in fact responsibility was more diffuse). At that point the Administration had filled most of the important jobs at the level of assistant secretary and above. For some of the remaining openings, he said, the political loyalty test could be relaxed. Then Meese brought the issue back to square one. "But remember," he warned, "we're not looking for people who don't support the President's program." The pep talk had little practical effect.

James, as he returned to private business, seemed frustrated about the record of minority hiring. But in retrospect, how high a priority had it been? Not very. James had been under some pressure to take on a few recruiters with specific experience in prospecting for minorities and women. "To me," he observed, "that smacked of discrimination. I elected not to bring in minority specialists although, politically, it would have been a good thing. In hindsight, I might have done it differently." James even proposed that the White House—to prove that it was not sexist—end the long practice of naming a woman as Treasurer of the United States (the official whose signature appears on the lower left side of currency). Angela M. ("Bay") Buchanan, an alumna of the Reagan campaign, got the post anyway.

In its small way, James's approach was a paradigm of the attitude of the Administration, from Reagan downward, to racial matters. There was no imperative, in raw political terms, to treat these issues urgently. Blacks had not elected Reagan in 1980 and would not reelect him if he ran in 1984. On the other hand, if Reagan—and by extension the party —were perceived as a sufficiently vivid enemy, that perception might serve as a rallying point to increase black and Hispanic turnout on the Democratic side. That, at least, was the view of some of Reagan's more pragmatic political advisers. The 1982 vote totals lent credence to that concern. Another consideration was the ruboff on Reagan's standing among more or less moderate whites. Suggestions of racism might scare off some centrist swing voters. Yet signs that Reagan was taking unusual steps to placate minorities in any important way caused immediate protest from the New Right. Thus the political considerations were something of a trade-off. If the GOP was to be in spirit and deed the "Party of Lincoln," as the platform every four years asserts, the impetus would have to come more from principle than from political necessity.

Reagan himself insisted, whenever the occasion arose, that his principles were perfectly sound. In his 1965 autobiography, *Where's the Rest of Me?*,[9] Reagan writes movingly about prejudice in Midwestern small towns when he was growing up. He recounts with pride the night his Irish father slept in a car rather than take a room in a hotel that barred Jews. When the Eureka College football squad played a game near Dixon and could not find a place that would put up its black players, young Reagan took those two teammates home with him for the night. Yet when he reconstructed that evening thirty-five years later for his book, he inadvertently provided a small example of his distance from contemporary racial concerns and sensitivity. The semantic evolution in the mid-sixties, when he wrote his book, was from "Negro" to "black." In Reagan's prose, the college players are "colored boys."

One reason, perhaps, that Reagan used his book to advertise himself as a foe of bigotry was his uneasiness with the popular connection between Goldwater conservatism and opposition to the civil rights movement. Reagan in early 1965 still was not an avowed candidate for office, but his tie to the Goldwater movement was strong and public. In that period of ferment and legislative landmarks, conservative Republicans of the Goldwater persuasion generally opposed the Johnson administration's civil rights bills on grounds of constitutional concerns and states' rights.

While campaigning for the GOP gubernatorial nomination in 1966, Reagan lost his temper on one occasion when his liberal Republican opponent implied that the Goldwaterites lacked sympathy for blacks. The accusation was based on the conservatives' opposition to Johnson's legislation. Reagan was still uncomfortable with the question as the 1980 campaign began. Late one night in his Pacific Palisades living room, I was attempting to make up for my own insufficient homework on his early record. Had he explicitly opposed the major civil rights bills of the 1960s? Reagan ducked the question: "I can't remember, I honestly can't."[10] But he must have felt that he could not let the cassette recording stand that way, so he continued: "But is it liberal or conservative to believe, as I do, that the federal government has a responsibility to protect the constitutional rights of even the least citizen among us, wherever he may be, if those rights are being unjustly denied him? And to enforce them at the point of bayonet, if necessary? And who is the man who enforced them at the point of bayonets? Dwight Eisenhower."* Even if he had a convenient memory lapse about where he had stood concerning specific bills, he observed that the 1965 Voting Rights Act had been "humiliating to the South." A year later, after the election, the same subject came up in the same living room, but this time there was no amnesia. "I was opposed to the Voting Rights Act from the beginning," he acknowledged, and went on to explain that he objected to the law's vindictive, selective application.[11] He ignored the fact that the same clause he found repugnant was used to monitor some Northern states as well, including parts of New York City.

Reagan would have voted "no" on the original Voting Rights Act had he been in a position to do so. He would eagerly give beds to black acquaintances barred from a hotel, but he had trouble with a public accommodations law making it a federal offense to exclude guests on the basis of race. As governor, Reagan would brag later, he appointed many blacks to patronage jobs. But at no time in Sacramento, in his campaigns, or in the White House did he ever have a black adviser close enough to him to be considered even moderately influential. The same can be said of women, with the single exception

---

* Reagan liked the bayonet image and used it periodically in the same context both during the campaign and after inauguration.

of Jeane Kirkpatrick, whose advice to Reagan never concerned matters of special relevance to women.*

Periodically Reagan's political advisers have fretted about his low standing among minority and women voters. The response has usually been a good public relations ploy. That accounted for Reagan's promise, during the campaign, to appoint a woman to one of the first openings on the U.S. Supreme Court. The idea came from Stuart Spencer, the political tactician, not from Reagan's advisers on judical affairs or from Reagan himself. (Later, however, it was Reagan who insisted that the pledge be honored at the first opportunity even though William French Smith had reservations about the quest until all concerned settled on Sandra Day O'Connor.) The O'Connor appointment was important in its way, but hardly indicated any serious effort by the Administration to bring more diversity to the federal judiciary as a whole. A survey by the Washington *Post* of other court appointments during the first nineteen months showed that sixty-eight of the seventy-two nominees were white men. Three new district judges were women. A single black showed up in the survey, a district judge who was promoted to the Circuit Court of Appeals.[12] Publication of that story prompted a statement from the Justice Department to the effect that it would try harder. Three months and eleven additional appointments later, the department responded to my inquiry by saying that there had been no more women or blacks named to the bench. Two persons of Hispanic descent and one Asian had been selected by the end of November 1982.

The contrast between the splashy O'Connor appointment and what occurred—or failed to—concerning the judiciary at large was reminiscent of what had happened during the campaign. The strategy team scheduled Reagan for two consecutive days of courting black groups. But just before he went to New York to address a meeting of the Urban League, he appeared at the Neshoba County Fair near Philadelphia, Mississippi, a region still considered a bastion of segregationist sentiment. Confederate flags snapped in the warm breeze, the band

---

* The highest-ranking woman on the White House staff during most of 1981–82 was Elizabeth Dole, who headed the liaison office which looked after relations with various interest groups. Like Helene von Damm, however, Dole had limited influence on important issues. In January 1983 Reagan chose Dole to head the Transportation Department when Drew Lewis resigned. Thus she became the Administration's first female department head.

The second, appointed later the same month, was Margaret Heckler, whose defeat in the midterm congressional election Reagan had lamented. Reagan named her Secretary of Health and Human Services when Richard Schweiker resigned. Schweiker, like Lewis, left of his own volition to take a highly paid post outside government.

played "Dixie," and Reagan told his enthusiastic white audience: "I believe in states' rights. I believe in people doing as much as they can for themselves." In political cryptography, those words—coupled with a strong denunciation of welfare bureaucrats—was a much clearer message than anything he would tell the Urban League two days later. Yet Reagan did not seem to understand why black organizations rejected his wooing.

A month after the Bob Jones furor, Deaver conducted one of his weekly meetings with his Communications Strategy Group. A few of his colleagues were surprised at Deaver's frankness. What we have to do, he said at that late date, is to sensitize the President to "urban blacks." He observed that Reagan still thought in terms of the few blacks he knew back home in Illinois and of black stars like Jackie Robinson. Deaver wasn't alone in that reading. After attending a White House luncheon with other black clergymen sympathetic to Reagan, Hosea Williams told reporters: "I do think Reagan has compassion, but one of his problems when it comes to relating to the poor is that the only black folks he really has ever associated with are people like Harry Belafonte, Sidney Poitier and Cicely Tyson."

Deaver tried to remedy that in the spring of 1982. Reagan visited a black high school in Chicago and charmed students and teachers alike. He spoke at a fund-raiser for Howard University in Washington. When the Washington *Post* did a piece about a black family that had been harassed after it moved into a suburban neighborhood just outside Washington, Reagan visited the family the same day. Melvin Bradley was promoted to be a special assistant to the President and assigned, in the words of the announcement, to study "the needs and priorities of the minority and disadvantaged communities." For the first fifteen months, no one in the White House carried that mandate. These minor steps produced no big breakthroughs in the way the Reagan administration dealt with minority groups. But at least most of Reagan's aides were learning to avoid obvious mistakes.

25

Of Leaks and Ears

The long Thanksgiving weekend, 1981, was to be private time at Reagan's sanctum, Rancho del Cielo. It is the place where he fortifies his serenity and the place where he least tolerates an alien presence. Reporters rarely make it through the gate. Nevertheless, ABC's proposition—an hour-long documentary to be broadcast during prime-time Thanksgiving night—was too promising an opportunity to refuse, even if it did involve a lengthy interview with Barbara Walters on the ranch. Deaver and Gergen knew that the invasion of privacy would be well worth it. The questions would doubtless be gentle and the overall effect, boffo.

They were correct in both judgments. Reagan was in relaxed good humor, to the point of playing along when Walters asked him about a childhood habit that annoyed his brother, Moon. The network audience learned that six decades earlier little Dutch pulled Moon's earlobe frequently. Further, this strange attraction for aural flesh persisted even in the White House, though the President now restricted himself to his own ear. Viewers were just recovering from this revelation when Walters asked what his biggest disappointment as President had been.

"I think," Reagan replied, "it has been the inability to control the leaks that just seem to constantly be coming no matter what efforts you make . . . I think the District of Columbia is one giant ear. No matter where you are and how few people [are present], you almost read [what was said privately] before you get home."

Reagan's shock over the metaphorical ear was more startling than his tweaking of the real thing. At the time, the country was sinking deeper by the week into recession. Reagan's grip on a working majority in the House of Representatives was slipping and he had been forced, just the day before the interview was taped, to cast his first veto. His national security adviser was under investigation. His budget director a fortnight earlier had become an embarrassment to the Administration because of the *Atlantic Monthly* article. Overseas, assorted serious problems were proving to be intractable. Nonetheless, near the end of his first year in office, Reagan's quick, instinctive response to a question about his biggest disappointment dealt with leaks and press coverage. Fully a year later, during his last conversation with me in connection with this book, Reagan brought up the subject in a similar manner. The specific question I raised concerned problems with the White House staff's performance. In his response, he mentioned just one difficulty about which he had "really stomped around a bit"—what he called "the leak situation."

Despite his easy affability with reporters, Reagan in fact was profoundly uneasy with the journalistic process. Even when the preponderance of coverage was favorable, he bridled at the publication of material that he (or any President) would prefer remain buried. To him it smacked of disloyalty on the part of the leakers and irresponsibility by those who trumpeted the news. A month after the ABC interview, he was back in California for another respite. I asked him what, specifically, so troubled him about leaks. His response:

Well, everything. These unnamed sources and administration aides or high-placed sources and so forth that are never named and I know that when you take over an administration you try to bring in people who are supportive of what it is you want to do, but you also—there are large layers of the bureaucracy that you cannot change, and there are many of them, I suppose, who are resentful and do not agree with what it is you are trying to do. Now maybe they are the ones that are the principal sources of the leaks.[1]

Yet in the very next exchange during that conversation, Reagan indicated that he knew better. Question: "But maybe not?" Smiling, Reagan replied: "Maybe not." He wasn't so innocent as to believe that only career civil servants talked loosely. He knew that his own people had interests to defend and axes to grind. The whole business offended him. Soon he would try to do something about it. He would make a stab at changing the way the news business worked in Washington, just as he was trying to alter basically the way government functioned.

The Reagans celebrated 1982's arrival in customary fashion, as guests at the Annenberg estate near Palm Springs. Spending New Year's in the desert is something of a ritual for the extended Reagan clan. Walter and Leonore Annenberg are friends of long standing.

Frank Sinatra's spread is nearby. Geography now divided the old bunch, with the Smiths, the Wicks and the Wilsons in Washington while those who retained civilian status—the Darts, Tuttles and Wrathers among them—remained on the newer coast.

Wealth and a connection with the Reagans had served as the group's glue for more than a dozen years. Now there was another bond, a shared elation. Their man had not only won power, but also wielded it successfully during a first year studded with drama. This reunion had all the makings of an emotional high.

Reagan went to one party after another during the long weekend and indulged his host by taking his annual stroll on the golf course. But distractions, along with more rain than the resort usually sees in a fortnight, marred the holiday. The President was having trouble with decisions about his first State of the Union speech, which would be given four weeks later. The recession was growing worse during this difficult winter and his advisers were pressing unpleasant budget choices on him. Overseas, most of the NATO allies hesitated when asked to unite on strong anti-Moscow sanctions in response to the suppression of Solidarity in Poland. Back in Washington, the national security bureaucracy sprang another leak of the kind that so irritated Reagan. Word got out that Reagan would finally end the Richard Allen affair by replacing Allen with William Clark. Further, Reagan had agreed to a major overhaul of the national security apparatus.

Though they violated no military or diplomatic secrets, these news accounts nettled Reagan. Yet again, unnamed "sources" had scooped him. The White House once more had lost control of the flow of information. Both the initial story and the follow-up pieces linked the changes to instability and factional rivalry. Reagan had to go over the issue with Clark and Deaver, who were in California. Meese, minding the shop in Washington, had to put up his own defenses because the news stories depicted him as a loser in the new order of things. The officials with Reagan remained inside the guarded gates of estates and private clubs in which they were housed. At the Gene Autry Hotel, my colleagues and I reluctantly put aside tennis rackets and other tools of entertainment. The new game: to cajole operators of the military switchboard serving the President wherever he is to put through our calls to his aides.

Leaks and the broader subject of general press coverage became an unseasonal staple of conversation between the President and his old pals that weekend. The tone of those talks, as recounted later by a participant, underscored a familiar little cleavage in our political culture. Democrats and liberals are more deft than Republicans and conser-

vatives in dealing with the national press corps.* The approach of the
right wing, traditionally, centers on alienation or confrontation. Further
left, the tactics tend to be fraternization and manipulation. The Goldwater campaign of 1964 and Richard Nixon's entire career as candidate and incumbent are extreme examples of the combative attitude,
but hardly unique. On the other side, such master masseurs of the journalistic ego as John and Robert Kennedy elevated their style to a
much-copied art form. As a green political reporter in New York
twenty-five years ago, I watched Nelson Rockefeller seduce as hard-bit-
ten a crowd of newsies as existed outside of Ben Hecht's imagination.
Rockefeller's technique was simple. He made sure that his underlings
fed reporters interesting information and decent food. When really intent on conquest, he would give you a one-armed hug and personally
confide something that your editor would be happy to print. Rockefeller, like Theodore Roosevelt a half century earlier, showed that a
Republican could waltz with, rather than wrestle with, reporters. Of
course it helped to be from the East, to be an activist, to be a progressive.

Ronald Reagan fell between these polar schools. As a Goldwater
man twenty years ago, he naturally distrusted the national press. But in
Sacramento Reagan got on well enough with state-house journalists.
His show business background had taught him the advantages of civil
dealings with reporters; his amiability worked against vendettas on either side. When he ventured East to challenge Gerald Ford in 1976, he
had some tense moments. "We were like strange dogs sniffing each
other," he said of his initial dealings with Washington-based writers.[2]
Four years later, as the primary campaign began, he still fretted about
being misunderstood. John Sears was attempting to plane the rough
edges off Reagan's persona, to eliminate the notion that his candidate
was either a Scrooge, a Strangelove, or both. It caused Reagan problems during the winter of 1979–80 as he tried too hard to avoid traps
and, worse, to step way from off-the-cuff remarks of the previous day,
or hour, which somehow hadn't come out right. He worried about the
"prejudice in the East" that painted him as "somehow harsh, unfeeling,
perhaps reckless." As a result: "Maybe I *am* a little gun-shy. I'm fearful that I'll find myself faced with a distortion of something that I
didn't even say."[3]

But a great deal had changed by 1980 in the ever-shifting relationship between pols and press. From the late 1960s through the
1970s, the cumulative impact of Vietnam, the Spiro Agnew crusade,
and Watergate created a skepticism almost as abrasive as the tradi-

* Defined here as the largest daily newspapers, most of them in the East, the
weekly magazines and the broadcasting networks.

tional self-image we previously enjoyed, while rarely acted out, in real
life. Jimmy Carter paid dearly because of that attitude during his
unhappy term. But this spasm of pugnacity was relaxing by the time
Reagan won office. Reporters occasionally dinged Reagan for his
bloopers and commentators challenged his policies during the early
months in office, but he knew—and acknowledged—that the coverage
of him was generally fair. Failed presidencies had lost their novelty
value after four consecutive flops.

Two forms of criticism, nonetheless, nibbled at Reagan's serenity. He
bridled at suggestions that Reaganomics actually hurt the least blessed
in society. And he was constantly angered by disclosures concerning
national security affairs, some of which dealt with personality conflicts
and some with policy controversies. He was all the more frustrated by the
fact that his own appointees in the White House and the departments
were the deepest reservoirs for these leaks. Sometimes he simply refused to accept that reality. On March 25, 1981, the day after Haig
testified on Capitol Hill about his opposition to Bush's designation as
chairman of the Crisis Management Team, Reagan chatted with reporters on the South Lawn. Haig's statement had been made in public
and his aides had spread the word that the Secretary of State considered resigning over the issue. What did Reagan have to say? "I don't
know whether you'd like my reaction," the President responded tautly.
"Well?" one of us said. "My reaction was that maybe some of you were
trying to make the news instead of reporting it."

That became a Reagan refrain. He found it easier to chastise those
who published unpleasant information rather than to deal with the
original purveyors or with the problems that had led to the leaks in the
first place. In October, just as the White House won the AWACS fight,
one of Reagan's friends planted a story about an imminent shakeup.
That version had Reagan on the brink of firing Allen, moving Meese to
the cabinet, and dumping Haig as well. Several of us heard this yarn
and CBS went with it, hard.

The next morning in the Oval Office, Reagan was angry. David Gergen, auditing the interview, fidgeted nervously as Reagan spoke: "That
is totally invented, and I don't believe there is an unnamed source responsible. I believe it is entirely blowing smoke on the part of whoever
carried the story or wrote the story. And I have no intention [of making important personnel changes]."

Reagan usually tolerates interruptions easily, but this time when I
tried to point out that the story was all over town, he leaned forward in
his chair and rushed on: "I think Al Haig has been doing a magnificent
job and he's going to continue to do that. And I'm satisfied with the

setup that we have here in the office and not planning any changes here in the White House staff."[4]

In fact, Reagan by this time was growing restless with the National Security Council staff operations. Mike Deaver, as we have seen, was already attempting to bring Clark into the White House. But it was also true that Reagan then had no desire at all to force out either Meese or Haig. The temptation to go with stories of dubious authenticity isn't resisted often enough even though, in most cases, there are sources more or less worthy of that tired adjective "reliable." Reagan's annoyance was typical of Presidents who find themselves in these situations, which is to say nearly all Presidents. Like cockroaches and humidity, it is a problem that one lives with in Washington.

Not Reagan, however. He saw the leaks threatening to become a flood. They rankled him and rattled him. As he talked with his friends over the long New Year's weekend in Palm Springs, he found his feelings reinforced. The Washington press was after him, they said; he should fight back. He had been too agreeable. He had mistaken the honeymoon period, and the extension of it following the attempted assassination, for permanent civility. Now the wolves were showing their fangs and should be dealt with. Bill Clark, though himself an adroit operator with reporters when he thought it served Reagan's or his own interests, agreed that it was time to make a stab at protecting sensitive information. If some mechanism could be found for reducing disclosure of what was merely embarrassing, so much the better. The theme of this talk was an almost perfect reversion to Republican old-think concerning the press. It dovetailed with advice that Richard Nixon had been passing along through Lyn Nofziger's political liaison office.

The President returned to Washington determined to do something concrete. At his regular morning meeting with the troika, he reviewed his reasons for annoyance and pointed out that the Palm Springs crowd agreed with him. Even Walter thought that the national press was way out of line, and Walter should know. (Annenberg had once been publisher of the Philadelphia *Inquirer,* a paper which rose from mediocrity to excellence after he sold it. He kept *TV Guide* and the *Daily Racing Form.*) At a cabinet meeting that first week of 1982, Reagan complained again. He displayed a copy of the January 6 Washington *Post.* Two stories dominated the top of the front page, both of them "it-was-learned" pieces about the prospective fiscal '83 budget. Below the fold, under a more modest headline, was an article on Reagan's meeting with Helmut Schmidt, a session which the White House considered a success. At the same time, the White House learned that *Time* was about to break a story describing the latest U.S. approach to Peking on the delicate question of arms sales to Taiwan.[5]

Reagan had had enough. He proposed nothing less than a revolution in press relations for the executive branch of government. The main problem, Reagan said, was the loose talk by officials at all levels of government. Most of these conversations were conducted on a "background" basis—that is, with the official remaining anonymous. Throttle most of these background interviews, Reagan reasoned, and we will have gone a long way toward a solution. The troika was astonished, though Clark thought that the idea might work. Baker and Deaver composed counter-arguments while a draft directive was begun. Its main provisions would have limited those permitted to talk on a background basis in the White House to just half a dozen: Meese, Baker, Deaver, Clark, Gergen and Speakes. In the cabinet departments, only the secretary and his principal press relations aide would be authorized to speak from behind a mask. Everyone else would either have to speak on the record—with the permission of his boss—or give up dealing with reporters.

Fearful that Reagan might actually go ahead with the scheme, causing a real confrontation with the entire national press corps (not to mention all the expense-account restaurants that live off "source" meals), Baker and Deaver sought a way out. Deaver proposed a compromise: forcing all interviews to be coordinated by the press office of the agency involved. Baker argued that the Reagan approach, after causing a great deal of ill will and negative publicity, would prove to be unenforceable.

Reagan soon cooled down. He agreed to settle for an "NSDD" (National Security Decision Directive) drafted by Clark as one of his first acts in his new White House post. The order, dated January 12, was an attempt to limit the access of officials to classified material. It also set up a check on interviews. The operative paragraph:

All contacts with any element of the news media in which classified National Security Council matters or classified intelligence information are discussed will require the advance approval of a senior official. An Administrative memorandum will be prepared as soon as possible after the contact, recording the subjects discussed and all information provided to the media representative.

The White House statement summarizing the NSDD also threatened that the government would use "all legal methods" to discover the perpetrators of "unauthorized disclosures of such information." If actually enforced, the directive would have intimidated middle-level officials throughout the government, discouraging the dissemination of all kinds of information, sensitive or otherwise. For instance, while the January 12 order was being drafted, the Agriculture Department circulated an

internal memorandum saying that all interviews of consequence by
agency officials would have to be cleared by the White House.[6] That
document was, of course, promptly leaked and then quashed. When
Clark later produced the detailed procedures necessary to carry out the
January 12 directive, they turned out to be less fierce than the original
document. The White House, in effect, stepped back from a direct confrontation that would have caused more problems than it solved. Nonetheless, a point had been made. Some bureaucrats were discouraged, at
least temporarily, from dealing with reporters. Covering the State Department and the Pentagon became slightly more difficult. But serious
leaks continued apace concerning the same subjects—national security
policy and the budget-making process—that Reagan found unsettling.

Reagan suggested the possibility of a new crackdown again from
time to time, but halfheartedly. A full year later, after his 1983 New
Year's break in Palm Springs, Reagan's indignation overflowed again
largely because of embarrassing disclosures concerning his budget
plans. He signed another directive aimed at controlling conversations
between reporters and White House officials. This order set up a cumbersome procedure before interviews could take place. Reagan and
Clark still hoped, in vain, to discourage "background" discussions. In
fact, more serious obstacles already had been constructed elsewhere in
the Administration.

At the Justice Department, the Pentagon, and the Central Intelligence Agency, systematic efforts began soon after Inauguration Day to
dam the flow of information. Leaks weren't the issue in these situations. Rather, these agencies attempted, with some success, to alter established procedures under which scholars and journalists could gain
access to documentary material. At the CIA, Director William Casey
drastically restricted the practice of providing special briefings for reporters or others who demonstrated a legitimate need for information.
Previously, for instance, a correspondent about to take up a new post
abroad could fill a notebook or two at the CIA's Langley headquarters
before leaving. Casey, who during 1980 often complained that campaign organization officials wasted far too much time talking to journalists, concluded that the CIA had no business briefing reporters. He
also eliminated the agency's separate press operation, ending what little
independence it had enjoyed.

Both the CIA and the Defense Department were eager to reduce proceedings brought under the Freedom of Information Act (FOIA).
First enacted in 1968 and then expanded in 1974 as part of the post-
Watergate reforms, FOIA provides a legal mechanism through which
citizens can obtain certain types of information which government
agencies choose to keep secret. While the Administration requested

amendments in Congress which would drastically weaken the statute, the Justice Department sought the same ends by changing guidelines issued to executive agencies. The standing instruction to departments that FOIA applications should be honored unless doing so clearly harmed the public interest was simply withdrawn. Democratic Senator Jim Sasser of Tennessee wrote of this trend: "The stakes in this matter are very high—a question of whether the public has a right to know what its government is doing."[7]

The White House adroitly kept its direct involvement in this controversy to a minimum. Reagan's advisers were too shrewd to allow the President to be cast personally on the wrong side of an argument over freedom of the press. Nonetheless, as almost always happens after the first few months, day-to-day dealings between the White House and the press corps that covers it routinely became increasingly abrasive. Some of the face-offs forced by the reporters were over relatively petty questions concerning reportorial ego and convenience rather than the grand stakes Sasser talked about.

Routine coverage of the White House has changed dramatically during recent administrations because of the growing importance, and physical presence, of television operations. John Kennedy skillfully exploited his televised news conferences and the occasional speeches he made, but his Press Office's day-to-day operations were aimed primarily at print rather than video. Not a single television camera was present in the Oval Office when Lyndon Johnson held his first "impromptu" press conference soon after Kennedy's death. Today at least five TV camera crews and twelve to fifteen broadcast correspondents are present whenever the President is in the White House. The appetite for footage adaptable for evening news spots of 60 to 120 seconds or longer pieces on the morning shows is insatiable. The competition among network correspondents when they do their "standups" on the White House lawn is keener than the rivalry among soccer teams in Latin countries.

This situation led to the comic but distracting "war of the photo ops." In the prehistoric era of the Speed Graphic, a White House "photo opportunity" was simply a chance for still photographers to get a few quick black-and-white shots for use by wire services and daily newspapers. That minor practice evolved into a major operation because of television. But silent footage is of limited value and the temptation to ask a sharp question or two which might help the correspondent scoop out a few precious seconds of air time is difficult to resist.

Initially, Reagan reacted with a reasonable degree of patience, often trying to reply to abrupt inquiries regardless of the questions' bearing on what he happened to be doing at the moment. But the President and his staff both began to resent—even fear—these quickie interrogations. When they took place in the presence of a foreign leader, they could be embarrassing. Since no President—and it surely was not one of Reagan's habits—could be briefed constantly on all subjects that might be asked, Reagan was at risk of being shown on television with no information or the wrong information. Further, a few of his interrogators took to treating him with roughly the same degree of respect that a sportswriter shows to the day's goat in locker room banter after a game. ABC's Sam Donaldson specialized in that sort of thing. After a minor event in the East Room on March 10, 1982, Reagan was passing the press pool and trying to give deft no-comments to sensitive questions about his policy in Central America. Donaldson barked at him: "Do you want to overthrow the Nicaraguan Government? Tell the truth now!" Reagan merely shrugged in response.

Because of such incidents, Deaver had been trying since midwinter to ban questions at photo ops. Gergen, however, feared the wrath of broadcast and wire service correspondents and resisted the change. Finally Deaver prevailed. The number of correspondents present at routine Oval Office events would be reduced to the wire services, one broadcaster, and one newspaper or magazine writer. In exchange, Reagan would hold more frequent Q and A sessions at which there could be an orderly exchange. These would supplement, rather than replace, the monthly formal press conferences. It seemed a reasonable trade-off, but no one was satisfied. The magazine writers were irritated because they lost their separate pool slot as a result of a fight that had nothing to do with them. The networks were upset for obvious reasons. The White House enjoyed only a limited victory because the smaller number of correspondents continued to pepper Reagan with questions. The prevailing sentiment in the Press Room was that Reagan was becoming invisible.

Even if that notion were true, it would not have been particularly relevant. There is no direct correlation between a President's exposure to questions and the discovery of useful information. In any event, apart from the period in which he was convalescing after the attempt on his life, Reagan was usually accessible. He could hardly be expected to maintain the pace of his first four weeks in office, when he held a formal press conference and gave separate interviews to a sextet of columnists, a quartet of television commentators, a sophomore from the *Harvard Crimson,* two Washington *Post* reporters, an NBC correspondent, and the man from *Time.* But he continued to do well enough in terms of frequency of exposure.

The content of these exchanges was another matter. Any politician rating even journeyman status will try to slide under the tag of difficult questions, but Reagan is a particularly tough interview subject. He has a talent for drifting away from the nub of an inquiry so that pursuers feel that they are chasing smoke with a net. Only with a great deal of time for persistent follow-up can Reagan be surrounded. This is usually impossible. A typical bit of give-and-take occurred at Reagan's press conference of October 1, 1981.

Question: Mr. President, as I think you're aware, a number of black leaders in this country have expressed some reservations about your policies, not only economic policies, but other policies, and I wonder if you might have something to say today to reassure the blacks in this country concerning your attitude and your policy. Specifically, sir, whether or not you're in favor of extending the Voting Rights Act as it is now constituted?

Reagan: I have not had an opportunity—the report that I've been waiting for is on its way to my office and didn't get here before the press conference, but I am wholeheartedly in favor, let's say, in principle of the Voting Rights Act because I believe very deeply that we've had experiences in this country, and not alone on a racial basis, of both fraud and discrimination and that's a sacred right that must be upheld and I will uphold it.

I think that possibly there are some leaders of organizations in the black community who have followed the lead of others and have been attacking from the very beginning our programs, but I have been gratified by the support that is evidenced to me through mail, through calls, through personal meetings with members of the black community that have told me they believe in the programs. I had one letter just a few days ago from a sixteen-year-old boy who identified himself as black. And he said, "I am wholeheartedly behind what you're trying to do and I think it means much for my own future." I had another from a young black man who had just become the father of a baby girl. And he was telling me that he—and he had come all the way over from being a die-hard Democrat to support this program—and he said "because I think it means a better world for my daughter."

At that point, black support for Reagan had diminished from low to virtually nil and the Administration was about to attempt—unsuccessfully, as it turned out—to weaken the Voting Rights Act. Reagan's response had little bearing on either the feelings among blacks, the policy being refined in his Justice Department, or the impact of his budget changes on the poor. The fact is that a news conference makes news in the headline sense only when the White House has determined in advance that it should do so, or when the President goofs. Otherwise these encounters are a form of political theater, occasionally valuable for showing what the President does—and does not—know on a particular day. They add to the public's general impressions of the man at the top, though in a diffuse manner. The cognoscenti parse nuances, count boners, award points or grades. Usually the scorecard done in Washington bears little resemblance to the echoes one gets from the country. More importantly, if the best definition of covering the President is to report on what he and his advisers are doing, or failing to do, for the nation, then the Chief Executive's public sparring matches with reporters are about as revelant as Memorial Day parades are to the country's real military strength.

The actual contest occurs on another level, daily, between the President's staff and the reporters who attempt to get beyond the window dressing and the showroom into the policy factory where the patterns are cut and the fabric stitched. This is a separate game, to which the White House devotes enormous energy and considerable personnel, and to which we will now turn.

26

Tall's Tales

At the end of a workday, David Gergen went through a fixed routine. Whether alone in his office or in the company of a reporter, he turned on his television set with a remote control device, then flipped from channel to channel to catch each network's White House coverage. His eyes darted from the visitor to the screen. If the quick images confirmed his intention for the principal Reagan story of the night, he would grin or even chortle. "See that? Aha . . . that's nice." If the screen told him something else, he tended to be silent. His companion would imagine that Gergen was wondering what went wrong, how he could do it better tomorrow.

According to the organization chart, Gergen, whose title was Assistant to the President for Communications, ran all the megaphones. The Press Office, the speech writers, the public affairs shop and related offices—forty-six souls in late 1982—all reported to him. He was hardly a sedentary bureaucrat. Gergen conducted briefings on some of the more complex issues. He appeared on television occasionally either to promote an Administration position or to defend against attack. When high-level coordination with the National Security Council staff or the principal spokesmen at State and Defense was necessary, Gergen involved himself. He spent a few hours each week in earnest, separate conversations with correspondents of the more influential news organizations. "The Tall One" (sometimes called "Tall" for short) is six feet, five inches of restless intellectual energy. If an eyelid showed the strain by twitching now and then, or if the words tumbled out so quickly that they collided with each other, the tension was easily understood.

The organization chart, nonetheless, was misleading. In the Reagan

White House, the entire senior staff was engaged in getting out the message. Quite apart from Reagan's own preoccupation with the honing and delivery of the Word in public presentations, the President's men were keenly sensitive to public relations. Meese, Baker and Deaver each saw reporters one-on-one frequently. Clark played hard to get, but planted stories deftly when in the mood. Darman and Fuller, though less visible, often shaped the written "guidance" circulated among officials for use in responding to reporters' questions. They also starred in Deaver's long-range PR planning committee.

Permitted to attend a few troika breakfasts and the larger staff meetings that followed, I found myself afterward with notes on a score of different subjects. But one concern permeated all those sessions: how events had played or would play on the air and in print. What items on the schedule should be turned into "photo ops"? Should the President have a question period with the press today? If he does, what story should be "sold"? Is the briefing material ready to prepare Reagan for his next magazine interview? Murray Weidenbaum wants a consensus position for replying to a critical statement by a number of Republican former cabinet officers; Darman quickly sketches out a response. The Administration has been taking heat in the press about its latest proposed reduction in the Medicare budget; Darman thinks that the story should be allowed to sink if possible, but he hands out a fact sheet for use as a talking paper in case it doesn't.

The question of who has been bad-mouthing William French Smith comes up; Baker warns his colleagues to be discreet on that subject. He mentions a rumor that the Washington *Post* is putting half a dozen reporters on the story of Smith's financial dealings. Speakes detects a yen within the press corps to link the relatively petty Smith affair with the much heavier Ray Donovan investigation. Gergen worries aloud more about the pack's pursuit of Donovan. New inflation figures will come out this day; how should they best be described?

Later the visitor inquires whether this fare is typical of staff meeting agendas or whether some coincidence has bunched these items into a few sessions. Answers from three of the participants are unanimous: that was standard. One of the things this White House understood well was the connection between perception and political power. Another was the possibilities of modern polling techniques. Funds channeled through the Republican National Committee permitted Richard Wirthlin's firm, Decision Making Information, to conduct the most active (and most expensive) continuous opinion survey operation ever undertaken on behalf of a President. Wirthlin's sophisticated tracking and analysis of the popular mood was a constant factor in the private deliberations of Reagan's strategists. Occasionally, as we have seen, Wirthlin's findings influenced presidential decisions. One of his former DMI associates, Richard Beal, was given a staff job whose duties include the assimilation of polling data. Gergen himself had been a founder and editor of *Public Opinion,* a thoughtful quarterly devoted to the same subject.

This high level of attention to press relations and polling gave birth to a minor myth about the White House's prowess in shaping perceptions. One serious journal headlined an analytical article, "How the White House Cons the Press,"[1] and attempted to prove that Reaganaut guile had turned journalistic tigers into tabbies. In another article, Sidney Blumenthal, a student of political image-making, argued at length that the smoothies in the White House seemed to be succeeding, as the headline put it, in "Marketing the President."[2] Gergen was the principal source for Blumenthal's story. That probably accounts for the erroneous assertion in it that after the troika no one in the White House had more access to Reagan than Tall himself. *National Journal,* a weekly devoted to coverage of the federal government in minute detail, contributed to the myth with its gee-whiz stories on the Reaganauts' skills in orchestrating information.[3] On any day around the White House Press Room, you could hear grumbling from some of the regulars about efforts to manipulate them. Often this talk was glazed with a certain grudging admiration for at least a few of the ostensible manipulators, particularly Baker, Deaver, Clark and Gergen.

There are several reasons for this fairy tale's currency. Because turnover in the press corps is rapid and memories are short, every White House staff is compared with its immediate predecessor. Jimmy Carter's people were maladroit in their PR efforts, allowing heavy-handed gimmicks to become visible to the press. Hence the short-lived verb "to Rafshoon," as in Jerry Rafshoon, the advertising man brought in to polish Carter's image. More experienced and subtle, Reagan's people benefited from this comparison.

Then there is the disorder that might be described as access-envy. Many reporters covering national political campaigns or incumbent administrations suffer from this malady. No matter how accessible he may attempt to be, the candidate who prospers in the primaries inevitably becomes a more distant figure as the press group covering him grows. Once in office, he is insulated by the trappings of the modern presidency. Problems became more complex, the pace of events quickens, personalities clash, alliances change. The journalist trying to track all of this must rely more and more on the handful of campaign strategists or White House aides who are on intimate terms with the candidate/incumbent. The more information a staff member has, or seems to have, the more influence he appears to wield. Reporters in this situation are always in danger of accepting these few lieutenants' evaluations of their own worth to the captain, and of their own wizardry. Access-envy, as much as anything else, accounts for the legends that grow up around some of the more deft political managers and White House retainers.

The largest flaw in the myth about image-making on Reagan's behalf shows up in the bottom line. If Gergen and the others had the magic touch often attributed to them, Reagan, first, should have been relatively free of criticism. Second, when the news started to turn bad, he should have been insulated from the political impact. Neither of these results occurred. Because of his personality and because of his cultivated talent as a messenger, his personal standing remained higher than those of his policies. But that was Reagan the man at work, not his magicians. Further, the same distinction was present during the first half of Carter's term. To the extent that Reagan enjoyed a generally favorable press during 1981, the reasons were clear: a desire to reverse the trend of failed presidencies, a sentiment to which editors and reporters were not immune; the attempt on Reagan's life and the grace with which he responded to it; a disorganized opposition; the fact that he was on a legislative win streak for nearly a year, making it difficult to quarrel with success.

But even in those first months, there was steady criticism of Reagan's ability in the national security field. On Sunday, October 4, James Reston's New York *Times* article on the subject was headed "Squabble and Wobble." Joseph Kraft's piece the same day on the same subject in the Washington *Post* bore the caption "General Muddle." That was typical of much of the commentary. If the Reaganauts were such wizards at shaping public opinion, Louis Harris' survey in mid-1981 would not have picked up clear evidence that Reagan even then was losing the "fairness" argument just as his economic program was being enacted.[4] And a year later one would have imagined that, at the very least, Reagan and his partisans would be getting credit among the citizenry for having reduced inflation drastically. In fact, the opposite was happening. In the late spring of 1982, pollsters discovered that public confidence in the Republicans' ability to control inflation had declined ten points in thirteen months—the same period in which inflation itself was falling rapidly.[5] Further, many of those polled denied that the rate of price increases had declined. Some magic.

The argument here isn't that the White House staff never pulled off a cute trick, or that it lacked skill and imagination in salesmanship. Of course it sought to polish Reagan's persona in small ways and large, sometimes at the expense of the truth, and occasionally we fell for it. When the White House won the AWACS vote, word was put out that Reagan's instant reaction when he got the news in private was to exclaim: "Thank God!" I used that in my account, as did some other reporters. In fact, I learned later, Reagan's initial response was to tell a little joke about feeling relief after a painful process. The punch line: "It's like shitting a pineapple."*

More importantly, the Reagan White House showed a good flair for political theater. Deaver was particularly adept at picking interesting settings for Reagan's appearances, backdrops that made for good television footage. Nor was the staff ever bashful about demanding network prime time for Reagan at critical moments even when the purpose was crassly political. On October 14, with the midterm election less than three weeks away, Reagan got free time on NBC and CBS in which he delivered a blatant defense of his economic policies. Only ABC had the courage to turn down the request on that occasion. In general, television is much more susceptible than print to White House exploitation. But that was hardly unique to the Reagan years. Every politician attempts to milk television; that is a given. It is up to broadcast executives to resist the squeeze not only when free time is at issue for a speech, but also in terms of routine coverage. Apparently the producers of the regular evening news believe that no program is complete without at least one report from the White House lawn, regardless of whether there is important information to convey that night. This mentality, more than any machinations by the President's minions, allows the manufacture of favorable images.

Special occasions provided Gergen & Company with larger opportunities. It was a shrewd decision, for instance, to send Reagan to Capitol Hill on April 28, 1981, for the speech celebrating his recovery from the shooting. Reagan seized that televised opportunity to promote his budget proposals, which just happened to be approaching a critical test at the time.

Unlike the Carter or Ford strategists, Reagan's people demonstrated a talent for sustaining themes. This is an element in effective leadership; it is then up to the press to judge for itself whether the themes are valid or not. For instance, in the early spring of 1982—rather belatedly —the political council decided that strong stuff would be needed to counteract the growing anti-nuclear movement, along with the idea that Reagan couldn't handle foreign affairs. A sequence of speeches and events was laid out stretching from early April through mid-June to take advantage of Reagan's first trip to Europe as well as the UN special session on disarmament. The peace offensive plan was executed

---

* He used that analogy on a few other occasions. One was during his "summit" meeting with Speaker O'Neill in April 1982, when Reagan was trying to indicate how difficult it was for him to meet the Democrats' demands.

with considerable dexterity for both the domestic and the international audiences.

Still, the hazards of attempting to fine-tune press coverage were shown in the very first step of that peace promotion. The opening number was planned to coincide with another first, the premiere of the informal Q and A sessions that were supposed to end the photo-op war. It took place in the Oval Office on April 5. Reagan was to await the right question and then make the headline desired: a challenging invitation to Leonid Brezhnev to attend the June UN session along with Reagan. This would allow the two leaders to have their first meeting, though it would be something less than a full-dress summit. Until that point, pressure for a summit conference from the Kremlin had been deflected in the White House.

Reporters, however, have a way of frustrating such plausible PR plans. Questions during that session wandered over the several topical subjects, starting with combat in the Falkland Islands, moving on to the budget, and then getting around to controversial statements Reagan had made previously about comparative U.S.-Soviet nuclear strength. That last topic might have been a place for Reagan to wedge in his news, but he missed the chance as reporters put him on the defensive.

Time was running out when a reporter asked: "What about a summit meeting with the House and Senate leadership on the budget?" The word "summit" seemed to trigger Reagan's memory. "I think," he started to reply, "that will be a part of the procedure before we finally arrive at a budget. Let me just say in closing, though, since we can't take any more questions here . . ." And he went on to challenge Brezhnev to come to New York. By this time, however, the subject had become submerged in other material. The White House failed to get the clear news gong it had hoped for.

Frustration of that kind happens frequently despite all the high-level attention to press relations. During the same period in which Reagan was trying to seize the peace issue, the White House was also attempting to placate the New Right by showing interest in the conservative "social issues" agenda. An odd legal case arose in which a state court was asked to rule on the withholding of special medical treatment necessary to save the life of a Mongoloid infant. The parents did not authorize required surgery and the hospital chose to honor the parents' wishes. The White House's connection with this issue was nil, but it seemed to be an opportunity to show sympathy for the Right to Life position. A presidential memorandum to the Department of Health and Human Services was drafted. It pointed out that HHS might withhold federal funds from hospitals that fail to protect innocent life. Instead of simply announcing the memorandum through the Press Office, thereby putting the White House into the middle of a delicate issue, a series of evening phone calls was made by the Office of Policy Development, bringing the memo to the attention of news organizations. The ploy was so subtle that it resulted in no news coverage at all.

Still eager to show presidential action on domestic issues of interest to conservatives, the White House in late May cobbled together its position on the latest version of legislation intended to stiffen the federal criminal code. A bill with bipartisan support was coming up before the Senate Judiciary Committee. The Administration favored most of the provisions, which generally followed a law-and-order theme, and the point of the exercise was to draw attention to the White House's strong views on the subject. But Reagan was again en route to California for a few days off. Those reporters who stayed behind were attending briefings organized by the Administration in anticipation of Reagan's trip to Europe the following week. No one seemed to notice the statement on criminal justice revisions even though Gergen's aides phoned reporters individually—a rare service usually reserved for important news breaks. The brief stories finally published were routine, concentrating on the Senate committee rather than the White House.

Flanking maneuvers were often more successful than that. Further, when the big guns of the White House staff lined up for concentrated public relations volleys, they did attract attention and affect the tone of coverage. But the bulk of the wordage sent over news wires from the White House daily comes from a more prosaic process: the routine briefings given by the principal spokesman, the handouts distributed frequently, quick conversations conducted al fresco in the West Wing driveway with congressional leaders and others visiting the White House. The jam of interpretation or insight that can be spread on this bland, official white bread is expected to come from the press secretary, the main front man readily accessible to the entire White House press corps. In this department the Reagan White House got itself in trouble at the beginning and had failed to sort things out midway through the term.

The problem started during the transition with a decision by the troika that the press secretary, once Deaver had declined the honor, would not be a member of Reagan's closest circle. This was a change from the original concept in Sacramento. In the early gubernatorial days, Lyn Nofziger, a former political reporter, stood at Reagan's elbow both literally and metaphorically. Over the years the combative Nofziger drifted in and out of the Reagan entourage. During the 1976 primary campaign, his replacement, James Lake, was a senior member of the hierarchy and maintained that status in the preliminary rounds of 1980's combat until he was fired along with John Sears. After that, the chief press aide would at best rank high in the second tier. That became painfully clear to Nofziger when he returned in June for his penultimate tour of duty—he would resign and be called back for different duties yet one more time, after the election—and found his influence distinctly limited. Ed Meese and Bill Casey, in charge of the power cupboard from March through November of 1980, had no desire to thin the soup at the captain's table. Besides, both of these conservatives were leery of the press and, by extension, suspicious of those who made their career dealing with reporters. After the election, as the new triumvirate was aligning itself, those at the top felt that three was already a crowd.

In fact, Reagan's managers were reverting to a more or less traditional arrangement. The Carter setup, in which Press Secretary Jody Powell had an intimate, almost filial relationship with the boss and participated in much of the decision-making, was highly unusual. Nonetheless, Powell was the most recent precedent. White House reporters loved the idea that the staff member assigned to treat with them routinely not only knew his principal well but also attended the most important private meetings. Powell would not or could not tell you everything he knew, but at least he *knew*. When he did speak, he had credibility. For that reason alone, he would be a difficult act to follow.

Thus when Baker and Deaver started to look around for a press secretary, they got refusals from the first three outsiders whom they approached. James Brady, meanwhile, was serving as transition spokesman, making no secret of his availability for the permanent assignment. When it became general knowledge that he was not the first choice, his position became thoroughly uncomfortable. But he was patient. An affable, shrewd political survivor, Brady had joined the Reagan troupe after John Connally's nomination campaign folded. He lacked strong connections with Reagan personally and with the heavyweights. On the plus side, Brady had rapport with many political reporters and knew the town. His long experience and quick intelligence allowed him to grasp complex policy issues. The White House spokesman's job was the zenith of his trade, he explained over lunch during December, and thus was worth the suspense he was enduring while waiting for the right phone to ring.

Gergen wasn't interested in the post at that point. He was an even later arrival in the Reagan ranks, having been brought in by Baker after the election, and lacked strong conservative credentials. Gergen had been a Democrat until his late twenties and now, at thirty-eight, he was considered by the hard-core Reaganauts to be a squishy, cerebral moderate whose real loyalty was to Jim Baker, or George Bush, rather than to the President. He came from Durham, but only because his father taught at Duke University. In his genes Gergen was still of New England, where his family came from. Whatever Southern intonations had been picked up in his North Carolinian boyhood were squeezed from him at college (Yale) and law school (Harvard). It was a mark of Gergen's brash ambition that he aspired to become head of the International Communication Agency in an administration pledged to converting ICA into a heavy ideological weapon.

By the time the troika agreed to give the spokesman's job to Brady, virtually all the important staff appointments had been announced. Brady clearly needed some puffing up if he hoped to have sufficient credibility. Not only was he an outsider who was being given the job late, but gossip central had distributed the rumor that Nancy Reagan thought this balding, bulky stranger with a taste for disrespectful wisecracks lacked the proper image. For that reason, Reagan was asked to announce the appointment personally, which he did outside Blair House on the chilly morning of January 6.

"Do you think," a reporter asked, "that Brady is good-looking enough?"

Reagan dropped his smile when he replied: "That question leads to a story that has been written concerning Nancy which was a total invention out of whole cloth, and there have been several more of those and I'm getting to be an irate husband [because of] some of the things that I am reading, none of which are true, and Nancy couldn't be more delighted and thinks he's absolutely handsome."

The ploy of having Reagan announce the designation failed to solve Brady's credibility problem, and at the same time created another difficulty. Reagan simultaneously announced the appointment of Karna Small, who had previously worked at the Chamber of Commerce, to be Brady's deputy. The White House wanted to show that it was giving a few visible posts to women. This was a humiliation for Larry Speakes, who was serving as Brady's assistant at transition headquarters. Speakes would have to wait a couple of days for his appointment to be made official, and would have to wait six months for Small to be eased out of the post for which she was ill-suited to begin with. For Speakes, this was part of an unfortunate pattern of put-downs that chipped at his stature and hampered his performance.

An alumnus of small-town newspapers in his home state of Mississippi, Speakes came to Washington as an aide to Senator James Eastland. Later he held minor press posts on the Nixon and Ford staffs, then waited out the Carter years as a vice-president of Hill & Knowlton, the public relations firm. Blond and boyish, Speakes looked younger than his age (forty-one) and far less intense than others in his trade. He seemed to absorb slights with an aw-shucks grin and to tolerate his position on the periphery of influence with gratitude that he was in the game at all. In fact, his pride suffered constantly. When the *Newsweek* bureau invited Brady and Small to a private luncheon, Speakes quietly conveyed his indignation at having been left out. Soon after, *Newsweek* made up for the lapse by asking Speakes to come in with James Baker.

The press operation in the initial months of the new administration couldn't quite find its bearings. Gergen then bore the title of Assistant to the President and Staff Director. He obviously outranked Brady, though he had no direct responsibility for press relations. Nonetheless, many reporters sought out Gergen for private guidance if they couldn't see Meese, Baker or Deaver. Brady constantly tried to prove that he was indeed an insider in the Reagan White House. In public, his wit helped a great deal. Sitting down to breakfast with a group of us, he feigned shock that the first question came in hard. He projected his heavy-lidded, wry look, accompanied by a soundless chuckle. Then: "Whatever happened to foreplay?" Privately, however, Brady resented the fact that some reporters in the early days went around his flanks or over his head. He also felt—correctly—that the troika's habit of conducting press relations on its own did little to buttress his position.

Brady was working his way into the inner loop when he was shot. The bullet that felled him also raised him above the petty rivalries and pecking-order distinctions common in any White House. Yet that same slug created new confusion in the press operation. At George Washington University Hospital on that tense day, Nofziger rather than Speakes served as spokesman. When Speakes did appear back in the White House Briefing Room, Al Haig raced up from the basement with clarifications.

When it became clear that the miracle of Brady's survival would not be topped by the second miracle of an early, full recovery, titles and assignments were rearranged. Gergen became Director of Communications and Speakes, Principal Deputy Press Secretary. Speakes resented the divided turf, believing that in Gergen's absence he would have become the acknowledged chief spokesman. This idea was incorrect; the troika considered shopping outside for a new press secretary but finally decided that Brady should hold the post indefinitely and in absentia. For a time Gergen chose to conduct the routine press briefing on alternate days. He clearly operated on a longer tether than Speakes enjoyed, a fact that naturally irritated Speakes. Tension between the two, and their subordinates, became an unpleasant fact of life in the West Wing.

More importantly, it became obvious that even Gergen was running into access problems. Though he was on excellent terms with his patron, Baker, Gergen's relationship with Meese was distant and with

Deaver, ambiguous. Further, he made the mistake of getting on the wrong side of Darman, whose influence rose steadily as the months passed. The result was that sensitive matters—Haig's resignation, for instance—were sometimes kept from Gergen until literally the last moment, a lapse that would cost the White House dearly from time to time.

One vivid example occurred when the Richard Allen case broke on Friday, November 13, 1981. The news came early in the morning in the form of cryptic wire service stories from Tokyo. Initially, these bulletins said that an unnamed senior American official was the subject of an investigation that had reached all the way to Japan. The inquiry about the $1,000 "payment" from Japanese journalists to a White House personage had been going on for two months. But Gergen was unaware of it, as he would be kept ignorant of certain other delicate items. Leaning heavily on White House Counsel Fred Fielding, Speakes put out some of the facts, but clearly he knew little about the situation. Then Allen and Speakes appeared before reporters together. By this time the newsies smelled a hot one. Speakes interrupted the crosstalk and tried to cool things by saying:

> I'm trying to make a statement here. My statement is that the matter has been investigated thoroughly at the request of the White House and there had been no evidence of any violation of law or regulation.

That was a blunder. The Justice Department would not complete its official "review" of Allen's affairs for nearly two months. Gergen and Speakes, having been kept in the dark, were now inadvertently creating the impression that the White House was trying to cover up something significant. Gergen appeared in the Press Room and initially repeated the misinformation first cited by Speakes. Peppered with specific questions—Who found the money? Who called the FBI? Was any name on the envelope?—the chagrined Gergen could only reply, "I don't know," several times. Finally, in exasperation, he carped: ". . . I guess we don't find this whole story quite as exciting as you do." Before the end of the day, Gergen had to return to the lectern for a teatime snack of crow. Speaking as if each word was costing him, Gergen conceded:

> This morning when we issued a statement on the matter it may have created an impression which we wish to correct. And that is with regard to the status of the matter at this time . . . One could well have read into the statement that the matter was completed and wrapped up, and we want to correct that impression . . . We are advised that the Justice Department has the matter under review . . . Let me make clear that Fred Fielding who drafted that statement today did so based upon the information which he had at hand and which he obtained from within the White House . . .

Quite understandably, this failed to satisfy the pack, which continued to torment Gergen. Finally he had to plead: "I'm dealing with second-hand information." The following week Gergen had to correct himself again. Reagan, it turned out, had known about the investigation since mid-September, whereas Gergen initially said the President learned of it only on November 13. Though the intrinsic events were petty, the case was a challenge to reporters. For weeks they sought firsthand material, keeping the story alive as new tidbits surfaced, showing that the White House had withheld some information. What did not come out at the time was the fact that Allen, with Meese's support, was arguing against any disclosures except for his increasingly vehement self-defense. The Allen affair could have been a brief shower of bad publicity, but it turned into a rainy season lasting until the new year.

The episode rattled both Gergen and Speakes for obvious reasons. To their credit, however, they resisted the human temptation to turn nasty when on the defensive. Their experience during Watergate, their common sense, or both, served them well. To convert jousts with the press into personal friction is usually a losing proposition from the politicians' viewpoint. In fact, the Reagan crew learned healthy lessons from the mistakes of both the Nixon and Carter staffs. In Nixon's time, the press was a natural enemy to be evaded or attacked as the situation dictated. Under Carter, the press was a philandering lover, to be made to feel guilty or foolish or both with each frequent "transgression." The Reagan people were too sensible and mature to harbor either of those attitudes. Junior staffers in the lower Press Office, just off the Briefing Room, were under instructions to be helpful, even cheerful, under all circumstances. A bright and sunny bunch, they usually complied, even when dealing with journalists who were skewering the President or senior staff. If there was to be a fight, as far as the troika and Gergen were concerned, it would be conducted on a professional level.

When Reagan himself let his indignation boil over with his "South Succotash" blooper, on March 16, 1982, his advisers suggested that he make a public act of contrition, which he did almost immediately in the form of a planned ad-lib during a speech to an audience itself unfriendly to the press.[6] "Presidents," he said, "even Thomas Jefferson, have their moods just like everyone else, including members of the press. Some of the things we say and do regarding each other may cause a little momentary frustration or misunderstanding, but that's all it is. So I hope that I didn't touch a nerve with any of the press . . . I think that most of the time the overwhelming majority of them do a fine job, and as a former reporter, columnist and commentator myself, I know just how tough their job can be."

Conciliatory personal words, however, hardly meant lasting peace in institutional terms. The following month Gergen learned that CBS was planning a documentary demonstrating, with intimate case histories, how the recession and Reagan's economic program were causing suffering among the poor. By the spring of 1982 that subject had become a journalistic genre. Publications as dissimilar as *Newsweek* and *The Wall Street Journal* did major articles on the hardship theme, as did many local newspapers and stations. The CBS program "People Like Us," to be broadcast in prime time, promised to have special impact. Further, the network was not at all interested in broadcasting any statement giving the Administration's side of the argument either during the documentary or after it.

CBS made previews available to television critics, following normal custom, and the reviews published in advance of the April 21 broadcast reinforced the attack on the Administration's policies. Gergen, in an open letter to CBS News President Van Gordon Sauter, protested that the network had denied the White House even an advance transcript, as well as a list of the unfortunates whose plight was to be described. In fact, that point was disingenuous. The White House, through a back channel, had obtained the names several days earlier. A former associate of Deaver's with friends at CBS performed that minor bit of genteel espionage. Nonetheless, Gergen's letter charged: "We asked that we have in advance the names of the individuals whose cases were presented so that we could review those cases internally to determine whether they were accurately presented. That request was refused." The Administration ended up doing nothing with the names it had obtained.

What it did do, the morning after the broadcast, was to renew the request for rebuttal time and to carp that some of the incidents had been depicted in a misleading way. The first point seems fair enough at first glance. However, the networks supply so much free time on demand to the President and his spokesmen that broadcasters surely are entitled to an uncluttered presentation of their own now and then. The second point was more valid. Every large welfare system, no matter how liberal in concept or how flush with cash, commits blunders that affect some individuals adversely. Zeroing in on a few eccentric cases can make for heartrending reportage, but it has as much relevance to national policy as Reagan's believe-it-or-not tales about tricksters who abuse the dole.

Nonetheless, it is one of journalism's jobs to underscore the mistakes of government. It is one of the rights of incumbents to defend themselves vigorously. By the end of Reagan's first year this traditional adversarial relationship was in full play. Each side occasionally was guilty of minor excess, but neither seemed eager to return to the kind of bitter combat that had raged intermittently since Lyndon Johnson's final agony. Reagan's second year brought more severe tests in the form of worsening economic problems and new alarms abroad. Commentators inevitably pointed out the White House's responsibility and examined more closely Reagan's personal failings. Only a saint in the Oval Office could resist totally the temptation to blame the press for some of his problems. Still, the exchanges were conducted within certain bounds of civility. In this matter, as in some others, Reagan helped restore a piece of the past.

27

The Sleaze Factor

When picture editors retrieved the photograph nearly three years after it was taken, one could read into it a marvelous sense of prescience. Frank Sinatra and Raymond J. Donovan on the left, Nancy Reagan in the middle, and William E. McCann on the far right are all throwing wide grins at the lens. Portly and gray-haired, with the map of Ireland clearly visible in his genial features, McCann seems particularly merry. Standing between his wife and McCann, however, the fifth person in the photo, Ronald Reagan, appears much less jolly. His smile is grudgingly small, the kind extracted by social duress. Perhaps Reagan was tired that evening, reluctant to put on his tuxedo and fraternize with political contributors. Maybe his allergies were acting up; September is a bad month for pollen in New Jersey. Surely Reagan could not have known that he was in a bad place, with people who would later cause him embarrassment. Surely no one could have predicted that the photo would eventually turn up in a sober publication like *Fortune,* illustrating an article headed: THE PAYOFF CHARGES AGAINST REAGAN'S LABOR SECRETARY.[1]

The event was a $500-a-head dinner at the Fiddler's Elbow Country Club near Newark on September 30, 1979. Donovan's firm, the Schiavone Construction Company of Secaucus, owned the country club. As he had in 1976, Donovan was doing all he could to advance the Reagan candidacy. McCann, another nouveau Irish Republican in a state where the GOP was dominated by older money and WASP's of genteel moderation, was also pitching in to capture Jersey for the Western challenger. The state's Republican hierarchy had held firm for Gerald Ford four years earlier. Now there was some sentiment for George

Bush, but the elders were weakened by other forces and the climbers, like Donovan and McCann, provided wind for the new wave. It was fitting that Sinatra supplied the entertainment for the Fiddler's Elbow evening. Like Raymond Joseph Donovan, who came up from Bayonne, Albert Francis Sinatra of nearby Hoboken had risen from a hard-luck, hard-knocks "Joisey" town to the top of his field. Now Donovan was using his new acquaintances, the Reagans, to gain a different level of respectability on the national scene. Frank's old ties with his pals Ron and Nancy would pull him back to the White House stage.

The irony in the cases of Donovan and McCann was that their political efforts turned into nightmares for them. The President would personally announce McCann's nomination to be ambassador to Ireland, making McCann the only prospective Reagan envoy so honored. But the Administration then had to drop him, with a thud that stunned the insurance company executive and his family, rather than face an investigation of McCann's business dealings. Donovan, after being confirmed by a reluctant Senate, became the subject of one of those long-run inquiries that tar the individual irreparably and damage the Administration. For eighteen months the Labor Department lacked effective leadership as Donovan thrashed about in self-defense. The Administration's relations with big labor, poor to start with except where the Teamsters Union was concerned, grew still worse.

If you judged only by the headlines, the Reagan administration supplied as much grist as the scandal mills of Washington could handle. In December 1981 alone, there were new revelations in the Donovan case and the Justice Department appointed a special prosecutor. The department was also winding up its inquiry into the affairs of Richard Allen. The business dealings of William Casey were referred to Justice by a Senate committee that had raised skeptical questions. The White House tried to appoint a Watergate casualty, Maurice H. Stans, to a minor post. December was a busy month in this unseemly regard, but hardly unique. Journalistic fingers kept poking for sleazy patches in the Reaganaut mantle and often found one.

Yet these weak spots, inspected closely, consisted more of attitude than of deed. Reagan and some of his most important subordinates are men with an ethical code which sometimes verges on the moralistic when sniffed by Eastern establishment nostrils. It comes across as a law 'n' order credo when the subject is street crime or pornography or use of marijuana. No one high up on the Reagan White House staff was likely to be accused of inhaling cocaine.

Serious contradictions turned up, however, in the crucial, amorphous realm of the private standards of public officials. To the old Reaganauts and certainly to the old man himself, a person demonstrating certain central virtues, such as loyalty to traditional ways, to the program, to his family, was marked okay-plus. If that person had seemed to stray in other respects, well, he was probably a victim of idiotic government regulations or of prying reporters or of jealous rivals. That person's privacy had probably been violated. The fact that public officials, particularly in the world after Watergate, must meet different standards than entrepreneurs competing for contracts was a constant affront to many of Reagan's people. And that blind spot became a chronic cause of trouble for the Reagan White House.

Aficionados of red-meat scandal had to be disappointed. During the first two years, at least, we could find no influence-peddling in high places. No one personally close to the President, like a Harry Vaughan or a Sherman Adams, had to pack his vicuña coat and leave. No intimate of the President, in the manner of Bert Lance, was driven from office because of past performance (though Donovan was a near-miss). No fraternal black sheep was suspected of grazing on the pasture of an unfriendly foreign power. No world-class swindler on the order of Billy Sol Estes could be found enjoying the benign neglect of a cabinet department. And there was no coverup on a grand scale, nothing approaching a Watergate mystery. (How much fire of malfeasance lay behind the smoke of misfeasance at the Environmental Protection Agency was unclear in early 1983.)

The Donovan case had fragrant and bizarre ingredients, to be sure, what with the Godfatherly roster of informants, the body of a potential stoolie found in the trunk of a car, and the Schiavone Company's bold use of a private detective to investigate the Senate investigators. But the collective hanky-panky detectable in this administration, relative to the lulus of the past, was as hubcap theft is to bank robbery. And nearly all the hubcaps in question involved matters that had taken place before the incumbents assumed office.

The Reaganauts, then, could claim to be running an operation relatively free of real knavery at the top. They could make no such claim when it came to foolishness that closely resembled knavery, however. Nor could they get many points for attempting to elevate, or even maintain, standards of public service. In fact, they displayed a chronic discomfort with the stringent demands for public disclosure that had been imposed in the post-Watergate period. Attorney General Smith and Ed Meese, not to mention Reagan himself, agreed that those reforms had gone too far. They chafed under what they perceived to be the difficulties of the Freedom of Information Act (though the Administration failed to get Congress to dilute it in any important way). They attempted to undermine the Foreign Corrupt Practices Act, which crimps bribery as a tool of the export trade. They complained about the inconveniences of the 1978 Ethics in Government Act, which requires detailed financial reporting by senior appointees.

Reagan hardly favored bribery abroad any more than he favored air pollution at home. Yet he was eager to attack restraints on both in order to defend what he considered more important principles—in this case, the need to unleash business. At the same time, he and his advisers shared a firm belief that law enforcement and intelligence agencies also needed a freer rein—even if that had the paradoxical side effect of giving retroactive approval to unlawful acts.

Early in his term Reagan gave a clear signal of his particular approach to crime and punishment when he became personally involved in the case of W. Mark Felt and Edward S. Miller. Felt and Miller were the two highest-ranking FBI officials brought up on criminal charges in connection with illegal break-ins by Bureau agents during the bad old days of 1972–73. They took the fall for having authorized procedures that violated the Fourth Amendment shield against arbitrary search and seizure. Eventually they were convicted in a U.S. District Court trial the same month Reagan was elected. Several former FBI agents immediately got in touch with the President-elect, asking sympathy for the two, who meanwhile appealed the verdict. Reagan naturally turned to Meese, whose first job in Sacramento included reviewing executive clemency petitions for the governor. Even before the inauguration Meese began to gather material on the subject.

The first few weeks in office are naturally frantic for any President, and Reagan was personally caught up in a detailed budget review as the Administration rushed to complete its economic program. Nonetheless, Reagan, ever the caseworker, kept the plight of Felt and Miller in mind. On the morning of February 12, when the agenda was crowded with heavy items, Reagan asked Meese what was taking so long. "Don't we have to goose them a bit?" the President asked. Neither wanted to elaborate on this sensitive subject because I happened to be present. But Reagan was clearly impatient as Meese cryptically explained that these things take time. Two months later, just after Reagan returned from the hospital to complete his convalescence in the White House, he granted full, unconditional pardon to Felt and Miller.

Later in the year Reagan would destroy the Professional Air Traffic Controllers Organization and fire all the strikers, arguing that the law is the law. Addressing a convention of police officials, he would bemoan permissive courts (". . . right and wrong matter, individuals are responsible for their actions, retribution should be swift and sure for those who prey on the innocent"). But now, in the Felt-Miller matter, his rhetoric was different:

Their convictions . . . grew out of their good faith belief that their actions were necessary to preserve the security interests of their country. The record demonstrates that they acted not with criminal intent, but in the belief that they had grants of authority reaching to the highest levels of government. America was at war in 1972, and Messrs. Felt and Miller followed procedures they believed essential to keep the Director of FBI, the Attorney General and the President of the United States advised of the activities of hostile foreign powers and their collaborators in this country. They have never denied their actions, but, in fact, came forward to acknowledge them publicly in order to relieve their subordinate agents from criminal actions . . .

The announcement caused a minor stir in the civil liberties crowd. G. Gordon Liddy, after all, believed that the Watergate burglary and the attempt to circle the White House wagons afterward were in the public interest. As the wagon master with the most true grit, he served fifty-two months in prison, acting out with grim fortitude a rationale rejected by the national consensus that drove Richard Nixon from office. Compared with the eccentric foray against the Democratic National Committee organized by Liddy and Howard Hunt, the pursuit of radicals, bomb throwers, and those suspected of subversive acts by the FBI was a comprehensive, organized assault against legal procedure.

Of course the passage of years cooled some of the passion. Felt and Miller had lost their jobs and had suffered through lengthy litigation. Reagan's formal pardon statement could have been read as a boon to two offenders who had paid a high-enough price for their offense. But it was also ambiguous enough to be read the opposite way, that no price should have been exacted in the first place. The next day, Larry Speakes was questioned on this point in the White House Press Room. Does Reagan think that they never should have been prosecuted? The response: "Well, he didn't make a statement along those lines but he clearly felt . . . that the decision of the jury, the decision of the court, was not correct."

That the White House willingly advertised Reagan's role in the pardon was unusual. As a rule the President was kept insulated from potential controversy when possible by the simple device of having the announcements come from the departments, or in the form of bland notices in the Federal Register. That approach kept criticism down. More important, perhaps, was that Watergate was slipping from the collective memory. The burglary's tenth anniversary, in June 1982, provoked retrospectives in print and on television, but these treatments, no matter how well done, made those awful events seem prehistoric. As time is measured in Washington, they were. When criticism of the

Reaganauts' attitudes did show up, the voices seemed lonely, detached from current issues. Law Professor Archibald Cox, whom Nixon had fired for trying to do his job as Special Prosecutor too well, lamented to an interviewer: "My view is that the measures adopted by Congress and the Executive Branch as a result of Watergate saved us from sinking into a moral abyss in the conduct of government . . . They expressed a level of concern that government should be open and not only honest, but honorable. I think the sum total of the criticisms being leveled today by members of the present administration amounts to saying that we don't care about ethics and honesty in government. It's not just the criticism of particular measures, but what energizes it. It shows a lack of concern."[2]

Jeremiads from people like Cox and his friends at Common Cause had little impact. Certainly there was a lack of concern when Reagan decided to throw a bone to a faithful old Republican dog of war, Maurice H. Stans.* Reagan had no personal tie to Stans and owed him no political debt. A financier who had served in the Eisenhower and Nixon administrations, Stans in 1972 left the cabinet to take charge of fund-raising for Nixon's reelection campaign. Two years later he was acquitted of perjury and conspiracy charges, along with John Mitchell, in one of the showiest of the Watergate trials. But in 1975 Stans pleaded guilty to five misdemeanor counts involving improper handling of campaign contributions. Two of the donations had been illegally given and three others had gone unreported. Stans claimed at the time, as well as later, that he had been exonerated of guilt for any of the major facets of Watergate. He also argued that the criminal justice system abused him. In fact, cash raised surreptitiously by the Committee to Reelect the President was used, in part, to finance the Watergate coverup.

Almost as soon as Republicans recaptured the White House, Stans got in touch with friends in Washington, letting it be known that a federal appointment would finally clear his name. A few Senate Republicans told the White House that they agreed with Stans's request for rehabilitation. Richard Allen intervened vigorously on Stans's part as well, recommending that he be made an ambassador. The troika felt that would be going too far. But Reagan fully agreed with the basic premise. Stans, by then seventy-three, deserved at least a symbolic appointment. One presidential aide involved in the conversations recalled: "The President felt that here was a man who had worked hard

* The White House Press Office was sufficiently self-conscious about the Stans nomination that it put out the word late on Friday afternoon, December 4, 1981. That is the preferred timing for news that the Administration would prefer to bury.

for his country and his party, a decent man who had suffered a lot."
Deaver was assigned the task of finding a suitably obscure post. It
turned out to be a seat on the Overseas Private Investment Corporation, which promotes U.S. investment abroad. Though only a part-time
job, membership on the OPIC board requires Senate confirmation. The
nomination made few ripples when announced in December, but Majority Leader Howard Baker then discovered that approval could not
be obtained without a difficult committee hearing and floor debate.
Even then the issue would be in doubt. Did the White House really
want to make that kind of investment? It did not. On the morning of
May 24, the troika informed Reagan that the Stans nomination was
dead. With a reporter present, Reagan confined his reaction to a frown
and a grumble: "Boy oh boy."

Reagan's less inhibited reactions in other sticky personnel situations
tended toward indignation. Max Hugel, a businessman whom Casey
had named chief of covert operations at the CIA, was an early casualty. His appointment was controversial initially because he lacked experience in the field. Thus, when Hugel's former business associates
leaked derogatory information about him to the Washington *Post* in
July, there was a ready market on Capitol Hill for his head. Reagan
objected privately that Hugel was getting a raw deal. He was to some
extent a victim of Casey's own lack of support in the Senate, where
members expert in intelligence, such as Barry Goldwater, were openly
skeptical about the director's handling of his job. But the White House
staff decided that Hugel was a high-priced liability and that his resignation should be elicited promptly. Casey complied, and the brouhaha
soon died.

The President also bridled when McCann's nomination had to be
abandoned. In that situation, Reagan himself inadvertently caused the
problem while exchanging toasts with the Irish ambassador, Sean
Donlon, on St. Patrick's Day, 1981. Reagan brought along to the
Donlon residence for that holiday luncheon a Waterford crystal jar
filled with green jelly beans and an interesting bit of information—his
intention to nominate McCann for the Dublin embassy. "Bill, why
don't you stand up," Reagan said. Delighted, McCann took a bow. In
mid-March of 1981, however, the background investigation on
McCann was incomplete. There wasn't anything sensational in the dossier after it was finished, but one item would catch the eye of any investigator. Ten years earlier, when Senator John McClellan's Permanent Subcommittee on Investigations was looking into suspect
Teamsters Union insurance systems, the name of the New Jersey insurance company headed by McCann came up in an unflattering way. The
reference made a connection between that company and an operator

with a bad record for constructing dubious insurance schemes. A Senate subcommittee report summarizing these findings appeared in 1977.[3]

There was no allegation against McCann personally. But by the late spring of 1981, when the Donovan case was twitching again, the White House staff had no appetite for another protracted inquiry that might attempt to link one of its appointees to irregular union practices. When this was put to Reagan, his instinctive response was to stick with McCann. Here was another striver, the author of his own success story, a Korean War veteran, active in local affairs back home in Short Hills. Can't we fight this one out? Reagan wanted to know. Maybe, the troika responded, but it will be a mess.

When Reagan agreed to squelch the nomination, McCann was irate. He had already made preparations to move to Ireland. He had scouted schools for his children. His New Jersey friends and associates all knew of his good fortune. How would he explain the sudden demotion to civilian life? He found a sympathetic ear in Helene von Damm, who had run fund-raising for Reagan in the New York–New Jersey area and who had been helped considerably by both Donovan and McCann during the 1980 campaign. During the transition she did personnel work for the Reagan group. Much later she succeeded Pendleton James as director of personnel for the White House. So McCann took his complaints to her. He even asked if some other, less visible, job could be found for him so that he could at least erase the impression that the White House was rejecting him outright. She understood, she said, but she could do nothing.

If the Hugel and McCann matters could be marked off as unlucky accidents for all concerned, the same could hardly be said for Donovan. Donovan was named to the cabinet with the knowledge that his record was vulnerable to attack. Before the Senate Labor Committee's confirmation hearings on the Donovan nomination in January, the FBI, the White House, and the committee itself were all aware of raw investigative data putting the construction company official in a bad light. Informants had told FBI agents investigating the nominee that he had associated with known mobster characters. One tale placed Donovan at a luncheon table where a payoff was supposedly given to a corrupt union official, for instance. But the sources of these reports were themselves tainted. Donovan stoutly denied the unsubstantiated allegations. The FBI official who testified in those early hearings backed Donovan.

But the rumors continued to circulate, and to grow. It turned out that the transition headquarters office tracking clearance procedures neglected to press for an intense investigation when the first red flag appeared. Then FBI headquarters discovered that additional information unfavorable to Donovan had remained in a bureau field office when it should have been sent to Washington. The Donovan saga became one of those investigative onions with many layers. One of the most redolent was peeled off in June 1982, when the body of a professional thug, Fred Furino, was found in Manhattan. At first sight, the only thing unusual about the killing was that the corpse's head contained just one bullet. As a rule, the gunmen in such situations are more extravagant in their use of ammunition. Then, however, one of my investigative colleagues at *Time* discovered that Furino had been questioned extensively by Leon Silverman, the special prosecutor looking into the Donovan case. *Time* reported that Furino had repeatedly flunked a lie detector test when questioned about any association he had had with Donovan.[4]

While no one connected that murder, or the anonymous death threats received by Frank Silbey, the chief investigator for the Senate Labor Committee, with Donovan himself, the atmosphere surrounding the case became increasingly tense. Senate Democrats demanded that Donovan step aside until Silverman's work was done. He refused to do so. Members of the White House staff talked privately about the inevitability of Donovan's departure, the sooner the better, they said. In late June, Paul Laxalt and Stuart Spencer, in separate conversations, warned Reagan that he should end the problem decisively. He demurred.

Hoodlums' gossip, Reagan said, was hardly sufficient to force out a cabinet officer. Ray deserved better than that. The investigation would run its course. On June 28, Silverman released his 708-page report, plus appendices, which recounted the allegations about Donovan's purported associations with gangsters. Silverman even uncovered additional slurs, previously unreported. But the sum of this, Silverman concluded, was "insufficient credible evidence" on which to seek an indictment of Donovan. The White House chose to interpret this finding as vindication. Donovan remained in office while the brouhaha seemed to diminish. Yet before the summer was out another set of allegations against Donovan surfaced. Silverman reopened his inquiry. He also requested the FBI to investigate a second murder in New York City. The victim in that killing was the son of a gangster who had been interrogated earlier by the same special prosecutor. In mid-September Silverman ended his effort with a repetition of what he had said in June. The accusations were "unproved." Again, there was "not sufficient credible evidence." Case closed, at least in the legal sense. The White House staff quietly gnashed its teeth because of the Labor Secretary's continued presence in the cabinet.

The situation of William Casey, while far less catchy in the headlines, was more typical of the attitudes of some of the Reaganauts con-

cerning routine disclosure of information. Eventually the Justice Department would conclude, as it did in Richard Allen's case, that the
lapses were inadvertent. In the interim, the Administration suffered
prolonged embarrassment. A wealthy lawyer with long experience in
both government and private enterprise—and one whose complex business affairs had been the subject of previous investigations—Casey of
all people should have had his accountants prepare meticulously comprehensive reports for the Senate and the Office of Government Ethics.
Instead, the Republican-controlled Senate Select Committee on Intelligence found:

> The original answers omitted at least nine investments valued at more
> than a quarter of a million dollars, personal debts and contingent liabili-
> ties of nearly $500,000, a number of corporations or foundations on
> whose boards Mr. Casey served, four civil lawsuits in which he was in-
> volved in the last five years, and more than seventy clients he had
> represented in private practice in the last five years. Among the clients not
> disclosed to the committee were two foreign governments, the Republic of
> Korea and the Republic of Indonesia, and an oil company controlled by
> the latter, Pertamina of Indonesia. Mr. Casey's representation of In-
> donesia in 1976 raised a question of whether he should have registered
> under the Foreign Agents Registration Act . . .[5]

Though one of the richest men in an administration studded with
millionaires, and though he held one of the most sensitive posts in the
government, Casey declined to put his assets in a blind trust. That device had come into vogue during the 1970s as a means of insulating an
official from the management of his investments. With a professional
trustee running the portfolio, the possibility of conflict between the
official's private financial interests and his decisions on public policy is
reduced. The Carter White House directed that all officials at the cabinet secretary and deputy secretary level with personal assets of
$250,000 or more use the blind-trust device. Senior White House staff
members were included in the order. Reagan's lawyers during the transition and afterward made no such demand.* Further, when wealthy
appointees produced lists of their holdings for Fred Fielding and his
subordinates, the scrutiny for possible conflicts was lax. The attitude
was that these matters had to be reviewed for the record, but let's not
fret about them.

This cool approach showed up in the actions of another of the cabinet's millionaires in a highly sensitive position, Attorney General

---

* According to the Office of Government Ethics, only eighteen people in the
highest echelons did so voluntarily, including Reagan, Bush and Haig, during the
Administration's first year and a half. Thus many other wealthy members of the
Administration avoided the procedure.

Smith. After his selection in 1980, he accepted an unusually large severance bonus, $50,000, from a steel company which he had served as a board member. Then, operating outside his blind trust, he invested in tax shelters of the most venturesome variety which promised a write-off of four dollars for each dollar put at risk. Tax-avoidance schemes of that magnitude are frequently challenged by the Internal Revenue Service. These facts came to light in May 1982, when Smith filed his annual disclosure form with the Office of Government Ethics. When the news caused a fuss, Smith prudently decided to return the $50,000 and to limit his tax break to a one-for-one basis. Before Smith announced that decision—to "dispel all of the concerns raised in the press," he said—Reagan betrayed a strange innocence of such matters. Questioned by reporters on May 24, Reagan said of Smith's tax strategy: "I don't think the point has been made by anyone that the so-called 'tax-shelters' are things passed by Congress to encourage investment or speculation in certain undertakings. And a tax shelter is only a shelter if you lose your investment. You actually enter it with the hope or the prospect that you'll earn additional money from that investment, in which case you'd owe additional tax." In fact, a well-designed tax shelter pays off immediately for the investor in a high tax bracket, regardless of whether the venture ever earns a dime. The payoff comes from the U.S. Treasury, which is one reason why the Reagan administration was attempting as a policy matter to discourage the use of shelters.

For a politician so skilled in presenting his ideas, and himself, in positive ways, Reagan was astonishingly unconcerned about displaying a keen sense of propriety. After the Smith story broke, Reagan in private was not at all irritated about the latest annoyance caused by a pal, this latest reminder that his wealthy friends knew how to avoid the pinch of hard times. Instead, Reagan was ticked off by published criticism of Smith attributed to unnamed "sources." One morning he told the troika "I know it isn't any one of you, but if I find out who's been bad-mouthing Bill, I'm going to kick his ass out of here."

Repeatedly, when choices arose, Reagan elected to go with his own instincts of fair play toward the person under attack rather than submit to demands for the person's head. He refused to budge when his old friend Barry Goldwater wanted him to oust his much newer friend, William Casey. Reagan stuck it out with Donovan and Allen longer than other Presidents would have and longer than his advisers thought wise. He tried to give Stans a job though there was nothing in it for the White House except risk. On a couple of occasions people very close to him suggested that perhaps it was a bad idea to entertain Frank Sinatra at the White House in so public a way. The singer, after all, was a walking public relations problem. Reagan would not even discuss the matter; he considered Sinatra a friend much abused by the press and a do-gooder whose work for charity had been ignored.

According to conventional wisdom, shared by his political advisers as well as the commentators of the national press, decisions of that kind should have injured Reagan's personal standing. He should also have paid some price for his administration's attempt to chip away at the Watergate reforms. Yet the results seemed otherwise. In early June of 1982, when the Donovan case was building toward a climax, the firm of Yankelovich, Skelly and White conducted one of its periodic opinion surveys for *Time*. The poll found that Reagan had lost support on a number of subjects. However, one of the questions asked was whether Reagan had made a good start on "providing moral leadership." On that item, 67 percent of the respondents answered yes, an increase of six points over the previous September.

28

Husband, Father, Brother

Photographers were summoned to the spot on the South Lawn where the President normally bids Godspeed to foreign visitors. This was a different sort of farewell to be performed in front of scores of lenses: Reagan was seeing his wife off to the wedding of Prince Charles and Lady Diana in July 1981. A smile, a wave to the press, then a clinch, a kiss, more kisses. In both duration and intensity, the embrace was several degrees beyond what film directors thought decent thirty years before, when Nancy Davis and Ronald Reagan smooched antiseptically on camera.

This time they were not acting. After three decades of marriage, Ronnie and Mommy, Rawhide and Rainbow, still had a romance as well as a partnership going. The prospect of a week-long separation affected them both.* She wept most of the way to Andrews Air Force Base. He moped a good deal while she was gone. It had been Reagan's idea that she go to Britain and make a holiday of the invitation to a royal wedding; he thought she needed diversion after the assassination attempt. As it turned out, however, the trip added to her burden in another way. The British press, ever eager to torment the aristocracy of either side of the Atlantic, took its cue from the way the Colonials had been covering their First Lady and mocked her as a frivolous partygoer.

* Ever eager to exploit the First Couple's togetherness, the White House put out the word that this was the longest Mister and Missus had been apart during their marriage. Later Nancy told me that there had been a few longer separations in the mid-fifties when he toured GE plants and she stayed home with their young daughter, Patti.

Nancy Reagan's first year in Washington gave her a jolting case of déjà vu. As the governor's wife in Sacramento she absorbed some hard shots from the press. She was alternately depicted as a size-six vessel of ice water and as an ambitious schemer who manipulated her husband's policies. She was even given credit—or blame, depending on the commentator's perspective—for Reagan's conservative conversion. Those last two bits of piffle induced the Reagans and their retainers to create a counter-myth: that Nancy knew nothing about politics and cared less; that she had no influence whatsoever on the Master's decisions concerning policy or administration; that she was Superwife pure and simple. By the 1980 campaign, Nancy was an easy, even irresistible, target for every woman journalist assigned to do a piece on her. She became all the more wary and controlled, and thereby invited still more acidic coverage. This carried through the transition and their first year in the White House. "You know," she remarked during her second spring in Washington, "eighty-one was a terrible year, an awful year. It took me a long time to get over that whole thing [the assassination attempt]. And then—and then—I was unprepared for a whole lot of things. Despite Sacramento, I was unprepared for the scrutiny and for the, uh, remarks and so on. I never really had been used to . . ."[1] Her voice trailed off, as it often did when the subject was painful. She gave a little shudder, accompanied by a wordless appeal, conveyed by her large hazel eyes, for the reporter to move on to something else.

It was tempting in moments like that, as it was in the aftermath of the shooting, when Hinckley's bullet pierced her spirit as surely as it penetrated Reagan's lung, to treat Nancy Reagan as if she were a damsel in distress. You wanted to pat her hand reassuringly, dash off a let's-hear-it-for-Nancy story and second the motion when her husband declared indignantly: "There's been an awful lot of false image-building . . . She's a warm and generous person, and vulnerable to the kind of unjust criticism that comes this way . . . You'd find that she is very much beloved by all the women who know her."[2]

To succumb to that urge, however, would do violence to more than the truth, because she brought some of her troubles on herself. It would also be a disservice to the damsel to treat her as an innocent in need of champions. In fact, she is a strong and complicated woman, with an interesting mix of acuity and blind spots, who has played an unusual role in her husband's life. That she made foolish mistakes as First Lady is hardly astonishing. Most incumbents have suffered some difficulty in that amorphous post. That she recovered her balance is characteristic of her resilience. That their relationship has endured with such remarkable cohesion through the ordinary quirks of life and the abnormal demands of world-class politics says a great deal about the two of them.

Perhaps the only really proper preparation for First Ladyship is to be the daughter or widow of an earlier President. Having been an ordinary political spouse is good experience only in theory. The wife of a governor or senator is expected to be loyal, cheerful, discreet and as decorative as her Maker and hairdresser permit. The wife of a President in the media age is supposed to be all that and a national emblem as well. To earn straight A's she must symbolize virtue, concern, intelligence. The persona should also contain some recognizable facsimile of what the ordinary citizen thinks she would be like had she married the right comer many years earlier. The First Lady compiles no objective scorecard as the months pass, no list of bills enacted, economic statistics improved, treaties signed. She succeeds to the extent that a fickle public finds her worthy of respect and affection.

Nancy's earlier life did not exactly prepare her for this subtle challenge. Rather, it was a search for security and protection, which were amply provided by the two strong men in her life. When she was born in New York her name was Anne Frances Robbins. Her father, an automobile salesman, promptly left his wife and infant daughter. Mother was an actress, Edith Luckett, who went back to the stage to make a living. The child picked up Nancy as a permanent nickname and an aunt in Maryland as a temporary parent. Once in a while she went by train to New York when her mother appeared on Broadway. Salvation from this difficult arrangement came when the actress married Loyal Davis, a wealthy Chicago neurosurgeon, who not only adopted Nancy but also provided all the comforts that go with the position of rich man's daughter.* Later, after studying drama at Smith College, Nancy was assisted into professional acting by her mother's old friends. Eventually that led to Hollywood, roles in some marginal films and an encounter with Reagan in 1951, which she says she contrived.[3] When they married the following March, Reagan was forty-one, with a daughter and an adopted son by his earlier match to Jane Wyman. Nancy, ten years younger, had never been married and was eager for children of her own. She soon left acting and never missed it, she would insist later: "It was my choice. Ronnie never asked me to give up my career, ever. That was my choice. That was what I wanted to do. I think there has been a whole misunderstanding about it."[4] Feminists, including some of the feature writers who have done profiles of her, never forgave her for that, or for her occasional declarations that "My life really began when I married Ronnie."[5]

* Loyal Davis died in 1982.

She did not exactly leave the glamour of the movie lot for barefoot pregnancy in the kitchen. Though his career suffered a few bumps during this period, circumstances never compelled Nancy to learn to cook very well or endure other mundane housewifely burdens. Motherhood came early but hard. Patti was born in October by Caesarean section. Later there were two miscarriages and while pregnant with Ron her confinement was difficult. Otherwise, Nancy lived the comfortable life of an upper-class matron, Junior League and all, and provided her husband with a single-minded adoration. In the four years before they met, Reagan had endured reverses that jangled his self-confidence for the first and last time. Wyman had booted him, his film career had gone terminally stale, his life had been disrupted by the Hollywood union and Red-scare wars that cost him friends and serenity. With Nancy he regained the peace of mind that was so important a cylinder in his engine before and after.

As Reagan became increasingly involved in Republican politics and with the conservative businessmen who would promote his gubernatorial candidacy, Nancy found herself in a new role. During her brief acting career, she had been no one special in Hollywood, a contract player with no grand successes or prospects, an awed admirer of the really famous. She could be bobby-soxish about a Frank Sinatra or a Charlton Heston. Later, when Sinatra was exiled from the Kennedy circle and discovered his affinity for Republicans, Nancy was delighted that the change of orbit brought him together with the Reagans more often.

At the round table of their actor friends in the first few years of the marriage, Reagan was a junior knight in decline as the film industry measured things. William Holden, John Wayne and Jimmy Stewart were true barons of the box office while Reagan was perfecting his speech on the General Electric plant circuit. Within the other circle of friends, the Jorgensens and the Wilsons, the Bloomingdales and the Darts, the balance was different by the mid-sixties. They had the money but the Reagans had the persona. The Reagans were the ones to be coddled. The Jorgensens and the Wilsons started a tradition of throwing a lavish birthday party for Nancy each July, a custom that would continue in Washington.

One of those able to watch at close range from the early sixties onward described Nancy's ambivalent transit: "Sometimes she resented having to share him so much. She always worried about the demands on him, whether it was the kids, the speaking dates or politics. Everybody wanted a piece of him, the way she looked at it. But she knew that he needed something else to do and in her own way she kind of enjoyed being a star. Now she could be a star by promoting him. It was a pretty good solution. It was a lot more classy than being the wife of the guy introducing 'Death Valley Days.' "*

Classy certainly, but more difficult as well. In the 1966 campaign and during the early Sacramento years, Nancy gagged on some aspects of politics. Bitchy commentary on her drove her, literally, to tears. Harsh criticism of him drove her to vengeful anger; once Reagan had to tell her that he could not order the arrest of a radical merely for abusive language.[6] One of Nancy's habits which attracted ridicule was dubbed "the Gaze." When she was present at any of her husband's public appearances, she would stare at him with total awe. She seemed to be watching a miracle performed for the first time.

During this period some of the couple's differences in temperament became obvious to outsiders. At home, she was the disciplinarian with the children, while he was prone to benign leniency. Concerning political business, she was a detail hound, occasionally making life difficult for the staff, while he winked at little gaffes. Poison arrows from political opponents or journalistic critics usually bounced off him while they stuck in her skin long enough to fester.

That pattern held in 1980 and afterward as well. During the campaign, when one woman writer did a savage (and inaccurate) story depicting Nancy as intimidating reporters on the plane, the ostensibly hard-hearted manipulator wept on and off for two hours. At the University of Oregon, Reagan faced hostile questions from a group of students. He handled himself well, humorously giving as good as he got. On the platform she stared with undisguised loathing at the unfriendly interrogators.

Then, as later, she almost never involved herself in her husband's positions on issues. That much of the myth about her staying out of "business" was accurate. However, she was very much a part of decisions concerning his staff. In the weeks before the John Sears group was dismissed from the campaign organization, she attempted to work out a compromise. At a later stage, she was a full party to the move by Spencer and Deaver to make Baker, rather than Meese, the White House Chief of Staff. When there was some indecision about the initial appointment of a press secretary, she came down in favor of Brady, who got the job. In mid-1981, when it became clear that Brady could not recover sufficiently from his wound to return to the Press Office, she opposed the vague arrangement that left Larry Speakes in the post. On that one Reagan fended her off for a time, as he had when she wanted Dick Allen removed immediately after the controversy about him broke.

---

* The TV show on which Reagan appeared regularly after his contract with General Electric was canceled.

She would talk about her role in none of these matters, partly out of concern for the individuals' feelings but also because she had an almost irrational fear of being seen as influencing Reagan's decisions. The fact that her instincts concerning personnel were usually quite sound was irrelevant from her viewpoint. She would rather be known for her discrimination in selecting the menu for state dinners or bric-a-brac for the executive mansion.

On one occasion I pointed out to her that rumor central already had a fix on her ability to work as a quality control inspector concerning the staff. She looked embarrassed, tried to change the subject and finally relented to an extent. She would confess, in the fall of 1982, that she—along with Deaver—was trying to interest the President in a reorganization after the midterm election. "Only in a very general way," she insisted. "I've said to Ronnie that normally after the election that's the time you want to take a second look and see if people should be changed around or let go or whatever. That seems the normal time to do it and I think it would be a good idea for him to do that."[7]

He was not enthusiastic about facing the problem. It was not merely his disdain for detail. Just as important was his habit of blinking away unpleasantness. That was another difference between husband and wife. Nancy knew little about economic theory, geopolitics or living conditions among the underclass. But she had an almost reportorial interest in human conflict and tragedy. Once the Reagans dropped by the White House tennis court on a pleasant autumn Sunday afternoon while eight officials and reporters were playing round-robin doubles. They chose to kibbitz the game for a while, chatting with the four of us who were between matches. Deaver interrupted with some grim news. The daughter of old California friends had committed suicide and Deaver suggested that Reagan make a condolence phone call to the bereaved parents.

Returning from that chore, Reagan told his wife about the sad conversation. They talked about the dead woman's three small children, what grief it must be for them. Then there was an awkward silence. Reagan seemed to be groping for a way to restore cheer. At that point Nancy asked: "How did she do it?" It was a perfectly logical question, one that usually occurs to people upon hearing of an unexpected death. But Reagan, startled, replied, "What do you mean?" Nancy was matter-of-fact. "You know," she replied, "how did she *do* it?" Her husband confessed no such curiosity: "Gee, I don't know. I didn't ask." Nancy, I suspected, would have found a way to ask.

Much more than her husband, Nancy was subject to the normal range of emotion. By her second year in Washington she began to display her human qualities more often as her tension spring uncoiled.

She could even laugh—with genuine rather than feigned amusement—when a parody newspaper published a "scoop": the President, in making staff changes, was going to hire a new First Lady. During 1981 the giggle would have been forced because she appeared to be on an endless losing streak.

First there was her impatience, during the transition, about having full access to the White House so that she could begin redecorating quickly. That chance remark made in private took on exaggerated proportions. Then there was the problem of the designer dresses which she accepted gratis from her acquaintances in the fashion industry. No one on her staff had the information or the nerve to point out the ethical considerations involved. She also wore jewelry lent her by two firms. From the viewpoint of the designers and the jewel merchants, it was priceless publicity to have fashion writers mention who was adorning the First Lady. When the details leaked out, the White House finally announced that the intention all along had been to give the frocks to fashion museums, as Nancy had done earlier with some of her own clothing before the inauguration.* The entire procedure was billed as an altruistic effort to help the fashion industry. As a result of the negative publicity, however, the practice was stopped.

By itself, the design caper might have been only a fleabite to Nancy's image. Trouble was, it came in tandem with her redecorating binge and the purchase of new china for the White House. All that was done with donated money—mostly from wealthy Republican contributors—rather than federal funds. But the contributions were tax deductible, so that the Treasury was paying half the cost indirectly. Nancy argued that the place needed fixing up, and she had a point, though not a strong one. And then there were the friends she was often photographed with in public—wealthy Californians, for the most part, who had either inherited or married money and spent most of their time enjoying it. Unlike duchesses of East Coast society, Nancy's set seemed little involved with grand philanthropy or capital "C" culture. That may have been why Nancy enjoyed the company of Jerome Zipkin, whom she fancied to be a sophisticated tutor. A New Yorker with inherited wealth and vague connections to international café society (geriatric division), this short, stocky, aging bachelor constantly popped up at social events organized by Nancy's pals. When I ran into him at a Sunday brunch in Georgetown during the transition, he was wearing a Tiffany's shopping bag and a languid look. "What's in the

* For 1981, the Reagans took a deduction from taxable income of $4,180 for non-cash contributions to the Fashion Institute of Design and Merchandising Museum. The gowns were given on January 5, 1980, two weeks before Reagan took office.

bag, Jerry?" "My lunch, darling, *my lunch*." What was Jerry Zipkin doing in a First Lady's entourage? Why were her interior decorator and personal hairdresser visible in the retinue so often?

Nancy followed four White House wives—Lady Bird, Pat, Betty and Rosalynn—who, whatever their weak points, had the decency to seem ordinary once in a while. They looked as if they could remember what it was like to check the accuracy of a grocery bill. (That Lady Bird had never been required to do so was irrelevant.) They also looked as if they knew what it was to struggle up the ladder alongside their men. Thanks to her mother's good marriage to Loyal Davis and her own to Ronald Reagan, Nancy had no adult memory of material adversity. Nor did she think it important to change her privileged habits.

Washington's caterers, jewelry merchants, florists and importers of caviar were frequently quoted exulting over the return of "glamour" and "class" to the capital. What they meant was that big spending was chic again on the party circuit. The Kennedys had carried it off quite well in their day, and with more snobbery in the bargain. So why not a return to conspicuous consumption with the White House leading the way? The answer was the same that explained why Reagan's tax bill could not work nearly as well as the one Kennedy promoted: times had changed. The Reagan White House became a symbol of the New Extravagance at the moment it was asking Americans to make do with fewer government benefits. And before long the deep recession arrived, making the contrast between high times in Washington and hard times in the country all the more stark.

Nancy initially bore much of the burden because of the pattern of press coverage and because her husband had a knack of identifying himself with Main Street while she could not. Besides, he wasn't photographed by *Women's Wear Daily* kissing Jerry Zipkin. When *Newsweek* at the end of 1981 commissioned a Gallup survey on Nancy, the results were predictable.[8] She was seen as callous toward the poor and excessively concerned with "style and elegance."*

Nancy, ever vulnerable, found critiques of this kind personally painful. She was even more disturbed by the notion that she was doing damage to her husband's political interests. Most of all, she reproached herself for not having sought better tactical advice. She had consulted

* Two thirds of the respondents found her more preoccupied than her predecessors with matters of style; 62 percent said this was excessive (compared with 30 percent who approved) and 61 percent said she was less sympathetic to the underprivileged than other First Ladies had been while only 16 percent found her more sympathetic. On the general question of "favorable impressions," she trailed Jackie Kennedy, Rosalynn Carter and Betty Ford. However, Nancy fared much better in later surveys.

no one, she told me, about her dealings with the designers, and later realized that was a mistake. When I asked if she hadn't given Administration critics openings to attack on the "fairness" issue, she replied: "I suppose I did, but I didn't realize it. In the beginning, there wasn't that feeling [that the Administration lacked compassion], at least as I look back on it . . . No one knew there was going to be a recession or anything of the kind."

On one item she would yield no ground at all: her choice of pals. Of Sinatra, she said: "But he is an old friend. So do you drop your old friends just because [they are controversial]? I don't think you do." She talked about Zipkin as if he were a family member of whom one had to be proud: "He's a very good friend, very, much more than I think people realize. A very bright man. You go to a museum with Jerry Zipkin, it's really great, because he knows everything. He knows all the painters. He knows everything. He's got a wonderful, inquiring mind . . . Plus he's wonderful to your children. He'll break his back for your children." Besides, Nancy insisted, she had lots of friends, including ordinary salt-of-the-earth types and nobody wrote about them.[9] Of course, no one saw these simple folk at Nancy's glitter events either.

Though unwilling to desert her friends, Nancy was eager to change the picture. Her special project all along had been a leftover from California, the foster grandparent program. This brought elderly people seeking constructive activity together with retarded youngsters in need of affectionate attention. Nancy periodically provided some publicity. The only thing wrong with the foster grandparent scheme was that the national press found it dull. Nancy stuck to it, but her advisers decided that she needed an additional, more dramatic personal mission. They settled on drug and alcohol abuse. Now and then Nancy would travel to a community where she drew attention to volunteer organizations involved with prevention programs or rehabilitation of youthful addicts. This worked well in two ways. It attracted favorable coverage, as intended, and she discovered that she was also quite good at it because she enjoyed it.

She fought a counteroffensive on yet another front when she set out to prove to the Washington press corps that she had both heart and a sense of humor. With the help of a White House speech writer, Landon Parvin, she began to respond to criticism with quips. When a parody postcard appeared depicting Nancy with a crown, ermine robe and scepter, she said she could never wear a crown because it would muss her hair. In response to ribbing about the new place settings for state dinners, she called the executive mansion "the Nancy Reagan home for wayward china."

A breakthrough of sorts occurred at the Gridiron dinner in March

1982. She and her aides planned an elaborate response to a skit that would satirize her expensive tastes. After that number, she appeared dressed as a bag lady and to the tune of "Second Hand Rose" she sang:

> Second hand clothes, I'm wearing second hand clothes,
> They're all the thing in the spring fashion shows;
> Even my new trench coat with the fur collar
> Ronnie bought for ten cents on the dollar . . .*

The performance drew raves. It was all the more remarkable because, despite her show-biz background, she was generally reticent in front of a microphone and rarely gave formal speeches if she could avoid them. Privately she continued to feel insecure about how she was perceived. She wondered aloud about how to improve her technique in interviews. But she was able to choke down those doubts in 1982. Her pride demanded that she recoup and so, she felt, did her duty to Reagan. The salvage operation succeeded. By the middle of '82 she was more comfortable in the job of First Lady, and the critical audience sensed it.

Somehow she was also more at ease in her role of mother. In the annals of presidential families, the Reagans will doubtless appear as a study in separation of the generations. Never in the last half century at least have the First Offspring been so distant from the White House orbit. This was partly a result of geography; Maureen, Mike and Patti continued to live in California during 1981–82 while the youngest, Ron, though based in New York, was prisoner of a busy schedule that took him on the road a good deal. Age was another element. By the 1980 campaign, all four were adults engaged in their own pursuits. But aside from those objective circumstances, there had been for many years an emotional distance that was unmistakable.

The divorce was hard on Maureen and Mike when they were youngsters. Their mother's career was active and successful, their father was in constant motion. Though they spent some weekends with him and Nancy, the teenagers were sent to out-of-state boarding schools. Maureen ended up at college in the Washington area, dropping out, dashing through two brief early marriages and experimenting with different occupations. She became a confirmed Republican before her father did and maintained a strong interest in politics, though Reagan hardly encouraged it. An intelligent, strong-willed and mercurial woman, Maureen Reagan could not quite disguise the coolness that

---

* It went on in the same vein. The gag lyrics were written by Parvin and Sheila Patton Tate, Nancy's press secretary.

existed between her and Nancy. Reagan himself, at the apex of this triangle, was typically insensitive to the emotions at play.

She was a grown woman, after all, having turned forty just before
the inauguration, and there was no point in raking over the anger of
her adolescence at never having had enough of her father. Reagan as a
youth had been self-sufficient, and as a young man was mentor to his
older brother and protector to his middle-aged parents. He made no
demands on his own children, expected none from them when they
were old enough to fend for themselves. When Maureen and Mike
needed money, they were each given a loan from the Reagan trust administered by Lawyer Smith and were charged interest. Before Reagan
was shot, Maureen was planning her third marriage, to take place in
early spring. The Reagans were to attend. Nancy wanted to clarify the
arrangements but, as usual, wasn't eager for a discussion with
Maureen. So she asked a mutual friend to act as go-between (and was
turned down).

Once wed, Maureen, along with several other California Republicans, decided to run for the Senate seat held by the elderly S. I.
Hayakawa. She would be a long shot of course, but given the state's
proclivity for electing amateurs to high office, her candidacy was plausible. She had been a political activist for twenty years, followed public
issues and was articulate. Her first task was to establish herself as a legitimate prospect though she had never held public office. In August
1981, when she was doing serious planning and beginning to raise
money, reporters asked her father whether he thought she would actually run. His whimsical response: "I hope not. I don't know. I know
she's talked of it. I don't know how serious she is about it."

She was, in fact, deadly earnest. Reagan's offhand reply, which got
wide attention in California, made her task all the more difficult. Understandably, she was angered by this latest example of paternal
indifference. It would have been inappropriate, of course, for Reagan
to promote her candidacy directly or indirectly. Instead of benign
neutrality, however, she got harpoons from her family and from the
White House. Uncle Neil, still interested in the state party affairs,
loudly announced his preference for one of her rivals for the GOP
nomination, Mayor Pete Wilson of San Diego. He also questioned his
niece's qualifications. Ed Rollins, the White House political liaison
chief, thought he was speaking off the record when he told a California
reporter that Maureen's organization lacked enough steam to get anywhere. Instead of being handled with delicacy, Rollins' appraisal was
published as the White House view. That put still more sand in her engine. In tears, Maureen called her father several times and demanded

that Rollins be fired. The talkative adviser merely got a dressing down. Maureen finished fifth in the primary, with just 5 percent of the vote.

Mike, four years younger, was more relaxed about his relationship with his father and also more candid. Like Maureen, he was interested enough to do some dutiful campaign appearances for their father during 1980, something Patti and Ron avoided. Though clearly in awe of his father, Mike did not have to be prodded to reveal scar tissue. "We always felt that we were sharing him with others," he remarked in one interview. "We were basically raised by nannies and maids."[10] As youngsters, he recalled, Maureen and he understood that Dad was a busy man. Still, many years after the fact, Mike sounded uncomprehending when he talked about his prep school athletic career. It was the early sixties and the father was between major engagements— done with the GE connection but not yet immersed in his own political career. The son was winning distinction on the football and baseball teams at the Judson School in Scottsdale, Arizona. He was good enough to be named player of the year in his school's football division and to be offered an athletic scholarship at Arizona State (which he turned down). Despite his own abiding interest in sports, Reagan never saw his son play a single game. Later, when Mike tried professional speedboat racing, the father missed those contests too. Jane Wyman attended an occasional varsity game at Judson. Even Edith and Loyal Davis, Nancy's parents, showed up to cheer occasionally. But the most important fan never made it to the stadium. "You'd like the recognition of your family," Mike said during one of our conversations. "I think I'll raise my family the opposite way. I'll give up things to spend more time with my children."[11]

Like the other three, Mike dropped out of college. His first marriage ended quickly and his racing career terminated in a crackup that caused him serious injury. He sold boats for a time, married again and fathered a son, Cameron, who was two when Granddad won the presidency. Reagan rarely saw his only grandchild. Mike tried a few business ventures which did not quite click. In 1981 he caused some embarrassment when he invoked his father's name in a sales promotion letter to government purchasing agents. Though he tolerated journalists with much more patience than any of his siblings, even Mike began to complain about what he considered unfair press coverage.

Patti, who was twenty-eight at election time, inherited her father's height, her mother's good looks and an appetite for show business. She studied drama at the University of Southern California but did not hold out for a diploma. "I thought he was a great actor," she once said of her father. "Because I was interested, I always had this fantasy that I could act with him in a film someday."[12] When we talked, she sounded

almost sorry that Dad had gone into politics. That arena held no interest for her, though she occasionally participated in anti-nuclear demonstrations. She couldn't be sure, but she thought that she missed the opportunity to vote for her father in the 1976 and 1980 California
primaries because she was enrolled as an independent.

There was a more dramatic disconnection in the mid-seventies when
Patti went with a rock musician (and had one of the songs she wrote
recorded by his band, the Eagles). Parents and daughter were estranged during this period. Nancy was particularly bitter about the separation as well as her daughter's rebellious lifestyle. Later on, Patti returned to the fold, at least partially; she moved back to the Pacific
Palisades house while struggling to get an acting career going.

"Young Ron is Nancy's last hope," a sympathetic friend said during
the campaign year. "He's smart, stable and in some ways the most mature of the four. The others caused problems, complications. She sort
of looked to Ron to make up for that." Of the four, he had spent the
most time during childhood with his parents. Governor Reagan kept
regular hours. Patti, six years older than her kid brother, was away at
boarding school and Ron would recall feeling like an only child who
saw Dad at dinner almost every night. Tall, lean and attractive, he
found himself a freshman at Yale with little inkling of why he was
there. The more he thought about it, the more he realized that his real
fascination was ballet. One night he called his father and announced
that he wanted to leave college in order to become a professional
dancer. Typically, that was news to Reagan; he'd had no idea what was
on the boy's mind. Also typically, he raised no serious objection.

After studying in Los Angeles for a time, Ron accepted a scholarship
from the Joffrey Company in New York and eventually worked his way
up to Joffrey II, a kind of ballet farm team for aspirants.* Though his
father once saw him in a class when Ron was breaking in, Reagan did
not watch his son perform for more than two years after the dance became the boy's occupation. Unlike Mike, Ron insisted that he understood. "I was just starting out," he said later, after his father became
an occasional spectator at performances. "I was getting more than my
share of attention, more than I deserved from a dance standpoint
anyway. To have them show up at the performance [with a crowd of
reporters] would have been unfair to the company and to me in
particular."13

* Late in 1982, he was accepted into the main company, an unusual achievement for someone who started serious study relatively late. The company was in
recess while Ron awaited his new status and, like other dancers, he was technically laid off. He was photographed waiting in line for an unemployment insurance application. Later he decided to quit professional ballet.

Originally reticent about her son's sudden career decision, Nancy was positively disturbed by the way he was living in New York. He was living with his girlfriend, Doria Palmieri, an editorial researcher seven years older than he. She came from a homespun Italian-American family. Mommy thought that it was the wrong match at the wrong time for Ron, who was then twenty-two. Three weeks after the election, while the Reagans were relaxing in California between forays to Washington, the wire services announced that Doria and Ron had been married in a civil ceremony conducted by a New York judge and witnessed by the Secret Service detail.

Nancy was astounded by both the fact and its circumstances. When she left the house that day, she brushed off reporters' questions but her eyes revealed that she had been crying. An aide confided that she thought Ron had made a serious mistake. Of course her feelings were crushed at not having been informed in advance. A few days later Mike Reagan observed: "The Secret Service knew about it before we did." He called his father when the first bulletin arrived. "Congratulations," he said. "You're a new father-in-law." He recalled Reagan's laconic reply: "That's what I hear."

Tension remained between mother and son for two or three months. On Inauguration Night, Nancy wanted the young couple to tour all the inaugural balls with her and Reagan. Ron would consent to go to only one. He thought he should spend the rest of the evening with his wife's family. As usual, he prevailed. Soon after, however, Nancy made peace with the situation. She confected a little story about the suddenness of the wedding. The youngsters had not intended to have the ceremony that day, she said, merely to get a license. They got carried away somehow. Ron remembered it a little differently: "I just don't think we owed anybody any explanations or any advance notice, so we didn't give any."

Despite that collision, Nancy got used to the idea quickly enough. Ron and Doria, living in New York, became the most frequent White House visitors among the offspring. Nancy looked for excuses to go to Manhattan as well. After the shooting particularly, she found herself leaning on Patti, Ron and Doria for moral support. When the shock of the assassination attempt began to wear off, the warmth remained. "She needs a friend more so now than ever," Ron observed. "Life is not too easy for her, being in the White House and everything. In that way, it has sort of brought us closer together. I call her every week. She wants someone to talk to. She wants family."

Reagan in the White House felt no increased need for filial or fraternal devotion. His relations with his children barely changed. He enjoyed their company now and then. He liked swapping stories with

Mike, his rival as a collector of anecdotes and quips.* He kept in touch with Patti's progress, or lack of it, as she tried to establish herself as an actress under her mother's maiden name. He rarely let irritation show when one or another of the four did something controversial.

Yet there remained an intangible barrier, particularly where the older two offspring were concerned. In the early years especially Nancy would have liked to forget that there had been another woman in Reagan's life, a beautiful and successful woman at that. Maureen, with her facial resemblance to Jane Wyman and her mother's strong-willed ways, made forgetting impossible. Nancy regarded Mike's publicized difficulties the way she would the errors of a political aide; she resented the bother it caused.

For Reagan, the distance was also part of his conflict-avoidance mechanism. Ron, a perceptive observer of the relationship, put it this way: "As far as Michael and Maureen go, they can sometimes make it very difficult for him to be around them, you know. They're always kind of harping on one thing or another. They find it difficult I think to sort of be with him and have a good time. Maureen is always beating him over the head with this or that issue . . . Michael complains [in interviews] about Dad not going to see him play football, this, that and the other thing. They make themselves real scarce, too. They make no effort to come and see my folks." Ronald Reagan does not like to be harped at or beat over the head, certainly not by his children.

Reagan, as with all emotional subjects, rarely discusses the matter. He did acknowledge once, however, that he saw strong glints of his father in his own performance as a parent. "Yes," he said, "and maybe sometimes too much so."[14] As Reagan remembered it, that meant giving great independence to the youngsters. His brother Neil, two years older, went along with that in a separate conversation. The consensus was unusual because Moon and Dutch usually clashed in their recollections. But Neil went further, pointing out that it was much more than a question of freedom to make decisions. Jack Reagan, a semiprofessional ballplayer as a young man, waited until the very end of his sons' high school careers before attending a football game in which either boy played. Ronald Reagan, a versatile athlete and professional sports announcer, skipped Michael's competitive appearances altogether. "It's the way we were raised," Neil said.[15]

And it was the way Reagan lived—a convivial loner with few ties to anyone. As candidate, governor and President, Reagan was personally

---

* It was Mike who first told his father the infamous "Polish duck" story, an ethnic joke which Reagan imprudently repeated to a few reporters during the New Hampshire primary campaign. Word of that got out, to Reagan's great embarrassment, and he had to squirm his way through a quasi-apology.

close to very few of his subordinates. Even Deaver, with whom he had the strongest bond, recognized an invisible boundary that was not to be violated. If some rare moment aroused emotion, better to suppress it. Reagan was saddened by Deaver's self-exile from the organization between the fall of 1979 and the spring of 1980. Deaver had been ill-used; all the principals knew that. When Deaver returned to the entourage, he caught up with the candidate's party at a hotel. He went to the room assigned to him and waited. David Fischer, whom Deaver had originally brought into the circle, phoned at last: "The Governor would like you to come by for a drink." Deaver didn't know quite what to expect. When they finally saw each other for the first time in a few months, Reagan served him a screwdriver and said, deadpan: "Where have you been, Mike?" That was the extent of Deaver's welcome-home.

Reagan was as reluctant to demonstrate wrath as he was to show affection. At times this narrow emotional band added to the impression of passivity in a man who could in private be tough or generous as the occasion demanded. The roots of this contradiction remained buried. Reagan declined to delve very deeply into intimate matters and pop-psych isn't one of my fields of expertise. But it isn't unreasonable to speculate that Reagan, growing up in hard times with a good-natured alcoholic for a father, decided early on that playing his own hand his own way was essential, that he should not demand much of others, that giving free rein to feelings set him up for cruel disappointment.

At various stages in their lives, the Reagan brothers helped each other in important ways. It is interesting to recall that in their Illinois years it was the younger who led the way. Dutch went to college first, then lured Moon away from dead-end menial work and eased his way into Eureka. A few years later Moon followed Dutch into broadcasting in Iowa, where he started what turned out to be a solid career in advertising, with a heavy slant toward radio and television. It would be Moon, the successful agency executive and producer, who in the 1960s arranged Dutch's stint on "Death Valley Days" when the kid brother needed the work. In 1964 Neil was more heavily involved with the Goldwater campaign than Ronald was, and then played a part in the early phase of Reagan's 1966 race.

Yet the two were never exactly friends, rarely sought each other's company when both lived in the Los Angeles area for many years, barely acknowledged each other's assistance. Once I asked Neil if they had ever been close. For the first time in that long conversation he paused, turned the question over and finally answered with some hesitation:

Well, it depends how you mean "close." We're pretty much the same beneath the skin. Neither of us really shows much emotion on anything. He blows his stack once in a while and so do I. Maybe the best way I can put it is that you'd never know it unless you became a "victim" of it but we're both very soft touches. Yet we both work overtime, I guess, even unconsciously, trying not to show that—to each other, or to friends or to outsiders.

Dutch does better at the ruse than Moon. He would not admit it, but on Election Day 1980, when the good news was in, Neil Reagan found a private corner in the Pacific Palisades house and celebrated the victory by blubbering with joy into a large handkerchief. Deaver, who discovered him, recalled Neil's great embarrassment. And occasionally Neil would recall, with gruff pleasure, some small, fleeting show of affection from his brother. That he gave voice to the recollection, of course, was the equivalent of blinking in the game of chicken. You found no such flinching by the younger brother.

An anecdotalist in his brother's big league, Neil told one elaborate, bittersweet tale that revealed a good deal about the two of them. After the war, when both were established and affluent in Los Angeles, Neil concocted a complicated Christmas present for Ronald. Through a friend in the county welfare department, Neil was put in touch with a down-and-out family—an alcoholic father, youngish mother, three-year-old son. Neil and his secretary took an afternoon off, drove the mother and child to Sears and conducted a buying spree of clothing and toys. They even bought an outfit for the absent father, who was at home sleeping off a bender.

The "present" to Ronald was the news that this had been done in his name and for his sake. Neil even wrote a poem about it. The symbolism, in view of their own childhood, was as rich as it was unmistakable. Finally Neil worked his way to the punch line, which was Ronald's reaction to this most unusual Christmas gift. "His remark was something like, 'Gee, that's keen.' Now if that had been you [hearing that response], not knowing him, you would have turned around and walked away and said, 'Well, that son of a bitch, that went over [badly].' But sure enough, a couple of weeks or months later, a friend of his told me, 'Well, you gave your brother one hell of a Christmas present. He almost cried when he told me about it.'"

In telling that story, Neil in effect flinched. He could not disguise the fact, thirty years later, that he had felt pleasure in penetrating Reagan's emotional armor. It was almost impossible to elicit a similar concession from the younger brother. When you drew an occasional mention of Neil from him, the allusion was most often a jocular putdown. A poignant example of that concerned Neil's Catholicism. Their father was a

Roman Catholic of unsteady devotion, their mother a devout member
of a liberal Protestant denomination now called the Christian Church
(Disciples of Christ). Neil as an infant was baptized Roman, but not
informed of that act. Growing up, both boys followed their mother,
Nelle, in her affiliation. Then, as Neil told it, he became restless about
religion. He visited other churches, including a Roman Catholic one,
and decided to seek instruction in that faith. The priest's first question
to him: are you doing this because you're seeing a Catholic girl? No,
Neil replied, he was not "keeping company" with anyone at that time.
The instruction proceeded and Neil remained a practicing Catholic the
rest of his life, attending Mass weekly.

The story stuck in my mind because it had been recalled with obvious feeling. It had been a big thing in his life, particularly when he told
his mother about what he thought was his conversion. Whereupon she
informed him that, technically at least, he had been a Catholic since infancy. A year after hearing the story I happened to be seated at the
President's table for an informal White House dinner. Someone
brought up religion and Reagan reminisced about his family's church-
going habits. Of Neil he said: "He converted for a very good reason.
He was seeing a Catholic girl." Then he laughed and provided the
kicker: "But he ended up going with a Protestant."

I never chased down the truth of the matter, which is irrelevant anyway. The point is that Reagan trashed his brother's version as if by
reflex, turning what he must have known was a heavy bit of sentiment
into just another one-liner. That, in turn, sent me back to notes of
earlier conversations with Neil. Sure enough, he had already provided a
kind of explanation: "There's a game we play back and forth. I don't
give him credit for taking a deep breath and he won't give me credit for
taking a deep breath." Though Moon could play the game in hardball
fashion now and then, deftly puncturing some of the kid brother's float-
ing illusions, Dutch scored more points.

Reagan seemed capable of genuine and consistent softness with only
one person, Nancy. It was as if she had totally exclusive rights to his
emotional reservoir. Not even his children could drink there. Where
she was concerned, he would sound like a love-struck sophomore to
anyone who asked, and act that way as well. A few people who know
them well and are willing to tell tales out of school on assorted intimate subjects could recall no instance of Reagan doing or saying anything insensitive or inconsiderate concerning Nancy. Neil at his most
acerbic could dump effectively on his brother, nieces and nephews in
two short sentences: "He's not a disciplinarian. If he were, he would
have broken their heads a long time ago." But if Neil knew anything

that cast doubt on the sentimental solidity of his brother's marriage, he was silent about it.

Following that emotional chain brings us to the intersection of Nancy Reagan and the next election. At the beginning of his third year, many professional spectators contended that Reagan might well be a one-term President by choice. It is easy to argue that case by merely listing a few objective facts: the man's age, the demands of the office, his lack of the power imperative most incumbents possess, the present condition and future prospects of the economy, the habit Americans have developed in the last fifteen years of losing patience with their leaders. To this roster the Washington cognoscenti add a clincher: Nancy will beseech him to quit. This last is a reversal of the earlier assumption, that "Queen Nancy" was so enamored of her scepter that the voters would have to pry it from her hand.

His political strategists to a man denied all of this for the usual reasons. To do otherwise would impose a lame-duck status that would cripple the balance of his term and cause disruptive competition within the party. Therefore they predicted that he would make the run. Nancy kept her own counsel, during the fall and winter, simply denying that she and her husband were ready to discuss the issue even between themselves.

When we had our final conversation on the subject just before the congressional election, she allowed that if her husband told her the next morning he had decided not to run, she would assent without argument.

But he is a competitor, I remind her.

"You're right. He is competitive. He doesn't like to lose or be regarded as a loser. I think probably that it might rest an awful lot with me, unfortunately—'unfortunately' because I don't know how I feel. I mean, I have very mixed emotions."

What is the positive side?

"Well, I think there is a danger of getting into only having one-term Presidents, which I don't think is good. I think that he's doing something that's necessary and will be good for the country . . ." She goes on to gush about her man and his value to the country, winding up this phase of the talk nonetheless with a sentimental evocation of the bliss of privacy recaptured in the twilight years.

One got the feeling listening to her, and to a few of the Reagans' intimates, that Nancy was creating a kind of fallback position. Her worry wasn't that the presidency was consuming her man, or that another four years would be killing. Clearly in the winter of 1982–83 he was still bearing up well, enjoying himself more often than not, despite his good-natured grousing about the constraints of having to "live over the store," as he put it. For her part, Nancy had learned the most difficult parts of her role.

What gnawed at her then was the thought of a grinding reelection campaign with defeat the most probable outcome. The idea of watching his career ending in humiliation was almost impossible for her to contemplate. Thus if the tide later ran strongly against him, if the quest began to seem truly quixotic, she could be counted on to compose a variety of strong arguments in favor of voluntary retirement.

Auguries immediately after the 1982 election pointed in that direction. A lame-duck session of Congress turned out to be a cranky standoff. Unemployment remained close to 11 percent in the Christmas season and stories of workers losing their homes to foreclosure proceedings became a nightly news staple. The mid-December Gallup Poll reported that either John Glenn or Walter Mondale could defeat Reagan easily if the election were held then.[16] Nancy could be imagined honing her westward-ho case.

The new year, however, brought a new mood. Reagan's resilience as well as his luck reasserted themselves yet again. Just as the country seemed to lose all patience with the recession, a convincing recovery began in late winter. Just as the Democrats thought to capitalize on their improved numbers in the Ninety-eighth Congress, the White House undertook a series of deft maneuvers under the rubric of bipartisanship that kept O'Neill off balance and showed that Reagan could still exert leadership. Overseas, German voters contributed their own good news by retaining in power the conservative Kohl government, with which Reagan felt comfortable. This verdict, Washington hoped, would induce Moscow to make concessions in the INF negotiations.

Reagan now acted like a President totally confident that he could avoid the familiar third-year doldrums. When his political capital was at a low point, he refused to take a defensive crouch. Instead he campaigned across the country, sounding very much the candidate as he preached that "America is on the mend." Achievement of the grandest items on his agenda would have to wait as he reconstructed his base.

"One of the beauties that come along with the years," Reagan remarked in a benign tone, "is the ability not to get impatient."[17] We were talking about 1984 and the line expressed by a few commentators that he was finally beginning to show his age. There was talk of closet crankiness and further deterioration of his hearing. He has been partly deaf in his right ear for decades and sometimes has difficulty when acoustics are poor. "My goodness," he went on cheerfully, "I've got people in the cabinet and on the staff who are a lot younger than I am wearing hearing aids. My doctor has still insisted that I don't require a hearing aid."

If the age issue were to be used against him in 1984, he indicated, he would deflect it as genially as he had in 1980. "Right now," he said in the fall of 1982, "I'm doing everything I did before." Actually, he was doing more in the way of physical exercise since the shooting. Proud of his regimen, he once flexed his arm with the mock order: "Feel this bicep." Complying, I found the muscle laudably firm, just as I've found his hearing acute enough in normal conversation.

What any person's health will be in a year or a month is imponderable. Reagan had other things on his mind looking toward the next election. The voters let you know, he frequently said, whether you should try again or pack your bags. That was his way of parrying the big question. He had his own ample love of solitude and leisure. From the moment he arrived in Washington one part of him yearned for the freedom of civilian status. He fled to California as often as public relations considerations allowed.

But another part of him seemed dominant. If he had learned anything in two years, it was that four years would not be enough to do what he had come to do. "This is the thing," he said in a ruminative tone, "it has been a long time since we had . . . stability in government."[18] By that he meant a two-term President, but not merely a steward. He meant an eight-year regime that accomplished its progenitor's goals.

Reagan was sufficiently at peace with himself to know that he did not need another electoral victory to certify his personal worth. Rather, another election doubtless would be necessary to give his *ideas* the full test he thought they deserved. The recession and the difficulties he encountered—in fact helped create—in the foreign affairs field had slowed everything down. Now, with just a bit more of the famous Reagan luck, favorable economic trends would begin having palpable effect in time for 1984. Yuri Andropov might in the end prove agreeable to a deal, or at least to a continued abstention from urgent confrontation.

Reaganism was still only an interesting beachhead on the coast of American public life. Its creator still yearned to strike inland. His premature withdrawal, he knew, would cause havoc in the party, even more than his challenge to Ford in 1976 had created. There was no single logical heir, certainly none Reagan trusted to administer his still-fragile legacy. With nomination fever on both sides dominating 1984, that year would be lost to effective governance.

If Reagan continues to defy the biological clock, one can easily envision an evening in mid- or late 1983 when he tells his wife that he must run again. Having never thwarted him on an important matter, Nancy Reagan will reply that she understands. Then Rawhide and Rainbow will take one last grand gamble together.

Notes

CHAPTER 1

1. Interview with the author, November 8, 1982.

2. *The American Spectator,* March 1982.

3. New York *Times* Op-Ed page, October 14, 1982.

4. From the "Final Report of the Initial Actions Project," January 29, 1982 (a confidential report drafted by several of Reagan's aides).

5. Interview with Donald M. Rothberg of Associated Press; it appeared March 1, 1982.

6. From Von Hoffman's witty diatribe "Contra Reaganum" in *Harper's,* May 1982. The title of one of his books indicates his orientation: *Make-Believe Presidents: Illusions of Power from McKinley to Carter;* Pantheon, 1978.

7. Wright, who was serving his fourteenth term in Congress when he wrote this, made portions of his journal available to David S. Broder of the Washington *Post.* The paper published it in its Sunday *Outlook* section, December 13, 1981.

8. *The American Spectator,* March 1982.

CHAPTER 2

1. Barber gave his initial verdict on Reagan in an interview published in *The Wall Street Journal,* September 17, 1980. Reagan's first eighteen months in office, Barber later told me, confirmed his judgment.

2. The conversation at Camp David took place July 24, 1982.

3. The interview was March 23, 1982; transcript provided by the White House.

4. "Money Income and Poverty Status of Families and Persons in the United States," Series P-60, No. 134, U.S. Census Bureau, July 1982.

5. Interview with the author, November 3, 1982.

6. Interview with the author, December 29, 1981.

7. Interview with the author, October 15, 1982.

8. Interview with Roger Rosenblatt of *Time* and the author, December 2, 1980.

9. *The New Republic,* April 7, 1982.

10. The "South Succotash" phrase popped out when Reagan talked to three staff members of the *Daily Oklahoman* while visiting Oklahoma City on March 16, 1982. Transcript provided by the White House.

CHAPTER 3

1. *New York Review of Books,* May 13, 1982.
2. Arthur E. Rowse, *One Sweet Guy and What He's Doing to You: The Promises and Perils of Reaganism;* Consumer News Inc., 1981.
3. Robert Lekachman, *Greed Is Not Enough: Reaganomics;* Pantheon, 1981.
4. Kevin P. Phillips, *Post Conservative America;* Random House, 1982.
5. Interview with the author, December 29, 1981.
6. George Gilder, *Wealth and Poverty;* Basic Books Inc., 1981.
7. Rowland Evans and Robert Novak, *The Reagan Revolution;* E. P. Dutton, 1981.
8. Interview with the author, September 4, 1981.
9. Interview with the author, July 24, 1982.

CHAPTER 4

1. Interview with the author, September 4, 1981.
2. Interview with the author, March 5, 1982.
3. Ibid.
4. Ibid.
5. "Cabinet and Subcabinet Personnel Selection in Reagan's First Year: New Variations on Some Not-So-Old Themes," a study by G. Calvin Mackenzie prepared for the September 1981 meeting of the American Political Science Association.

CHAPTER 5

1. *Time,* December 29, 1980.
2. Washington *Post,* November 19, 1980.
3. *Time,* December 1, 1980.
4. Interview with the author, October 10, 1981.
5. Interview with the author, September 30, 1981.
6. Telephone interview with the author, November 24, 1981.

CHAPTER 6

1. *Newsweek,* September 7, 1981.
2. Interview with the author, September 24, 1982.
3. Washington *Post,* January 8, 1982.
4. *Time,* July 12, 1982.
5. Interview with the author, April 14, 1982.
6. Interview with the author, May 6, 1982.
7. Interview with the author, May 7, 1982.

CHAPTER 7

1. Interview with the author, December 29, 1981.
2. Interview with the author, April 2, 1981.
3. Interview with the author, April 3, 1981.
4. Patrick E. Tyler and Bob Woodward of the Washington *Post* broke the

story December 13, 1981. The White House never confirmed it officially, but those familiar with the incident acknowledged privately that the newspaper's account was correct.

5. Interview with the author, July 21, 1982.
6. Interview with the author, August 19, 1982.
7. Interview with the author, December 29, 1981.
8. Interview with the author, September 15, 1981.
9. Interview with the author, August 18, 1981.

CHAPTER 8
1. "Current Population Reports/Consumer Income," Series P-60, No. 134, U.S. Census Bureau, July 1982.
2. *The Wall Street Journal,* February 1, 1982.
3. "The Stockman Recession: A Reaganite's Account," *Fortune,* February 22, 1982.
4. Interview with the author, February 16, 1982.
5. Ibid.

CHAPTER 9
1. Speech to the Massachusetts Democratic State Committee, March 12, 1981; text supplied by the Speaker's office.
2. New York *Times,* March 7, 1981.
3. Interview with the author, May 5, 1982.
4. Interview with the author, February 8, 1982.
5. Ibid.
6. Ibid.
7. Interview with the author, May 5, 1982.
8. Interview with the author, October 31, 1981.

CHAPTER 10
1. Interview with the author, October 2, 1981.
2. *Congressional Quarterly Weekly Report,* August 1, 1982.

CHAPTER 11
1. Interview with the author, August 24, 1981.
2. Interview with the author, October 10, 1981.
3. Washington *Post Outlook* section, September 20, 1981.

CHAPTER 12
1. *Time,* February 16, 1981.
2. Ibid.
3. Interviews with the author, October 10 and October 31, 1981.
4. Telephone interview with the author, August 16, 1982.
5. Ibid.

CHAPTER 13
1. Interview with the author, May 7, 1982.
2. White, his foreign service career over, published a long condemnation of Reagan's Central American policy in the New York *Times Magazine,* July 18, 1982.

3. The exchange took place February 27, 1982. Transcript supplied by the State Department.

4. The *Harvard Crimson*, March 23, 1982.

5. Interview with the author, July 21, 1982.

6. *U.S. News & World Report*, March 8, 1982.

CHAPTER 14

1. Interview with the author, July 21, 1982.

2. Interview with the author, August 13, 1982.

3. Interview with the author, September 29, 1982.

4. The interviewer was Philip Geylin of the Washington *Post*, which published the text September 13, 1981.

5. Interview with the author, September 29, 1982.

6. *Human Events*, January 30, 1982. Similar attacks appeared in several other publications, though few were so blunt and personal.

7. New York *Times*, January 17 and 18, 1982.

8. Washington *Post*, June 28, 1981.

9. This off-the-record conversation took place November 13, 1981, while Allen was still in office. Later he approved use of some of the material discussed.

10. Ibid.

11. Haig's remarks here and the passages immediately following are from an interview with the author, March 5, 1982.

12. Interview with the author, July 24, 1982.

13. Interview with the author, September 24, 1982.

14. Haig's statements in the balance of this chapter, unless otherwise indicated, were made in an interview with the author, September 29, 1982.

15. Interview with the author, July 31, 1982.

16. James Reston's column in the New York *Times*, December 9, 1981.

17. Interview with the author, October 2, 1982.

18. The issue date was June 7, 1982, but the edition appeared the preceding Monday, May 31, the same day Haig and Kirkpatrick saw Reagan separately.

19. That conversation at Camp David took place July 24, 1982. Like all journalists' interviews with the President, it was taped and transcribed by White House personnel. The quotations here are from that verbatim transcript, with the bracketed phrases added by the author for the sake of clarity.

20. Interview with the author, October 29, 1982.

CHAPTER 15

1. The September 20, 1982, issue of *Fortune*, for instance, carried an article written in the tone of an exposé. It criticized Deaver for cooperating with an "influential cadre of liberals" such as William Verity, Jr., chairman of Armco Steel, and John Filer, chairman of Aetna Life & Casualty, both of whom were active in the White House program.

2. *Time*, December 14, 1981.

3. Interview with the author, December 12, 1981.

4. Ibid.

5. Interview with the author, December 4, 1981.

6. Interview with the author, April 14, 1982.

7. Interview with the author, December 12, 1981.

CHAPTER 16

1. *Time,* June 22, 1981.

2. Haig was talking to reporters on July 20, 1981, in Ottawa, during the Economic Summit meeting.

3. Reagan addressed a B'nai B'rith conference in Washington, D.C., September 3, 1980.

4. Interview with the author, October 5, 1982.

5. Congressional Record (Senate), May 15, 1978.

6. Interview with the author, November 7, 1981.

7. *Time,* November 9, 1981.

8. Ibid.

9. The New York *Times* published a transcript of Begin's statement, December 20, 1981.

10. Meese spoke on "Meet the Press," December 20, 1981; transcript provided by NBC.

11. Interview with the author, September 29, 1982.

12. Interview with the author, October 5, 1982.

13. Interview with the author, September 14, 1982.

14. *Time,* September 13, 1982.

15. BBC aired the interview September 13, 1982. Transcript provided by the U.S. Foreign Broadcast Information Service, September 14, 1982.

CHAPTER 17

1. Quoted By William G. Hyland in his similarly pessimistic article "US-Soviet Relations: the Long Road Back," *Foreign Affairs,* Winter 1981.

2. Interview with the author, September 29, 1982.

3. *Time,* August 30, 1982.

4. New York *Times,* October 18, 1982.

5. From a speech to several European audiences during the week of October 4, 1982, shortly before Pipes left the NSC staff to return to Harvard. Text provided by the White House.

6. *Time,* January 4, 1982.

7. *Newsweek,* January 18, 1982.

8. *The Washington Quarterly,* Spring 1982. Davies, a career Foreign Service officer before he retired in 1980, had held senior posts both in Moscow and Warsaw. He was ambassador to Poland, 1973–78.

9. This passage and the one following are from an interview with the author, July 24, 1982, when both the INF and START sessions were underway.

10. *Time,* March 29, 1982.

11. "Brezhnev's Peace Offensive, 1981: Propaganda Ploy or U.S. Negotiating Opportunity?"; Congressional Research Service, Report No. 82-96S, published May 17, 1982.

12. *Commentary,* January 1982.

13. Interview with the author, July 21, 1982.

14. Interview with the author, November 3, 1982.

15. Quoted in the New York *Times,* January 23, 1982. Rostow spoke at a Washington meeting of the Committee for a Free World, a neoconservative group.

16. A relatively cryptic story on the secret probe appeared in the Chicago *Tribune,* October 22, 1982, but it contained no details and attracted little attention.

17. Interview with the author, November 3, 1982.

18. Tass distributed a translation of the speech, which was published in the New York *Times,* October 28, 1982.

CHAPTER 18

1. Clark's recollections about his earlier life here and in the balance of this chapter are from an interview with the author, March 13, 1982.

2. *Time,* February 15, 1982.

3. The audience was assembled by the Georgetown University Center for Strategic and International Studies on May 21, 1982. The rest of the speech was an attempt to describe the Administration's global defense strategy. Clark's staff tried to promote press attention, but the talk was opaque and raised more questions than it answered.

CHAPTER 19

1. Federal Reserve Banks no longer publish "real" interest rates. The calculations here are derived from data supplied by the Federal Reserve Bank of St. Louis at the author's request.

2. *Time,* December 28, 1981.

3. Interview with the author, December 29, 1981.

4. Interview with the author, January 23, 1982.

5. Domenici spoke to the Conference Board on February 23, 1982. Text supplied by his office.

CHAPTER 20

1. *The Wall Street Journal,* April 30, 1982.

2. Telephone interview with the author, September 24, 1982.

3. This account of the April 28 meeting is drawn from interviews with several of the participants conducted by four *Time* correspondents: Evan Thomas, Neil MacNeil, Douglas Brew and the author. Much of the material appeared in *Time,* May 10, 1982.

4. *Congressional Quarterly Weekly Report,* June 22, 1982.

5. *The Wall Street Journal,* October 12, 1982.

CHAPTER 21

1. Interview with the author, March 12, 1980.

2. *Texas Monthly,* May 1982.

3. Ibid.

4. That monologue was delivered the night of March 11, 1980, as Bush flew from Springfield, Illinois, to Houston with a few aides and reporters.

5. Interview with the author, August 16, 1981.

6. *Human Events,* February 28, 1981.

7. Washington *Post,* March 13, 1981.

8. Interview with the author, August 15, 1981.

9. Interview with the author, May 28, 1982.

CHAPTER 22

1. Interview with the author, June 26, 1982.

2. Washington *Post,* May 2, 1982.

3. Darman's collaborator was Lawrence E. Lynn, Jr., professor of public pol-

icy at Harvard. The book, edited by John T. Dunlop, was published by Harvard University Press. It also contained a chapter by George P. Shultz.

4. Darman's quotes in the rest of this chapter are from interviews with the author, September 5, 1981, April 3, 1982, and October 10, 1982.

5. Interview with the author, October 9, 1982.

6. Ibid.

CHAPTER 23

1. From the "Final Report of the Initial Actions Project," a document drafted by Reagan's advisers at the end of the transition and described in Chapter 5.

2. He was talking to editors of the *Daily Oklahoman* during a visit to Oklahoma City, March 16, 1982. A transcript of the interview was issued the next day.

3. The calculation was made by the Urban Institute for its study *The Reagan Experiment,* published by the Urban Institute Press in September 1982.

4. New York *Times Magazine,* January 17, 1982.

5. New York *Times,* May 8, 1982.

6. Universal Press Syndicate, August 3, 1982. Kilpatrick picked up the story, with appropriate attribution, from the Charlottesville *Progress.*

7. "Regional Impacts," Muller's chapter in *The Reagan Experiment.*

8. Including the author, in a *Time* analysis article February 1, 1982; Robert B. Reich, in an essay in *The New Republic,* September 20, 1982; and Kevin P. Phillips in *Post Conservative America,* Random House, 1982.

CHAPTER 24

1. Interview with the author, January 22, 1982.

2. Associated Press, January 18, 1982.

3. New York *Times,* January 19, 1982.

4. Interview with the author, January 22, 1982.

5. New York *Times,* March 27, 1982.

6. *National Journal,* March 27, 1982.

7. U.S. Commission on Civil Rights, Clearinghouse Publications, No. 71, June 1982.

8. Interview with the author, May 7, 1982.

9. Written with Richard G. Hubler and brought out in a new edition by Karz Publishers in 1981.

10. Interview with the author, January 26, 1980.

11. *Time,* January 5, 1981.

12. Washington *Post,* September 10, 1982.

CHAPTER 25

1. Interview with the author, December 29, 1981.

2. Interview with the author, January 2, 1980.

3. Interview with the author, January 26, 1980.

4. Interview with the author, October 28, 1981.

5. The story appeared in the issue of *Time* available January 11, dated January 18, 1982.

6. Washington *Post,* January 15, 1982.

7. Washington *Post,* December 20, 1982.

CHAPTER 26

1. *The Washington Monthly*, January 1982.
2. New York *Times Magazine*, September 13, 1981.
3. *National Journal*, July 25, 1981, and April 17, 1982.
4. Chicago *Tribune* Syndicate, July 10, 1981.
5. CBS/New York *Times* Poll conducted May 19–23, 1982 and published May 28, 1982.
6. Reagan addressed the National Association of Manufacturers on March 18, 1982, a time of friction between the White House and the press corps.

CHAPTER 27

1. *Fortune*, May 31, 1982.
2. Washington *Post Outlook* section, July 15, 1981.
3. Supplemental Staff Study of Severance Pay–Life Insurance Plans Adopted by Union Locals; Permanent Subcommittee on Investigations; Government Printing Office, March 21, 1977.
4. *Time*, June 28, 1982.
5. Report of the Senate Select Committee on Intelligence, December 2, 1981.

CHAPTER 28

1. Interview with the author, April 20, 1982.
2. *Newsweek*, December 21, 1981.
3. That account has appeared in several places, most recently in *Nancy*, the autobiography written with Bill Libby; William Morrow & Co., 1980.
4. Interview with the author, October 15, 1982.
5. *Nancy*, op. cit.
6. Lou Cannon, in his biography *Reagan* (G. P. Putnam's Sons, 1982), recalls that and similar occasions on which Nancy displayed a thin skin. The offending radical in this instance was Eldridge Cleaver.
7. Interview with the author, October 15, 1982.
8. *Newsweek*, December 21, 1981.
9. Interview with the author, April 20, 1982.
10. *Time*, July 14, 1980.
11. Interview with the author, November 11, 1980.
12. Interview with the author, June 25, 1980.
13. Ron Reagan's remarks in the balance of this chapter come from a telephone interview with the author, July 7, 1982.
14. In an interview with Roger Rosenblatt and the author, December 2, 1980. when we were collaborating in preparation for *Time*'s Man of the Year story on Reagan, which appeared in the issue of January 5, 1981.
15. Neil Reagan's remarks here and in the rest of this chapter are from interviews with the author, September 28 and November 25, 1980.
16. New York *Times*, January 6, 1983.
17. Interview with the author, November 3, 1982.
18. Ibid.

Index